Handbook of Organizational Behavior Management

Handbook of Organizational Behavior Management

LEE W. FREDERIKSEN
Editor
*Virginia Polytechnic Institute
and State University*

A Wiley-Interscience Publication
John Wiley and Sons
New York • **Chichester** • **Brisbane** • **Toronto** • **Singapore**

Library of Congress Cataloging in Publication Data:

Main entry under title:

Handbook of organizational behavior management.

   "A Wiley-Interscience publication."
   Includes indexes.
   1.   Organizational behavior—Addresses, essays,
lectures.   2.   Management—Addresses, essays, lectures.
I.   Frederiksen, Lee W.
HD58.7.H36   658.3'12   82-4741
ISBN 0-471-09109-X   AACR2

Printed in the United States of America

10 9 8 7 6 5 4 3 2 1

Contributors

FRANK ANDRASIK
State University of New York at Albany

JOHN A. FAIRBANK
VA Medical Center and University of Mississippi Medical Center

LEE W. FREDERIKSEN
Virginia Polytechnic Institute and State University

GLORIA GASPAROTTO
West Virginia University

E. SCOTT GELLER
Virginia Polytechnic Institute and State University

THOMAS F. GILBERT
Performance Engineering Group

JOHN W. GUNKLER
Wilson Learning Corporation

BRANDON L. HALL
Wilson Learning Corporation

JUDY STANLEY HEIMBERG
State University of New York at Albany

BILL L. HOPKINS
University of Kansas

R. W. KEMPEN
Western Electric

JUDITH L. KOMAKI
Purdue University

JON E. KRAPFL
West Virginia University

ROBERT KREITNER
Arizona State University

GARY P. LATHAM
University of Washington

FRED LUTHANS
University of Nebraska

ROBERT MIRMAN
General Mills, Inc.

PHILIP M. PODSAKOFF
Ohio State University

DONALD M. PRUE
VA Medical Center and University of Mississippi Medical Center

PAUL C. ROSS
American Telephone and Telegraph Co.

W. E. SCOTT, JR.
Indiana University

JUDITH SEARS
University of Kansas

BETH SULZER-AZAROFF
University of Massachusetts

MALCOLM W. WARREN
Performance Technologies, Inc.

RICHARD A. WINETT
Virginia Polytechnic Institute and State University

RONALD E. ZEMKE
Performance Research Associates

*To Candace, whose unending
patience and support
made this happen*

Preface

American business is in trouble, we are told. Long the preeminent industrial power in the world, we are now in the midst of a productivity crisis. Although the average person may not know exactly what "productivity" means, he or she is liable to be well aware that it is declining. There is undoubtedly a multitude of reasons for this difficulty. Unfair foreign competition, over-regulation, inflation, a changing workforce: the list of contributing causes is a long one. However, as almost everyone who has given the problem a serious look concludes, at least part of the solution lies in the more effective management of our workforce. This is a task for which Organizational Behavior Management (OBM) is well suited.

Even in view of the need for more effective human resource management, some might respond that the last thing we need is another new approach to managing people. If you ask managers to list their pet peeves, you are likely to find remarkable consistency. Close to the top of the list, somewhere near high taxes and red tape, will be theories of human behavior. Managers are accustomed to hearing lofty sounding, impractical advice on how they ought to manage people. These theories are typically abstract, complex, and contradictory. Who can blame a manager for simply doing what feels right and letting it go at that?

Part of the reason for this unfortunate state of affairs undoubtedly centers around the way new approaches are developed. Frequently, they are based on the work and experience of a single individual. Some approaches have also evolved from a single technique, assessment instrument, or model of human behavior. Only after the approach has been developed, publicized, and promoted does anyone get around to testing it (if they ever do). The trend seems to be theory first, data second.

The development of OBM has taken quite a different course. First, no single individual "invented" the approach. Rather, a broad range of individuals, working quite independently of one another, have evolved similar approaches to the management of behavior in organizational settings. The extent of this independent development became evident in the process of assembling this volume. As I queried a range of individuals to identify leaders and innovaters in the field, I came up with lists that were largely nonoverlapping. Likewise, it was not uncommon for an author to be acquainted with only a small number of the other contributors to the current volume. Clearly, OBM belongs to no individual or small group.

Second, OBM is data centered, not theory centered. It is true that many of the pioneers of this approach share a common perspective on human behavior. That perspective recognizes that the context of behavior makes a difference. Behavior is determined by the nature of the situation and the individual's experience in similar circumstances. However, this shared view of behavior has not been central. The critical element seems to be the insistence on looking at what people *actually do* and the *results* of their behavior. OBM has arisen not from speculation and theoretical abstraction but from the reality of day-to-day organizational life. Techniques have evolved on the basis of whether they work rather than whether they fit into a preconceived theoretical system. In short, the approach has been data first, theory second.

Few people working in the field would maintain that OBM has all the answers. Rather, they would argue that OBM represents a scientifically sound and extremely practical approach to finding solutions to particular problems. The principles that have evolved can aid in the selection of tentative solutions. However, each solution must stand the ultimate test of whether or not it produces the desired results.

OBM has been approaching a turning point in its development. For a number of years, researchers and practitioners had been publishing a growing volume of studies describing the application of OBM to specific problem situations. While each individual study can answer only a small question, the cumulative impact of these data has been growing. Yet if OBM is to have maximum impact, it must become an overall approach to management of human resources rather than an isolated problem-solving technique. I think the contents of this book support the argument that OBM has entered that second stage of development.

The volume has been organized into four parts. Part 1 presents a perspective on OBM. It places the field in historical context, outlines some underlying assumptions, and reviews common misconceptions and ethical concerns. Part 2 focuses on techniques for analyzing and assessing behavior. These techniques have, in a very real sense, formed the foundation of OBM. They have supplied the data from which it has evolved. Part 3 focuses on the techniques used in the management of behavior. These range from techniques for self-management to approaches to entire organizational systems. The fourth and final part is perhaps the most exciting. It consists of seven chapters that review specific applications of OBM to important problems. These applications represent a sample of what has been done and point the way to future development. In addition, each chapter presents an action plan to guide the manager in tackling his or her particular situation.

It almost goes without saying that this volume could not have been assembled without the help of a great many people. The authors of individual chapters have made their obvious and essential contributions.

Their task was not a small one. There are also a great many individuals who have made less obvious but equally important contributions. A number of people helped set the tone and aided in the selection of chapter authors. Among the most helpful of these people (listed in alphabetical order) were Karen Brethhower, Thomas Gilbert, Brandon Hall, Robert Mager, Donald Prue, and Ronald Zemke. Also of great help were Bridget Simmerman and Patricia Watkins, whose long and thankless hours helped translate lofty plans into concrete action and ultimately manuscript pages. I would also like to acknowledge the people at Wiley for their patience and consistent support. Of particular note are the contributions of Catherine Dillon, John Mahaney, and especially Walter Maytham for taking a chance on this project. And last, but certainly not least, I'd like to thank a number of individuals (who shall go nameless) whose discouraging comments absolutely convinced me that I was on the right track.

LEE W. FREDERIKSEN

Blacksburg, Virginia
June 1982

Contents

PART 4.   APPLICATIONS AND RESULTS, 361

Handbook of Organizational Behavior Management

PART

Perspectives

Organizational Behavior Management (OBM) is more than a group of the latest techniques for managing people at work. Rather it represents a very different approach to understanding, measuring, and managing behavior in organizational settings. In short, it's a totally new perspective. The purpose of the current section is to capture that perspective.

As with any new approach, OBM cannot be understood apart from its historical context. We need to know what it actually is, how it differs from other approaches, and what are its unique contributions. For some readers the concepts and language will seem familiar. Yet concepts and terms that sound familiar may be defined and used in somewhat novel or unfamiliar ways. OBM also has long been subject to misconceptions and conflict. It is not uncommon to hear it simultaneously criticized for being impossibly simplistic and devastatingly effective.

Each of the four chapters in this first section helps the reader gain some perspective on the field. In combination they provide a comprehensive picture of what OBM is, where it has come from, and what its major contributions are; and they set the stage for exploring its future potential.

Chapter 1 presents the broadest overview of the field. It starts by defining OBM and tracing the growth of the field. Next its major contributions, including its unique perspective, methods used for assessment and analysis, and techniques developed for behavior change, are reviewed. Finally, areas in which OBM has seen its greatest application and some of the prospects and preconditions for future development are discussed.

Chapter 2 covers the topic of behavioral systems analysis. It represents the general theoretical perspective from which OBM has developed. Many managers are justifiably skeptical about another theory of human behavior, having been led down the garden path many times only to find another hierarchy of inner needs. These managers will undoubtedly find behavioral systems analysis, with its emphasis on the observable, controllable, and practical, to be a refreshing change. Krapfl and Gasparotto present behavioral systems analysis as developing from behavior analysis and general systems theory. They review some of the basic concepts associated with each field and show how they have been combined into a usable approach to behavior in organizations. They also point out the difficulties inherent in such a synthesis and problems yet to be overcome.

Chapter 3 extends this theoretical perspective to some traditional concerns of managers. Built around the cornerstones of leadership and supervision, this chapter by Scott and Podsokoff examines the unique contributions of a behavioral approach to these topics. Leadership is viewed as behavior designed to control the behavior of others rather than some vague personality construct. Some basic behavioral principles are then reviewed in detail. Based upon this analysis prescriptions for effective leadership are offered. These suggestions cover topics as diverse as directing subordinates, making decisions about hiring, training, maintaining desirable performance, and preventing or eliminating problem behavior. The chapter concludes with a discussion of the implications of this approach for developing subordinate self-control.

As with many radically different approaches to important topic areas, OBM has a controversial history. Chapter 4 attacks this controversy head on. Kreitner reviews the heritage of OBM with special attention to topics such as radical behaviorism, Skinner's treatment of freedom and dignity, and questionable applications of behavior modification. He then turns his attention to problems associated with terminology such as "control," "punishment," and "negative reinforcement." Finally, some commonly held misconceptions about OBM are debunked, and frequently raised ethical issues are discussed.

By some measures, the chapters in this first section are the least practical in the entire volume. Yet they provide the context for what is to follow. They provide the perspective of theory that leads to the emergence of practical and effective approaches to difficult organizational problems.

1

Organizational Behavior Management: An Overview

LEE W. FREDERIKSEN

Virginia Polytechnic Institute and State University

The behavioral sciences have promised a lot to managers. The ability to understand people, to select the right person for the job, to help people to be both productive and satisfied with their job, to be more creative, and to help resolve interpersonal conflict are only a few examples of these alluring promises. Yet, along with several decades of growing influence, there is also growing disillusionment. Many managers have put down a book or come away from a seminar filled with enthusiasm and insight into the nature of people. They might feel that they have gained new understanding of people's basic needs and motivations or are now able to categorize and label behavior in new and useful ways. Filled with enthusiasm and this newfound insight, they return to work on Monday morning only to find the same problems they left behind. Attempts to change people may meet with only limited or transitory success. Before long, the particular theory or technique is relegated to the status of "I tried that; it didn't work." In short, the promise of the behavioral sciences has been largely unfulfilled.

It would clearly be a mistake to say that the behavioral sciences have added nothing to the prediction and management of behavior in organizational settings. Yet their impact has been sharply limited by one overriding failing, that is, their inability to specify techniques and procedures that result in clear, well-documented improvements in performance. It is this simple point, the ability to produce measurable changes in important behavior, that has been the stumbling block for a seemingly endless parade of insights, theories, and approaches.

The past decade has seen the growth of an exception to that trend. That exception has been the application of specific principles and procedures of behavior modification, developed in laboratory and clinical settings, to the improvement of performance in organizational settings. While a whole host of labels have been used to describe this approach, the term "organizational behavior management" (OBM) is probably the single most widely accepted one. The paramount strength of OBM has been its ability to produce documented increases in human productivity.

The purpose of the current chapter is to present an overview of OBM. How did the field develop? What are its major contributions? Where has it been applied?

THE DEVELOPMENT OF ORGANIZATIONAL BEHAVIOR MANAGEMENT

What Is OBM?

An appropriate starting place for understanding OBM is to look at how it has been defined. A recent survey of OBM practitioners (Frederiksen and Lovett, 1980) asked individuals to give their own definition of the field. Based on their responses, a consensus definition began to emerge:

> OBM is the application of principles of behavioral psychology and the methodologies of behavior modification/applied behavior analysis to the study and control of individual or group behavior within organizational settings. (Frederiksen and Lovett, 1980, p. 196)

A less formal but perhaps more descriptive definition of the field was offered by Hall (1980). Writing in an editorial for the *Journal of Organizational Behavior Management*, he explains:

> The field of OBM consists of the development and evaluation of performance improvement procedures which are based on the principles of behavior discovered through the science of behavior analysis. These procedures are considered to be within the scope of OBM when they focus on improving individual or group performance within an organizational setting, whether that organization be a business, industrial setting, or human service setting, and whether that organization was established for profit or not.

> The goal of the field of OBM is to establish a technology of broad-scale performance improvement and organizational change so that employees will be more productive and happy, and so that our organizations and institutions will be more effective and efficient in achieving their goals. (p. 145)

These two definitions share a number of common characteristics. First, there is clear agreement on the *subject matter* of the approach. The focus is on the behavior of both individuals and groups in organizational settings. These settings can include businesses, industries, schools, government, community organizations, hospitals, or human services. Likewise the behavior can be quite diverse. Absenteeism, the completion of assigned tasks, unit production per hour, quality, safety, and customer service are just a few examples. In short, the focus is on almost any behavior that affects productivity or satisfaction in the work environment.

There is also agreement on the *purpose* of OBM. The purpose is not simply the description or academic understanding of behavior. While such an understanding may be a necessary prerequisite for change, the primary focus is on the improvement of performance and satisfaction. It is not enough simply to describe, classify, or label behavior. Rather the goal is to make organizations more effective at achieving their goals through improving the performance of both workers and managers. In this respect OBM is very much a practical, action-oriented endeavor.

A third important feature of OBM is its *theoretical or conceptual basis*. While a variety of different terms, such as behaviorism, behavioral psychology, operant psychology, or behavior analysis have been used, the thrust is the same. The primary emphasis is on the behavior of individuals rather than their personality, attitudes, perceptions, needs, deep-seated motives, or other things that supposedly go on beneath the surface. Rather than inferring these internal states from behavior, the focus is on the behavior itself.

There is a parallel focus on the role that the environment plays in shaping that behavior. Attention is paid to the role of events in the setting that set the occasion for certain types of behavior. There is an equally strong emphasis on the consequences of behavior, or put another way, the context in which behavior occurs. A host of theoreticians and researchers have contributed to this perspective, as will be discussed later.

A final important characteristic of OBM is the *methodology* employed. Methodology refers to the techniques used for assessing and analyzing behavior. The methodology used in OBM differs from that traditionally used to study individuals or groups in organizations in two important respects. First, there is the ongoing and direct observation of behavior as it occurs in the organization. Rather than focusing on what people tell you about how they act or feel, OBM actually looks at what they do. This doesn't mean that an individual is never asked about feelings or perceptions, but rather that actual accomplishments are more important than internal feelings. This focus is ongoing: rather than basing assessments on one-time surveys, collecting repeated observations over time becomes important. In other words, there are repeated measurements of what people are actually doing over time rather than a one-time assessment of how they feel about what they are doing. A second important characteristic of the methodology is the use of within-group comparisons of performance. What this means is that a single individual or groups of individuals are observed over time as the conditions are changed. Employees' current performance is compared to the baseline of their past performances as programs are introduced or other conditions changed. This contrasts with the traditional approach of comparing different groups of individuals. It

forces one to look for practical significance rather than statistical significance as the criteria for improvement. This is an important consideration,
since sometimes a statistically significant change in behavior may be of
little or no practical significance to the organization. There are many
variations on this within-group methodology that will be covered later in
this volume.

In summary, OBM concerns itself with the behavior of individuals and
groups in organizational settings. It is very much concerned with improving performance in a way that makes organizations more efficient in
achieving their objectives. These two characteristics are not particularly
new. What is new is the theoretical perspective and methodology that
OBM brings to these tasks. It takes a perspective of behavioral psychology
and uses the related methodology in its attempt to understand and improve
performance. What further distinguishes this approach is that it works.

The Growth of OBM

OBM represents a convergence of two fields: organizational behavior and
behavior modification. While they have shared some common influences,
OBM has developed somewhat independently in the two areas. Only
within the past decade has any significant cross-fertilization occurred. To
understand this convergence, it may be helpful to first view some developments in each area.

The field of organizational behavior has its roots in the development
of management theory. Frederick W. Taylor's early work on improving
the efficiency of certain production tasks was instrumental in starting the
scientific management school of thought (Carroll and Tosi, 1977; Weissenberg, 1971). The work of Taylor strongly influenced Munsterberg's
(1913) seminal text concerning the application of psychology to industrial
management. Subsequent work by Henri Fayol and Chester Barnard also
furthered the field through the development of administrative theory.

The behavioral sciences took on a larger role in the management of
human resources subsequent to the well-known Hawthorn studies conducted at Western Electric (Roethlisberger and Dickson, 1939). However,
probably the most widely recognized influence of psychology on the field
of organizational behavior has been Abraham Maslow's work. The extent
of his influence is hard to overestimate. There are probably few managers
who have received formal training since World War II who have not been
exposed to Maslow's concepts, such as the hierarchy of needs, as pop-
ularized by theorists such as Herzberg (1966) and McGregor (1960). The
legacy of this influence has been a generation of managers, consultants,
and academicians who have been oriented towards thinking in terms of
people's internal needs, desires, perceptions, and so on. In short, the focus
was on the "internal person."

To a great extent, psychology shared the emphasis on inferred internal
states. However, this was not universally the case. There is a thread run-

ning through psychology that has consistently emphasized the observable behavior of individuals and the influence that the environment has in shaping and strengthening that behavior. This tradition has served as the basis for the development of behavior modification.

The work of the Russian physiologist Ivan Pavlov and American psychologists John B. Watson and Edward L. Thorndike served as some of the early foundations for these developments (Hersen, Eisler, and Miller, 1975; Franks, 1969). Watson is perhaps the most widely recognized pioneer in the field of behaviorism, that is, a concern with the behavior of the individual rather than with the individual's thoughts, feelings, or needs. Thorndike is widely recognized for the emphasis he placed on the consequences of behavior. His famous Law of Effect pointed out that behavior that led to certain positive consequences tended to be strengthened. However, it was probably the work of B. F. Skinner that has been most influential. He not only presented the scientific rationale for studying observable behavior and the environment (Skinner, 1953) but also pointed out the practical implications and ramifications of his theory (Skinner, 1948, 1971). Undoubtedly Skinner is the most widely known and controversial contemporary psychologist.

The decade between the mid-sixties and mid-seventies was a period of much conflict surrounding the development of behavior modification and its application to clinical problems. However, there has been a gradual acceptance of behavior modification as a useful and effective approach to understanding and ameliorating human problems (Hersen et al., 1975; Redd, Porterfield, and Anderson, 1979).

About two decades ago, the first visible signs of OBM began to appear. In 1961, Aldis published an article in the *Harvard Business Review* entitled "Of Pigeons and Men," in which he argued for using varying schedules of reinforcement in industrial settings. Another development within the field of organizational behavior was some of the early work on programmed instruction and behavior management procedures in business settings conducted at the University of Michigan in the early sixties (Cornellan, 1978). In short, people working within an organizational context were beginning to apply some of the principles of operant psychology to the problems they were encountering.

The decade of the sixties was also a very active one for behavior modification. As people began to apply principles of behavior modification to clinical and school populations, they began to encounter problems in the implementation of programs. In many cases there were difficulties in getting staff to actually carry out the program as designed. Hence a number of people began to turn their attention to using the principles of behavior modification to get the staff to perform their assigned duties. It was speculated that the principles and procedures of behavior modification that were so effective with disturbed populations and children might also be applicable to increasing the performance of normal adults in their work setting. In summary, the sixties was a decade of early experimentation with cross-fertilization. However, what was missing was some clear demonstration that this cross-fertilization was indeed worthwhile.

That deficit was partially filled with the publication, in the early seventies, of the Emery Air Freight experience. Edward Feeny reported that by the use of some behavioral principles (charting specific performances, social praise, and performance feedback) the Emery Air Freight Company was able to sharply improve productivity. The end result was an annual savings of hundreds of thousands of dollars. This result was widely reported in the business press (At Emery Air Freight, 1973; Performance Audit, 1972) and probably remains one of the most widely known applications. While it was certainly not the first systematic application of OBM, it served to spur a good bit of interest in the approach and its applicability to a range of organizational concerns.

The decade of the seventies was a period of accelerated growth and integration of the field. Besides a continued flow of publications advocating or criticizing this kind of development (e.g., Bobele and Buchanan, 1975; Conversation with B.F. Skinner, 1973; Hamner and Hamner, 1976; Kreitner, 1975; Nord, 1969), there were also a number of other indications. These include the inevitable appearance of literature reviews (Andrasik, 1979; Babb and Kopp, 1978; Schneier, 1974), bibliographies (Prue, Frederiksen, and Bacon, 1978), and books (Brown and Presbie, 1976; Connellan, 1978; Gilbert, 1978; Luthans and Kreitner, 1975; Miller, 1978). Perhaps the most convincing signs that the field is taking on its own identity was the appearance of a professional journal devoted entirely to the topic of OBM (Journal of Organizational Behavior Management) in 1977, as well as the beginning of a professional association (the OBM Network) in the late seventies.

If the observable signs are any indication, OBM has enjoyed a marked increase in its use and acceptance in the past decade. Surveys of both practitioners (Frederiksen and Lovett, 1980) and the literature (Andrasik, Heimberg, and McNamara, 1981; Frederiksen and Johnson, 1981) indicate that the future of OBM is extremely promising, in terms of both performance improvement and its apparent broad applicability. However, OBM is at something of a crossroads. Many of the early applications were small-scale or short-term demonstration projects aimed at showing that OBM could be applied to important organizational concerns. By and large, these early efforts were successful. With these documented successes and growing acceptance, OBM must now be judged on its applicability to a wider range of organizational problems as well as its place in the management of the organization as a whole. Put another way, we might say that OBM is entering its second stage of development. Its first stage consisted of early suggestions, demonstrations, small projects, and the development of a track record. In the second stage, it will increasingly be called upon to function as an integral part of the overall management approach.

MAJOR CONTRIBUTIONS

The understanding and management of people in the work place is not a new topic. OBM represents a very promising approach to the effective management of behavior in organizational settings. What then are the unique contributions of OBM? What can the approach really offer to management? I will consider three major areas: perspectives, methods for assessment and analysis, and techniques for behavior change.

Perspectives

Historically the predominant approaches to the behavior of individuals in organizations have been internal in their orientation (Carroll and Tosi, 1977; Luthans and Kreitner, 1975; Weissenberg, 1971). Theorists, consultants, and managers have been urged to look within the individuals for the source of problems and solutions. We have attempted to identify individuals' needs, modify their satisfaction, change attitudes, and generally get beneath the surface. While this approach has legitimized the whole notion of looking at employees as people rather than as inanimate objects, it has also led us astray. In the rush to change attitudes, perceptions, and personalities, we have overlooked two important facts. The first of those is the behavior of the employee. We have sometimes acted as though changing attitudes is an end in itself, not a means to change behavior. In our rush to get to the deeper cause of problem behavior, we have often overlooked the behavior itself. It can also be argued that an employer has a right to expect certain kinds of performance and accomplishments from an employee. On the other hand, the employer does not have a right to expect certain kinds of internal attitudes, perceptions, and personality characteristics. In short, we can think of employment as buying a person's behavior but not the person.

A second perspective has been the role of the environment. We have often looked at behavior as somehow springing from within the individual. While the role of the environment in controlling behavior has often been acknowledged, it has somehow been deemphasized. The environment has been taken as a given. When performance is substandard, the blame falls on the individual and his or her attitudes or personality. This is unfortunate, for the environment clearly has a strong impact on behavior. Behavior occurs within a context. To attempt to remove that behavior from its context is a mistake. Both controlled research and the application of OBM to significant organizational problems indicates that changes in the environment can have a profound impact on improving the performance of groups and individuals. Further, the work environment is something that the employer has legitimate control over, whereas he or she has no claim to the employee's internal thoughts, feelings, perceptions, and attitudes.

OBM's primary focus is on the behavior of people and what they do, rather than who they are. This does not mean that OBM is unconcerned with people's satisfaction, perceptions, attitudes, or the like. The goals of OBM are to increase both productivity and satisfaction, not one at the cost of the other; it does not focus exclusively on internal events to the exclusion of performance. OBM also places a great deal of emphasis on the environment or the context in which behavior occurs. It recognizes that events that immediately precede behavior (antecedents) as well as events that follow behavior (consequences) have a profound effect on individual performance. While these perspectives may seem simple and straightforward, they are powerful in their simplicity. They have helped uncover basic principles of behavior, and they serve as a foundation for effective procedures for behavior change.

Methods for Assessment and Analysis

As helpful as perspectives (theory) may be, they do little unless they can be translated into action. Methodology is important in that it is the translation of a perspective into concrete action. Put another way, methodology is how one goes about assessing and actually analyzing the behavior of the individuals and groups. Not surprisingly, methodology is related to one's perspective. In many traditional approaches to organizational behavior, the methodology is based on surveys, questionnaires, and ratings. Large groups of individuals are surveyed about their attitudes, personality, expectations, perceptions, or the like. These data are then often subjected to statistical analysis to try to classify individuals as to the personality, likelihood of success, and so on. When a new technique is proposed, it is usually evaluated by looking at group comparisons. The new technique is used with one group and not with a second group. The person asking the question then looks for difference in the average between the two groups. The criterion for the importance of the difference is whether it is statistically significant rather than of important practical value. Differences between individuals are treated as error in the measurement system. The methods of assessment and analysis used in OBM differ from this pattern in two main respects.

First, OBM emphasizes the direct and ongoing measurement of actual behavior as it occurs in context. Let's take the example of wearing protective safety equipment to illustrate this point. Traditional methods may do things such as asking workers their attitude about safety, asking them to estimate how often they wear their safety equipment, asking the supervisors to rate them on safe performance, or the like. An OBM approach, by contrast, would be more likely to actually observe the workers during the performance of their duties to determine what proportion of the time they are actually wearing the required safety equipment. This observation would be done on an ongoing basis, not just a single occasion. In this way it would be possible to determine what the workers are actually doing and whether that changes over time. This does not imply that one might not also determine the workers' attitudes about safety, the supervisor's perspective, and so on. Rather it is to imply that the primary focus is on the behavior as it occurs in context.

Second, OBM differs in the type of methods used for evaluating the effects of programs. Here the focus is looking at how individuals change across time or how they are affected by a particular program or procedure. By combining these single-case designs with the continuous measurement described above, one can determine whether a particular program has the desired impact on the behavior (Komaki, 1977). There are at least two major types of designs. One allows for the introduction and subsequent withdrawal of a program after a stable baseline level of performance has been determined. The other design allows for the sequential introduction of programs across different individuals, groups, or kinds of behavior. These designs will be described in detail later in this volume. However, suffice it to say that they allow the manager to determine the effects of the program in a way that is both practical and logically sound. They also pay close attention to the differences in individual performance rather than treating them as "unwanted error" and focusing on the practical significance of changes rather than their statistical significance.

Techniques for Behavior Change

A final important contribution has been the techniques for behavior change that have been developed within OBM. Theoretical perspectives and refined methodology are of limited value if they don't ultimately result in effective techniques for improving performance. With this focus on behavior and the environmental factors that influence it, OBM has been particularly successful in developing performance improvement techniques. OBM has been closely associated with improvements in the techniques used for training new skills as well as in the ongoing performance of those skills. OBM has also led to the development of fairly specific techniques for self-management.

With its emphasis on the environment, it is not surprising to see that many of the techniques for behavior change involve changing some aspect of the work environment. These techniques can include changing what precedes behavior (antecedents) or what follows it (consequences). These changes may occur on a very individualized basis as in a self-management program or on a more systematic large-scale basis. Examples of these larger-scale techniques include performance feedback systems or incentive systems.

Many of the techniques may sound familiar. Managers often talk about giving people feedback or providing incentives. However, while the language is common, OBM offers more than a simple restatement of time-worn techniques. Because of the perspective and methodology, it allows the manager to be much more precise in knowing what kind of feedback to be delivered, when it should be delivered, in what form, how often, and to whom. It also guides the development of incentive systems with regard to when the incentives should be delivered, how large they should be, on what basis, and so forth. Importantly, because of the methodology for assessment and evaluation, the manager is also in a position to determine whether a behavior change technique is in fact working. The selection of techniques can be based on their proven effectiveness rather than their apparent plausibility or the persuasiveness of the person advocating the technique.

AREAS OF APPLICATION

OBM has been applied in a wide range of organizational settings, including businesses, industries, health care organizations, governmental units, social service agencies, schools, mental health institutions, and volunteer organizations. Within these settings it has also been applied to a wide range of problem areas. The purpose of the current section is to enumerate some of these. This effort should be viewed as illustrating the range of topics in which OBM has been applied rather than an exhaustive list of all possible applications.

Production-Task Completion

Probably the single largest area of application for OBM has been increasing worker performance or task completion. This trend is evident in both practitioners' surveys (Andrasik, McNamara, and Edlund, in press; Frederiksen and Lovett, 1980) and systematic literature reviews (Andrasik, 1979; Andrasik, Heimberg, and McNamara, 1981; Frederiksen and Johnson, 1981). The target of somehow improving either the quantity, timeliness, or quality of employee output cuts across virtually all organizational settings and virtually all intervention techniques. Examples include performance feedback and supervisory praise to improve factory worker output (Chandler, 1977; Emmert, 1978), financial incentives to increase seedling planting in the forest product industry (Yukl and Latham, 1975; Yukl et al., 1976), and monetary rewards to increase output in manufacturing facilities (Orpen, 1974). Social praise and monetary reinforcement have also been successfully employed to improve task completion in human service settings (Montegar, Reid, Madsen, and Ewell, 1977; Hollander and Plutchik, 1972; Pommer and Streedbeck, 1974). Given the consistency of improvement found across organizational settings, it does not seem unreasonable to conclude that OBM has wide applicability for performance improvement (Frederiksen and Johnson, 1981).

Training and Development

Principles of OBM have also had a heavy influence on how training is conducted. One of the most important trends has been the development of programmed instruction as an approach to training. Babb and Kopp (1978) argue that programmed instruction probably represents the single largest application of behavior modification principles to business settings. It has been used in a variety of America's largest corporations to teach a range of skills such as blueprint reading, basic electronics, office procedures, industrial safety, keypunch operation, computer programming, communications, statistics, management decision making, increased product knowledge, and sales. Programmed instruction involves breaking the material into small, discrete units of ascending difficulty. This allows for self-paced individualized instruction with frequent feedback and mastery of the material.

Another area where OBM has had an impact is in the social skills training. Examples of this training include providing feedback to a subordinate, handling interpersonal conflict, delegating authority, and interviewing (Eisler and Frederiksen, 1980; Goldstein and Sorcher, 1974). Here again, an OBM approach takes a basic skill and breaks it into its component parts. These component parts are then taught using a combination of background rationale and specific instructions, demonstrations or modeling of appropriate behavior, actual practice of the targeted behavior, and praise and feedback (sometimes employing videotape or audiotape replays). Although meager, the available research seems to support the efficacy of this approach (Frederiksen and Eisler, 1980; Kraut, 1976). Its acceptance also seems to be growing. Moses (1978) reports that over 10 thousand managers have been trained using this basic approach at the Bell Systems and General Electric alone.

Absenteeism and Tardiness

Reduction of absenteeism and tardiness represents another area where OBM has been used extensively. The procedures often involve some combination of rewards for attendance and disapproval or punishers for non-attenders. Some examples of these programs include the use of small monetary bonuses (Hermann, deMontes, Dominguez, Montes and Hopkins, 1973) or lottery incentive systems (Pedalino and Gamboa, 1974) to increase attendance in industrial work forces. One of the largest controlled studies was reported by Kempen and Hall (1977). This study involved 7500 production workers at two factories. Intervention included a two-pronged approach that both specified disciplinary action for excessive absences as well as installing a reinforcement program for good attendance. As attendance improved, workers could earn privileges such as freedom from punching the time clock, time off with pay, and the like. The results of this study indicated both improvement in attendance as well as acceptance by management and union employees.

Sales Management

The area of improving sales presents an interesting challenge. On one hand, some aspects of sales are not under control of the individual employee (e.g., economic conditions, nature of the product, pricing considerations). On the other hand, the behavior of the individual sales person is amenable to change. However, "sales behavior" can be difficult to accurately measure. These problems notwithstanding, OBM has made some important progress in the modification of sales-related behavior. Gupton and LeBow (1971) reported an early study designed to change the selling patterns of two part-time telephone solicitors. These solicitors had to sell both new and renewal service contracts. The intervention consisted of setting up a schedule in which the opportunity to sell renewal contracts was made contingent upon placing five new service calls. This contingency resulted in an increase of both types of sales.

Another approach has been to look at customer service behavior. In a recent study (Komaki, Blood and Holder, 1980), feedback and management recognition were used in a systematic way to increase friendliness in a fast food franchise. The authors specified what constituted friendliness (e.g., smiles at the appropriate time), and measurements were taken. The introduction of the technique resulted in a marked increase in friendliness in one area and a partial increase in another. A similar approach was used to improve several aspects of customer service behavior in a large department store setting (Brown, Malott, Dillon, and Keeps, 1980). Again the targeted behavior was defined and baseline measurements taken. A training program was first provided and found to result in only minimal increases in targeted behavior. However, when a behaviorally based feedback system was introduced, behavior showed marked improvement. These few examples certainly don't represent the last word in modifying sales behavior. However, they do stand in marked contrast to prevailing approaches that emphasize internal motivation, the selection of individuals who have "natural talent," and sales training.

Safety

Safety, or the reduction of accidents, also presents a difficult challenge. Accidents tend to occur at a relatively low frequency. However, when they do occur they can be associated with injury, death, or disability. Rather than focusing on accidents *per se*, OBM has generally focused on improving compliance with safe practices. There are a number of examples in the literature. Most have employed programs in which safe performances were specifically targeted, measured, and some sort of feedback or incentive provided for safe performance. The settings in which these programs have been used are diverse. They include a commercial bakery (Komaki, Barwick, and Scott, 1978); research laboratories (Sulzer-Azaroff, 1978); coal mines (Rhoton, 1980); manufacturing plants (Komaki, Heinzmann, and Lawson, 1980). In each of these diverse settings an OBM approach has been associated with either reduction in identifiable hazards or an increase in safe performance.

Conservation

In the era of rapidly accelerating energy costs, conservation takes on increasing importance. While there is clearly a role for technological in-

novations and capital expenditures in this area (e.g., improving insulation, streamlining manufacturing processes, developing more efficient power sources), there is also an important role for behavior change. It seems that the single most cost-effective way to reduce expenditures on energy-related cost is to promote changes in certain types of behavior patterns (Stobaugh and Yergin, 1979). It is in this area, the promotion of behavior change, that OBM has made its major contributions to conservation. Examples include feedback and incentives to modify driving in a way that produces increased fuel mileage in a trucking fleet (Runnion, Watson, and McWhorter, 1978) as well as the development of strategies that help people comfortably adapt to working in warmer or cooler environments (Winett, Hatcher, Leckliter, Ford, Fishback, and Riley, in press).

PROBLEMS AND PROSPECTS

Some Limitations

As the above sampling indicates, OBM is being applied to a wide range of problem areas. While these successes are indeed encouraging, OBM is not a panacea. It is subject to a number of constraints.

In the first place, OBM encounters the same kind of difficulties common to any type of organizational intervention. Even under the best of circumstances, it is not a simple matter to make a fundamental change in the way an organization is managed. The same kinds of constraints apply to techniques of a more limited scope. People are often reluctant to make changes in established routines. This is true even when the change might result in a more pleasant or productive work environment. Further, some of the changes might involve costs to specific individuals, and hence they may resist it. Overcoming these constraints to organizational change is a task faced by any kind of organizational intervention.

OBM also faces other constraints. Some of these relate to the language that is often used in OBM. Terms such as "control," "contingency," or "behavior modification," and concepts such as the systematic use of rewards and punishments may be threatening to some individuals. Similarly, some individuals raise questions regarding the ethics of using behavior modification techniques (Locke, 1977). These issues will be addressed in more detail later in the current volume.

Finally, OBM must be concerned about the choice of behavior selected for modification. Since behavior change programs may be expensive in both direct and indirect costs, it behooves the manager to select the objects of the change wisely. If a program is developed, it should be one that has a good likelihood of favorable return on investment. Fortunately, OBM is becoming more sophisticated in developing procedures for selecting appropriate behavior for modification (Gilbert, 1978). However, this remains a special concern for OBM, since the techniques are intended to change specific kinds of behavior.

On the Future

The development of OBM has been an evolutionary process. In the early stages its proponents were concerned with demonstrating that OBM had something to offer. Many of the early efforts could best be labeled demonstration projects. They tended to be on a relatively small scale and confined to an isolated problem (e.g., a difficult employee, an isolated production problem, or a group showing low attendance). When the problem had been identified, the task was to apply the principles and procedures of OBM to its solution. To a great extent, these early demonstration projects were remarkably successful (Andrasik, 1979; Frederiksen and Johnson, 1981; Luthans and Kreitner, 1975). Individuals were reporting that techniques based on OBM were cost-effective ways to modify important work-related behavior.

One can of course argue that there was an understandable tendency to only report successful efforts. Individuals are often reluctant to publicize mistakes and failures. Likewise professional and trade publications are not known for the dissemination of unsuccessful projects. On the other hand, surveys of OBM practitioners (Andrasik et al., in press, Frederiksen and Lovett, 1980) seemed to indicate that there were a good many successful or partially successful projects being conducted that never attained wide dissemination. Even if many techniques were not successful, it does not change the basic point that there is a growing body of systematic and objective documentation showing that OBM is an effective procedure for changing important work-related behavior. This trend stands in marked contrast to most of the literature on human resource management. While it is common for proponents of certain approaches to make claims about that approach's effectiveness, it is relatively rare to see such claims documented by a body of systematic case studies and scientific experiments.

The next logical step in the evolution of OBM is its extension to broader areas of organizational functioning. This too has been happening. A growing number of reports have appeared in the literature and popular press describing broader scale applications of OBM. These have included developing a behaviorally based system for managing the functioning of a multiplant textile manufacturing firm (Bourdon, 1978), reorganization of professional service delivery systems (Frederiksen, 1978; Turner and Lee, 1976a, 1976b), and the organization of a small manufacturing facility (Luthans and Schweizer, 1979). However, these are only the published examples of larger-scale intervention techniques involving the entire organization or at least a significant subunit of it. The survey data seem to indicate that these larger scale applications are more common than reported (Frederiksen and Lovett, 1980).

As OBM develops, it becomes necessary to integrate it with the entire functioning of the organization. This means that OBM must become part of strategic planning for the development and effective use of human resources. It must involve attention to all levels of the organization. It is not enough to simply have OBM used as an isolated procedure with lower-level organizational participants. It becomes increasingly necessary to *view OBM as the way the organization is managed* rather than an isolated technique that is used in specific situations. For it to function most effectively, the system must be interlocking. Line employees must be accountable to their supervisors, who are in turn accountable to successive management levels, all the way up to the chief operating officers. In short, OBM must become the way that a company is managed (Gilbert, 1978; Hall, 1980).

OBM is entering a new phase of its development. It has already compiled an impressive track record of successes in circumscribed situations. Additionally, the prospects for its expansion to broader areas of the organization seems excellent. However, it also faces a number of challenges. Just as other attempts to change organizations face resistances, so too does OBM. The installation of an OBM system of management requires the same kinds of talents and interpersonal skills as are required of individuals trying to install any other comparable approach to human resource management. However, the prospects do not seem bleak. OBM has a firm foundation upon which to build. This includes not only its theoretical and conceptual base, but more important, its useful, workable methodology and an arsenal of techniques that have already proven successful. And finally, there is the need. Few would argue that there is not room for improvement in our ability to manage human resources in a way that increases both productivity and the quality of working life.

SUMMARY

OBM is the application of the principles and techniques of behavior modification to the management of behavior in organizational settings. As such, it represents a convergence of the fields of organizational behavior and behavior modification. While the roots of OBM go back to developments in the early part of the century, its emergence as a separate field has only been within the last two decades. The available indications seem to show an ever-increasing rate of growth. The major contributions of OBM are threefold. First, it provides a theoretical perspective that focuses on the behavior of individuals (as opposed to unobservable thoughts and feelings) and how that behavior is affected by the environment. Second, it provides a methodology that focuses on the ongoing analysis of behavior as it actually occurs in organizational settings. Finally, it provides a series of techniques for behavior change that have already been demonstrated to be effective. OBM has begun to amass a track record of successful techniques in areas as diverse as production and task completion, training and development, absenteeism and tardiness, sales management, safety and conservation, to name a few. The field is not without its limitations. While it shares the problems inherent in any attempt to change the way organizations are managed, it also has some unique problems related to the language used to describe it, the selection of appropriate targets for change, and so on. Still, the future of OBM looks promising. While early efforts focused on limited demostration projects, there is a growing need to view OBM as an approach to the management of all human resources within an organization, rather than an isolated technique. At this point, OBM seems to be in a position to accept that challenge.

REFERENCES

Aldis, O. Of pigeons and men. *Harvard Business Review*, 1961, *39*, 59–63.

Andrasik, F. Organizational behavior modification in business settings: A methodological and content review. *Journal of Organizational Behavior Management*, 1979, *2*, 85–102.

Andrasik, F., Heimberg, J. S., and McNamara, J. R. Behavior modification of work and work-related problems. In M. Hersen, R. M. Eisler, and P. M. Miller (Eds.), *Progress in Behavior Modification*. New York: Academic Press, 1981, *11*, 118–161.

Andrasik, F., McNamara, J. R., and Edlund, S. R. Additional future directions for OBM. *Journal of Organizational Behavior Management* (in press).

At Emery Air Freight: Positive reinforcement boosts performance. *Organizational Dynamics,* Winter 1973, 41–50.

Babb, H. W., and Kopp, D. G. Applications of behavior modification in organizations: A review and critique. *Academy of Management Review*, 1978, *3*, 281–292.

Bourdon, R. D. A token economy application to management performance improvement. *Journal of Organizational Behavior Management*, 1977, *1*, 23–37.

Brown, M. G., Malott, R. W., Dillon, M. J., and Keeps, E. J. Improving customer service in a large department store through the use of training and feedback. *Journal of Organizational Behavior Management*, 1980, *2*, 251–266.

Brown, P. L., and Presbie, R. J. *Behavior modification in business, industry, and government*, 1976, Available from Behavior Improvement Associates, P.O. Box 296, New Paltz, New York 12561.

Carroll, S. J., and Tosi, H. L. *Organizational behavior*. Chicago: St. Clair Press, 1977.

Chandler, A. B. Decreasing negative comments and increasing performance of a shift supervisor. *Journal of Organizational Behavior Management*, 1977, *1*, 99–103.

Connellan, T. K. *How to improve human performance: Behaviorism in business and industry*. New York: Harper and Row, 1978.

Conversation with B. F. Skinner. *Organizational Dynamics*, 1973, *1*, 31–40.

Eisler, R. M., and Frederiksen, L. W. *Perfecting social skills: A guide to interpersonal behavior development*. New York: Plenum, 1980.

Emmert, G. D. Measuring the impact of group performance feedback vs. individual performance feedback in an industrial setting. *Journal of Organizational Behavior Management*, 1978, *1*, 134–14.

Franks, C. M. Behavior therapy and its Pavlovian origin: Review and perspectives. In C. M. Franks (Ed.), *Behavior therapy: Appraisal and status*. New York: McGraw-Hill, 1969.

Frederiksen, L. W. Behavioral reorganization of a professional service system. *Journal of Organizational Behavior Management*. 1978, *2*, 1–9.

Frederiksen, L. W., and Johnson, R. P. Organizational behavior management. In M. Hersen, R. Eisler, and P. Miller (Eds.), *Progress in Behavior Modification*. New York: Academic Press, 1981, *12*, 67–118.

Frederiksen, L. W., and Lovett, S. B. Inside organizational behavior management: Perspectives on an emerging field. *Journal of Organizational Behavior Management*, 1980, *2*, 193–203.

Gilbert, T. F. *Human competence: Engineering worthy performance*. New York: McGraw-Hill, 1978.

Gillen, R. W., and Heimberg, R. G. Social skills training for the job interview: Review and prospectus. In M. Hersen, R. M. Eisler, and P. M. Miller (Eds.), *Progress in Behavior Modification*. New York: Academic Press (in press).

Goldstein, A. P. and Sorcher, M. *Changing supervisor behavior*. New York: Pergamon, 1974.

Gupton, T., and LeBow, M.D. Behavior management in a large industrial firm. *Behavior Therapy*, 1971, *2*, 78–82.

Hall, B. L. Editorial. *Journal of Organizational Behavior Management*, 1980, *2*, 145–150.

Hamner, W. C., and Hamner E. P. Behavior modification and the bottom line. *Organizational Dynamics*, Spring 1976, 3–21.

Hermann, J. A., de Montes, A. I., Dominguez, B., Montes, F., and Hopkins, D. K. Effects of bonuses for punctuality on the tardiness of industrial workers. *Journal of Applied Behavior Analysis*, 1973, *6*, 563–570.

Hersen, M., Eisler, R. M., and Miller, P. M. Historical perspectives in behavior modification: Introductory comments. In M. Hersen, R. M. Eisler, and P. M. Miller (Eds.), *Progress in Behavior Modification* (Vol. 1). New York: Academic Press, 1975.

Herzberg, F. *Work and the nature of man*. New York: World Publishing, 1966.

Hollander, M. A., and Plutchik, R. A reinforcement program for psychiatric attendants. *Journal of Behavior Therapy and Experimental Psychiatry*, 1972, *3*, 297–300.

Kempen, R. W., and Hall, R. V. Reduction in industrial absenteeism: Results of a behavioral approach. *Journal of Organizational Behavior Management*, 1977, *1*, 1–21.

Komaki, J. Alternative evaluation strategies in work settings: Reversal and multiple-baseline designs. *Journal of Organizational Behavior Management*, 1977, *1*, 53–77.

Komaki, J., Barwick, K. D., and Scott, L. R. A behavioral approach to occupational safety: Pinpointing and reinforcing safety performance in a food manufacturing plant. *Journal of Applied Psychology*, 1978, *63*, 434–445.

Komaki, J., Blood, M. R., and Holder, D. Fostering friendliness in a fast foods franchise. *Journal of Organizational Behavior Management*, 1980, *2*, 151–164.

Komaki, J., Henzmann, A. T., and Lawson, L. Effect of training and feedback: Component analysis of a behavioral safety program. *Journal of Applied Psychology*, 1980, *65*, 261–270.

Kraut, A. I. Developing managerial skills via modeling techniques: Some positive research findings—A symposium. *Personnel Psychology*, 1976, *29*, 325–328.

Kreitner, R. PM—a new method of behavior change. *Business Horizons*, December 1975, 79–86.

Locke, E. A. The myths of behavior mod in organizations. *Academy of Management Review*, 1977, *2*, 543–553.

Luthans, F., and Kreitner, R. *Organizational behavior modification*. Glenview, IL: Scott, Foresman, 1975.

Luthans, F., Schewizer, J. OB Mod. in a small factory: How behavior modification techniques can improve total organizational performance. *Management Review*, September 1979, 43–50.

McGregor, D. M. *The human side of enterprise*. New York: McGraw-Hill, 1960.

Miller, L. M. *Behavior management: The new science or managing people at work*. New York: John Wiley and Sons, 1978.

Montegar, C. A., Reid, D. H., Madsen, C. H., and Ewell, M. D. Increasing institutional staff-to-resident interactions through inservice training and supervisor approval. *Behavior Therapy*, 1977, *8*, 533–540.

Moses, J. L. Behavior modeling for managers. *Human Factors*, 1978, *20*, 225–232.

Munsterberg, H. *Psychology and industrial efficiency*. New York: Houghton-Mifflin, 1913.

Nord, W. R. Beyond the teaching machine: The neglected area of operant conditioning in the theory and practice of management. *Organizational Behavior and Human Performance*, 1969, *4*, 375–401.

Orpen, C. The effect of reward contingencies on the job satisfaction-task performance relationship: An industrial experiment. *Psychology*, 1974, 9–14.

Pedalino, E., Gamboa, V. U. Behavior modification and absenteeism: Intervention in one industrial setting. *Journal of Applied Psychology*, 1974, *59*, 694–698.

Performance audit, feedback, and positive reinforcement. *Training and Development Journal*, November 1972, 8–13.

Pommer, D. A., and Streedbeck, D. Motivating staff performance in an operant learning program for children. *Journal of Applied Behavior Analysis*, 1974, *7*, 217–221.

Prue, D. M., Frederiksen, L. W., and Bacon, A. Organizational behavior management: An annotated bibliography. *Journal of Organizational Behavior Management*, 1978, *1*, 216–257.

Redd, W. H., Porterfield, A. L., and Anderson, B. L. *Behavior modification: Behavioral approaches to human problems.* New York: Random House, 1979.

Rhoton, W. W. A procedure to improve compliance with coal mine safety regulations. *Journal of Organizational Behavior Management*, 1980, *2*, 243–249.

Roethlisberger, F. J., and Dickson, W. J. *Management and the worker.* Cambridge, MA: Harvard University Press, 1939.

Runnion, A., Watson, J. O., McWhorter, J. Energy savings in interstate transportation through feedback and reinforcement. *Journal of Organizational Behavior Management*, 1978, *1*, 180–191.

Schneir, C. E. Behavior modification in management: A review and critique. *Academy of Management Journal*, 1974, *17*, 528–548.

Skinner, B. F. *Beyond freedom and dignity.* New York: Bantam, 1971.

Skinner, B. F. *Science and human behavior.* New York: Macmillan, 1953.

Skinner, B. F. *Walden Two.* New York: Macmillan, 1948.

Stobaugh, R., and Yergin, D. (Eds.) *Energy future: Report of the energy project at the Harvard Business School.* New York: Random House, 1979.

Sulzer-Azaroff, B. Behavioral ecology and accident prevention. *Journal of Organizational Behavior Management*, 1978, *2*, 11–44.

Turner, A. J., and Lee, W. E. Motivation through behavior modification, Part 1: The job contract. *Health Services Manager*, 1976a, *9*, 1–5.

Turner, A. J., and Lee, W. E. Motivation through behavior modification, Part 2: Evaluation. *Health Services Manager*, 1976b, *9*, 1–4.

Weissenberg, P. *Introduction to organizational behavior: A behavioral science approach to understanding organizations.* Scranton, OH: Educational Publishers, 1971.

Winett, R. A., Hatcher, J., Leckliter, I. Fort R., Fishback, J. F., and Riley, A. Modifying perceptions of comfort and electricity used for heating by social learning strategies: Residential field experiments. *ASHRAE Transactions*, (in press).

Yukl, G. A., and Lathma, G. P. Consequences of reinforcement schedules and incentive magnitudes for employee performance: Problems encountered in an industrial setting. *Journal of Applied Psychology*, 1975, *60*, 294–298.

Yukl, G. A., Latham, G. P., and Purcell, E. D. The effectiveness of performance incentives under continuous and variable ratio schedules of reinforcement. *Personnel Psychology*, 1976, *29*, 221–231.

2

Behavioral
Systems Analysis

JON E. KRAPFL

and

GLORIA GASPAROTTO

West Virginia University

This chapter is designed to explicate the general viewpoint from which the *Handbook of Organizational Behavior Management* was written. The overall purpose of this book is to bring the theory and perspective of behavioral psychology to bear on the problems of managing behavior in organizations. Before analyzing the various topics covered in this text from a behavioral viewpoint, the viewpoint will be discussed in sufficient detail to bring some continuity to chapters that follow.

Why should a behavioral point of view be adopted for a volume of this sort? One advantage is that this book seeks to be practical, objective, and results oriented rather than abstract, conceptual, or concerned with ivory-tower issues. Behavioral theory too is practical, objective, and results oriented. It is not characterized by a great deal of abstract reasoning nor by elaborate conceptual or theoretical structures. The behavioral perspective is an outgrowth of pragmatic philosophy, a decidedly American philosophy that was as important to the development of American business organization and productive capacity as to the development of a theory of behavior associated with a rigorous experimental method and careful scientific measurement and observation. As is the case with all pragmatic points of view, behavior theory changes with the times. The viewpoint is easily modified as data and scientific facts demand. More hypothetical theories tend to be more complex and are not so easily modified.

Second, the viewpoint of this book is scientific, and behavior analysis is a scientific theory. The principal feature of a scientific perspective is that it demands more than folklore or commonly accepted beliefs as the basic datum for the development of its position. Further, scientific viewpoints may be counter-intuitive. That is to say, scientific viewpoints may go beyond common sense in some specific and practical way. The theory of behavior analysis is consistent with this scientific point of view. Behavior theory has come out of a natural science tradition and helped to establish psychology as a scientific discipline.

Finally, the focus of this book is on people. Specifically, we are interested in the behavior of people in the organizational environment. Social organizations do not exist in the natural environment; they are a product of people's behavior. Whatever is done to develop, dissolve, or in any way change an organization is always done by people. It is the behavior of people that makes organizations change. Therefore, a theory of behavior is an appropriate perspective from which we can analyze organizations.

WHAT IS BEHAVIORAL SYSTEMS ANALYSIS?

The topic of this chapter, behavioral systems analysis, is a perspective shared by most of those contributing to this book. Behavioral systems analysis comes from a synthesis of the fields of behavior analysis and systems analysis. Certain features of each of these approaches have been incorporated into the behavioral systems analysis perspective. Although we will provide a more detailed and sophisticated definition of behavioral systems analysis later, the reader might find it useful to have a working definition while reading through the chapter. For now, we can define behavioral systems analysis as the analysis of behavior that occurs in complex and organized social environments. Certain characteristic features of behavioral systems analysis constitute a common perspective shared throughout the book. Among those features are the following.

First, there is a focal interest in behavior. As has been discussed previously, it is behavior that creates organizations, develops them, and changes them. When we look at behavior we are looking at the force that moves the organizational environment. Here, when we talk about behavior we are talking about any activity of the person. Ordinary common sense views of behavior usually include such activities as talking, running, eating, and drinking, but behavior as defined here includes such activities as thinking, deciding, and choosing.

In a behavioral model the focus is on behavior and not on phenomena likely to be related to behavior. Most organizational analyses concern themselves with phenomena presumed to exist and to be responsible for behavior such as attitudes, feelings, or mental states, of which behavior is assumed to be a product. Much of the research in organizational performance has to do not with target performance itself, but with people's reactions to that performance. Often data are collected on what people think good performance might be or on opinions about what might constitute good performance. The behaviorist would argue that it is often useful to collect such data, but that reports of attitudes should be analyzed as behavior, themselves. Given the lack of direct evidence to support the existence of internal cognitive phenomena, the behaviorist's point of view is that directly observable verbal responses are subject to control by the external environment in the same manner as are overt nonverbal responses. Thus overt behavior is the focus of a behavioral systems perspective.

The second focus of behavioral systems analysts is on the environment. Traditional concepts of environment most often include the physical environment and little else. The behavioral systems analyst's definition of environment is considerably more broad. To the behavioral systems analyst, the environment includes any thing or event with which the behavior might come in contact. For the behaviorist, the term "environment" includes not only such things as rocks, chairs, and buildings, temperature and weather conditions, but also the genetic environment that may define certain biological characteristics and capacities of the person, and influence the nature of its interaction with the external environment. Perhaps more important, the term environment includes the social environment, that is, the environment that consists of the behavior of all other people with whom an individual may come into contact. People, if not inherently social, are certainly heavily influenced by the behavior of other people. In fact the environment most often found to be of interest and importance in analyzing organizational performance is the environment that consists of social relations.

The third principal interest of the behavioral systems analyst is in functional analysis. Functional analysis means simply that we analyze a behavioral phenomenon in terms of its function in influencing the environment and in being influenced by that environment rather than in terms of its structure. When we analyze structure we measure things in terms of their physical characteristics, their height, their weight, their depth, temperature, or velocity. When we analyze phenomena functionally, we analyze them in terms of their effect or in terms of their relations to other phenomena. In a sense, this can be considered the analysis of purpose. Because we conduct analyses that are functional rather than structural, we must look at phenomena as they interact with one another. We cannot study phenomena in a static state or in a vacuum. For the behavioral systems analyst, behavior cannot be studied independently of its controlling environment. No assessment of environment is possible without a corresponding analysis of the behavior affected. When we conduct a functional analysis, we look at the ongoing flow of behavior as it occurs across time, and analyze it in terms of its relation to a changing environment. The effect that behavior has on the environment is to change it. Furthermore, the effect that the environment has on behavior is to change it. Behavior and environment are both phenomena in a continuous state of change. As behavior and environment change, they interact. The importance of their interaction is that they affect one another. In a functional analysis what we seek to understand is the relationship between changing behavior and changing environments.

What a system perspective adds to a behavioral point of view is basically an analysis of more complex behavior-environment relations. Behavioral systems analysis is a blend of behavior analysis and systems analysis perspectives in that the environment of interest for the behavioral systems analyst is generally a complex environment. In this book the organizational environment is of principal concern, and the behavior of interest is that which is controlled by that organizational environment. Further, it is not one or two kinds of behavior in the organizational environment that are of interest, but the behavior of many persons across relatively long periods of time in that environment. The behavior of one person in an organization serves as the controlling environment for the behavior of another person in the organization. For example, the behavior of a supervisor serves as part of the controlling environment for the behavior of an employee, and vice versa. Thus, in the behavioral systems analysis context, we study the behavior of many persons in a complex environment and analyze how combinations of behavior interact to make an organization function, develop, or change.

Finally, we should say what behavioral systems analysis is not. It is not behavior modification as applied to the individual case. Rather it is an extension of that technology to modify the maintaining environment. It is not thought control or mind control. It is not the study of the mind or the self. It is not the study of attitude or opinion. It is the application of a philosophical, theoretical, and technical body of knowledge to systems and organizational problems. Before further articulating this point of view, it will be useful to review the fields of systems analysis and behavior analysis in order to see what perspectives were merged into a behavioral systems viewpoint.

BEHAVIOR ANALYSIS

The term "behavior analysis" refers to analytic and technological practice based upon the psychological theory of behaviorism. Behaviorism is a natural scientific theory of behavior. Scientific approaches to other disciplines (e.g., physics, chemistry, and biology) have proved fruitful in understanding those subject matters. Behavioral theorists, most notably B.F. Skinner (1953), contend that studying human behavior within a natural science framework will provide us with levels of understanding similar to those of other natural sciences. Within this framework the behavior of organisms is seen as a subject matter amenable to empirical (scientific) investigation. Much of behavior is observable and thus can be subjected to systematic observation and manipulation, the fundamental characteristic of scientific investigation. A wide range of basic research accomplished in well-controlled laboratory settings is the foundation of behavioral theory. In addition, and of most relevance to this book, many of the principles derived from such basic research have been applied to everyday, nonlaboratory settings, where they have been determined to hold true.

The most general tenet of behavior analytic theory is that the frequency of occurrence of behavior is a function of: (1) the consequences of past occurrences of similar behavior, and (2) the similarity of the prevailing environment to that which exists when certain kinds of behavior were followed by particular consequences. Thus each individual's current behavior patterns are a result of his or her unique history, in combination with currently existing environmental conditions. In this way we are all unique, as we have all experienced a lifetime of unique interactions with our environment.

Certainly these propositions may seem to some as mere simplistic common sense. Behavior analysts, however, distinguish themselves from those of other psychological persuasions in that they attempt to use the basic tenet of behaviorism to analyze and extrapolate upon a far wider range of psychological phenomena than would those others. For example, the phenomena that cognitive psychologists call "thinking," "remembering," "attitude formation," or "feeling" are viewed by many behaviorists as complex forms of behavior, the most important aspect of which are as observable as any other type of behavior (see Skinner, 1969, for a detailed analysis of these points).

Behavior analysts have found a certain model useful in depicting the basic unit of analysis from a behavioral perspective. Figure 2-1 illustrates the basic model.

The three-term contingency relationship illustrated in the model includes a response, or unit of behavior, with certain defined characteristics. The nature of events immediately preceding and immmediately following behavior (i.e., stimuli and consequences) determine whether there is a high or low probability that behavior of the same class will again occur. In the presence of a particular set of environmental stimulus conditions—*antecedent stimuli*—a response of certain topographical characteristics

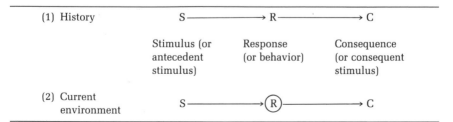

FIGURE 2-1.   Essential components of the most basic unit of analysis—the contingency relationship—from a behavioral perspective. ® is the response under analysis for purposes of this illustration.

may occur with increasing frequency over previous rates. We may then say that the past consequences of an occurrence of that response when stimulus conditions were present have been *reinforcing consequences*. In contrast, if behavior occurs with decreasing frequencies in the presence of a particular stimulus condition, we may say that past consequences under similar conditions have been *punishing consequences*. It is important to note that we may not define a consequent stimulus condition as a reinforcing or punishing one except in retrospect. It is also important, for the sake of precise analysis, to understand that neither antecedent nor consequent stimuli are static conditions but *stimulus changes* (Michael, 1975). For example, a certain consequent stimulus may on one occasion contribute to future occurrence of the immediately preceding behavior (i.e., a reinforcing consequence) and on another occasion result in fewer occurrences of that behavior (i.e., a punishing consequence). What is essential to know is the nature of historical conditions existing prior to the consequent stimulus. For instance, a certain frequency of praise for an accomplishment is likely to be reinforcing for staff performance if it represents an increasing frequency over past levels of praise. On the other hand, the same frequency may be punishing if it represents a decrease over past levels of praise. The precision with which a response is defined should depend upon the precision of the analysis required. A fine-grained breakdown of the response class—a specified category of behaviors which are topographically similar—contributes to a more precise identification of the numerous controlling variables (i.e., stimuli and consequences) involved. The various aspects of the environment, or the controlling variables, which influence the response class of "managing" may best be understood if managing is broken down into its component response classes (e.g., specifying staff performance, praising accomplishments).

For example, in any given organizational setting, the administration may direct middle managers to specify staff performance as part of their management duties. This direction, generally a verbal instruction, may be considered an antecedent stimulus for the response class of specifying staff performance. Any type of approval by the administration for having specified staff performance, then, might be considered a consequent stimulus for that response class.

On the other hand, the stimuli and consequences for the manager's praising of staff accomplishments may be very different from those that are associated with specifying staff performance. For example, the antecedent stimulus most frequently preceding the praising of staff accomplishments might come from the staff members themselves. The staff member might ask "How did I do on the job yesterday?" Following some words of praise by the manager, the staff member might respond with a "Thank you." The "Thank you" is a consequent stimulus for the manager's praising of accomplishments. These different contingency analyses for the two separate response classes (i.e., specifying staff performance, praising accomplishments) are illustrated in Figure 2-2. The point is that if an anal-

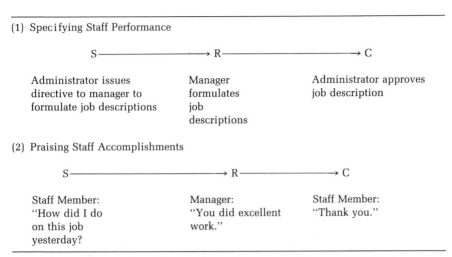

FIGURE 2-2. Contingency analyses for two types of managerial behavior.

ysis of the variables controlling managing or any other grossly specified response class are to be identified, that response class must be broken down into finer-grained components if it is suspected that different stimuli and consequences have been associated with different components of that larger class of behavior.

To the extent that a class of behavior occurs in the presence of one set of stimulus conditions and not in the presence of another set of dissimilar stimulus conditions, we may say that the process of *stimulus discrimination* has occurred. For example, an employee may be more diligent at work in the presence of one manager than in the presence of another. When a class of behavior occurs in the presence of stimulus conditions under which that class of behavior has *not* previously been followed by reinforcing consequences, we say that *stimulus generalization* has occurred. For example, an employee may work diligently in the presence of a new supervisor, even though the employee has had no previous interactions with that supervisor. Generalization, therefore, is a lack of discrimination. We might say that the employee assumes that he or she will be treated in a similar way by both supervisors, even though the employee has had no history of reinforcement in the presence of the new supervisor. The degree of discrimination or generalization of a class of behavior has been shown to be dependent upon the similarity of one set of antecedent stimulus conditions to those conditions existing when behavior has been followed by reinforcing consequences. In the above example, generalization may have occurred because the employee has been reinforced in the past for diligent work in the presence of those individuals introduced as supervisors. The same relationships hold for punishing consequences. That is, the greater the similarity of current antecedent stimulus conditions to those under which a particular behavior was previously punished, the less likely that behavior will occur under present conditions. The following is a list of definitions for some of the basic concepts of behavior analysis:

Term	Definition
Response (or behavior)	Any action of any living organism.
Antecedent stimulus (or stimulus)	Any set of changes in the environment (internal or external to the organism) that immediately precedes a given response.
Consequent stimulus (or consequence)	Any set of changes in the environment (internal or external to the organism) that immediately follow a given response.
Reinforcing consequences	Any consequent stimulus that *increases* the future probability of occurrence of a response that it has immediately followed.
Punishing consequence	Any consequent stimulus that *decreases* the future probability of occurrence of a response which it has immediately followed.
Stimulus discrimination (or discrimination)	The phenomenon of a class of responses occurring in the presence of one set of stimuli and not in the presence of another set of dissimilar stimuli.
Stimulus generalization (or generalization)	The phenomenon of a class of responses occurring in the presence of a set of stimuli under which that class of responses has not previously been reinforced.

The basic unit of analysis—the contingency relationship—illustrates the functional nature of a behavioral analysis. That is, behavior is discussed not only in terms of its topographical features (its physical structure) but also in terms of its history, i.e., its relationship to past and present antecedent and consequent stimulus conditions associated with behavior. All events can be defined in terms of their structure and function. For example, a truck can be described structurally as a vehicle with four or more wheels, a steering wheel, motor, and bed for putting things in. Functionally, a truck is a vehicle for moving something from one location to another.

Behavior is defined topographically in terms of what it looks like, just as with the truck. To know the function of behavior we look to its relationship to the environment, i.e., to past and present antecedent and consequent stimulus conditions. To define function we must see what the behavior does or accomplishes and under what conditions it occurs. Attention to the structure of behavior is important in determining how a particular behavior developed, insofar as we must define a behavior according to its structure before we are able to determine specific conditions under which responses of that structure occur. In a functional analysis, the important question is not *what* behavior occurs at any given moment, but *how* it came to occur. If the eventual objective of a psychological analysis is to modify behavior, we must understand something about how that behavior came about in the first place. The importance of a functional analysis is that the relationship between a class of behavior and its antecedent and consequent stimulus conditions, or controlling variables, may then be modified in order to produce desirable changes in the frequency of behavior.

SYSTEMS ANALYSIS

Systems analysis is a term that has frequently been identified with military and industrial operations research, which used such language to describe their applied technology. The creation of RAND and similar nonprofit corporations that study strategies and tactical problems of the military was a result of the merger between computer technology and systems theory. In his book *The Systems Approach*, Churchman (1968) pointed out how scientists began to use something called a systems approach as their perspective was forced to become more broad. Early attempts at systems analysis were designed to allow for the most logical and coherent decision making as it affected a wider and wider group. In time the military began to see the advantages of the approach, and it was originally adopted by the Department of Defense and later on by other departments of government and industry as well. The systems approach that was being adopted was simply a way of thinking about problems in terms of the interdependency of parts and how they worked in concert to achieve an objective. Although its origins were in biology, systems analysis has received most of its emphasis from the field of engineering. The systems approach has been extensively used to provide a way of thinking about hardware systems such as missile systems, ship building, computer systems, and so forth. Much less attention has been focused on the human components of systems. More recently, organizations have become explicitly concerned with the role of the manager and executive in relation to the total organizational structure and function. One consequence of this greater concern has been the overuse of the language and methods of hardware systems in dealing with social problems. The use of traditional systems terms in conceptualizing organizational problems involving human behavior helps perpetuate the belief that concepts from engineering will prove to be beneficial when applied to situations far beyond their original intended usage. To the behaviorist, systems language seems needlessly obscure. Nevertheless, many of the concepts of systems have proven useful in the development of behavioral systems analysis.

While the study of systems and the process of systems analysis make important contributions to behavioral systems analysis, the systems analysis model is not altogether synchronous with a behavioral systems viewpoint. Systems analysis will be reviewed here in order to illustrate the similarity between systems analysis and behavior analysis and, further, to reveal those features of systems analysis that have been incorporated into a behavioral systems viewpoint.

To begin, two definitions are necessary. Separate definitions are required for "system" and for "systems analysis." "System" is a term with a very broad definition. Webster (1977) defines it as "a regularly interacting or interdependent group of items forming a unified whole." This broad definition is then followed by specific definitions for a variety of systems. For example, gravitational systems are defined as interacting bodies influenced by related forces and thermodynamic systems as assemblages of substances that tend toward equilibrium. Perhaps the most important definition offered for our purposes is that which defines systems as an organization that forms a network to serve a common purpose.

"Systems analysis" is defined as the act, process, or profession of studying an activity in order to define its goals and purposes and to discover operations and procedures for accomplishing them most efficiently. The critical terms are "network" and "purpose." If a social system consists of a network or requires that something be organized, it clearly implies that more than one person is involved. Thus a clear feature of systems analysis is that it is an analysis that involves the behavior of more than one person. Second, the notion of common purpose or common objective means that all persons involved in a network are to some extent under the control of the same reinforcers, or put another way, after the same effects. An overly simplified analysis could be troublesome here, and more on the issue of common purpose will be discussed in the following section on behavioral systems analysis.

There are additional concepts in systems thinking that will assist in the understanding of a general systems perspective and in knowing how systems function. A subunit within a system that has all the characteristics of a system itself and could be analyzed as a system is called a subsystem. Whether a unit is analyzed as a system or a subsystem depends on the question raised. For example, if the purpose of our analysis is to determine the efficiency of the operation of a manufacturing firm, a manufacturing facility within the firm becomes a subsystem. However, if our focus is on the improvement of the efficiency of a single manufacturing facility, that plant would now be called a system. It can be seen, therefore, that definitions in systems are functional as they were in the earlier section on behavior analysis. We cannot define events or phenomena in systems in terms of an analysis of their structure, but must do so in terms of the functional relations between the event or phenomena to be defined and all other events that relate to the question we ask or to the goal which we seek.

A related concept in systems analysis is the concept of the boundary. A boundary is that specification of systems that distinguishes it from other systems. When one crosses a boundary, one leaves the system in question and enters another system. Sometimes the boundaries can be physically defined. However, sometimes they defy physical definition, as would be the case in the law enforcement system, e.g., a conglomerate of many governmental agencies. A boundary is nothing more than a specification of what constitutes a system and what does not constitute a system. The boundary of a system is a matter of convenience. It is a specification that defines the scope of an analysis.

Input is an additional concept to be considered in any systems analysis. The inputs are all those factors that enter a system, such as dollars, people, clients, and so on. The input consists of the resources that are somehow acted upon or transformed into the output of a system.

Process is that element in a system that is responsible for changing resources into output. For example, in a manufacturing system budget, raw materials are converted into finished products.

The *output* in a system is what the system produces. When the basic resources entering a system in the form of input are processed or transformed by the system, what emerges is output. In a manufacturing operation, employees and machinery, facilities, and operating capital work on raw material and transform it into widgets. The widgets are the systems output.

Inputs and outputs always cross systems boundaries. The resources used by the system, whether it be raw material in a manufacturing plant or clients in a service oriented operation, cross the system's boundary and enter as input into the system. Similarly, when the system processes a client or transforms the raw material, the changed client or changed raw material is sent out of the system into another system as output.

If we used only the concepts we have discussed so far in defining systems operations, we would end up with static systems. But most systems are not static systems; rather they are dynamic systems. Dynamic systems are systems that operate on themselves to correct errors or to increase efficiency. This self-corrective feature of systems is known as feedback. Feedback consists of information that indicates how well the system or some specific subsystem is working. The feedback can come from several sources. Feedback from the processing subsystem will tell you something about the efficiency or perhaps even the cost efficiency of the processing or transformation subsystem. Feedback from the output subsystem provides information on the quality of the output or on the extent or quality of the objectives achieved by the system. If the feedback indicates that the system or subsystem is performing appropriately, it is termed positive feedback. If the feedback indicates that the system is in error or that some change is necessary, it is called negative feedback. Feedback in turn is directed to the processing component and input so that necessary changes may be made to produce acceptable outputs.

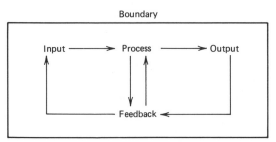

FIGURE 2-3.   Basic systems model.

Figure 2-3 illustrates the basic systems model. The concepts of systems boundaries, input, output, process, and feedback are incorporated, and function as described above.

Another important feature of systems is permeability. Systems are often described as open or closed systems. When we speak of a system as open or closed, we are generally speaking of the ease with which the system boundary can be crossed or the extent to which stimuli external to the system, as defined by our boundary, control what is going on in a system. A corporation that is part of a larger conglomerate is likely to be more permeable in the sense that the conglomerate can control policies of the corporation.

BEHAVIOR SYSTEMS ANALYSIS

Historically, behavior analysts have focused most of their research and applications in a limited number of areas for some very practical reasons. Basic research in the analysis of behavior has relied heavily on the availability of well-controlled laboratory settings. Nonhuman organisms have been employed in order to limit the extent of control over behavior of antecedent and consequent stimulus conditions other than those under investigation. Behavior having topographically simple characteristics have been the focus of attention (e.g., the keypeck of a pigeon or the level pull of a human). Consequently, the generality of the effects of certain contingency relationship—relationships between the individual and environment—to situations involving more complex responses would be uncertain without explicit testing. The area of applied behavior analysis developed in response to this need.

Applied behavior analysis refers to the use of basic principles arising from a functional analysis to solve important societal problems. While early work in this area focused upon problems that would lend themselves to the generality testing of a specific principle, e.g., a relatively well-controlled environment such as that of a mental institution patient, the topic of an increasing amount of applied research is guided by the importance of the problem. As more complex problems are undertaken, principles are often combined to produce a "package" of procedures aimed at solving the problem of concern. Referenced literature consists most often of other applied behavior analytic research, rather than literature in the experimental analysis of behavior. Thus the generality of principles defined in the laboratory has already been shown in many applied settings. Generality across different applied settings, determined by the importance of a problem, is currently the main focus of applied behavior analysis. There is an increasing rate of shift from the laboratory to more complex settings. In addition to generality being demonstrated, these settings are also developing new and interesting technologies appropriate to the setting under investigation.

An important advantage of the aforementioned shift in the field of behavior analysis is that the demands for demonstrations of the utility of basic principles are satisfied to a greater extent than before. The danger of such an approach is that it is more difficult to retain a precise behavioral perspective when dealing with complex contingency relationships. It is easy for the behavior analyst in such a situation to be influenced by nonbehavioral concepts that have developed from nonbehavioral approaches to the problems under investigation. For example, the terms "prompt" and "feedback" to describe complex sets of antecedent and consequent stimulus conditions may lead the behavior analyst to forego a thorough analysis of the nature of those conditions. A prompt or feedback in one setting may be distinctly dissimilar in terms of its functional relationship with certain behavior from a prompt or feedback in other settings. Developing a set of principles based upon the effect of prompts or feedbacks, then, is likely to be a futile attempt. Rather an attempt to clearly describe the functional components—antecedent and consequent stimuli—involved in prompts and feedback in each setting is required.

As the generality of a number of basic principles has been shown across a great number of human settings, behavior analysts have come to involve themselves in settings of greater social complexity. The solutions to problems in these settings require analyses of large numbers of contingency relationships, as the behavioral units to be modified are numerous. In complex organizational systems, the danger of shifting away from a behavioral approach is greater than in more well-controlled settings. Nevertheless, the importance of the problems to be solved merits attention by behavior analysts.

The term "behavioral systems analysis" has come to refer to the practice of identifying relationships among complex sets of social contingencies. The traditional systems approach has been directed toward this very task. The uniqueness of a behavioral systems approach, however, lies in the emphasis upon an analysis of individuals in identifying variables that control organizational behavior. A behavioral systems analysis perspective focuses upon an analysis of how the behavior of individuals combines to form a social organization. A melding of the two approaches is the objective in behavioral systems analysis.

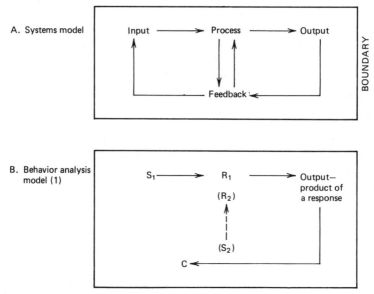

FIGURE 2-4. One interpretation of the correspondence between the systems model and the basic model of behavior analysis. The basic behavior analytic model has been supplemented to better illustrate its relationship to a systems model.

Figure 2-4 illustrates the correspondence between the behavior analysis and systems models for the purpose of illustrating the functional nature of both approaches. By functional, again we mean the viewpoint that neither systems processing nor the behavior of an individual may be thoroughly studied without considering the relationships to those events by which they are affected.

In this comparison, antecedent stimulus condition may be compared with the inputs of a system. The processing of inputs may best be related to those responses of an individual that are followed by a change in antecedent conditions from prevailing conditions. The consequences of behavior may be related to feedback in a systems model.

Finally, the output in a systems model can be compared with the product of behavior, or the changes in the environment that occur when some behavior is acted out. While the product of behavior is not included as a separate component of the behavior analysis model, it is implied in the term response (R). Certain consequences may be seen as an important component of a functional analysis to the extent that they consistently follow the emission of a response. If a particular consequence occurs *only if* a particular response is emitted, we say that the consequence is *contingent* upon the emission of a response. Contingent consequences occur not in response to behavior, but in response to the environmental changes that occur when behavior is acted out. We might say therefore that contingent consequences are those that occur only when a certain response occurs.

There are two main differences between a systems model and the model of behavior analysis currently in use, i.e., S $\longrightarrow$ R $\longrightarrow$ C. First, the behavior analytic model does not include a loop to illustrate the point that consequent stimuli themselves serve as antecedent stimuli for future behavior. The consequences of one response may be considered as inputs for a second response. This loop is included in Figure 2-4 to indicate the point at which it would occur if made explicit by the model. This function is considered implicit by most behavior analysts, and is a minor difference between the two models.

A second and very important difference between models is illustrated by the fact that a direct link between feedback and input included in the systems model is absent in the behavior analytic model. From a behavioral standpoint, this aspect of the systems model is inappropriate for an analysis of individual behavior. No change in input as a function of feedback may exist without an additional response on the part of an individual. For example, changes in raw material to be processed must be made only by a response on the part of a supervisor. Thus an additional behavioral contingency analysis would be required to determine why the supervisor alters the systems input. As can be seen, the behavior analysis model is a more refined model, which specifies what must be done with people to change the system. In this sense the system model and the behavior analysis model may be viewed as dealing with different dimensions of organizational functioning. While the systems model deals with an analysis of the overall functioning of an organization, the behavior analysis model focuses on the behavior of individuals within each component of the systems model. Many individual contingencies (the components of a behavior analysis model) may exist within each component of the systems model. A behavioral systems perspective holds that both levels of analysis are necessary, and in fact complementary.

In a behavioral systems analysis, the response class of concern is complex and involves the behavior of more than one individual. While each component behavior of the response class may be independently analyzed, it is often functional to take a more molar view at first. For example, the analyst might first ask whether there exists any reinforcing consequences for good managerial behavior in general, before engaging in an analysis of fine-grained components of managerial behavior. In order to determine which individual behaviors to facilitate, the analyst must determine whether conditions in the larger social system will maintain such behavior. For example, it is probably useless to train managers to identify poor staff performance if administrators will refuse to support managers in remedying that performance (e.g., reprimanding a poor performer).

From a behavioral systems perspective, it is critical to identify the general objective toward which all members of a social system are likely to be working. That is, the common reinforcers or common purpose must be determined. If an organizational environment can be structured so as to increase the personal benefits to each organizational member for working toward the common purpose of the organization, then that organization will be a stable, self-corrective one. Certainly the common purpose itself may be modifiable if more individual reinforcers are available under the new system than were available under the old system. A profit-sharing program, for example, may bring in line some of the personal goals of each worker (i.e., to earn a living) with the formal objective of the organization (i.e., to make money by producing a product).

Some traditional analytic concepts of social interaction (e.g., cooperation and competition) may be useful in developing the behavioral systems analysis perspective if viewed from a behavior analytic rather than cognitive framework. We might view cooperative behavior, for example, as behavior that must be explicitly reinforced rather than behavior occuring as a result of "attitude" changes or innate tendencies alone. Likewise some traditional practices in the area of organizational management may be useful if analyzed from a behavioral and functional approach (e.g., planning, decision making, development of information systems, policy making). Planning may be analyzed in a manner similar to a behavior analytic view of self-control. According to this analysis, planning involves structuring the current environment so that certain responses to future situations will likely occur. In planning, certain objectives are specified so that future behavior will be emitted in response to those objectives rather than only to stimulus conditions that would provoke actions having more short-term reinforcing consequences. A behavioral perspective then implies that much control over organizational behavior is in the hands of the manager and administrator. Successful systems intervention may thus be achieved in areas in which other analytic approaches have not been so successful.

Conclusion

This chapter is an attempt to illustrate the benefits of an integration of a traditional behavior analysis perspective with a traditional systems analysis approach. It is hoped that both those with backgrounds in behavior analysis and systems analysis will benefit from exposure to additional, not alternative, viewpoints. For the behavior analyst, it is hoped that the main benefit will be a concern with analyses of those environments maintaining behavioral changes that are a product of direct intervention. Unless the larger system is considered, those changes may be short-lived, and the benefits of a behavioral approach will not be seen. For the systems analyst, the adoption of an empirical and functional approach to analyzing human performance may lead to more productive techniques at the systems level. The behavior analytic point of view certainly conflicts with long held assumptions regarding the nature of human behavior, in that it emphasizes the role of an individual's history of interaction with the environment. Given the past successes of this perspective, however, it seems worthwhile to consider its application to problems of complex human interaction.

SUMMARY

The present chapter suggests that a behavioral systems analysis perspective is appropriate for analyzing and modifying organizational management practices. As behavioral systems analysis is an integration of behavioral theory and systems theory, the main concepts of each of these theories first is described. Second, those concepts borrowed from each theory to comprise a behavioral systems analysis perspective are identified.

In behavioral theory, a focus on the observable behavior of individuals is emphasized, in contrast to a focus on attitudes and feelings and other unobservable states of mind as the important topics of analysis. With a focus on observable behavior, the effects of intervention techniques may be assessed within a scientific framework. Manipulable events (the antecedents and consequences of behavior) are seen as the most important variables affecting the occurrence of behavior in various situations. Thus behavioral theory is a theory about the individual.

Systems theory is based on the proposition that no system or organization can be successfully analyzed without also analyzing the interaction of its subsystems. The way in which an input subsystem affects the processing subsystem is an example of such an analysis. Systems theory then is a theory about organizations.

The functional nature of both behavioral and systems theories is their most common element. A functional approach is one in which the behavior of individuals or the processing system within organizations is analyzed in terms of its relationship to other events with which behavior or processing systems come into contact.

Behavioral systems analysis borrows the emphasis on the individual from behavioral theory, and the emphasis on organizations from systems theory. The setting in which a behavioral systems perspective is appropriate is in organizations that are complex because many individuals are involved, rather than one in which primarily mechanical systems are involved. Social or behavioral systems cannot be sufficiently analyzed without considering the manner in which collections of individuals affect and are affected by other individuals within an organization. The behavior of interest is observable, and so scientific methods of the analysis of behavior within social systems are borrowed from behavioral theory.

REFERENCES

Churchman, C. West. *The systems approach.* New York: Dell Publishing Co., 1968.

Michael, J. Positive and negative reinforcement, a distinction that is no longer necessary; or a better way to talk about bad things. *Behaviorism*, 1975, *3*, 33–44.

Skinner, B.F. *About behaviorism.* New York: Alfred A. Knopf, 1974. *Webster's new collegiate dictionary. Springfield, MA; G. & C. Merriam Co.,* 1977.

Skinner, B.F. *Contingencies of reinforcement: A theoretical analysis.* Englewood Cliffs, NJ: Prentice-Hall, 1969.

Skinner, B.F. *Science and human behavior.* New York: Macmillan, 1953.

Skinner, B.F. *Verbal behavior.* New York: Appleton-Century-Crofts, 1957.

3

Leadership, Supervision, and Behavioral Control: Perspectives from an Experimental Analysis

W. E. SCOTT, JR.
Indiana University

and

PHILIP M. PODSAKOFF
The Ohio State University

Persons appointed to leadership positions have always been held accountable for the behavior of their work groups. But aside from the formal assignment and good wishes, little has been offered in the way of useful advice or training. Indeed it has only been recently that we have recognized that leadership is behavior that could be analyzed, described, and developed.

Much of our early leadership research was dominated by variations of the "great man" theory (Carlyle, 1841), which assumed that effective leaders were those who possessed certain unique characteristics or traits that distinguished them from nonleaders or ineffective leaders. Trait theories naturally gave rise to numerous studies in which one trait after another was examined, but the net return from this extensive research effort[1] has not been encouraging. To be sure, some correlations between trait mea-

---

[1]Although it is doubtful that a complete account of this effort has been compiled, in two reviews Stogdill (1948, 1974) references nearly 300 traits studies.

sures and indexes of leadership effectiveness have been found. But Gibb (1947) and Stogdill (1974), among others, have concluded that no one trait or combination of traits has been found to consistently distinguish leaders from nonleaders.

Perhaps it is just as well. Traits are presumed to be enduring if not innate characteristics of individuals, more generally viewed as causes of behavior rather than behavior itself. In the unlikely event that a pattern of traits had been found to distinguish effective leaders from all others, we would neither have been moved to discover what it is that leaders do when they direct or otherwise effectively control the behavior of others nor to attempt to *develop* leadership effectiveness.

The poor return from trait studies led some theorists to conclude that situational variables had to be taken into account, though most did not suggest that traits, whatever they might be, were unimportant. Rather it was proposed that the leader's style[2] must match the setting, if the would-be leader is to be effective. Situational variables that were suggested as important in the outcome of this matching process included but were not limited to the nature of the tasks performed by group members, the ability, training, and prior experiences of group members, the position power of the leader, and the structure of the organization.

Situational theories are obviously more complex than trait theories since, at a minimum, they suggest that both traits (or styles) and a wide variety of situational factors must be taken into account. But it is not merely their complexity that has been criticized. They too have accomplished very little in the way of identifying specific acts, practices, and methods that might have a significant impact on the behavior of group members in a given situation or in all situations.

The shortcomings of trait and situational approaches to the study of leadership have led some to despair. McCall (1976) concluded that "after 40 years of accumulation, our mountain of evidence about leadership seems to offer few clear-cut facts." Janda (1960, p. 347), after surveying the study of leadership in sociology and social psychology, was equally pessimistic in concluding that "these disciplines have distinguished themselves more by accumulating *studies* of leadership than by accumulating *knowledge* of leadership."

There is reason to be more optimistic. Though our earlier theories did in fact turn our attention away from what leaders actually do, it is possible that something useful can be gleaned from this literature. Traits at least imply behavior, and if one goes beyond the trait names, culling and reinterpreting as necessary, one can find some clarification of effective leader behavior in our trait studies. Situational theorists, on the other hand, reminded us, if nothing else, that environmental variables must be taken into account if we are to provide a comprehensive treatment of leadership. Thus it is reasonable to suppose that our earlier theories gave rise to the

[2]"Style" was most often conceived as an enduring predisposition to behave in a given though ill-defined way. As such, styles differ very little from traits.

notion that "leadership is behavior which makes a difference in the be-havior of others" (Bowers and Seashore, 1966).

LEADERSHIP AS BEHAVIOR

Bowers and Seashore were not the first to conceive of leadership as be-havior. Even as trait studies were being conducted, Bogardus (1928) con-cluded that leadership could be fruitfully viewed as "the creation and setting forth of exceptional behavioral patterns in such a way that others respond to them." Sometime later Hemphill (1949) also defined leadership as "the behavior of an individual while he is directing group activities." The idea did not immediately catch on, possibly for two reasons. First, there was widespread objection to the implication that leaders are those who *control* the behavior of others, and more generally, to the notion that human behavior can be controlled. We preferred to think of leaders as those who guided or influenced the behavior of others through inspiration and persuasion.[3] A second reason was that an experimental analysis of human behavior was still in its infancy. It is unlikely that the notion of leadership as behavior would be regarded as important if there was also no convincing evidence that human behavior in general was amenable to a scientific analysis.

We now recognize of course that human behavior is susceptible to a scientific analysis, and that we have come a long way in analyzing it. Therefore, the conceptualization of leadership as behavior that makes a difference in the behavior of others is an idea whose time has come. While many still prefer to limit the term leader to those who do *not* employ coercive methods, it is widely recognized that effective leaders exercise a great deal of control over the behavior of others. It is also clear that leadership, as a kind of human behavior, can be accounted for just as we account for other classes of human behavior. That is to say, we can study it, come to understand the circumstances under which it arises and is maintained, and ultimately to describe its more effective forms. The anal-ysis is far from complete, but it is fair to state that we have advanced well beyond the vague and sometimes useless rules of thumb of yesteryear.

AN OVERVIEW OF BEHAVIOR PRINCIPLES

Before turning to leader behavior in particular, we must review the prin-ciples that have evolved from the experimental analysis of behavior in general. These principles in the form of descriptions of the functional relations between behavior and environmental events provide, as we shall see, a reasonably coherent account of leadership. But one can also derive from them some invaluable suggestions as to how leaders should behave if they are to be effective.

---

[3]When we carefully examine such terms as "inspiration" and "persuasion," controlling practices are revealed, though they appear to be in more palatable forms.

Respondent Behavior

Human behavior, like infrahuman behavior, falls into two broad classes. The first to be discussed is respondent or phylogenic behavior. The human organism comes with a ready-made physiology, which is particularly sensitive to certain classes of stimuli. When those stimuli occur, behavior classified as respondent will be automatically *elicited*.

We must not define the respondent repertoire too narrowly. We are all familiar with the automatic respondents such as salivation, but human organisms exhibit other types such as species-typical approach and consummatory responses and withdrawal and defensive reactions. Examples of the former are the visual tracking and the sucking response, while the so-called startle response is an example of the latter. Another respondent pattern is not readily observed without instrumentation. And for want of a better term, we shall call them psychoneural respondents or patterns of respondent activity observed in various structures that comprise the central nervous system. It has been found, for example, that a wide variety of stimulus events will elicit responses in the reticular arousal system and hypothalamus when initially presented. Activity in the reticular arousal system may be described by the human adult as a feeling of alertness when a moderate level has been elicited, as boredom when occurring at a low level, and as feelings of tension or anxiety if environmental events have elicited a high level of arousal. Respondent activity elicited in certain portions of the hypothalamus may sometimes be described as pleasant or as a feeling of satisfaction, while activity in other portions of the hypothalamus is sometimes described as unpleasant or painful. Needless to say, psychoneural respondents figure importantly in discussions of emotions such as joy, elation, satisfaction, frustration, anger, and rage.

As we have noted, respondent behavior is automatically elicited by specific features of the environment when they are first introduced or encountered. But repeated presentations of, or continuous exposure to, those events will elicit less and less of the respondent pattern that was elicited when the stimulus event was first introduced.

When a stimulus event that for any reason does not elicit respondent behavior is paired with one that does, the formerly neutral stimulus will come to elicit a portion of that respondent pattern. This classical conditioning is the method by which additional stimulus events gain control over respondent behavior during the lifetime of an organism.

There has been a tendency to relegate respondent behavior to a position of minor importance in human affairs. But as we shall see, respondent behavior cannot be ignored if we are to achieve a comprehensive understanding of human behavior, whether it be that of the leader or the led.

Operant Behavior

The second class of behavior is referred to as operant or ontogenic behavior. Unlike respondent behavior, operant behavior produces changes in the environment and is particularly sensitive to those changes. That is to say, the environmental effects generated by an operant determine the form of that operant and the probability that it will occur again. The relations between operant behavior and its consequences have been studied under a wide variety of conditions with both infrahuman and human subjects. Descriptions of those relationships in their most basic form are given below.

Principle of Positive Reinforcement.   If, in a given setting, an operant of a given topography is followed by a stimulus consequence identified as a positive reinforcer, there will be an increase in the probability that operants of that topography will occur again in that setting. The reinforcement contingency may be depicted symbolically as follows:

$$Ss : Rx \equiv Sc+$$

where Ss = the ambient stimulus setting
  : = sets the occasion for
  Rx = the designated operant
  $\equiv$ = is followed by or produces
  $Sc+$ = a positive reinforcing stimulus (or reward)

Principle of Extinction.   If, in a given setting, an Rx of a given topography is followed by a reduction in, the withdrawal of, or the absence of a positive reinforcer, there will be a decrease in the probability that Rx's of that topography will occur again in that setting. Symbolically,

$$Ss : Rx \equiv \overline{Sc+}$$

where the only new term, $\overline{Sc+}$ = a reduction in, withdrawal of, or absence of a positive reinforcer.

Principle of Punishment.   If, in a given setting, an Rx of a given topography is followed by a stimulus consequence identified as a negative reinforcer, there will be a decrease in the probability that Rx's of that topography will occur again in that setting. Symbolically,

$$Ss : Rx \equiv Sc-$$

where $Sc-$ = a negative reinforcing stimulus (a "punitive" or aversive stimulus)

Principle of Negative Reinforcement.   If, in a given setting, an Rx of a given topography is followed by a reduction in, the withdrawal of or absence of a negative reinforcer, there will be an increase in the probability that Rx's of that topography will occur again in that setting. Symbolically,

$$Ss : Rx \equiv \overline{Sc-}$$

where $\overline{Sc-}$ = a reduction in, the withdrawal of, or absence of a negative reinforcer.

Descriptions of relations in this form, like all empirical generalizations, leave out many details that must be added if the principles are not to be misunderstood. Obviously not all of them can be taken up here, but to provide some of the more basic examples, the extinction principle does not indicate the manner in which Rx was strengthened in the first place. Perhaps there is no need to state that it was strengthened by contingent applications of the very Sc+ that is now withdrawn, but the manner in which this was accomplished is important. If only a few operants of a given topography are reinforced on an intermittent schedule, many more operants will occur during extinction than will occur if the same number of responses were reinforced on a continuous schedule. Moreover, the rate of decline does not always show a predictably simple pattern. In fact, the rate of Rx often increases before declining and it is also quite likely that other responses, both operant and respondent, will be observed after the Sc+ has been withdrawn.

In a similar fashion, the punishment principle does not indicate how Rx was strengthened in the first place, nor does it indicate that the rate of decline will differ when the Rx has been strengthened by applications of the negative reinforcement principle as contrasted with the positive reinforcement principle. It seems likely that the effect of Sc-ms on Rx will differ in the two instances, but in neither case is a simple decline likely to be observed. In fact some radical behaviorists hold that the effect of a contingent Sc− is merely a temporary suppression of Rx rather than a permanent reduction in its rate. There can be no doubt that there is at least a momentary (and often an abrupt) reduction in the frequency of Rx to zero, but some attribute this effect to the fact that an Sc− *elicits* respondent behavior (freezing, crouching, and other species-typical avoidance and defensive reactions) that are incompatible with Rx. When the Sc− is withdrawn, therefore, the Rx is predicted to bounce back, and of course it does on some occasions. Others have advanced the hypothesis that the more longlasting effects of an Sc− are due to the development and reinforcement of incompatible escape and avoidance operants. The Sc− is correctly assumed to be classically paired with features of the setting in which it occurs, and operants incompatible with the punished Rx are then reinforced by the reduction or elimination of those classically conditioned Sc−'s. This "avoidance theory of punishment" also allows for the recovery of Rx and thus stands in opposition to the notion that a contingent Sc− decreases the probability of Rx just as a contingent Sc+ increases its probability. Since operants incompatible with the punished Rx avoid the Sc−, the classically conditioned Sc−'s undergo extinction. The incompatible operants are thereby weakened, and the punished Rx is predicted to emerge again, conceivably at full strength. No doubt something like this does happen on occasion, but the explanation cannot account for the fact that under some circumstances a contingent Sc− produces a rapid and, it appears, permanent reduction in Rx, not merely to baseline but to zero. Thus the issue of whether the effect of a contingent Sc− is simply opposite to that of a contingent Sc+ cannot be easily resolved. We are quite inclined to believe that the validity of the punishment principle remains intact, but in the meantime it is clear that setting factors have to be taken into account before we can accurately predict the effects of a contingent Sc− on a given Rx.

Eliciting Properties of Reinforcing Events

The principles of operant behavior in their unelaborated form also do not tell us how to identify reinforcing events before the fact. One could simply try out stimulus events of all sorts and develop a catalog of those that were found to effect operant responses, and we have been doing just that. But we have also begun to realize that events that serve to reinforce operant behavior, human and otherwise, have something in common. In fact any stimulus event that serves as a reinforcer has also been found to elicit a constellation of *respondents* including psychoneural responses (arousal activity and activity in the pleasure and punishment centers of hypothalamus), concomittant autonomic responses such as changes in salivation, heart and respiratory rates, and sweat gland activity, and species-typical approach and consummatory responses or escape and defensive respondents. These three types of respondents do not vary together in some fixed pattern, and in fact a stimulus may serve as a powerful reinforcer, though it does not elicit respondent behavior that can be easily observed at the periphery of the body. But we can be certain that a reinforcing event will elicit respondent behavior, and for that reason we must add another detail to our basic principles. Thus we have:

$$Ss : Rx \equiv Sc \rightarrow r$$
where r refers to the respondent(s) elicited by (→) the Sc.

The addition of the fourth term has several important ramifications. The most obvious one is that when an operant (Rx) is followed by a reinforcing event (Sc), certain features of the setting (Ss) will be effectively paired with the Sc. For that reason various features of the Ss will come to elicit some portion of the respondent pattern (r) elicited by the Sc. For example, if the behavior (or the results of the behavior) of a group member is especially reinforcing for the leader, the behavior of that group member and other features of the setting will come to elicit respondents in the leader that could be described as feelings of satisfaction, admiration, or attraction toward the group member. If the leader in turn administers positive consequences to the group member, the leader's presence will elicit the same sort of respondent reactions in the group member. Conversely, if the group member's operants or the results of his or her operants are aversive to the leader, the mere presence of the group member and other features of the setting will come to elicit respondents in the leader that could be described as tension, anger, and dislike of that group member. The leader will not readily approach the group member and may show a tendency to turn away from, avoid, or show hostility to him or her, though the latter behavior is likely to be learned operant behavior rather than elicited respondent behavior. If the leader administers aversive events (negative reinforcers or punishment) to the group member, then the leader may be one who is avoided and who will otherwise elicit the same pattern of respondents in that group member. (An effective leader will be required to administer punitive consequences on occasion, but as we shall note, this can be accomplished without establishing strong or longlasting respondent reactions such as tension, anger, or avoidance.)

The conjunction of behavioral and environmental events we have just described may lead one to the conclusion that features of the setting, including the presence of others, come to elicit conditioned respondents that serve as "causes" of operant behavior. Laymen and scientists alike have from time to time proposed that satisfaction or attitudes cause performance. However, we know that is not the case. Conditioned respondent behavior has been observed to occur after and during operant behavior as well as before it occurs. But the fact that conditioned respondents are merely collateral responses does not mean that important interactions do not occur. Respondent behavior elicited by reinforcing stimuli or by features of the setting in which those stimuli are introduced may facilitate or be perfectly compatible with ongoing operant behavior. On the other hand, respondent behavior, conditioned or otherwise, may be so prominent as to disrupt or intrude upon a given operant and much of the individual's operant repertoire, particularly in those settings in which a powerful negative reinforcer has been applied.

Antecedent Stimulus Control

There is yet one other detail to be supplied before an analysis of leadership can be undertaken. The principles of operant behavior in their unelaborated form also do not indicate that operant behavior is importantly affected by specifiable *antecedent* events as well as by those that come after it. But the operant behavior of both leaders and other group members is clearly controlled by stimulus events that precede it. They are sometimes difficult to spot, and it is of course true that a given operant may be under the control of multiple stimulus events, but we can usually spot them if we look hard enough.

The control of operant behavior by antecedent stimuli arises as a consequence of conditioning. The most fundamental statement one can make about antecedent stimulus control is that when an operant (Rx) of a given form or topography is followed by a reinforcing event (Sc) in a given setting (Ss), some feature or features of the setting gain a measure of control over the Rx. We refer to the controlling feature as a discriminative stimulus or S_D, and evidence for its controlling effect is found in the observation that when the S_D is presented, the Rx occurs or is *evoked*. However, the control exerted by discriminative stimuli over operant behavior is distinguishable from that exercised by prior stimuli over respondents. Under some circumstances, the occurrence of the S_D virtually guarantees the appearance of the operant, but for many reasons, the S_D does not always appear as coercive as the antecedent stimulus in the respondent case. It is therefore said that the S_D increases the probability that the operant will occur, but if prior conditioning hasn't been complete, the probability may be less than 1.00.

Our studies of the development of stimulus control have shown that operant behavior can be brought under the exclusive control of very subtle features of the environment. It has also been demonstrated that where the position of the S_D is varied, the behaving organism eventually learns to "scan" or otherwise investigate the setting until it produces (sees, hears, or encounters) the S_D, which then evokes the operant that is subsequently reinforced. When, for example, the lowly cat can only gain access to food through a red door, and the position of that door is moved to various locations, the cat will first scan the setting until its scanning operants have produced the red door. The pigeon whose pecking behavior has been reinforced only when it pecks a key under the one light (of a series of lights) that is flickering will eventually attend to the lights and nothing else in the setting. It will also be observed to scan or orient its visual receptors toward first one light and then the other, until one begins to flicker.

Although we did not recognize it immediately, the study of the development of stimulus control was also the study of problem solving operants. When we alter the contingencies so that behavior previously reinforced in the presence of a given stimulus is no longer reinforced (pecking at a key that had been flickering but is no longer flickering), we pose a problem for the behaving organism. And when the pigeon subsequently learns to behave so as to produce an S_D that evokes reinforced behavior, it has learned to solve the problem. Human beings acquire basic problem-solving operants in the same manner. Scanning, turning and looking, listening, and so on are prototypical problem-solving operants that are under the control of altering or novel settings and that produce S_D's. If the S_D then evokes an operant that is reinforced, the problem is resolved.

But the human organism is capable of much more. A class of S_D's of awesome significance in human affairs are verbal stimuli (auditory or visual) in the form of words, sentences, or propositions. From shortly after birth on, most parents not only attempt to teach the child how to speak (the shaping of a verbal operant repertoire), they also attempt to bring the child's developing nonverbal operant behavior under the control of verbal stimuli. A classic example is "come to Daddy," which initially serves as the controlling S_D for the behavior of crawling or otherwise approaching the male parent. "Go to your room," "button your coat," "look," "run," and "pick up your toys" are further examples of verbal stimuli that come to serve as S_D's. Later, when the child's nonverbal operants are brought under the control of its own self-produced verbal stimuli, he or she then has the capability of solving its own problems. When a large verbal operant repertoire has been shaped and when much of the child's nonverbal behavior has been brought under the control of verbal stimuli, the child is capable of being instructed and of instructing himself or herself. In the latter case, it is simply a matter of behaving so as to produce additional S_D's (in this case, verbal), which then serve to evoke solution operants.

Self-controlling operants of this type may easily become covert, and indeed they most often occur at the covert level. Another observer cannot readily observe them, and in fact the behaver himself or herself may neither observe nor be able to describe them. This is why there is currently so much mystery surrounding the operant behavior we commonly refer to as "thinking" and problem solving. But just because it is not readily observed does not mean that it is ruled out in an experimental analysis of leadership. Leaders will of course be faced with many problems, as will their group members. When, e.g., a leader is confronted with a group member whose behavior has been dysfunctional, and the leader behavior evoked in that setting has proved unsuccessful in modifying the group member's behavior, the leader may seek advice from a variety of sources. Seeking advice may be nothing more or less than engaging in verbal operant behavior ("Can you tell me what to do") or by consulting a book of this sort. The behavior of seeking advice produces verbal S_D's evoking leader behavior that proves to be effective in changing the behavior of the recalcitrant group member.

Organizational leaders often solve group member problems simply by describing behavior that is or may be effective in that setting. When the leader also has control over consequences that are reinforcing for a group member, the leader's description is usually called a "command" or a "directive." When the leader has no control over the consequences, it is likely to be called "advice." In either case, the leader behaves so as to produce verbal S_D's, which may serve to control the behavior of a group member. And like all S_D's, they may quickly lose their effectiveness in evoking behavior when important reinforcing consequences ($Sc+$ or $\overline{Sc-}$) do not occur.

The above principles and their corollaries obviously provide us with important suggestions for leading effectively, but they also serve us in another way. When we recognize leadership for what it is—behavior that makes a difference in the behavior of others—we also see that leadership itself can be accounted for by the same principles that govern other classes of human operant behavior. Leadership operants, like other classes of operants, are shaped and maintained by their consequences. They are also brought under the control of (evoked by) various features of the organizational setting. When, e.g., leaders are appointed rather than emergent, several features of the formal designation may serve as S_D's for leader operant behavior. The formal designation may include a job description, policy statements, and other types of written or verbal instructions that describe or imply the behavior of both the leader *and* group members. If the instructions are specific with respect to the behavior of the appointed leader, then we have some basis for predicting the leader's behavior. But in the typical case, the instructions that may serve as S_D's are either incomplete or vague. Therefore the appointed leader is "left to his own devices," as we say.

Whether emergent or appointed, many leader acts eventually come under the control of S_D's in the form of the behavior of group members. Initially the presence and behavior of group members will evoke leader behavior described or implied in instructions and other operants conditioned in previous social settings. As interaction continues, however, the leader's behavior comes under the more precise control of the behavior of members comprising the present group. For example, unproductive or dysfunctional behavior on the part of a group member may evoke leader operants in the form of "corrective action." Group member behavior "above and beyond the call of duty" may serve as an S_D for leader operants in the form of delivery of praise, recognition, or other reinforcing events.

A variety of nonbehavioral stimuli may act as S_D's that control or evoke leader operants. The *environmental effects* of a group member's behavior rather than the behavior itself may serve as S_D's for leader operants. A flawed product may evoke leader expressions of criticism or encouragement to do better, whereas output that consistently meets specification might evoke leader expressions of appreciation and promises of other rewards.

Leaders will inevitably encounter a variety of complex contingencies that may evoke multiple but incompatible operants (one is "torn between doing this or doing that"), operants that fail to produce reinforcement ("now what do I do"), and respondent behavior sometimes described as frustration, anger, or depression. Various features of the problem setting then come to serve as S_D's for a variety of problem-solving operants in the form of "reviewing the circumstances," consulting superiors and "experts," and other behavior traditionally described as thinking, problem solving, and decision making. This behavior in turn produces additional verbal S_D's that, though they may be covert, serve to evoke more effective leader behavior.

Leader behavior is strengthened and maintained by a variety of reinforcing consequences, the most fundamental of which is the behavior of group members or the environmental effects of their behavior. (We are reminded here that stimulus events that serve as reinforcers *may* also serve as S_D's evoking other operants, but the dual effect is not inevitable.) Changes in group member behavior in the form of increased or sustained high levels of productivity as well as reductions in dysfunctional group member behavior are powerful reinforcers of any leader operants that produce those effects.

Another class of reinforcing events for leader operants is provided by group members. When the leader has been effective in directing or otherwise strengthening group member behavior that is consistently reinforced, they may in turn provide added reinforcement for that leader. Recognition dinners, certificates, special celebrations honoring the leader, gifts, and other expressions of appreciation are sometimes bestowed upon leaders by those who have been led effectively.

A third class of reinforcing events are those extrinsic reinforcers provided by the leader's superiors. Appointed organizational leaders are "held accountable for results," which is to say that their own leaders typically reinforce them with recognition, pay increases, bonuses, and advancement to higher level positions. These reinforcing events, and the contingencies implied, are quite powerful, so powerful in fact that the leader must be careful that they do not cause trouble. Appointed leaders are frequently reinforced by their own superiors not for developing a strong group but for getting the work done at the lowest possible cost. When leaders are also reinforced for conserving resources, they may apply less positive reinforcement than they should, granting only small and infrequent pay raises or none at all, failing to order and provide necessary tools or supplies, or reverting to punitive practices.

Turning now to leadership operants themselves, we find that even the trait literature is helpful. Stogdill (1974, pp. 35–156) concluded that effective leaders are observed to be more active, persistent, talkative, and able to maintain a high rate of physical activity. But merely being active is not of course sufficient. The trait literature suggests that only certain classes of leader behavior will prove to be effective in influencing the behavior of others. Characterizations of effective leaders as "showing a long duration of verbal excitation" and as "verbally fluent or expressive" suggest that a very large class of leader operants are comprised of verbal responses that serve as S_D's for the behavior of group members. As we have noted, it is altogether possible to control the behavior of others simply by describing or clarifying the relationship between their behavior and its reinforcing consequences, even though the leader has little control over the consequences. This type of controlling practice, however, is more certain if the leader also has control over reinforcing consequences and is therefore able to make certain that reinforcing events follow the behavior that is evoked by those descriptions.

The characterizations of leaders as "socially expansive," "sensitive and insightful," "tactfully considerate of others" and as those who "sustain interaction with most members of a group" implies that the effective leader's stimulus control practices are widely directed in the group. However, stimulus control cannot be maintained unless important consequences follow the behavior evoked. For that reason, the effectiveness of the leader's stimulus control practices depends upon the nature and scheduling of reinforcing events contingent upon group member behavior. An important class of leader behavior therefore produces or mediates reinforcing events for group members.

Finally, trait descriptions of leaders as "knowledgeable," "able to diagnose situations," and as "keenly alert to the surrounding environment" suggest that effective leaders monitor their environment and engage in a variety of problem-solving operants when problems arise or are anticipated.

SOME PRESCRIPTIONS FOR EFFECTIVE LEADERSHIP

Trait descriptions provide some important clues about the behavior of effective leaders. But the behavior of effective leaders needs to be described more precisely. In what follows, we attempt to provide a more comprehensive description of leadership operants, and as the reader will note, most of our prescriptions are in the form of applications of the behavioral principles discussed above.

The Specification of Group Member Operants

Collections of individuals come together and begin to behave "co-operantly" for one primary reason: By behaving in concert, they can produce reinforcing consequences that far exceed the sum of the consequences that can be produced if each behaved independently (Skinner, 1953, p. 312). As groups form and become successful in this regard, the role behavior of each member emerges and becomes more precisely determined by the prevailing reinforcement contingencies. But this process takes a long time, and in any case, the unanalyzed contingencies may shape and strengthen behavior, which is by no means the most effective in maximizing the group's success. The behavior of the emergent leader in these cases is interesting as well as informative. By virtue of their "superior knowledge" of the behavioral requirements, they respond differentially to the behavior of the other group members, attempting to modify ineffective forms and promoting the development of the more effective forms.

This means, among other things, that effective leaders are able to identify and specify the kinds of subordinate role behavior that are likely to maximize the group's effectiveness. Whether emergent or appointed, leaders who do not respond differentially to variations in subordinate behavior cannot effectively strengthen the more appropriate forms and may indeed reinforce inadequate or dysfunctional subordinate behavior.

The identification of effective subordinate operants is relatively straightforward in a *simple* group, in which the role behavior of each member is the same or very similar. It is even more straightforward when the appointed leader has had the opportunity to acquire the requisite behavior through "experience" or formal training or both. However, it becomes more complicated in the case of a *complex* group, in which the role behavior of each group member may be different in some respects from that of every other member. In this case, leaders who have been appointed from the ranks have a significant advantage if they have had the opportunity to acquire the different operants required of each member.

Under these circumstances, the reinforcing practices of the leader are likely to be under the control of the behavior of each subordinate as they carry out their roles. But it still remains for the leader to *describe* the behavior of each subordinate if they are to train new members, to direct the behavior of subordinates, and to appropriately reinforce the new effective forms. In this regard a job analysis is very helpful. Job analyses may be accomplished by the leader or by a staff expert, but in either case the end result is a verbal description of each subordinate's primary role behavior which then serves as a guide for training or otherwise strengthening and maintaining that behavior.

All is not lost if the appointed leader is unable to specify the primary role behavior of each subordinate. Under these circumstances, the leader's reinforcing behavior can be under the control of "results" or the products of each subordinate's behavior. A supervisor can, e.g., reinforce the secretary who types letters that are consistently error-free, or criticize him or her when they are not. The leader may thus strengthen effective forms of typing behavior and punish ineffective forms, though it may be impossible for him to specify or model effective forms. Nevertheless, the leader remains at a serious disadvantage when things go wrong, unless he or she delegates the function of developing and strengthening effective typing behavior to others in the group. There is nothing wrong with this procedure, so long as it is recognized that the appointed leader is then a leader of leaders and now must specify, direct, and maintain *their* behavior. Ultimately, therefore, the leader who wishes to be effective cannot avoid the responsibility of analyzing, specifying, and responding differentially to subordinate behavior.

The behavior of group members should not be defined too narrowly. Katz (1964) has pointed out that behavior other than that required in the primary role are essential if the group is to remain successful. A cohesive group is one in which interpersonal relationships are mutually reinforcing. This condition can be brought about when group members sustain and reinforce the behavior of each other, provide aid to others when they encounter difficulties, and promote the development of more effective forms of co-operant behavior. Such behavior is rarely if ever specified in the description of primary role behaviors, but as Katz notes, it is the very life blood of an effective group. The effective leader cannot legislate such behavior and may not formally specify it, but he or she should be able to recognize its various forms and to powerfully reinforce it when it occurs, if not to evoke or encourage it through instruction.

The task of determining and clarifying the behavior of subordinate group members is a continuing process. Once behavior has been specified, developed, and maintained by the leader's reinforcing practices, they become standard forms consistently displayed in the group setting. But every human adult comes to the group setting with a different prior reinforcement history, and for that reason the prevailing contingencies do not always have the same behavioral effects. Variations in standard forms are often observed, and some may prove to be more effective, in which case they then become specified as the desirable form as the process continues. The prevailing contingencies may also change, and behavior once effective must then be replaced by operants that will meet the requirements of the new contingencies. Effective leaders strive to anticipate such changes when possible, but in any event, they are required to determine and specify ever more clearly the new, more effective forms.

It is not the case that leaders must perform this function unilaterally. On the contrary, they need all the help they can get, including that which may come from group members themselves. Thus a class of co-operant behavior that may be specified by the leader that is important for group effectiveness might be described as the behavior of experimentation. The leader identifies some of the basic forms of experimentation, then encourages subordinates other than new members to study or observe their surroundings, to systematically vary their behavior while noting the effects, or to otherwise think about and suggest alternative approaches (behavior) that might prove more effective.

Finally, the behavior of determining and controlling their own behavior can itself be specified and then effectively promoted by the leader. Group members are often able to behave effectively, though that behavior has not been identified through experimentation or specified by either the leader or the subordinate. In such cases the leader and subordinate may sit down and specify goals or objectives to be met while leaving the manner (the behavior) in which those goals are to be achieved in the hands of the subordinate. Needless to say, it is important that the leader consistently reinforce subordinates when the goals are met. In doing so, effective subordinate behavior, while not specified nor possibly observed, is nevertheless strengthened. This may be the only approach available to the leader who cannot, for one reason or another, identify, model, or describe the behavior required. Again, however, the leader in these circumstances is not as effective as he or she could be, for when the objectives are not realized, the leader is in no position to evoke and promote behavior effective in achieving those goals.

Selection Decision Making

Whatever the origin of the group, its membership will almost certainly change over time. Some members will leave the group for higher level positions in other groups or to seek membership in other groups, some may suffer major illnesses or death, and some may retire. Thus, leaders are faced with the necessity of recruiting and selecting new group members periodically.

If the leader was required to shape the role behavior of a new member from ground zero, replacement would be a problem of monumental proportions. Many and perhaps most roles require behavior that can only be shaped in a step-by-step fashion by conditioning procedures that would require months if not years to administer. If the group is to survive, the only alternative is to seek out human beings whose reinforcement histories have been such that at least some of the operant behavior required for effective role performance has already been shaped and brought under the control of verbal stimuli. Then it is a matter of evoking and sequencing the operants in their approximate forms through instruction and improving their skill properties through appropriate reinforcement.

However, selection is still a complicated and important process. It is by no means the case that all human beings are equally capable of acquiring the behavior required in a given role. We have found that early conditioning treatments importantly determine the rate at which the nervous system develops after birth, so that even if we could assume an intact physiology at the time of birth, the child might not fully benefit from the later exposure to parental and educational reinforcement contingencies. And of course the developing child might never be exposed to the contingencies responsible for shaping those operants. Human adults therefore show wide variations in those special operant repertoires that are often called aptitudes or special abilities and that may be required for effective role performance. Whether these operants can be shaped at maturity is still an open question, but our research has indicated that they change very little over the lifetime of the human adult. And in any event, it is impossible for leaders to design and administer the extensive conditioning procedures that only *might* develop those operant repertoires.

The leader therefore is confronted with the problem of accurately discriminating between those applicants who are likely to behave effectively in a given role after reasonable exposure and those who will fail to do so. One apparent way to resolve this problem is simply to expose applicants to the prevailing contingencies and observe their behavior for some period of time. If effective behavior is evoked and sustained, the new member is granted permanent membership status. If not, he or she is rejected. Thus we can see that in this case the behavior of discriminating is merely delayed, and while this procedure may be necessary on occasion, it is undesirable when it becomes customary. Group effectiveness is always impaired during the trial period, and those who subsequently fail and are rejected may be devastated.

A much more desirable approach is to attempt to discriminate before the fact. The behavior involved in making these discriminations is complex and never perfectly accurate, but in general the leader or other group members gather extensive information about a prospect that serves as S_D's evoking a decision to invite the applicant to become a member or not.

Standard procedures facilitating this behavior have evolved and are reasonably useful when the information thus procured is relevant or valid. Application blanks upon which applicants may describe their prior behavioral (work) histories and educational treatments can be useful. Structured interviews in which the leader or staff specialist obtain and record descriptions of other facets of the applicant's prior reinforcement history have also been applied with some success. Psychological tests can be especially useful when it is ascertained that they are reliable measures of those special operant repertoires that are required for effective performance.

The leader may delegate some responsibility for selection decision making to a specialized subgroup. In the larger formal organizations, e.g., one is likely to find that a personnel staff has been appointed to develop and maintain contact with individuals who may be prospects for group membership. They also develop and administer procedures for selecting group members and study the validity or effectiveness of these procedures. An effective leader, however, always plays an important role in this process, and may in fact be more capable of making accurate discriminations than anyone else.

Training and Orientation

Most individuals bring a large number and variety of kinds of behavior with them to the organization when they join it. If the selection decision making procedures employed by the leader are reasonably valid, much of the behavior required in the work setting will have been shaped and brought under the control of verbal instructions. But most functional operants will not be strong in the new setting, or if evoked by features of the group setting, they will not occur in the proper sequence nor in the most effective forms. Organizational leaders will therefore be required to evoke approximations of the required operants through modeling and verbal instructions, and to enhance the skill properties of such operants through the careful reinforcement of ever-closer approximations of the final form. This is typically accomplished by means of on-the-job training and on occasion by means of formalized classroom procedures.

Training is a process of establishing skilled behavior that is functional to the organization now or at a future time. When effective, the consequences of training produce many special advantages to the leader and other group members. Training can convert a newly hired individual into a useful, productive group member who contributes to the effectiveness of the group and the organization as a whole. Moreover, training prepares group members to perform more effectively on their tasks and therefore increases the probability that they will maximize their reinforcement through prolonged group membership. Finally, because training not only results in the evocation of functional group member operants but also in the specification of the conditions under which these operants are appropriate, it releases the leader from continually having to watch over his or her subordinates in order to insure they will behave appropriately.

The training procedures utilized in organizations have often been equated with the behavioral shaping process. In shaping, successive approximations of an operant with an initially low or zero probability are differentially reinforced until the desired response is evoked in its final form.

But shaping is only a part of the total training process and may prove to be of limited value in organizational settings. This is not to deny that shaping is important in the development of an individual's behavioral repertoire. The shaping process plays a vital role in the way children learn to walk, stand erect, talk, and acquire other motor and verbal operant skills. But training is largely a function or result of improving or refining the skill properties of operants and bringing them under the control of specific stimulus events, not developing them in raw form. In organizational settings we generally assume that many if not most of the operants that are functional or desirable have already been inserted into the individual's behavioral repertoire, and that these operants can be brought under the control of stimuli in the task environment or properties of the task itself. Thus the problem faced by leaders in training group members has less to do with shaping new responses than it does with evoking operants that may be of low probability and bringing them under the control of appropriate stimuli. In these situations other methods of behavioral change, most of which require the leader to manipulate S_D's for group member behavior, are more likely to prove effective. A supervisor may instruct a new employee, "In the presence of a red light on panel A, press button number 1 down to release the pressure so that the boiler does not explode." In this example the S_D takes the form of a verbal instruction, as well as a *warning* or *threat* that specifies how to respond in an effective manner and to avoid an aversive situation. Instructions comprise an important class of *contingency-specifying* discriminative stimuli. Other important forms often utilized in organizational settings include policy statements, written procedures, directions on how to perform a task, and the advice of peers. Each of these are utilized in organizations to specify responses and their probable consequences. Job descriptions, e.g., specify the behavior considered appropriate for performing tasks within a given job. In so doing, they may induce those responses required to perform one's job and minimize the necessity of producing such responses by differentially reinforcing successive approximations to the "target" or desired response. Contingency-specifying discriminative stimuli therefore are of considerable importance in developing appropriate forms of group member behavior.

Of course not all discriminative stimuli are verbal in nature. Some stimulus events acquire discriminative properties as a result of an individual's exposure to the contingencies that prevail when they are present. A special case of nonverbal S_D's deserves mention here because of its ability to evoke operants, which can subsequently be refined and brought under the control of task-relevant stimuli. These S_D's have their characteristic effects on behavior, because individuals learn that certain properties of the behavior of others frequently set the occasion upon which *imitative behavior* on their part is likely to be reinforced. A young child who sees his brother rewarded with candy from an uncle for turning a somersault may imitate his brother's behavior, because he has learned that such behavior on his part is also likely to be rewarded by candy. The behavior of his brother has become a stimulus that has acquired discriminative properties, so that it sets the occasion upon which imitative behavior is likely to be reinforced. This of course is not the limiting case. The behavior of others can also set the occasion upon which imitative behavior is punished, produces the removal of an aversive stimulus, or is followed by the removal of a positive reinforcer.

With adults, a very extensive imitative repertoire has typically been previously shaped and is under the control of stimuli in the form of the behavior of others. Thus in an organizational system we might find some workers imitating the behavior of a peer who frequently receives reinforcement from his supervisors. Benefits would accrue to the group depending on whether the modeled behavior was productive or not. But a more direct application of this form of discriminative stimulus can be utilized by a supervisor when training workers to do a particular task by simply modeling the desired task behavior himself. In this case the supervisor's task behavior sets the occasion upon which similar behavior by the worker is reinforced. Modeling as a form of stimulus control appears therefore to be another alternative to the shaping of appropriate forms of organizational behavior, or at least enable leaders to short circuit an extensive shaping process.

Regardless of whether the behavior evoked in training is imitative or results from verbal S_D's in the form of instructions, descriptions, advice, and so on, the leader should take care to monitor and reinforce functional operants when they are first emitted by new group members. Behavior that is characterized by its skill properties is often under the control of rather subtle environmental contingencies that may go unnoticed by new group members and may lead therefore to considerable delays in reinforcement. Since the operant behavior evoked in training may only be approximations of the final form, it is quite important to continually monitor the behavior and provide reinforcement without delay. Delays may be particularly dysfunctional because the behavior only in its approximate form may be strengthened and interfere with later transitions into its more effective form. Thus the leader's attention to the details of the training process is vitally important in the initial stages, and the leader is advised to observe group member behavior closely at this point and reinforce functional behavior appropriately.

Employee training may be an ongoing process if the skill requirements of a particular job are complex or if an individual's job is altered or changed frequently. But training usually becomes less problematic, the longer an individual works for the organization. New group members present particular problems to leaders because they are the least familiar with their jobs and the organization itself. For this reason an integral part of the training process in many organizations is an orientation program designed to help the new subordinate settle into the job. Whether these programs are successful or not may have a substantial effect on the training program as a whole.

Individuals who are relatively new on the job seldom lack motivation.

In fact, rather than lack motivation, they may suffer from too much of it. Novel, new, or unfamiliar surroundings generally produce numerous emotional respondents, many of which are incompatible or may otherwise interfere with functional group member operants. The effects of these novel stimuli are often compounded or made more acute because many organizations conduct intensive sessions for new group members in order to provide them with information not only about their job but also about the company, its history, the products it sells, and so on, long before the high level of respondent behavior elicited by novel features of the setting has subsided. To be sure, complete information regarding the group member's role is necessary, but organizational leaders are well advised to provide training in the primary role behavior immediately and orientation training later.

It is only when the new member has become accustomed to his task environment that questions are raised about the meaning and significance of his particular role. Depending on the complexity or novelty of the tasks to be learned, this may not come until after a few months, a year, or even longer. Only when these questions are raised will the group member generally benefit from a more general orientation procedure. At this time a rather comprehensive discussion of how the group member's specific job fits into the total picture, the history of the company, the products it sells, and the markets sold will prove useful.

Training new employees may be time consuming, and for this reason leaders may wish to delegate part of the orientation and training procedures to someone else. Leaders can obviously delegate the responsibility of subordinate training to another group member or to a formal trainer. But regardless of whether or not these duties are delegated or performed by the leader, they should not be left to chance.

Evoking and Maintaining Subordinate Behavior

If the group is to remain successful, subordinate operants must be brought under the control of task stimuli and maintained at reasonable levels. An effective leader therefore is one who is able to identify stimulus events that will serve as positive reinforcers, and who sees to it they follow upon group member operants with some degree of consistency.

Stimulus events that have been found to serve as positive reinforcers for human beings can be conveniently grouped into two broad classes. The first to be considered are referred to as *intrinsic* reinforcers. It has been found that virtually any stimulus change will serve as a positive reinforcer when first introduced, so long as it is not too novel or intense. They are called "intrinsic reinforcers" largely because they are inherent in the design of the task and include any sort of change in the task setting produced by task operants. Flipping a switch to turn on a motor or a light is reinforced by the hum of the motor, the appearance of the light. The operant behavior required for the manual assembly of a water pump is reinforced by the changes in the structure of the water pump as it nears completion, just as the behavior of a carpenter or a typist is reinforced by the stimulus changes their behavior produces. Intrinsic reinforcers must be regarded as relatively weak unless they are paired with other reinforcing events, because they show rapid habituation effects. That is to say, they will serve as positive reinforcers when they first appear, but will lose that property rather quickly with repetition. On the other hand they regain their reinforcing potential when they have been withdrawn or have not occurred for some time. The leader must therefore be aware that the nature of the subordinate's task is important in maintaining functional operants. Some tasks may be structured so that over time multiple operants, each producing different stimulus changes, are required. Since these response-produced changes occur in some temporal sequence, they are likely to maintain their reinforcing potential and thus effectively maintain the behavior which produces them. Other tasks, however, may require a limited number of operants that produce few changes in the environment. Those changes will quickly lose their reinforcing properties due to habituation and will be relatively ineffective in maintaining the task operants which produce them.

Organizational leaders usually cannot do very much about the technology, and hence the task structure, in the short run. On the other hand, jobs can be enlarged in a number of ways without significantly changing the technology. Since the manner in which a job is defined is often arbitrary, subordinates can be assigned a greater variety of tasks, as in job rotation. The effective leader will look for ways to increase the intrinsic reinforcing properties of group member roles when they are lacking. If none can be found, he or she must necessarily turn to the more careful administration of *extrinsic* reinforcers.

Extrinsic reinforcers are events that are mediated or delivered by a leader, and include pay, smiles, nods, compliments, praise and other types of acknowledgements of good work. They may be regarded as powerful reinforcers for most human beings for two reasons. In the reinforcement histories of human beings, they are paired with a variety of other reinforcing events and continue to be paired with them in adulthood. Second, they are not often delivered on a continuous basis and for that reason do not suffer habituation effects. Monetary reinforcement in all its forms (wages and salaries, bonuses, periodic increases in pay, promotions, fringes) is a very powerful *generalized* reinforcer because it continues to be paired in incremental amounts with a host of other reinforcing events in adulthood, and it is never delivered on a continuous basis. It is something that most human beings never "have enough of."

It has occasionally been said that extrinsic reinforcers are not very effective. The implication is that they simply do not serve as reinforcers for some or all human beings. However, it is almost inevitably the case that when extrinsic reinforcers seem to be ineffective, it is because they are not administered properly by organizational leaders. The most common problem is that there is no clear-cut relation between functional subordinate behavior and the occurrence of extrinsic reinforcers. Supervisors might supply extrinsic reinforcers on the basis of perceived need, or to avoid respondent and operant aggression elicited or evoked by the absence of positive reinforcement, or on the belief that rewarded group members will *subsequently* produce, although they were not behaving effectively at the time the reinforcement was delivered. In all such cases, it is not that the events are not reinforcing, but rather that they are likely to be contingent upon and therefore strengthen any behavior *but* functional subordinate operants.

A second problem is that the leader's administration of extrinsic reinforcers is often inconsistent. All of us are typically conditioned to reinforce another whenever they behave in a manner that is reinforcing to us, and leaders are no exception. When the leader reinforces a group member without awareness, he or she may reinforce subordinate behavior that is pleasing but possibly not required for group effectiveness. This is merely another example of obscure or irrelevant contingencies discussed above. But leaders are inconsistent in their delivery of extrinsic reinforcers in other ways. Their administration takes time, a valuable resource, and in the case of pay, the dispensing of a valuable resource that can be utilized in other ways. As a consequence, reinforcers may be delivered after a long delay or too infrequently to sustain behavior. In this regard organizational leaders must be careful not to strain ratios. It is rather easy through the careful scheduling of a reinforcing event to get more and more for less and less. Moreover, organizational leaders are often powerfully reinforced for conserving resources such as money. It is therefore tempting to get as much work out of their group members at the lowest possible cost. There is inevitably an upper bound limit, however, and both pigeons and human organisms exhibit a breaking point at which functional behavior ceases, emotional respondents set in, and operant aggression as well as other forms of counter control are likely to be observed. In these cases the organizational leader has not only failed to maintain functional subordinate operants, he or she has also evoked dysfunctional or disruptive behavior that may become commonplace.

A third problem arises from the amount of control exercised by organizational leaders over certain types of extrinsic reinforcers such as pay. A great deal is lost when wages are "negotiated" or when other organizational leaders unduly constrain a supervisor in the administration of those events. Under these circumstances praise, recognition, and other positive acknowledgements provided by a supervisor will not in fact serve as effective reinforcers. On the other hand, when an organizational leader has unilateral control over monetary reinforcement, virtually any act on the part of that leader may serve as a powerful reinforcer. As a consequence, the leader may inadvertently reward or punish a group member, and of course reinforcing events that are inadvertently administered may not be delivered contingently.

One might conclude that the leader's behavior of maintaining functional subordinate behavior is impossible or at least hopelessly complex. But while it is a difficult chore, it can be done and it must be if the leader is to be effective. As a matter of fact, a number of useful suggestions can be derived from our discussion of the problems that have been observed, but rather more specific prescriptions can be offered.

First, organizational leaders should take steps to determine how much control they may exercise over extrinsic reinforcers—pay increases, promotions, bonuses, and the like. When they have little or no control, they should take steps to gain some measure of control. If they cannot, it would be unwise to accept a management position or to remain in the position for very long, for they would then have to rely upon punishment (discharge or threats of discharge) and applications of the negative reinforcement principle in maintaining behavior. This may be effective in the short term, but it spells disaster over the long term. Organizational leaders do not require unilateral control over such reinforcers, but it is necessary that they have some voice or "upward influence" in determining the magnitude and timing of extrinsic reinforcers. Otherwise leaders cannot possibly effectively reinforce functional subordinate behavior by the contingent delivery and scheduling of pay, nor will it be possible to reinforce through praise, commendations, and other personal acts.

Second, organizational leaders are much more likely to maintain functional subordinate operants when they administer reinforcing events consistently. They are in a much better position to do this when they have specified the more effective forms of group member behavior and can respond differentially to effective and ineffective forms, as we have noted. But beyond this, they must identify those events serving as reinforcers, and deliver them frequently and without too much delay. The leader is not required to continuously monitor group member behavior and "zap each member with a pay increase, praise, or a carrot" each time functional operants have occurred. On the contrary, supervisors may administer reinforcers contingent upon the production of results (quality and quantity indexes, reduction in waste, good housekeeping, no accidents or injuries, reports by one group member that another "helped them out," and so on) without monitoring their behavior as such. Moreover, reinforcing events can be effectively delivered after some delay so long as the supervisor is also careful to supply S_D's that describe the behavior or accomplishment that needs to be strengthened and maintained. Examples include statements such as "I want you to know that I think you did an outstanding job in putting together the Davis contract last month" or "I want to thank you for your help in preparing the budget," or "I am recommending a __ percent increase in your pay for the following reasons: (1), (2). . . , (N)."

It is not possible or necessary to administer reinforcement continuously. Intermittent schedules of reinforcement have been shown to be far more effective in maintaining behavior than continuous schedules. But it is usually the case that organizational leaders do not reinforce frequently enough, especially when the given task structure is such that intrinsic reinforcers are ineffective in maintaining behavior. A rather crude but useful guideline is to look for instances of functional operant behavior (or results) on each occasion the leader has other reasons for being present or for a total of at least one hour a day, and to deliver social-evaluative reinforcers when functional behavior is occurring or has obviously occurred. A record of the administration of reinforcers proves especially instructive to the leader in at least three ways. Group members whose names are missing from this record will indicate that either they could benefit from further instruction or that the supervisor has simply not reinforced the individual enough. It will also provide a guide for changing the frequency of reinforcement (usually an increase) if the individual's functional behavior is not being effectively maintained. Finally, it provides a general guideline in the supervisor's determination of *equity*. Equity or the determination of each member's *appropriate* share of the group's consequences is rarely achieved when each member receives an equal share. Equity is a condition that is met only when the magnitude of reinforcement is contingent upon and proportionate to each member's contribution to the group's effectiveness. Questions of equity and the problems attendant with inequities do not often occur in the case of social-evaluative reinforcers because they are difficult to "count up." But they certainly arise in the case of monetary reinforcement, where even slight variations can be observed. Even a very large increase in pay may serve as an aversive stimulus when another group member gets more but is believed to be contributing less.

The establishment of equity is never easy, but it can be reasonably achieved in complex groups through the use of job evaluation techniques that help determine the criticality of the role in the group's success and by means of adequate methods for observing, recording, and appraising the degree to which functional behavior within each role has occurred.

Our prescription for effectively maintaining functional subordinate operants is obviously time consuming if not complex. Effective leaders recognize, however, that it is one of the most important, if not the most important, behavioral requirements of a leader.

The Prevention and Elimination of Dysfunctional Behavior

Subordinates may behave in ways that are dysfunctional, unproductive, or unsafe to themselves or others. Ignoring or paying little attention to safety rules, interrupting the work of peers, playing practical jokes, using machinery in need of repair, and driving vehicles in a reckless or unsafe manner are examples of undesirable employee operants. If such unwanted behavior results in receiving aversive stimulation from the physcial environment or social sanctions from one's peers, it may be eliminated or reduced without the intervention of the leader. But there is little reason to expect that all undesirable and dysfunctional subordinate operants can be reduced or precluded in this fashion. It is inevitable therefore that organizational leaders will encounter situations in which the use of aversive events or punishment is appropriate.

Several social scientists have suggested that punishment is among the most widely employed procedures of behavioral control in organizational settings. One reason for this, as we have noted, is that managers who employ little control over traditional organizational rewards find it necessary to revert to punishment and coercive procedures in their attempts to eliminate dysfunctional behavior and to maintain more functional group member behavior. Another reason is that the use of punishment is seductive. The effects of punishment are frequently much more dramatic than that of positive reinforcement. Aversive events almost immediately reduce the frequency of the behavior upon which they are made contingent. For this reason some leaders utilize the punishment and negative reinforcement principles almost exclusively in their attempts to influence group member operants.

Aversive control is not only frequently relied upon, it is also typically administered ineffectively. A common practice employed by many managers when they punish group members is called "bagging it." Supervisors who "bag it" avoid dealing with dysfunctional group member behavior directly when they observe it by depositing the incident into an imaginary bag that they carry on their back. As the incidents of undesirable behavior accumulate, the manager's "bag" becomes more and more difficult for them to carry. Then one day, usually without much warning or provocation, the manager "unloads the bag" on a group member. As one might expect, the result of this emotional display by the supervisor is seldom very functional. Initially many group members respond to such an outburst by the supervisor with bewilderment and surprise. They find it difficult to understand why the manager has overreacted so much. But eventually the surprise may turn to anger, frustration, and other negative emotions, as well as a variety of counter controlling practices on the part of subordinate group members.

Leaders of course cannot always avoid the use of punishment. It may be necessary to use aversive events in some cases to eliminate unsafe or unproductive group member behavior. But punishment need not produce dysfunctional consequences. Although the effects of punishment are quite complex, there are several prescriptions derived from recent research on the administration of aversive events that, if followed, can improve the leader's ability to administer punishment more effectively. We now turn to those prescriptions.

Punishment should be delivered as quickly after the undesirable response as possible. Any delay between the occurrence of dysfunctional behavior and the administration of punishment increases the probability that other, more desirable forms of behavior will unintentionally be punished. Some managers make a point of reprimanding an individual's dysfunctional behavior only during formalized performance evaluation meetings, even when the behavior in question may have occurred days, weeks, or months earlier. The problem with this approach is that the behavior has continued and quite probably has been strengthened in the interim.

In order to be maximally effective, punishment should be administered at a reasonably high level of intensity from the very outset. Aversive events applied in a sequence of gradually increasing intensities permit habituation effects that may nullify the effectiveness of the punishment administered. In the case of adult human beings not all aversive events have to be physically intense in order to be effective. Expressions of disapproval, reprimands, threats of the removal of privileges, and other forms of negative evaluative statements frequently serve as effective punishers if they have been paired over time with other aversive events. No doubt very loud or shouted warnings or reprimands that are physically intense may be used as aversive events. But verbal stimuli of moderate or low intensities may be more effective as long as the leader does not use them indiscriminately.

To the degree possible, those environmental events sustaining undesirable behavior should be eliminated. This may be accomplished by identifying and removing or withdrawing those reinforcing events maintaining the dysfunctional behavior. In general, the use of the extinction procedure in conjunction with the administration of punishment increases the effectiveness of both of these procedures in eliminating undesirable responses.

Punishment should be directed at specific responses and should never be employed by a supervisor in order to "get even" with an employee. As noted earlier, many managers often overlook initial offenses by a group member in hopes that the problem behavior will go away, or in order to avoid the unpleasant feelings that often accompany having to tell someone he or she is making a mistake or performing poorly, only to become emotionally upset with the employee and berate him or her severely after repeated rule violations have occurred. Such emotional outbursts on the part of the supervisor are likely to be viewed as a personal attack by the individual who is punished, and he or she may respond in kind with a similar emotional onslaught, or by utilizing various counter control techniques in order to pay the supervisor back. In order to avoid this problem, punishment should be administered in a consistent fashion and should focus on the behavior considered dysfunctional, not at the individual being punished.

The reason for the punishment should be clearly explained to the individual being punished. In order for punishment to be effective, the group member whose behavior is being punished should be told why the punishment is occurring. As a part of this process, the leader should identify the dysfunctional behavior of the subordinate, explain why such behavior is aversive to the leader or why it impedes the progress of the group, and explain that continuation of such behavior is likely to lead to more serious consequences. Once the aversive event has been administered, it is also generally an excellent opportunity for the leader to use S_D's to suggest more acceptable behavior and also to perform a useful diagnostic activity. It may, e.g., be beneficial to ask the group member to examine his or her own behavior to determine why he or she responded dysfunctionally and how such responses can be avoided in the future. Such behavior by leaders may help them to better understand the causes of the behavior in question. It may also benefit the subordinate because it will provide S_D's for them to respond in a more appropriate manner.

Caution should be exercised so that punishment does not signal positive reinforcement. Aversive stimuli differentially associated with reinforcing events may acquire discriminative as well as secondary reinforcing properties. In such cases the frequency of the punished response may actually increase rather than decrease. For the child whose father spanks him for saying a curse word, but who is comforted immediately afterward by his mother because she feels sorry for him, the spanking received may acquire the properties of conditioned reinforcer or a discriminative stimulus, which signals that crying or looking sad will be followed by the mother's affection and attention. Increases, rather than decreases, in cursing or other undesirable behavior may result when they are followed by a spanking. Similarly, employees who are "chewed out" by their supervisors for "goofing off" may increase the undesirable behavior because of the attention they get from their peers when the boss gets angry. For this reason a time-out or extinction procedure should always follow the presentation of an aversive event. Punishment in this instance becomes a signal that reinforcement will not be forthcoming for some period of time, and the elimination of the undesirable response should be enhanced as a result.

In summary, then, an effective leader will apply a punishment procedure when necessary, but he or she will apply it only when necessary and only in conjunction with other behavioral control techniques. Certain limited classes of behavior may be regarded as so dysfunctional that both the behavior and the punishment are specified in a rule. The supervisor's behavior in these circumstances is unequivocal. He or she delivers the punishment, and it is usually harsh, typically immediate dismissal. However, it is generally wise to suppress the tendency to write a rule describing every potential transgression and the punishment to be administered for it, for then the leader becomes a punitive agent and not much else.

When behavior distasteful or repugnant to the leader occurs, the first question to be asked is whether the behavior is replacing more effective behavior or is merely a personal reaction of the leader and of no consequence to group effectiveness. If it is the former, the leader should proceed without delay to describe the behavior to the subordinate and to seek out the reasons for its occurrence. (If operant behavior, however dysfunctional, is occurring, it is occurring for some reason. Either it is being effectively evoked and maintained by positive reinforcers, or it is avoidance behavior maintained by a reduction in or the avoidance of aversive reinforcers. In either case, both the leader and the subordinate involved might identify the supporting reinforcing events and work towards the elimination of both the behavior and its support.) The leader's investigation, however straightforward, will constitute a punishment procedure which, though it is a mild form of punishment, is likely to have a significant effect. In fact the behavior may be eliminated at that point, never to appear again. However, the effective leader is guided by the general principle that the important thing to recall when an individual misbehaves is *not what they are doing or have done*, but what they are *not* doing. A most important strategy to employ in conjunction with a punishment procedure is to evoke functional behavior incompatible with the transgression and to see that it is powerfully reinforced.

THE DEVELOPMENT OF SUBORDINATE SELF-CONTROL

All of our prescriptions for effective leadership are descriptions of behavioral control techniques. They describe or imply leader operants, which will either change or evoke and sustain group member behavior.

Individuals who have emerged as leaders in group settings or who have been effective as appointed leaders will have little difficulty with the notion of leaders as behavioral control agents. It is likely, however, that they will feel that something is missing, and indeed there is. The leader who unilaterally determines and prescribes the behavior of subordinates, who has near-complete control over potent reinforcing consequences, and who has learned how to manage the reinforcement contengencies of others can in fact produce behavior according to plan. The real danger, however, is that group members will come to depend too much on the leader. They will behave according to the plan, doing nothing more no less than what has been prescribed and reinforced by the leader. This condition, if put into effect, is problematical even when the leader's plan is the best that could be devised. Though by definition the group continues to be maximally effective, the leader under these circumstances tends to get most of the credit, while other group members may get less and less. The net effect is that no deviations in prescribed behavior are reinforced (and are likely to be punished), but in addition, *prescribed* group member behavior may be tentative or weak in the absence of the leader and his or her blessing. Ultimately, therefore, the group may fail even though the plan is a good one.

A more serious problem is that the leader's plan is likely to be imperfect or at least incomplete. If it is imperfect, the group will fail to achieve the level of effectiveness it could otherwise have realized if a better plan, possibly developed with the assistance of other group members, had been implemented. When it is incomplete, behavior not prescribed by the powerful leader but necessary for group effectiveness simply does not occur.

The wise leader recognizes these dangers and attempts to preclude them by encouraging the development of subordinate self-control. Most group members and certainly most of those who have been on the scene for some time are capable of some degree of self-determination. When we speak of self-control or self-determination, we are not referring to "inner will" or some other mysterious process. Rather we are referring to operant behavior on the part of a group member that serves to evoke or sustain his or her own behavior. In other words, when the group member exercises control, he or she is behaving just as the leader might behave.

There are many forms of self-control that a leader promotes simply by reinforcing the individual when they have occurred. For example, when effective group member behavior has already been identified (the subordinate knows what to do) but is not being maintained at a reasonable rate, at least some group members may strengthen this behavior by telling themselves to "get with it" or by establishing for themselves a quota, after which they promise themselves a break. Self-controlling operants of this sort are automatically reinforced by the leader, if they occur, when he or she consistently reinforces a high and sustained rate of behavior, though the leader may never observe the self-controlling behavior.

There are other, possibly more important forms of self-control that a leader can and should promote. Some, though probably not all, of the group members may be as capable as the leader of identifying and describing methods and behavior that would serve to make the group more effective. At the very least they might be capable of identifying and describing alternative modes of behaving from which the leader might select those most likely to maximize the group's success. Effective leaders often promote or evoke and then reinforce participative decision-making behavior of this sort, and it has several advantages. When group members participate in the design of their own contingencies, they are likely to specify behavior that has been made a part of their repertoire, and in some cases at least, it may prove to be more functional than behavior that the leader could identify. Second, group members who are encouraged to design their own reinforcement contingencies are typically more committed, which is to say that the behavior specified is likely to be maintained at a high rate by the self-controlling operants of the members themselves. The reason for this is not that human beings naturally and inevitably prefer to exercise some control over their own destiny but that they often receive a greater (or fair) share of the reinforcing consequences when they are successful. Also they rather than the leader will be punished when they are not successful. For this reason, some members, especially the new and inexperienced, will not benefit from this type of controlling practice and may reject it. The strategy for the effective leader is to *gradually* promote this form of self-control among group members.

As a final form of self-control, leaders may encourage experimentation by their subordinates. As noted earlier, contingencies that prevail in a particular environment may change over time, and as they do, it is possible that behavior not specified by the leader may be effective. In such cases leaders can encourage group members to experiment with the environment; that is, to observe and study the contingencies that prevail, try out new behavior, and note its consequences. Of course, a leader too can experiment with new contingencies. But in a changing environment other group members may engage in functional behavior not performed by the leader and in such instances may be more effective than the leader is. Under these circumstances the leader may find it particularly useful to permit these group members to participate in the experimentation process also.

Whenever leaders undertake to develop and sustain subordinate self-control, they are not themselves denying or refusing control. They are merely engaging in behavior and controlling operants of a different sort or establishing an environment that will promote different operants that may be critical to the success of the group in the future. Leaders control the behavior of others and should promote the development of self-control. But in no case should the leader exercise control or seek control for its own sake. Leaders are only as strong as the group they lead, and behavior that strengthens the group also strengthens the leader so that he or she is able to behave effectively with respect to the prevailing contingencies and to those that arise in the future.

SUMMARY

A recurring theme throughout the leadership research conducted over the past 80 years is that leaders are individuals who direct the efforts of others. It is only recently that a description of leadership as "behavior that makes a difference in the behavior of others" has been taken seriously. In this chapter we have explicitly assumed that leadership is operant behavior, and that leaders are behavioral change agents. Proceeding from these basic assumptions, we have discussed the principles that have evolved from an experimental analysis of behavior and from these principles have derived several recommendations for improving a leader's effectiveness.

The acceptance of managers as behavioral change agents is salutary, for with it, the use and problems of behavioral control can be frankly and objectively treated. Extensive research on animals on virtually all branches of the phylogentic tree, including human beings, has shown that behavioral control procedures are quite powerful. Because of this power we recommend that leaders implement such procedures only after a reasonable grasp of the basic principles has been obtained. Nothing is more hazardous or more irresponsible than jumping into behavioral control programs without a prior and careful consideration of what behavior is and what remains to be learned about it. It has been our purpose here to provide a reasonably comprehensive treatment of how behavioral control procedures may effectively be administered by leaders. We have not been able to discuss all of the complex reinforcement contingencies that exist or can be devised. We feel, however, that leaders must move from an understanding of basic principles to more complex ones if they are to control behavior effectively.

Behavior control cannot be made to disappear by a process of wishful thinking. Nor can we guard against abuses by continuing to deny that behavior can be and is controlled. Effective leaders control behavior and promote the development of self-control, but they do not weaken individuals by despotic or Machiavellian practices. On the contrary, they are always seeking ways to strengthen the group, for after all, leaders are only as strong and effective in dealing with their world as the groups they lead.

REFERENCES

Bogardus, E. S. World leadership styles. *Sociological and Social Research*, 1928, *12*, 573–599.

Bowers, D. G. and Seashore, S. E. Predicting organizational effectiveness with a four-factor theory of leadership. *Administrative Science Quarterly*, 1966, *11*, 238–263.

Carlyle, T. *Heroes and hero worship.* Boston: Adams, 1841.

Gibb, C. A. The principles and traits of leadership. *Journal of Abnormal and Social Psychology*, 1947, *42*, 267–284.

Hemphill, J. K. The leader and his group. *Journal of Educational Research*, 1949, *28*, 225–229.

Janda, K. F. Towards the explication of the concept of leadership in terms of the concept of power. *Human Relations*, 1960, *13*, 345–363.

Katz, D. Motivational basis of organizational behavior. *Behavioral Science*, 1964, 134–146.

McCall, W. W., Jr. Leadership research: Choosing gods and devils on the run. *Journal of Occupational Psychology*, 1976, *49*, 139–153.

Skinner, B. F. *Science and human behavior*, New York: Macmillan, 1953.

Stogdill, R. M. *Handbook of leadership: A survey of theory and research.* New York: Free Press, 1974.

Stogdill, R. M. Personal factors associated with leadership: A survey of the literature. *Journal of Psychology*, 1948, *25*, 35–1.

4

Controversy in OBM: History, Misconceptions, and Ethics

ROBERT KREITNER
Arizona State University

Human action can be modified to some extent, but human nature cannot be changed.

Abraham Lincoln

A scientific view of man offers exciting possibilities. We have not yet seen what man can make of man.

B. F. Skinner

Organizational behavior management (OBM) is an area of theory and practice ripe for controversy, for a number of reasons. Its association with the name B. F. Skinner, the emotion-laden term "behavior modification," and the notion of systematically controlled behavior virtually assure the regular renewal of long-standing questions about how, why, and to whom. Making matters worse is the problem of confusing terminology. OBM, like its predecessor operant conditioning, has its own unique technical jargon. Even proponents of OBM cannot agree on a generally acceptable label for their field. The application of Skinnerian operant conditioning to job performance has been variously labeled applied behavior analysis, behavior technology, organizational behavior modification, and organizational behavior management. (The latter term is used here to avoid needless confusion.) Added to these historical and terminological problems are a number of popular misconceptions about the nature of OBM. It has come to mean many things to many people. A number of fundamental philosophical and ethical issues guarantee that OBM will be the object of controversy for a long time to come. The purpose of this chapter is to unravel and clarify these sources of controversy so that the reader can form personal judgments about where and how to best apply OBM in a constructive and ethical manner.

A CONTROVERSIAL HERITAGE

Instead of suddenly springing up sometime during the 1970s with a distinct identity of its own, OBM is the product of an evolution that dates to the nineteenth century (Kazdin, 1978). This evolution started with Russian physiologists such as Ivan M. Sechenov, Ivan P. Pavlov, and Vladimir M. Bechterev, who attempted to demonstrate what they considered to be the essentially reflexive nature of behavior. The Russian physiologists' reflexology, a discipline devoted to experimentally discovering the external causes of objective (or observable) behavior, stood in marked contrast to structuralism and functionalism, two schools of psychological thought popular at the turn of the century. Structuralist psychologists attempted to identify the components of thought or, in effect, the structure of the mind. In contrast, the functionalists analyzed the operations of consciousness. Both schools of psychology relied upon introspection for evidence. By rejecting introspection and embracing the experimental observation of actual behavior, a legacy of the Russian reflexologists, an American psychologist named John B. Watson introduced behaviorism to the domain of psychology.

A couple of decades later (1930s), another American psychologist, B. F. Skinner, redirected Watson's preoccupation with observable behavior and its environmental causes into a behavior control technology called "operant conditioning." Eventually, during the 1950s and 1960s, operant conditioning techniques were transferred from animal-research laboratories to human application under the heading of behavior modification. Misbehaving school children, mentally handicapped children and adults, and prison inmates became the favorite targets of pioneering behavior modifiers.

It was well into the 1970s before behavior modification was seriously considered as a useful human resource management tool for improving job performance. Unfortunately, modern managers who embrace OBM, the product of a long and complicated evolution, also inherit a disproportionately large amount of controversy and debate. Brief discussion of four major historical tap roots of that controversy follows: radical behaviorism; Skinner's treatment of freedom and dignity; questionable applications; and technical jargon.

Radical Behaviorism

Some psychology historians humorously note that John B. Watson made psychology lose its mind. In actual fact, what he attempted to do was to get psychologists to be more scientific by relying less on subjective introspection and more on objective behavior. In Watson's words:

> Why don't we make what we can observe the real field of psychology? Let us limit ourselves to things that can be observed, and formulate laws concerning only the observed things. Now what can we observe? Well, we can observe *behavior—what the organism does or says* (Watson and MacDougall, 1929, p. 18)

Naturally Watson's prescription for dealing with only exterally controlled observables was extremely unpopular among his colleagues, who were busily probing the structure and function of the mind.

Those who have followed in Watson's footsteps, such as B. F. Skinner, have been labeled radical behaviorists because they ignore internal states and processes. While Skinner disagrees with Watson's insistence that every behavioral response is caused by a prior eliciting stimulus (Skinner says that behavior also can be a function of its consequences), he has embraced the Watsonian disregard for dealing in terms of unobservable inner states. According to Skinner (1953):

> The objection to inner states is not that they do not exist, but that they are not relevant in a functional analysis. We cannot account for the behavior of any system while staying wholly inside it; eventually we must turn to forces operating upon the organism from without. (p. 35)

Similar to Watson's fate, Skinner has been roundly criticized by humanistic psychologists and philosophers who prefer to describe the internal causes of human behavior in terms of will, purpose, attitudes, needs, drives, or expectations. Regarding the extension of behaviorism to the work place, Locke (1977) has written:

> While Skinner does not openly deny that people have minds, he does assert that the environment is the ultimate cause of all thinking and action. *But if the mind is an epiphenomenon, then for all practical purposes, it does not exist.*

> Only if humans were by nature limited to the perceptual level of functioning, like dogs or cats, could one reasonably argue that they were passive responders to outside influences and that they would do nothing that they were not conditioned to do . . . .

> Since people can choose to think (a fact which can be validated by introspection), the behaviorist view of human nature is false. Thus the claim that behaviorism, taken literally, can serve as a valid guide to understanding and modifying human behavior in organizations is a myth. (pp. 550–551)

So it seems that managers who follow in Skinner's behaviorist footsteps, like Skinner who followed in Watson's behaviorist footsteps, can expect to be criticized for dehumanizing people.

While failing to once and for all resolve the behaviorism controversy, Luthans and Kreitner (1975) have framed a workable compromise:

Switching from an internal to external perspective is not an attempt to completely disregard the hypothetical *causes* of behavior. Rather, the point is to use workable behavioral *control* techniques for more effective human resource management while the search for causes continues. A comprehensive *combination* of cause and control is a desirable goal for better understanding of human resource management, but for pragmatic prediction and control of organizational behavior, the practitioner should turn more to the concepts and principles embodied in [OBM]. (p. 189)

As OBM grows in popularity, the battle of behaviorism will inevitably rage. After all, two very different philosophies of human nature are at stake: free will and self-determination, on the one side, environmental determinism, on the other. This philosophical debate is picked up later in the chapter.

Skinner's Treatment of Freedom and Dignity

For many years discussion of Skinner's unique deterministic approach was pretty much limited to academic circles, primarily within the discipline of psychology. Although Skinner's novel *Walden Two* (1948), broadened his notoriety, it was the publication of *Beyond Freedom and Dignity* in 1971 that catapulted Skinner into the public limelight. Suddenly even those who never before heard of Skinner or fully understood his work debated, editorialized, and criticized points he made in *Beyond Freedom and Dignity*. Most of the things said about Skinner's behavioristic formula for the survival of our culture have been strongly negative.

The following selections from *Beyond Freedom and Dignity* help demonstrate why so many people from so many different walks of life have accused him of deviously undermining individual dignity:

A culture is like the experimental space in the study of behavior. (p. 173)

Consciousness is a social product. It is not only *not* the special field of autonomous man, it is not within the range of solitary man. (p. 183)

Autonomous man is a device used to explain what we cannot explain in any other way. (p. 191)

Man is a machine in the sense that he is a complex system behaving in lawful ways, but the complexity is extraordinary. (p. 193)

Machan's (1974) scathing assessment of *Beyond Freedom and Dignity* is a typical reaction:

The mistake is that Skinner has allowed his name to give weight to very questionable politics, ethics, and philosophy. He has denounced freedom, dignity, human rights, democracy, and other human achievements that have brought happiness and security to millions of people everywhere. Being wrong in his attack, and out of his specialty to boot, cannot easily be chalked up as simple misfortune. (p. 113)

From the standpoint of OBM, it is prudent to recognize that Skinner's contributions, spread over a 40-year career, are not an indivisible lump. One can appreciate the practicality of Skinner's operant conditioning without necessarily embracing his philosophy of applying it on a culture-wide basis. Obviously one's own value system must be the final arbiter of whether or not, and if so how, one applies Skinnerian operant conditioning to human resource management.

But once again, as with the Watsonian heritage, those who use techniques associated even indirectly with the name B. F. Skinner will fall heir to a legacy of controversy.

Questionable Applications of Behavior Modification

When specific behavior modification techniques derived from Skinner's operant conditioning were taken out of animal laboratories and used on subnormal and deviant humans, more fuel was added to the fires of controversy. Despite a great many success stories reported by teachers, mental health technicians, social workers, and prison administrators, a number of highly publicized misapplications of behavior modification have clouded its reputation in the public eye. Vance Packard (1977) detailed one such horror story regarding the modification of prisoner behavior with drugs:

> Anectine [a derivative of the poison curare] takes the misbehaving inmate to Death's Door. It paralyzes his muscles for breathing. He is suffocating but fully conscious. It is during this suffocating phase that the therapist reminds him of his inappropriate behavior and that this kind of aversive therapy may be helpful in enabling him to behave more appropriately in the future. Once the terror-stricken prisoner seems to get the point, the drug's effect is counteracted. (p. 81)

While this scenario, straight out of Burgess's *A Clockwork Orange* (1963), has virtually nothing in common with OBM-type intervention, those outside the discipline do not always discern a difference.

To many observers, such grotesque scenes are what behavior modification is all about. Those who apply behavior modification can expect negative comments from those who put all behavior modification techniques, both punitive and positively reinforcing, in one undifferentiated basket. If the application is positive and constructive in nature, as it should be, then a straightforward explanation of the program will help defuse misinformed criticism. A general prejudice against anything associated with the term behavior modification will certainly persist for some time to come. This unfortunate state of affairs owes to both real and fictional tales of abuse.

Technical Jargon

Like any evolutionary technology, OBM has inherited its own strange language. Managers who readily use terms such as attitude, need, and motivation sometimes recoil from terms such as modification, control, contingent reinforcement, extinction, and shaping. However, these latter terms are fundamental to the teaching and practice of OBM. An American Psychological Association Commission, convened in 1974 to consider ethical issues in behavior modification, summed up why technical jargon is a problem in behavior modification:

> Complaints have been voiced about the technical terms used by behavioral professionals—words like *modification, shaping,* and *control*—because of their manipulative connotations. On the other hand, the complaint has also been made that the technical language of behavior modification—words like *time out* and *aversive stimuli*—can be used euphemistically to cover up harsh procedures and to provide professional legitimation of ugly techniques. (Stolz and Associates, 1978, p. 11)

As with the other controversial aspects of OBM's heritage, generalized bias against the technical jargon of operant conditioning and behavior modification will continue to be a problem until public opinion is tempered by the constructive results of ethical applications.

Because OBM has its own unique and sometimes confusing language, the following section is devoted entirely to sorting out and clarifying some important terminology.

A TERMINOLOGY JUNGLE

Discipline-specific terminology represents an interesting dilemma. On the one hand, those within a specific discipline converse more easily and parsimoniously because of a common technical language. On the other hand, those from other disciplines tend to be confused and even alienated by unfamiliar terminology. So it is with the extension of behavior modification to the work setting. While discussing this language problem, Luthans and Kreitner (1975) have noted:

> Whether we are aware of it or not, most of us speak the cognitive language of the internal approach to explaining human behavior. Not surprisingly, it is simply the result of steady exposure to the language of the psychoanalytic and cognitive schools of thought—the internal approach. (p. 5)

By familiarizing themselves with key OBM terminology, managers will not only break down prejudicial barriers, they will open exciting new doors to personal and organizational effectiveness as well. The glossary of OBM terms in Figure 4-1 is intended to be a helpful starting point.

As with any applied technology, the OBM terms in Figure 4-1 represent precise processes rather than vague generalities. For example, the term "positive reinforcement" is not necessarily synonymous with the commonly used term "reward." Also, although positive and negative reinforcement may eventuate the same behavioral outcome, each goes about it in a very different way. Finally, negative reinforcement and punishment, in spite of typically being confused, are very different processes with

Term	Definition
Organizational Behavior Management (OBM)	Organizational behavior management (OBM) involves the process of making specific job-related behavior occur more or less often, depending on whether it enhances or hinders organizational goal attainment, through the systematic management of (1) antecedent conditions that serve as cues, or (2) immediate pleasing or displeasing consequences.
Positive reinforcement	Positive reinforcement is the process of encouraging the reappearance of specific behavior by conditionally granting a favorable consequence (e.g., praising a co-worker's cooperation to help insure that it will continue).
Negative reinforcement	Negative reinforcement is the process of encouraging the reappearance of specific behavior by conditionally terminating an unpleasant situation (e.g., a manager stops criticizing a subordinate for loafing only when that subordinate starts working again).
Extinction	Extinction is the process of discouraging specific behavior by ignoring it (e.g., the office clown eventually stops telling racist and sexist jokes when co-workers no longer laugh).
Punishment	Punishment is the process of discouraging the appearance of specific behavior by either conditionally presenting an undesirable consequence or conditionally withdrawing something of value (e.g., a manager can punish a tardy individual by either assigning him or her to a dirty job or docking his or her pay).
Shaping	Shaping is the process of making simple behavior more complex by making positive reinforcement contingent upon progressively more complex behavior (e.g., a committee chair shapes a timid committee member into a regular contributor by first praising any contribution at all and later praising only valuable contributions).
Modeling	Modeling is the process of getting people to behave in a desired manner by (1) exposing them to an appropriately behaving individual with whom they identify, and (2) positively reinforcing them for successful imitation (e.g., an office manager gives a raise to a clerk who successfully operates a word processor after having observed a demonstration by a manufacturer's representative).

FIGURE 4-1. A Glossary of key OBM terminology.

opposite behavioral results. With an eye toward setting the record straight, each of these three areas of terminological confusion will be examined more closely.

Positive Reinforcement versus Reward

The distinction between positive reinforcement and reward, relative to OBM, is an important one because it separates objective fact from subjective good intentions. More specifically, a consequence is positively reinforcing if it demonstrably causes certain behavior to occur more often. In other words, consequences must prove their worth in an objective manner before earning the label "positive reinforcement." This amounts to after-the-fact definition. Rewards, in direct contrast, are subjectively defined in the eye of the giver, while positive reinforcement is defined in the behavior of the receiver. For example, a well-intentioned supervisor who rewards an employee who greatly dislikes physical contact with a pat on the back will likely hinder rather than encourage good performance. Similar treatment with a more gregarious employee, however, might turn out to be excellent positive reinforcement if subsequent performance improves.

Managers who fully appreciate this distinction between positive reinforcement and rewards are less likely to be trapped into narrowly believing that blanket rewards (money, for instance) will automatically improve job performance. Sheer human diversity guarantees that many rewards will not qualify as positive reinforcement. Consequently, the more tailor-made the reward scheme, the greater the reinforcement effect.

Positive versus Negative Reinforcement

As briefly mentioned earlier, both positive and negative reinforcement have the same impact on behavior. Each is capable of making the behavior to which it is conditionally tied occur more frequently. However, despite this common end, the means are very different. With positive reinforcement, one is encouraged to behave in a given manner to gain access to a desired consequence. Oppositely, with negative reinforcement, one is encouraged to behave in a given manner to escape an undesirable circumstance. Auto manufacturers have made good use of negative reinforcement to get us to buckle our seat belts, because the only way to terminate the annoying buzzer is to buckle up. (Of course some people illegally disconnect the buzzer; this is termed "avoidance" behavior in OBM.) Both escape and avoidance behavior tend to be counterproductive on the job because the employee spends more time watching out for negative circumstances than tending to the job at hand.

This distinction between positive and negative reinforcement brings to the surface an important point regarding the management of job behavior. It involves the old adage, "You can catch more flies with honey than, with vinegar." Those who are exposed to a positive reinforcement strategy become the active pursuers of consequences that they desire; those who are exposed to a negative reinforcement strategy become the reluctant escapists of annoying circumstances. This latter situation amounts to coercive social blackmail (Luthans and Kreitner, 1975, p. 112). Since most of us tend to resent coercion, managers who rely on negative reinforcement instead of positive reinforcement can expect to cope with emotional side effects on the part of employees.

Negative Reinforcement versus Punishment

Perhaps it is because the word "negative" conjures up visions of punishment that so many people tend to equate negative reinforcement with punishment. But the two processes, as indicated in Figure 4-1, are quite different. Both the means and the ends of the two processes differ. Negative reinforcement is used to strengthen or encourage behavior, while punishment is used to weaken or discourage behavior.

Another source of confusion between these two processes stems from the fact that they are often closely paired. For example, an angry boss who berates an uncooperative employee and continues to do so until he or she begins to cooperate is relying on punishment and negative reinforcement in such rapid succession that the two processes are easily confused. The key to unscrambling this little scenario is to view the employee's uncooperative and cooperative behavior as incompatible. In other words, one cannot be both uncooperative and cooperative at the same time. The boss applied punishment to the uncooperative behavior, and it was replaced by an incompatible behavior, cooperation, which was in turn negatively reinforced by the termination of the berating. It turns out that the berating was punishment when it was applied and negative reinforcement when it was removed. One needs to find out whether a condition was presented or withdrawn and whether a behavior was discouraged or encouraged before determining whether punishment or negative reinforcement has been used.

One thing that negative reinforcement and punishment have in common is the tendency to prompt dysfunctional side effects due to their inherently coercive nature (Luthans and Kreitner, 1975, pp. 117–123). Positive reinforcement is a much more effective and socially acceptable way to improve on-the-job behavior.

SOME COMMON MISCONCEPTIONS ABOUT OBM

Misconceptions about OBM abound. This is not a surprising state of affairs considering that the field has such a controversial heritage and possesses its own strange language. Unfamiliar disciplines are always much easier to criticize than one's own. But if OBM is to play a significant role in human resource management, a number of widespread misconceptions about it need to be cleared up first. As Alfred North Whitehead once remarked, "Not ignorance, but ignorance of ignorance, is the death of knowledge." Hopefully, by dispelling some common misconceptions about OBM, the way can be paved for a productive exchange of interdisciplinary information. As long as these misconceptions persist, many who would otherwise benefit won't give OBM a second look. The six misconceptions addressed here include: (1) the S-R misconception; (2) the animal research–human application misconception; (3) the puppet-on-a-string misconception; (4) the piece rate misconception; (5) the Big Brother misconception; and (6) the three-easy-steps misconception. Each represents a prejudicial barrier to the understanding and application of OBM.

The S-R Misconception

OBM is consistently confused with the stimulus-response (S-R) model. A familiar S-R connection is when a doctor taps (stimulus) an individual just below the kneecap and the lower leg reflexively jerks upward (response). This S-R model plays a relatively small role in complex, mature human behavior. Much of our everyday behavior is the product of operant conditioning, not classical (S-R) conditioning.

The fallacy of assuming that all conditioning involves S-R connections in the classical Pavlovian tradition may be countered by referring to Skinner's (1938) 40-year-old distinction between respondent and operant behavior. Respondent behavior is reflexive. Genetic predisposition permits the healthy individual to respond reflexively when presented with environmental stimuli. Thus prior environmental stimuli *elicit* unlearned, reflexive responses. As a result, the S-R model adequately explains the connections between a tap on the knee and a leg-jerk response, a puff of wind and an eye blink, or the touch of a hot object and the quick withdrawal of the hand. But because relatively little adult human behavior satisfies the S-R criteria of prior eliciting stimulus and subsequent reflexive response, it is unproductive and misleading to subsume all behavior under the S-R model.

Convinced that the S-R model did not adequately explain the learning of complex behavior, Skinner formulated the *operant* model. Skinner relegated the S-R model to the relatively minor role of explaining unlearned, reflexive behavior. In contrast, individuals *learn* through operant conditioning. Learning amounts to the behavioral adaptation to changing circumstances.

The operant conditioning model is a three-term model that explains how organisms learn through environmental experience. According to Skinner (1969):

> An adequate formulation of the interaction between an organism and its environment must always specify three things: (1) the occasion upon which a response occurs, (2) the response itself, and (3) the ... consequences. (p. 7)

Stated another way, the operant model's three key components are: Antecedent→Behavior→Consequence. Translated to convenient shorthand form, an A→B→C model emerges (Luthans and Kreitner, 1975, pp. 42–44). Both the A's and C's reside in the environment, while the B's are observable behavior. Antecedent conditions (A's) in the immediate environment do not reflexively elicit behavior as in the S-R model; they simply increase the probability that certain behaviors (B's) will appear. From that point on, the frequency or strength of a particular behavior (B) is controlled by the nature and scheduling of its immediate consequences (C's). Simply stated, OBM involves control of B's by managing A's and C's. Favorable or encouraging antecedents and consequences serve to strengthen behavior (see Situation 1 in Figure 4-2). Unfavorable or discouraging antecedents and consequences serve to weaken behavior (see Situation 2 in Figure 4-2).

Thus, operant conditioning and OBM are not adequately explained by Pavlovian classical conditioning or the S-R model. To confuse the S-R model with the operant model is to miss entirely the key to explaining how we learn complex behavior through experience.

The Animal Research–Human Application Misconception

This second misconception notes that the operant conditioning principles that underlie OBM were derived from animal research. People are not rats or pigeons. Therefore, operant conditioning and OBM are inappropriate for human behavior (Fry, 1974). This deceptively enticing syllogism has led to some unfortunate confusion about behavior modification. After labeling behavior conditioning techniques as "applied ratamorphism," Hammer (1971, p. 529) concluded that: "Any theory of behavior which effectively equates man with lower animals will . . . be incapable of dealing with the vast majority of human behavior that has no parallels in the subhuman world."

True, normally functioning adult humans have little in common with relatively simple subhuman species such as rats and pigeons. But the proponents of OBM do not pretend that they are equivalent. Both behavior and environmental antecedents and consequences differ vastly between lower animals and man. Nonetheless, behaviorists have found strikingly similar parallels in the ways in which the environment controls lower animal and human behavior. Thus, although the behavior and antecedents and consequences vary significantly, the organism-environment interaction is virtually identical. Whether it is a pigeon pecking a colored disk 100 times to gain access to a grain hopper, or a sales person attempting to contact a potential buyer for the third time in order to close a sale, behavior is subject to control by the immediate environment.

A corollary point remains. When one stops to think about it, the transition from animal research to human application in operant conditioning is consistent with one of the basic traditions of science. Chemical compounds are normally tried out on animals prior to clearance for human consumption, and animals were rocketed into space prior to manned space flights. Behaviorists have merely followed in the footsteps of toxicologists, space scientists, physicians, pharmacologists, and other scientists. A tradition of animal research does not necessarily preclude the use of operant conditioning in human organizations.

	Antecedent (A)	→ Behavior (B)	→ Consequence (C)	=	Result
Situation 1 A discouraging antecedent combined with a discouraging consequence	Boss (skeptically): "I suppose you haven't finished the Jones report yet?"	Clerk (somewhat angrily): "No, in fact, it's not. It still needs some work."	Boss (sarcastically): "Thanks, we'll probably both be looking for a new job next week."		Angered and frustrated by the boss's sarcastic treatment, the clerk has no incentive to promptly finish the report. Instead the clerk turns to a coworker to complain about their boss.
Situation 2 An encouraging antecedent combined with an encouraging consequence.	Boss (in a friendly manner): "How are things going with the Jones report?"	Clerk (proudly): "Fine, it's just about done. I need about an hour to put on the final touches."	Boss (appreciatively): "That's good news! I really like the way you've handled this tough project."		The clerk enthusiastically returns to the work at hand and finishes the report within the hour.

FIGURE 4-2. How antecedents and consequences strengthen or weaken job performance.

The Puppet-on-a-String Misconception

Some critics contend that behavior modification reduces people to passive slaves of someone else's bidding. This line of reasoning raises the specter of *Brave New World*, *Nineteen Eighty-Four*, and *A Clockwork Orange*. Interestingly enough, the puppet-on-a-string misconception generously overstates the case for behavior modification. While some subhuman species may be almost mechanically controlled through operant conditioning, adult human beings in loosely controlled environments are in little danger of puppet-like control. Emotion appears to override practical fact as far as this misconception is concerned.

Through the phenomenon of *countercontrol* (Skinner, 1974, pp. 190–196), the controlled individual in turn controls the supposed controller. First, it must be recalled that a behavior modifier only indirectly controls behavior by managing the antecedent and consequent elements of an individual's immediate environment. Behavior subsequently adapts to the rearranged environment. Thus we come to realize that if the behavior fails to fall into line, the controller must retreat and try another arrangement of the environment. For this very reason, some of the best behavior modifiers are children and pets. In fact, one group of researchers has reported the modification of teacher behavior by students (Gray, Graubard, and Rosenberg, 1974).

Robot-like control of complex organizational behavior would be extremely difficult if not impossible. OBM is an unlikely candidate for achieving an Orwellian world in today's work organizations.

The Piece Rate Misconception

It is common today to hear individuals claim that OBM involves nothing more than a return to piece rates (the payment of a fixed amount of money per unit of output). While it is true that OBM proponents strongly recommend that pay and performance be closely linked to achieve an incentive effect, OBM offers managers many options above and beyond piece rates for reinforcing good job performance. One alternative set of options involves the timing or scheduling of reinforcement. Research (Luthans and Kreitner, 1975, pp. 49–52) indicates that intermittent reinforcement on an unpredictable schedule (e.g., a slot machine) encourages more durable behavior than continuous reinforcement for every single response (e.g., a piece rate). Another alternative set of reinforcement options involves the granting of nonmonetary rewards. Typical examples of nonmonetary rewards are praise, formal and informal recognition, time off, feedback, rotation to favored jobs, and increased responsibility. Yet another set of OBM options includes the creation of antecedent conditions, such as enriched jobs, flexible work schedules, or participative schemes like quality control circles, that in effect set the stage for improved job performance. When intermittent schedules of reinforcement, nonmonetary rewards, and time, task, and participative rearrangements are taken into consideration, the claim that OBM is little more than a scheme for dispensing piece rate payments rings hollow. OBM permits managers to administer a vast array of work improvement techniques in a rational and efficient manner within the A-B-C context.

The Big Brother Misconception

Because OBM often involves the monitoring and recording of behavior, some critics have suggested that such close scrutiny takes us one step closer to George Orwell's Big Brother. Within a free society, scientific rigor in behavior management is easily confused with restrictive control. Americans seem to be particularly sensitive to close scrutiny. However, the practical limitations of constantly observing such complex human activity as job performance preclude effective Big Brother scrutiny. Busy supervisory personnel typically do not have the time, patience, or desire to surreptitiously peer from behind file cabinets and machinery.

How then can the practicing manager collect behavioral data of sufficient specificity and validity for OBM? *Random time sampling* and *performance sampling* are two workable alternatives (Brandt, 1972). From a busy manager's standpoint, each is time efficient. Random time sampling involves brief periods of observing actual job behavior. Performance sampling, in contrast, involves recording critical incidents of job behavior over extended periods of time. Examples of behavior suitable for performance sampling include instances of interpersonal conflict, suggestions offered, relevant questions asked, and "great" ideas. Another viable alternative is self-observation through personal record keeping. With time and performance sampling and self-observation, necessary behavioral data can be collected without undue or unethical "snoopervision." When the monitoring of actual behavior is not feasible, managers can fall back on the strategy of tracking "hard" results such as keystrokes per hour, units of output completed, claims settled, or problems solved as indicators of effective or ineffective job behavior.

The Three-Easy-Steps Misconception

Unlike the other misconceptions discussed here, this one comes from the OBM camp. A few overzealous proponents of OBM have created some unrealistic expectations with exaggerated claims of simplicity and efficacy. OBM is not a panacea; it is a tool—a tool derived from years of empirical laboratory and field research of the environmental determinants of behavior change. Like any tool, OBM may be improperly or inappropriately used. OBM requires hard work, objectivity, experimentation and subsequent adjustment, consistency, and persistence. On again off again, half-hearted attempts at OBM are doomed to failure.

On-the-job application promises to give OBM its supreme test. In the contemporary work environment, unionization, worker alienation, and vague performance-reward contingencies, among other factors, have rendered money and other contrived rewards practically useless from a motivational standpoint. Ways must be found to put specific job performance more directly under the control of potent reinforcing consequences. A return to piece rates is certainly not practical and probably not even possible in most cases. Fortunately, OBM appears to hold the key, by first requiring the identification of a wide variety of encouraging antecedents and rewarding consequences, and second, providing the operational blueprint for their use. The requisite techniques are specific and demand systematic and consistent application. Three easy steps will not get the job done.

Hopefully, addressing the foregoing misconceptions about OBM, has helped to put it into a clearer and more realistic perspective. The application of OBM to a large extent is limited only by the practicing manager's problem solving ability and desire to improve upon the past in an ethical manner.

ETHICAL ISSUES

Broadly defined, ethics is "the study of right and wrong, usually including the determining and encouraging of what is right" (Brown, 1976). Debate over right versus wrong is especially vigorous in management circles these days. Prompted by highly publicized evidence of illegal political campaign contributions, untruthful advertising, discriminatory hiring and promotion practices, price fixing, and foreign bribery, the search is on for a moral philosophy of management (Bowman, 1976). As OBM becomes more prevalent, it too, because of its controversial heritage, will rate a place on management's ethical agenda. The ethical debate over OBM in the organization management literature has been somewhat limited to date. Meanwhile, however, the use of behavior modification in applied settings such as schools, prisons, and mental health institutions has raised a number of ethical questions that can be extrapolated readily to the organizational context. Braun (1975) has outlined the ethical domain of behavior modification in the following terms:

> The subject of behavior control has, throughout history, given rise to discussions of the ethical use of power. The central problem has continually been: how to use power justly. The questions asked have always been: Who shall have power? Toward what ends shall the power be used? By what means shall the power by regulated? (p. 51)

Operating from this base, the following discussion examines three areas with ethical implications: (1) the legitimacy of behavior modification as a human resource management tool; (2) the means-ends relationship; and (3) the matter of accountability on the part of organizational behavior modifiers. The purpose of raising these issues is to get present and future OBM practitioners to consider the ethical implications of their actions and decide how best to proceed. All too often, questions concerning ethics are not asked by those caught up in the expedient application of a promising new technology.

Is Behavior Modification a Legitimate Human Resource Management Tool?

Exploring the ethical dimension of OBM is like peeling an onion. No matter how one goes about it, the core of the onion always remains the same. Similarly, if one probes any ethical question about OBM deeply enough, the core philosophical debate over whether humans are autonomous or environmentally determined beings always surfaces. This is particularly true relative to the legitimacy issue. It stands to reason that those who do not accept Skinner's deterministic view of the individual certainly will not accept its application to human problems. The following point-counterpoint debate helps demonstrate why philosophy and application are inextricably intertwined when it comes to OBM.

Point: Behaviorism Has No Place in Management   One of the most outspoken critics of OBM-related concepts and techniques is Edwin A. Locke (1977; 1979). As the following excerpt indicates, Locke (1979) is philosophically opposed to OBM:

> I am unalterably opposed to behaviorism, not because I am biased, but because it flies in the face of the most elementary and self-evident facts about human beings: that they possess consciousness and that their minds are their guides to action, or more fundamentally: their means of survival. I am not against the judicious use of contingent rewards and punishments; it is the behaviorist philosophy of man that I oppose.

Along a somewhat similar line, Scott and Hart (1979) take managers who have adopted the Skinnerian philosophy to task for embracing the assumption of human malleability:

> Managers, as the elite of advanced industrial society, have set the tone of that society and established its cultural pace by their influence on values. Since managers control all modern organizations, they can write programs of social control for people who cannot hope to accede to managerial power but whose support is absolutely necessary for maintaining the managerial regime. . . . The inescapable fact remains that management scholars and practitioners accepted the premise of innate human malleability without a trace of philosophical reflection. That demonstrates an appalling philosophic bankruptcy. (p. 61)

The foregoing criticisms of Skinnerian behaviorism unequivocally make the point that managers should reject it as a legitimate management tool because it is philosophically unsound. According to this line of reasoning, to adopt such a demeaning and dehumanizing view of human beings is to stunt human growth and development.

Counterpoint: Behaviorism Belongs in Management.   Proponents of OBM have an interesting way of justifying its legitimacy in productive organizations. Rather than taking the philosophical issue head on, they conveniently sidestep it by claiming that managers are already behavior modifiers, though somewhat haphazard ones. So, they contend, why don't managers adopt behaviorism and start modifying employee behavior in a conscious and forthright manner? Connellan (1978) has articulated this position in the following way:

> Although the idea of behavior change is anathema to many managers, they engage in this technique every day whether they are aware of it or not. . . . The thought of modifying behavior deliberately and systematically appears to many to smack of manipulation and control, or it seems to be degrading to the individual whose behavior is being changed. (p. 29)

> No matter how we look at it, management is getting other people to do things that have to be done. It is clearly a practice that implies we are going to have to manage other people's behavior (p. 30). . . .

> Managers who deliberately set out to change employee behavior and admit this are much farther ahead of their colleagues who motivate employees to "change their attitudes" or "affect their personalities." . . . Managers who use behavioral technology to get their staff to do the job are merely doing with foresight and in a carefully planned fashion what they formerly did haphazardly—changing employee behavior. If we examine other methods people use to influence employee behavior, we see they are actually trying to change that behavior, even though they may not call it that. (p. 32)

In short, advocates of OBM pragmatically challenge managers to do what they already do, just more systematically. In no way does this tack resolve the underlying philosophical issue. By appealing to management's pragmatic and characteristically shortsighted quest for results and techniques that "work," OBM proponents have attempted to win the legitimacy debate by default. But as history has so often demonstrated, ignored philosophical questions are remarkably persistent. Disagreement in this area promises to be around for a long time.

To What Ends Will Managers Use Behavior Modification as a Means?

Those who view behavior modification as philosophically illegitimate and have trouble getting their point across to pragmatists have a second line of defense, namely, to what *ends* will employee behavior be modified? Managerial pragmatists are quick to reply that the organization's overall purpose is the rational focal point for all individual and collective objectives, techniques, and activities. Of course this response often prompts a fundamental query about the ultimate purpose of the organization in question. For instance, what is General Motors' ultimate purpose, to provide transportation or to produce a profit for its stockholders? The stock reply one hears most often from the business community is that it is a combination of both. After all, they argue, how can General Motors make a profit if it fails to meet the demand for transportation? For present purposes it is sufficient to simply raise rather than attempt to finally resolve this underlying question about the ultimate purposes of organizations. Suffice it to say that OBM proponents see behavior modification as a common means to many ends, whatever purpose the organization may have. They claim that OBM, like any tool, can be used in a constructive and socially responsible manner or in a destructive and antisocial manner. But critics detect a disturbing ethical "loose end" here.

Within the foregoing context, the question of ends is really an economic one. At least within the private business sector, the marketplace is the ultimate arbiter of which products and services are sold and which are not. Firms producing salable goods and services tend to survive to do business another day, while those left with unsalable items face bankruptcy. But closer examination shows the situation to be less than clear-cut. Unfortunately, mass advertising, government subsidies, and other exogenous factors have a tendency to bias the free market mechanism, so that organizations can end up pursuing some rather unwholesome and socially irresponsible ends. For example, as a long-time proponent of OBM, I had serious second thoughts after hearing a glowing report about the enhancement of productivity through behavior modification in a cigarette manufacturing firm. Considering that cigarette smoking is a proven health hazard, the reader is left to ponder along with the author the societal value of this particular means-ends arrangement. From an ethical standpoint, it is imperative that every prospective user of OBM consider the ultimate ends of its use in terms of the general well-being of society rather than from solely the myopic standpoint of "will it sell?"

Shifting the focus from organizations to society in general opens the door to some rather sinister claims about the ultimate impact of behavior modification. Scheflin and Opton (1978) have expressed the following concern about where Skinner's contributions will lead:

> Some social planners have realized that people may be conditioned over time passively to accept increasing restrictions on their liberty. . . . But more important than the conscious designs of social planners is the unplanned drift of our modern industrial state. We think it likely that current mind-control techniques both reflect and advance an evolutionary development toward a mechanized culture. As a by-product of increasing automation and industrialization, people are coming to resemble the automatic machines which they use to sustain their lives. (pp. 11–12)

This generalized fear takes on added legitimacy in light of Scott and Hart's (1979) observation about today's well-intentioned managers:

> The power of the modern organization is such that it has reformed the qualitative expectations we have for our lives and reordered the priorities we assign to our values. Invariably, organizational values will take precedent over individual values. *The individual is now being made for the organization rather than the organization for the individual* . . . .(emphasis added)

The decent intent of managers has its origin *within* the justificatory value system of modern organizations, to which they owe their loyalty. Thus, their very definitions of "good" and "bad" are predicated upon their prior acceptance of the values of the organizational imperative. (pp. 30–31)

Despite the difficulties of being thrust into a position of appearing to bite the hand that feeds one, present and future users of OBM have a moral obligation to consider and frankly discuss the question "to what end?"

Who Will Control the Controllers?

This third and final ethical issue is one that haunts the critics of behavior modification, because, they contend, it puts those in authority in the position of playing God. They see great potential for abuse of power when the very same person or persons defines good-versus-bad behavior and uses behavior control technology to encourage the good and stamp out the bad. Skinner (1974) has fallen back on the notion of countercontrol, as discussed earlier in this chapter, to allay fears of this form of Big Brotherism. He contends that citizens living in a democracy collectively decide through their laws which kinds of behavior deserve rewarding and which require punishment. Those who dispense the rewards and punishments are merely society's agents and ultimately accountable to society for exercising their control prerogatives responsibly. In Skinnerian language, both leaders and followers in a democratic arrangement control each other's behavior very effectively through contingencies of reinforcement.

On an organizational level, Luthans and Kreitner (1975) have addressed the issue of controlling the controllers by pointing out that every organization operates within a larger sphere of control.

. . . top management is responsible to the board of directors in a corporation and is controlled by organizational consequences such as survival, growth, share of the market, and rate of return on investment. In addition, direct and indirect control comes from stockholders, unions, customers, suppliers, government, and general social, economic, and technological conditions. (p. 180)

According to this perspective, managers are not free agents who can do as they please. They serve many masters. Given these circumstances, the argument goes, any gross misues of OBM would eventually work against management's interests.

Summarizing, although some aspects of these ethical issues might seem a bit exotic or far removed from the daily practice of management, each raises important questions that will not be dismissed easily. The most important thing a manager can take away from this discussion of OBM's ethical implications is the realization that it is a powerful tool for altering the human condition, and as such, it must be employed responsibly and with careful forethought of its potential impact on society at large.

SUMMARY

Organizational behavior management (OBM) is controversial because of association with B.F. Skinner's operant conditioning and the label "behavior modification," its somewhat confusing terminology, some popular misconceptions about what it actually involves, and its philosophical and ethical implications. Present and future users of OBM need to consider these sources of controversy so they may apply it constructively and ethically.

With its roots in nineteenth-century reflex physiology and twentieth-century behaviorism, OBM has a unique heritage with several lingering sources of controversy. Radical behaviorists like John B. Watson and B. F. Skinner stirred vigorous debate by concerning themselves with the environmental control of observable behavior while ignoring inner states. At the heart of this continuing debate is the philosophical issue of environmental determinism versus free will. Highly publicized abuses of primitive coercive techniques labeled behavior modification with captive mental patients and prisoners have served to alienate many people from anything remotely associated with the term "behavior modification."Moreover, operant conditioning's legacy of technical jargon including such terms as "behavior control" and "shaping" has added fuel to the fires of controversy.

One constructive approach to breaking down prejudicial barriers to adopting OBM is to become familiar with its key terminology. First, the terms positive reinforcement and rewards are not synonymous. Next, although positive and negative reinforcement both have the same strengthening effect on behavior, they achieve that end in opposite ways. Finally, negative reinforcement and punishment, although typically equated, have opposite effects on behavior.

If OBM is to play a significant role in human resource management, some widespread misconceptions about what it involves need to be cleared up. It is important for managers to recognize that: (1) OBM involves more complex learning processes than simple stimulus-response (S-R) reflexes; (2) a history of animal research does not preclude the application of operant conditioning to mature humans; (3) countercontrol protects individuals from puppet-like behavior control; (4) OBM involves a great deal more than piece-rate pay schemes; (5) OBM actually is an ineffective way to achieve Big Brother control over people at work; and (6) OBM is not a panacea that can be implemented in three easy steps.

Because of the obvious ethical implications of behavior control, OBM will continue to undergo close scrutiny by those concerned with managerial misconduct. Some critics flatly reject OBM as a legitimate management technique because they claim its underlying assumption of environmental determinism is dehumanizing. Proponents of OBM counter by observing that managers already engage in primitive and often punitive behavior control, so they should adopt OBM and start managing behavior systematically and positively. Critics also are concerned about the ends to which OBM will be used and who ultimately will control the controllers. OBM advocates claim that market forces and group dynamics are dependable safeguards against abuse of behavior management in the work place.

REFERENCES

Bowman, J. S. Managerial ethics in business and government. *Business Horizons*, 1976, *19*, 48–54.

Brandt, R. M. *Studying behavior in natural settings*. New York: Holt, Rinehart, and Winston, 1972.

Braun, S. H. Ethical issues in behavior modification. *Behavior Therapy*, 1975, *6*, 51–62.

Brown, M. A. Values—A necessary but neglected ingredient of motivation on the job. *Academy of Management Review*, 1976, *1*, 15–23.

Burgess, A. *A clockwork orange*. New York: W. W. Norton, 1963.

Connellan, T. K. *How to improve human performance: Behaviorism in business and industry*. New York: Harper and Row, 1978.

Fry, F. Operant conditioning and O. B. Mod.: Of mice and men. *Personnel*, 1974, *51*, 17–24.

Gray, F. P., Graubard, P., and Rosenberg, H. Little brother is changing you. *Psychology Today*, 1974, *7*, 42–46.

Hammer, M. The application of behavioral conditioning procedures to the problems of quality control: Comment. *Academy of Management Journal*, 1971, *14*, 529–532.

Kazdin, A. E. *History of behavior modification*. Baltimore: University Park Press, 1978.

Locke, E. A. The myths of behavior mod in organizations. *Academy of Management Review*, 1977, *2*, 543–553.

Locke, E. A. Myths in "The myths of the myths about behavior mod in organizations." *Academy of Management Review*, 1979, *4*, 131–136.

Luthans, F., and Kreitner, R. *Organizational behavior modification*. Glenview, IL: Scott, Foresman, 1975.

Machan, T. R. *The pseudo-science of B. F. Skinner*. New Rochelle: Arlington House, 1974.

Packard, V. *The people shapers*. Boston: Little, Brown, 1977.

Scheflin, A. W., and Opton, E. M. *The mind manipulators*. New York: Paddington Press, 1978.

Scott, W. G., and Hart, D. K. *Organizational America*. Boston: Houghton Mifflin, 1979.

Skinner, B. F. *About behaviorism*. New York: Alfred A. Knopf, 1974.

Skinner, B. F. *The behavior of organisms*. New York: D. Appleton-Century, 1938.

Skinner, B. F. *Beyond freedom and dignity*. New York: Bantam, 1971.

Skinner, B. F. *Contingencies of reinforcement*. New York: Appleton-Century-Crofts, 1969.

Skinner, B. F. *Science and human behavior*. New York: Free Press, 1953.

Skinner, B. F. *Walden two*. New York: Macmillan, 1948.

Stolz, B. S., and Associates. *Ethical issues in behavior modification*. San Francisco: Jossey-Bass, 1978.

Watson, J. B., and MacDougall, W. *The battle of behaviorism*. New York: W. W. Norton, 1929.

PART

Techniques for Assessment and Analysis

Managers have always had a need to assess and analyze performance. How are people performing? Is there a better way of doing the job? Why aren't people doing what I told them to do? Is the new program really changing anything? Is it worth the cost? These are just some of the questions managers face every day.

In the past these answers have often been based on limited information, bias, or hunches. For some decisions this has been good enough. However, a host of factors, ranging from equal opportunity pressures to a more competitive economic environment, have fostered a need for greater objectivity and precision. The margin for error is narrowing.

Among the most important contributions of OBM are the techniques used for assessing and analyzing performance. These techniques form the groundwork for applying behavior change techniques to important organizational problems.

The first chapter in this section, authored by Gary Latham, focuses on behavior-based assessment strategies. He starts by reviewing the importance of assessment and some of the criteria that a successful system must meet. Different approaches that have been taken to assessment are then critically reviewed. From this review it is clear that a behaviorally based assessment strategy offers the greatest promise. The discussion then turns to how one actually goes about developing such an assessment system based on a comprehensive job analysis. Finally, he reviews how these systems can be used to address such critical organizational problems as selection, performance appraisal, training, and employee motivation.

Given that performance can be changed, the question becomes "which performance should be changed?" Chapter 6, authored by Tom Gilbert,

tackles this important topic. He starts with the basic economics of organizations and discusses how we can measure the productivity of their two
most fundamental assets, capital and people. He then discusses how these
measures can be combined to provide an overall understanding of how
well the organization is doing. Through the mechanism of an actual case
study he demonstrates how such an analysis can yield some eminently
practical and often surprising information. The behavior that has the greatest impact on productivity is often quite different from the behavior we
originally thought needed to be changed. Finally he discusses a procedure
for determining how to go about improving the relevant performance in
ways that are both effective and cost efficient. The reader who can't benefit
from Gilbert's analysis will be rare indeed.

Making judicious decisions about the effectiveness of various programs
and procedures is no easy task. Chapter 7, by Judi Komaki, presents a tool
that can make the job a lot easier. Traditionally, effectiveness has been
evaluated using some kind of between group design. Single-case designs,
as presented in this chapter, offer an innovative and practical alternative
way to draw conclusions about actual job performance. After contrasting
them to traditional approaches, she presents two types of single-case designs, reversal and multiple baseline. The requirements and essential features of each design are reviewed and examples of their application presented. Advantages and limitations are also discussed. For the individual
who thinks that important questions about actual performance in real life
organizational settings just can't be answered, single-case designs present
a breath of fresh air.

Each of the three chapters in this section covers a different aspect of
understanding and measuring performance. Together they offer a wide
range of useful tools for the difficult tasks of performance assessment,
determining targets for change, and assessing the effectiveness of performance improvement programs.

5

Behavior-Based Assessment for Organizations[1]

GARY P. LATHAM
University of Washington

The assessment of people is probably the most important decision-making process in which an organization engages. This is because it is people who advocate ways of increasing productivity; it is people who recommend ways of slashing costs; it is people who decide where capital should be invested. And it is people who decide what technology should be developed and used in responding to opportunities for improving productivity and decreasing costs. If the wrong people are making these assessments, the consequences can be disastrous for the organization.

Certainly the assessment of people forms the core of an organization's human resource system. For example, the purpose of a *selection* system is to correctly assess who is the right person to perform a given job. Properly developed selection systems increase productivity because they can be designed to screen out applicants who engage in unacceptable work behavior. The amount of money saved by correct assessments can be enormous. One company found that it costs more than 16 thousand dollars over a six-month period before a machine operator is performing at the same level as a skilled predecessor (Latham and Wexley, 1981). This figure is based on the assumption that the right person is selected as the replacement. If the wrong person is chosen, this cost figure increases dramatically. Thus assessments as to who should be hired or rejected can literally make or break an organization.

In order to be certain that staffing assessments are truly identifying the

---

[1]This chapter is based in part on the book, *Increasing productivity through performance appraisal*, by G.P. Latham and K.N. Wexley (Reading, MA: Addison-Wesley, 1981).

right people to do the job, the *validity* of the assessments must be demonstrated. This is done by determining whether there is a significant correlation between the assessments of applicants at the hiring stage and assessments of them performing the job. If the correlation between the two assessments is significant, the hiring assessments are said to be valid (Arvey, 1979).

Assessments of employee job performance are commonly referred to as *performance appraisal.* Such assessments often influence who will be promoted, demoted, transferred, terminated, or admitted into a training program. However, if performance assessments are biased or inaccurate, no degree of care in the development of selection instruments will improve selection and staffing decisions. This is because the validity of staffing decisions is determined by correlating the assessment decisions of applicants with their performance on the job. Therefore, to the extent that the performance assessments are biased, the effectiveness of the selection instrument is reduced. Moreover, biased assessments that adversely affect people of a specific race, age, or sex can lead to costly litigation battles. Without admitting guilt, AT&T agreed in court to compensate women with payments that are estimated to run between 12 to 15 million dollars (Miner, 1974). The payments are intended as retroactive compensation to those who in the past may have been victims of discrimination in promotions, transfers, and salary administration.

No approach to selection assessments is foolproof. Therefore, once a person has been selected for a job, the problem becomes one of monitoring and maintaining a high level of performance. This is where performance appraisal plays a critical role.

A properly developed appraisal instrument serves as a contract between the organization and its employees in that it makes explicit what is required of them. Assessing performance is necessary because it serves as an audit for the organization about the effectiveness of each individual. Such a control system enables a manager to specify what the employee must start doing, stop doing, or continue doing. It is the combination of performance feedback and the setting of specific goals based on this feedback that enables performance assessment to fulfill its two most important functions, namely, the counseling (motivation) and development (training) of employees (Latham and Wexley, 1981).

When making assessments of performance, the manager may determine that the person is not fulfilling job responsibilities or behaving in a satisfactory manner due to a lack of knowledge or skill. Where this is the case, *training* that actually brings about a relatively permanent change in an employee's behavior is critical for effective human resource development. On the other hand, to the extent that a person has both the knowledge and skill to do the job, but is doing it in an unsatisfactory manner, the problem may be one of *motivation.* Two key components of effective motivation strategies include feedback of assessments, which allows an employee to learn how well he or she is doing, and the setting of specific goals on the basis of the assessments (Latham and Locke, 1979).

In summary, assessments of people are a fundamental requirement for improving the productivity of an organization's human resources, because it is through assessments that each individual's productivity is evaluated. Assessments serve as the basis for counseling and developing an individual to maintain or increase productivity. Performance assessments are critical to selection systems because, as stated previously, it is the correlation of assessments of applicants on a selection instrument (e.g., interview) with the assessments on the appraisal instrument after they have been hired that determines whether the staffing decisions are valid. After the individuals have been on the job, the performance appraisal identifies who is in need of training or motivation.

The purpose of this chapter is to discuss ways of improving employee assessments so as to increase productivity. Specific attention is given to three different ways of making assessments, a job analysis procedure on which the assessment instruments can be based, and the application of assessment decisions to improving an organization's approach to selection, performance appraisal, training, and motivation.

ASSESSING PERFORMANCE

The problem of assessment may be approached from one of three perspectives. That is, the person may be evaluated on the basis of personality or traits, economic indexes or "results," or through the observation of behavior. The perspective one takes is important from both a management and a legal standpoint.

Traits

An advantage of this approach is that trait scales that define acceptable employee behavior can be developed quickly. It does not take considerable time or imagination to brainstorm a set of words that are considered positive, complimentary, and necessary for all employees (e.g., aggressive, decisive, dependable). A second advantage is that they can be used across jobs. Thus the organization only has to use one assessment scale. Everyone is evaluated on the same basis. But these two advantages are illusory for the following reasons.

First, feedback and training must be specific if they are to bring about a relatively permanent change in an employee's behavior. Traits such as creativity, loyalty, integrity, and the like are words surrounded with ambiguity. Telling a person to be a better listener or to show more initiative may be good advice, but it doesn't tell the individual what to do to accept this advice. These words must be defined explicitly for the employee if they are to have a beneficial effect.

Second, the assessments must be related to critical or important aspects of the job if they are going to meaningfully affect an employee's performance. What is truly critical or important in one job is not necessarily critical or important to the same extent in other jobs.

Third, the dependability of these assessments is questionable. "On each particular characterization of persons, two raters typically correlate with each other on the order of 0.25" (Fiske, 1979, p. 25). Thus two or more people are likely to disagree in their assessments of the same person when traits are used.

Finally, whenever assessments are challenged in court due to alleged discrimination on the basis of race, sex, or age, the court has almost always found the assessors guilty when the assessments were based on traits. For example, in Wade v. Mississippi Extension Service (1974) the court ruled that what the organization called an objective assessment of job performance was in fact based on supervisory ratings of such general characteristics as loyalty, public acceptance, attitude, appearance, and personal conduct.

> As may be readily observed, these are traits which are susceptible to partiality and to the personal taste, whim, or fancy of the evaluator. We must then view these factors as presently utilized to be patently subjective in form and obviously susceptible to completely subjective treatment. (p 1427)

Economic Indexes

Cost-related results have historically been the preferred method of assessment by industrial psychologists because they are concrete tangible measures. Such objective measures were believed to eliminate errors in observation and judgment that often occur when ratings are used. Further, quantitative measures such as profits, costs, and returns on investment serve as excellent indicators of an organization's effectiveness. Nevertheless, they are generally inadequate indicators by themselves of an individual's job effectiveness for several reasons.

First, economic indexes or performance results do not eliminate errors in observation and judgment. Observation is a necessity for evaluating the meaning of cost-related results such as tardiness, absences, and accidents. "Human judgment enters into every criterion . . ." (Smith, 1976, p. 757).

Second, cost-related results are difficult to obtain on an individual employee in most jobs. For example, a cost-related measure of a typist's performance might be the number of words typed per minute. But what cost-related measures exist for the individual personnel manager, engineer, or newspaper reporter?

Third, cost-related measures are almost always deficient in that they often omit important factors for which a person should be held accountable (e.g., team playing as defined by a manager in one district loaning people or equipment to a manager in another district). This deficiency is a major criticism of management by objectives (MBO). Many employees argue that they are not measured on nor do they receive credit for important aspects of their job if they cannot be spelled out in quantitative terms.

Fourth, such measures are often excessive in that they take into account factors for which the individual cannot or should not be held accountable.

This is true where an employee's performance is affected by the performance of others. Thus the employee is evaluated on factors that are beyond his or her control.

Fifth, the sole use of cost-related measures can encourage a results-at-all-costs mentality that can run counter to an organization's corporate ethics policy. Moreover, a results-at-all-costs mentality can run counter to the overall productivity of the organization. For example, loaning equipment or people to a fellow manager may hurt the monthly cost sheet of the loaner, but it may significantly increase the productivity of the organization as a whole. Nevertheless, the person whose performance assessment is based primarily on minimizing costs is unlikely to loan the equipment or people unless coerced to do so by a supervisor.

Sixth, reasons four and five can lead to litigation suits to the extent that a person believes he or she was penalized unfairly due to measures beyond his or her control. Costly litigation suits are also likely if the results-at-all-costs mentality leads to unethical behavior (e.g., price fixing, bribery).

Seventh, and most importantly, cost-related measures or performance results by themselves do not inform employees what they need to do to maintain or increase productivity. Cost-related measures may indicate whether an employee is or is not meeting a set of objectives, but the answers to the questions of how or why can remain elusive.

Finally,

> the perception of poor performance may lead to inaccurate appraisals and points of conflict . . . the data suggest that supervisors make attributions and responses partly as a function of the seriousness of the outcome. In work settings these outcomes may be completely out of the subordinate's control (e.g., whether a patient falls out of bed when the railing is down) . . . supervisors would be more efficient if they concentrated on trying to change the behavior that caused the incident rather than focusing on the outcome. . . . when poor performance occurs but the outcome is not serious, the supervisor is more likely to overlook the problem. This strategy can lead to serious negative consequences at some later time and is clearly not an effective means of feedback. To change behavior we must focus on the behavior not the outcome. (Mitchell and Wood, 1980, p. 138)

Behavioral Assessment

Behavioral measures overcome the limitations of trait and economic measures in that they are specific, they are observable, they dictate exactly what the individual is to do on the job, and they are under the individual's control. The correlations among observers as to whether a behavior occurred are often above 0.90 (Fiske, 1979). When based on a systematic job analysis, the assessment instrument is neither excessive nor deficient. A job analysis, to be discussed later, identifies the critical acceptable (legally and ethically) behavior that a person must demonstrate on the job to complete assignments successfully. Some examples of behavioral measures are:

1. Checks statements to insure that bills are not overpaid.
2. Meets deadlines in making bank deposits.
3. Explains why a change is necessary.
4. Uses ear plugs in designated areas.
5. Responds to a customer request within 20 seconds.

Note that behavioral measures can encompass cost-related measures. For example, in the game of baseball, coming to the ball park, striking out, and hitting a home run are all performance results. Similarly, reducing costs by 10 percent, selling 52 cars in a month, and turning a report in on time can be considered performance results. Each of these statements also constitute behavioral measures. What makes behavioral measures more comprehensive than cost-related or economic measures is that behavioral criteria not only measure the individual on factors over which they have control, but they also specify what the person must do or not do to attain these results.

In summary, behavioral assessments pinpoint the strategies necessary for employees to affect the bottom line. The bottom line defined in cost-related terms is a primary measure of an organization's effectiveness. The purpose of behavioral assessment is to specify what each employee needs to do to influence that bottom line. Behavioral assessments will do this to the extent that the measurement criteria are based on a systematic job analysis.

JOB ANALYSIS: DEVELOPING BEHAVIORAL ASSESSMENTS

A job analysis is a systematic procedure that identifies behavior critical for performing a job satisfactorily. It forms the basis for making behavioral assessments.

One of the most frequently used job analysis procedures for developing behavioral criteria is the critical incident technique (CIT) first described by Flanagan (1954). The CIT requires observers who are aware of the aims and objectives of a given job and who see people perform the job on a frequent basis (e.g., daily) to describe to a job analyst incidents of effective and ineffective job behavior that they have observed over the past 6 to 12 months. Thus supervisors, peers, subordinates, and clients may be interviewed about their observations of the *critical requirements* of the job. The specific steps in conducting a job analysis based on the critical incident technique are as follows:

1. *Introduction.* I am conducting a job analysis to determine what makes the difference between an effective and an ineffective (supervisor, dentist, secretary). By effective performance I mean the type of behavior that, when you saw it occur, you wished all employees would do the same thing under similar circumstances. By ineffective performance I

mean behavior that, if it occurred repeatedly or even once under certain circumstances, would make you doubt the competency of the individual.

I am talking with you because you are aware of the aims and objectives of the job, you frequently observe people in this job, and you are able to discern competent from incompetent performance. Please do not tell me the names of any individual to whom you are referring. (Note: Job incumbents are not interviewed concerning their *own* behavior. This is because incumbents are usually objective in describing their *effective* but not their *ineffective* behavior, Vroom and Maier, 1961).

2. *Interview.* I would like you to think back over the past six to 12 months of specific incidents that you yourself have seen occur. (Note: The emphasis on the past 12 months is to insure that the information is currently applicable. For example, behavior that was critical for a sales person in the 1950s may no longer be critical in the 1980s. Moreover, memory loss may distort the facts if the analysis is not restricted to recent incidents. The requirement that the interviewer report only first-hand information maximizes the objectivity or factual nature of the information to be reported.)

Can you think of an incident? (Note: If the answer is no, the following comments may stimulate recall.)

    (a) Write down the five key things that an employee *must* be good at in this job. What is the first thing you wrote? Can you think of an employee who within the past year demonstrated that point? What was the second thing you wrote? The third, etc.?

    (b) Tell me the first initial (in order to maintain anonymity) of the most effective person you know in this job. Suppose I stated that this person is ineffective. What incidents can you cite to change my opinion?

You have thought of an incident. Good. For each incident you recall, I am going to ask you the same three questions, namely:

    (a) What were the circumstances surrounding this incident? In other words, what was the background? What was the situation? (Note: This question is important because it establishes *when* a given behavior is appropriate.)

    (b) What exactly did the individual *do* that was effective or ineffective? (Note: Generally effective incidents are requested before ineffective incidents. There is no empirical evidence to support this decision. However, experience indicates that when effective incidents are requested first, the interviewee does not feel that the information is being obtained for a "witch hunt." The purpose of this second question is to elicit information concerning specific *observable* behavior.)

    (c). How is the incident you described an example of effective or ineffective behavior? In other words, how did this affect the task the individual was performing?

Generally an interviewee is asked to report five effective and ineffective incidents. Attention is given to both effective and ineffective incidents because an effective incident is not necessarily the opposite of an ineffective incident. For example, setting a specific goal was found to be effective for increasing the productivity of loggers, but not setting goals by no means led to bankruptcy (Latham, 1969).

A total of 10 incidents are collected because they can usually be collected within one hour. This is the maximum time period that many employees can be away from the job without disrupting their work day. No more than 10 incidents are collected from any one individual, so that the data are not biased by talkative people. In order to obtain a comprehensive sample of incidents it is recommended that at least 30 people be interviewed for a total of roughly 300 incidents.

The interviewer must be skilled in collecting information describing observable behaviors. If the interviewee says, "The employee really showed initiative in solving the problem," the interviewer must ask, "What exactly did the individual do that indicated initiative?"

APPLICATION OF BEHAVIORAL ASSESSMENTS

Selection

The interview is the selection tool used by virtually every company in North America. In fact the *Wall Street Journal* (Lancaster, 1975) reported that as a result of federal legislation in the United States regarding hiring procedures, a majority of companies are relying solely on the results of an interview for making hiring decisions.

What makes the reliance on the interview for making selection decisions alarming is that a person's behavior in an interview is seldom indicative of that person's behavior on the job. There are several reasons for this. First, the questions asked are frequently not related to the job. Second, the person generally can determine from the wording of the question what is considered to be a socially desirable answer. Third, the interview frequently focuses on traits. As noted earlier, two or more people who assess a person at the same point in time often come up with different conclusions when assessments are based on traits. Fourth, the trait measures are often correlated with on-the-job measures of the person's traits. The lack of reliability in the two sets of trait measures makes prediction all but impossible. Fifth, the organization may try to correlate trait measures in the interview with economic indexes on the job. This can be analogous to attempting to match apples with oranges.

A behavioral assessment procedure that overcomes these issues is the situational interview (Latham, Saari, Pursell, and Campion, 1980). The situational interview is based on the critical incident technique. The steps are as follows:

1. Performance dimensions or behavioral criteria (e.g., planning, cost

control, interactions with subordinates) are identified from the job analysis. This is determined by reading the critical incidents and clustering or grouping those incidents that are similar, if not identical, in content.

2.   At least one critical incident that aptly describes each dimension is chosen by job experts. The experts are typically supervisors of the people who perform the job in question.

3.   Literary license is used in turning each incident into an interview question in which applicants are asked to explain how they would behave in a given situation.

4.   Each answer is rated independently by two or more interviewers on a 5-point scale.

5.   To facilitate agreement among interviewers, job experts develop behavioral statements that are used as benchmarks or illustrations of 1, 3, and 5 answers. Thus the benchmarks serve as a scoring key.

6.   The results of the interview are correlated with behavioral assessments of the person on the job. The outcome is high agreement among interviewers, and a significant relationship between what a person says in an interview and how that person behaves on the job. The procedure has proven effective for predicting the performance of blacks and females in entry-level jobs as well as people in a supervisory position (Latham et al., 1980).

The following is an example of how a critical incident was used for developing a question for assessing the performance dimension "Attendance":

An example of a critical incident describing ineffective behavior of an employee was:

> The employee was devoted to his family. He had only been married for 18 months. He used whatever excuse he could to stay home. One day the fellow's baby got a cold. His wife had a hangnail or something on her toe. He didn't come to work. He didn't even phone in.

This incident was rewritten by the job experts (managers) in the form of the following question:

> Your spouse and two teenage children are sick in bed with a cold. There are no relatives or friends available to look in on them. Your shift starts in three hours. What would you do in this situation?

Each member of the group was then asked to independently benchmark a 5 answer, that is, "Things you have actually heard said in an interview by people who subsequently were considered outstanding on the job"; a 3 answer, that is, "Answers that you have actually heard said in an interview by people who as a result got hired and turned out to be mediocre performers"; and a 1 answer, that is, "Things that you have actually heard said in an interview by people who as a result got hired but turned out to be very poor performers." For job experts who did not have extensive interviewing experience (e.g., line managers), these instructions were modified to read, "Think of people you know who are outstanding, mediocre, and poor on the job. How do you think they would respond to this question if they were being interviewed?"

Each manager then read his or her answers to the other job experts. After group discussion, consensus was reached on the answers to use as benchmarks. The three benchmarks for the above question were: (1) I'd stay home— my spouse and family come first; (3) I'd phone my supervisor and explain my situation; and (5) since they only have colds, I'd come to work.

The answers to this and similar questions were found to correlate significantly with how the person actually behaved on the job (Latham et al, 1980).

Performance Appraisal

As stated in the introduction of this chapter, the validity of selection decisions is established by showing that there is a significant correlation between how people perform on the selection instrument and how these same people perform on the job. The validity of the situational interview has been established by showing that there is a significant correlation between what people say in response to interview questions and what people do in response to job requirements. Job performance was assessed by a series of instruments known as behavioral observation scales (BOS).

The specific steps required for developing BOS are as follow:

1. Critical incidents that are similar, if not identical, in content are grouped together to form one behavioral item. For example, two or more incidents concerning a supervisor who compliments or rewards employees for doing a good job were used by Latham, Fay, and Saari (1979) for writing the item, "Praises or rewards subordinates for specific things they do well."

2. Behavioral items that are similar are grouped together by job incumbents or analysts to form one BOS criterion. For example, the above behavioral item was grouped together with similar items (e.g., counsels employees on personal problems) to form the criterion, "Interactions with subordinates."

3. Interjudge agreement is assessed to determine whether another individual or group of individuals would have developed the same behavioral criteria from the critical incidents obtained in the job analysis. After the incidents have been categorized, they are placed in random order and given to a second individual or group, who reclassify the incidents according to the categorization system established in step 1. The ratio of interjudge agreement is calculated by counting the number of incidents that both groups agree should be placed in a given criterion divided by the combined number of incidents both groups placed in that criterion. Thus if one group of judges classified incidents 4, 7, 8, 9, and 17 under

one criterion, while another group of judges classified only incidents 7, 8, and 9 under the same criterion, the interjudge agreement would be 0.60

$$\left[\frac{(7, 8, 9)}{(4, 7, 8, 9, 17)}\right] = \frac{3}{5} = 0.6.$$

An a priori decision is usually made that the ratio must be 0.80 or higher for a behavioral criterion to be acceptable. If the ratio is below 0.80, the items under the criterion are reexamined to see if they should be reclassified under a different criterion, or if the criteria should be rewritten to increase specificity.

4. The BOS criteria (e.g., interactions with peers, safety, technical competency) are examined regarding their relevance or content validity (Nagle, 1953). Relevance or content validity is concerned with the systematic evaluation of appraisal instruments, by people who are intimately familiar with the job, to see if they include a representative sample of the behavioral domain of interest as defined by the job analysis (Anastasi, 1976). Two tests for content validity are described below:

(a) Prior to the categorization of the critical incidents, 10 percent of the incidents are set aside. After the categorization is completed in Step 1, these incidents are examined to see if any of them describe behavior that has not yet appeared. If this examination necessitates the development of a new behavioral criterion, or the formation of two or more behavioral items under an existing criterion, the assumption that a sufficient number of incidents have been collected is rejected.

(b) The second test of content validity involves recording the increase in the number of behavioral items with the increase in the number of incidents classified. If 90 percent of the items appear after 75 percent of the incidents have been categorized, the content validity of the BOS is considered satisfactory.

5. The appraisal instrument is developed by attaching a 5-point Likert scale to each behavioral item. Only five numbers are placed under each behavioral item because research shows that there is little utility in adding scale values beyond five (Jenkins and Taber, 1977; Lissitz and Green, 1975).

Observers (e.g., peers, supervisors) are asked to indicate the frequency with which they have observed a job incumbent engage in each kind of behavior. Here is an example of a BOS for a public affairs manager:

Interactions with the Public

1. Identifies community and special interest groups or organizations that can influence directly or indirectly company operations.

Almost Never   0   1   2   3   4   Almost Always

2. Directs the public to the local superintendent for questions, support, or assistance so that the superintendent is looked upon favorably by the community.
Almost Never   0   1   2   3   4   Almost Always

3. Asks for and listens openly to criticisms of the company.
Almost Never   0   1   2   3   4   Almost Always

4. Can explain the company's rationale for engaging in policies that irritate or concern local residents.
Almost Never   0   1   2   3   4   Almost Always

5. Follows up on complaints lodged against the company to see if the company's explanation is understood.
Almost Never   0   1   2   3   4   Almost Always

6. Can explain the basis for controversial company actions without irritating or offending the listener.
Almost Never   0   1   2   3   4   Almost Always

7. Knows the opinions of each member of the city council on issues that do or could impact the company.
Almost Never   0   1   2   3   4   Almost Always

8. Knows the mayor(s) on a first name basis.
Almost Never   0   1   2   3   4   Almost Always

9. Can formulate a response compatible with the company's philosophy during a crisis situation (e.g., 22 people injured minutes ago).
Almost Never   0   1   2   3   4   Almost Always

10. Develops and implements surveys on community attitudes that do or could impact region operations.
Almost Never   0   1   2   3   4   Almost Always

11. Insures that opinion makers in the community (e.g., members of the Chamber of Commerce) are invited to functions that may be of interest to them.
Almost Never   0   1   2   3   4   Almost Always

12. Knows the county commissioners on a first name basis.
Almost Never   0   1   2   3   4   Almost Always

13. Using NEWSLINE or region newspaper explains both sides of an issue factually without offering an opinion.
Almost Never   0   1   2   3   4   Almost Always

14. Provides information and background to region and corporation on need to support political candidates.
Almost Never   0   1   2   3   4   Almost Always

Employees receive a 0 if they have been observed engaging in a specific kind of behavior 0–64 percent of the time, 1 for 65–74 percent of the time, 2 for 75–84 percent of the time, 3 for 85–94 percent of the time, and 4 for 95–100 percent of the time. These percentages, corresponding to the five points on the Likert scale, can change depending upon the job and organization involved. In some cases the behavioral items are stated in terms of ineffective behavior if that is the way the incidents were described by the interviewees during the job analysis.

6.   Many items on the BOS, although critical in terms of defining highly effective or ineffective performance, occur either so frequently or infrequently that they do not differentiate good from poor job incumbents. For example, of 90 supervisors rated on "has the smell of liquor on his/ her breath," Latham et al. (1979) reported that 85 received 4 (almost never), 4 received a 3 (seldom), and 1 person received a 2 (sometimes). A major purpose of a performance appraisal instrument is to differentiate between good and poor performers. The above item does not meet this requirement, since almost every supervisor received the same rating. Therefore, these types of items are eliminated by conducting an item analysis. This statistical procedure involves correlating the scores on each behavioral item with the sum of *all* items so that each section on the appraisal instrument is unambiguous to the appraiser.

Latham et al. (1979) compared the frequencies of supervisors in five categories (e.g., superior, excellent, full) on an original BOS with a revised BOS (after item analysis). The effect of removing undifferentiating items spread out the total ratings.

7.   If there are approximately three to five times as many individuals to be rated as there are behavioral items, a factor analysis can be conducted. A factor analysis groups behavioral items together on the extent to which they correlate with one another to form different behavioral criteria (e.g., interaction with peers, organizational commitment). This grouping removes the need for two groups of judges to categorize the incidents into overall categories, because the factor analysis performs this step for them. This is one reason why factor analysis rather than judges should be used to group the items into behavioral categories; it saves time. Further, it insures that the different behavioral criteria will be independent of one another and thus contain the minimum number of items on which an employee should be evaluated.

The advantages of using BOS for conducting performance appraisals include the following:

BOS are developed from a systematic job analysis supplied by employees for employees. Thus understanding of and commitment to the use of the appraisal instrument are facilitated. The frequently heard complaints from both managers and subordinates that the items on the appraisal instrument are either sufficiently vague to defy understanding or completely inappropriate for the individual's appraisal are minimized. Thus BOS satisfy the requirement of the 1978 Civil Service Reform Act to allow employees to participate in identifying the critical requirements of their job.

BOS can either serve alone or as a supplement to existing job descriptions in that they make explicit what kinds of behavior are required of an employee turnover and job dissatisfaction (Wanous, 1973). They can assist "job preview" for potential job candidates by showing them what they will be expected to do. Job previews are an effective means of reducing employee turnover and job dissatisfaction (Wanous, 1980). They can assist candidates in making a decision as to whether they would want to consistently demonstrate the behavior described on the BOS.

BOS are content valid in the sense that the behavior differentiating the successful from the unsuccessful performer are included on the instrument. Appraisers are forced to make a thorough evaluation of an employee rather than emphasizing only what they can recall at the time of the appraisal. The typical supervisor simply does not have time to record systematically instances of adequate and inadequate behavior. Thus the behavior that is recorded, both effective and ineffective, is unlikely to be a representative sample of the employee's behavior (Feldman, 1979). The BOS approach specifies to both the supervisor and the employee exactly what must be observed.

BOS facilitate explicit performance feedback in that they encourage meaningful discussions between the supervisor and the employee of the latter's strengths and weaknesses. Generalities are avoided in favor of specific overt behavior for which the employee is praised or is encouraged to demonstrate on the job. Explicit performance feedback using BOS combined with the setting of specific goals has been shown repeatedly to be an effective means for bringing about or maintaining a positive behavior change (Dossett, Latham, and Mitchell, 1979; Latham and Yukl, 1975a; Latham, Mitchell, and Dossett, 1978). BOS procedures request the supervisor to record incidents describing the employee's behavior. We have found, however, that supervisors often ignore this request and base their feedback on the numbers that they have circled under each behavioral item. The behavioral items not only focus the supervisor's attention on what to look for during an appraisal period, but also facilitiate recall in discussing the results of the appraisal with the employee.

BOS can satisfy EEOC guidelines in terms of validity (relevance) and reliability. The content validity, interjudge agreement of the categorization system, and the internal consistency of the criteria are usually found to be satisfactory. In previous studies (Latham and Wexley, 1977; Latham, Wexley, and Rand, 1975; Ronan and Latham, 1974) the test-retest and interobserver reliability, as well as the validity of the BOS in indicating employee attendance and productivity, were demonstrated.

Finally, BOS measure the production level of the individual employee. Just as one measures the production level of a machine in terms of machine rate, in the area of human resources one can measure the production level of human beings in terms of response rate. A response rate is defined as the frequency over time with which a person exhibits behavior critical to performing a task or series of tasks. Critical job behavior is that which affects the bottom line. Output/input measures and safe working environments do not occur through osmosis. Someone must do something to bring about maximum output through minimum input. It is that measure of "do something" that is critical to measuring accurately the productivity or efficiency of an employee. BOS, based on a systematic job analysis, provide a comprehensive assessment of an employee's job performance.

Training

Training is defined as a set of procedures that bring about a relatively permanent change in a person's behavior as a result of practice (Wexley and Latham, 1981). A problem with most training programs is that they are not evaluated as to whether they attain the objectives for which they were designed. Consequently, no one knows whether the training should be continued, modified, or abandoned. Straightforward ways for assessing the effectiveness of training programs have been discussed elsewhere (Wexley and Latham, 1981).

Of importance to this discussion is that even when training programs are evaluated, they are often evaluated on the wrong criteria. That is, they are often assessed in terms of cost-related measures. Unless the gap between what an individual does (e.g., cutting down a tree) and the cost-related measure or outcome (e.g., cords per hour worked) is small, the conclusion on training effectiveness is likely to be erroneous. As noted previously, cost-related measures are usually excessive in the sense that they are influenced by conditions beyond the control of the individual (e.g., changes in technology, access to capital, marketing conditions, weather). These factors may mask the true effects of a training program by exaggerating or clouding training results. Training is done to inculcate or sustain effective job behavior. Training effectiveness therefore should be assessed primarily in terms of its influence on employee *behavior*. It is true that behavioral measures based on a job analysis correlate positively with cost-related measures (Latham and Wexley, 1981). This is because good cost-related results do not occur through osmosis. They are good because a person or persons engaged in appropriate behavior. But the correlation is seldom 1.0 for the reasons just cited.

For example, measures that concentrate solely on end results may be insensitive to performance changes on the part of employees. In a preventive maintenance study, Komaki et al. (1980) found that the condition of the vehicles, an end-result measure, was affected by such factors as the age of the vehicles, the supply system, variations in their size, the availability of funds—in addition to the preventive maintenance behavior demonstrated by the employee(s). Behavioral measures are just what the term implies, namely, measures of an employee's behavior. By using behavioral measures one can determine what percentage of maintenance costs, if any, are due to inappropriate employee behavior. If the inappropriate behavior occurs because of a lack of knowledge or skill on the part of the employee, a training program is in order.

An advantage of using behavioral measures is that they specify the steps that must be followed to obtain desired performance results. This has been found to be particularly effective in training the hard-core unemployed (HCU). For example, Schneier (1973) found that many HCUs in a company training program dropped out before the training tasks were mastered. To increase the training success rate, he specified the behavioral components of the various tasks. A trainee was praised for mastering the individual behavioral components. The result was a significant increase in training sucess.

In short, the key to effective training is to conduct a job analysis to identify job behavior critical for impacting the bottom line. Training is conducted for those people who lack the knowledge or skill to demonstrate these kinds of behavior. Training effectiveness is assessed by determining whether these people can demonstrate the appropriate behavior to master the job after completing the training program. BOS are excellent tools for assessing training effectiveness.

Motivation

Once effective performance has been defined, and employees have been given the opportunity to learn the behavior necessary for performing the job, the issue of motivation can be addressed directly. A fundamental concept indigenous to most, if not all, theories of motivation is goal setting (Locke, 1978); that is, specifying exactly what it is the individual is to do on the job.

In short, goal setting is effective because it clarifies exactly what is expected of an individual. As several engineers have commented, "by receiving a specific goal from the supervisor we are able to determine for the first time what that *** really expects from us" (Latham, Mitchell, and Dossett, 1978). Moreover, the process of working against an explicit goal injects interest into the task. It provides challenge and meaning to a job. Through goal attainment, feelings of accomplishment and recognition (from self or supervisor) occur.

Although feedback by itself has no effect on performance unless it affects the person's goals (Latham et al., 1978), feedback is a necessary condition for the effectiveness of goal setting (Locke, Shaw, Saari, and Latham, 1981). Because the emphasis of this paper is on assessment rather than goal setting, the remaining section of this paper focuses on three factors (Johnston, Duncan, Monroe, Stephenson, and Stoerzinger, 1978) that need to be taken into account before assessment can play a contributory role in motivation.

First, in order for feedback to be of value, it must be accurate. A fundamental limitation of behavioral assessments is that their effectiveness or accuracy is dependent upon the objectivity of the observer. Observers are prone to recording errors that the observer is frequently unaware of making. For example, halo error occurs when an observer is so impressed by the frequency with which a person engages in appropriate behavior in some context that the observer erroneously records the person engaging in appropriate behavior in all contexts. Contrast-effects errors occurs when a person's behavior is evaluated relative (in contrast) to another person rather than against the job requirements. First-impressions error refers to the tendency for observers to record data that support an initial favorable or unfavorable impression.

Latham, Wexley, and Pursell (1975) developed a training program to teach observers (managers) ways of minimizing observational errors by increasing their objectivity in recording their observations of an employee's behavior. The program has been shown to be highly effective in both selecting (Pursell, Dossett, and Latham, 1980) and appraising (Fay and Latham, in press) employees. In brief, the program teaches people to recognize the multidimensionality of work performance, and to specify the target behavior (effective or ineffective) that is to be observed and recorded.

.Related to the issue of accuracy is determining who is a credible source for recording observations of the person's behavior. In general, the people who record behavioral observations should be those who are aware of the aims and objectives of the person's job, who routinely see the person performing on the job, and who are capable of discerning competent behavior. Generally such people include supervisors, peers, subordinates, the employee himself or herself, and customers or clients. Of these five groups, peers whose recordings are anonymous frequently provide the most reliable and valid observations. This is because peers generally have more data than the other sources. They see how a peer interacts with the supervisor, subordinates, clients, and they themselves (Latham and Wexley, 1981).

The motivational value of peer assessments is similar to that of sensitivity training. The goal of sensitivity training is to make the individual sensitive to how he or she is perceived by others. This increase in sensitivity allegedly leads to an increase in interpersonal effectiveness on the job. Unfortunately, this goal is seldom achieved in practice (Wexley and Latham, 1981). A major reason why the goal is not achieved is because the assessments are infrequently job related. The group is allowed to provide feedback regarding any aspect of a person's behavior; moreover, the assessments are often based primarily, if not solely, on the behavior exhibited by the person during the training session.

Peer assessments based on BOS have the same goal as sensitivity training. The difference between this approach and the former approach is that the peer assessments are based on behavior identified through a job analysis. Thus the assessments are not only job related but they evaluate behavior critical to fulfilling job responsibilities. Each person, in a group setting, receives feedback in terms of an arithmetic mean as to how he or she was rated by the group. Discussion follows on what this person can do in the future to maintain or increase a score on the BOS items. The person then sets specific goals in terms of the behavior that need to be changed. The advantage of using BOS coupled with group discussion is that the person knows fully, precisely, and clearly what is expected of him or her on the job.

A second consideration regarding an assessment system is its frequency. Some authors have argued that the measurement system, ideally, should be continuous and routine (Johnston, Duncan, Monroe, Stephenson, and Stoerzinger, 1978). This recommendation is based on the assumption that knowledge of a deviation will lead to immediate correction of the behavior.

This consideration is a pragmatic one where counters, timers, and other detection and recording devices can be used. For example, Lise Saari and I had counters hooked to machines in a sawmill that repeat a particular action. The result was an immediate increase in the productivity of the unionized employees who operated the machines. The increase in productivity occurred although management neither praised nor threatened people regarding productivity after the counters were installed.

Where counters are neither applicable nor feasible, providing employees with specific praise is effective for bringing about and maintaining desired work behavior. The praise must be specific for at least three reasons. First, if the praise is specific it increases the probability that the behavior will be repeated. If the praise is general, the employee may not only be unaware of the specific behavior that resulted in the praise, but he or she may interpret the praise as reinforcing the very behavior that the person who gave the praise wished would change. Second, making praise specific increases the probability that it will be considered sincere by the listener. The listener knows that he or she engaged in given behavior; the only surprise is that someone not only noticed the occurrence of the behavior, but time was taken to actively comment on them. Third, it decreases the probability that the praise will be perceived as a sign of favoritism. The minimizing of this perception is important in both unionized and nonunionized work settings. This perception is minimized to the extent that the praise is given to everyone who exhibits the behavior.

The schedule or frequency of the assessments should be continuous for people in a learning or training mode. But once the behavior is learned, the frequency with which the behavior is emitted is often greater when the assessments are provided on an intermittent schedule (Latham and Dossett, 1978).

There are several explanations for the effectiveness of an intermittent schedule. From the standpoint of an assessment, a person who is praised on a continuous schedule may become satiated with the praise. For example, a person who is always complimented for each and every meal, assuming that the cooking is indeed satisfactory, may not work as fast or as hard in preparing subsequent meals as the person who is intermittently reinforced for the way in which a meal is prepared. A letter of commendation from a vice president in which an employee is recognized and appreciated may be much more reinforcing if it is sent once in a while rather than every single time the employee demonstrates outstanding behavior.

A third factor regarding assessments is their display and interpretation. As Johnston et al. (1978) have noted, the most revealing data are of no value if they are not displayed in a way that encourages the proper interpretation and uses of them. Graphs are among the simplest and most straightforward approaches in that they facilitate the daily plotting of data, they are easy to understand, and they encourage simple and frequent comparisons of data from all aspects of the business. A further benefit of graphs is that they often serve as a key ingredient in a feedback system, which in turn affects performance through its effects on goals.

A colleague and I recently designed a study to investigate the effects of monetary incentives on the attendance of female workers in a nursery. Before the incentive was implemented, baseline data were collected on each employee. The data were posted publicly by employees. The result was a significant increase in attendance. The increase was so significant that the monetary incentive study has never been implemented. This increase in attendance occurred even though the employees knew that it would result in the abandonment of the incentive study. It occurred even though the employees were members of a strong union. Moreover, the employees lived in a rural area where management had little alternative to employing them.

Similar results have been obtained with unionized male truck drivers regarding their truck loads (Latham and Baldes, 1975) and truck turn-around time (Latham and Saari, 1981). In the latter study, the drivers insisted that the management continue to post the results whenever management attempted to discontinue the practice.

SUMMARY

A straightforward approach to employee assessment is to define performance behaviorally. Effective assessment requires a manager to identify and define specific behavior that is required of the employee on the job. A job analysis procedure that yields this information is the critical incident technique. BOS can serve as a performance assessment instrument for counseling and developing an employee.

The critical job behavior on the BOS should be specific to the extent that they are observable. "Showing initiative" is not sufficiently specific. "Calling on a customer without being asked to do so by anyone" is specific. The ability to specify behavior in observable terms is the first skill people must acquire before they can assess employee performance accurately. Moreover, it forces someone who is dissatisfied with an assessment of an employee to analyze the source of their dissatisfaction to the point of identifying the specific behavior they would like to see changed. By pinpointing these kinds of behavior, feedback and the setting of specific goals in relation to this feedback can bring about a rapid change in employee behavior.

Selection instruments should be designed to predict who is likely to *behave* appropriately on the job. Instruments designed to predict a person's traits or cost-related results are unlikely to be as effective as those that are designed to predict on-the-job behavior. This is because behavior is largely under the control of the individual. Cost-related measures, although affected by a person's behavior, are also affected by a wide variety of other factors beyond the person's control. Traits are generally poorly defined and difficult to measure. Thus they are frowned upon by the courts.

For these same reasons, the effectiveness of a training program should be assessed in terms of its effects on employee behavior. If the training brings about a relatively permanent change in employee behavior, it is effective.

Motivation is defined as the frequency or rate with which an employee exhibits critical job behavior. Three factors need to be taken into account before behavioral assessments can play a contributory role in motivation. First, in order for the assessments to be of value, they must be accurate. Second, the assessments, ideally, should be continuous and routine. After the behavior has been learned, the feedback can be given on an intermittent basis. Third, consideration must be given to the display of the assessments. The most revealing data are of no value if they are not displayed in a way that encourages proper interpretation.

REFERENCES

Anastasi, A. *Psychological testing.* New York: MacMillan, 1968.

Arvey, R. D. *Fairness in selecting employees.* Reading, MA: Addison-Wesley, 1979.

Dossett, D. L., Latham, G. P., and Mitchell, T. R. The effects of assigned versus participatively set goals, KR, and individual differences when goal difficulty is held constant. *Journal of Applied Psychology,* 1979, *64,* 291–298.

Fay, C. H. and Latham, G. P. Effects of training and rating scales on rating error. *Personnel Psychology,* in press.

Feldman, J. M. Beyond attribution theory: Cognitive processes in employee performance evaluations. Paper presented at the annual meeting of AIDS, New Orleans, 1979.

Fiske, D. W. Two worlds of psychological phenomena. *American Psychologist,* 1979, *34,* 733–739.

Flanagan, J. C. The critical incident technique. *Psychological Bulletin,* 1954, *51,* 327–358.

Jenkins, G. D., and Taber, T. A. A Monte Carlo study of factors affecting three indices of composite scale reliability. *Journal of Applied Psychology,* 1977, *62,* 392–398.

Johnston, J. M., Duncan, P. K., Monroe, L., Stephenson, H., and Stoerzinger, A. Tactics and benefits of behavioral measurement in business. *Journal of Organizational Behavior Management,* 1978, *1,* 164–178.

Komaki, J., Collins, R. L., and Thoene, T. J. *Behavioral Assessment,* 1980, *2,* 103–123.

Lancaster, H. Failing system: Job tests are dropped by many companies due to antibias drive. *Wall Street Journal,* September 3, 1975, p. 1.

Latham, G. P. The development of job performance criteria for pulpwood producers in the southeastern United States. Unpublished master's thesis, Georgia Institute of Technology, 1969.

Latham, G. P., and Baldes, J. J. The "practical significance" of Locke's theory of goal setting. *Journal of Applied Psychology*, 1975, *60*, 122–124.

Latham, G. P., and Dossett, D. L. Designing incentive plans for unionized employees: A comparison of continuous and variable ratio reinforcement schedules. *Personnel Psychology*, 1978, *31*, 47–61.

Latham, G. P., Fay, C. H., and Saari, L. M. The development of behavioral observation scales for appraising the performance of foremen. *Personnel Psychology*, 1979, *32*, 299–311.

Latham, G. P.,and Locke, E. A. Goal setting: A motivational technique that works. *Organizational Dynamics*, Autumn 1979, 68–80.

Latham, G. P., and Saari, L. M. Improving productivity through goal setting with union workers. Technical Reports, Office of Naval Research, April 1981.

Latham, G. P., and Yukl, G. A. A review of research on the application of goal setting in organization. *Academy of Management Journal*, 1975, *18*, 824–845.

Latham, G. P., Saari, L. M., Pursell, E. D., and Campion M. A. The situational interview. *Journal of Applied Psychology*, 1980, *65*, 422–427.

Latham, G. P., Wexley, K. N., and Pursell, E. D. Training managers to minimize rating errors in the observation of behavior. *Journal of Applied Psychology*, 1975, *60*, 550–555.

Lissitz, R. W., and Green, S. G. Effect of the number of scale points on reliability: A Monte Carlo approach. *Journal of Applied Psychology*, 1975, *60*, 10–13.

Locke, E. A. The ubiquity of the technique of goal setting in theories and approaches to employee motivation. *Academy of Management Review*, 1978, *3*, 594–601.

Locke, E. A., Shaw, K. N., Saari, L. M., and Latham, G. P. Goal setting and task performance: 1969–1980. *Psychological Bulletin*, 1981, *90*, 125–152.

Miller, L. M. *Behavior management: The new science of managing people at work*. New York: Wiley, 1978.

Mitchell, T. R., and Wood, R. E. Supervisor's responses to subordinate poor performance: A test of an attributional model. *Organizational Behavior and Human Performance*, 1980, *25*, 123–138.

Nagle, B. F. Criterion development. *Personnel Psychology*, 1953, *6*, 271–289.

Pursell, E. D., Dossett, D. L., and Latham, G. P. Obtaining validated predictors by minimizing rating errors in the criterion. *Personnel Psychology*, 80, *33*, 91–96.

Schneier, C. E. Behavior modification: Training the hard-core unemployed. *Personnel*, 1973, *50*, 65–69.

Smith, P. C. Behaviors, results, and organizational effectiveness: The problem of criteria. In M. D. Dunnette (Ed.), *Handbook of industrial and organizational psychology*. Chicago: Rand McNally, 1976.

Vroom, V. H., and Maier, N. R. F. Industrial social psychology. *Annual Review of Psychology*, 1961, *12*, 413–446.

Wade v. Mississippi Cooperative Extension Service, 372 F. Supp. 126 (1974), 7 EPD 9186.

Wanous, J. P. Effects of realistic job previews on job acceptance, job attitudes and job survival. *Journal of Applied Psychology*, 1973, *58*, 327–332.

Wexley, K. N., and Latham, G. P. *Developing and training human resources in an organization*. Santa Monica, CA: Goodyear Publishing, 1981.

6

Analyzing
Productive Performance

THOMAS F. GILBERT
Performance Engineering Group

Productivity is the big word these days, and I use it because it *is* the big word—even though it is ill chosen for what I think people in organizations really want to be talking about. Why ill chosen? Its connotations, rooted in our language, are those of activity (specifically, generative activity) more than of worthy performance. It suggests quantity more than quality—getting the *most* rather than the *best* out of people. It is better applied to the novelist who writes a best-selling gothic romance every year than to the person who writes only one book, but one so profound that it greatly affects millions of lives. Finally, and most pertinent here, the word promotes an already well-established tendency of managers to think that they will best improve organizations by cutting personnel, and demanding high levels of almost panic-driven activity ("look like you're busy!").

Worthy performance—competent performance—is what we really want to be talking about: getting the *best* out of people and not necessarily the most; getting the greatest net worth. Worthy performance connotes the highest reasonable standards of quality results, the necessary standards of quantity results, and the wisest use of resources to get both kinds of results. It does not suggest activity at all. So when I use the big word, I will mean worthy performance—human competence—and I will define it rigorously.

Because organizations are enormously complex, however, we need some way to organize how we look at them. A good way to begin is to ask ourselves this question: What is a marvelously competent person really like?

First, we might imagine, such people have a remarkable fix on their values. They know what they are after and what it is worth to them; and they can gauge their decisions against this measure. As they work toward achieving their mission in life, they always have accurate information about their progress, so that they know exactly where they are at all times. With such a sense of direction and such information, they don't waver; they are "double-minded"; and they seldom fool themselves.

Next, we can suppose that these extremely competent people have goals—the results—they must obtain; and that they have set their priorities for these results against the measure of their values. They have also, we assume, set exemplary standards of performance for themselves; and they can measure their progress in accomplishing their results against these standards.

Finally, they must create the behavioral conditions that will permit them to accomplish their mission. They arrange to have: the best training they need; the finest tools, resources, and procedures to pursue their objectives; and adequate and timely data to give them direction and to confirm how well they are performing. They also avoid hidden incentives that would waylay their journey, or create superstitious behavior to counter their achievements. And they make certain that the mission they have adopted is not beyond their capacity or their motives to achieve.

Overall, we can see that their performance is measured along three dimensions: establishing their values, defining their accomplishments, and controlling their behavior. By doing these three things well, they can become—with a little luck—truly worthy performers. Admittedly, such a high state of virtue is a bit hard for us hapless individual human beings to achieve. But organizations *can* attain this state of grace, and through one principal mechanism: the productive management of the same three dimensions of worthy performance. They are, as we shall see, the only dimensions that managers can assuredly control.

But before focusing on the details of how we can really assess and manage organizations, I will describe the economics of an organization, because ultimately, worthy performance in organizations is an economic issue.

ECONOMICS OF ORGANIZATIONS

The program of assessing and improving human performance in organizations, which I call "performance engineering," relies upon two fundamental measures of the productivity of people. These two basic measures recognize that productivity is the result of managers' two essential assets:

1. Capital, in the form of equipment, goods and services, materials, energy, plant, and the like.
2. People, both management and nonmanagement. This is just another

way of saying that the ideal manager is one who gets the *best*, both from his or her people and from his or her capital assets. And notice, once again, that I do not say the *most*. Driving a government meat inspector to the point of inspecting as much meat per day as possible may be, and actually is, counterproductive. Instead we want to create inspection systems that assure the highest probability of safe meat with the least possible inspection, since the very act of inspection slows the productivity of processing meat. And driving a salesman to sell as many trucks as possible may only encourage him to practically give them away. Similar differences between optimal and maximal performance exist in the management of capital assets.

In this section I will first describe how best to measure the capital productivity of an organization; next, how best to measure the productivity of the people in that organization. Then I will explain why another measure is needed, combining these two indexes, and I will point out the pitfalls and obstacles that confound our attempts to measure the productivity of an organization.

Measuring Capital Productivity

Accountants have given us ample indexes of capital productivity—the penultimate coefficient being some variant of return on investment (ROI) or its controllable correlates, like return on assets (ROA) and net profits.[1] ROI, when properly used, is an ideologically free measure that need not reflect any commitment as to how profits are to be distributed. Whether you view capitalism as a spur to productivity or as a mammoth organization of thieves is not relevant so far as the usefulness of this coefficient is concerned. Nor does it matter whether you view socialism as a benevolent context for productivity or as oppressive slavery. The net return on useful commodities and services as a proportion of what we invest to get that return can be applied in any kind of organization. And those who find the notion of profits either distasteful or invigorating confuse productive return on efforts with the way these returns are distributed.

Of course coefficients like ROI, ROA, and net profits are frequently

[1]For the novitiate, ROI is a ratio of return—net contribution, or net profits—to the net worth of an organization. Net worth is obtained by subtracting the liabilities (such as debt) from the total value of the assets of the organization.

ROA is the ratio of net profits to the total value of assets. The value of the assets are such things as the value of inventory, fixed assets such as buildings and grounds, work in process, accounts receivable, and cash and securities in the bank.

Net profits as a percentage of revenues is a very misleading measure of economic health. If I sell $1,000 worth of gee-gaws at a profit of $200, the 20 percent return sounds good. But if I have assets with an average value of $100,000 invested in this business, then my return on my assets is only two-tenths of one percent. I would do much better to sell my assets, and put the money in the bank.

misapplied—but more about that later. The point is that the ratio of our net profit to the assets we employ is simply a fundamental measure of capital productivity. The greater that proportionate return, the more wisely we have used materials and energy to create more goods and services for people to use. Nonproductive assets subtract from the total of human capital, and they deny people productive jobs.

Measuring the Productivity of People

I call the penultimate index of the productivity of people the PIP—Potential for Improving Performance.[2] To assess how well we are getting the *best* out of people, we compare their performance with that of the best. If we say that the best reasonably possible performance is exemplary, then we can compare the exemplary standard with typical, or average, performance.

If the least wasteful tailor scraps only two yards for every hundred yards he or she produces while making a dress, and the average tailor scraps six yards for every hundred he or she produces, then an average tailor has at least the potential for tripling his or her scrap performance. Theoretically, an average tailor could do as well as the best, and it would be unrealistic to expect more than that. His potential for improving performance is:

$$PIP = \frac{TYPICAL\ WASTE}{EXEMPLARY\ WASTE} = \frac{6}{2} = 3$$

But exemplary performance need not be defined as the performance of the *historically* best performers. For example, if we should observe that even our best performer uses an inefficient pair of shears, guaranteeing twice the scrap as a really good pair, then we might conclude that our PIP is really 6—that the typical tailor could waste a sixth as much if he cut as well as the best *and* used a decent pair of shears. Part of the art of performance engineering is to establish reasonable standards of exemplary performance.

Here is another example. If the best dress salesperson sells 500 dresses a day, and the average sells 200 a day, so far as sales quantities are concerned, the potential for improving average performance is:

$$PIP = \frac{EXEMPLARY\ SALES}{TYPICAL\ SALES} = \frac{500}{200} = 2.5$$

It means that the typical performer has the potential for improving sales quantities by two and a half times. And you will note that in computing the PIP, the larger number is always in the numerator. But that is only a

[2]For a detailed discussion of the PIP, see Chapter 2 of Gilbert (1979).

peculiarity of arithmetic. It happens because we always write our equation to show the potential for improvement.

There is also some latitude in the format. I defined the PIP as a ratio. But that is only for the sake of convenience. We could with equal validity define it as a difference:

EXEMPLARY PERFORMANCE — TYPICAL PERFORMANCE = PIP

However, ratios are conceptually more useful because they supply numbers we can compare. And this does not become obvious until we attempt to interpret the PIP. For example, if our exemplary seamstress makes 36 dresses a year compared with an average of 24, the ratio is 1.50 and the difference is 12. But the difference between the performance of the exemplary tailor who creates 24 men's suits and the average tailor who creates only 12 suits is also 12. Yet the ratio between the exemplary and the average tailor is 2.00, indicating that tailors have even greater potential for improvement than average seamstresses (whose PIP is 1.50).

Having studied PIPs in many types of human endeavor, I have arrived at these general conclusions:

1. *The larger the PIP, the easier it is to improve performance.* When you first think about this, it seems like a paradox. After all, the PIP is really a measure of human competence: The larger the PIP, the more incompetent the typical performer. So my conclusion really means that the more incompetent people are, the easier it is to improve their performance. But that only sounds like a paradox, since we are used to equating competence with such things as how "bright" people are. But notice, in our examples we are measuring *performance*, that is, results, not behavioral traits such as intelligence, whatever that is.

Think about it. If, among our tailors, we have a PIP of 1.01, then the best performer is only 1 percent better than the average. Since it is almost certain that someone will always excel by at least a little bit, it would be extremely difficult to make the average tailor perform as well as the best reasonably possible. But if our average tailor wasted a hundred times as much cloth as the best, what he or she is doing wrong must be so palpably obvious that even an idiot could find a way to improve such a performance.

This characteristic of the PIP has been very useful to my clients and me. We look for large PIPs for two reasons: Not only does this potential for improving productivity mean a great deal, but it is almost always easy to do something about.

2. *The PIP is a measure of potential, and only a guide to opportunity.* If we define opportunity as a reasonable prospect for realizing a part of what is the potential, we can see that we will not often be able to reduce PIPs to 1. Suppose we were to select the most able people, train them extremely well, and provide them the finest tools, the best data, the right feedback, and great incentives. Under these, the best conditions,

some will still have more flair, ambition, sharpness, fear of failure, or something. But this should not discourage us. With all too little effort, PIPs as large as 3 or 4 can be reduced to about 1.2 or 1.3. As a general rule, I would say that the larger part of most PIPs represents genuine opportunity.

3. *Often the opportunity is larger than the PIP seems to be.*   This only means that the historically exemplary performer can usually be improved. Travel with the best salesperson in an organization, and you will inevitably observe that the existing sales management systems either fail to give him or her optimal support and recognition, or else they go to the other extreme and downright mislead him or her into an exaggerated notion of his or her efficiency. Find out how you can provide better supports for the best salesperson, and you can redefine exemplary standards.

4. *The more complex the job, the higher the PIP is likely to be.*   PIPs among clerks and semiskilled workers run low—around 1.5 to 1.75. PIPs in complex jobs, like managing, selling, and research, run 2.00 and above— even as high as 10 or 100. But if we set our sights to reduce any meaningful PIP to, say, 1.25, we are likely to meet considerable success.

Athletic PIPs, on the whole, are unusually low. This is because most athletic tasks are fairly simple—and because great and instant rewards are made contingent upon success. The best professional swimmer or golfer performs only about 5 percent better than the average professional competitor. Baseball PIPs are higher, though; hitting a ball traveling 90 miles an hour with a round bat is harder than hitting a still ball with a flat surface.

These and other conclusions about the PIP are useful in interpreting it as a guide to performance engineering.

THE NEED FOR AN ULTIMATE PRODUCTIVITY MEASURE

But taken by themselves, both the ROI class of measures and the PIP can be useless or downright misleading in interpreting true productivity. Let's look at some real examples.

I know an organization whose net profits after taxes run around 30 percent of sales; its return on investment exceeds 60 percent. Is it productive? Comparatively, no. This organization has a great product, but little competition. Easy success has made it lax and complacent. It could easily double its productivity, however. And if it did, its personnel would not have to work nearly as hard as they do now (they would have to work smarter, though). It could also bring its product to its customer for a much lower price, and without sacrificing its returns. This is one way ROI measures can mislead: ROIs can be high even when PIPs are high.

There is another, even more common way that ROI measures can mislead. Most businesses calculate their profits through an instrument called a "financial statement." But financial statements are drawn up by accountants for one or both of two purposes: either to arrange the facts to their best tax advantage, or to impress the stockholders. (Sometimes two statements are used for these too often contradictory purposes.) However legal these accounting fantasies may be (and I am assured that most conform to a magical standard called GAAP—Generally Accepted Accounting Principles—they are nevertheless designed to create pictures. And often these pictures are at odds with the truth about an organization's productivity. Let's take an example, which is just one of countless examples I could give.

For tax purposes, a dealer who sells trucks depreciates his or her lease and rental fleets by the double-declining-balance method, which is one of several options under GAAP. This means that he or she declares a tax-deductible loss of half the remaining value of his or her trucks each year. This leaves the book value of the rental trucks at zero when five years have passed. At that time the dealer turns these "worthless" trucks over to the used-truck department. Disregarding inflation, a truck that sells for $20,000 new now sells for $5,000 used. It is clearly an asset of some value. But by writing off the entire value of the truck as a loss, the dealer makes his or her profits appear less for tax purposes. And by counting the truck as having zero asset value, he or she improves the picture of the return on assets to the stockholders. Meanwhile there is $5,000 worth of iron sitting in the inventory. And even though these trucks sit in the yard as unused assets if they are not sold quickly, they do not show up as a mark against productivity.

This, as I've said, is just one tiny bud of an example plucked from the accountants' gardens, where many flourish. Indeed a number of my clients have financial statements that indicate a return on investment of over 30 percent, when a truer evaluation of assets shows a return of less than 10 percent.[3] It is not as if these were shrewd managers outsmarting the Feds; they are managers being fooled by the same instruments they use to fool others (legally of course). When true productivity is low, everyone suffers—owners, managers, employers, and customers alike.

The PIP also can mislead when taken in isolation from a larger picture. One example should suffice.

A certain manufacturer carefully measures variances in labor productivity (a form of the PIP), and rewards and punishes his or her line supervisors accordingly. With unrelenting pressures on the supervisors to get the most (not the best) out of their people in labor hours, the line supervisor's labor PIPs are very low; even the average does nearly as well as the best in labor hours required per parts produced. (The parts are automobile doors.) Upon further examination, however, we find a negative correlation between labor use and scrap: Those using the most labor per

---

[3]This means that they could sell their assets and put their money in the bank and do better, while more productive people would have access to their capital.

part tend to scrap fewer doors. Little reflection is required to see why it takes extra labor to salvage a door. But application of that labor to salvage is by far the more productive use of assets. Because when you scrap a door, you also scrap all the earlier labor that went into it, as well as the use of expensive materials, energy, and machinery. By using labor as the measure of productivity, then, management encourages nonproductive work strategies.

It may be surprising that managers in so sophisticated an operation as auto manufacturing can measure productivity in such an unsophisticated way, yet at the same time busy themselves trying to learn how to simulate Japanese styles of production. But in my considerable experience, such practices are the rule, not the exception—at least in North American industry.

So we can see that an organization can boast of its high ROI even when its PIPs are also high, or of its efficiency (low PIPs) even when its ROI is low. What clearly is needed is an ultimate measure of productivity that gives a truer picture of competent performance. To arrive at this ultimate measure, we need to put the two concepts, ROI and PIPs, together to be able to see how well an organization is fulfilling its productive potential.

Approaches to Achieving the Ultimate Measure of Productive Potential

Let's examine some of the ways we might more systematically marry these already complexly intertwined concepts of productivity—capital and people.

One obvious way to combine ROI and the PIP is by a simple act of multiplication. Suppose I, as a manager, boast of an ROI of 18 percent (higher than average, let us say); but I am managing my people so poorly that I am only getting a third of the value from their efforts that they have the potential for (a PIP of 3.00). Then my boast of high productivity is a hollow one indeed. It is equally vain for me to boast that I have so well managed my people that I'm getting very close to the best from them (a PIP of 1.20) if I have so squandered my capital by frivolous spending, stupid use of assets, failure to provide the marketing force, and poor financing that my ROI is only, say 7.2 percent. In either case, I have similar effects on my implied social contract to operate a productive organization. In the first case I can hardly be serving well the consumers of my products or services. In the second, I am threatening the very livelihood of those who work for me.

Let's look at another approach. One theoretical measure of how well or poorly I am realizing my productive potential could be my the ratio of my ROI to my PIP. We might call this the ROP— the Realization Of Potential:

$$ROP = \frac{ROI}{PIP}$$

In the first case I have just described, my ROP would be 6 percent, or

$$\text{ROP}_1 = \frac{18\%}{3} = 6\%$$

What it means is that I have not realized my potential any better than in the second case, when my ROP is also 6 percent, or:

$$\text{ROP}_2 = \frac{7.2\%}{1.2} = 6\%$$

A ratio like the ROP is by no means an accounting number; it reflects a concept.[4] It might be roughly interpreted (in the two examples) as saying that no matter what my ROI is, I only deserve to get a 6 percent return on my investment. Or it might be interpreted as the ROI I would get in a world in which my competition was perfectly productive, or if consumers demanded exemplary productivity.

Unfortunately, the ROP is too simple a number to be very parctical for measuring the productivity of organizations. If all organizations were as simple as the one imagined here, that would be different— because in the one I've imagined, I am the one and only manager. All the other people are wage earners, say, a hundred dressmakers, with all my dresses already sold by contract. My ROI is easily measured, as are the PIPs of my dressmakers. But then I begin to add supervisors, sales reps, purchasing agents, and shipping clerks; retail outlets; additional product lines; machinery promising greater speed, but permitting greater scrap and requiring additional training; a credit office; and so on. Now the simple correlation I once could make between my ROI and the PIPs of my dressmakers are no longer clear. And my beast continues to grow—accountants, lawyers, engineers, training people, and organizational development specialists (experts on the beast itself). And the beast begins to swallow other beasts, and it is soon so large that it is difficult to trace the connections between its still small brain and the feet that move it. We continue measuring the ROI of the whole and the PIPs of simple performance dimensions of the principal wage earners. Indeed whole departments are devoted to these measurements, but certainly not to the measurement of my ROP.

There are plenty of other measures, all right: great mounds of computer printouts, whose individual numbers I understand, but whose real meaning I barely comprehend—a lot of data, but so little information. And performance appraisals assure me that my people have the right attitudes, are flexible, are well motivated, come to work on time, take initiative, and so on. But they leave me wondering whether all that nice, admirable behavior has anything to do with my ROP. Other reports proudly announce that the training department has even more people spending even more

---

[4]The ROP could be developed into an accounting number, however.

time in even more courses; that the legal department has grown and is wrestling with more and more legal issues; that more computers are being added to spew out even larger mounds of paper; that credit managers are finding even better ways to deny more customers credit. They leave me to wonder if I don't want *fewer* of these things, not more of them. But still no measure of my ROP.

Then I realize that some huge contradictions are built directly into my beast. I have experts trained to prove to the tax authorities that we are not very profitable, and to prove to the stockholders that we are; I have managers trying to prove during performance reviews that their departments could not be more effective, and during budget reviews to prove that they cannot possibly be effective with the support I give them. But no one mentions our ROP. Our ROI, alas, is less than the prime interest rate.

It is time to stand back and wonder if there is a more systematic way to look at our performance and relate its component PIPs to its ROI—to see how well we are realizing our potential. So I call a meeting of all our top managers and experts, and I tell them I believe we are not as productive as we might be and I ask them why. Compiling a list of the reasons they give, I narrow them to eight:

1. Rising energy costs.
2. Scarcity of raw materials.
3. Aging plant.
4. International competition.
5. Government regulations.
6. High interest rates.
7. Inadequate labor market.
8. Loss of the work ethic.

I really should list the eighth as number one, since that is the one most frequently mentioned, though weakly documented. Overall, though, my managers do well in defending and documenting their reasons. But not a single manager points the finger of blame at himself or herself, and rarely at management.

Then I suddenly have an insight: There is not a damn thing of any real significance that my managers can do about any of these problems that they are not already doing. And many other managers I have known have already come to the conclusion that they are no longer sure of controlling the organization they presume to manager, and that they are frequently involved in issues they cannot help.

Obviously, before we can begin the search for the ultimate measure of productivity, combining both the ROI and the PIP, we need to identify what managers can realistically do to control the productivity of their organizations.

THE THREE BASIC DIMENSIONS OF PRODUCTIVITY

I have identified three conditions or dimensions that I believe have tremendous leverage for improving organizational performance, and for which only management can be held accountable. They are the same dimensions that an individual must control in order to be truly competent.

These are the three most important questions that managers should always be asking themselves:

1. *What* are we trying to accomplish, and how well are we doing it?
2. *Whose* performance is in the greatest need of improvement?
3. *Why* is performance less than exemplary?

Put another way, the three reasons that performance at all levels of an organization is less than exemplary are:

1. *Information* is frequently inadequate, and often downright misleading; managers often don't really know how well people are performing.
2. *Job models* seldom exist to tell people precisely what important results they are supposed to accomplish, how those results are measured, and what standards of performance are expected of them.
3. *Behavioral conditions* for performance are rarely well supplied by management to see that people have the best data, feedback, resources, procedures, incentives, and training in order to meet exemplary standards.

Before discussing these three controllable contributions to low productivity, I will give examples through a case study based on a real and only slightly disguised organization—a large truck dealership.

THE SEIDLER TRUCK CASE: A PERFORMANCE INVENTORY

The Seidler Truck Company is one of a hundred dealerships spread throughout the country to sell a line of commercial trucks manufactured by the Rise Corporation. Larry Peet is Seidler's general manager, and he oversees operations that sell both new and used trucks, rental trucks, and parts and service. Seidler is a subsidiary of a Seidler Machinery Company, an extremely profitable operation—except for its truck subsidiary, which annually returns about 1 percent on sales and 4 percent on the investment in it (or so the accountants say). When Larry Peet recently became the truck general manager, he decided to conduct a "performance audit" to help him understand how he might improve the subsidiary's performance. He began by evaluating the integrity of the information he currently has to tell him how good a job Seidler Truck is doing.

Seidler's Information

First, Larry made a list of those beliefs that are widely held among Rise Truck dealerships. Since he knows that well-established beliefs are often generated by the data at hand, and that those data are frequently misleading, he wants to give them a critical look. Here is a partial list of those cherished beliefs:

1. Used trucks are highly profitable.

2. New trucks are losers.

3. New trucks sold to key users—businesses with larger fleets—are especially unprofitable.

4. Rental trucks are highly profitable.

5. The parts department is the most profitable operation in Seidler Truck.

6. Allied lines—small, specialty trucks not manufactured by Rise—are very profitable.

When Larry completed his analysis, he discovered that these six cherished beliefs had one thing in common: They were all disastrously wrong.

But the data Larry has on hand tended to support these beliefs. His principal document is a monthly financial statement, prepared through the great computer and accounting facilities of both Seidler Machinery and the Rise Corporation. Larry knows that the financial statement was designed from a tax-accounting viewpoint, designed to "fool" the tax authorities, although quite legally. But he suspected that any set of data designed to fool one group of people might also fool him. He also knows that the statement was put together by people who have never managed truck sales, and who have few insights into the kind of data such management needs.

For example, the financial statement tells Larry that the gross profits[5] on used trucks are over twice those for new trucks. But it tells him nothing about the net profits realized on used trucks when all the expenses are figured. Indeed all descriptions of expenses simply lump together the used, new, and rental trucks. The statement also tells him that he spent $570 on excise tax on the tires for his service trucks (accountants think about taxes), but it does not tell him what his warranty costs for used trucks were—and they are sizable. For all Larry knows, his sales reps may be far too generous when they warranty used trucks. So Larry decided his financial statement is nearly worthless as a management tool, and he determined to create his own economic model for the truck subsidiary. His procedure for doing this was to conduct a *performance inventory* (PI).

A PI is nothing more than a very simple economic model that factors in both profit contributions as they are, and PIPs (as described earlier) to

---

[5]Gross profit = sales price, less the cost of purchase of the truck, before expenses are figured.

show a manager what his ROI *might* be if business were practiced in an exemplary fashion.

To conduct the PI, Larry started with some simple worksheets—one each for new-truck sales, used-truck sales, rental sales, service, and parts. In each left-hand column he identified various categories of the business in that area. For example, in the lefthand column of his used-truck worksheet, he identified and listed both used-truck markets and methods of getting used trucks. He did this because it occurred to him that it might be more or less profitable to sell used trucks to, say, retail purchasers rather than to wholesale customers; or that trucks purchased on trade-ins might be less profitable than those obtained after their leases had expired.

On the top row of his worksheet he listed the categories of expenses required to do business. When he finished, his used-truck worksheet looked something like the segment shown in Figure 6-1. Larry knew that if he could fill this table in with reliable numbers, he would understand exactly how profitable his used-truck operation is and with what kinds of trucks and to which customers.

But here is the rub: Where can he locate the data to tell him what ROI he is getting from his used trucks? When Larry gave this worksheet to the Accounting Department, *they could not supply numbers for a single cell.* And not only for this worksheet, but they were also unable to help with any of the others. Yet these are the kinds of data he needs to assess his own performance. Should Seidler be selling used trucks to wholesalers at the present time or not? Is Seidler acquiring trade-in trucks at a reasonable price? Is Seidler warranting trucks sensibly? Does Seidler's rental fleet contribute to its used-truck profits? The answers to these and other questions would tell Larry how productive his used-truck management really is.

In other areas, Larry does not know such important things as whether his new-truck leasing operation is profitable or not—perhaps he should be encouraging his sales reps to sell almost nothing but capital leases;[6] or perhaps he should be discouraging them from leasing at all. Are large "key user" customers more or less profitable than ordinary customers? How should his sales reps be spending their time? And so on. The list of unanswered questions relative to key management decisions is very long indeed.

So, since such vital data are not to be found in the huge stack of computer printouts that Larry receives each month, he had no choice but to generate the data himself. This was an especially painful conclusion, since he had just read an article in a major business magazine describing how the Rise Corporation is considered one of corporate America's exemplars of smart management. When he went to the data people at Rise, however, not only were they unable to answer his questions, but they also looked at him as if he had taken leave of his senses.

---

[6]Where the buyer does not own part of the truck at the end of the lease period.

Used Truck Categories	Revenues	Cost of Trucks	Gross Profits	Sales Rep Compens.	Super-visor Costs	Clerical Costs	Warranty	Total Costs	Profits	1%
Retail Buyer, with Warranty										
Trade-in acquisition										
Rental retirement										
Lease expiration										
Purchased outright										
Purchased wholesale										
Total warranty sales										
Retail Buyer, No Warranty										
Trade-in acquisition										
Rental retirement										
Lease expiration										
Purchased outright										
Purchased wholesale										
Total nonwarranty sales										
Wholesale Purchasers										
Trade-in acquisition										
Rental retirement										
Lease expiration										
Purchased outright										
Purchased wholesale										
Total wholesale sales										
TOTAL USED-MACHINE SALES										

FIGURE 6-1. Segment of used-truck PI worksheet.

"And they use Rise in the Harvard Business School as a case study of one of the magnificent users of data in the world," Larry moaned.

He then proceeded to get the data for his worksheet in three ways:

1. *He Counted.* In some categories, he went to original data sources and added up figures, either for a whole year or by sampling. For example, he took all of his sales contracts and sorted them by category, and then he added up the sales commission paid in each category.

2. *He Estimated.* For example, by interviewing his personnel, he arrived at an estimate of supervisory costs for used trucks: 15 percent of his time, 100 percent of the used-truck manager's time, and 20 percent of the sales manager's time.

3. *He Allocated.* He reasoned, for example, that supervisory time spent will be correlated with the number of sales reps.

So he allocated that time to customer categories accordingly. Some expenses he allocated by proportionate revenues, some by number of units sold, some by numbers of personnel, and so on, according to the logic suggested. As Larry found, this was no job one could turn over to a clerk, and it required many hours of management time to dig through data sources, determine their integrity, choose samples, and make empirically based estimates. So much management time was required, in fact, that it became clear that the exercise would have to yield considerable results to justify the effort. It did. For the first time, Larry understood the economic characteristics of his business. Indeed he was the first Rise dealer ever to understand it. What did he find?

First, he discovered that what his accountants had told him—that the new-truck business was unprofitable—was true only in the sum. New trucks sold in fleets on closed bids to very large customers were so unprofitable as to make the total new-truck business a net loss. But new Rise trucks sold any other way were quite profitable. Those sold to key users— larger customers who did not buy under closed bids—were even more profitable than average; and trucks sold as capital leases (and especially to key users) were exceptional earners.

DISCUSSION: A PERFORMANCE INVENTORY

But before we continue with Larry's findings, let's pause a minute to see what this has to do with human productivity, and not merely with the fulfillment of greed for profits.

Some five years ago, Larry's service department had purchased an automatic welding (AW) facility to sell welding services. Last year an accountant had explained to Seidler's managers that AW was an unprofitable operation. As a result, the company ceased to promote AW services, and was even thinking of selling the facility.

But Larry's PI showed that the AW shop was the single most profitable operation in Seidler trucks. What happened was that the accounting department had used t'is entity as a place to dump certain expenses on paper, for accounting, not for management reasons. Thus several hundred thousand dollars in assets sat increasingly idle, two servicepeople lost their jobs, and customers needing automatic welding services had to go greater distances to get it.

Larry's new-truck analysis also spoke to sources of human unproductivity. It simply was not good for jobs, customers, or the use of valuable assets for sales reps to spend as much time selling a small truck to a small user as it was to provide such time and expertise to larger users. Return on investment is a measure of human productivity, whether in private business or in public institutions.

The list of Larry's significant findings—those that told him how to manage his business to get the best out of his people and assets—was long indeed. For example, the cherished belief that used-trucks sales were the most profitable part of Seidler's business turned out to be almost completely false. Larry discovered what seemed obvious only after this discovery: It cost him a lot more to handle used trucks than new ones. As it happened, few used trucks were sold retail without warranty, but they were very profitable. All others yielded large net losses. It became clear that Seidler's used-truck department was acquiring used trucks at much too high a price, and it was warranting them far too readily. In plain English, it was buying too much junk and too easily guaranteeing its operation.

Although Larry's findings eventually led him to completely reorganize the way Seidler Truck did business in all areas—new, rental, used, and parts and service—we will restrict the rest of this case study to the used-truck operation, largely because it is easier for most readers to follow. It also illustrates so well the three controllable conditions for productivity.

Now, unenlightened management might easily jump to the conclusion that Seidler's incompetence in used trucks was the direct responsibility of Al Drobney, Larry's used-truck manager. But Larry was becoming enlightened faster than Custer at Little Big Horn. That the first controllable condition for management performance—the possession of quality information— did not exist at Seidler, cannot be placed on Al Drobney as a fault before upper management is asked to account for this failure. Larry appropriately pointed the finger at himself.

To complete his PI, Larry restructured his economic models to reflect what his business might look like if conducted in an exemplary manner. The details of how he did this are beyond the scope of this treatise. Suffice it to say that he identified the major PIPs (e.g., acquiring and warranting used trucks), and he assessed his opportunities to improve them. His ideal economic model, estimating what his business would be like if practiced sensibly, showed no need to leave the used-truck business; he could convert a net loss of 7 percent return on revenues to a plus 4 percent profit, which would translate into about 24 percent ROI on his used-truck operations alone. That is more than you can make (in 1981) by investing in Treasury bonds.

Larry's use of PI revealed the first and foremost cause of low management productivity: the frequent and widespread absence of clear, accurate, and performance-based *information* (data there is plenty of) to make sensible decisions about managing a business. Seidler's misinformation was sowed by top management itself, from Larry on up to the chief executive officer of the Rise Corporation. As it turned out, every one of Rise's dealerships had much the same information as Seidler, and that could not be corrected by turning the matter over to accountants and computer specialists. And my own rather extensive experience tells me that the situation in Rise is the rule in North American organizations, not the exception. Indeed I have yet to find an exception where most of an organization's management have the information they really need and *could* get in order to manage in an exemplary fashion. Computers could help, but they alone will not solve this problem.

We might well ask, Why are these organizations able to compete? The answer is simply that their competitors battle in the same data jungle, without the information *they* need.

But information alone is not enough. It is nice to know where and why you are not very productive, but you also need to do something about it. Larry realized that he was responsible for establishing the second controllable condition for productivity: He had to establish models to elucidate for his people what they were supposed to accomplish, how they would be measured, and what standards he would expect of them. We will pursue how he did this for Al Drobney.

THE SEIDLER TRUCK CASE: PERFORMANCE-BASED JOB MODELS

At 42, Al Drobney has been with Seidler Truck for 15 years. He had started in the service department and afterwards managed the used-truck department for five years. He knows trucks with the same intimacy that a brain surgeon knows the corpus collosum. Not only is he knowledgable, but he cares about his job. Indeed for five years everyone above him has congratulated him for running such a profitable operation, and Al talks about his work with the gleam of love in his eye. Also Al disproves any premise that the work ethic does not exist in his small department. He works long hours, as do his subordinates. And enthusiasm has been the mark of Al et al.

Who else *could* you want? A bright man with great knowledge of his operations, who works like Sisyphus and with the dedication of Madame Curie. He is also loyal, flexible, and loved by sales reps, customers, sources of supply, and managers alike. And he has twice won Rise's annual award as the top used truck manager in the country. The suggestion that Al Drobney is a counter-productive, incompetent employee is unthinkable.

But he is. Then Larry showed Al the results of the performance inventory, revealing that Al has run his operation at such a loss that the profitability of the dealership has been pulled down, and now the owners want to get out of it, thus dissipating valuable assets and destroying 120 jobs. Al seemed to be a defeated man. He has all those marvelous qualities of behavior that performance assessment programs find so rewarding, yet his accomplishments are miserable.

Larry Peet quickly tried to convince Al that he is not at fault, but that Larry himself and Al's other managers have "lied" to him with misleading data, and they have set poor objectives for him. (Seidler of course had been using MBO for several years.)

"Just think of your potential, Al. We're going to establish a sensible job model for you, and you will become the exemplary used-truck manager in the country," Larry promised.

They began the job modeling procedure by using a performance table. A simplified version appears in Figure 6-2. If you study the figure, you will see that Larry and Al identified Al's mission as disposing of used trucks, and the first two major responsibilities as establishing an acquisition price for used trucks, and determining the condition of their sale— e.g., whether to warrant them or not.

It obviously was not an arbitrary decision to give these accomplishments major priority; the PI revealed that they must do this because these were the two areas where Al could have the greatest effect on the economic health of the company. It becomes the first rule of performance-based job

Accomplishments	Requirements		Present Measures	Measures to Be Developed	Standing
Mission					
Disposal of used trucks	1.	Volume	Sales revenues	None	$1.5 million
	2.	Return on assets	None	Return on assets tracking system	12% ROA (30% ROI)
Major Responsibilities					
1. Establish acquisition price of used trucks	1.	Accuracy	None	Seidler acquisition formula	To be set
	2.	Timeliness	Time to quote	None	Within 48 hours
2. Determine whether trucks should be sold with warranty, as is, wholesale, or as scrap	1.	Accuracy	None	Seidler classification system	To be set
3. Etc.					

FIGURE 6-2. A simplified version of the performance table used to create Al Drobney's job model.

modeling that the accomplishments to be identified as major are those whose genuine economic stakes lie in good performance.

Notice too that the worksheet identifies accomplishments—results— and not behavior: what *should* get done, and not how. Al also has significant control over the accomplishments. If he does them well, they will not compete with other things the company is trying to accomplish; and they are all measurable.[7]

Measurable, yes, but not necessarily measured. As we see in the worksheet, Al's two most important accomplishments are not now measured, and no standard can be set for them until they are. Larry then decided that he must create such measures. He knows that all performance can be measured—*if* you keep your eye on accomplishments, not behavior.

Let's take one example of establishing measures for Al's performance; measuring how well he *acquires* used trucks. In interviewing Al, Larry asked him what he looks at to determine the value of a used truck that a customer offers on a trade-in.

"I don't know," said Al. "It's not something you can measure. You just develop a feel for it. So many factors are involved."

"Yeah," Larry frowned. "But we don't seem to have the *right* feel. We're paying too much. Let's try to list the really important factors we should look at."

After some discussion, Larry and Al identified at least two such factors that determine the proper acquisition price of a truck. First is the price objective for a particular truck. For example, if you know that an average four-year old Model X will sell for about $10,000, then you should buy it for $8,000 if your objective is to realize a 25 percent gross profit on the truck—assuming you can sell it without much ado. And, in Larry's ideal economic model, he estimated that his gross profits would have to average about 25 percent. So if the selling price objective were the *only* factor, the formula for determining acquisition price would be:

$$\text{Acquisition Price (AP)} = 0.80 \times \text{Selling Price Objective (SPO)}$$

But normally you can't sell a used truck without repairing it. So your estimated repair costs (Re) becomes another factor in determining a sensible acquisition price. A good used truck manager, Al argued, must consider the repair estimate. Larry, whose algebra is better than Al's, then expanded the formula.

"If you can sell it for $10,000 and it costs a $1,000 to repair it, you want to buy it for the $8,000 less the $1,000 repair cost. So you buy it for $7,000," he reasoned. His new formula looked like this:

$$\text{AP} = (0.80 \times \text{PO}) - \text{Re}$$

[7]For the five characteristics of a good accomplishment description, see the ACORN TEST, in Gilbert (1979, pp. 150–156).

"But that isn't *all*," said Al, warming to the task. "A Model X is so popular you can sell it the week you buy it. But a Model 192–7 is going to sit in our inventory for six months before we get rid of it. Don't we have to factor out those estimated inventory costs?"

So Larry figured two other factors. The longer the time the truck is estimated to take to sell (Ts), the more it is going to cost by tying up Seidler's money. And how much that time-in-inventory will cost will depend upon the interest rates—the cost of money (m). With a little algebra, Larry derived this formula, the one they finally settled upon:

$$AP = \frac{0.80\ PO\ -\ Re}{1\ +\ m\ Ts}$$

Voila! A performance formula is born. Not so elegant or general as $E = MC^2$, it nonetheless accomplishes two things for Al Drobney and Larry Peet that can mean a great deal to their productivity. The acquisition formula becomes, one, a means of rather precisely measuring Al's acquisition performance, which is the most important accomplishment of his job; and two, a job aid to guide Al in making these important decisions. He no longer has to wander blindfolded in this competitive jungle.

Al wondered out loud, though, if the formula would convert him from a reasoning human being into an automaton.

"A computer could acquire these trucks with this formula," lamented Al.

"Not really." Larry replied. "Don't you see? The formula frees you to do what you do best—make deals and work with sales reps on trade-ins. And it lets you know at all times how well you are doing this. You don't have to meet the AP objectives on *every* purchase—just cumulatively through the year. On any given important deal you can give a little, and you'll know how much you have to make up on other deals. And if we can't meet the objectives we've set, we'll soon know it, and we can reduce our sights a little. You won't have to fight with the sales reps so much either—because everyone will know what your objective is, and what you're up against. Now you can work smarter, and not so hard."

Emboldened by one performance formula, Larry and Al tackled the problem of deciding whether to sell a truck wholesale, retail as-is, or retail with a warranty. And they came up with another formula that could serve both as a measure and as a job aid to help Drobney make these decisions.

After completing their performance table, Al Drobney and Larry Peet were able to write a summary performance-based job model for used-truck management. Figure 6-3 is almost an exact copy of the job model the real Al Drobney uses today (with a few simplifications for the reader) as he runs a truly profitable, productive used-truck department with the same pride, enthusiasm, dedication, flexibility, and all those marvelous qualities he always exhibited—except now reality cannot sneak up on him and tell him he has been fooling himself. The desire to be competent in this life is wondrous to behold; its actuality is even more so.

Responsibility	Standards	Conditions
1. Will determine acquisition price of all used trucks.	Average price will not deviate more than 2% from acquisition formula. Response will be within 48 hours.	1. Field inspection system to be installed. (N) 2. New inspection rating scale for specific judgments. (R) 3. Cumulative acquisition formula feedback. (N)
2. Will determine whether used trucks should be sold as is, under warranty, scrap, or wholesale.	Average deviation from classification system will be no more than 10% warranty/as is. 0% scrap or wholesale no more than 10% inspection outside yellow area.	1. Installation of classification system. (K) 2. Classification system feedback program. (N)
3. Will contact the maintenance and turnover of used inventory.	Average turnover 45 days; no unit in stock more than 6 months.	1. Formal reporting system on dollar turnover to be initiated. (N) 2. Exception report on unit turnover to be installed. (N) 3. Feedback program on dollars and unit turnover reports. (N) 4. Lost sales report system to be installed. (N)
4. Will conduct a promotion and advertising program for used equipment.	Budget = 0.5% of sales (2% for unique offerings) Response standards to be set.	1. Initiate, set up, and maintain advertising log that will report on response ratio. (K) 2. Establish practices for direct mail. Establish rules for sampling. (N) 3. Acquire and use memorex typewriter. (L) 4. Set up procedure for acquisition of labels. (N)

FIGURE 6-3. Al Drobney's final performance-based job model: used truck manager.

DISCUSSION: A PERFORMANCE-BASED JOB MODEL

The third column of the job model in Figure 6-3 is yet to be explained, and we will do this shortly. First, readers will want to examine the model closely. Those who have never seen typical job descriptions will not be able to appreciate what the experienced reader can so easily see: that this is a paragon of simplicity and precision as a job description. It describes precisely what Drobney is responsible for; how he will be measured; the standards to which he will be held accountable; and the conditions his management must provide in order to help him meet those standards. It says nothing vague about his behavior, nothing about "monitoring this" or "coordinating that" or "showing creativity." As a job description, it is coherent, simple, and useful.

Now let's understand the third column of Figure 6-3, representing a summary of the conclusions that Larry Peet arrived at when he decided to become responsible for creating the third condition that management can control if it is to assure the productivity of organizations. Larry recognized that it is not sufficient to establish the goals and standards for job performance: He must also provide the behavioral supports required to help incumbents meet their standards.

THE SEIDLER TRUCK CASE: BEHAVIORAL SUPPORTS

Larry Peet assessed the behavioral changes needed to assist Al Drobney by using a device I call the Behavior Query, a series of questions generated by a model[8] for assessing the behavioral conditions under which employees work.

First, Larry was able to see quite easily that Al Drobney at least has an adequate repertory. He has the knowledge, skills, capacity, (mental, physical, and emotional), and the motives needed to do a good job. But when Larry asked his questions about Al's environment, he came up short of important answers.

Larry proceeded in this way: He asked a series of questions about each major responsibility in Al's Job Model (Figure 6-3). For example, the first responsibility Al has is to acquire used trucks at the right price. Larry asked some 17 questions about the adequacy of the data Al has to do this job well, questions such as these:

1. Are the data reasonably adequate to direct an experienced person to perform well?
2. Are they accurate?
3. Are they simple to find, that is, accessible and not buried in a lot of extraneous data?
4. Are they timely?

As he asked these questions, he noted on a separate worksheet any question to which he answered "No." These items were a barrier to good performance, and some behavioral support would be needed to overcome it.

If you will recall, Al needed four kinds of data to make acquisition

---

[8]The behavior management model, which is a refinement of Chapter 3 of the behavior engineering model. See Gilbert (1979) for a detailed explanation.

decisions: Price objective, repair estimate, expected time in inventory, and the cost of money. When Larry asked the first question (are the data adequate?), he concluded that there are sufficient data to help Al do an excellent job of setting the price objective and estimating the time in inventory. (Rise monthly publishes an average price list of every kind and age and turnover of used trucks.) And cost of money information is available from the daily newspaper.

But the data Al needs to make repair estimates are decidedly not adequate or accurate. Typically, a sales rep will call Al about a trade-in opportunity and ask for an acquisition quote. Al's question is, "What condition is it in?" The sales rep will perhaps answer "Fair" or "Good," and he or she may give further descriptions. But Larry knows from his PI that these estimates are not good; and by merely asking the questions, he begins to see why. First, most of the sales reps are not really equipped to make such judgments accurately. Next, what one rep means by "fair" another would call "good," since there are no standards for these descriptions. Finally, the reps have a great incentive to overestimate the quality of the condition of a used truck; they want to quote as low as possible on the trade-ins, to make it easier to sell the new trucks. So Larry entered into the behavioral conditions worksheet the description of this behavioral barrier to Al's good performance. Then he and Al then discussed the conditions that they might create to remove the barrier.

They first decided that they needed to set some definite standards for estimating the repair condition.

"What we need," Al suggested, "is a sheet of paper that lists the definitions of excellent, good, fair, poor, and junk. For example, we could have an inspection rating scale that "fair" means from 4–6 thousand hours of use, ruined paint, minor dents, minor parts missing, and so on. Then the sales reps could simply check off these descriptions and come up with a rating. Every rep would then mean the same thing by "fair."

"Great," said Larry, "I'll have Rob design an inspection rating scale." (Rob is Larry's parts and service manager.) Larry entered this condition into his behavioral conditions worksheet.

But still they weren't satisfied. If the truck is a candidate for a warranty contract, the sales reps' judgments are not good enough. So Larry, after a little figuring, concluded that it would be cost-effective to send out field service reps to examine all such candidates and supply qualified repair estimates. He entered "field inspection system to be installed" in his worksheet, and delegated the responsibility for its development and implementation to his general sales manager.

Larry then went on to further questions. And he concluded that, for acquiring trucks, Al needs a feedback system that will show him daily, on a *cumulative* basis, how well his acquisition performance holds up against the standard set for him in the job model. He also concluded that Al has a real incentive to underestimate the acquisition price to accommodate the sales reps who put great pressure on him to quote low. Larry decided he need not do anything about this now, since he thinks the feedback program may counter this motive against doing well. Besides, he has decided to put Al on a bonus program keyed to his sales and profit performance.

When Larry asked all the questions in the behavior query about each of Al's responsibilities, he summarized in the job model (Figure 6-3) the behavioral conditions he must create if Al is to meet the standards of exemplary performance. If you will study Figure 6-3, you will see an initial written after each of these conditions in column 3—those are the initials of the managers he has assigned the responsiblity for creating those conditions. Al's job model is now complete; he knows precisely what is expected of him and why, and what his management has committed to do to help him—all on one page. Few incumbents of any job are so fortunate.

DISCUSSION: BEHAVIORAL SUPPORTS

As a sequel to the Seidler Truck story, Al Drobney has been working for a year (as this is written) with his new job model. He has exceeded the standards set for him, mostly because the company did not lose used truck sales as was expected when it set higher acquisition price and warranty standards. The sales reps are given Al's job model and job aids, and they quickly learn to sell a bit smarter instead of "giving away the store." And Al is not required to work harder; it is easier not to work in the dark.

But it is important to realize that the conditions Larry Peet found with Al Drobney generalize to all people who work. They bring a repertory of behavior into a behavioral environment, which includes their knowledge and skills, their capacity to learn and to adapt to the work, and some degree of motive. But this repertory is only one of the two factors in the behavioral equation. The other factor—and the one management has the greatest potential control over—is the behavioral environment: the data, tools, resources, and incentives that people need in order to perform. This distinction between behavioral repertories and behavioral environments is an important one, especially because managers are so adroit at laying the causes of low productivity on the repertories of their employees. In truth, however, the greatest potential for improving performance lies in improving behavioral environments, as Larry Peet found in the case of Al Drobney.

Managers have more opportunity to get leverage by improving data than by training people to operate in environments lacking good data; more leverage by improving tools and resources than by trying to improve people's capacity to learn and adapt; more leverage in supplying decent incentives to work than by trying to heighten people's intrinsic motives to work. It is not that people's motives and capacity are not important; it is simply that managers cannot do much about them.

THE BEHAVIOR MANAGEMENT SYSTEM

A brief explanation of the behavior management model will help you see where Larry got his behavioral questions. This model plots the two major facets of behavior, people's repertories and environment, against the three classes of things that can be done to modify behavior. They are:

1. Improve the information ("inputs" or "stimuli," as they are called in some circles) that people have to perform—both the information that gives direction to performance, and the information feedback that condirms good performance.
2. Improve the instrumentation required for good performance ("processes" or "response conditions," as some call it)—the use of tools, procedures, and resources.
3. Improve the consequences of good performance ("outputs" or "reinforcement," as it is sometimes called)—supplying effective incentives and counteracting punishment.

Figure 6-4 is a summary outline of the behavior management model, showing six general ways we can look at behavior. It makes some interesting distinctions. For example, it shows that information should not be confused with data; data are only the environmental aspect of information. Without the skill to interpret or discriminate data, people do not become informed. And if the data are absent, confusing, or misleading, there can be misinformation regardless of the skills a person has. Information, then, is the product of data and the ability to process it. This cannot be said any more concisely than in a verse I once wrote:

HAYSTACKS

> Data, like the hay, is usually dry
> And piled in stacks, and measured by the bit.
> But how like the needle information is: It
> Always has a point and needs an eye.

Similarly with motivation, which is the product of both incentives in the environment and the motives in people's repertories. Even with great motives to do a job, people are unlikely to work if there are no incentives, e.g. if they are not paid to work. And if they have no interest in the incentives, they are unlikely to work. Most people, simply by entering the job, show evidence of the motive to perform; managers then have the responsibility to provide the incentives that will match these motives.

The behavior management model represents six different ways we can look at behavior; and each of the six cells of this model allows us to generate questions we can ask about the sufficiency of behavior to support competent performance. These questions and answers make up the be-

		E (behavioral environment)		P (behavioral repertory)	
		1. Data		2. Knowledge	

S	I N F O R M A T I O N	a. DIRECTION
		  1. Accurate and adequate
		  2. Parsimonious
		  3. Timely
		  4. Unequivocal (not confusing)
		
		b. CONFIRMATION
		  1. Work related
		  2. Immediate
		  3. Selective and specific
		  4. Educational
				a. INDUCTIVE
				  1. Consequential
				  2. Contextual
				
				b. THEORY (Concepts)
				  1. Mediating
				  2. Domain relevant
				
				c. SKILLS
				  1. Cognitive
				  2. Motor	

		3. Instruments		4. Capacity	

R	I N S T R U M E N T A T I O N	a. TOOLS
		  1. Available
		  2. Efficient
		
		b. PROCEDURES
		  1. Efficient
		  2. Nonrepetitious
		  3. Free of interference
		
		c. RESOURCES
		  1. Adequate
		  2. Efficient
				a. PERCEPTUAL
				  1. Accurate
				  2. Sensitive
				  3. Quick
				
				b. COGNITIVE
				  1. Integrative
				
				c. MOTOR
				  1. Timely
				  2. Accurate
				  3. Strong	

		5. Incentives		6. Motives	

Sr	M O T I V A T I O N	a. INTRINSIC
		  1. Adequate
		  2. Contingent
		
		b. SECONDARY
		  1. Valence
		  2. Contingent
		  3. Periodic
				a. PRIMARY
				  1. Adequate
				  2. Enduring
				  3. Relevant
				
				b. INDUCED
				  (same as primary)	

FIGURE 6-4. The behavior management model.

havior query; and the whole package—model, query, behavior supports worksheet, and materials created to support each cell of the model—I call the behavior management system (BEMANS).

PERFORMANCE DIMENSIONS

I have argued that there are three conditions for competent performance that managers are principally responsible for and capable of controlling: (1) developing information about the true worth of what an organization is trying to accomplish; (2) designing accomplishment-based job models, with measures and standards; and (3) creating the behavioral conditions for good performance. There is a basic formulation, a definition, of worthy performance that ties these three conditions together. The most fundamental of economic concepts relates net worth to the value and cost of doing business. Worth (W) can be described as the difference between Value (V) and Cost (C), or more generally, as the ratio of value to costs:

$$W = \frac{V}{C}$$

We can translate this formula into performance terms. We should easily see that performance (p) is the transaction that occurs when behavior (B) leads to results—accomplishments (A), or

$$P = B > A$$

We should also see that it is accomplishments that we value, and behavior that costs us. We have to pay for hard work, motivation, and knowledge. Thus worthy performance (W) can be described as the ratio of valuable accomplishment to costly behavior, or:

$$W = \frac{A}{B} = \frac{V}{C}$$

Thus to obtain high productivity—very worthy performance—we need to do three things:

1.   Develop the information that can help us decide how worthy the performance (W) of an organization is now, and what potential we have to improve that worth. We do this through economic modeling and the analysis of both ROI and PIPS.

2.   Decide what the truly valuable accomplishments (A) on a job are, how they can be measured, and what are the exemplary standards. We do these through accomplishment-based job models, using worksheets such as the performance tables.

3.   Create the behavioral conditions (B) for good performance. We do

this by assessing the behavioral barriers to good performance, and designing the conditions to counter them.

Only when we have done these three things well should we worry about energy shortages and the work ethic. These, as you may recall, are the three characteristics that define the rare competent person—we hapless folks won't make it. But organizations can maximize human beings. This hope may explain why we mere mortals invest so much in the organizations we work for. The productivity of these places becomes a symbol of our own worth. The Al Drobneys of the world await managers who will make themselves more productive in order to be able to show us how productive their organizations can be.

SUMMARY

This chapter defines productivity and describes the three basic dimensions of productive performance, which managers can control. They are:

1. Determining how well an organization is performing up to its potential (principally through certain economic models); then creating strategies for realizing opportunities for improving both its business practices and its people.
2. Creating performance-based job models, describing the accomplishments, measures, and standards of jobs.
3. Using a behavior managing model to identify the barriers to exemplary performance, and then determining how to overcome them.

A case study was included to illustrate how these basic points can be applied.

REFERENCE

Gilbert, Thomas F. *Human competence*. New York: McGraw-Hill, 1979.

7

The Case for the Single Case: Making Judicious Decisions about Alternatives

JUDITH L. KOMAKI

Purdue University

Management today can choose among a bewildering number of alternative methods for solving organizational problems. Some are old standbys, others are relative newcomers. Proponents for each strategy herald the organizational streamlining and increased profits their method would realize if it were enacted. How to select judiciously among the available choices, the topic of this chapter, has become a critical task for the resource-conscious consumer. If one can distinguish effective means from fads before launching a new system, one has a greater likelihood of achieving success and avoiding unwarranted risks.

CLIMATE OF UNCERTAINTY

Unfortunately, the painful lack of evaluative data about the various methods of effecting organizational change makes it difficult for any decision of this kind to rest on a sound empirical basis. Motivational programs, training innovations, policy revisions, personnel reshuffling—changes such as these are continually introduced into the ebb and flow of organizations in the hopes of improving aspects of the existing system. More often than not, however, these changes are not carefully and specifically evaluated to determine their effectiveness (Staw, 1977). Instead they are assumed to be naturally beneficial, or their effects are only cursorily examined, with management accepting testimonials from nonneutral parties as primary evidence. Goldstein (1980), in a comprehensive review of training

145

in work organizations, acknowledges this unfortunate situation, noting that most "decisions are based upon anecdotal trainee and trainer reactions" (p. 238). Given such uncertainty, it is no wonder that decisions in this area are little better than shots in the dark.

CONFOUNDING FACTORS

Even when more precise information is provided, few guidelines exist to aid in discriminating among choices. How does one separate fact from fantasy in claims like:

150 percent jump in productivity.

Significantly fewer grievances.

$2 million annual savings.

District-wide sales increases.

Accidents cut in half.

The most common pitfall is to take claims like these on face value, trustfully believing that the improvements described are directly attributable to the particular modifications advanced as their cause. This leap of faith is especially tempting when the proposed change fits one's own predilections, when the results produced are exactly what one would like to see, and when immediately comprehensible before-and-after comparisons (e.g., a 150 percent *increase* in productivity over previous levels) are provided.

While evidence based on before-and-after comparisons is surely better than none at all, it is not sufficient to support a verdict that the plan being credited is truly responsible for the positive results described. Before any improvements can be attributed to a particular change, other plausible alternatives must be ruled out. Let's say that information was collected about sales for a certain product in a certain region, a program was introduced to bolster sales, and sales doubled. Given this information, one might want to conclude that the program was responsible for the dramatic improvement. Upon further probing, however, one may discover that sales figures for all products were on the rise during the same period in the same region. This calls into question whether the economy or the program was responsible for the increase in sales.

A variety of reasons other than instituted changes can explain why certain results occur. Events other than the experimental program (*history*) might make the difference, events as varied in scope as:

A supervisory change.

The threat of an economic recession.

A technological advance.

The provision of new procedures.

Increased pressure from top management.

A new influx of trained personnel.

Sometimes improvements reflect changes that occurred merely through the passage of time, such as a worker becoming more expert at a particular task or growing acclimated to the work environment (*maturation*). In cases in which employees have been selected because they have done relatively poorly on a pretest measure, improvements sometimes reflect the effect of *regression artifacts*, that is, the tendency for individuals with extreme scores to move toward the mean of the population from which they were selected. Such pseudo-shifts have nothing to do with whatever improvement program may be under evaluation, but their effects can make the program seem more successful than it is in fact.

ESTABLISHED EVALUATION METHOD

How then can one rule out such a myriad of potential influences? How does one definitely determine whether or not a particular program resulted in the desired improvements?

The established way is to use what are referred to as between-group or control-group designs. In the simplest case, persons are assigned by lot to one of two groups. One is labeled the treatment group; the other, the control group. Persons in the treatment group are exposed to the program, whereas persons in the control group are not. Other potential factors have been effectively ruled out because random assignment equalizes both groups on all dimensions except the treatment; it is, for example, just as likely that one group will experience a significant event (history) or will get more practiced at a task (maturation) as it is than the other group will. If improvements occur in the treatment group and not in the control, one can confidently say that the program was responsible for the improvements. For a further description of these designs and potentially confounding effects, refer to the classic text by Campbell and Stanley (1963).

Although control-group designs are widely acknowledged to be *the* way to rule out alternative hypotheses, suitable control groups are difficult to arrange in most work settings. Rarely, outside of laboratories, can one randomly assign persons to different groups with the purpose of exposing only one of the groups to a change. Persons in production typically stay in production; persons in marketing stay in marketing. Seldom can individuals from two such departments be reassigned by lot so that some in marketing are now in production and vice versa, and persons in newly formed Group 1 are exposed to the new policy change, whereas persons in newly formed Group 2 are not. Despite the importance of precise evaluation, it is a simple fact of organizational life that presently constituted groups tend, rightfully, to be left intact.

Yet even if persons could be assigned by lot to one or another group, problems sometimes occur because of the nature of the procedures being introduced. A job enlargement program made differentially available to one group might cause production disruptions. Similarly, a change in incentive plans might produce troublesome inequities between treatment and control groups. Consequently control-group designs are rarely used in organizational settings because of the problems their implementation involves.

Occasionally a nonequivalent control group design is used in which one intact group (marketing) is exposed to a program and another (production) is not. Using intact rather than randomly constituted groups, however, also presents problems. The groups frequently differ from one another in significant ways, such as background, seniority, supervision, job task, or baseline level. So if a change is introduced in one group and that group improves, the improvements can very plausibly be attributed to any number of potentially justifiable reasons. As a result, one cannot be sure in such instances about results attributed to one specific change.

RECOMMENDED ALTERNATIVE

Fortunately, a valuable alternative exists. Called within-group or single-case designs, these methods are frequently used by persons in the area of behavior analysis to assess the effectiveness of changes introduced in applied settings (Hersen and Barlow, 1976).

Instead of comparing a treatment group with a control group, comparisons are made within the group under study; that is, the group serves as its own control. The advantage is that one can draw sound conclusions about the effectiveness of changes without having to create a control group.

In the remainder of the chapter, the two most widely known and suitable single-case designs—reversal and multiple-baseline—are described and the rationale behind them explained. Examples are also presented, demonstrating how these designs have been and can be used in work settings to improve decision making.

REVERSAL DESIGN

In its simplest form, the reversal design includes three phases:

1. *Baseline (A).*   During this phase information is collected regularly over a period of time prior to the institution of any change.
2. *Intervention (B).*   The program or intervention is introduced, and information continues to be collected regularly over a period of time.
3. *Reversal (A).*   During this phase one returns to baseline conditions, discontinuing the program introduced previously, but still collecting data.

Rationale

Performance levels are examined to see if they fluctuate with the different conditions the design establishes and measures. If performance markedly improves when the intervention is in effect and worsens during the reversal phase, then one can say that the improvements resulted from the intervention and not from other extraneous variables.

The more times one can demonstrate that performance changes as the intervention is introduced and reversed, the more convincingly one can argue that the changes were caused by the intervention. A highly recommended extension of the reversal design includes a baseline (A), intervention (B), reversal (A), and then a reintroduction of intervention (B) phase. The reintroduction of intervention phase strengthens the claim that the instituted modification, and nothing else, caused the observed change.

Example of ABAB Reversal Design

An ABAB reversal design was used to determine whether or not an intervention was responsible for the improvements in the performance of a game room attendant (Komaki, Waddell, and Pearce, 1978). Initially the owner of the game room threatened to discharge the attendant if his performance did not show "visible" improvement. After desired on-the-job performance was defined, the percentage of time the attendant spent working was assessed three to five times each week for a total of 27 observation sessions over a seven-week period. Attempts to upgrade on-the-job performance were made during the intervention phase (B) using a contingent pay system. During the reversal and reintroduction of intervention phases, the intervention was discontinued (A) and reintroduced again (B).

Figure 7-1 shows the percentage of time the game room attendant spent working during the four conditions. The attendant averaged 63 percent, sometimes dropping as low as 40 percent during baseline. During intervention his performance increased dramatically, with a mean performance level of 93 percent. When conditions were reversed, the attendant's performance reverted to baseline levels, averaging only 62 percent. However, during the reintroduction of intervention phase, the attendant's mean performance level again increased to over 90 percent.

Because performance dramatically increased when the intervention was in effect, declined to baseline levels when the treatment was discontinued, and then increased again when the experimental modification was reintroduced, it was concluded that the intervention was responsible for the evident improvements. *History* was dismissed as a possible factor because it was not likely that another significant event would occur and then reoccur in precise time with the introduction and reintroduction of the intervention. *The Hawthorne effect*[1] was similarly ruled out. If the Haw-

---

[1]For a description of the study that gave rise to the term, Hawthorne effect, and an account of how this effect came to be recognized as a potential source of confounding, refer to Roethlisberger and Dickson (1939) and Homans (1965).

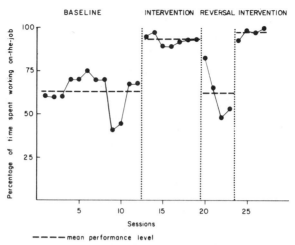

FIGURE 7-1. Example of ABAB reversal design. Percentage of time a game room attendant spent working on the job over a seven-week period during the four experimental conditions: baseline (12 sessions over a three-week period), intervention (seven sessions in a two-week period), reversal (four sessions in one week), and reintervention (four sessions in one week). From Komaki, Waddell, and Pearce (1977). Copyright 1977 by Academic Press, Inc. Reprinted by permission.

thorne effect accounted for the changes in performance, then one would assume that the attendant's performance could be maintained during the last three phases when he was aware of the experimental manipulation. However, during the reversal phase his performance declined to baseline levels, *and* it was only when the reinforcement contingencies were reinstated that his performance improved. The results were also not attributable to *maturation*. If maturation were the primary reason, then one might expect that performance would gradually increase as time passed. However, there was a sharp drop during the reversal phase, and it was only when the intervention was reintroduced that the percentage of time spent working improved.

Regression *artifacts* were also dismissed because regression effects (once again, the tendency of extreme scores to move toward the mean) would be likely to appear in any series of repeated measurements and not just after the introduction and reintroduction of the intervention. In fact, because regression effects are usually a negatively accelerated function of elapsed time, that is, more likely to occur after the second, third, and fourth observations than after the twelfth, thirteenth, and fourteenth, or the nineteenth, twentieth, and twenty-first (the first and second intervention points), it is even less likely that regression effects were responsible for the improvements during the two intervention phases.[2]

---

[2]*Selection*, another possible source of confounding, is not a problem with reversal or multiple-baseline designs because comparisons are not made between groups but rather within

Essential Feature

The *reversal* phase, as its name would imply, is crucial to the reversal design. Without the reversal phase one is left with an AB or a before-and-after comparison design. With an AB design all one can say is that changes occurred. One cannot make causal statements about the changes and the modification because one cannot rule out potentially confounding factors such as the rate of unemployment, new hires, or pending policy revisions.

To set up a reversal design, one should collect baseline data before the change, continue to collect data while the change is in effect, and then revert to baseline conditions at least once. To restore baseline conditions, the active components of the program are either discontinued or removed. If the program involves supervisors providing daily feedback, then the graphs can be left as is, but the feedback must be discontinued. If, however, the program consists of posting job openings at different locations, then the information should be removed. The intentional removal or discontinuation of a program's active components constitutes a reversal. This should not be confused with a situation in which the active components have not been discontinued or removed but the intervention appears, for unknown reasons, to have lost its effectiveness.

Use of Reversal Designs

In Various Organizations.   The reversal design can be used to evaluate changes in a variety of work settings. The effect of a group response-cost procedure on cash shortages was assessed using an ABAB reversal design in a family-style restaurant (Marholin and Gray, 1976). When it was found that employees regularly ended the day with cash shortages, a group response-cost policy was instituted, by which cash shortages were subtracted from the six employees' salaries on days in which the shortage exceeded 1 percent of total daily sales. Following five days of baseline, the response-cost procedure was introduced for 12 days, removed for three days, and then reintroduced for the final 21 days of the experiment. As shown in Figure 7-2, the magnitude of daily shortages sharply decreased when the group response-cost procedure was in effect.

In a sales setting, a procedural change in the selling of contracts was assessed using an ABA Reversal design (Gupton and LeBow, 1971). During baseline, which lasted 10 sessions, no constraints were placed on the types of calls or sales made. When it was found that warranty sales were much lower than renewal sales, renewal sales were made contingent upon

---

groups. As a result, one need not be concerned with biases that can be introduced when selecting persons for comparison groups. Likewise *testing* is usually not a problem because it primarily has reference to personality or paper-and-pencil tests, a relative rarity in any repeated measures design. *Differential mortality* can be a problem if subjects drop out of the intervention phases more or less often than they do the baseline or reversal phases. In assessing the results, one should be aware of this potential source of confounding.

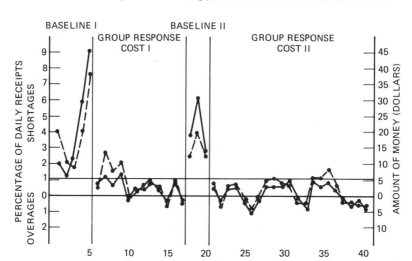

FIGURE 7-2.   Example of ABAB reversal design. Percentage of daily shortages by restaurant employees over a 40-day period. The program was introduced on day 6, removed on day 18, and reintroduced on day 21. From Marholin and Gray (1976). Copyright 1976 by the Society for the Experimental Analysis of Behavior, Inc. Reprinted by permission.

the successful completion of warranty sales. That is, when telephone solicitors made one warranty sale (a lower-probability behavior), they were then given five renewal customers to call (a higher-probability behavior). Intervention lasted for 10 sessions and resulted in a substantial increase in the number of warranty sales. For the reversal phase, lasting five sessions, the experimental contingencies were withdrawn and the solicitors again began to make more renewal than warranty sales.

In another sales organization, Kreitner and Golab (1978) used an ABA reversal design to evaluate the effectiveness of a monetary refund on the frequency of field sales staff telephone calls to the home office. Baseline information was collected for eight work days. Then a memo describing the new reimbursement plan was distributed to the entire sales staff. After nine work days, the plan was withdrawn. Both the number of sales persons calling in at least three times a day and the total number of calls increased measurably when the refund was in effect.

With Large Groups.   Although reversal designs are referred to as single-case designs, they are *not* restricted to individuals or small groups. The reversal design can be used in plant operations with hundreds of employees. Pedalino and Gamboa (1974) used an ABA reversal design, e.g., to evaluate the effectiveness of a lottery incentive system on workers' absenteeism in a large manufacturing and distribution center. Following 32 weeks of baseline conditions, the incentive system was introduced and then discontinued with a group of 215 workers within the center.

By Taking Advantage of Interruptions.   Generally the reversal phase is planned. Sometimes, however, disruptions occur which result in the intervention being temporarily interrupted. Instead of regretting these interruptions, one can take advantage of them and incorporate them into one's evaluation strategy. In a study aimed at increasing attendance at self-help meetings (Miller and Miller, 1970), the reversal phase coincided with the period of time that the person responsible for implementing the intervention and obtaining the supplementary reinforcers discontinued her attendance at the meetings due to major surgery. In the Pedalino and Gamboa study on absenteeism (1974), further evidence of the efficacy of the program was provided when unanticipated circumstances resulted in no incentive program being put into operation for three weeks.

In Combination with a Control Group.   Although the reversal design alone permits one to assess the efficacy of a program, a control group provides further confirmation of its efficacy. Hermann and his associates (1973), e.g., used an ABABAB reversal design, in combination with a control group, to evaluate the effectiveness of an incentive procedure on the punctuality of workers in a manufacturing company. Twelve chronically late male workers were assigned, in order of their appearance on the company payroll, to either a treatment or a control group. For the

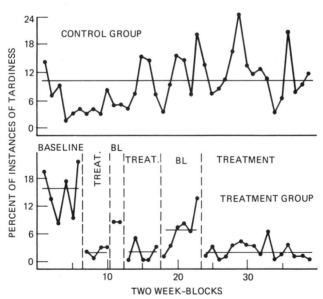

FIGURE 7-3.   Example of ABABAB reversal design in combination with a control group. Upper graph presents percentage of instances of tardiness of control group during 77-week period. Lower graph presents same for treatment group. Incentive procedure was introduced after 12, 24, and 46 weeks, whereas the reversal phases occurred after 20 and 34 weeks. From Hermann, deMontes, Dominguez, deMontes, and Hopkins (1973). Copyright 1973 by the Society for the Experimental Analysis of Behavior, Inc. Reprinted by permission.

treatment group, baseline and intervention conditions were rotated a total of three times. After 12, 24, and 46 weeks the workers were told they would receive a 2.00 pesos bonus for every day they arrived on time. During return-to-baseline conditions (after 20 and 17 weeks), each worker was told that the payment for punctuality was going to be suspended. As the lower graph of Figure 7-3 shows, the percentage of time the workers were tardy fluctuated with the different conditions. Performance markedly improved when the treatment was in effect, resulting in late-arrival averages of only 2.5 percent, 1.8 percent, and 2.0 percent during the three intervention conditions. In contrast, during the baseline and reversal phases, the mean percentage of tardy arrivals was 15 percent, 8 percent, and 6.5 percent, respectively.

On the other hand, the control group was not told about the incentive procedure and, as the upper graph of Figure 7-3 shows, did not experience the performance fluctuations shown by the treatment group. Although control groups are not necessary to ensure sound conclusions with reversal designs, they provide supplementary evidence and, where feasible, are highly recommended additions.

Advantages and Limitations

The reversal design provides an attractive alternative to control-group designs in that one can infer cause-effect relationships from them without a traditional control group. Another benefit is that one can examine trends over time and make revisions based on ongoing information. In all single-case designs, data are collected regularly, i.e., three times a week. Because up-to-date information is available, one can readily determine whether a particular program is having its desired effect. If plans are not progressing as expected, alterations can be made quickly. There is no need to wait until the posttest data are analyzed and interpreted.

The main drawback of the reversal design is that it requires a reversion to baseline conditions. Sometimes it is impossible to do this. Training situations in which people learn new information or acquire new skills are examples of this.

Other situations arise in which it is impractical to return to baseline conditions. Once progress is being made in desired directions, persons implementing programs are sometimes reluctant to return to baseline, where conditions are likely to worsen and perhaps interfere with future performance. Even persons who institute reversal phases sometimes cut them short. One department manager, upon seeing the performance of his group worsen, felt that he could not afford to let performance return to baseline levels, so he restored the feedback program after only 11 days (McCarthy, 1978).

The reversal design is also not a wise choice when harmful or dangerous conditions are involved. One would not want to remove safety guards or reinstall faulty equipment, for example. When problems exist with reverting to baseline conditions, one should consider the design discussed in the next section, the multiple-baseline design.

MULTIPLE-BASELINE DESIGN

The multiple-baseline design is highly recommended for work settings. As its name indicates, it involves the collection of data on two or more baselines. The second characteristic of this design is that the intervention is introduced in a staggered fashion across the baselines. In a multiple-baseline design across groups, e.g., the treatment is first introduced with one group. When the desired change has occurred (or a certain amount of time has passed, or a number of data points accumulated), the treatment is begun with the second group. Again, following an observed change, the treatment is introduced with the next group, and so on until the intervention has been introduced with all of the groups.

Rationale

The rationale underlying the multiple-baseline design, similar to that for the reversal design, is that performance levels can be compared within rather than between groups. Comparisons are made between baseline and intervention phases *and* the results are checked to see whether effects are replicated at different times.

To assess whether a particular procedure is responsible for a change, one must examine whether performance changes after the intervention is introduced, and whether other groups that have not yet received treatment continue at their baseline rates. If performance improves during, and not prior to, the intervention phase, *and* this result occurs each time the treatment is introduced, then one can conclude that the experimental manipulation is responsible for the changes.

Example of a Multiple-Baseline Design across Behavior

A multiple-baseline design across behavior was used to assess whether or not an intervention was effective with personnel in a neighborhood grocery store (Komaki, Waddell, and Pearce, 1977). Data were taken daily during a 12-week period on three different desired kinds of activity: (1) remaining in the store, (2) assisting customers, and (3) stocking merchandise. After 18 observations, the treatment was introduced with the first behavior. For the intervention, the desired tasks were clarified in a 30-minute training session and several potentially reinforcing consequences were arranged for desired performance. Workers were given time off with pay contingent on performance. In addition, the clerks were given daily feedback and agreed to self-record their own behavior eight times each day. When improvements had been noted in the percentage of time spent in the store (after 24 observations), the intervention was introduced with the second kind of behavior. When the clerks had begun regularly assisting

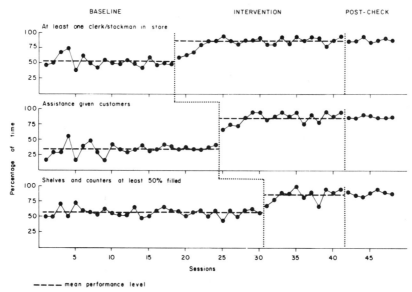

FIGURE 7-4. Example of multiple-baseline design across behavior. Percentage of time the
three target actions were performed by grocery personnel during a 12-week period of time.
The first intervention took place after 18 sessions (three weeks), the second after 24 sessions
(four weeks), and the third after 30 sessions (three weeks). Post checks were carried out
during the last four weeks. From Komaki, Waddell, and Pearce (1977). Copyright 1977 by
Academic Press, Inc. Reprinted by permission.

customers and had continued to remain in the store (after 30 observations),
the clerks were presented with the treatment for the third goal.

The performance of the clerks is shown in Figure 7-4. When the intervention was introduced, performance on the first kind of behavior steadily increased, so that by the second week the criterion of 90 percent was
being met regularly. The second and third activities, however, remained
at baseline levels. When the experimental manipulation was introduced
for the second activity, it improved dramatically. At the same time the
first one continued at its postintervention level, while the third remained
at baseline levels. Only when the intervention was introduced for the
third kind of behavior did it improve. During baseline the mean performance level of the three behaviors was 53 percent, 35 percent, and 57
percent, whereas during the intervention phase the means were 86 percent, 87 percent, and 86 percent, respectively.

It was concluded that the changes in performance were a function of
the experimental manipulation because performance improved only after,
and not prior to, the introduction of each intervention. After sessions 18,
24, and 30, respectively, the first, second, and third kind of behavior could
have increased, decreased, or remained the same. However, in each case
increases followed the introduction of the intervention. One might expect
that if workers spent more time in the store (the first kind of behavior),

customer assistance (the second kind of behavior) and mechandise supply (the third kind of behavior) might also improved. However, it was not until the intervention was implemented for the second and third activities that these areas began to improve.

History was ruled out as an alternative explanation for the results. Although an extraneous event could have coincided with the introduction of the treatment for the three activities and had a similar effect on the activities in the exact same order, this is unlikely. The outside event not only would have had to occur on three different occasions, but would also have had to coincide in timing, order, and effect. *Maturation* was also dismissed. If processes operating as a function of the passage of time or practice effects were responsible for the change, then you would expect that performance would steadily increase. However, the three kinds of behavior did not gradually improve throughout the study. Rather they improved only after 18, 24, and 30 sessions when the intervention was introduced. The improvements were not likely to be a function of regression artifacts, because regression effects would be seen in any repeated measurements and not just after the experimental manipulations.

Essential Features

An integral feature of the multiple-baseline design is that *two or more baseline measures are taken at the same time*. In the above study, data were collected on three activities of the store clerks. Doing this made it possible to assess the effect of the program three times. When the same effect occurs each time the program is introduced, the method's conclusion gains credibility; one can argue more convincingly that improvements must be attributed to the program. Because of the importance of replicating the results, one baseline is not sufficient. In fact Hersen and Barlow (1976) recommend three as a minimum. In general, the more baselines one can obtain the better, and the more certain are the conclusions one can draw.

Another crucial feature of the multiple-baseline design is the *introduction of the treatment at staggered intervals*. In the study above, the program was introduced after 18 sessions for the first activity, 24 for the second, and 30 for the third. By introducing the program at different points in time, one can not only assess *whether* performance changes but also determine *when* performance changes. If the program is introduced at different times *and* performance changes only after the program is implemented, then one can more assuredly rule out alternative hypotheses. It is unlikely that an extraneous event would coincide and have a similar effect on the first, second, and third activities at approximately the same times in exactly the same order. Similarly, it is unlikely that practice effects would measurably influence the first behavior at time 1, the second at time 2, and the third at time 3. In contrast, if the program is not staggered but is introduced simultaneously in both departments, then the situation is similar to the before-and-after design with all of its attendant problems.

Outside events, practice, and regression effects become more plausible explanations in such a case. By staggering the treatment and demonstrating that performance improves only when the experimental modification is introduced, one can rule out these potential sources of confusion.

Types of Multiple-Baseline Designs

Across Behavior.   The multiple-baseline design can be readily adapted to a variety of work situations. It can be arranged *across behavior* as in the example above, *across groups*, and *across settings*.

For the multiple-baseline design *across behavior*, two or more activities are selected to be measured throughout the duration of the study. Sample behavior for grocery store clerks have already been discussed. For secretarial and clerical personnel, suitable activities might be: turning out clean copy, correcting errors, returning copy promptly, and taking accurate phone messages. For hospital emergency room staff, they can be: maintaining complete emergency room records, verifying the accuracy of these records, and being helpful to patients.

Lamal and Benfield (1978) assessed the impact of a self-monitoring system on a draftsman who had problems with tardiness and "goofing off" at work. The two kinds of behavior were: arriving at work punctually, and working a greater percentage of time while on the job. On day 11, the draftsman was asked to keep track of the first action and on day 16, the second action. An independent assessment of his behavior showed that his performance improved measurably after he began to monitor each of the respective actions himself.

The behavior chosen for the multiple-baseline design *across behavior* can be descriptive of on-the-job performance, as the previous examples indicate. Another possibility that has yet to be fully explored is for the behavior examined to be different components of a training package. Miller and Weaver (1972) performed such a study when they evaluated an instructional package they designed. First, they divided the content area into five subsections and devised a series of comprehensive tests on each subsection:

1. Research methods.
2. Reinforcement.
3. Stimulus control.
4. Conditioned reinforcement.
5. Aversive control.

For 14 consecutive weeks, students took a different version of the test. After one week of baseline, the teaching package for the first subsection of the course was introduced. Two weeks later materials were presented for the next subsection, and so on until the instructional package had been introduced for all five subsections. When they found that scores for the last two subsections had not improved as dramatically as they had on the previous three sections, as shown in Figure 7-5, they revised those sections of the teaching package.

Across Groups.   Among single-case designs, the multiple-baseline *across groups* design is probably the most suitable to work settings, because it makes use of already existing groups and administrative units. The groups can consist of:

Different units within a single company (e.g., live dock, evisceration, chill and pack, and shipping departments in a processing plant).

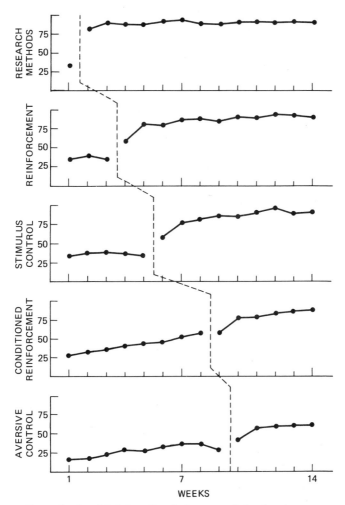

FIGURE 7-5. Example of multiple-baseline design across behavior. Average scores on each subsection of an achievement test over 14 weeks. Teaching package introduced on each of the five subsections at approximately three-week intervals. From Miller and Weaver (1972). Reprinted by permission.

Different branches in a statewide organization (e.g., Northern, Bay, Central, Los Angeles, Orange, and Border).

Different divisions within a city government (e.g., public works, parks and recreation, property and code enforcement).

Different shifts in one section of an organization (e.g., nurses on the 7–3, 3–11, and 11–7 shift).

Hospital personnel (Panyan, Boozer, and Morris, 1970; Quilitch, 1975) used the multiple-baseline design *across groups* to assess whether management procedures improved staff performance. The groups consisted of staff assigned to different living units within the institutions. Panyan et al. (1970) collected baseline data on the percentage of training sessions

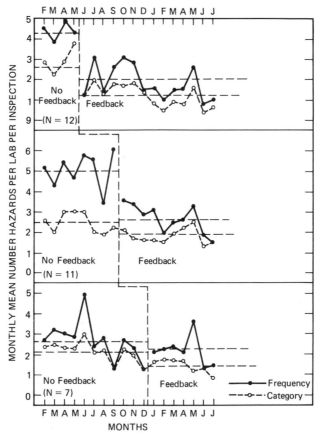

FIGURE 7-6. Example of multiple-baseline design across groups. Number of hazard categories and hazards in each of three different groups of university laboratories over an 18-month period. Safety program was introduced in the first, second, and third groups in May, September, and December, respectively. From Sulzer-Azaroff (1978). Copyright 1978 by Behavior Systems, Inc. Reprinted by permission.

conducted by staff on 11 units. In eight of the halls, a feedback system was introduced immediately. In three of the halls (Halls E, O, and C), feedback was given after 4, 8, and 38 weeks, respectively. Only when the feedback was initiated did the percentage of training sessions conducted increase.

In two recent studies, Sulzer-Azaroff used the multiple-baseline design *across groups* to evaluate a safety program in six production departments of an industrial organization (with de Santamaria, 1980) and in 30 university laboratory facilities (1978). In both studies, she grouped the units. In the 1978 study, she combined the 30 laboratories into three large groups, comprising 12, 11, and 7 laboratories, respectively. The feedback program was initiated following baselines of five, nine, and 12 months. Following the delivery of feedback, safety hazards were substantially reduced, as Figure 7-6 shows.

Even larger groups have been used in *across group* designs. Kempen and Hall (1977) assessed the absenteeism rates of from six thousand to eight thousand hourly employees at two plants of a manufacturing company. In Plant A, baseline rates were obtained for 34 months; the implementation of an Attendance Management System followed. In Plant B, a similar system was introduced almost nine months later. As Figure 7-7 shows, absenteeism decreased considerably in both plants following the introduction of the system.

Because comparisons are made within rather than between groups in the multiple-baseline *across groups* design, it is not necessary to ensure through random assignment that the groups are more or less equivalent. In fact the more the groups differ from one another in such factors as age, educational background, training, job description, supervision, and job task, the more that can be said for the general nature of the results.

Across Persons.   The multiple-baseline design *across persons* is similar to the multiple-baseline design *across groups*. Instead of different groups, the focus shifts to different individuals. The persons can be parts of groups as varied as:

Loan officers at a local bank.

Plant managers in different locations.

Members of an accounting firm.

Tool-and-die operators on machines 1, 2, and 3.

Teachers in the same school district.

To assess the effectiveness of various procedures on the performance of individual teachers in classroom settings, several investigators (Cooper, Thomson, and Baer, 1970; Cossairt, Hall, and Hopkins, 1973; Van Houten and Sullivan, 1975) have used the multiple-baseline design *across persons*. Cossairt et al. (1973) observed and recorded the number of intervals each teacher devoted to those students who were working and those who

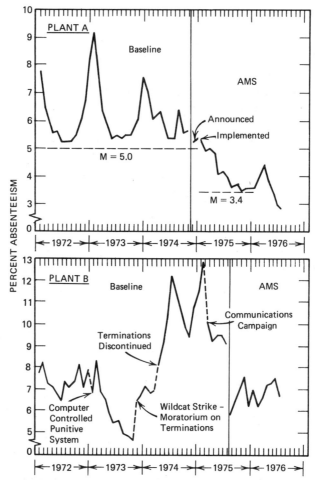

FIGURE 7-7.   Example of multiple-baseline design across groups. Absence rates for hourly employees at experimental plants over a five-year period from 1972 to 1976. Program was introduced in Plant A in late 1974 and in Plant B in mid 1975. From Kempen and Hall (1977). Copyright 1977 by Behavioral Systems, Inc. Reprinted by permission.

were not. Three conditions were introduced at different points for each teacher. When the first and second conditions—instructions and feedback, respectively—produced inconclusive results, feedback plus social praise was introduced, insuring more positive teacher response to students' attentive behavior.

Across Settings.   The multiple-baseline design across settings can be used when one is interested in performance in different situations or circumstances. This method can work in a wide variety of settings. For example, management trainees can be evaluated:

1. In role-playing sessions during training.
2. On the job in the presence of the training director.
3. On the job on their own.

Stock brokers may be observed as they interact with:

1. Same-age, same-sex clients.
2. Same-age, opposite-sex clients.
3. Different-age, same-sex clients.
4. Different-age, opposite-sex clients.

Or fast-foods employees can be monitored for friendliness at different areas within the store:

1. At the cash register.
2. At the pick-up counter.
3. In the dining area.

In a recent study (Kirchner, Schnelle, Domash, Larson, Carr, and McNees, 1980), the residential burglary deterrent effects of a helicopter patrol procedure were investigated in four separate areas in the Nashville metropolitan area:

1. High density area I.
2. High density area II.
3. Low density area I.
4. Low density area II.

The police chief decided how long the helicopter would remain in a given area but was asked, for evaluation purposes, to leave the helicopter in one area for at least 10 days. Figure 7-8 shows that the helicopter procedure resulted in a lower average number of daily burglaries during helicopter patrol periods for the two high density areas.

For the two low population density zones (not shown), however, the program did not deter burglaries. Thus it could be concluded that the program was effective for one type of area but not for another.

Uses of Multiple-Baseline Designs

Evaluate Training Programs.   Multiple-baseline designs are particularly appropriate for assessing the effects of training programs, a common internal intervention in work settings. Unlike reversal designs, multiple-baseline designs do not require a return to baseline conditions to determine whether a change results in improvements. Rather a manager or

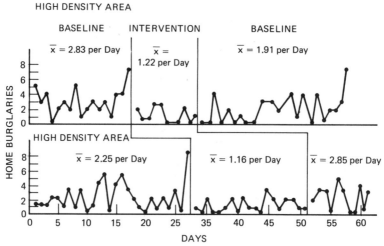

FIGURE 7-8. Example of multiple-baseline design across settings. Number of home burglaries in two high-density areas over a two-month period. Helicopter patrol was introduced in the first and second areas after 2½ and four weeks, respectively. From Kirchner, Schnelle, Domash, Larson, Carr, and McNees (1980). Copyright 1980 by the Society for the Experimental Analysis of Behavior, Inc. Reprinted by permission.

supervisor can collect information on two or more baselines and then introduce the training in steps.

Let's say that a manager is conducting a 12-week training course on the processing of wire to 25 new employees and wishes to evaluate whether the training is having the desired effect. He or she could use a multiple-baseline design *across behavior* as Miller and Weaver (1972) did (see the preceding section). The manager would first divide the content area into components, such as: the coating, the drawing, and the annealing of wire. He or she would then repeatedly assess how well the new employees performed on each of the components, and then introduce the training, one component at a time. After assessing knowledge and skill in these three areas, the manager would present the instructional package for the first component, the coating of wire. Once the trainees demonstrated a mastery of the first component, the manager would introduce the second one. If the employees demonstrated mastery of the second component and were still able to score well on the first, then the manager would introduce the third and last one.

Another possibility is to use a multiple-baseline design *across groups.* A manager could take trainees from two sections of the plant, collect baseline information on both groups, and then train the first group for the entire 12 weeks. Once the first group demonstrated improvements, then he or she would train the second group and assess whether they too improved.

With Addition of Reversal Phase. One can beneficially add a reversal phase to the multiple-baseline design. A multiple-baseline design across groups with a reversal component was used in a recent safety study (Komaki, Barwick and Scott, 1978). The multiple-baseline design was used to assess whether or not a behavioral safety program was effective with personnel in two accident-ridden departments of a wholesale bakery. After a safety observational code was devised, information was collected about the workers' safety performance four times a week over 25 weeks.

During baseline the wrapping department was more or less stable, performing 70 percent of its tasks safely, as shown in Figure 7-9. After 5½ weeks, training and feedback were introduced in the wrapping department. Within the first week, the percentage of incidents performed safely increased dramatically. After the second week, the department was regularly obtaining scores of at least 90 percent. In contrast, in the make-up department, which remained under baseline conditions during the same period (Sessions 20–49), no improvements were noted, and performance remained more or less at its baseline rate. After the program was introduced in the make-up department, however, scores immediately rose to 100 percent and, with one exception, continued at this level. It was concluded that the changes in performance were attributable to the program, because performance improved only after and not prior to the introduction of the program.

A reversal phase was added to demonstrate to management the importance of continuing the program. After the program had been in effect 11 weeks in the wrapping and three weeks in the make-up department, the observers stopped observing and providing feedback. To assess the effect of this reversal phase, observations were reinstituted five weeks later for a period of four weeks. Performance declined to baseline levels (71 and 72 percent). As soon as the president saw the results of the reversal phase, the training of on-site personnel began. Within a year, the number of lost-time accidents decreased fivefold, and the plant moved from last to first place in the company standings.

The reversal phase also made it possible to assess whether reactivity of measurement was a potential source of confounding. If performance levels were primarily a function of the presence or absence of the observers, then one might expect that performance would continue during the reversal phase at its high program rate. Because performance declined to baseline levels during the reversal phase, when the observers were not only present but the workers knew what was expected, it is unlikely that the observers alone served as a cue for safe performance. As a result, it was concluded that reactivity of measurement was not a plausible alternative explanation of the improvements obtained.

Advantages and Limitations

As can be seen, the multiple-baseline design is extremely versatile. One distinct advantage is that it is not necessary to return to baseline conditions for the design to be effective. As a result, the multiple-baseline design can be used when evaluating techniques involving instructions, the clarifi-

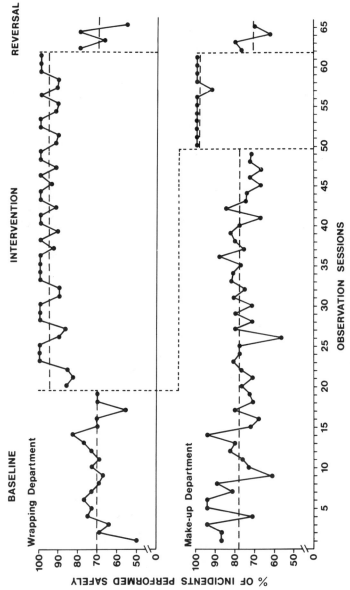

FIGURE 7-9. Example of multiple-baseline design across groups with reversal component. Percentage of incidents performed safely by employees in two departments of a food manufacturing plant during a 25-week period. The behavioral safety program was introduced in the first and second departments after 5½ and 13½ weeks, respectively, and discontinued after 16½ weeks. From Komaki, Barwick, and Scott (1978). Copyright 1978 by the American Psychological Association. Reprinted by permission.

cation of desired performance, or the learning of new information or skills. It can also be used when participants are concerned about returning to baseline conditions that are potentially harmful or dangerous.

Because the multiple-baseline design includes the collection of data on two or more baselines, it is almost always necessary to plan for it in advance, particularly when a manager uses observational measures rather than already existing archival records. On the other hand, the staggering of the techniques is relatively easy to arrange:

> Different groups can almost always be scheduled to receive the intervention technique at different points in time, thus resulting in a multiple-baseline design *across groups.* The rationale: The program can be introduced on an experimental basis in one group. If the program works in the first group, then any wrinkles in it can be ironed out before it is introduced in the next group. If the program does not work as desired, then revisions can be made and tested, thus sparing additional groups the trouble of being guinea pigs for an ineffective treatment.

> A recommended training strategy is to introduce components individually, making sure that trainees have mastered each kind of behavior as it is offered before being allowed to proceed to the next. This "natural" spacing of the technique is ideal for the multiple-baseline design *across behavior.*

> Likewise, if a manager is interested in generality across settings, he or she can introduce the treatment first in one setting, and once the behavior has been established there, he or she can introduce the intervention in the next setting, producing a multiple-baseline design *across settings.*

The main limitation to the multiple-baseline design is that the manager must be careful to select behavior, settings, and persons or groups that are independent of one another so that an intervention technique in one will not affect the others. If the technique on the first kind of behavior has a simultaneous facilitative effect on the second kind, it is difficult to interpret the results. When setting up a multiple-baseline design *across behavior,* one should avoid closely related behavior, for example, carrying out variations of the same accounting method or maintaining similar pieces of equipment. Similarly, one should avoid arranging multiple-baseline designs *across persons or groups* in which the persons subject to the first technique are likely to communicate with persons scheduled to participate in the experiment at a later date.

BEHIND THE SCENES

The choice and execution of a manager's research design is critical to the quality of the conclusions he or she will be able to draw about improvement efforts. These decisions, however, are affected by a number of factors such as:

The feasibility of randomly assigning persons to groups and making available the treatment to only one group.

Control over the timing of the introduction of the program.

The regular collection of information on the area(s) of interest.

The possibility and suitability of reverting to baseline conditions.

The independence of the baselines.

Unfortunately, discussions of these behind-the-scenes decisions rarely appear in print to guide persons who wish to evaluate the efficacy of programs in applied settings. An example from the author's recent work will be used here to illustrate how a multiple-baseline design across groups was chosen to evaluate a preventive maintenance program in the U. S. Marine Corps and how the design was implemented (Komaki, unpublished study). The factors considered in this case are typical of those that come into play in work settings.

The Scene

The long-range goal of the research was to develop a behavioral program that would improve the preventive maintenance of heavy equipment in ongoing Marine Corps units. A PM program was devised, implemented, and tested in a heavy artillery Battery at Camp Lejeune, North Carolina. The focus was on the performance of approximately 60 Marines in two sections: ordnance, with six medium-sized howitzers, and motor transport, with approximately 15 pieces of rolling stock. The two performance areas were:

Detecting deficiencies: The accuracy with which first echelon maintenance personnel identify items needing repair, adjustment, or replacement during weekly maintenance checks.

Follow through: Corrective and timely action taken on the above items by first and second echelon maintenance personnel.

Retired Marines were scheduled to go on site and collect information weekly in the two sections on the two performance areas. The PM Program consisted of two major components:

Specification of desired performance for first and second echelon personnel, as well as their supervisors.

Provision of feedback each week to the above personnel and monthly to management personnel.

Design Possibilities

Both between-group and within-group designs were considered in assessing the effectiveness of the PM program.

Control Group.   The control-group design was ruled out because it was impossible to randomly assign persons in the ordnance section to motor transport and vice versa. Since persons could not be assigned by lot to one group or the other, the fact that the groups might be significantly different from one another could not be ruled out. Thus if the program was introduced to ordnance and improvements resulted, factors other than the program could not be ruled out as possible causes. For example, Marines in ordnance might be better trained or might receive closer monitoring.

Reversal.   The reversal design was also rejected. It was not possible to revert to baseline conditions, because the program consisted of two components, specification and feedback, one of which was impossible to "reverse." A manager or supervisor could discontinue the feedback, but he or she could not revert to a situation in which personnel were not aware of what they were supposed to do. If the program was introduced at the same time in both groups for both behaviors, and if there was no reversal phase (an AB design), a manager could assess only whether improvements occurred. One could not determine whether the program was responsible. Other plausible reasons—an increased emphasis on maintenance by upper-level management, preparation for a period of heavy equipment use in the field, a disturbing trend in the percentage of operable equipment, anticipation of a maintenance inspection—might be responsible and would be difficult to rule out.

Multiple-Baseline across Behavior.   The multiple-baseline design *across behavior* was considered, but was eventually passed over in favor of the multiple-baseline *across groups*. Two out of three requirements were met in that:

> Information could be collected regularly on two activities of the same group.
> The program could be introduced in steps with the first activity and then with the second.

Baseline data could be collected on the two performance areas, detecting deficiencies and follow through, in both ordnance and motor transport. The PM program could be introduced first for detecting deficiencies in both groups, and after improvements occurred, for follow through. However, questions arose about the third requirement: whether the two activities were sufficiently independent of one another. If the program were introduced for detecting deficiencies, a carryover effect might result in improvements in follow through, because first echelon personnel might begin to take action on the detected deficiencies and might also goad second echelon personnel into doing their share. If these carryover effects occurred, then it would be difficult to assess whether the program or some other event was responsible for any changes.

Multiple-Baseline across Groups.   The multiple-baseline design across groups was the eventual choice. All three requirements were met in that:

Information could be collected regularly on two groups.

The program could be introduced in a staggered manner, first to one group and then later to the other.

The groups were independent of one another.

Baseline data could be collected on two existing groups. After an assessment of the initial level of performance, Marines in ordnance could be exposed to the program. Following improvements in ordnance, the same program could be introduced in motor transport. Although both groups belonged to the same battery and worked in the same general area, there was no overlap in personnel assignments, and the supervisory structures were entirely separate. Thus it was thought that changes in the performance of those in the first group would not be likely to affect the performance of those in the second group.

Design Execution

Implementation of Data Collection.   Figure 7-10 shows how the multiple-baseline design *across groups* was actually implemented. Plans were made to collect information weekly on both kinds of behavior in both groups. However, a number of developments prevented the strict following of these plans. There were weeks when a substantial portion of Camp Lejeune was on leave, weeks when the entire regiment was engaged in field exercises, weeks when personnel in one entire section had other commitments, weeks when equipment was unavailable for assessment, and weeks when no deficiencies were accurately detected, thereby precluding an assessment of follow through. As a result, baseline information was collected over a fairly lengthy period of time (e.g., 14 weeks in ordnance) to insure a representative picture of the initial level, and the effects continued to be monitored over 11 months.

Step-Wise Introduction of Intervention.   Few problems were encountered in arranging for the introduction of the program at staggered intervals. On-site personnel were eager to begin, particularly after seeing the baseline data, and initially wanted the program to start in both groups at the same time. After some discussion, however, they agreed to begin with one group. The author allowed on-site personnel to select the group, and they chose ordnance. Both the author and on-site personnel had wanted to begin with motor transport because its data had been more stable and its performance more in need of immediate improvement. Ultimately, however, on-site personnel suggested beginning with ordnance because of its being better organized and having more stable personnel. Once improvements were forthcoming in ordnance, the author had little trouble

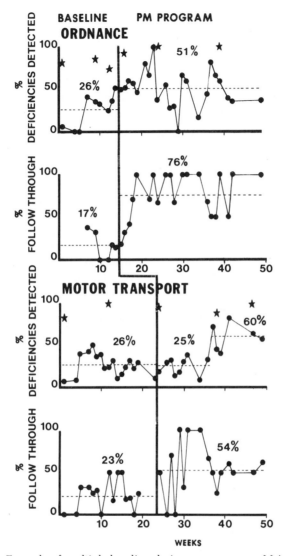

FIGURE 7-10. Example of multiple-baseline design across groups. Maintenance performance in two areas, detecting deficiencies and follow through, in two sections of a heavy artillery Battery in the U. S. Marine Corps over an 11-month period. PM Program was introduced after 14 and 22 weeks. From Komaki (unpublished).

convincing on-site personnel to allow a similar program to be introduced in motor transport eight weeks later.

The only problem that occurred involved the difficulty of postponing the intervention when the data or the data collection went awry at the last moment. Intervention dates were arranged in advance around other commitments. During the twelfth week, e.g., it was decided that ordnance personnel would receive the explanation of the program on Monday of the fifteenth week, and that the program would officially begin then. It was impossible to change this schedule when the upward trend for detecting deficiencies become apparent on Friday of the fourteenth week. Similarly, although the data in motor transport continued to be more stable than that in ordnance, various events prevented data from being collected in follow through the three weeks before the intervention.

Benefit of Repeated Measurement.   The fact that up-to-date information was available, however, did enable me to determine whether the program was having its intended effect. When plans were not progressing as expected, I could immediately alter them instead of having to wait until the posttest data were analyzed and interpreted to see what could have been improved. After four weeks of the program in motor transport, e.g., steady progress was being made in follow through but not in detecting deficiencies. The results looked bleak in the latter category, with the data hovering around the baseline mean with no sign of improvement. I tried to determine what the problem might be. Two differences finally became apparent between ordnance, where the program was successful, and motor transport: (1) the weak supervisory structure in motor transport as opposed to ordnance with its two layers of supervision, and (2) the fact that the recommended supervisory procedures were not being followed in motor transport. I began working immediately with on-site personnel on the suggested scheduling and quality control procedures. When the data showed no improvements for the following two weeks, I renewed my efforts to insure that supervisory personnel knew what to do and carried out the procedures. The percentage of deficiencies detected eventually doubled from 25 to 60 percent, as Figure 7-10 shows, once the recommendations were finally implemented.

Conclusions

Substantial improvements occurred in both measured areas after the program was introduced in ordnance, and in follow through when it was introduced in motor transport (Figure 7-10). Thus the program appeared promising, particularly for ordnance and for follow through. The improvements were sustained in ordnance for a fairly long time, despite the group's numerous other commitments. It cannot be said that the program, as it was originally introduced, was effective in motor transport, where improvements did not occur in detecting deficiencies. However, the eventual improvement in motor transport underscores the importance of the supervisory aspects of maintenance efforts. Plans were made to account for this factor in the next program refinement.

Comparing Within-Group and Between-Group Designs

Differences in Comparisons.   The main difference between within-group designs and traditional control-group designs is their manner of comparison. In the reversal and multiple-baseline designs, comparisons are made *within* groups or within a specific individual's range of behavior. That is, each person or group serves as its own control. In contrast, with control-group designs, comparisons are made *between* groups, with at least one group serving as the control.

Ability to Draw Causal Conclusions.   Although the comparisons are carried out differently, one can draw causal conclusions from either design. That is, one can say with a degree of certainty that the program did or did not produce the desired results. The primary advantage of the reversal and multiple-baseline designs is that they enable one to establish causal relationships without having to create a control group. In fact, with the multiple-baseline design *across groups,* intact groups can be incorporated as an integral and valuable part of the design.

Frequent Data Collection.   Another important benefit of within-group designs is that data are collected regularly over a specified period of time. Instead of assessing a group once before and once after the treatment, as is typically done with control-group designs, one collects data repeatedly during each phase. The repeated measurements provide a descriptive record over the entire course of the experiment, allowing one to examine trends over time and make adjustments accordingly.

Differences in Degree.   Other differences between control-group and single-case designs have been pointed out. These differences are ones of degree rather than kind. One of the most frequently cited differences involves the number of subjects. Reversal and multiple-baseline designs, sometimes subsumed under the rubric of single-case, $N = 1$, or intensive designs, are said to be different from control-group designs because individual entities comprise the entire sample. Although reversal and multiple-baseline designs are sometimes used with only one person, they are *not* limited to single individuals or small groups. The performance of large groups of people can and has been assessed by means of single-case designs (e.g., Kempen and Hall, 1977).

Another frequently mentioned difference between these designs centers on the relative external validity of their results. In particular, questions have been raised about the extent to which results obtained through single-case designs can be generalized to the rest of the population. Naturally, when small numbers of subjects are involved in a design, one should be cautious about drawing general conclusions. Questions of external validity, however, are *not* inherent in reversal and multiple-baseline designs, nor are they effectively answered by using a control group or a large number of subjects. The only way of extending external validity is to carry out a series of related experiments in which the populations, settings, response variables, *and* intervention strategies vary from study to study (Runkel and McGrath, 1972). Unless the findings are replicated with persons in different organizations using different treatment strategies and response measures, it is not clear to what extent any one set of results are unique to the specific individuals, organizations, intervention strategies, or response measures involved, *regardless* of the design used.

Another difference concerns the use of statistical analyses. Statistical analyses, to date, are rarely used when interpreting the results of reversal or multiple-baseline designs. Instead the data are visually inspected, as this chapter describes. Recently, however, as settings become more open and the desired improvements less dramatic, statistical techniques are being used with increasing frequency. In a recent study (Komaki, Heinzmann, and Lawson, 1980) an analysis developed for time-series data called an Autoregressive Integrated Moving Averages (ARIMA) analysis was used in addition to a visual inspection of the data. This analysis was employed to confirm that changes which took place between two conditions were significant in one case and not in another.

An ARIMA analysis transforms data, using the least squares solution, to remove serial dependencies within the data (a potential problem with regularly collected information about the same group) and performs a statistical test (a t–test) on the transformed data to compare changes in the slope and level of scores across conditions. For a comprehensive discussion of this and other newly proposed techniques, refer to the recent article by Hartmann et al. (1980). Thus, although statistical analyses are not yet the norm, they are being used with increasing frequency, as circumstances dictate.

SUMMARY

Management today can choose among a bewildering number of alternative programs for solving organizational problems. Because of the range of forces influencing behavior in the work place, however, determining whether a particular program produced its intended results is not a simple task. Between-group or control-group designs—in which individuals are assigned by lot to one of two groups, one of which is treated and the other not—are the standard means of measuring program effectiveness. However, because of specialized skills and job characteristics in most work settings, suitable, randomly selected control groups are nearly impossible to arrange in that context.

Fortunately, a valuable alternative to control-group designs is available. Single-case or within-group designs are frequently used by behavior analysts to evaluate the effectiveness of changes introduced in applied settings. Instead of comparing a treatment group with a control group, these designs make comparisons within the group under study; that is, the group serves as its own control. Consequently, one is able to draw sound conclusions about effectiveness of organizational changes without having to create a control group. This chapter described the two most widely known and suitable single-case designs—reversal and multiple-baseline—and explored the rationale behind them. Examples were presented, demonstrating how these designs have been and can be used in work settings to improve decision making.

The reversal phase is both the strongest point and greatest drawback of the reversal design. Reverting to baseline conditions allows one to rule out alternative explanations for improvements, such as the Hawthorne effect, reactivity of measurement, history, maturation, and regression artifacts. The problem with the reversal phase, however, is that it is sometimes impossible or impractical to effect.

The multiple-baseline design is a highly recommended alternative when this is the case. It involves the collection of data on two or more baselines and the introduction of the treatment in steps. Its strong suit is its adaptability to a variety of work situations; it can be arranged across behavior, across groups, and across settings. Because it does not require a return to baseline conditions, the multiple-baseline design is particularly useful in assessing the effects of training programs, a common internal technique in work settings.

Because single-case designs can verify cause-effect relationships without using control groups and are able to document and trace shifts in behavior over specified spans of time, the chapter argued for their singular appropriateness to the work place and the importance of their being given increased opportunities to display their effectiveness there.

REFERENCES

Campbell, D. T., and Stanley, J. C. Experimental and quasi-experimental designs for research on teaching. In N. L. Gage (Ed.), *Handbook of research on teaching.* Chicago: Rand McNally, 1963. Reprinted separately as *Experimental and quasi-experimental designs for research.* Chicago: Rand McNally, 1966.

Cooper, M. L., Thomason, C. L., and Baer, D. M. The experimental modification of teacher attending behavior. *Journal of Applied Behavior Analysis,* 1970, *3,* 153–157.

Cossairt, A., Hall, R. V., and Hopkins, B. L. The effects of experimenter's instructions, feedback, and praise on teacher praise and student attending. *Journal of Applied Behavior Analysis,* 1973, *6,* 89–100.

Goldstein, I. L. Training in work organizations. *Annual Review of Psychology,* 1980, *31,* 229–72.

Gupton, T., and Lebow, M. C. Behavior management in a large industrial firm. *Behavior Therapy,* 1971, *2,* 78–82.

Hartmann, D. P., Gottman, J. M., Jones, R. R., Gardner, W., Kazdin, A. E., and Vaught, R. Interrupted time-series analysis and its application to behavioral data. *Journal of Applied Behavior Analysis,* 1980, *13,* 543–560.

Hermann, J. A., de Montes, A. I., Dominguez, B., Montes, F., and Hopkins, B. L. Effects of bonuses for punctuality on the tardiness of industrial workers. *Journal of Applied Behavior Analysis,* 1973, *6,* 563–570.

Hersen, M., and Barlow, D. H. *Single-Case Experimental Designs: Strategies for Studying Behavior Change.* New York: Pergamon Press, 1976.

Homans, G. Group factors in worker productivity. In H. Proshansky and B. Seidenberg (Eds.), *Basic studies in social psychology.* New York: Holt, Rinehart, and Winston, 1965.

Kempen, R. W., and Hall, R. V. Reduction of industrial absenteeism: Results of a behavioral approach. *Journal of Organizational Behavior Management,* 1977, *1,* 1–22.

Kirchner, R. E., Schnelle, J. F., Domash, M., Larson, L., Carr, A., and McNees, M. P. The applicability of a helicopter patrol procedure to diverse areas: A cost-benefit evaluation. *Journal of Applied Behavior Analysis,* 1980, *13,* 143–148.

Komaki, J. A behavioral approach to preventive maintenance: A case study in the Marine Corps (unpublished).

Komaki, J., Barwick, K. D., and Scott, L. R. A behavioral approach to occupational safety: Pinpointing and reinforcing safe performance in a food manufacturing plant. *Journal of Applied Psychology*, 1978, *63*, 434–445.

Komaki, J., Heinzmann, A. T., and Lawson, L. Effect of training and feedback: Component analysis of a behavioral safety program. *Journal of Applied Psychology*, 1980, *65*, 261–270.

Komaki, J., Waddell, W. M., and Pearce, M. G. The applied behavior analysis approach and individual employees: Improving performance in two small businesses. *Organizational Behavior and Human Performance*, 1977, *19*, 337–352.

Kreitner, R., and Golab, M. Increasing the rate of salesperson telephone calls with a monetary refund. *Journal of Organizational Behavior Management*, 1978, *1*, 192–195.

Lamal, P. A., and Benfield, A. The effect of self-monitoring on job tardiness and percentage of time spent working. *Journal of Organizational Behavior Management*, 1978, *1*, 142–149.

McCarthy, M. Decreasing the incidence of "high bobbins" in a textile spinning department through a group feedback procedure. *Journal of Organizational Behavior Management*, 1978, *1*, 150–154.

Marholin, D., II, and Gray, D. Effects of group response-cost procedures on cash shortages in a small business. *Journal of Applied Behavior Analysis*, 1976, *9*, 25–30.

Miller, L. K., and Miller, O. L. Reinforcing self-help group activities of welfare recipients. *Journal of Applied Behavior Analysis*, 1970, *3*, 57–64.

Miller, L. K., and Weaver, F. H. A multiple baseline achievement test. In G. Semb (Ed.), *Behavior analysis and education—1972*. Lawrence: Support and Development Center For Follow Through, Department of Human Development, University of Kansas, 1972.

Panyan, M., Boozer, H., and Morris, N. Feedback to attendants as a reinforcer for applying operant techniques. *Journal of Applied Behavior Analysis*, 1970, *3*, 1–4.

Pedalino, E., and Gamboa, V. U. Behavior modification and absenteeism: Intervention in one industrial setting. *Journal of Applied Psychology*, 1974, *59*, 694–696.

Quilitch, H. R. A comparison of three staff-management procedures. *Journal of Applied Behavior Analysis*, 1975, *8*, 59–66.

Roethlisberger, F. J., and Dickson, W. J. *Management and the worker*. Cambridge, MA: Harvard University Press, 1939.

Runkel, P. J., and McGrath, J. E. *Research on human behavior*. New York: Holt, Rinehart, and Winston, 1972.

Staw, B. M. The experimenting organization: Problems and prospects. In B. M. Staw (Ed.), *Psychological foundations of organizational behavior*. Santa Monica: Goodyear, 1977.

Sulzer-Azaroff, B. Behavioral ecology and accident prevention. *Journal of Organizational Behavior Management*, 1978, *2*, 11–44.

Sulzer-Azaroff, B., and de Santamaria, M. Industrial safety hazard reduction through performance feedback. *Journal of Applied Behavior Analysis*, 1980, *13*, 287–296.

Van Houten, R., and Sullivan, K. Effects of an audio cueing system on the rate of teacher praise. *Journal of Applied Behavior Analysis*, 1975, *8*, 197–201.

NOTE: Chapter preparation and research in the area of preventive maintenance were supported by the Naval Personnel Research and Development Center under Contract No. N00014–79–C0011 (Judith Komaki, principal investigator). Many thanks to all of my co-authors at Georgia Tech and San Jose State University; to Lee Frederiksen for his collegiality and the chapter's title; to Anthony DeCurtis for his fine grasp of the language; and to Diane Robertson and Diane Stewart for their typing and deciphering skills.

PART

Techniques for
Behavior Management

A critical part of most manager's jobs is managing behavior. Accomplishing things through other people is a common view of what managers do. Sometimes the management of other people is very direct, such as giving specific instructions or meting out consequences for subordinate's actions. At other times it is more indirect, such as through the use of training programs. Likewise the management of behavior may vary on the scale of the change desired. On some occasions the manager may be interested in altering the behavior of a single individual with whom he or she works closely. At the other extreme a manager may be interested in improving the performance of a large group of individuals, most of whom he or she has never met. The chapters in the currect section cover a range of techniques and procedures that are applicable to managing behavior in this range of situations.

Most people recognize the need for managers to have technical competence in certain areas of expertise. Likewise the ability to manage the behavior of others is also widely recognized. Less frequently acknowledged is the manager's need to manage his or her own behavior; thus self-management is also covered in this wide-ranging section.

Training is probably one of the most widely recognized procedures for changing behavior. Chapter 8, authored by Paul Ross, tackles this important topic. When a manager encounters a performance problem, one common response is to call for a training program. However, as Ross points out, training is often not the best solution and may even be a costly mistake. The author first presents an overview of training, covering such topics as its cost and the historic development of modern training methods. He then goes on to present a strong case for front-end analysis and the systematic development of training programs. Some behavior-based strategies for making training more effective and a systematic approach to training development are also discussed. Finally he presents an approach to insure that training is actually translated into on the job performance improvement, a critical consideration.

Chapter 9 covers the important but often overlooked topic of self-management. Authored by Andrasik and Heimburg, the chapter starts with a discussion of what self-management is and is not. They then go on to present a catalog of behavioral self-management methods including self-analysis, modification of behavioral antecedents, modification of consequences, reordering behavioral routines, and contracting. They also cover the important topics of evaluating the effectiveness of a self-management program and maintaining it over time. Through the use of numerous examples and a specially developed program planning guide, they have made their presentation both clear and extremely practical.

Managers are often faced with performance problems for which traditional methods are woefully inadequate. In Chapter 10 Fred Luthans presents a behavioral problem-solving model for tackling performance problems. This structured five-step model presents a systematic way of improving performance. The model starts with the task of identifying and defining critical problem behavior. Step 2 involves the careful pinpointing and measuring of problem behavior. Careful measurement not only provides a basis for later change but may also indicate that the supposed problem is really no problem at all. A careful functional analysis of the factors maintaining the problem behavior is the purpose of Step 3. Step 4 involves developing an intervention strategy. Luthans reviews a range of potential intervention techniques along with specific examples and practical suggestions. The final step involves a careful evaluation of the program. The chapter also features illustrations and examples of how this model has been successfully applied to boost productivity in a range of different organizations.

Perhaps the single most common technique used in OBM is performance feedback. Part of its appeal undoubtedly lies in the dual advantages of relatively low cost and an impressive track record of effectiveness. In Chapter 11, Fairbank and Prue discuss how to develop such a system. The authors recognize that much remains to be learned about why feedback systems work and how to make them more effective. Yet, based on our current knowledge, they have come up with a series of practical guidelines and rules for developing a workable system. Starting with a determination of suitability of a feedback system for the organizational problem of interest, they cover the important topics of selecting appropriate performance measures and deciding on the parameters of the system. They also present a series of specific guidelines to aid in the design of the system and illustrate the process that one might go through in making the series of necessary decisions.

The first four chapters in this section focus on specific techniques for analyzing and managing performance-related behavior. The emphasis is on the technique and not on how it is integrated into the overall organization. By way of contrast, the final two chapters in this section focus more on strategic or organizational level considerations. Chapter 12, authored by Brandon Hall, discusses planning and implementing organization-wide productivity improvement programs, while Chapter 13 reviews ways to overcome constraints to organizational change that are inherent in virtually any intervention.

Hall starts his chapter by acknowledging the problems inherent in the quest for quick fixes for difficult organizational problems. If a program is going to have any long-term impact on human productivity, it must have full management support and an organization-wide commitment. His approach involves four critical steps. The first is developing an organizational mission statement with specific goals projected at least five years into the future. Second, there must be an agreement on what constitutes ideal management practices. The third step involves a thorough assessment of current management practices. This requires an unflinching look at how things are actually done as compared to how they should be done. Finally, there is a need for detailed planning regarding a program to help move the organization from where it is to where it should be. For each of these steps the author gives specific suggestions on how it can be implemented and examples of what the final product might be like.

The final chapter in this section is authored by Prue and Frederiksen. It starts from the premise that, no matter how good an intervention technique, it is of no value unless it is actually implemented. Based on a review of the literature and practical experience, they identify a series of constraints to organizational change. These constraints can arise from sources as varied as organizational structure, employee concerns, the behavior of the consultant, external rules and regulations, and so on. The identified constraints are then organized within four prototypical stages of organizational interventions: entry, preparation for change, initiation of change, and maintenance of change. At each stage of the intervention the authors identify specific actions that can be taken to increase the likelihood that the change will be adopted and maintained.

The chapters in this section are diverse, yet they share some important elements. First, all the authors share a common view of behavior. We must look closely at what people do and not simply what they say about what they do. Second, the authors recognize that the key to managing behavior is attention to its context. We must carefully attend to the events that precede behavior and the consequences that follow it. Third, the maintenance of behavior must also be carefully planned for and not left to chance. Finally, the success of our efforts must be carefully assessed and not just assumed. The net effect of this approach is to provide the manager with specific, workable suggestions rather than global unattainable admonitions.

8

Training: Behavior Change and the Improvement of Business Performance

PAUL C. ROSS

American Telephone and Telegraph Co.

The assertion that good training makes good business sense somehow has never had the ring of credibility. Perhaps this lack of a credible claim comes from our social and cultural bias, which does not value education as much as other endeavors. We can see this in the pay scales for teachers versus engineers or the salaries we pay for marketing professors versus those we pay marketing specialists, who are usually their students. Or perhaps, as business people, we tend to see training as a component of operating cost rather than as an investment in productivity improvement.

In this chapter I will present a case for viewing training as an investment device for the improvement of productivity and profit. I will argue that training represents a means for investing in human capital, and that the modern manager and executive must begin to ask questions about how this investment will yield a return. The chapter will examine some of the economic implications of training and provide a frame of reference for asking "smart" questions about how the training investment in your business is managed for profit. I believe that any business that has a training organization, or is about to establish one, must approach the function from a sound business viewpoint. This means that the business need must be carefully developed, and then the successful training organization must carefully arrange their resources so as to meet this need in the most cost effective way. For most industry, but by no means all, these needs can be developed in economic terms. Therefore, I will begin this chapter with a brief review of some of the economic issues that touch the training system.

The economics of training are not easily identified. My own experience is probably as good a starting point as any. In the period between 1967 and 1976, I and my colleagues conducted several studies aimed at estimating the cost of training in various departments of our company. The results were often disappointing because we could not agree on a common definition of what training was, where it was conducted, or what it was intended to accomplish, and so on. After several attempts to develop cost estimates for training, I began to examine common findings as orders of magnitude issues rather than as precise information about cost or benefit. This approach led to some estimates of how we were spending the training dollar. While the specific figures varied from organization to organization, an overall pattern began to emerge from these studies.

Figure 8-1 shows an estimated breakdown of how the training dollar was spent. While the percentage for salary, development, training center cost, and miscellaneous expenses may vary from one organization to another, I found that overall development was about ⅕ of training center cost, and that trainee salary and loading were usually more than twice the training center cost.

These rough percentages were useful in helping us estimate our overall training cost and in contrasting these training costs with other operating expenditures so as to establish an order of magnitude view of training and other business expenses. Over the years, these estimates were used by various people to help plan for the centralization of our training effort, first by major departments, and later integrating these departmental efforts into a human resource department for the corporation.

One of the driving forces during this period was for consolidation and control of cost. Duplication of effort and the control of visible cost, e.g., leased classroom space or the use of outside professionals to deliver train-

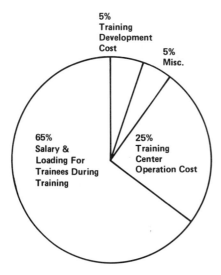

FIGURE 8-1. How the training dollar is spent. This figure represents a summary of several studies of training costs conducted between 1970 and 1976.

ing, were often sufficient reason to drive the corporation towards the centralization of all training. It would not be incorrect to say that during this period more concern was focused on where training was given and by whom than upon what the training accomplished or how it was developed. This driving concern, supported by fragmented data, tended towards the view that training costs must be managed; to some this meant minimized.

If this view seemed unbalanced, it was because training professionals were unable to make a cogent case for training benefits. Measurement problems and a performance-based view of training were in their infancy, leaving only the cost tip of the training iceberg visible to the eye of the astute manager. What was clearly absent in this period was a means for relating training to some meaningful estimates of business performance such as overall sales or profit. What was needed was a shift in emphasis from viewing training as an overhead cost to viewing training as an investment opportunity. Unfortunately, credible data to support the benefits of training was not generally available at that time. Throughout this period, the absence of credible data about the overall cost of training or information about the benefits of training reached a climate in which cost-control management assumed a much more prominent role than did cost-benefits management. In the hope that better information would lead to a better climate, I and my colleagues continued to do studies of training.

In one analysis I examined the business opportunity potential for training for the Fortune 500 companies based on reported 1979 sales, profits, and personnel. This analysis was based on some assumptions drawn from some of my work in the communications industry. Before going further, I will readily concede that this analysis is not an accurate one beyond the order of magnitude. That is, I am confident that the Fortune 500 companies are spending tens of billions of dollars, not hundreds of millions of dollars for training. Furthermore, throughout the analysis, conservative assumptions were used. For example, in estimating the increased efficiency for applying systematic training development methodology, a high of 20 percent and a low of 10 percent are used. My own experience suggests that systematic development can lead to improvements in efficiency of 50 percent or more in training time and substantial improvements in end-of-course performance. For the purpose of this analysis, we assumed no improvement on performance.

Even with these conservative assumptions, we found some extraordinary opportunity values for the Fortune 500 companies. The analysis suggests that if we increase spending for training development cost by 50 percent, as we apply modern systematic development methods, and we assume that we will obtain an increase in efficiency of 10 percent, then the return on investment (ROI) would be more than 400 percent. If that 50 percent increase in spending for development yielded a 20 percent improvement in efficiency, the ROI would be more than 800 percent. That is, for each additional dollar invested, a return in reduced operating cost (trainee time and training center utilization) of $4 to $8 might be expected. Although this analysis was based on conservative assumptions, there is some research that would support the view that large increases in training efficiency can be achieved through the investment in development methodology. Jeon and Branson (1981) examined the relative efficiency of various instructional media and found that efficiency gains of about 37 percent were achieved when careful instructional design criteria are employed. This study also reports improved performance on a performance test. These findings are not an isolated incident. Similar improvements in instructional efficiency are reported by Shoemaker (1976), who describes a 33 percent increase in instructional efficiency that is attributable to systematic instructional design. In an unpublished study, Williams (1980) compared computer-based training to conventional training and reported efficiency gains of 25 to 30 percent over conventional instruction. In this study some of the gains are thought to be in part due to the individualization of training that is achieved when a computer delivers the instruction. In any event, it is worthwhile to note that individualization of instruction alone can result in significant improvements in training efficiency.

If we consider only the gains that we may achieve in improved efficiency (reduced training time), then clearly the business opportunity potential for investing in training is substantial. And when this opportunity is examined in comparison to overall business profitability, it is clearly of significant proportions. On the basis of a conservative analysis, I have estimated that for the Fortune 500 companies (based on 1978 and 1979 earnings), a modest improvement in training efficiency of between 10–20 percent due to improved development can yield between 1.44 and 9.53 billion dollars in reduced labor and training costs. Expressed as a percentage of 1979 profits, these values translate into 1.8 to 12.17 percent of total 1979 profits for these corporations. Clearly, an analysis of business opportunities in the training area shows that there are some significant gains to be made. Their attainment, however, will require an investment.

All of this argument rests upon an investment in systematic development methodology. What it is, where it came from, and how you can use it will concern us throughout the rest of this chapter.

SYSTEMATIC DEVELOPMENT METHODOLOGY

I could have referred to this methodology by several other names: "Programmed instruction," "instructional technology," "instructional systems methodology," "instructional systems development," "training technology," and so on. I have chosen to call it "systematic development methodology" because I want to call attention to the methods of development, NOT the product produced. In my experience, the need to separate these two issues is important if we wish to avoid confusing means and ends. For example, most people tend to think of programmed instruction as a book in which statements are made, questions are asked, and the learner can check the answer. Fewer people (within and outisde of the training profession) would recognize that a programmed instruction (PI) unit may appear in various media, e.g., books, slides, tape, video. Still fewer people would recognize that PI is a development methodology that assures learner competency through successive approximation, shaping, and the feedback of test results. Regardless of what name we call the discipline, one very important assumption sets this approach apart from other forms of training. This assumption is best summed in this phrase: "If the learner didn't learn, then the training didn't teach." Underlying all that we do in systematic development is the responsibility that the instructional developer readily accepts for learner performance. In short, the instructional developer attempts to engineer learner performance. And the learner, even a low ability one or one who shows limited interest in the material, is treated as a condition that is engineered as part of the overall design. In this sense the instructional designer assumes a responsibility for motivating the learner through a design that is carefully tailored to the needs of the learner.

Only a small portion of the people that I talk to in industry realize that programmed instruction is a process of development that includes systematic techniques for determining what should be taught. I believe that these characteristics of programmed instruction probably stem from the various stages through which this methodology evolved. And so, in this next section, I will present a brief and incomplete history of modern training methodology.

A Short History of Modern Training Methods

Modern training methods have roots in several disciplines. One major root goes back to concern for how learning is measured. This root stems from a concern for improving ways to conveniently test students. In the early 1920s, Sidney L. Pressey of Ohio State University began to apply mechanical devices for administering and scoring objective tests (multiple-choice tests). Pressey saw these devices as useful aids in teaching. They could be used to help teachers with routine drill and practice assignments because they allowed the student to respond to a question and instantly let the student know if the choice answer was correct or incorrect (Porter, 1960).

Dr. Pressey found that by carefully breaking an instructional unit into multiple choice questions or true and false questions, a simple device could be used to teach. Pressey pursued the development of these devices and was guided by the principles of learning theory as it was then formulated. With the advent of World War II, these devices were used by the Armed Forces as simple training machines. After the war, these machines played a central role in establishing the basis for more complex teaching machines and their present counterpart, computer based instruction (CBI). Some called this approach "programmed instruction" or "adjunctive autoinstruction."

Another important root for modern training stems from the work of Dr. B. F. Skinner of Harvard University. He significantly advanced the state of training art in two important ways. First, Skinner developed an answer device that freed the machine from a multiple choice format and allowed the student to compose an answer (and be confirmed of its correctness). Second and more importantly, Skinner focused attention upon the organization of the subject matter and the way it is sequenced for the learner. Skinner introduced the idea that instruction should be designed in successive steps, in which later material is based on earlier material. He organized these steps into "frames," which were small enough to insure that learning is gradual from frame to frame and that errors would rarely occur. The amount of information in each frame came to be called "step size" and was determined through a careful analysis of the subject matter. As the learner moved through each frame, a question was posed and answered. Each answer was confirmed before moving on. In this way Skinner applied the principles of reinforcement that he and other psychologists were developing in the research laboratory.

The pioneering work of Pressey and Skinner established the basic elements for systematic development methods in training. The essential elements are:

1. Dividing the subject matter into small testable units (Pressey).
2. The importance of immediate knowledge or results (Pressey).
3. The way content is selected and organized into a sequence (Skinner).
4. The application of the principles of reinforcement so that errors are minimized and correct responses are positively reinforced to enhance learning (Skinner).

Today practitioners of instructional technology often confuse these four elements. Knowledge of results (confirming responses) are often confused with reinforcement and sequencing. Much research has been devoted to these issues. As a result, we now have a body of useful theory concerning instructional effectiveness based upon Pressey and Skinner's work. In short, we have the beginnings of a technology of instructional development. It is a crude and incomplete technology, yet it is serviceable and it can be applied to yield important practical business results.

As we have expanded our view of this infant technology, we see that some of our early concerns like immediate knowledge of results can be understood in terms of more recent theories, e.g., cybernetic theory and particularly the notion of feedback and control. Content selection, sequence, and step size is better understood today in terms of specification of objectives (what will be taught) and instructional strategy (how it will be taught). So far in this short history of modern training, I have traced the early concern with testing devices, the contributions of the early learning theorists, and our present acceptance of cybernetic theory and its usefulness in instructional design and development. I would now like to turn to some other forces that I see influencing modern training.

The issue of determining content was most pressing not in education but in military and industrial training. And it was in the military that systematic methods of studying jobs (job task analysis) were most conspicuously applied. In the military, these methods (job task analysis) were applied to training development, and significant economies were obtained. These economies resulted from the careful determination of what should be taught for specific jobs. For example, when we began to apply these methods to industrial training, we found we were able to reduce training time by removing nonessential content. In some of these cases we reduced the content by as much as 75 percent. We often found we were not only training people on nonessential tasks, but more importantly, we were *not* training them on essential ones. Job task analysis provided us with a tool to make important content decisions.

Another force that has substantially influenced modern training is the recognition that there is an optimum sequence for developing training. This approach has been called systematic development or instructional systems development. This approach describes a process in which a job is analyzed into its component parts before instructional content and media decisions are made. In this approach a road map is laid out for instructional development. The map begins with task analysis and ends with training that carefully builds the trainee's ability to perform on a job. Figure 8-2 shows a general version of this approach.

Before going on with our description of modern training, I would like to discuss some of the organizational constraints that affect how training is developed in the business environment. This discussion is important because training development is subject to all of the pressures that influence all business systems. Concern for general business issues, managerial influence, and sensitivity to the political realities of the organization are all represented in the training organization. The next section of this chapter will briefly examine some of these organizational issues.

The Training Departments and Systematic Training Development

Although most training organizations acknowledge that a careful determination of training needs should be made before undertaking a training development project, in my experience the practical constraints of time, people, skill level, and organizational mission conspire to make it more likely that training will be developed whether it is needed or not. This may appear to be a harsh indictment of current training organizations, yet it adequately reflects my experience working with large corporations and government agencies. Training, like any human endeavor, requires collaboration and cooperation. The training organization is an organizational

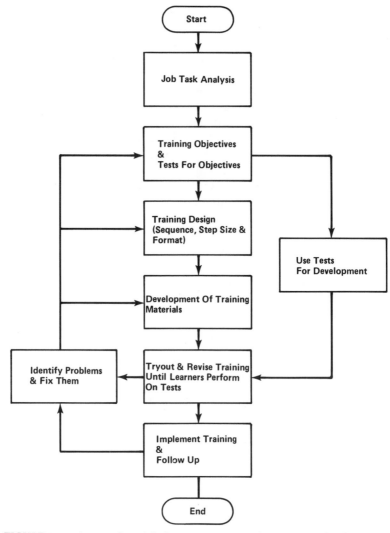

FIGURE 8-2. A general model of a systems approach to training development.

means to bring about this cooperation. And like all organizational forms, it is a political mechanism through which decisions are reached through compromise. The role of power and influence often guides these compromises. Sometimes the power and influence stems from powerful managers who see training as a means of influencing others; sometimes power and influence has its focus in the training organization; and they are evident concerns in planning how to sustain funding and growth of the training organization.

For example, although centralizing training in a department or incorporating it in a human resource department has been promoted as a means to achieve management control over the cost of training, I believe the centralization of training may have in some cases actually increased the cost of training. There are at least two major reasons, and possibly a third, why this increase might occur.

1. *The removal of training responsibility from operating management.* To the operating manager, training is a means for developing the competencey of the employee. Training is not an end in itself. Consequently the operating manager tends to act to minimize training cost in preference to other options, i.e., training time is viewed as unproductive time. The centralization of training brings with it organizational objectives for how much training should be done, when, and to whom. Sometimes the net effect of these objectives is to increase the level of training.

2. *Centralized training organizations tend to adopt a training delivery mission over a broad human performance mission.* They tend to measure their performance in trainee days delivered, not contributions to operating performance, and they often neglect other cost-effective alternatives to formal training. For example, while we tend to acknowledge the cost-effective role that job aids can play, more often than not the development of such aids is viewed by trainers in centralized organizations as beyond their responsibility. In a system that focuses on delivery of training, there is usually no way to count and credit job aids. Trainee days and seats filled are more easily identified measures of the training function and therefore are more readily measured.

3. *Large centralized training organizations can become very efficient in delivering training, even when it is not needed.* The training departments' own objectives, measurements, budgeting, and even the social relationship that trainers establish among each other can all conspire to bring about a condition in which the training organization drifts increasingly from its corporate mission. The role of training in a business system must be carefully managed to assure overall business performance. One way to offset some of these problems is to define training in a way that focuses attention on how well it serves the overall business needs. Training might be defined as a system that enables human performance by developing relevant skills and instituting programs for the maintenance of these skills within the organization. Focusing on enabling the overall business mission makes it much more difficult for the organization to pursue a course in which power and influence takes precedence over performance. Modern performance-based training contains the tools to achieve this purpose. Whether it is achieved will be determined by how management positions the training function within the overall organization. In the next section I will examine some tools that a performance-based training organization can use to insure that the organization's business needs are met.

PEFORMANCE ANALYSIS, TRAINING NEEDS AND
TRANSFER OF TRAINING

One of B. F. Skinner's contribution to modern training technology was the emphasis that he gave to the selection and sequencing of content. This emphasis placed a responsibility upon the training developer for organizing the instructional material in learner relevant terms. The application of task analysis in military training added another dimension, the relevance of the content to a set of job requirements. Thus far, two types of analysis are incorporated into modern instructional technology: analyzing job and tasks, and analyzing learner requirements.

A third type of analysis came into use in the early 1970s. This type of analysis has been called by several names e.g., needs analysis, performance analysis, front end analysis) and was an attempt to apply systems analysis methods to the training process. The application of systems analysis to training was an attempt to link training not only to a job but to business performance. Gilbert (1967) set the stage for doing this by relating training cost to business value, using a concept called worth. Another important early contributionn to this effort was 'Mager and Pipe's (1970) book *Analyzing Performance Problems*. In this book a problem-solving approach was developed that helps the trainer sort out problems in behavior due to skill versus problems due to other factors (e.g., punishing appropriate behavior).

Concurrently, T. F. Gilbert began to introduce the concept of "accomplishment," which, when coupled to Mager and Pipe's problem solving approach, provided a sound systems-based framework for examining performance in terms of the business purpose.

Gilbert's concept of the accomplishment, I believe, is one of those simple yet significant steps in the evolution of a discipline. Gilbert was concerned about how we could distinguish between behavior (what one does) and performance (what is achieved that is valued by the organization). The notion of the accomplishment is equivalent to the system's notion of output, i.e., the focus is upon what is produced as contrasted with the steps or process used to produce it.

This concept (accomplishment) was important because it clarified several major issues that arose in the early application of task analysis to training. First, a task analysis yields a description of the steps in a job. The level of detail of the analysis has always posed a problem for the analyst. Should the tasks be described in terms of large steps, or should they be described in terms as fine as motor movements of the hand? Second, whenever we specify a task sequence for performing a job, we presume that that sequence is optimal. This presumption may be accurate for some jobs that involve largely motor tasks, such as the assembly of a device. For other jobs such as sales work, supervision of subordinates, or customer complaint handling, the presumption of a fixed or correct sequence may actually lead to a decline in performance, i.e., a concern for "the right" way may lead to the elaboration of the trivial. Third, task analysis yields some kind of description of the job such as a flow diagram of the steps in a job. What we often forget is that the description or flow diagram is a representation of the job. It is a model of the job, not the job itself. And it is important to remember that models have utility because we can use the model to make predictions about the job. Models also have their limitations. Because models are approximations of events and relationships, they can only approximate performance. Consequently, some models yield better approximations of a performance than others. For example, a flow diagram of how a sales person sells a high technology device is not the same as how he or she actually sells it. Yet by reviewing the model, we can trace each step of the sale. In so doing, we can draw some conclusions about the sales process. But the model is not the job, and we need to be sure, especially in complex verbal jobs like supervising subordinates, that the conclusions reached are true for the real job is well as for the model. Finally, models are creatures of the process used to develop them. Most models are constructions of what someone sees. However, the very process of seeing implies that we experience something filtered through our unique history and our present vantage point. In short, we interpret what we see, and we filter what we describe. Our descriptions include not only the properties of the event, but they also include our individual understanding of those events. Models that we develop based upon job analysis alone, while often useful, can sometimes yield marginal and even foolish training. For example, I have seen how a task analysis resulted in management training on ways to empty your in box, and sales training that focused on questioning techniques to the exclusion of closing a sale.

The concept of the accomplishment or output provides a basic reference for focusing upon the business need. Gilbert has argued that if accomplishments are identified, we can assess the organizational value of the work. In this way we can sort out the important from the unimportant and relate training to business purpose. Using accomplishment as a reference point, we can arrange tasks into sequences that optimally meet the organization's needs. We can also use accomplishments to evaluate alternatives, so that we select those that make the most business sense. At the end of our project, the accomplishments enable us to establish a meaningful basis for evaluation.

If this discussion seems overdrawn, it is because the distinction between output and behavior has escaped the attention of much of the literature on training. Goldstein (1980), in a major review of the literature, has highlighted various disciplines that are part of the training process including work and organization analysis, task analysis, and person analysis. Goldstein, however, seems to ignore either accomplishments or output analyses as a relevant discipline in training development. Consequently, when he describes various issues related to how we can evaluate instruction to assure its quality, the implications of accomplishment-output analysis are ignored. Goldstein suggests that the criterion test be based on the task analyses, a common practice. However, when applied to non-routine cognitive jobs (e.g., sales, supervision) we run the risk of placing equal emphasis upon the trivial and the critical. Unloading your in box can be treated with the same importance a planning a budget.

In short, transferring a skill from a learning situation to on-the-job performance can be either helped or hindered by other events that occur in the job. For example, sales people may know how to schedule their day's work in the most efficient way. But knowing how doesn't always translate into doing what is known. A performance analysis should uncover not only the accomplishment output for a job, it should also uncover what job conditions exist that can reinforce (reward or punish) desired work behavior. Properly used, the performance analysis helps you plan for these conditions in your training design.

The utility of the accomplishment can best be seen by comparing it to a job task analysis approach. Figure 8-3 shows this comparison as it might have occurred for a electronic technician repair job. In this case, inspection of the list of job tasks does not show how they are organized into events that are of value to the employer. For example, "reads a circuit diagram" has no inherent value to the repair business. The boss would not pay the technician to sit around and read circuit diagrams. The reading of diagrams is clearly part of some valued result. In contrast, the output analysis shows two valued outputs. First, diagnosing repair problems and rendering an (accurate) estimate is a tangible product produced by the repair person. Since many repair services charge for this estimate, an economic value can be attached to it. It is unlikely that a technician can produce this output without being able to read a circuit diagram. It is also apparent that the technician will need to use complex test equipment in order to diagnose the problem, so that an accurate estimate can be given to the customer.

In this example, a performance analysis is also shown. The performance analysis has identified several performance problems and the probable reason for these problems. The performance analysis enables the analyst to pinpoint problems and to classify these problems in a way that leads to a solution. In this situation only one training problem was identified. The analyst recommended that training be given on the use of the ABC scope to test XYZ sets. The other performance problems, pricing of estimated work and inaccurate circuit diagrams, are corrected through the use of a checklist (job aid) for pricing and a new updated circuit diagram for XYZ sets.

In this example of a performance analysis, we see how the training specialist can make recommendations that lead naturally to the enhancement of overall business performance.

In the next section we will explore how this analysis is combined with the step shown in Figure 8-2, so that we can develop training that is cost effective in meeting the business purpose.

Some Typical Tasks	Typical Accomplishments (Outputs)	Performance Analysis			
		Deficiencies	Reason	Business Impact	Proposed Solution
Job: electronic technician Tasks: Trouble shoots electronic equipment Reads circuit diagrams Solders components Reads test instruments Use hand tools Replace components Maintains a clean work area	Job: electronic technician outputs 1. Malfunctioning electronic equipment; diagnosed and repair estimate rendered. Steps: Trouble shoots equipment Identifies nature of malfunction Writes up estimate form	Three out of 10 pieces of equipment are misdiagnosed. Typically XYZ sets are misdiagnosed	Circuit diagrams for XYZ sets are out of date	Lost revenue when set estimate is underpriced A real performance analysis would detail out the loss in dollars	Provide updated diagrams for XYZ sets
	2. Malfunctioning equipment repaired Steps: Defective component replaced. Equipment tested and performance specifications measured calibration and adjustments made to meet performance specification. Service orders prepared and priced.	ABC scope not used properly on XYZ sets Errors on service order pricing	Technician not familiar with use of scope on XYZ set Doesn't include all work operations to fix set	Excessive test time and service cost overcharge to customers Lost revenue Customer irritation	Training on how XYZ set is to be tested using ABC scope Provides checklist of service operations for repair person

FIGURE 8-3. How a task list might differ from an accomplishment analysis of a electronic repair technician's job. A performance analysis of the outputs is also shown.

Performance-Based Training

The application of task analysis to training proved to be a very useful was to develop training content. Through this analysis, the training designer could learn as much as was needed about the task. The training designer is not required to be a subject matter specialist. In fact, for many types of development work, a training designer who is not a subject matter expert is preferred. This may at first appear odd, but sometimes knowing little or nothing about a task allows you to see the obvious. Through a systematic task analysis, even a person with no prior exposure to the job can quickly learn enough to begin to develop a trial or test version of the training course.

Training, however, is a solution to some problems, not all problems. Training is appropriate when there is a real skill or knowledge deficiency. Training is not a solution when the problem is caused by poor management, lack of proper tools, incorrect or missing measurements, poorly organized work, poor job methods, and so on. Unfortunately, at the beginning of a training project, you really don't know exactly what is underlying a problem. And if you behave the way most effective managers are expected to behave, you may begin a task analysis for training without really checking to see if the problem belongs elsewhere. In some organizations, action and the appearance of movement sometimes is rewarded more strongly than results. A little analysis up front can save much effort later if we can pick out training from nontraining problems. For example, in one organization, when they began to screen their training requests using performance-based methods, they found that more than 80 percent of the problems that were said to be training problems were in fact due to other factors. In the past they would have developed training for all requests. In other words, they would have developed training for the 80 percent of the requests that were not really training needs along with the 20 percent that were.

Performance-based training begins with the analysis of the training request. Before any task analysis work is performed, the performance-based approach leads to a business analysis of the problem. In this section I will present a process for developing performance-based training that integrates systematic training development (the first generation systems approach to training) with performance analysis.

The Armed Forces' Instructional Systems Development Model (ISD) represents one point of origin for the model that is presented here. The performance analysis methodology as developed by T. F. Gilbert (1967) represents a second point of origin. Finally, my own experience in attempting to apply curriculum concepts to training and career pathing (Ross, 1979) played an important role in the evolution of this model. Beyond these direct contributors, the model benefits from the work of my colleagues who have struggled with the problem of developing effective instruction for specific organizational needs. Figure 8-4 shows the overall sequence of steps that I propose.

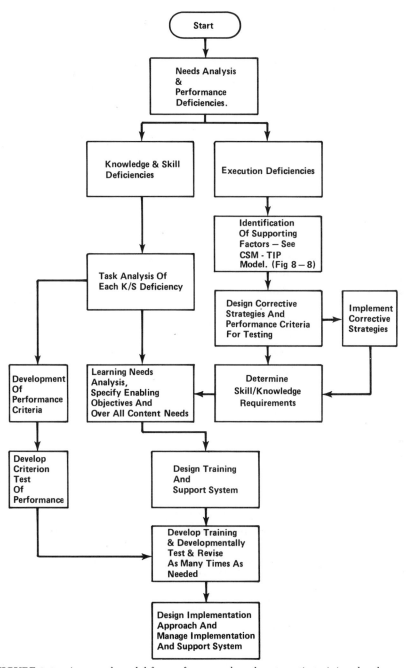

FIGURE 8-4. A general model for performance based systematic training development.

This model, like most models of training, rests upon some important principles of effective training. These principles combine the experience of several disciplines that support our ability to develop effective instruction. This approach places heavy emphasis upon the analysis of business needs and performance deficiencies. It integrates nontraining and training solutions, and finally, it provides for managing and tracking not only the training but also the support system and the business performance that it was designed for.

Instructional Effectiveness and Efficiency

Figure 8-1 (at the beginning of this chapter) highlights the significance of labor cost in the overall training budget. In discussing this point, noted that training development can exert a significant influence upon labor cost. I have suggested that merely converting a unit of instructions from group-paced to self-paced will result in some saving in training time. Our factor in achieving this improvement is of course the reading speed of the trainee. And reading speed is likely to be influenced by trainee characteristics that are evaluated when people are tested during the employment process. In one study I found a significant relationship between job selection test scores (a verbal ability test) and time to complete a job-related self-paced technical training course (Ross, 1973). I found that time to complete the training could vary on the order of 15 to 20 percent, if average test scores were allowed to vary by plus or minus one standard deviation. In practical terms this variability in time amounted to a whole day of instruction. On the basis of this study, I concluded that there is significant economic advantage for controlling trainee characteristics at entry. In short, entry-level characteristics of the trainee can influence training costs (e.g., time in a self-paced course). At the time, a colleague of mine conducted an unpublished study in which she attempted to assess the degree to which several instructional variables could influence performance on self-paced text (Dockery, unpublished). She found that varying the number of objectives given to the learner accounted for less variability in learner performance than did a general ability measure. She found that the second best predictor of learning outcome was the learner's expression of interest in the subject matter (on a single item seven-point scale). Both of these studies, my colleague's and my own, seemed to support the view that learner characteristics are important in facilitating performance in training.

Although these findings were consistent with the research literature, we wanted to examine them from a business point of view. When we adopt a business viewpoint, we typically ask questions about where we can have the most impact. From the business viewpoint, we want to know where we can get the most return for an investment of effort. In practical terms, we want to determine how to allocate our limited resources among selection testing, training development, training delivery, organization and management development, and so on. We observed that in the absence of credible and useful information, the allocation of resources seems to be influenced by popular fads, trends, and the reaction we have to the subsystem that shouts the loudest. Although there indeed was an absence of hard credible data, it is not unreasonable to believe that if we look in the right places, we might develop some soft credible data to help us make these kinds of business decisions.

Soft data rarely finds its way into journal articles or other easily accessible media. Much of it comes from our first-hand experience of working with people in training development projects. What follows is based on my own experience.

One such form of soft data is a demonstration that I conducted and replicated several times as part of a workshop on instructional design. During this workshop I had the class develop a task analysis for a trainer to set up and show a 16mm sound movie. Next I had the class develop a lesson for teaching someone to set up and operate the 16mm sound projector. Finally, I had them try out the lesson on a person, usually a clerk or secretary who had never used a 16mm projector before. In every session—more than eight that I have records of—the time to conduct the training ranged from 25 minutes to 50 minutes. That is, to teach the trial subject to perform the task without error required between 25 and 50 minutes. In every case, the lesson plan that the class developed followed all of the steps in the task analysis. Each time I replicated this demostra-tion, I found that the lesson plan produced by the class relied upon a lot of verbal instructions. The trial subject was directed through *each* step in the task in the order in which the task was to be performed. They began with a discussion of how the film reel was to be mounted on the projector and ended with a discussion of how the switches operate the projector. In general, the instruction that was developed in the workshop was effective. The trial subjects seemed to be able to perform well on a performance test, i.e., set up a projector and show the film, then take it down, all without any prompting.

Effectiveness and efficiency, however, are not the same thing. One way to access the economic impact of training is to compare the efficiency of two forms of equally effective training. That is what I did next. I invited another subject in and taught that subject to perform the task to the same level of effectiveness on the test. However, I was able to achieve this in four to seven minutes. In other words, I was able to produce instruction that was equally effective, yet was between six and seven times more efficient. This demonstration was very convincing to my workshop participants. It demonstrated in a convincing manner how the selection of an instructional approach can influence efficiency and training cost.

Now if I consider this demonstration alongside the studies of learner characteristics that my colleague and I had performed, I can draw some conclusions about the relative potential contribution of training design versus learner characteristics to instructional efficiency. In the learner characteristic study we found efficiency gains that were fractional improvements in performance on the order of 15 to 20 percent. In the demonstration that I used in the workshop, the gains in efficiency were on the order of 600 to 700 percent. Clearly, by changing something in the teaching process, I was obtaining an order of magnitude difference in an economically relevant variable (time to teach to a performance criterion).

The contrast of the relative impact of these two sets of studies piqued my interest in the instructional design process. I concluded, and I still maintain, that substantial economic benefits are to be obtained through the careful application of instructional design methods. What I did in my demonstration that seemed to make such a marked difference was to utilize the most powerful instructional strategy that I know. I merely demonstrated, without comment, how I set up the projector and how I took it down. Through elaboration of movement, I called attention to the critical discriminations—the upper gate loop, lower gate loop, and the auditory cue that shows that the film is properly positioned in the track behind the lens. All of my subjects were able to perform to criterion with an observation trial. Some needed minimum prompting while they did it, but they all performed faultlessly on a performance test. Technically, this powerful strategy is called modeling, and it is a distinctly human quality. We can learn by imitation of what we see.

Modifying Behavior through Observation and Modeling

Learning to do things through observation and imitation is an example of how complex integrated human behavior really is. Learning theorists for the most part have tended to avoid dealing with observational learning, and as a consequence, much of what training technologists did tended to avoid holistic learning strategies in favor of teaching the elements of a task. Programmed instruction clearly shows this preference for teaching small units of behavior as opposed to teaching large complete behavioral units that we might think of as styles. One early behavioral theorist, E. C. Tolman (Tolman, 1967), in a series of studies using rats, demonstrated otherwise. Tolman found that subjects not only acquire specific skills that are reinforced but acquire more generalized understandings of the relationship between goals and the ways to reach them. Tolman asserted that "knowing," or I might add "learning," involves two important elements: a readiness or expectation, and a verification of the expectation. Tolman's work pointed to the importance of those internal processes that enables the subject to grasp a set of environmental events and to behave in some organized manner.

Tolman anticipated much of what we now call cognitive psychology. Tolman's analysis placed emphasis not on microbehavior, but upon purposeful behavior and how the subject can organize events in terms of purpose. Observational learning, i.e., acquiring a knowledge or a skill through observing, in recent years has come to play a very important role in both cognitive psychology and in social learning theory. One important viewpoint shared by cognitive psychology and social learning theory is the recognition that is given to the role played by internal symbolic processes, i.e., mental process. For example, Albert Bandura, one of the leading researchers in social learning theory, has demonstrated how the learning of a skill is under the control of different variables from the performance of a skill. He has shown that learning can occur when the events are consistent with the observer's attentional state, whereas performance of a learned event will depend upon reinforcement conditions.

In the example of the 16mm motion picture projector discussed above, I found that for a simple motor task, like setting up the projector to show a film, modeling, i.e., showing how it is done, was a far more efficient approach to instruction than was a step-by-step instructional approach. In Tolman's terms, the modeling established a set of expectancies about the "means" (steps to set up the projector) and the "ends" (showing the film). Clearly in simple tasks modeling can be a powerful approach for teaching. However, can it also be used for training people in more complex tasks?

In recent years this approach has given rise to many applications in which social skills are taught through modeling. For example, in the mid 1960s, job interview skills were taught to hardcore unemployed with substantial success. Modeling and role playing methods were used to teach adolescents conversational skills and comfortable ways to interact with members of the opposite sex. Modeling was used to teach police officers complex social skills that enable them to deal with confrontations or hostile situations. Similarly, in industry, modeling methods are used to teach supervision and interpersonal skills.

Goldstein and Sorcher (1974) have described how modeling can be and was used to train business supervisors in social skills. Specific skills included: giving directions and assigning work, discussing performance problems, and discussing undesirable work habits. When evaluated, however, not all industrial training programs utilizing modeling approaches were found to be effective. Burnaska (1976) and Moses and Ritchie (1976) have each cautioned that long-term developmental experiences and role models encountered in the job may be more important than the types of training that people get. These researchers have raised this concern because of the impression that proponents of modeling seem to generate, that is, that modeling is a new "panacea."

Unfortunately, modeling, like programmed instruction and other techniques, are often presented as the single best approach, a claim they can almost never live up to. Modeling, like any other instructional approach, must be used where it is appropriate, and the way to make that determination is in the context of a complete performance-based analyses of the specific business needs and the specific performance problems of the people in the targeted jobs.

As a manager, it is important not to confuse means and ends. As a training technologist it is important to have many means available for any set of client ends. As powerful as modeling is, it is but one means to the end of better performance.

Before going on, it is appropriate to try to summarize what performance-based systematic training development is all about. Clearly it represents an integration of education and training ideas, theories from psychology, and concepts and methods used in business consulting and systems development. In this summary the process of development will be described as a series of steps along with the underlying principles that govern that step. The summary in the following section is intended to be used in conjunction with the questions in Figure 8-5, the Manager's Training Audit. Understanding each step in this process and understanding how the questions in the audit are used can help you in examining how well your training organization is meeting your business needs. The Manager's Training Audit can also be used in helping you manage the work of outside consultants and contractors who are developing or delivering training for you. An understanding of the whole process and the questions in the Manager's Training Audit can help you in defining business problems that your training department can help you solve.

Introduction to the Manager's Training Audit

The management audit questions are based on a six-step training development process. Each step represents a link in a chain that begins in the job and ends in the job. In between, a chain of events enables us to engineer a course or training program that is optimally cost-effective for that job. Each link in that chain rests upon important principles that are research based. In turn, each link requires people who are skilled at applying the various disciplines called for in that link. The cost effectiveness of the final course will depend upon how strongly we forge each of these links. If the chain we build is to yield optimum cost-effective performance, then it can be only as strong as its weakest link.

Directions

Answers to the following questions will give you a quick estimate of the overall probable quality of your training courses. Refer to the discussion of PBSTD for a description of each step. In general use, the more yeses that apply to a given course, the more reasonable it is to have confidence in the quality and effectiveness of that course.

Step 1   Needs Identification and Analysis

Questions in this step apply to any training that you plan to offer. Training should always be targeted to real business needs.

1. Are training needs generated from present or anticipated business performance need? .... Yes   No

2. Are these training needs based upon an analysis of the factors that underlie the business need? .... Yes   No

3. Have alternatives to training been considered? .... Yes   No

4. Are the performance needs reflected as deficient outputs? .... Yes   No

---

FIGURE 8-5.   Manager's Training Audit (copyright 1981, Instructional Systems Associates Morris Plains, NJ).

FIGURE 8-5 Continued.

5. If there is a business performance need, can you as a manager tell
   when that need will be met? .... Yes   No

6. Have the affected performers been identified (e.g., entry level skills,
   abilities and numbers)? .... Yes   No

7. Has any foreseeable change in skill, ability, size, or work redesign for
   this population been identified? .... Yes   No

8. Have critical or key implementation requirements been identified (e.g.,
   packaging-format, key opinion headers)? .... Yes   No

Step 2   Needs Identification and Analysis

Questions in this step apply to courses that are either being developed for you or are offered
to you as job related training. The purpose of the task analysis is to zero in on the most
important training content.

1. Has a task analysis been made of each training need?................ Yes   No

2. Are both training and nontraining requirements identified? .... Yes   No

3. Has the training need been positioned within a context in which all
   methods-practice-work designs or rearrangement requirements are
   identified? .... Yes   No

4. Are job task requirements and standards identified or set? .... Yes   No

Step 3   Training Design

This step assures you that the training is as cost effective as possible and that it is clearly
linked to your business needs and the skill and ability level of your people.

1. Are all tasks selected for training reflected as training objectives?....... Yes   No

2. Do the objectives match the task analysis?........................... Yes   No

3. Are there clear performance standards for the trainees on each
   objective? .... Yes   No

4. Are these trainee standards consistent with the job task requirements?   Yes   No

5. Does the training design reflect the most efficient training strategy?..... Yes   No

6. Have career pathing and curriculum needs been considered?........... Yes   No

7. Have entry skills and ability for the target population been
   incorporated into the design?..................................... Yes   No

8. Has the design considered cultural or preference factors identified
   among the target population, management, others? .... Yes   No

Step 4   Training Development and Trial

Good training should be validated to your needs. This step is where validity is established.
Questions in this step are related to the validation process, which in turn determines how
well your business needs will be met.

1. Has the development step been based upon the objectives and overall
   design? .... Yes   No

2. Have changes in the content, objectives, or design been based upon
   careful tryout with appropriate learners? .... Yes   No

FIGURE 8-5 Continued.

3. Has there been a clear reduction in learner error or problems to negligible levels from first to last trial? .... Yes   No

4. Have all support materials (AV material, Leader Guides, etc.) been through a test and revise process?................................... Yes   No

5. Have nontraining supports been developed or tested and installed (e.g., boss information packages, job rearrangements, measurements)?........ Yes   No

6. For public courses, are the credentials of the course leader relevant to your business needs, and are they credible to your people? .... Yes   No

Step 5 Production

Packaging and final production, along with the means for distribution, must be carefully considered, since they can affect acceptance.

1. Have cost-effective decisions guided the production process? .... Yes   No

2. Have packaging-production decisions reflected concern for organizational acceptance? .... Yes   No

3. Have final production decisions been made that are consistent with the results of the trials (Step 4)?...................................... Yes   No

4. Have distribution mechanisms been developed?...................... Yes   No

Step 6 Implementation and Management

Effective training requires effective implementation, assessment, and management over time. These questions reflect some of those critical concerns.

1. Has an implementation plan been developed? .... Yes   No

2. Is the plan sensitive to the organization's needs (e.g., timing, rate of training, calendar schedule, key influences)?........................ Yes   No

3. Does the plan contain provisions for on-line evaluation of the training against business needs? .... Yes   No

4. Does the plan integrate the training with other performance-enhancing approaches?.. Yes   No

5. Is there clear responsibility, authority, and accountability for the implementation of the training?.................................... Yes   No

PERFORMANCE BASED SYSTEMATIC TRAINING DEVELOPMENT: A SUMMARY

Six interlocking steps (or links) made up the PBSTD approach. The outcome of each step is the input to the next. Consequently, from the point of view of project planning, cost estimating and project management, the steps represent useful reference points where intermediate products may be evaluated and project management decisions can be made.

In this section, each step in the PBSTD will be described. It may be helpful to read each step and then review the manager's audit questions for that step. Each step begins with a brief description of its purpose followed by the principles that are applied, followed by a brief description of the approach used. Incorporated in the principle and approach are references to the kinds of technical disciplines needed to carry out the step.

Step 1: Needs Identification and Analysis

The first link between the business system and the training process is forged in this step. Here business needs that may be met through training solutions are identified and analyzed.

1. *Principle.* Training should be developed *only* when there is a present or anticipated job performance problem, which is caused or supported by the performer's lack of knowledge or skill. A good rule to follow is: if it ain't broken, don't fix it.

2. *Approach.* Surveys, forecasts, and performance analyses are combined to detect needs and to determine their extent, and determine whether there are significant performance problems that may be resolved through training.

Step 2: Task Analysis

In this step the job or parts of jobs that have performance problems are examined in more detail.

1. *Principle.* The requirements for training must be clearly based upon the job requirements, and they must be integrated with other job requirements so that performance is facilitated on all relevant and important job outputs.

2. *Approach.* Job task analysis through some combination of observation, survey, or simulation and modeling of the job leads to a specification of behavior and the sequences of behavior for all relevant outputs. In this step, new job procedures and methods or work designs are often developed along with new or revised job performance aids such as guides, references, checklists, templates, and so on. These must be developed, tested, and revised to meet performance needs before training requirements can be clearly defined. We must also develop test specifications for what the trainee will be able to do at the end of training. This test is called a criterion test or criterion performance specification. Through this test or specification, we will be able to determine if the training and other performance improving methods in fact improve the targeted performance.

Step 3: Training Design

In this step we forge another link between our training and business performance. This link is made of two things, our end-of-course objectives and the mastery tests for each objective. The end-of-course objectives must match the performance results identified in the needs analysis. The mastery tests will become the targets toward which the instructional materials must carry the learner. In turn they are linked to the criterion test—a test of job performance as best as we can simulate it. It is in this step that important decisions about instructional efficiency are made. It is also at this step that career path and overall curriculum needs are examined and integrated into the training design.

1. *Principle.*   Training objectives and mastery tests must be performance based and relevant to the job (linked to the tasks and outputs). The training design should be selected with concern for efficiency and effectiveness in meeting these objectives and test standards. In general, a design calling for a high rate of learner responding is preferred.

2. *Approach.*   Instructional design, like any design activity, is a planning process in which a set of behavioral specifications (objectives) are set and measures are established (mastery tests), followed by a plan to meet these objectives. This plan must take account of the learner needs (learning requirements), the organizational context, the entry level skills of the learner, and the principles of instructional design that enable us to *efficiently* develop learner competence on the objectives.

Step 4: Development of Instructional Materials and Testing

In this step all of the previous analytic work is integrated in the form of instructional materials for the learner. These materials include leader notes, study guides, reference materials, resource documents, job performance aids, directions, text, scripts for any audio or visual treatments and specification of media, group size, and other instructor or delivery needs.

1. *Principle.*   Material should be developed in very lean form—objective and test with minimum of instruction to prompt the learner. These materials begin through a process of trial and revision, and are gradually developed as early as possible with one or two trainees. All subsequent development is directed at enabling trainee performance on the objective. The principles of destructive testing are used in the step. Find out where it fails and fix it! Through a careful analysis of trainee failures, improvements are made to the sequence and content of the training.

2. *Approach.*   This step is a series of trials in which the training material is tried out on samples of trainees. The failure points are noted, and the materials are redeveloped and improved. Each trial should be directed at improving learner performance on the objectives, as measured by the mastery tests. In this step, the training developer needs patience and personal discipline. The developer needs to establish an open and professionally uncritical climate that lets the trainee guide development. Throughout the three to five trials (normally required) before field testing, the developer should be aware of both efficiency-oriented decisions and decisions affecting media and production cost.

Step 5: Final Production

Production of the final course presents the designer with many options that influence efficiency, cost, trainee acceptance, and management acceptance as well as the esthetic appeal of the finished product.

1. *Principle.* Production decision should reflect concerns for implementation, distribution, and acceptance by management and trainees, credibility, cost, and future maintenance needs.

2. *Approach.* Knowing the climate of the organization in which the training will be used is very important. Some organizations want to look "lean and mean," while others are very conscious of appearance, style, and format. A package done in very high quality binding and printing will probably be viewed as a gold plating job in the lean-mean organization, whereas in another organization these same attributes may be major factors in its acceptance. The rule to follow here, as in all development steps, is "let form follow function."

Step 6: Implementation and Management

The success of all that was done up to this point new rests upon how the training is introduced, delivered, and managed. What was learned in Steps 1 and 2 about who are the key influencers, decision makers, and opinion leaders can be incorporated into a plan for implementation. The plan should contain provisions for evaluation of the training against business needs and provisions for redirecting the training as business conditions dictate.

Principles. Regardless of how good the training might be from a technical viewpoint, poor implementation and training management can undermine all of the good work done up to this point. Training must be integrated with other performance supporting programs, and it must be managed from a client-focused point of view. One important rule to follow in this step is; the user organization should have a strong sense of ownership in the product and a stake in its successful application.

There are many adjustments that we must make in this development process. Reality is a cruel task master. Sometimes we can't spend 60 percent of our project time doing Steps 1, 2, and 3 (analytic work). Sometimes we need to have a short turnaround time on a course under development. Sometimes we need to produce training for a nontraining problem, because it is the only solution that is acceptable to the organization. Sometimes we need to establish our credibility fast. Sometimes we need to get members of the organization involved at each step. As a business manager we must recognize that each step in the PBSTD model represents a series of trade-offs between training product efficiency on the one hand, and development efforts and cost on the other. No business system is ever free of constraints of money, time, or people. These constraints must all be resolved in an accommodation plan for any given project. In short, any given project is a compromise of several business and technical issues. Having a process like this one should make clear just what trade-offs are achieved in the inevitable compromise.

What's a Training Technologist?

Before leaving PBSTD, I would like to comment on the training professionals and what they do. A quick reading of the history of the training business suggests that it has evolved in close step with the development of psychology. Educational and industrial psychologists are conspiciously present in this field. In the last 15 years several universities have established departments and programs of instructional technology, as distinct from audiovisual or media based programs. Graduates of these programs have either master's or doctoral degrees and are usually well equipped to support your business training needs. Beyond the formally credentialed members of this community, the largest pool of resources are people who have earned their spurs in the hard world of consulting or the training departments of large corporations and government agencies.

One way to tell who the training technologists are is to ask them about their membership in national or state associations. As a group, training technologists tend to affiliate with associations that espouse behavioral or performance-based views. The most notable among this group of associations is the National Society for Performance and Instruction (NSPI). Apart from their professional membership and academic training, most performance-based training professionals will at the drop of a hat tell you about how they changed someone or some group's behavior, improved results, or otherwise contributed to a business or organization. The themes you will hear are distinctly different from the more interpersonal helping themes that other training practioners might offer. I don't intend this to be a statement of how hardheaded training technologists are versus how softheaded other trainers are. There is, however, a distinct difference. The training technologist will look to and speak about behavior theory, modern systems theory, and cognitive and social learning theory. The nonperformance-based trainer will likely talk about the adult learner and their needs, motivation, interpersonal communications, and the techniques of experiential learning. In practice, both will seek to place their skills and approaches in the service of your business needs. However, these different themes are best seen in the degree to which the training technologist readily accepts responsibility for learner performance. The true training technologist does not attribute performance in training (e.g., learner failure) to the trainee; he or she accepts the trainee as a package of abilities, skills, strengths, and weaknesses, and then engineers training that bridges the performance gap between the trainee package and the performance the business system needs.

Employing a highly trained and experienced training technologist in your business is one way that your business can utilize these capabilities. There is another approach that we have only hinted at until now. Performance-based training can be done for you. When it is done for you, a contractor is retained to investigate a business need and recommend a solution strategy that may involve training. The contractor, if he or she is an instructional technologist, will follow a process like the PBSTD. They will begin with an analysis of your need, and if a training course is developed, they will provide you with information about its validity (effectiveness). Figure 8-5, the Managers Training Audit, can be a useful checklist to help you manage this kind of project.

Using an outside contractor to develop your training can have several important advantages.

1. You can obtain high-quality training resources to work on your business needs without expanding your staff.

2. Using a reputable contractor, especially if you are new to performance based training, can allow you the time and opportunity to develop your organization readiness for performance-based training.

3. In the course of managing the contractor's work, you will learn how to manage a performance-based training function.

Establishing and managing a training development contract requires managerial competence and good business sense. Although there are many technical training issues that you will need to cope with, neglecting basic business concerns can be devastating. Remember, the training contractor is a vendor of services. You will need to have a clear statement of the scope of the work, the products produced, the time frames, and the roles to be filled by the contractor and yourself. In short, a contractual agreement must be drawn up between you and the vendor. As a general rule, it should be a fixed price contract with the product or service clearly identified, and you should have appropriate oportunity to review, accept, or reject products produced. Finally, it is important to remember that the contractor and the client relationship works best when this is a partnership as opposed to an advisory relationship.

PERFORMANCE BASED TRAINING AND ON-THE-JOB DEVELOPMENT OF PERSONNEL

Earlier in this chapter, I presented an overall approach to developing training (PBSTD) that is useful if we have lots of people to train in relatively stable jobs, i.e., jobs that are not likely to change much over a period of several years. Now I would like to discuss the problems we have in developing and managing individual employee performance. To do this, I will extend the performance based training approach and show how it can be used by the line manager to change, improve, and manage the behavior of subordinates. I will develop this discussion around some of the experience I have had in getting field managers to use performance-based concepts in their organization. When I began to work directly with field managers, I used to think that all that managers needed was to apply reinforcement strategies to shape or extinguish various kinds of behavior. In that period, the mid 1960s, I believed that significant improvements in performance could be achieved if we could only apply learning theory to the management of people. What I didn't see very clearly was just how complex human behavior in an organization can be. My work during this period—and I know others were having similar experiences—focused on workshops for managers that were full of legendary stories about pigeons, rats, dogs, and how their behavior could be shaped through reinforcement.

Often these stories were used as a background for a scheme to get children to do homework or play the piano through the clever use of reinforcement. Somehow I'm always taken by surprise when some veteran manager would ask a stupid question like "What do you reinforce someone with in business?" "Doesn't this mean you have to pay them more?" "When are you going to talk about the use of punishment?" "Won't this approach take a long time?" And the classic question, "How do you know people will behave like pigeons?"

After several such encounters, it gradually dawned on me that I somehow was not connecting up with the world of the business manager. When I took a hard look at how unsuccessful I had become, I began to be aware that I was offering a solution to managers without understanding their problem. I was teaching managers how to change behavior without clearly identifying what behavior needed changing.

When I began to work directly with line managers, e.g., sales managers, I found that they could do a much better job of developing their people if they could learn to pinpoint specific behavior that was keyed to job performance. As I worked with sales managers, I began to see a pattern that set effective managers apart from ineffective ones. The ineffective managers seemed to make snap judgments about the problems that their people were having. They tended to label them as motivational or training problems. In contrast, the more effective managers seemed to dig a little deeper. They were more likely to identify specific behavioral problems that the sales person had, e.g., they could more readily identify problems in incomplete recommendations, poor use of the customer information file, skill deficiencies in making a proposal, or a lack of flexibility in talking to the customer. The better sales managers, as a group, seemed to more ready to identify a sales person's behavior that was correctable through some kind of on-the-job training. In short, the way they labeled a problem seemed to lead them (the sales managers) to some corrective action. On the other hand, the poorer sales managers seemed to label the problem in a way that made it difficult to correct. Problems like motivation and lack of formal training all seem to place the responsibility for correcting the problem outside of the sales manager's domain.

At this point in my observations, I might have concluded that I was working with stupid sales managers and intelligent sales managers, and what was needed was a better selection system so that we got more intelligent ones. I considered this view at the time. But when I stood back and examined what I saw, I concluded that effective sales managers (good ones) seemed to be looking at their subordinates in a way that helped them pinpoint problems that they could correct. They seemed to have a clear understanding of what their people were doing and what they should be doing. The effective managers seemed to be examining the performance of their subordinates in terms of expected and actual behavior. Shades of T. F. Gilbert! They, the good sales managers, were focusing on accomplishments not behavior.

The poorer managers seemed to be making more generalized and more abstract judgments about what they thought they saw. Consequently the labels they attached to what they saw were also more abstract and general, e.g., motivation. A simple diagram was developed from these observations that seemed to describe how effective managers develop their subordinates.

In this diagram, the employee is behaving and the boss is observing, and since they presumably share a goal, the difference in their vantage point (doer versus observer) allows the boss to generate information about the performance that the employee would otherwise not have.

Clearly this simplified representation implies that the boss and subordinate share a common objective, and that the presentation of information to the subordinate is in a form, rate, and proximity that can be used to improve performance. In this model they share a common objective, and it is assumed that they both want improved performance.

If performance is to improve, the boss must have a means to classify what is seen in a way that allows the generation of information that the subordinate can use. Managers don't get very far by calling the behavior stupid or unlucky. What the boss seemed to need was a simple guide that directed his or her attention to the critical parts of the sales process. From the boss's point of view, we established a three-step process and taught the boss to use it. First, we taught the boss to describe performance prob-

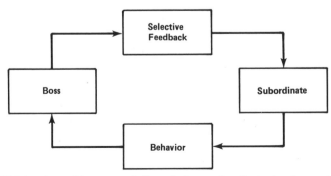

FIGURE 8-6. A graphic representation of a boss-subordinate development system.

lems as a difference between what is desired and what is achieved. Second, if the performance problem was of sufficient priority, we taught the boss to classify it at two levels: Was it a knowledge or execution problem? and what kind of knowledge or execution problem was it? Third, we taught the boss how to work with the subordinate to correct the problem. The second step was the bridge between the problem and the kind of action that the boss could take to fix it.

In summary then, an event occurs in the sales contact. The boss and subordinate attend to the event according to a set of rules, and the boss provides corrective feedback to the subordinate.

Events, perception, decision rules, behavior, and results are one useful set of ideas that can help us examine and classify the complex world of job performance. In my experience these ideas, when understood and applied to a field management situation, receive much acceptance. And more importantly, these ideas have been demonstrated to contribute to improved business performance in both sales and nonsales situations (Ross et al. 1980).

In working with the process in many different settings, I found that the development of individual performance, just like the development of a large training system, must carefully follow from an assessment of need. Some form of systematic problem identification and analysis must be a part of any process that we use for developing individual performance.

Where we can clearly specify (in advance) all of the job requirements, we can develop a needs identification and analysis process that is very efficient for that particular job. This is precisely the approach I followed with our sales managers. I began with a detailed analysis of the sales job. All of the critical decision points were identified, and the sales manager was taught to use a set of diagnostic questions to help uncover the job requirements that were not met. Depending on the pattern of answers to the diagnostic questions, the manager was guided to various types of remedies.

A generalized version of this process is shown in Figure 8-7. In this version the manager is directed to answer a set of questions about what is expected in performance and what is actually happening. You may want to try to use this guide for your own job. It is intended to be a useful job aid for any manager familiar with the underlying performance theory. The underlying theory is called Cognitive Systems Theory. The theory integrates both behavioral and systems concepts into a useful model for managing people in a business. Figure 8-8 shows how this theory is represented as a model called The Cognitive Systems Model. In this form the Cognitive Systems Model is used to diagnose performance problems in an operating business system.

Together, Figure 8-7 and 8-8 are aids that are used in a workshop to teach managers how to pinpoint and correct business performance problems (Instructional Systems Associates, 1981).

The Cognitive Systems Model Illustrated in Figure 8-8 is used as a

Troubleshooting Guide	
Conditions	Action
1. What do I expect?	Describe what's expected in behavioral terms, i.e., state the conditions, actions, and results desired.
2. What do I get?	Describe what was done.
3. If there's a difference between 1 and 2 (above), is it critical?	If the difference is very small or if the difference is not critical to overall performance, move on to another situation.
4. If there's a difference that you want to pursue, could the person ever do it?	If the person has actually done it in the past, and the event occurs with some reasonable frequency, then the present performance is not likely to be a training problem (see the C.S.M. TIP, Figure 8-8).
5. Determine if the person *can do it*, but doesn't know *when* to do it.	Consider *discrimination training:* practice in recognizing when to do something. Sometimes sales people have difficulty recognizing an objection to price, even though they can meet the objection when they recognize it. Giving the sales person a list of typical objections to practice on can help in this situation.
6. Determine if the person doesn't know *what to do.*	Consider *response practice:* For simple tasks, practicing the correct response under a relevant set of conditions can usually correct this type of problem, e.g., role play, demonstration and practice. For a more complicated response in which many elements are required, it may be more useful to break down the response into the parts and train on each part separately before allowing the person to practice the whole response.
7. Determine if the person can do it, but the response is poorly organized.	Consider *integrated practice and guidance:* sometimes complex verbal or motor responses need to be carefully practiced before the person can smoothly perform, e.g., driving a car requires practice with guidance. Over many practice sessions, the guidance is reduced until the person is able to drive on their own.

FIGURE 8-7. Troubleshooting on the job training needs by the boss may be facilitated by addressing these seven conditions in the order that they are presented. The Action column suggests what the boss might do for each condition. Copyright 1981, Instructional Systems Associates, Morris Plains, NJ.

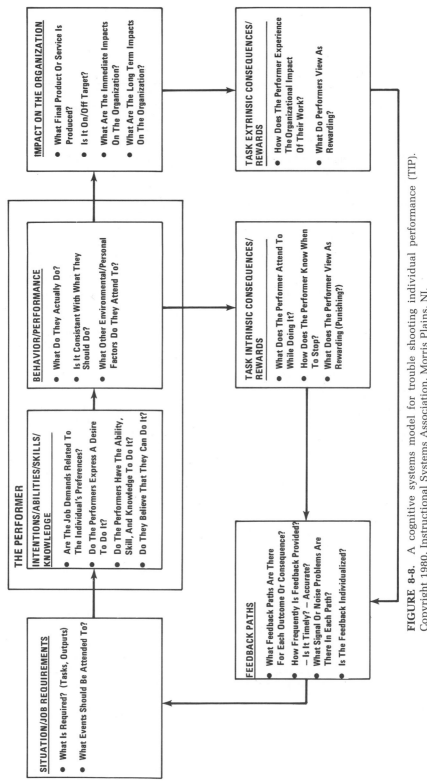

FIGURE 8-8. A cognitive systems model for trouble shooting individual performance (TIP). Copyright 1980, Instructional Systems Association, Morris Plains, NJ.

road map that helps the supervisor break down a performance problem into a number of components. Breaking down the problem into components helps the boss isolate various kinds of action that might be taken. Training on the job is only one of several options open to the boss. Some of the other options that this model leads to are rearrangements of work or job assignments, improved or different performance information, and changes in the types of rewards that occur in the job.

Together, these two aids (Figures 8-8 and 8-7) can open new ways to improve performance. These aids, properly used, help the supervisor apply the following techniques:

Clarify the relevant feedback that the employee gets.

Set up opportunities for guiding the employee through a difficult task.

Develop useful job aids for the person to use in performing the work (e.g., a worksheet or checklist).

Have a person help the person do the task.

Develop rules and procedures for the work.

Get outside help when it is needed (e.g., work redesign or formal measurements).

In my experience, this type of framework really helps the supervisor figure out effective ways to improve and maintain high level performance. Old labels like motivation and training are replaced by new labels that lead the supervisor to take specific and effective action. The old labels merely hung a name on a problem; they didn't solve it.

In summary, the boss's role in developing and improving performance rests on his or her ability to clearly define what's wanted, what people are doing, and how important is any difference. To do this, the boss needs a simple means for classifying problems into various types that are soluble. A diagnostic framework like the Cognitive Systems Model for Trouble Shooting Individual Performance is important because it can open up new possibilities for improving performance. Finally, the boss needs to integrate any direct action (such as improving the performance information to the employee) with the employee's skill and ability. In most cases this means some form of on the job training, usually given by the boss.

In practice the boss will use both Figures 8-7 and 8-8. A nontraining need is identified (Figure 8-7), which leads to a diagnosis using the CSM-TIP (Figure 8-8), which results in a plan to change the measurements in the job, which in turn lead back to Figure 8-7 because we need to determine if the person can understand and use the new measurements without training.

The performance-based approach reflected in the two Figures (8-7 and 8-8) integrate problem detection, diagnosis, solution planning, and implementation into an overall employee development approach.

Systems to Support Performance

Integration, however, comes at a price. Performance-based training in a line organization is a disciplined approach to job management. In my experience the organization has to support this approach through its management structure. Although the line supervisor can learn to use this approach in a short workshop, whether it gets applied back on the job will depend upon how strongly the organization supports that application. If the dominant management philosophy is inconsistent with a performance-based approach to training, the intangible network of supporting opinion and multilevel commitment necessary for this approach to succeed will be undermined. We know that when the supervisor's boss doesn't support this approach, the supervisor soon loses interest in applying it. Supervisors seem to "respect what their bosses inspect." In actual use I found that early multilevel commitment must exist for tangible results to occur. The task of implementing this approach is not a training task. It is, in most organizations, an organization development effort of substantial proportions. The nature of this effort is to effect a change in the "culture" of the organization. It is not a task in which performance-based methods are overlaid on some existing management framework. Modern training merges with organization development, and we are on the leading edge of redefining both training and organization development in performance-based terms.

Some Speculation of Where Performance-Based Training Might Be Going

Performance-based training has had its roots planted firmly in the behavioral sciences, particularly behavioral learning theory, systems theory, and more recently cognitive and social learning theory. Initially the focal concern in the field was on how to enhance learning through the use of the behavioral sciences. Over time, however, the methods of investigation used in performance-based training began to reach out into the work environment. Today these methods are used to analyze work systems and improve business performance. Credibility and acceptance has been established for performance-based training because it works. With increasing acceptance comes an increasing demand for performance-based services. Today these services seem to offer a significant enhancement to more traditional organization development approaches. In short, I believe that we are now seeing the beginnings of a role for performance-based training in which the training role is integrated into a broadly based form of organization development. This new organizational development role utilizes performance-based methods to analyze and act upon significant business performance issues that involve the strategic business environment, the organizational structure, the arrangement of work, and the development of human resources. The cognitive systems approach presented in this chapter is an example of how a psychological perspective can help us understand and deal with basic business issues. The important premise underlying this approach is that business performance results from the performance of individuals. The cognitive systems approach clearly positions the individual as the unit of study.

Another area of future growth, I believe, will be the forging of stronger links between performance-based training and employee selection methods on one hand, and upon employee appraisal methods on the other. The link is performance analysis and job models. The need for these linkages in part stems from the growing concern for improving the predictive validity of selection devices as a result of increasing federal government's attention to labor practices. Performance-based studies yield useful criterion data for both selection methods and appraisal methods. Performance-based training, when validated to acceptable standards, may prove useful as an economic criterion for selection instrument validation (Ross, 1973).

Finally, as I have tried to show in this chapter, performance-based training methods can play a significant role in helping the line manager or supervisor manage business performance. In this role, performance-based training influences not only the skills and techniques that supervisors use but the way they construe a business system and how they see their role in that system. Over time, I expect this trend to continue.

Performance-based training has provided both a methodology and the energy for forging a more integrated approach to the utilization and development of human resources. The behavioral and cognitive systems theory upon which it rests provides a compelling basis for refocusing attention upon the criticality of the human performer in a complex organization. It is this person that development activity focuses on and from whom the organizational processes unfold. To develop the person is to develop the organization. Consequently, the distinction between organization development (OD) and training is beginning to merge.

Before concluding this chapter, I would like to return to my concern for the economics of business training. We have the ability to manage training as a profitable undertaking. The full realization of this potential, I believe, comes not from developing ever more centralized training profit centers within a corporation but from an alternative strategy that seeks to drive training through an informed and knowledgable line management that directly controls training cost and directly receives the training benefit. Formal corporate schools modeled after colleges may not produce the most cost effective results for the operating system. A distributive delivery network with centralized quality assurance, when used by knowledgeable field managers, may yet prove more cost effective by insuring the integration of training into overall business performance.

After all, that's what it's all about!

SUMMARY

How to obtain productivity improvement through the application of modern performance-based training methods was the central theme of this two-part chapter.

First came a discussion of how formal training can improve business performance. This discussion addressed the issues of training effectiveness and efficiency, principles that underly modern performance-based training, and the economic implementation of modern training, such as how much does business spend on formal training and how might this investment in people be made to result in improved business performance. Some of the organizational issues that result from the concentration of training resources into a centralized function were discussed. The role of the training technologist, their services, and the direct benefits to your business were also discussed. Finally, this portion of the chapter presents an aid for the manager for evaluating their own training organization.

The second major part of the chapter took up the techniques and principles used in performance-based training and showed how they could be extended into useful tools and aids for the line manager. In this role, performance-based methods are used to develop and improve the performance of subordinates. A practical problem-solving approach was presented and supported with a set of aids to help line managers or supervisors improve their ability to pinpoint specific problem areas in the job. There use, when carefully followed up, can result in improved productivity and job performance. The problem-solving approach and aids presented in this part of the chapter evovled over many years of work with a wide range of supervisors and managers in many different work settings.

The chapter attempted to show how training methods and behavior change methods can improve business performance at two levels: first, where the organization invests its resources in the development of its people (i.e., through formal programs of training); second, at the level of the field or line manager, where the process of ongoing personnel development is a day-to-day responsibility for all management and supervisory levels. The common theme throughout the chapter was the role that modern performance-based training plays in both formal training and in individual employee development.

REFERENCES

Bandura, A. *Principles of behavior modification.* New York; Holt, Rinehart, and Winston, 1969.

Branson, R. K. Military and industrial training. In L. J. Briggs (Ed.), *Instructional design: Principles and applications.* Englewood Cliffs, NJ: Educational Technology Publications, 1977.

Burmaska, R. F. The effects of behavior modeling training upon managers behavior and employee perceptions. *Personnel Psychology,* 1976, *29,* 329–335.

Dockery, P., Unpublished study, undergraduate thesis, Pace University, 1974. Available from author c/o Am. Tel. & Tel. Co. 1776 On The Green, Morristown, NJ

Gilbert, T. F., Praxeonomy: A scientific approach to identifying training needs. *Management of Personnel Quarterly* (now called *Human Resources Management*) 1967, *6*, 20–33.

Goldstein, A. P., and Sorcher, M. *Changing supervisory behavior.* New York: Pergamon Press, 1974.

Goldstein, I. L., Training in work organizations. *Annual Review of Psychology*, 1980, *31*, 229–272.

Instructional Systems Associates, Workshop on Performance Problem Solving, Instructional Systems Associates. Morris Plains, NJ, 1981

Jeon, U. H., and Branson, R. K. Performance and simulated performance test results as a function of instructions by still and motion visuals. *Journal of Educational Technology Systems*, 1981–1981, *10*, 33–44.

Mager, R. F., and Pipe, P., *Analyzing performance problems or "you really oughta wanna."* Belmont, CA: Fearon Publishers, 1970.

Moses, J. L., and Ritchie, R. J. Supervisory relationships training: A behavioral evaluation of behavior modeling program. *Personnel Psychology*, 1976, *29*, 337–343.

Porter, D., A critical review of a portion of the literature on teaching devices. *Teaching Machines and Programmed Learning: A Source Book.* Washington, DC: National Education Association 1960.

Praxis Corporation. Performance Analysis Workshop. Praxis Corporation, New York, 1971.

Ross, P. C. A relationship between training efficiency and employee selection. *Improving Human Performance: A Research Quarterly*, 1974, *3*, 108–117.

Ross, P. C. Curriculum management: A career development approach to training. *TRAINING/HRD*, December 1979, 61–66.

Ross, P. C., Tighe, P. D., Westover, C. P., Houtz, J. C., and Denmark, R. A. Problem-solving management training effects on sales productivity and job satisfaction. Paper presented at The American Psychological Association Meeting, Montreal, Canada, September 1980.

Shoemaker, H. A. The pay-off of instructional technology. *Improving Human Performance Quarterly*, 1976, *5*, 47–61.

Tolman, E. C. *Purposive behavior in animals and men.* New York: Irvington Publisher, 1967

Williams, J. R. *Residence Computer Assistance Instruction Study, Draft Report.* Training Research Group, Training and Education Division, Human Resources Department Am. Telephone & Telegraph Co. Morristown, NJ, September 1980.

9

Self-Management Procedures

FRANK ANDRASIK

and

JUDY STANLEY HEIMBERG
State University of New York at Albany

A manager is expected to plan, set priorities, direct others, mediate between supervisors and subordinates, and most importantly, execute his or her responsibilities in a way that produces the desired results. At times when all goes according to plan, when tasks are competently completed when delegated, when interruptions are minimal, and when the work is rewarding and stimulating, managers have little or no need for self-management. The environment is operating to encourage and reward productivity. However, few if any environments function in that manner. One might find that the task to be accomplished is lengthy and boring; insufficient information is available to complete critical sections; the telephone rings constantly; and just as it appears that progress is possible, notification arrives concerning a shift in priorities. The person attempting to resolve the emerging crises abandons all hope of conforming to initial work plans.

In the face of competing demands on one's time, it is essential that a manager have clearly stated objectives. However, objectives alone are insufficient in the predictably unpredictable world of work. Behavioral self-management (BSM) is an approach that enables one to assess what is and isn't being accomplished, monitor the ways in which the environment is subverting one's well-laid plans, restructure one's environment to support identified goals or objectives, determine whether or not the intervention was successful, and refine or change the self-management program if necessary.

While we will be discussing specific self-management strategies, the primary aim of this chapter is to present something more than a list of techniques. We will discuss and give examples of self-management applications in business and will explain ways in which these or similar approaches can be adapted to the needs of individual managers. BSM is a personalized program for modifying one's own behavior. Its usefulness to a manager depends on that individualization.

It is only recently that practitioners of Organizational Behavior Management have begun to recognize the benefits to be derived by the manager well-versed in the ways of BSM (Luthans and Davis, 1979; Manz and Sims, 1980). These authors suggest that the use of BSM is particularly advantageous for several reasons: (1) management by self is less expensive than management by others; (2) since many individuals unknowingly engage in counterproductive self-management, knowledge of effective BSM strategies may enable these individuals to improve their situations; and (3) knowledge of BSM will enable the manager to instruct others in its use, thereby augmenting his or her effectiveness.

WHAT IS BEHAVIORAL SELF-MANAGEMENT?

BSM is the deliberate regulation of situations and events that lead a person to behave in a particular way. Events that lead up to an activity are called antecedent events. Events that follow an activity are called consequences. We assume that what someone does, at home or at work, is affected by antecedents and consequences that occur every day (see Figure 9-1). The ultimate goal in a BSM program is to change one's behavior to conform to personally identified goals. A BSM approach to behavior change entails the identification of the existing antecedents and consequences to an undesired behavior and the establishment of antecedents or consequences that will support and maintain a desired behavior (Watson and Tharp, 1981).

For example, Mr. X. arrives at work at 8:00 a.m. However, he is slow to gear up each morning; the hour between 8:00 and 9:00 is wasted day after day. Mr. X. identifies this wasted hour as a problem. He records his

Antecedents (A)	Behaviors (B)	Consequences (C)
When did it happen? Whom were you with? What were you doing? Where were you? What were you saying to yourself?	Actions, thoughts, feelings.	What happened as a result? Pleasant or unpleasant?

FIGURE 9-1.   Aspects to consider when identifying antecedents and consequences for behavior (from *Self-Directed Behavior: Self-Modification for Personal Adjustment, third edition,* by D. L. Watson and R. G. Tharp. Copyright © 1981 by Wadsworth, Inc. Reprinted by permission of the publisher, Brooks/Cole Publishing Company, Monterey, California).

activities from 8 to 9 every day for one week. He discovered that the hour was typically spent:

Walking down the hall for coffee and chatting with co-workers while hanging around the coffeemaker, 15 minutes.

Preparing his desk for the day's work. This included sorting through the clutter of the previous day and picking the least aversive project to tackle, 30 minutes.

Scanning the morning paper while awaiting the 9:00 arrival of his secretary, 15 minutes.

Mr. X analyzed his current behavior in terms of antecedents and consequences.

Antecedent	Behavior	Consequence
COFFEE		
Sees cup	Gets coffee	Pleasant conversation
Feels sleepy		Caffeine
DESK		
Messy desk	Sorting papers	Feels good about being organized
		Delays unpleasant job
WAIT FOR SECRETARY		
Sees newspaper	Reads	Entertainment
		Delays unpleasant job

Mr. X. now has a good idea about what is currently maintaining his behavior. The environment cues (leads) him to waste time, and the short-range rewards for time wasting are many. He might attempt any number of strategies to restructure his environment, focusing upon changing either the antecedents or the consequences so that they cue and support behavior are more consistent with his long-range goals. His continued assessment of his morning behavior will allow him to determine which strategies work and which strategies don't work for him. A summary of the basic steps in conducting a BSM program is contained in the following excerpt:

1. Selecting a goal and specifying the behavior needed to change in order to reach the goal. This is often called the *target behavior.*
2. Making observations about the target behavior. You may keep a kind of diary describing it or count how often you engage in it. You discover the events that stimulate your acts and the things that reward them.
3. Working out a plan for change, which applies basic psychological knowledge. Your plan might call for gradually replacing an unwanted action with a desirable one. You might change the way you

react to certain events. You might arrange to be rewarded for certain kinds of behavior.

4. Readjusting your plans as you learn more about yourself. As you practice analyzing your behavior, you can make more and more sophisticated and effective plans for change (Watson and Tharp 1981).[1]

WHAT BEHAVIORAL SELF-MANAGEMENT IS NOT

There are other ways of describing and labeling the problem of Mr. X. We could label him as unmotivated or as a slow starter, and describe his problem in terms of attitude. Some persons prescribe pep talks, attempting to change Mr. X's attitude toward his job. Still others might question how well Mr. X's basic personality conforms to the demands of his position. A BSM approach, however, makes no assumptions concerning personality or amibition. The behavior is both the identified problem and the target for intervention.

METHODS OF BEHAVIORAL SELF-MANAGEMENT

Our aim in this section is to acquaint the manager with the steps involved in establishing a BSM program and to present pertinent examples of the effective use of BSM. A number of other authors have written about various aspects of BSM. The interested manager is encouraged to consult the following texts: Foster (1974), Goldfried and Merbaum (1973), Mahoney and Thoresen (1974), Schmidt (1976), Thoresen and Mahoney (1974), and Watson and Tharp (1981); chapters; Kanfer (1980) and Mahoney and Arnkoff (1978); and articles: Luthans and Davis (1979), Mahoney (1972), and Manz and Sims (1980).

SELF-ANALYSIS

Pinpointing

This first step in any successful BSM program is to pinpoint the troublesome behavior in a manner that will allow you to notice it each time it occurs. For example, you might state that wasting time is a problem for you. At first glance the problem appears to be identified quite clearly. However, most people would find it very difficult to accurately count how often they waste time or how much time is wasted. The behavior must be specified more exactly. Let's consider some of the many kinds of behavior that might be involved: working on tasks that could be delegated to others, working on unessential or nonpriority projects, daydreaming,

[1]Copyright © 1981 by Wadsworth, Inc. Reprinted by permission of the publisher, Brooks/Cole Publishing Company, Monterey, California.

talking to unexpected visitors, traveling and moving from place to place during the day, correcting avoidable mistakes, and so on. The more specific you are in identifying a problem, the more likely you are to be able to resolve it. An example from Luthans and Davis (1979) will help to illustrate the procedures involved in pinpointing.

Luthans and Davis (1979) describe the BSM program of an assistant manager of a retail store who became disconcerted over her ineffectiveness on the job. An initial analysis of her work situation produced an awareness of her overdependence on her boss, an observation with which her boss agreed. Before proceeding further with her BSM program, the assistant manager recognized the need for pinpointing this troublesome behavior, as overdependence was vague and difficult to measure. A closer look indicated the one behavior most often giving rise to her feelings of overdependence was visiting her boss and asking him for assistance in decision making. Thus the working definition of overdependence became number of times the assistant manager asked for information from her boss. In this particular intervention program the assistant manager recruited her boss to record the frequency of questions she asked. In one sense it would appear that the assistant manager is no longer using a *self-management* program, because she is involving her boss in carrying out the program. However, this example illustrates that BSM programs needn't be conducted in isolation from others and may be formulated with or assisted by others. The distinguishing feature is that the decision to involve the boss in the intervention came at the instigation of the assistant manager, not the boss.

Some individuals may have difficulty pinpointing in a precise manner. In such instances, Watson and Tharp (1981) recommend that the individual cease conjecturing and begin self-observing. Note what it is you are doing in the problematic situation; define and redefine until the problem is acceptably defined. When possible, Watson and Tharp (1981) recommend pinpointing a behavior that you would like to increase, rather than one you would like to decrease.

If, e.g., you find that interruptions are adversely affecting your work, you might select uninterrupted writing or reading as your targeted behavior. As you begin to observe what happens when you try to write or read, the problem becomes clearer. In our hypothetical example, self-observation reveals that interruptions occur in a variety of forms and are more problematic at some times of the day than at others. An initial attempt at self-observation might reveal the following:

Periods of Uninterrupted Writing	Interruption
9:00–9:45	Received phone call from business associate (5 min.)
9:50–9:55	Co-worker stopped by to discuss World Series (15 min.)

Periods of Uninterrupted Writing	Interruption
10:10–10:15	Took a break to refill coffee cup (10 min.)
	Checked mail on return trip (1 min.)
	Opened and read mail (45 min.)
	Placed three nonbusiness phone calls (25 min.)
	Left for lunch

Work-related interruptions included unanticipated telephone calls and dealing with the morning mail. Personal interruptions included discussion with co-workers, a coffee break, and self-initiated telephone calls. Pinpointing the interruptions more specifically can help the manager decide which interruptions are the most troublesome and which could be targeted for modification.

Self-Monitoring

It is always tempting to move directly from problem identification to problem solving. This can be accomplished if you already know the severity or frequency of the problem, there is little or no possibility of gradual improvement or worsening (it is an all-or-nothing behavior), and if the solution is obvious. However, in most instances, monitoring the problem is essential, as we are often fallible in our estimates. For example, interruptions can seem more frequent on some days than on others, even when they in fact occur at the same rate. Also, through careful assessment you may find that the major sore spot is not the frequency of interruptions, but rather how long they last. Assessment serves many purposes; it can be used as an aid for (1) pinpointing the problem more clearly; (2) selecting the most workable intervention strategy; (3) determining whether or not your intervention was effective (eliminating the need for guesswork); (4) reminding you to implement the planned behavior change program; (5) recognizing gradual improvement (which in many instances can be quite rewarding); (6) evaluating the need to switch intervention plans; and (7) targeting what went wrong in a strategy that was ineffective. Obviously our bias is toward assessment. For these reasons it is necessary to provide a record for yourself of when, where, or for how long the behavior occurs or does not occur. This process is termed self-monitoring.

A number of methods have been developed for self-monitoring of behavior; the two most common are frequency of occurrence and duration of occurrence. Frequency measures, or how often a behavior occurs, are the most convenient to collect and are appropriate for use when the behavior under study has distinct starting and stopping points and occurs at relatively low rates. Behavior such as completing business letters, making suggestions during meetings, complimenting a co-worker, or arriving on time for work could all be counted and expressed as a frequency per unit of time (_____ times per _____). If the behavior does not occur in discrete units, or occurs at high rates, the individual may need to sample the target behavior on some periodic basis, e.g., every half hour record "yes" if the individual is engaging in the behavior and "no" if not. One use of sampling might be to provide an estimate of the amount of time one spends writing, as opposed to daydreaming or thinking with pen in hand. If one were to record "yes" for writing and "no" for thinking, using incoming telephone calls as a prompt to record the behavior, a reasonable estimate could be obtained of the time spent writing versus the time spent thinking.

Duration of the target behavior, or how long the behavior lasts, may be the preferred self-monitoring procedure for behavior of a more continuous (but variable) nature. Examples would be time spent on the telephone, in talking with co-workers or friends or in preparing project reports. In these instances recording of duration would be preferred, but such a method places increased demands upon the individual.

A third form of recording may be appropriate for behavior that varies in value or intensity. One might pinpoint as problematic an emotional reaction or feeling state (e.g., anxiety during board meetings, anger at supervisors) or the quality of an activity or product (e.g., clarity of a presentation, voice volume, quality of a report). In such cases the individual may want to record the feeling, behavior, or product in terms of a rating. For example, ratings ranging from 0 to 10 could be assigned to reflect variations in work quality (0 = very poor, 10 = excellent) or emotional state (0 = no emotional reaction, 10 = extremely anxious).

The three types of measures that we have discussed include how often an action occurs, how long it lasts, and how one rates it according to its intensity or quality. Once a manager decides what type of measure would be most useful, it is necessary to develop a way to record the behavior in a reliable or consistent manner. When deciding on a self-monitoring system it will be helpful to remember these guidelines (Watson and Tharp, 1981): (1) keep it simple; (2) try to fit it into your daily routine; (3) record the behavior as soon as it occurs, not later; (4) strive for accuracy; (5) keep written records; and (6) reward yourself for accurate record keeping if necessary.

A variety of recording procedures have been successfully used in self-management programs, including pocket notebooks or diaries, mechanical counters, and timing devices (Ciminero, Nelson, and Lipinski, 1977). Sometimes the behavior of interest involves making or using a product. In such instances, maintaining counts of these products, which are often referred to as traces, might serve as the simplest way to record progress. For example, if you wish to monitor writing productivity, you could count total pages written per day, number of ink cartridges used, or number of letters mailed per day. Trace measures will often allow you to monitor your behavior while exerting little extra thought of effort.

There may be situations in which it would be desirable to devise unobtrusive ways to keep track of the pinpointed behavior. For example, a manager who is assessing frequency of active participation in meetings could keep a tally of comments on a notepad, remove one match from a match book for each statement made, or transfer one paper per comment to a second stack of documents. Such strategies simply use immediately available materials to establish a temporary record of ongoing behavior.

How one behaves is affected by one's surroundings. Assessment of potentially influential situations is often essential to effective self-management. Attention to events regularly preceding the behavior of interest, termed antecedents, and regularly following the pinpointed behavior, termed consequences, will be helpful in developing your BSM program. Use of the diary format previously presented in Figure 9-1 is typically helpful in identifying these antecedent and consequence events.

Assessments should continue until you are reasonably sure that you are measuring the behavior at its typical level of frequency, duration, or intensity. Nevertheless, variations in the target behavior can provide useful information. What was occurring on the atypical days that may have positively or negatively affected the target behavior? This information could aid you in selecting an intervention strategy.

For example, a business executive who wishes to become more prompt in submitting a record of travel expenses may find that there is typically a one-week delay between the trip and the completion of the necessary paperwork. He or she usually travels alone, files receipts in a wallet, and prepares a written expense record from the stacks of receipts. However, on the two occasions that the executive traveled with co-workers, his or her written expense record was submitted within two days of the return home. When the executive evaluated the differences in behavior that occurred on those atypical days, he or she discovered that he or she had followed the example of the companions by keeping a daily diary as well as saving receipts. Compiling the expense record took less than one-half the usual time. The business executive may now hypothesize that his or her self-change program would be aided if he or she (1) traveled with colleagues, (2) carried an expense ledger, or (3) established some other reminder to help him or her record expenses as they occurred.

An Example of Self-Monitoring.   Lamal and Benfield (1978) describe one successful use of self-monitoring in a work setting. The subject of this investigation was a junior draftsman who frequently was tardy for work and once at work often spent excessive time off-task. Initial monitoring of the draftsman's target behavior was conducted without his knowledge. After this initial evaluation, or baseline assessment period, the draftsman's boss pointed out the importance of being at work and arriving at work on time, and requested that the subject begin to log his time in and time out each day on the recording form shown in the top portion of Figure 9-2. The draftsman was later asked to begin recording the amount of time spent

C CODE
0—PRELIMINARY
1—WORKING DWGS.
2—CONSTRUCTION

BEGINNING DATE ______
ENDING DATE ______
NAME ______

IN								
OUT								
IN								
OUT								
IN								
OUT								
TOTAL HOURS PER DAY								

PROJECT	JOB	C	MONDAY	TUESDAY	WEDNESDAY	THURSDAY	FRIDAY	SATURDAY	SUNDAY	TOTAL
OVERHEAD										
TOTAL										

FIGURE 9-2. Sheet for daily self-recording of arrival time, departure and return from lunch, departure from work, and amount of time spent on each job and time spent not working. (From Lamal, P.A., & Benfield, A. The effect of self-monitoring on job tardiness and percentage of time spent working. *Journal of Organizational Behavior Management*, 1978, *1*, 142-149. Reprinted by permission of the publisher, Haworth Press, Inc.)

working on each assigned job, as well as the time not working on an assignment, the second problematic behavior identified (see bottom portion of Figure 9-2). The effects this self-monitoring produced on the draftsman are shown in Figure 9-3 where considerable improvement is seen to occur once self-monitoring was begun for each of the target activities.

This example illustrates a number of important points about self-monitoring. First, the act of observing one's behavior may produce meaningful changes in the behavior being monitored, which is termed "reactivity." When reactivity occurs, the change tends to be in the direction desired or valued by the subject; there are increases for desirable behavior and decreases for undesirable behavior. Also performing the recording prior to performing the behavior often increases reactivity (Bellack, Rozensky, and Schwartz, 1974), as does displaying the self-monitoring counts in some public fashion (McKenzie and Rushall, 1974). In the example above,

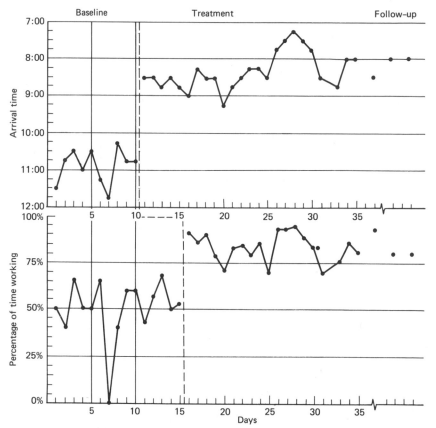

FIGURE 9-3. Subject's arrival time and time working during baseline and treatment. (From Lamal, P. A., and Benfield, A. The effect of self-monitoring on job tardiness and percentage of time spent working. *Journal of Organizational Behavior Management*, 1978, 1, 142–149. Reprinted by permission of the publisher, Haworth Press, Inc.)

the effects of self-monitoring appeared to endure, but research has shown the effects produced by self-monitoring frequently are short-lived (Mahoney and Arnkoff, 1978). The procedure utilized by Lamal and Benfield (1978) was not a "pure" example of self-monitoring, because the head draftsman regularly inspected the junior draftsman's records. One may speculate that the anticipation of some form of corrective action by the draftsman's boss contributed to the improvement observed as well.

Watson and Tharp (1981) estimate that self-monitoring alone may be sufficient for achieving the desired behavior change in as many as 15 percent of all self-management programs. This of course leaves the majority of problems unchanged. In the remaining sections we discuss three active intervention procedures that research has shown to be effective in self-management programs.

MODIFYING ANTECEDENTS

Events that reliably precede the pinpointed behavior will over time begin to serve as cues or signals for behavior, just as the red traffic light cues you to brake when driving. Knowledge of the cueing properties of events can be used in two basic ways by the manager interested in modifying particular aspects of his or her behavior. In some situations antecedents may signal the manager to behave in ways that are counterproductive. The goal in such instances would be to remove the antecedents, so that the undesirable behavior could be reduced or eliminated. Examples include having the switchboard operator hold calls during times when it is necessary to complete important paperwork (a ringing telephone invariably cues an individual to stop his or her present activity and to pick up the receiver) and removing from sight the day's newspaper, so as not to begin reading it. The manager may also want to establish signals to enhance the likelihood that a desirable pinpointed behavior will be performed. Examples include posting in the office a list of tasks to complete each day, clearing a space on an otherwise cluttered desk in order to facilitate the preparation of an important report, and engaging a co-worker to prompt you about performing certain duties.

An Example of Antecedent Modification

Another example from Luthans and Davis (1979) illustrates the positive effects obtained by the introduction of a cue. In this case the manager in question became dissatisfied with three separate kinds of behavior and set about to improve them one at a time. The second problematic behavior, discussed here, consisted of his leaving the office without informing others of his whereabouts. This precluded others from contacting him in times of need (while this may be considered desirable behavior by some managers at some times, the manager in question claimed that he did not regard his leaving in that light). Daily recordings of his behavior con ducted during the assessment period indicated that the manager left the office without informing others approximately five times per day. An in-out board attached to his office door was used to cue his behavior of notifying others of his time and destination of departure and expected time of return. Magnetized disks facilitated the manager's quick posting of the above information. Once this program was put into effect, the manager rarely forgot to notify others; no instances of the problematic behavior occurred on nine of 12 days. The manager also maintained a daily record of his pinpointed behavior, which almost certainly added to the success of the program.

Other applications are available to the manager knowledgeable of the role of antecedents, which will be briefly mentioned here. We have proposed that antecedents and consequences influence specific behavior, but it is also important to note that there are "chains of behavior." The behavior pinpointed will often occur at the end of a series of antecedent-behavior-consequence units, and therefore the manager may have to intervene at an earlier link to effect change. The manager concerned about time spent engaging in small talk at inopportune times will likely first identify the co-worker initiating the chit-chat as the antecedent for his or her behavior. The key for intervention might be found by examining an earlier step in the behavioral chain, which would be the manager leaving his or her door open. Here the open door serves as a cue for another individual to enter the office and begin conversing. One solution in this situation would be for the manager to break the chain by closing the office door when he or she does not want unwarranted intrusions.

The examples heretofore have concerned the removal or avoidance of cues prompting undesirable behavior and the introduction of cues to help prompt desirable behavior. In certain situations it may be impractical or impossible for the manager to avoid the antecedents of his or her undesirable behavior. This occurs frequently in dysfunctional interpersonal encounters, in which certain statements or acts of a co-worker serve as antecedents for the manager to become upset and possibly retaliate with negative comments. The manager might again look forward in the response chain to find ways to interrupt the usual series of events. One could attempt to modify the co-worker's behavior by rewarding him or her for a kind of behavior less combative than the one that usually cues the adverse reaction by the manager (i.e., modify the typical course of the behavior chain). Also the old adage of "counting to ten" before responding is a technique supported in the literature, because pauses also are occasionally effective for disrupting dysfunctional behavior chains.

MODIFYING CONSEQUENCES

Considerable attention has been focused on the role of consequences for perpetuating behavior. Three types of consequences have been used to increase the occurrence of pinpointed behavior: (1) positive self-reward, (2) negative self-reward, and (3) reordering of behavior.

Self-Reward

Of the above techniques, the application of positive self-reward is certainly the most familiar to the manager. This technique involves the self-delivery of a pleasant consequence after the occurrence of desirable behavior. These self-administered consequences may, but need not, be tangible. There is a body of research indicating that the self-presentation of pleasant consequences, either verbally or in imagination, can strengthen desired behavior considerably (Cautela, 1973; Wisocki, 1973). A personal example illustrates the application of a self-applied consumable reward for improving performance. One of the authors went through a period during which the reading of technical articles became less and less frequent, even though the importance of reading these materials remained constant. Cups of coffee, highly desired by the author, were used to reward reading a specified number of pages each day. This program worked quite well and quickly reinstated reading to the desired level.

Negative self-reward differs from positive self-reward, in that an unpleasant consequence is removed or avoided when desirable behavior occurs. An example common to most of us will help illustrate how negative reward operates. Nagging is perhaps the most frequent occurrence of negative reward because the unpleasant event, nagging, is stopped only when the person being nagged complies with our wish. Negative self-reward can be used as a self-management strategy, as illustrated in the following example. The manager may "nag" himself or herself by establishing a program whereby the removal of an uncomplimentary poster positioned in plain sight is made contingent upon the completion of a certain amount of paperwork (most managers would find this tolerable). Although negative reward can be effective in changing behavior, this technique's dependence upon aversive consequences limits its utility as a self-management procedure. The more aversive or unpleasant the consequence, the less it is likely that the self-management program will meet with success. Persons will act to avoid unpleasant consequences, but in a self-administered program at least two options avail themselves to the manager. One option is to perform the pinpointed behavior, but a second option is to abandon the BSM program. A highly aversive program could doom itself to failure.

An Example of Reward. This application, described by Kreitner and Golab (1978), was conducted with 14 field sales representatives employed by a paper products company. An integral part of each sales person's job was to place three daily calls to the home office in order to receive information about prospects for new customers and repeat sales, customer complaints, requests for service, and emergency situations. During assessment, it was discovered that few staff were completing this job function (see Figure 9-4). Management decided at that juncture to reimburse the sales staff for half of the expenses incurred by contacting the home office. When this policy was put into effect, the number of staff complying with the phone policy increased approximately twofold (see phase labeled

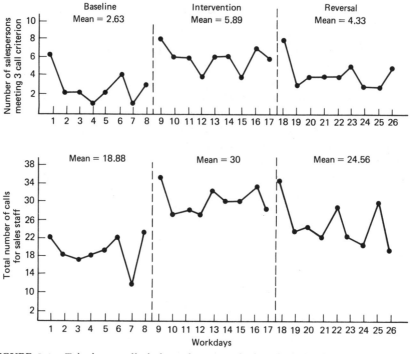

FIGURE 9-4. Telephone calls before, during, and after the refund intervention. (From Kreitner, R., and Golab, M. Increasing the rate of sales person telephone calls with a monetary refund. *Journal of Organizational Behavior Management*, 1978, 1, 192–195. Reprinted by permission of the publisher, Haworth Press, Inc.)

"Intervention"). For experimental reasons, the monetary refund was stopped after a certain period of time (labeled "Reversal" in Figure 9-4); the number of phone calls quickly became less frequent, which further demonstrates the effectiveness of the reward program. Although the above study was not designed as a *self*-reward program, the manager should be able to envision ways to capitalize on this type of an approach from a BSM perspective (e.g., rewarding yourself for completing necessary job duties).

REORDERING OF BEHAVIOR

Every manager is faced with a number of duties daily, which vary considerably in their frequency, urgency, and desirability. Problems arise when the manager puts off until later those tasks that need to be completed on a more frequent basis, or those tasks found to be undesirable. For these situations, knowledge of the Premack Principle (Premack, 1963) may be especially advantageous to the manager desirous of improving his or her work situation.

Consider that a manager has two tasks that require completion on a regular basis. Task A involves opening and reading mail and is completed on a very frequent basis, while Task B, which involves the completion of necessary but tedious paperwork, is regularly put off and therefore occurs with a low frequency. The Premack Principle states in essence that a low likelihood behavior, Task B in this case, can be increased by making the higher likelihood behavior, Task A, contingent upon it. Here high-frequency behavior serves as the reward. To apply this principle to the example at hand, the manager would establish a program whereby mail could not be opened and read until a certain amount of paperwork was completed.

In choosing high-frequency behavior for use in a reordering of behavior BSM program, consideration of the following will be helpful. First, any action that is performed frequently can potentially be used to reward behavior that occurs with less frequency, e.g., socializing, snacking, drinking, walking to the water cooler, reading the newspaper, or phoning home. How does one choose when faced with multiple high-frequency behavior? One way to determine the high-frequency behavior most appropriate for use in a contingent manner is to select for use the action you typically perform *instead* of the pinpointed behavior. The final consideration concerns pitfalls. Some highly frequent actions may be poor choices because they entail aversive or distasteful aspects (e.g., maintaining a log of the time spent on certain tasks). Use of high-frequency behavior that the manager would promptly stop if possible will all but guarantee failure and should be avoided.

The following program was designed and applied to employees by someone else—supervisory staff. However, since the procedures utilized in this study could just as easily have been applied within a BSM framework, this study has important instructional value and will be reviewed here.

An Example of Reordering of Behaviors

This intervention technique, described by Gupton and LeBow (1971), was performed with two part-time workers hired to solicit both warranty contracts and renewal service contracts by telephone. Initial monitoring of percent of contracts sold revealed higher amounts for the renewal contracts than for the warranty contracts (see Phase 1 of Figure 9-5). In Phase 2, warranty sales were made contingent upon renewal sales according to a specified ratio in order to achieve a more desirable rate of warranty sales. Reexamination of Figure 9-5 reveals that both solicitors increased the number of warranty sales (for Subject 2 this was especially so) when reordering of behavior was put into effect. When the reordering of behavior program was terminated in Phase 3, warranty sales quickly dropped to 0.

Our success with reordering of behavior programs, combined with their proven utility for a variety of problems, leads us to endorse this approach most highly. Such programs have much to offer the manager, because in most cases the behavioral reordering can be incorporated into the manager's routine easily and with minimal disruptions and costs.

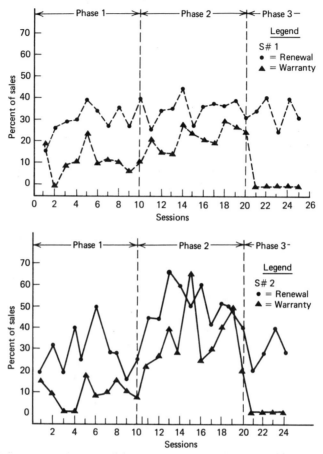

FIGURE 9-5. The percentage of sales for renewal and warranty contracts during each three-hour session for both subjects. (From Gupton, T., and LeBow, M. D. Behavior management in a large industrial firm. *Behavior Therapy*, 1971, *2*, 78–82. Reprinted by permission of the publisher, Academic Press, Inc.)

CONTRACTING

We have reviewed some ways in which managers can modify their behavior by changing the environment. Specifically we have discussed measurement systems and modifying both antecedents and consequences. Knowing what to do to effect a behavior change does not guarantee that the knowledge will actually be employed. When the novelty of the BSM program wears off, it's easy to "forget" to self-monitor, to delay in administering the planned consequence, and to lapse into old habits. One way a manager can protect against "forgetting" is to establish a contract. The contract is an antecedent to implementing the BSM program; it will prompt the manager to follow through on the planned course of action.

Contracts for BSM programs are basically contracts with self, although the participation of another person will probably improve the contract's effectiveness. In any event, a written contract is recommended, and it should be posted in a highly visible place to serve as a prompt. Consult the following list to determine the elements of an effective contract:

1. A clear detailed description of the required instrumental behavior should be stated.
2. Some criterion should be set for the time or frequency limitations that constitute the goal of the contract.
3. The contract should specify the positive reinforcements, contingent upon fulfillment of the criterion.
4. Provisions should be made for some aversive consequence, contingent upon nonfulfillment of the contract within the specified time or with the specified frequency.
5. A bonus clause should indicate the additional positive reinforcements obtainable if the person exceeds the minimal demands of the contract.
6. The contract should specify the means by which the contracted response is observed, measured, recorded; a procedure should be stated for informing the client of his achievements during the duration of the contract.
7. The timing for delivery of reinforcement contingencies should be arranged to follow the response as quickly as possible (Kanfer 1981, p. 35).[2]

If the self-modification program depends upon the cooperation of others, consider the impact on them of fulfilling the terms of the contract. It will be easier for a friend to deliver a pleasant consequence than an unpleasant one, but the same friend may be unwilling to withhold an unearned reward. A sample contract will be presented in a later section of this chapter (see Figure 9-8).

An Example of Contracting

There exists no straightforward example of formal contracts actually employed in self-management programs in work settings. However, a fascinating, although unverified, anecdote from the life of the novelist Victor Hugo makes an effective point. In an effort to establish an environment conducive to writing, Hugo enlisted the aid of his valet in a somewhat unusual way. He confined himself to his study by surrendering all clothing to his servant for the course of his work day, ordering (contracting with) the servant to withhold the garments until a specified time (Wallace and Pear, 1977). Although we cannot recommend the Hugo strategy for increasing writing time, the example is presented to illustrate the role that

[2]Reprinted with permission from *Helping People Change: A Textbook of Methods*, 2nd. ed., F. H. Kanfer and H. P. Goldstein, Copyright 1980, Pergamon Press, Ltd.

others can serve (on a contractual basis) to aid adherence to a BSM program.

EVALUATING PROGRAM EFFECTIVENESS

If the target behavior was specified in a measurable way, the goal was stated clearly, and self-monitoring was accurately conducted, progress toward meeting the goal will be obvious. When individuals are satisfied with their progress, they may not question the source of the behavior change. It's possible, however, that something other than the BSM program was responsible for the change in behavior. There are situations in which making that determination might be important. The self-monitoring system or the selected intervention strategy might require time or money that would preferably be spent elsewhere.

Consider the following example, based on the experience of one of the authors. This author chose as a goal to increase the amount of time spent reading current publications. This author measured minutes of reading per week and found that during the initial three-week assessment period, an average of 30 minutes per week was spent reading. After the five-week intervention period, the author had reached the goal of two hours per week. This author had instituted a procedure of having all telephone calls held for a two-hour period each Friday, hoping that the freedom from interruptions would prompt reading. When this progress was graphed, it was noted that reading time did not improve until the seventh week of the BSM program (See Figure 9-6). The author doubted that the BSM program accounted for the change in behavior.

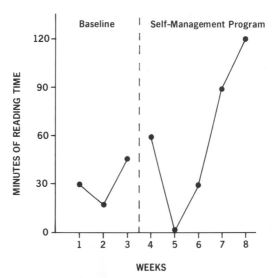

FIGURE 9-6. Time spent reading prior to and after implementing a self-management program.

In situations such as the one described above, two options exist for determining whether or not the program was responsible for the effects. One option is to cease the intervention while continuing to measure the target behavior. If the behavior returns to its preintervention level (amount, frequency, or duration), the previous improvement was probably the result of the intervention. A second way to test the effectiveness of an intervention is to attempt to obtain similar results by applying the same intervention to a second behavior.

MAINTAINING THE DESIRED CHANGE

Some behavior changes are maintained because they become habitual. What does that mean? It probably means that a person has effectively changed the environment so that a calendar, a secretary, a co-worker, or other aspects of the work world now prompt the desired behavior. It may also mean that the person is coming in contact with naturally occurring rewards.

Maintaining the desired behavior is not always (or even usually) the automatic result of having successfully made the initial change in behavior. Just as booster shots may be needed to maintain the effectiveness of certain vaccinations, so may the BSM program require occasional help.

When a behavior is established, the environment can once again be changed to support behavior maintenance. First of all, self-assessment must continue on at least an intermittent basis. Second, the frequency with which desired behavior is rewarded might be revised. For example, whereas a manager initially allowed 15 extra minutes per day at lunch as a daily reward, the reward could be revised to an extra free hour on Fridays for five hours work over the week. Similarly, a week's vacation may be awarded for meeting a year-long goal.

In general, desired behavior will be maintained if it is intermittently followed by pleasant consequences. A maintenance program requires increasing work to achieve the same payoff or a gradual lengthening of the delay between the behavior and the consequence.

ESTABLISHING A BEHAVIORAL SELF-MANAGEMENT PROGRAM

In the final section of this chapter we present a step-by-step guide for developing an individualized self-modification program. We have also included a "troubleshooting" section to help diagnose some of the more commonly encountered pitfalls to successful behavior management.

Program Planning Guide

Pinpointing the Problem.   Selecting and defining an action or series of actions that one wants to change can require much more time and effort than one might think. Precision is crucial. Pinpointing refers to a process whereby vague, often unobservable concepts are simplified until they can be observed and counted. The person measuring the behavior must be able to note with little ambiguity whether the behavior did or did not occur. The following questions were designed to help clarify a problem area and select a specific, measurable behavioral goal.

1. I'd like to exert more self-control over the following area of my work:

    _____

    _____

2. I'd like to increase or decrease the following specific behavior.
    Increase   Decrease

    _____   _____

    _____   _____

    _____   _____

3. Pick one kind of behavior that you would like to increase (increasing one kind of behavior can sometimes decrease its counterpart): I would like to increase _____

4. Can the behavior be measured as it is currently described? If not, restate the behavior so that it is countable.

    _____

5. I would like to increase the (select one)
    (a) frequency of _____
    (b) duration of   _____
    (c) amount of   _____
    (d) quality of   _____

6. I estimate that the behavior currently occurs at the level of
    _____ per day   _____ per month
    _____ per week   _____ per _____

7. I would like the behavior to occur at the level of
    _____ per day   _____ per month
    _____ per week   _____ per _____

Monitoring the Problem. How will you measure the pinpointed behavior? When you choose to count the number of times the behavior occurs, to time how long it lasts, to rate the behavior in terms of intensity or quality, or to employ some other unit of measurement, your decision will be based upon the behavior you have opted to change. The methods that can be used to record the behavior accurately are limited only by the bounds of the self-manager's creativity. The questions listed below may help you in designing an individualized system of measurement.

8. I think the best way for me to assess the current level of the behavior and any progress I make would be to count its frequency, duration, or amount every: hour _____ week _____ month _____ other _____

9. Label the graph in Figure 9-7 with the measurement unit you chose in Item 8.

10. Label the graph (Figure 9-7) with the behavior you will be measuring.

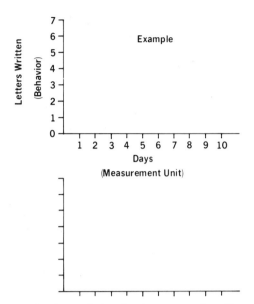

FIGURE 9-7. An example of a graph for charting progress in self-management programs.

11. Can the behavior be counted immediately after it occurs?_____
    If not, what is the most immediate way of noting that the behavior
    has occurred?_____

12. How many persons can possibly observe the behavior?
    self   _____   secretary   _____
    co-worker   _____   family member   _____
    supervisor   _____   other   _____

13. Who will record the behavior? Select one or more persons from Item
    12. _____   _____   _____

14. What arrangements must be made to establish your behavior record-
    ing system? (e.g., notepad by telephone, stopwatch on desk or pocket)

15. Make necessary arrangements.

16. Begin assessment, recording behavior on graph.

Selecting a Course of Action.   The steps you take to change undesirable
behavior to desirable behavior are partially determined by what you learned
while self-monitoring. Decisions include when and if additional actions
will be taken, whether antecedents or consequences will be modified, and
how the planned change program will be carried out. The following questions may serve as a guide in helping you make those initial decisions.

17. Consult your graph. Is the behavior changing in the desired direction?
    If so, you may not need to implement any strategy other than self-
    monitoring.

18. Is the behavior occurring at a constant level? If so, it is time to choose
    your course of action; continue following the action guide. If not,

continue to assess the behavior until it is occurring at a relatively constant level.

19. The behavior always (or almost always) occurs in the presence of the following prompt or antecedent (can be a situation, a person, an event, etc.) _____

20. The behavior never (or rarely) occurs in the presence of the following prompt antecendent: _____

21. Can you control the presence or absence of the above antecedents? If yes, consider modifying the antecedent as at least one component of your change program.
    If no, consider additional options outlined below.

22. The behavior is always (or almost always) followed immediately by the pleasant (unpleasant) consequence of _____
    _____

23. The behavior is never (or rarely) followed immediately by a pleasant (unpleasant) consequence. _____

24. Would it be possible for you to add (or remove) an immediate pleasant (unpleasant) consequence in your environment? _____
    If yes, consider modifying consequences as at least one component of your change program.
    If no, consider other options outlined below.

25. When you have some control over your time, are there work activities that are more likely to be performed than others? Name several of those more preferred tasks (opening mail, discussing ideas with others)
    _____

26. Is there behavior from Item 25 that usually precedes (or occurs instead of) the pinpointed behavior?
    If so, can your schedule be rearranged so that the more preferred behavior follows the performance of the pinpointed behavior?_____
    If yes, consider reordering behavior as one component of the behavior change program.

27. Summary of possible options.
    Which option(s) can be included in your behavioral self-management program?
    Adding antecedent _____   Removing antecedent _____
    Adding consequence _____   Removing consequence _____
                    Reordering behavior _____

28. What other factors must be considered? Which option is most desired in terms of
    Financial cost _____   Impact on others _____
    Personal effort _____   Other (   ) _____

29. Select at least one of the available options.
    _____

30. What specific antecedents, consequences, or behavior for reordering have you chosen? _____

_____

If you need help in selecting a pleasant consequence, consult the following questions posed by Watson and Tharp (1981):

1. What will be the rewards of achieving your goal?

2. What kind of praise do you like to receive, from yourself or from others?

3. What kinds of things do you like to have?

4. What are your major interests?

5. What are your hobbies?

6. What people do you like to be with?

7. What do you like to do with those people?

8. What do you do for fun?

9. What do you do to relax?

10. What do you do to get away from it all?

11. What makes you feel good?

12. What would be a nice present to receive?

13. What kinds of things are important to you?

14. What would you buy if you had an extra $20? $50? $100?

15. On what do you spend your money each week?

16. What behavioral acts do you perform every day? (Don't overlook the obvious or the commonplace.)

17. Are there any behaviors that you usually engage in instead of the target behavior?

18. What would you hate to lose?

19. Of the things you do every day, which would you hate to give up?

20. What are your favorite daydreams and fantasies?

21. What are the most relaxing scenes you can imagine?[3]

Contracting.   A self-management program need not be self-designed, self-implemented, and self-maintained. You may opt to involve others in your BSM plans whenever you believe that doing so would aid you in meeting your goals.

31. Will you involve other persons in your change program?
    Whether yes or no, consider developing a contract (see Figure 9-8).

[3]From *Self-Directed Behavior: Self-Modification for Personal Adjustment, Third Edition,* by D. L. Watson and R. G. Tharp. Copyright © 1981 by Wadsworth, Inc. Reprinted by permission of the publisher, Brooks/Cole Publishing Company, Monterey, CA.

Effective Dates: From _____ to _____ ._____

The following behavior will be monitored by _____ .
(Name of self or other(s))

Behavior: _____

_____

_____

Monitoring will occur _____
(When or in what situations)

Whenever _____ occurs at _____ ,
(behavior)   (specified level)

_____ will award _____ .
(self or other)   (consequence)

Whenever the behavior does not occur at the specified level, the following consequence will
occur _____ .

Contract may be revised on _____ .
(Date)

Signature(s)   _____

_____

_____

FIGURE 9-8.   Sample contract form.

32.   Implement your change program according to the terms of the contract.

Evaluating Program Effectiveness.   Evaluations of how well your program is working should be made regularly. Each time you add a point to
your graph, you make some judgment about whether or not the pinpointed
behavior is changing in the desired manner. A few simple pointers to aid
you in your evaluation are outlined below.

33.   Consult your graph. How well do your results compare with your
prespecified goal (indicated in Item 7)?
No progress? Check the trouble shooting section.
Continuing to see improvement? Extend the time line of the program.
Goal reached? Congratulations!

Maintaining Desired Change.   Old habits are sometimes hard to break;
and even when behavior is successfully changed, some backsliding may
occur. For this reason it's best to leave nothing to chance and plan some
strategies for supporting any gains you have made.

34.   How frequently will the pinpointed behavior be measured in the
maintenance phase of your program?_____

35.   Indicate any other changes in the way you measure the behavior.

36.   Select one (or more) maintenance strategies listed below

————   Reduce frequency of pleasant consequence (require more incidents of the pinpointed behavior to obtain the same reward). Change frequency to ————————.

————   Reduce intensity of pleasant consequence. Change intensity by ————————————.

————   Change form of consequence to conform with less frequent administration or reduced intensity. Change consequence to ————————————.

————   Change consequence to one more likely to naturally occur in the work environment (e.g., original consequence, dinner out with family; work-related consequence, lunch with amiable co-worker; naturally occurring consequence, consultation with knowledgeable co-worker).

Troubleshooting Guide: Common Problems and Likely Culprits

All programs occasionally encounter snags; unanticipated problems arise and intervention plans do not come off as planned. It's easy to become discouraged when initial plans go awry. However, after a little troubleshooting the revised program can be much better than its predecessor. We have identified three frequently encountered problems in BSM programs: (1) self-monitoring ceases, becomes sporadic, or is of dubious accuracy; (2) the intervention is not applied or is not sustained; and (3) the intervention is unsuccessful. For each problem, we have also identified some of the likely causes.

1.   Self-monitoring ceases, becomes sporadic, or is of dubious accuracy.

Likely Culprit	Possible Action
System is complicated or time-consuming.	Redefine problem into smaller components, pinpointing only one component for measurement or intervention.
System depends upon materials frequently unavailable.	Increase availability of materials. Revamp measurement system (see Section on "Monitoring the Problem," Items 8–16).
Delay between behavior and recording.	Select intermediate measurement system (i.e., use materials on hand for a temporary accounting of the behavior). Establish a prompt for measuring.

Likely Culprit	Possible Action
System yields unpleasant data.	Redefine goals to allow more immediate success (see Section on "Pinpointing the Problem," Items 1–7). Contract with another person to do the monitoring (see sections on "Monitoring the Problem," Items 12–13, and on "Contracting," Items 31–32).
Manager forgets to self-monitor.	Establish a prompt or a reward for self-monitoring. Contract with another.
System requires subjective evaluation of the occurrence or nonoccurrence of behavior.	Redefine pinpointed behavior until it can be objectively measured.

2. Intervention is not applied or not sustained over time.

Likely Culprit	Possible Action
Intervention is aversive to self or others.	Select a more positive prompt or consequence. Select a behavior to increase rather than one you wish to decrease.
Intervention creates problems in other areas of work or personal life.	Reevaluate pinpointed behavior. Choose a reward that does not interfere with other goals.
Resources are insufficient to apply intervention as frequently as planned.	Select different course of action (i.e., reordering behaviors). Consult the list in question 30 for selecting a different reward.
Application of intervention is dependent upon circumstances beyond manager's control.	Select different intervention or different form of the same intervention.
Manager forgets to implement the intervention.	Select a more positive consequence. Contract with another person to apply the intervention.
Pinpointed behavior does not occur (and therefore no consequence follows).	Select an initial behavior that is easier to perform; increase difficulty level later in the program.

3. The intervention is applied, but there is no change in the pinpointed behavior.

Likely Culprit	Possible Action
Consequence (or antecedent) modification was used alone.	Add a prompt (or a reward) to the intervention.
Pinpointed behavior cannot occur without performing earlier action(s).	Pinpoint the earlier action(s) for the self-change program.
The reward is used too frequently to be effective.	Use less potent form of the reward. Use multiple rewards on a rotating basis.
More rewards are available in the absence of the BSM program than are received in the program.	Select a component of the behavior to modify (make the initial goal easier to reach). Apply more potent rewards or apply the same rewards more frequently.
Consequence is applied whether or not the pinpointed behavior is performed.	Specify the consequence(s) more clearly for nonperformancce of the pinpointed behavior. Contract with another person to deliver the consequence.
There is a delay between the behavior and the consequence.	Reselect a consequence that can be applied more immediately.

4. Unanticipated difficulties.

We have two final troubleshooting hints for difficulties that we have not anticipated. First of all, consulting with another person about your BSM program may give you new ideas about what went wrong and how it can be changed. Second, it may be important to remember that while progress toward self-change can sometimes seem very slow, "Successful people use more techniques for longer periods of time" (Watson and Tharp, 1981). Be generous in your application of self-change procedures.

SUMMARY

The behavioral approach to self-management, termed behavioral self-management or BSM, was discussed in this chapter. In this approach, the individual alters problem behavior by actively changing the situations and events causing the problem. Four steps are involved in conducting a BSM program. The first step is pinpointing, which means the careful specification of the problem behavior so that the individual can easily notice each time the behavior occurs. Once the problem behavior is pinpointed, it is necessary to observe the behavior in order to identify the situations and events that lead the individual to behave in a certain way

(Step 2). Measures of (1) frequency, how often the behavior occurs, (2) duration, how long the behavior lasts, or (3) intensity are collected in this stage. These observations are necessary for discovering the situations that lead up to the problem behavior, called antecedents, and the events that follow the problem behavior, called consequences. In a small percentage of BSM programs, this intensive observation period is enough to correct the problem behavior. In most cases, however, a third step is needed that involves developing an action plan for changing the antecedents and consequences to the problem behavior.

In a BSM program antecedents may be added in order to cue or prompt wanted behavior to occur, or removed in order to make unwanted behavior less likely to happen. Consequences are used to enhance the chances of the individual completing a desired but infrequent or nonexistent behavior. When the consequence is pleasant the individual is using positive self-reward. Some individuals may choose to use negative self-reward, or the removal of something unpleasant when the behavior occurs, but this type of consequence is discouraged and should be reserved for special circumstances. A third way to make a desirable but infrequently occurring behavior more likely to happen stems from something known as the Premack Principle. To use this approach the individual would look for a second desirable behavior that already occurs with great regularity. By abstaining from the second behavior until the first behavior has been completed, the individual will likely increase the first behavior. Thus, in a Premack-based BSM program, regularly occurring behavioral acts serve as rewards for infrequently occurring behavior. Whatever action plan is selected, the BSM program can be facilitated by the use of a written contract or specification of the plan. This contract may and often does involve another person.

The fourth step in a BSM program concerns evaluating the plan to determine its effectiveness and making modifications to achieve the desired outcome. The preparation of a chart or graph is helpful at this stage. Insuring that the BSM program remains effective over the long term requires active planning as well. Resuming rigorous self-observation or changing the timing or amount of the self-reward are ways to prolong the effects of a BSM program.

The chapter concluded with a step-by-step "Program Planning Guide" to assist individuals in carrying out a BSM program. Even in well-formulated programs, problems sometimes occur. A troubleshooting guide is included in this last section to help the individual debug an unsuccessful BSM program.

REFERENCES

Bellack, A. S., Rozensky, R., and Schwartz, J. A comparison of two forms of self-monitoring in a behavioral weight reduction program. *Behavior Therapy*, 1974, 5, 523–530.

Cautela, J. R. Covert processes and behavior modification. *Journal of Nervous and Mental Disease*, 1973, *157*, 27–36.

Ciminero, A. R., Nelson, R. O., and Lipinski, D. P. Self-monitoring procedures. In A. R. Ciminero, K. S. Calhoun, and H. E. Adams (Eds.), *Handbook of behavioral assessment*. New York: Wiley, 1977.

Foster, C. *Developing self-control*. Kalamazoo, MI: Behaviordelia, 1974.

Goldfried, M. R., and Merbaum, M. (Eds.). *Behavior change through self-control*. New York: Holt, Rinehart and Winston, 1973.

Gupton, T., and LeBow, M. D. Behavior management in a large industrial firm. *Behavior Therapy*, 1971, *2*, 78–82.

Kanfer, F. H. Self-management methods. In F. H. Kanfer and A. P. Goldstein (Eds.), *Helping people change: A textbook of methods* (2nd ed.). New York: Pergamon Press, 1980.

Kreitner, R., and Golab, M. Increasing the rate of salesperson telephone calls with a monetary refund. *Journal of Organizational Behavior Management*, 1978, *1*, 192–195.

Lamal, P. A., and Benfield, A. The effect of self-monitoring on job tardiness and percentage of time spent working. *Journal of Organizational Behavior Management*, 1978, *1*, 142–149.

Luthans, F., and Davis, T. R. V. Behavioral self-management—the missing link in managerial effectiveness. *Organizational Dynamics*, 1979, Summer, 42–60.

Mahoney, M. J. Research issues in self-management. *Behavior Therapy*, 1972, *3*, 45–63.

Mahoney, M. J., and Arnkoff, D. Cognitive and self-control therapies. In S. L. Garfield and A. E. Bergin (Eds.), *Handbook of psychotherapy and behavior change* (2nd ed.). New York: Wiley, 1978.

Mahoney, M. J., and Thoresen, C. E. *Self-control: Power to the person*. Monterey, CA: Brooks/Cole, 1974.

McKenzie, T. L., and Rushall, B. S. Effects of self-recording on attendance and performance in a competitive swimming training environment. *Journal of Applied Behavior Analysis*, 1974, *7*, 199–206.

Manz, C. C., and Sims, Jr., H. P. Self-management as a substitute for leadership: A social learning theory perspective. *Academy of Management Review*, 1980, *5*, 361–367.

Premack, D. Prediction of the comparative reinforcement values of running and drinking. *Science*, 1963, *139*, 1062–1063.

Schmidt, J. A. *Help yourself: A guide to self-change*. Champaign, IL: Research Press, 1976.

Thoresen, C. E., and Mahoney, M. J. *Behavioral self-control*. New York: Holt, Rinehart and Winston, 1974.

Wallace, I., and Pear, J. J. Self-control techniques of famous novelists. *Journal of Applied Behavior Analysis*, 1977, *10*, 515–525.

Watson, D. L., and Tharp, R. G. *Self-directed behavior: Self-modification for personal adjustment* (3rd ed.). Monterey, CA: Brooks/Cole, 1981.

Wisocki, P. A. A covert reinforcement program for the treatment of test anxiety: Brief report. *Behavior Therapy*, 1973, *4*, 263–266.

10

Improving Performance: A Behavioral Problem-Solving Approach

FRED LUTHANS

University of Nebraska

Productivity in America is in trouble. In the period following World War II until the mid 1960s, productivity in this country increased almost 3 percent a year. Then it began to slide downward. Between 1966 and 1973 the average percentage increase fell to 1.6 percent, and for the rest of the 1970s the average increase per year was less than 1 percent. The prospects for the 1980s are not very encouraging. Everyone, from the person on the street to corporate managers to the President of the United States, now realizes that we must do something to increase productivity.

Obviously there are many contributing factors to the productivity problem. Double digit inflation and the rising costs of energy and government intervention are some examples. Besides these types of factors, which economists and the popular news media tend to give the most attention to, there seems little doubt that a major part of our productivity problem can be traced to the way today's organizations—both in the private and public sectors—are being managed. This management explanation applies all the way from the problems faced by Chrysler Corporation to the reason why John Q. Supervisor cannot get his employees to come to work on time (or even at all), follow simple safety procedures, and come anywhere near standards and goals regarding quality and quantity of performance.

Traditionally, the productivity problem has been viewed from a very general perspective, i.e, how can Chrysler Corporation be better managed. Solutions such as more and better plant and equipment, better computer systems, or strategic planning or matrix structures are usually offered. It is assumed that these technological or conceptual approaches are equated with better management and will in turn lead to a more effective operation and improved productivity. Few would argue that these things can help and need to be continually monitored and improved. However, in the meantime, regardless of the time, effort, and money that goes into improving the technological and conceptual aspects of management, John Q. Supervisor and other human resource managers in today's complex organizations still have problems effectively managing their people. The human side of management is being slighted when trying to attack the productivity problems plaguing modern organizations.

TRADITIONAL APPROACHES TO HUMAN RESOURCE MANAGEMENT

The usual approach to human resource management has and largely continues to be a matter of paying people well. The assumption is that this will make them motivated and satisfied, and this in turn will lead to high productivity. If pay alone won't do the trick, then better working conditions and fringe benefits can be added to get the job done.

Such an approach certainly hasn't hurt or detracted from performance improvement, but by the same token, it has been very costly and doesn't seem to have helped either. The track record speaks for itself. Wages, working conditions, and fringe benefits, although they can always be improved and employees will probably never be satisfied with what they have, are still relatively good in most organizations. Yet problems such as absenteeism, tardiness, and especially low quantity and quality of work are prevalent. These are the problems leading to low productivity. Furthermore, these problems cannot be solved by the traditional management prescription for more and better physical technology (e.g., plant and equipment or computer systems), conceptual approaches (e.g., strategic planning or matrix structures), or the traditional money, working conditions, fringe benefits approach to managing people.

AN O.B. MOD. PROBLEM-SOLVING APPROACH TO PERFORMANCE MANAGEMENT

New thinking and innovative application techniques are needed to more effectively manage problem employee behavior that is hurting productivity. The other chapters in this handbook as well as my own previous work (Luthans and Kreitner, 1975) suggest such a new approach and accompanying techniques. I have developed and extensively used and evaluated a five-step model that can be applied by practicing human resource managers to more effectively manage problem employee behavior. This is called the Organizational Behavior Modification or more simply O.B. Mod. technique. Figure 10-1 shows the O.B. Mod. model and the following discussion further explains its five steps.

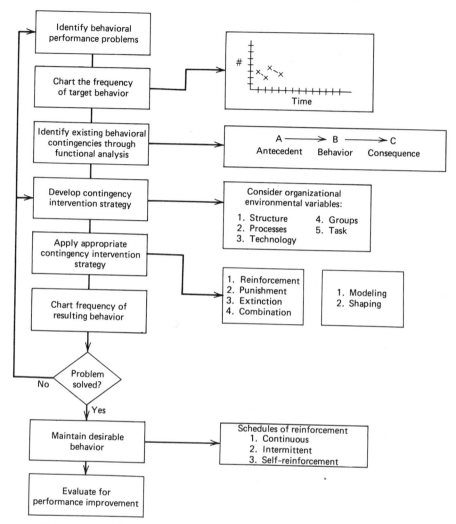

FIGURE 10-1.   O. B. Mod. problem solving model (Luthans and Kreitner, 1974).

Step 1: Identifying and Defining the Problem Behavior

As in any problem solving model, the first step—identifying and defining the problem—is critical to what follows. Most human resource managers have *solutions* to all their problems. Better wages, improved working conditions, a more comprehensive fringe benefit package, more effective communication, hiring better workers or firing those who don't produce—these are just a few of the numerous solutions that are on most managers' lists. Coming up with such solutions is easy. However, the critical question for performance improvement, which is much more difficult to answer, is: what is the problem?

Since O.B. Mod. is a behavioral approach, the problems facing the human resource manager must be put in behavioral terms. In other words, "poor attitudes" or "low morale" or other such internal motivational problems do not have a place in this O.B. Mod. approach. Neither do ambiguous but commonly identified problems such as employees who "goof off" too much. Only observable, countable kinds of behavior that are directly related to performance outcome measures are identified in this approach.

Examples of kinds of behavior identifiable as problems adaptable to the O.B. Mod. approach might be absenteeism, tardiness, unsafe behavior or not following safety procedures, staying at the work station, disrupting co-workers, and especially doing or not doing a particular task or procedure that leads to quantity or quality results. The following sections discuss some specific guidelines that can help in identifying and defining problem behavior suitable for the O.B. Mod. problem solving approach.

Be Sure the Identified Problem Behavior Is Related to Performance.   In every organization, regardless of type, size, or level, there are numerous employee actions occurring all of the time. Some of these actions have a significant, direct impact on performance, and some do not. Suppose that a supervisor identifies one of her subordinate's complaining behavior as a problem that needs to be changed. This constant complaining is extremely irritating and driving her crazy. In an O.B. Mod. approach, the first thing this supervisor must determine is whether this complaining behavior has anything to do with the performance of her unit. If the complainer is a good performer and the complaining is not disruptive to the operation of the unit, then it is not an appropriate behavior to change in the O.B. Mod. process.

The goal of this first step is to identify and define the critical performance behavior—that 20 percent of the behavior that may account for up to 80 percent of the performance in question. The 80 percent of behavior that accounts for only about 20 percent of the performance is not dealt with in this approach.

Ways to Help Identify the Critical Performance Behavior.   The guiding principle in identifying the problem behavior for an O.B. Mod. approach is a positive answer to the two questions: (1) Can it be seen? and (2) Can it be measured? If yes, then it must be ascertained that this problem behavior is in fact related to performance. This is the general approach that can be used in identifying the problem behavior. There are also more specific techniques that can assist in identifying the critical performance behavior.

One technique is to systematically survey (through questionnaires and interviews) supervisors and actual job holders on how they perceive the problems in their area. If this approach is used, it must be followed up and supplemented with actual on-the-job observations and archival data, e.g., industrial engineering or accounting data and reports. This multiple measures approach (Lockwood and Luthans, 1980) is needed to make sure the data generated by the survey is valid and real. This survey technique goes hand in hand with using O.B. Mod. as a problem solving approach for individual human resource managers. Its advantages are that the person who knows the job best can most accurately identify the critical behavior, and by participating, that person may be more committed to carrying the O.B. Mod. process to its successful conclusion.

Another technique that can help identify critical performance behavior is to conduct a behavioral audit. The audit could use internal staff specialists or outside consultants. The audit systematically analyzes each job in question, e.g., in the manner that jobs are examined in job analysis techniques used in personnel management. The advantages discussed above of using the job holder or the immediate supervisor can also be realized in doing the behavioral audit. In addition, the advantages of internal staff or outside consultant expertise and consistency can be gained. Such an audit approach has been successfully used by most consulting firms specializing in the behavioral approach (see Special Report, 1976, for a listing of such consulting firms). For example, in the widely publicized Emery Air Freight case (Performance Audit, 1972, and At Emery Air Freight, 1973) a behavioral audit determined that large container utilization for air freight shipments was a critical performance behavior.

Another suggested technique for identifying critical performance behavior is to work backward from an obvious performance deficiency. Just as not all behavior contributes to performance, as the example of complaining behavior had nothing to do with performance, not all performance problems can be traced to behavior. For example, the cause of poor performance of a production unit in a manufacturing plant may be faulty machinery, or poorly trained workers who do not know the proper procedures, or unrealistically high production standards. Each of these possible causes is not, at least not directly, a behavioral problem. The same is true of the person who does not have the ability to produce at an acceptable level. This is a selection problem, not a behavioral problem.

In general, nonbehaviorally related performance problems are the exception rather than the rule. Most organizations are not having problems with their technology or the ability of their people. When performance deficiencies are traced backward, a behavioral problem can usually be identified. Desirable performance-related behavior needs to be strengthened and accelerated in frequency, and undesirable performance-related behavior needs to be weakened and decelerated in frequency. An example of tracing back from a quality of performance deficiency occurred in one manufacturing plant. In this actual case it was determined that reducing the group scrap rate, decreasing the number of overlooked defective pieces, and reducing the assembly reject rate were critical to the quality of performance (Ottemann and Luthans, 1975). In another example, a large hospital found that each of the major departments were able to trace back to critical behavior as causing performance deficiencies (Snyder and Luthans, in press). In the medical records unit errors in filing were identified; in radiology the retake rate was identified; in the admitting office time (in minutes) to admit was identified; and in the pharmacy unit posting errors were identified. In both the manufacturing plant and the hospital, the deficiencies in performance were traced to employee behavior types of problems, not technology, ability, or training.

Identify the Incongruent Behavior.   Besides making sure that the behavior is performance related and utilizing certain techniques to help identify the problem behavior, you need to be sure that the incongruent behavior is also identified. In other words, employee behavior found in today's organization usually has two sides to it: desirable-undesirable, positive-negative, favorable-unfavorable. Examples would include absenteeism-attendance, safe procedures-unsafe procedures, high quantity-low quantity, high quality-low quality, good reports-poor reports, getting the work done on time-missing deadlines, and staying at the work station-absent from the work station.

If the incongruent pairs of the critical performance behavior are identified in this first step of the O.B. Mod. approach, then the following steps of measurement, functional analysis, and especially intervention becomes much easier. In essence, by identifying the behavior and its incongruent forms, the power and the effectiveness of the intervention strategy is doubled. The strategy would involve reinforcing the desirable and favorable aspects of the behavior and replacing or extinguishing or punishing the incongruent aspect of the behavior. These strategies will be discussed in more detail under Step 4, but in this initial step it is important to identify both the behavior and its incongruent form.

Step 2: Measuring the Problem Behavior

This second step of O.B. Mod. separates this problem solving approach from a more casual, off-the-top-of-the-head approach. Putting the identified problem behavior to the test of measurement makes this a more scientific, precise approach to behavioral change and performance improvement.

Preintervention or Baseline Measures.   The preintervention measurement, more commonly called the baseline measurement, is obtained by determining the number of times that the identified behavior is occurring under present conditions, either by observing and counting or by extracting from existing records. Often this baseline frequency is in and of itself very revealing. Sometimes it is discovered that the behavior identified in Step 1 is occurring much less or much more frequently than anticipated. The baseline measure may indicate that the problem is much smaller or larger than was thought to be the case. In some instances the baseline measure may cause the "problem" to be dropped because its low (or high) frequency is now deemed not to need change. For example, attendance may have been identified in Step 1 as critical behavior that needed to be changed. The supervisor reports that his or her people "never seem to be here, especially when I need them." The baseline measure, however, reveals that there is 90 percent attendance, which is deemed to be quite acceptable to this supervisor. In this example the baseline measure rules out attendance as being a problem. The reverse of course could also have occurred. Attendance may have been a much bigger problem than anticipated. In any case, the purpose of the baseline measure is to provide objective frequency data on the critical performance behavior. A baseline frequency count is an operational definition of the strength of the critical behavior under existing conditions.

During and Postintervention Measures.   The preintervention, baseline measurement serves as the benchmark in which to evaluate the effect of the intervention that is attempted. A careful analysis of the baseline measures may help identify the antecedents or consequences that are cuing and regulating the behavior, i.e., help in the functional analysis, which is covered next. For example, when problem behavior such as absenteeism is measured over time, certain identifiable patterns usually emerge. The measurement may show that certain employees or the group as a whole are absent much more frequently on Mondays, Fridays, paydays if the checks are mailed to the home, or some particular day of the month or year, such as opening day of hunting season. By analyzing this data, managers can identify antecedent cues that set the occasion for the absenteeism behavior. By the same type of analysis of the data, important consequences can also be identified. Where behavior frequencies are shown to be increasing, this indicates that reinforcers in the environment are encouraging the behavior. Where behavior frequencies are decreasing, this indicates that there is no reinforcement, or there are punishers in the environment. Identifying these existing consequences will greatly assist the development of an effective intervention strategy.

Once the strategy is applied, measurement becomes vital to see if it is having the intended impact on the targeted behavior. By comparing the frequency of the behavior before and after the intervention, it can be objectively determined whether the intervention is working. In a behavioral approach such as this, the only way that a reward becomes a reinforcer is by its accelerating effect on behavioral frequency. Thus the only way to determine if the intervention is in fact reinforcing is to carefully take a postintervention measurement of the behavior. Busy human resource managers may feel that they do not have time to objectively record behavioral frequencies, but at least initially, they must record them in order to effectively use the O.B. Mod. approach. The following discussion will give specific suggestions and techniques to ease the burden of measuring and point out how to minimize the problems and increase the effectiveness of this second step of O.B. Mod.

Guidelines and Techniques of Measurement.   The goal of the measurement step of O.B. Mod. is to obtain as valid and reliable data on the target behavior as possible. The following guidelines are offered to help meet this goal.

1. *Carefully Constructing a Simple Tally Sheet.* Since the critical performance behavior identified in Step 1 will be quite different in each case, a tailor-made tally sheet needs to be developed. A piece of notebook paper usually is sufficient. Figure 10-2 shows how a typical tally sheet looks. The form usually records behavioral frequencies (how often the behavior occurs) in relation to time. When at all possible, the frequencies are usually broken down in a yes-no format. The goal is to keep the recording as simple as possible. By the same token, however, it must be clearly understood what constitutes a frequency or occurrence of the behavior. For example, say that the critical behavior is tardiness in returning from breaks. A manager must decide exactly what is considered tardy. The definition of tardiness may differ from situation to situation, but say that five minutes or over is tardy. The observer-recorder then has a definite guideline in checking "yes" or "no" for frequency of tardiness behavior.

2. *Using the Appropriate Time Dimension.* The time dimension on the tally sheet can take several forms depending on the target behavior. One technique is called unit or continuous recording, in which the behavior is counted every time it occurs. Examples of target behavior that would be adaptable to unit recording would include tardiness, absenteeism, customers contacted, number of sales, or widgets produced. This unit recording is usually collected over a specified time period such as an hour or week. In most organizations this type of data is already being collected in the form of daily reports, production records or bogey sheets, sales figures, quality control reports, and all aspects of the extensive management information system (MIS).

In some situations, for some target behavior, unit recording would be too time consuming, impractical, or impossible. In these cases interval recording may be more practical. For example, behavior such as staying

Employee: _____		Behavior: _____							
Position: _____		Supervisor: _____							
	Monday		Tuesday		Wednesday		Thursday		Friday	
Times	Yes	No	Yes	No	Yes	No	Yes	No	Yes	No

FIGURE 10-2.   A simple example of a tally sheet.

at the work station may be checked at equal intervals (e.g., at the beginning of each hour) throughout the day. A major disadvantage is that the person being measured soon becomes aware of when the data is being gathered and behaves differently. This problem is overcome by random time-sampling techniques, an approach borrowed from work-sampling techniques that have been successfully used by industrial engineers for years. An example of a time-sampling approach would be to randomly select a time per each working hour to observe the target behavior. As in any sampling procedure, if the times are in fact random, confident generalizations can be made to the whole day. This random technique is most often used when original data must be generated.

3. *Charting the Data.* The old saying that a picture is worth a thousand words is quite true. In the case of an O.B. Mod. approach, a chart usually showing the frequency of the target behavior over time is worth pages of computer printout paper giving the same information. Most modern employees are overwhelmed by the increasing amounts of information they are receiving from computerized management information systems (MIS). The situation can be characterized as information overload. However, individual employees, the one (or ones) whose behavior is having a tremendous impact on performance, are either not getting the data, do not understand it, or are intimidated by the format in which it is presented to them, e.g., stacks of computer printouts. What is needed is a visual presentation of the data.

The data collected on the tally sheets should be transferred to a chart or graph like the one shown in Figure 10-3. As shown, the frequencies of the behavior identified in Step 1 are along the vertical axis, and time is on the horizontal axis. Percentage rather than raw frequency is usually used. The usage of percentage frequency simplifies the measurement process, because it permits a time or two to be missed during the day or even entire days without badly distorting the data. These frequency charts should be kept constantly up-to-date, and are kept for both the baseline period and after the intervention technique. Visual inspection will show if the intervention is having its intended effect, and of course the charts

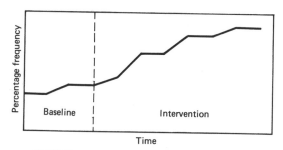

FIGURE 10-3. A simple example of charting.

themselves can become a feedback reinforcing mechanism for both the supervisor using this O.B. Mod. approach and the person whose behavior is targeted for change.

4. *Collecting the Behavioral Data.* How the data are collected becomes important not only to validity and reliability but to the credibility and ethics of the entire O.B. Mod. approach. There is a growing recognition in the entire behavior sciences that there has been too much dependence on just questionnaires and interviews in collecting data. The problem is that questionnaire and interview data are highly reactive; that is, they change the behavior being measured. However, if alternative observational measures are used, the mere presence of an observer may also badly distort the behavior being measured. For this reason, it is important that observational data be gathered as unobtrusively (inconspicuously) as possible.

By advocating unobtrusive observational measures I do not mean that hidden observers or hidden audio or video equipment should be used. Obviously such an approach would cause ethical and legal problems. With a few exceptions (e.g., reasons of security), such *hidden* or deceptive approaches cannot be justified. On the other hand, straightforward observational techniques that use common sense can minimize the reactive effects of those being measured. The observer should be completely open to any questions that the person being observed may have. Most employees in today's organizations are not sensitive to being measured, because industrial engineers and personnel specialists have been doing it for years. There have been abuses of this in the past, but hopefully the lessons have been learned and the abuses can be eliminated.

In addition to observational techniques of data collection, as mentioned earlier, many of the critical performance behavioral acts identified in Step 1 (e.g., absenteeism, quantity and quality data, or safety violations) are already being gathered by the organization in question. All that recorders have to do is retrieve these data; they do not have to intrusively intervene. In addition, some specific guidelines on "Tactics and Benefits of Behavioral Measurement in Business" (Johnston, Duncan, Monroe, and Stoerziner, 1978) have recently been offered. There are several ways to effectively observe, record, display, interpret, and in general assure the quality of behavioral measurement. For example, the use of equipment in any form, from simple clocks and counters to sophisticated numerical control devices, is helpful whenever feasible. Machine-measured data can eliminate human errors and give confidence that it is impartially derived.

What are sometimes called "response products" should be identified (Johnston et al., 1978). Instead of trying to measure the minute pattern of behavior as it occurrs, the product or outcome of this behavior is measured. Of course the measurer must be certain that the response product is the result of the behavior, i.e., there is a one-to-one or at least known correspondence between the behavior and the product. In addition, especially where more than one employee could be responsible for the product, the accuracy of the response authorship must be assumed. Most of the quantity and quality problems identified in Step 1 of O.B. Mod. utilize this response product approach to measurement.

Finally, another major dimension in collecting data in O.B. Mod. are self-recording and reporting procedures. The obvious advantage of self-generated data is the immediacy of the feedback it provides the person. In addition, the individual knows how the data was derived and where it came from, and thus has confidence in it. The foremost consideration in designing the self-recording format is to set up the observing and recording tasks so that they can be effectively carried out without any incompatibility with the person's important job requirements (Johnson et al., 1978). The biggest disadvantage of self-generated data is that the person knows that she or he is being measured, and therefore may distort the data to make him or herself look good. Because of this possibility, the measurer should always check the accuracy of self-reports by cross-validating them with other measures, i.e., take a multiple-measures approach (Lockwood and Luthans, 1980). There is some evidence to indicate that employees who are reinforced for keeping accurate and complete self-records will in fact be honest and reliable (Performance Audit, 1972, and At Emery Air Freight, 1973). The goal of Step 2 is to use as much self-recording as possible because the advantages outweigh the potential disadvantages.

Step 3. Functional Analysis of the Behavior

This third step of O.B. Mod. is at the very heart of the problem solving process. It prevents O.B. Mod. from being a simplistic list of steps instead of an analytical problem solving approach. The purpose of the functional analysis is to identify and understand the antecedent cues that emit the target behavior and sometimes control it, and the more important contingent consequences that are currently maintaining the target behavior. The consequences are the more important, because they give power to the antecedents. Under the operant paradigm, antecedents set the occasion for the behavior to be emitted; they do not cause (elicit) the behavior. Yet in terms of regulating and controlling behavior, antecedents become important and should be identified, understood, and sometimes managed.

In O.B. Mod. the functional analysis is simplified into an A-B-C format (antecedent-behavior-consequence). This A-B-C is derived from Skinner's (1969) original conception of a three-term contingency and has been featured in O.B. Mod. since the beginning (Luthans and Kreitner, 1975). Figure 10-4 shows a comprehensive functional analysis of attendance and absenteeism behavior.

Recently this A-B-C functional analysis has been defended as "the best technique for diagnostic evaluation of organizational behavior" (Luthans, 1980). The argument for the value of functional analysis is based on the goals of prediction and control of the critical performance behavior. By concentrating on the antecedent side of the functional analysis, it can be determined if the target behavior is under stimulus control. The popular

Functional Analysis of Attendance Behavior(s)

A ————————→ B ————————→ C

Antecedent cue(s)	Behavior(s)	Consequence(s)
Awareness of any consequence	Going to bed on time	Reward programs
	Setting the alarm	Contingent time-off
Advertising	Waking up	Gifts/prizes
Meetings	Getting dressed	Preferred jobs
Memorandums	Getting children off to school	Social
Orientation	Leaving home	Attention
Bulletin board	Getting a baby-sitter	Recognition
Observation of any consequence	Driving to work	Praise
	Reporting into work	Feedback
Social status and pressure		Data on attendance
Temporal cues		
Special events		
Weather		

Functional Analysis of Absenteeism Behavior(s)

A ————————→ B ————————→ C

Antecedent cue(s)	Behavior(s)	Consequence(s)
Illness/accident	Getting up late	Discipline programs
Hangover	Sleeping in	Verbal reprimands
Lack of transportation	Staying home	Written reprimands
Traffic	Drinking	Pay docks
No day-care facilities	Fishing/hunting	Layoffs
Family problems	Working at home	Dismissals
Company policies	Visiting	Social consequences from co-workers
Group/personal norms	Caring for sick child	
Seniority/age		Escape and avoidance of working
Awareness/observation of any consequence		Nothing

FIGURE 10-4. A comprehensive example of functional analysis. (From F. Luthans and M. Martinko, "An O.B. Mod. Analysis of Absenteeism," *Human Resources Management*, Fall, 1976, reprinted with permission.)

organizational development or OD approach provides an excellent example of how the understanding of the role of antecedents can have an important impact. Most of the OD techniques, e.g., job enrichment or team building, simply set the occasion or cue appropriate performance behavior. However, as was pointed out, these antecedents—an enriched job or a team concept—only become powerful and control behavior to the extent that reinforcing consequences follow the behavior that has been emitted. By recognizing this last point, it becomes clear why many OD programs seem to be only effective in the short run. The OD approach carefully structures the antecedent environment, e.g., provides an enriched task design or sets up mechanisms for conflict resolution or goal setting, and this sets the occasion for desirable employee behavior. However, this OD approach often fails to provide the contingent reward systems to reinforce these desirable kinds of behavior. With no reinforcement forthcoming, the OD program loses its controlling power to cause the desirable behavior and soon becomes ineffective.

Besides the importance of the antecedent or "A" side of functional analysis, identification and understanding of the consequence side or "C" is even more important. An actual example from a manufacturing plant points out why the analysis of the antecedents and consequences is so important to the O.B. Mod. approach. In this example, a production supervisor determined in Step 1 that the unscheduled breaks taken by his workers were a critical problem behavior detracting from the performance of his department. The workers were frequently wandering off the job; when they were not operating their machines, time was lost and productivity declined. In Step 2, when a baseline measure was taken, the data indicated that unscheduled breaks (defined as leaving the job for reasons other than taking a scheduled break or to obtain materials) were occurring in his department on a relatively frequent basis. This was translated into significant dollars lost in productivity. Next a functional analysis was performed to determine the antecedent(s) and consequence(s) of the unscheduled break behavior.

Analysis of the antecedent side showed that the clock served as the cue for the critical behavior to be emitted. The workers in this department started work at 8 a.m.; at 10 a.m. they had their first scheduled break; they had lunch at 12. They started work again at 1 p.m., had a formal break at 3 p.m., and quit at 5 p.m. The functional analysis revealed that almost precisely at 9, 11, 2, and 4 the workers were leaving their jobs and congregating at the restroom. In other words, the clock served as a cue for them to take an unscheduled break midway between starting time and the first scheduled break, between the first scheduled break and lunch, between lunch and the scheduled afternoon break, and between the afternoon break and quitting time. Remember that the clock did not cause the behavior; it only served as a cue to emit the behavior. On the other hand, the behavior was under stimulus control of the clock because the clock dictated when the behavior would occur. The consequence, however, was what maintained the behavior. The unscheduled break behavior was a function of its consequences.

The functional analysis revealed several consequences of the unscheduled break behavior. One was escape from a very dull, boring task, i.e., the unscheduled break behavior was being negatively reinforced. Another consequence was meeting with co-workers and friends to socialize and have a cigarette, i.e., the unscheduled break behavior was being positively reinforced. Still another consequence was the supervisor complaining and chewing out individuals and the group as a whole for taking all the unscheduled breaks. However, the data indicated that this last consequence had no impact. It was oncontingent, meaning the behavior did not depend on it. The competing contingencies of escape and socializing by having a cigarette were what was affecting the employees' behavior. Thus the functional analysis revealed what was cuing the behavior and what was maintaining the behavior. This provides invaluable information in order to develop intervention strategies in the next step.

Step 4: Developing an Intervention Strategy[1]

The first three steps in an O.B. Mod. approach are preliminary to this action step, the intervention strategy. The goal of the strategy is to strengthen and accelerate desirable critical performance behavior and weaken or decelerate undesirable critical performance behavior. Several strategies can be used, but the main ones are positive reinforcement, punishment with positive reinforcement, and extinction with positive reinforcement.

Positive Reinforcement Strategy.   Several other chapters in the handbook have devoted considerable attention to the concept of reinforcement. A *positive reinforcer* is defined as a consequence that strengthens the behavior and increases its subsequent frequency. Negative reinforcement, the termination or withdrawl of an undesirable consequence, has the same impact on behavior: it strengthens and increases subsequent frequency. Yet positive and not negative reinforcement is recommended as an effective intervention strategy for O.B. Mod. The reason is that positive reinforcement represents a form of positive control of behavior, while negative reinforcement and punishment represent forms of negative control of behavior. Negative reinforcement is actually a type of blackmail control of behavior; the person behaves in a certain way in order not to be punished. Most organizations today control participants in this manner. People come to work in order not to be fired, and look busy when the supervisor walks by in order not to be punished. Under positive control, the person behaves in a certain way in order to receive the desired consequence. Under positive control people would come to work in order to be recognized for making a contribution to their department's goal of perfect attendance, or would keep busy whether the supervisor was around or not in order to receive incentive pay or because they get self-reinforcement from doing a good job. Positive control through a positive-reinforcement intervention strategy is much more effective and long lasting than negative control. It creates a much healthier and more productive organizational climate.

Identifying Positive Reinforcers.   Again, a reward becomes a positive reinforcer only if, because of its presentation, the behavior increases in subsequent frequency. Thus some of the commonly used organizational rewards are ot necessarily positive reinforcers. This is why it is so vitally important t at the measures initiated in Step 2 be continued after the interventio The objective measures are the only way to tell whether an intervention is in fact a positive reinforcer.

There are several techniques available to help determine potential pos-

[1]The material discussed in this step is largely adapted from Luthans (1981, pp. 278–288).

itive reinforcers (Luthans and Kreitner, 1975). The most accurate but often difficult-to-accomplish method of identifying positive reinforcers is to empirically analyze each individual's history of reinforcement. Knowledge of what a particular person likes and dislikes gained through experience can help in this regard, and of course empirical evidence after intervention from the charting in Step 2 can be used to analyze the history of reinforcement. However, in an intervention measure, several self-reporting techniques can be used.

The most straightforward technique is to simply ask what the person finds to be rewarding. Although the person may not always tell the truth, it is nonetheless a logical point of departure for identifying potential reinforcers. Figure 10-5 gives an example of the types of questions that could be asked employees to help identify potential reinforcers. Employees could fill out such a form when they are hired or every year or so to help the manager find specific rewards for each employee.

A more formal approach is to use test instruments. For example, Milton Blood (1973) developed a test that helps identify the relative importance of several possible job-related reinforcers. Another possible method of identifying reinforcers is the use of contingency questionnaires (Reitz, 1971). The latter tests measure perceived performance-outcome probabilities and can help identify the important results (reinforcers) for employees.

Employee Reinforcer Survey

1. In my free time my favorite activity is _____

2. I would really like to visit _____

3. My favorite sports activity is _____

4. My favorite hobby is _____

5. Something that I really want to buy is _____

6. If I had fifty dollars to spend on myself right now I would _____

7. My job would be more rewarding if _____

8. If my manager would _____ I would enjoy working here.

9. I would work harder if _____

10. The place that I most like to shop is _____

FIGURE 10-5.   Examples of questions that could be asked in an employee reinforcer survey (Miller, 1978).

Still another way to help identify possible reinforcers is through self-selection techniques: the workers are allowed to select their own reinforcers from a variety of stated possibilities, sometimes called "smorgasbords" or "menus" or "cafeterias." The key to these approaches is that giving employees a "choice" may in and of itself be very reinforcing and may have a positive influence on performance (see Thoresen and Mahoney, 1974, pp. 3–5 for review of the literature on the impact of choice). This potentially significant impact of the choice aspect of administering rewards has been badly neglected to date.

Contrived Reinforcers.   The various techniques discussed above can be used to help identify reinforcers for the positive-reinforcement intervention strategy. Although reinforcers are highly individualized, research and experience have shown that most organizational participants find several rewards to be positively reinforcing. These can be classified as contrived and natural rewards. The contrived rewards are those that are brought in from outside the natural work environment and generally involve costs for the organization over and above the existing situation (Luthans and Kreitner, 1975). Examples would include the consumables, manipulatables, visual or auditory reinforcers, and tokens found in Figure 10-6. The two most widely used and effective contrived rewards are money and feedback about performance.

The literature on the impact that feedback has on organizational participants is not that clear. Feedback has played a key role in most of the reported behavioral management applications such as Emery Air Freight (Performance Audit, 1972, At Emery Air Freight, 1973). As pointed out earlier, there is little question that despite the tremendous amount of data being generated by computerized information systems in modern organizations, individuals still receive very little if any feedback about their performance. People generally have an intense desire to know *how* they are doing. There is some research evidence that feedback enhances individual performance; that the more specific it is, the greater its impact; and that the greater the delay between performance and feedback, the less the effect (Ammons, 1956, and Annett, 1969). Most consultants on behavioral management also suggest helpful guidelines in making feedback more effective. For example, Connellan (1978) suggests the following: (1) feedback should be specific in relation to a goal; (2) wherever possible feedback should be self-administered; (3) feedback should be expressed positively rather than negatively; (4) feedback should be as immediate as possible; and (5) relevant feedback should go to all levels of the organization.

Despite the general acceptance of feedback as an important intervention strategy, there is growing evidence that feedback should not automatically be equated with reinforcement. Although some studies have demonstrated that individual performance is directly related to the amount of feedback (Cook, 1968; Hundal, 1969; Anderson, Kulhavy, and Andre, 1971), but

Contrived On-the-Job Rewards				Natural Rewards	
Consumables	Manipulatables	Visual and Auditory	Tokens	Social	Premack
Coffee-break treats	Desk accessories	Office with a window	Money	Friendly greetings	Job with more responsibility
Free lunches	Wall plaques	Piped-in music	Stocks	Informal recognition	Job rotation
Food baskets	Company car	Redecoration of work environment	Stock options	Formal acknowledgment of achievement	Early time off with pay
Easter hams	Watches	Company literature	Movie passes	Invitations to coffee or lunch	Extended breaks
Christmas turkeys	Trophies	Private office	Trading stamps (green stamps)	Solicitations of suggestions	Extended lunch period
Dinners for the family on the company	Commendations	Popular speakers or lecturers	Paid-up insurance policies	Solicitations of advice	Personal time off with pay
Company picnics	Rings or tiepins	Book club discussions	Dinner and theater tickets	Compliment on work progress	Work on personal project on company time
After-work wine and cheese parties	Appliances and furniture for the home	Feedback about performance	Vacation trips	Recognition in house organ	Use of company machinery or facilities for personal projects
Beer parties	Home shop tools		Coupons redeemable at local stores	Pat on the back	Use of company recreation facilities
	Garden tools		Profit sharing	Smile	
	Clothing			Verbal or nonverbal recognition or praise	
	Club privileges				
	Special assignments				

FIGURE 10-6. Classifications of on-the-job rewards (Luthans and Kreitner, 1975)

recent comprehensive analyses point out the complexities of feedback and conclude that blanket generalizations about the reinforcing properties of feedback are too simplistic (Ilgen, Fisher, and Taylor, 1979). For example, after reviewing the existing research literature on feedback, Nadler (1979) concluded that its impact is contingent upon factors such as the nature of the feedback information, the process of using feedback, individual differences among the recipients of the feedback, and the nature of the task. Despite such qualifications, as a general guideline, feedback about performance is suggested here as an effective intervention strategy for O.B. Mod.

Nonperformance-oriented feedback can also be used by human resource managers to clarify contingencies. An example of this use of feedback was the supervisor cited in the discussion of the functional analysis who had the problem with his people taking unscheduled breaks. In that case he could not change the antecedent cue (he could not change time), and he could not change the consequence by preventing his people from going to the bathroom. What he did do was calculate the exact cost for each worker in the unit (in terms of lost group incentive pay) every time any one of them took an unscheduled break. This information regarding the relatively significant amount of lost pay when any one of them took an unscheduled break was fed back to the employees in his unit. After this type of feedback intervention (i.e., clarifying another contingent consequence that was always there but not given attention by the employees), staying on the job increased in frequency and taking unscheduled breaks dramatically decreased. The feedback pointed out the contingency that staying on the job meant more money. At least in this case, the money proved to be a more contingent consequence than the competing contingencies of social rewards with friends at the restroom and withdrawing from the boring job. The feedback in this case clarified the monetary contingency.

Money as a Reinforcer.   Despite the tendency in recent years to downgrade the importance of money as an organizational reward, there is ample evidence that money can be positively reinforcing for most people. The downgrading of money is partly the result of some of the popular motivation theories such as those of Maslow and Herzberg, plus the publicity from surveys that consistently place wages and salaries near the middle of the list of employment factors that are important to workers and managers. Although money was probably overemphasized in classical management theory and motivation techniques, the pendulum now has seemed to swing too far in the opposite direction. Money remains a very important but admittedly complex potential reinforcer.

In terms of Maslow's hierarchy, money is often equated only with the most basic level of needs. It is viewed in the material sense of buying food, clothing, and shelter. Yet money has a symbolic as well as an economic material meaning. It can provide power and status and can be a means to measure achievement. In the latter sense, money can be used as an effective positive-reinforcement intervention strategy.

Accepting the importance of money as a possible reinforcer does not mean that the traditional techniques for dispensing it are adequate. Starting with the scientific management movement at the turn of the century, numerous monetary incentive techniques have been developed. The payment schemes can be classified into three broad categories (Flippo and Munsinger, 1975):

1. Base pay or salary that is given for a job regardless of how it is performed.
2. Variable pay that gives recognition to individual differences on the job.
3. Supplementary pay that is not directly related to the job or the individual.

The base-pay technique provides for minimum compensation for a particular job. Pay by the hour for workers and the base salary for managers are examples. The technique does not reward for above-average or penalize for below-average performance, and it is largely controlled by the job rather than by the person performing the job. The variable-pay technique attempts to reward according to individual or group differences and is thus more human than job-controlled. Seniority variable-pay plans recognize age and length-of-service differentials, and merit and individual or group incentive plans attempt to reward contingently on performance. Incentive plans pay personnel according to piece rate, bonus, or profit sharing. Supplementary monetary techniques have nothing to do with the job or performance per se. The extensive fringe-benefit package received by employees in most modern organizations is an example.

Further refined and newly developed variable-pay or contingent-pay plans seem to be necessary to the effective use of money as a reinforcer. The base- and supplementary-pay plans are adequate for their intended purposes, but the variable-pay plans do not seem to have the desired effects. After an extensive review of relevant research, the following problems with merit pay programs were found (Hamner and Organ, 1978):

1. Pay is not perceived as being related to job performance. For example, one survey of 600 managers found practically no relationships between their pay and their rated performance.
2. Performance ratings are viewed as being biased. Most employees feel that appraisals are based on subjective rather than objective performance measures.
3. The pay is not viewed as a reward. Pay represents more than money to the employee. For example, conflicting reward schedules, perceived inequities, or threats to self-esteem may negate a merit increase from becoming a reward.

4. Those who administer merit pay are more concerned with employee satisfaction than with performace. There should be variability in an effective pay plan, but many managers are overly concerned with the accompanying complaints.

5. There is little trust or openness about merit increases. For the merit plan to be effective, there must be an open climate, in which work and effort are valued and paid accordingly.

6. Pay is viewed as the primary reinforcer, and the job itself is ignored. Feedback and pay systems must be designed to both get things done and make the work enjoyable.

The above points indicate that incentive or merit pay plans are not a clear-cut way to contingently administer monetary rewards.

The following guidelines are offered by Webber (1975) as a way to make money more effective as a reinforcer. The individual must believe that:

1. Increased effort would lead to better performance.

2. Your employer can determine the improved performance.

3. Increased money will follow from this performance.

4. You would value the additional money because it would satisfy your needs.

5. You would not have to unduly sacrifice satisfaction of other needs for security, affiliation, and so on.

Analyses of the role of money, such as those made above, are usually couched in cognitive terms. However, from these cognitive explanations it is very clear that the real key for assessing the use of money as a reinforcer is not necessarily whether is satisfies inner needs but rather how it is administered. In order for money to be an effective positive-reinforcement intervention strategy for O.B. Mod., it must be administered contingently on performing the critical performance behavior.

About the only reinforcing function that pay currently has in most organizations is to reinforce employees for walking up to a pay window or opening an envelope every two weeks or month. With the exception of some piece-rate incentive systems and commissions paid to sales persons, pay is generally not contingent on the performance of critical behavior. One experimental study clearly demonstrated that money contingently administered can be an effective intervention strategy (Herman, deMontes, Dominguez, Montes, and Hopkins, 1973). A contingently administered monetary bonus plan significantly improved the punctuality of workers in a Mexican division of a large United States corporation. However, the mere fact that money was valued by the Mexican workers in this study does not mean that it would have the same impact on all workers. For example, in a society with an inflationary economy and nonmaterialistic social values, money may be much less likely to be a potential reinforcer for critical job behavior. Money certainly cannot be automatically dismissed as a positive reinforcer, but because of its complexity, it may also turn out to be a reward but not a reinforcer. Only postintervention measurement will determine if in fact money is an effective positive reinforcer for the critical behavior in question.

Natural Reinforcers.   Besides the contrived rewards that most human resource managers tend to depend upon, there are a host of overlooked natural reinforcers available in every organizational setting. Potentially very powerful, these are the rewards that exist in the natural occurrence of events (Luthans and Kreitner, 1975). Figure 10-6 categorized the natural rewards under social and Premack headings.

Social rewards such as recognition, attention, and praise tend to be very reinforcing for most people. In addition, few people become satiated (filled up) with social rewards. However, like the contrived rewards, the social rewards must be administered on a contingent basis. For example, a pat on the back or verbal praise that is randomly administered, as was the case under the old human relations approach, may have more of a punishing, boomerang effect than a positive reinforcement effect. But genuine social rewards, contingently administered to the critical behavior, can be a very effective positive-reinforcement intervention strategy. The added benefit of such a strategy in contrast to the use of contrived rewards is that the cost of social rewards to the organization is absolutely nothing.

Premack rewards are derived from the work of psychologist David Premack (1965). Simply stated, the Premack Principle is that high-probability behavior can be used to reinforce low-probability behavior. For example, if there are two tasks, A and B, and the person prefers A over B, the Premack Principle would say that the person should perform B first and then A. In this sequence, Task A serves as a contingent reinforcer for completing Task B, and the person will perform better on both tasks than if the sequence were reversed. In common practice, people often tend to do the task they like best first and put off the less desired task. This common sequence of doing things is in direct violation of the Premack Principle and can contribute to ineffective performance.

As an O.B. Mod. intervention strategy, the Premack principle would suggest that a natural reinforcer could always be found. Certain job activities could always be used to reinforce other job activities. No matter how much employees dislike their jobs, there will be some things they like to do better than others. Premack sequencing would allow the more desired activities to reinforce less desired activities. The rewards listed under "Premack" in Figure 10-6 can be used to reinforce the less desirable activities on a job.

A Replacement Strategy.   The discussion so far has emphasized that the positive-reinforcement strategy is the most effective intervention for O.B. Mod. Nothing has been directly mentioned as to how the undesirable behavior—that which detracts from or is dysfunctional for goal attainment—are handled. This is because a positive reinforcement strategy implies a replacement strategy for decreasing the undesirable behavior. Going back to the discussion in the first step on identifying the incongruent pair for each performance behavior, if the desirable behavior is being accelerated by the positive reinforcement strategy, then by definition, the incongruent undesirable behavior will be decreasing. In other words, by accentuating the positives, the negatives will take care of themselves.

This replacement approach is a deliberate strategy to reduce the undesired behavior. It is not, as many practitioners will try to interpret, simply ignoring the undesirable behavior. A replacement strategy attempts to deliberately decrease (not ignore) the unwanted behavior by avoiding the problems that accompany a punishment strategy for decreasing undesirable behavior. Only when replacement or extinction is not feasible should human resource managers using an O.B. Mod. approach resort to a punishment strategy.

A Punishment Strategy.   Realistically, we must recognize that in some cases the use of punishment to weaken and decelerate undesirable behavior cannot be avoided. This would be true of something like unsafe behavior that needed to be immediately decreased. However, as was pointed out above, so many negative side effects accompany the use of punishment that it should be avoided if at all possible. Punished behavior tends to be only temporarily suppressed; if a supervisor reprimands a subordinate for some undesirable behavior, the behavior will decrease in the presence of the supervisor, but will surface again when the supervisor is absent. In addition, a punished person becomes very anxious and tense; reliance on punishment may have a disastrous impact on employee satisfaction. Perhaps the biggest problem with the use of punishment is that it is very difficult for a supervisor to switch roles from punisher to positive reinforcer.

Some supervisors and managers rely on punishment so much in dealing with their subordinates that it is almost impossible for them to effectively administer positive reinforcement. This is a bad situation for the management of human resources, because the use of positive reinforcement and replacement strategy is a much more effective way of changing organizational behavior. If punishment is deemed to be necessary, the desirable incongruent behavior, e. g., safe behavior, should be positively reinforced at the first opportunity. By using this combination strategy, the incongruent desirable behavior will begin to replace the undesirable behavior. Punishment should never be used alone as an O.B. Mod. intervention technique. If it is absolutely necessary, it should always be used in combination with positive reinforcement.

Extinction/Positive Reinforcement.   If replacement can't be used, an extinction strategy is a much more effective way to decrease undesirable behavior than by punishment. Extinction has the same impact on behavior as punishment, although it does not act as fast; but extinction does not have the negative side effects of punishment. Punishment could be thought of as the application of a noxious or aversive consequence or the *deliberate withdrawal* of a positively reinforcing consequence that is already a part of the person's environment. Extinction involves the *withdrawal* of a desirable consequence that is contingent upon the person's behavior; this happens after the behavior takes place. More simply, however, extinction can be defined as providing *no* consequence. Obviously there is a fine line between extinction and the withdrawal of a positive-reinforcer type of punishment. In fact there is such a fine distinction between the two that some behaviorists do not even deal with extinction. They simply operationally define anything that decreases behavior as punishment. But the important point for an O.B. Mod. approach to human resource management is that undesirable behavior can be decreased without the accompanying negative side effects of punishment. This can be done by making sure there is no consequence for the undesirable behavior, i. e., putting it on extinction.

In the functional analysis performed in Step 3 of O.B. Mod., the consequences maintaining the critical behavior are identified. The extinction strategy would eliminate those consequences of critical behavior that were to be decelerated. For example, if complaining was the targeted behavior, and the functional analysis revealed that the supervisor's attention to the complaining behavior was maintaining it, the extinction strategy would be to have the supervisor cease giving attention to the complaints. The supervisor may be able to avoid the complainer. Walking away from the person when he or she starts to complain may be punishing; but if handled properly, i. e., in a nonobvious manner, it could be an extinction strategy without the negative side effects. Again, as with any intervention strategy, whether it was effective in reducing the behavior can be known only by what happened to the frequency measures after intervention. Also, like the punishment strategy, extinction should be used only in combination with positive reinforcement. The desirable alternative behavior would be positively reinforced at the first opportunity. The positively reinforced behavior would begin to replace the undesirable behavior. In the example of the complaining behavior, when the person did not complain, the supervisor would notice and give attention to the person for constructive comments and noncomplaining behavior.

Because most organizational behavior is being reinforced on intermittent schedules of reinforcement, which are very resistant to extinction, the use of the extinction strategy may take time and patience. But as a long-range strategy for weakening undesirable behavior and decelerating the frequency of occurrence, extinction can be effective. In general, the very simple rule of thumb to follow in employing an O.B. Mod. intervention strategy is to positively reinforce desirable behavior and make sure undesirable behavior is not reinforced. This simple guideline may have as big an impact on effective human resource management as any single thing the supervisor or manager can do to improve performance.

Step 5: Evaluating to Insure Performance Improvement

The O.B. Mod. approach has a singular purpose: to improve performance. The goal is not to change behavior for behavioral changes' sake. Rather the purpose is to improve the total effectiveness of the human resource manager who uses this model. In order to insure that this purpose is indeed being accomplished, systematic evaluation is built into the model in terms of this fifth and final step.

There is considerable evidence that most human resource programs are not systematically evaluated. For example, one comprehensive survey of 154 selected companies concluded that "most organizations are measuring *reaction* to training programs. As we consider the more important and difficult steps in the evaluation process (i. e., *learning, behavior,* and *results*) we find less and less being done, and many of these efforts are superficial and subjective" (Cantalanello and Kirkpatrick, 1968, p. 9). In another survey, it was concluded that the typical organization that uses job enrichment "believes it has benefited from improvements in employee performance and job satisfaction but has made little effort to formally evaluate the effectiveness of the program, depending on impressions and anecdotal evidence, rather than quantifiable data, for its conclusions" (Luthans and Reif, 1974, p. 33). These typical haphazard evaluations of human resource management techniques have led to credibility problems. Today all programs dealing with people, whether they are government welfare programs or human resource management programs, are under the pressure of accountability. The O.B. Mod. approach recognizes this and tries to do something about it.

All four levels of evaluation (reaction, learning, behavioral change, and performance improvement) are stressed. The *reaction level* of evaluation simply refers to whether the people using the approach and those having it used on them like it or not. If O.B. Mod. is well received, if there is a positive reaction to it, there is obviously a much better chance of its being used effectively. If it is not well received, there is little chance of its being used effectively. In other words, reaction is an important part of the evaluation step of O.B. Mod., but it is not enough. The second level of learning is also necessary. This learning level is especially important when first implementing an O.B. Mod. approach. Do the people using the approach understand the theoretical principles and underlying assumptions and the meaning and reasons for the steps in the model? If they do not, the model will probably not be used effectively.

Reaction and learning should be evaluated. However, the real test of the O.B. Mod. approach is whether the critical behavior identified in Step 1 have really changed in the desired direction, and even more important, whether "bottom-line" performance has improved. The measurement and charting process started in Step 2 will be able to determine the impact on behavioral change. The causal impact that O.B. Mod. has on overall performance usually requires a relatively sophisticated design.

A simple before and after analysis is usually used if overall performance is evaluated at all. However, this does not allow causal explanations that it was in fact the O.B. Mod. approach that caused the change in performance. Because there are threats to both internal and external validity (Campbell and Stanley, 1963) with a simple before and after analysis, there are many possible explanations for the results (e.g., a change in technology or an improvement in the economy). To overcome this problem, three basic designs are recommended.

First is the so-called reversal or A-B-A-B design. It is applied in the following manner:

1. First a baseline measure is obtained on the individual or group behavior in question. (A)
2. Then an intervention takes place, and the behavior is measured until the change stabilizes. (B)
3. Then the intervention is withdrawn, and baseline conditions are reestablished. (A)
4. Once the behavior under baseline conditions stabilizes, the intervention takes place again. (B)

Figure 10-7 shows an actual case in which this reversal design was used to assess the overall impact of an O.B. Mod. approach on absenteeism in a bank. A real advantage of this design was that the subject(s) served as their own controls. The problem of intersubject variability inherent in even a classic control group experimental design was eliminated. However, the disadvantage of this potentially powerful design is that it assumes that the behavior is able to be reversed when returning to baseline conditions. Other things taking place in the environment may take over to sustain the dependent variable and thus undermine this assumption. Some of our own applications of reversal designs indicate that the assumption

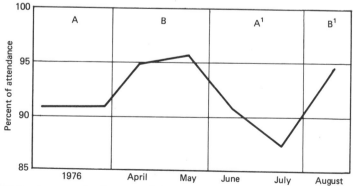

FIGURE 10-7. An example of a reversal design used to evaluate an O. B. Mod. program to increase attendance of bank employees (Luthans and Maris, 1979).

does not always hold. In a series of seven case studies that employed a reversal design to evaluate the impact of an O.B. Mod. approach to various kinds of performance behavior in a variety of settings, it was found that in all cases the behavior significantly improved, but in only four of the seven cases did a reversal take place (Luthans and Bond, 1977). In addition, a very understandable problem in using reversals is how to persuade results-minded managers to return to baseline conditions if an intervention is having the desired impact. Few managers are willing to sacrifice results in order to make a cause-and-effect evaluation of the program.

To get around some of the potential problems of reversals, especially the practical problem of reversing desired results, a multiple-baseline design is another approach that could be used. It is applied in the following manner:

1. Baseline data are obtained on two or more kinds of behavior (or individuals or situations).
2. An intervention technique is then applied to one kind of behavior, but baseline conditions are maintained on the other(s).
3. Once the behavior has stabilized after the intervention, the next kind of behavior becomes the subject of the intervention technique.
4. This continues until all the behavior is brought under control by the intervention strategy.

Figure 10-8 shows such a multiple baseline evaluation of an O.B. Mod. program in a small manufacturing plant. The left-hand portion of the graph depicts the average levels and variability of both quantity and quality of performance prior to intervention. The next segment of the graph displays the effects of a contingent time-off intervention on quantity when on consequences were being applied to quality. As evidenced by the changes illustrated, quantity improved with the application of the contingent time-off consequences, while the quality level, for which consequences were not changed, remained about the same. The third segment then demonstrates the positive impact of the contingent application of social reinforcers on quality, while the quantity levels remained about the same. Finally, the last segment demonstrates improved levels of both quality and quantity of performance under the control of a feedback system and contingent social reinforcement. This type of staggered intervention or multiple baseline design has advantages similar to the reversal, but at the same time eliminates the practical problem of reversing the behavior. It does, however, make the assumption of noninterdependence between the kinds of behavior being evaluated. In some cases changing one behavior (or individual or situation) may cause the other to change.

Besides the reversal and multiple baseline designs, the more traditional control group experimental design can be used to evaluate the O.B. Mod. approach. Figures 10-9 and 10-10 show two such evaluations. Figure

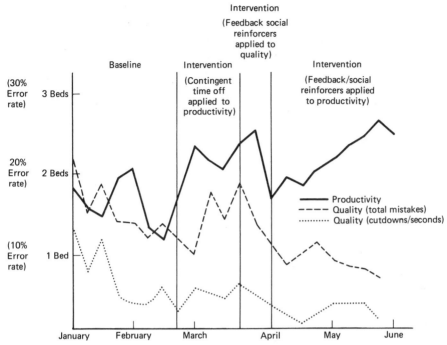

FIGURE 10-8. Multiple baseline design to evaluate the overall performance results of an O. B. Mod. program in a small factory (Luthans and Schweizer, 1979).

10-9 shows the results of the program in a manufacturing plant. The departments of experimental groups—those supervisors who used O.B. Mod. as outlined in the five-step model—clearly outperformed the control group's departments. All other variables except the O.B. Mod. approach were basically the same for both groups. The same is true for the evaluation shown in Figure 10-10. Retail clerks in a large department store who had an O.B. Mod. type of approach used on them significantly improved their

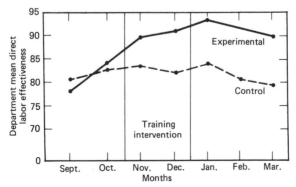

FIGURE 10-9. A control group design used to evaluate the impact of an O. B. Mod. program on the productivity of a manufacturing plant (Otteman and Luthans, 1975).

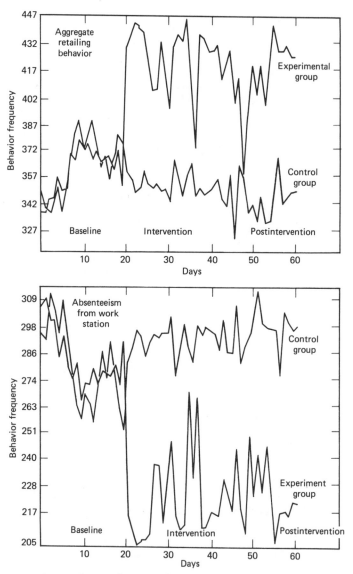

FIGURE 10-10. A control group design used to evaluate the impact of an O. B. Mod. program on sales persons' performance behavior (Luthans, Paul, and Baker, 1981).

performance behavior (increased aggregate retailing behavior such as selling and stockwork, and decreased idle time and absence from the assigned work area). With the control group of clerks, who had everything else basically the same but were not under the O.B. Mod. approach, performance remained the same.

Obviously most practicing human resource managers cannot be expected to do the extensive type of evaluation described above. However, the first three levels—reaction, learning, and behavioral change—should be constantly monitored by anyone using the O.B. Mod. approach. In addition, it is also recommended that if O.B. Mod. is implemented as an overall approach to improve productivity, then the reversal, multiple baseline, or control group designs be used to conduct an evaluation.

SUMMARY

Most of today's organizations are faced with the challenge of improving their productivity. Old, tried solutions from either the technological or managerial perspectives are not meeting this challenge. The time is ripe for new thinking and new approaches that work. A five-step problem solving model has been suggested here as one approach to help today's managers more effectively manage their human resources and improve performance.

The first step is to *identify* the critical behavior that will lead to performance improvement. Like any problem solving model, this initial step is vital to all that follows. It should be an observable behavior that has a direct, important impact on performance. Examples would include quality and quantity behavior, safety behavior, and tardiness-promptness or at-tendance-absenteeism behavior. The second step is to *measure* the performance behavior identified in Step 1. A baseline measure determines the frequency of the behavior under current conditions. Usually this measurement can be derived from existing data, but in some cases there must be a tailor-made measurement technique. Such a measurement approach assures that the O.B. Mod. approach is data-based and provides needed information for the subsequent steps of the model. Step 3 is to *analyze* the antecedents (e.g. standards, job instructions, equipment) and consequences (rewards, punishers, feedback) surrounding the behavior that has been identified and measured. The purpose of this third step is to gain a better understanding of what is going on and provide important information for developing an effective intervention strategy. The fourth step is to actually *intervene* with a strategy that will accelerate desirable, goal-oriented performance behavior and decelerate undesirable, dysfunctional behavior. Primarily a feedback-social reward intervention strategy is depended upon because of the problems associated with punishment. The fifth and final step is to *evaluate* to insure that the strategy is having its intended impact and performance is indeed improving.

This five-step model has been systematically evaluated by reversal, multiple-baseline, and control group experimental designs. The results are very encouraging. Managers who systematically follow the five steps of the O.B. Mod. model can not only help solve specific behavior problems they are faced with on a daily basis, but can begin to meet the overall challenges to improve productivity now and in the future.

REFERENCES

Ammons, R. B. Effects of knowledge of performance: A survey and tentative theoretical formulation. *Journal of General Psychology*, 1956, *56*, 279–299.

Anderson, R., Kulhavy, R., and Andre, T. Feedback procedures in programmed instruction. *Journal of Educational Psychology*, 1971, *62*, 148–156.

Annett, J. *Feedback and human behavior*. Baltimore: Penguin, 1969.

At Emery Air Freight: Positive reinforcement boosts performance. *Organizational Dynamics*, Winter 1973, 41–50.

Blood, M. R. Intergroup comparisons of intraperson differences: Rewards from the job. *Personnel Psychology*, Spring 1973, 1–9.

Campbell, D. T., and Stanley, J. C. *Experimental and quasi-experimental designs for research*. Chicago: Rand McNally, 1963.

Connellan, T. *How to improve human performance*. New York: Harper and Row, 1978.

Cook, D. M. The impact on managers of frequency of feedback. *Academy of Management Journal*, 1968, *11*, 263–277.

Flippo, E. B., and Munsinger, G. *Management: A behavioral approach* (3rd ed.). Boston: Allyn and Bacon, 1975.

Hamner, C., and Organ, D. W. *Organizational behavior*. Dallas: Business Publications, Inc., 1978.

Hermann, J. A., deMontes, A. I., Dominguez, B., Montes, F., and Hopkins, B. L. Effects of bonuses for punctuality on the tardiness of industrial workers. *Journal of Applied Behavior Analysis*, 1973, *6*, 563–570.

Hundal, P. S. Knowledge of performance as an incentive in repetitive industrial work. *Journal of Applied Psychology*, June 1969, 224–226.

Ilgen, D. R., Fisher, C. D., and Taylor, M. S. Consequences of individual feedback on behavior in organizations. *Journal of Applied Psychology*, 1979, *64*, 349–371.

Johnston, J. M., Duncan, P. K., Monroe, C., and Stoerziner, A. Tactics and benefits of behavioral measurement in business. *Journal of Organizational Behavior Management*, 1978, *1*, 164–178.

Lockwood, D. L., and Luthans, F. Multiple measures to assess the impact of organization development interventions. In *The 1980 Annual Handbook for Group Facilitators*. San Diego: University Associates, 1980, pp. 233–245.

Luthans, F. *Organizational behavior*. New York: McGraw-Hill, 1981.

Luthans, F. Resolved: Functional analysis is the best technique for diagnostic evaluation of organizational behavior. In Karmel, B. (Ed.), *Point and counterpoint in organizational behavior*. Hinsdale, IL: Dryden, 1980, 48–60; 81–83.

Luthans, F., and Bond, K. M. The use of reversal designs in organizational behavior research In R. L. Taylor et al. (Ed), *Academy of Management Proceedings*, 1977, 86–90.

Luthans, F., and Kreitner, R. The management of behavioral contingencies. *Personnel*, July-August, 1974, 7–16.

Luthans, F., and Kreitner, R. *Organizational behavior modification*. Glenview, IL: Scott, Foresman, 1975.

Luthans, F., and Maris, T. L. Evaluating personnel programs through the reversal technique. *Personnel Journal*, October 1979, pp. 692–697.

Luthans, F., and Martinko, M. An O.B. Mod. analysis of absenteeism. *Human Resource Management*, Fall 1976, 11–18.

Luthans, F., and Schweizer, J. How behavior modification techniques can improve total organizational performance. *Management Review*, 1979, *68*, 43–50.

Miller, L. M. *Behavior management*. New York: Wiley, 1978.

Nadler, D. A. The effects of feedback on task group behavior: A review of the experimental research. *Organizational Behavior and Human Performance*, 1979, *23*, 309–338.

Ottemann, R., and Luthans, F. An experimental analysis of the effectiveness of an organizational behavior modification program in industry. In A. G. Bedeian et al. (Eds.), *Academy of Management Proceedings*, 1975, 140–142.

Performance audit, feedback, and positive reinforcement. *Training and Development Journal*, November 1972, 8–13.

Reitz, H. J. Managerial attitudes and perceived contingencies between performance and organizational response. *Academy of Management Proceedings*, 1970, 227–238.

Skinner, B. F. *Contingencies of reinforcement*. New York: Appleton-Century-Crofts, 1969.

Snyder, C. A., and Luthans, F. The application of O.B. Mod. to increase the productivity of hospital personnel. *Personnel Administrator* (in press).

Special report: Performance feedback and positive reinforcement. *Training*, December 1976, 15–56.

Thoresen, C. E., and Mahoney, M. J. *Behavioral self-control*. New York: Holt, Rinehart and Winston, 1974.

11

Developing Performance Feedback Systems

JOHN A. FAIRBANK

and

DONALD M. PRUE

Jackson Veterans Administration Medical Center
and
University of Mississippi Medical Center

Ms. Jones, the general manager of the photofinishing division of a large newspaper and magazine publishing company, had been advised by corporate cost-efficiency analysts that, due to sudden unanticipated increases in the market value of silver, the cost of photographic paper coated with silver nitrate had increased dramatically. They warned that, at the rate at which the photofinishing division currently used silver nitrate photographic paper, the company stood to suffer a reduction in their annual profits of hundreds of thousands of dollars.

Determined to find a solution to this problem, Ms. Jones instructed her assistant to carefully monitor quantities of silver nitrate paper used by the division's three shifts of photofinishers. Results indicated that during a one-week period a total of 30 thousand sheets were used, but only 10 thousand pictures were printed, an unacceptably high waste-to-use ratio of photographic paper. Ms. Jones instructed her assistant to identify the specific factors responsible for high rates of waste. This analysis indicated that waste resulted from (1) repetitive and careless mistakes in exposure time, (2) unnecessary duplication of prints, and (3) loss due to soiling and spoilage as a function of improper handling or storage of paper. At a scheduled intradivisional management meeting, Ms. Jones informed her production manager and operations supervisors of the details of this problem. She instructed them to meet with each shift of photofinishers in order to encourage them to decrease current levels of photographic paper waste and to provide them with specific procedures for doing so. Subsequently, rates of paper waste decreased significantly, but several weeks later they returned to previous high levels.

Disappointed but undaunted, Ms. Jones began to meet with her production manager and operations supervisors on a biweekly basis for the purpose of providing them with feedback on the amount of paper wasted during the preceding two-week period. Waste decreased progressively over the next few weeks with no adverse side effects on photofinishing productivity rate or quality. After six months of regularly scheduled biweekly feedback meetings, Ms. Jones found that she could maintain low rates of waste by scheduling performance feedback meetings with her management staff at monthly intervals. Eventually Ms. Jones transferred responsibility for the waste-reduction performance feedback program to her administrative assistant with no loss in program effectiveness.

The above vignette describes an effective, relatively uncomplicated, and increasingly popular procedure for modifying behavior in organizational settings, performance feedback. Feedback intervention strategies, designed to provide information to individuals or groups about the quantity or quality of their performance, have been impressively effective in producing organizational change. Organizational problems such as waste (Eldridge, Lemasters, and Szypot, 1978), employee productivity (Parsons, 1974), absenteeism (Kempen and Hall, 1977), and supervisor effectiveness (Bourdon, 1977), to name but a few examples, have all been effectively modified using performance feedback techniques. Numerous other examples of the efficacy of performance feedback techniques are noted throughout this book.

The goal of the present chapter is to provide a framework for developing and implementing more comprehensive and effective performance feedback systems in organizational settings. An overview of performance feedback will first be presented, to be followed by a set of guidelines for evaluating the suitability of feedback techniques for organizational performance problems. Next, five parameters of feedback that require careful consideration when planning a performance feedback system will be discussed. Specific guidelines for developing feedback systems from among the numerous options available will then be offered. Finally, a summary section will discuss the implications of this chapter for future development of performance feedback systems.

OVERVIEW OF PERFORMANCE FEEDBACK INTERVENTION TECHNIQUES

Advantages of Feedback

Besides effectiveness, performance feedback systems have a number of other characteristics that make them attractive. One of the primary advantages has been their relatively low economic costs to organizations.

Feedback techniques have been reported to be less expensive to implement than other productivity-enhancement techniques (cf. At Emery Airfreight: Positive Reinforcement Boosts Performance, 1973). Significant investments of organizational resources into expensive accounting, legal, or other support systems are usually not required to implement and maintain effective performance feedback programs. Also organizations employing performance feedback systems do not have to rely upon often expensive employee incentive or reward programs.

Another advantage of performance feedback programs is simplicity of implementation. First, prolonged, cumbersome, and sophisticated training programs are seldom required to change target behavior (Sulzer-Azaroff and deSantamaria, 1980). Although managerial personnel sometimes receive detailed training in the technology of behavior analysis (Bourdon, 1977), simple instruction on how to provide positive feedback to employees is more often sufficient for managerial personnel to successfully implement feedback interventions. Second, although feedback interventions occasionally require the development of mechanisms to collect performance information, it is more often the case that organizations have existing information or accounting systems that offer easy access to performance data (Hall, 1979; Stoerzinger, Johnston, Pisor, and Monroe, 1978). In these latter cases the behavior analyst simply identifies relevant sources of performance information and then instructs organizational personnel on the use of extant sources to provide feedback.

Still another advantage of performance feedback techniques is decreased use of punishment procedures, such as unsystematic criticism, docked time, warnings, or other disciplinary action. Skinner (1953) has observed that punishment, or the threat of punishment, is the typical "control" procedure employed within organizations. For example, employees typically arrive at work on time to avoid the immediate aversive consequence of being fired from their jobs, not to earn the more distant positive consequence of their paychecks. In contrast, informal observations of the behavior and comments of workers in organizations that have employed performance feedback systems suggest that changes in worker behavior can be initiated and maintained without reliance upon the use of disciplinary procedures (Komaki, Barwick, and Scott, 1978).

Lastly, performance feedback techniques are attractive in organizations that may not have access to other intervention strategies. Many organizations find their ability to use monetary incentives or rewards for increased productivity restricted by factors such as union constraints. These organizations find that feedback techniques are one of the few options available to change employee behavior.

In summary, characteristics such as effectiveness, low cost, simplicity of implementation, and positive emphasis make performance feedback an attractive intervention technique for organizations. These advantages have permitted performance feedback programs to be implemented in organizations with varying resources, from small, owner-operated retail businesses with few employees (Komaki, Waddell, and Pearce, 1977) to large multidivisional corporations (Runnion, Watson, and McWhorter, 1978) and institutions with numerous employees (Prue, Krapfl, Noah, Cannon, and Maley, 1980).

Why Is Performance Feedback Effective?

Historically, changes in employee behavior that follow feedback intervention have been attributed to the effects of feedback as a reinforcer. A reinforcer is defined as any event that increases the probability of occurrence of behavior that it follows. The following example illustrates how performance feedback might be considered a reinforcer. The accounting department of a large metropolitan utility employs two shifts of keypunch operators. Although the personnel profiles (e.g., average age, sex, level of training, and experience) for employees on each shift are comparable in every way, the second shift makes significantly more programming errors than the first shift. In an attempt to increase the quality of performance of the second shift, management begins to publicly post a chart that compares the weekly percentage of correctly typed programs for each shift. After one month percentages of correctly typed programs increase for both shifts, with no significant difference between the two. Since increased production quality followed the feedback intervention, management might then consider feedback as a reinforcer. Yet, as straightforward as a reinforcement interpretation of feedback effects seems to be, it merely describes the more obvious changes in performance that follow feedback intervention. Elsewhere (Prue and Fairbank, 1981) we have argued that feedback intervention often produces additional subtle changes in organizational behavior that might contribute to the dramatic success of performance feedback systems, but have been neglected in prior interpretations of feedback.

One such effect occurs when performance feedback instructs employees in the behavioral requirements of their position. When a supervisor provides verbal feedback to an employee—"Tom, the mileage on your truck this week was over 10 m.p.g. That is 2 m.p.g. above our goal. Keep up the good work"—he or she is informing employees of job-related behavior of concern to the organization. These feedback-based "instructions" presumably specify job performance procedures or standards of importance to the organization. The instruction function of feedback may act much like a more formal change in an employees' job description or contract. Also, since feedback sessions typically are repeated over time, they continue to notify the employee of what their supervisors consider to be critical features of organizational functioning. The overall impact is to inform individuals or groups of workers at all levels of the expected or "now to be enforced" performance criteria operating within an organization. Evidence for this point has been provided by Locke and his colleagues (Locke, Cartledge, and Koeppel, 1968), who have argued that performance feedback always implicitly states a performance standard.

Another explanation of feedback effects, and one that appears to be especially important in organizations that rely upon public display of performance information, occurs when performance within an organization is below standard. Instruction regarding the feedback intervention, as well as the intervention itself, may lead individuals or groups within an organization to meet performance standards in order to avoid potentially aversive consequences associated with the public posting of low levels of performance. The aversive consequences may take the form of embarrassment over low productivity, or they may involve more tangible consequences such as supervisor or co-worker disfavor. For example, public posting of number of work days missed might act as an impetus for employees to decrease absenteeism to avoid supervisor or co-worker disfavor resulting from the perception that the individual is not doing a fair share of the work.

Performance feedback interactions may lead to other changes in the organizational environment that could account for some of the effects of feedback on behavior. One possible change would be modification of the manner in which people interact in an organization during a feedback intervention. For example, supervisors may begin to interact more, or perhaps differently, with workers as a function of feedback intervention. In addition, the quality of interpersonal interactions within levels of an organization may also change. For example, Prue et al. (1980) noted that the topic of conversation among employees seemed to increasingly center on job-related issues and activities during and following feedback intervention. Prue et al. (1980) suggested that some of the behavioral changes that followed the feedback intervention might have been related to these feedback-associated changes in the way organizational members interacted. Others (Parsons, 1974; Pedalino and Gamboa, 1974) have noted that competition, another form of interpersonal interaction often associated with performance feedback intervention, can play a significant role in motivating employee behavior change.

Finally, the effectiveness of feedback systems upon performance may be enhanced by increased job satisfaction during feedback intervention. For example, Sims and Szilagyi (1975) found that employees are more satisfied and report being more productive when they receive information based upon objective evaluations of their performance. Since the latter is the hallmark of feedback intervention, it is likely that feedback techniques are accompanied by increased employee satisfaction that might enhance performance apart from effects associated with reinforcement or other environmental changes.

The relative contributions of each of the above effects to the dramatic success of feedback intervention remains unclear at this time. However, the fact that feedback can play an instrumental role in organizational change, and that there are a number of likely interpretations of its effects, suggests that future feedback interventions should attempt to maximize both instructional and reinforcement effects of feedback.

DETERMINING THE SUITABILITY OF PERFORMANCE FEEDBACK INTERVENTIONS FOR ORGANIZATIONAL PROBLEMS

A careful analysis of organizational performance problems is mandatory when considering the application of performance feedback techniques. In point of fact, several authors (Ellsworth, 1973; Nadler, Mirvis, and Cammann, 1976; Oberg, 1972) have warned that performance feedback intervention can inadvertently boomerang, producing negative consequences such as low worker morale, when applied without an adequate a priori analysis of the organizational performance problem. Quite simply, not every organizational problem that results in a performance decrement represents an appropriate intervention for performance feedback. One situation in which feedback may not be appropriate is poor performance due to inadequate job skills. If workers have not received the specialized training required for adequate performance, then performance feedback intervention alone is not likely to lead to acceptable levels of performance. More subtly, when an employee lacks information on how to improve performance, feedback is unlikely to help him or her solve performance problems.

Another situation in which feedback might be inappropriate would be when structural characteristics of a task are at the root of the performance problem. For instance, extended restaurant turnaround time between when an order is received and when preparation of the meal is completed may be only partially related to the cook's performance. A more important factor might be the length of time it takes to cook food.

Finally, unknown, ambiguous, or unreasonable standards of performance also set the occasion for low rates of performance within organizations. Several investigators (Kim and Hamner, 1976; Locke, Cartledge, and Koeppel, 1968; Nemeroff and Cosentino, 1979) have shown that unspecified or unknown performance standards diminish the effect of feedback intervention. Consequently, when individuals at various levels within an organization fail to agree upon standards of performance, the effects of a feedback intervention upon performance are less likely to be predictable and positive.

The outcome of all these situations is generally a failure to improve performance with feedback alone. Additionally, extended periods of feedback on poor levels of performance may be aversive and lead to a number of unintended side effects, such as employees leaving the organization. The following are offered as task analysis guidelines for determining the suitability of performance feedback techniques for modification of organizational performance problems.

1. Determine if individuals within the organization possess the requisite skills for adequate job performance.
2. If workers do not possess the necessary skills for adequate job performance, implement appropriate training programs, personnel actions, etc.

3. After teaching the necessary job skills, reassess the need for performance feedback.

4. If lack of skills or knowledge was not a component of the performance problem, assess reasons for unacceptable performance. Identify the relative contributions of worker behavior and other factors (e.g., structural characteristics of the task) to the low performance level.

5. Determine the performance standards operating within an organization and their clarity. If performance standards are ambiguous or unreasonable, set new standards upon which an organizational consensus can be reached.

6. After performance standards are established, reassess the need for a performance feedback intervention.

SELECTING PERFORMANCE MEASURES

Once the suitability of performance feedback as an intervention technique has been established, the question of which measures of performance should be targeted for feedback can be addressed. For performance problems that are circumscribed to a specific individual or group within an organization, often a single measure of performance is sufficient to document an intervention effect. However, when performance problems are complex, or when they involve individuals or groups from diverse levels within an organization, multiple measures of performance are often more appropriate. The two types of performance measures that should be considered for inclusion in any feedback intervention are outcome and process measures (Gilbert, 1978; Nadler, 1979; Nadler et al., 1976). In general, outcome measures of performance refer to organizationally valued accomplishments of individuals or groups. Outcome factors are usually measures of individual or group performance that are directly related to the ultimate success or failure of the organization. Typical examples of organizational outcome measures include number of objects assembled per hour by line operators, total dollar amounts of sales by franchised dealers, and number of extended service warranty contracts issued by sales personnel. Many measurable outcome factors can be identified by using existing organizational data that document quantity, quality, time, or cost of performance. Examination of inventory control mechanisms, sales records, accounting practices, and so forth often provides a wealth of important organizational outcome data. In contrast to outcome measures, process factors refer to measures of compliance with organizational procedures, rules, or guidelines considered essential for the accomplishment of organizational goals. Process factors may also include measures of any other activities engaged in by workers during performance of their jobs (Mollenhoff, 1977). Common examples of organizational process measures are latency of report filing, numbers of telephone solicitations of potential customers, hours worked, frequency of intragroup communications, absenteeism, and orderliness of work areas.

In selecting between outcome or process measures of performance the primary requirement is to identify the important parameters of the organizational problem in question, as well as ways to measure these parameters. Generally it is more desirable to provide feedback on outcome measures. Results are what matter most to organizations, and therefore they should be the basis for performance measures. However, process measures are sometimes easier to obtain and are typically selected for use in feedback systems when results occur infrequently (e.g., number of industrial safety accidents) or are not easily measured (e.g., number of clients who show improved psychological functioning at the end of treatment), or when process measures relate directly to the attainment of important organizational results (e.g., number of suggestions for improvements in productivity).

PARAMETERS OF FEEDBACK INTERVENTIONS

Feedback systems can be implemented in a variety of different ways. Five parameters on which feedback interventions can vary are discussed in this section:

1. Recipients.
2. Content.
3. Temporal characteristics.
4. Mechanism.
5. Source.

The discussion of each parameter includes a brief description of possible variations.

Recipients of Feedback

An initial consideration in feedback intervention in organizational settings is to identify the intended recipients of the performance information. Studies in the feedback literature have provided information to both individuals and groups about their performance. Information distributed to groups has been further divided into data about the performance of individuals within the group, or about the performance of the group as a unit. Feedback can also be delivered either privately, when performance information is shared only with a targeted individual or group, or publicly, when performance information is shared with the targeted individual and also provided to other individuals. Factors to consider when choosing appropriate recipients of feedback include the generally greater success of public feedback (Welsh, Ludwig, Radiker, and Krapfl, 1973), the amount of resources available for the intervention (e.g., private feedback sessions are labor intensive), and the ability of organizational members to carry out the intervention (e.g., private feedback requires socially skilled managers to conduct sessions).

Content of Feedback

Another important parameter of feedback intervention systems is the specific content of the information provided to recipients. As noted above, feedback can focus on output or process measures of performance (Nadler, 1979; Nadler et al., 1976). The content can also vary with respect to how the performance measures are derived from available data. That is, feedback may include (1) comparison of an individual's performance with his or her previous performance; (2) comparison of an individual's performance with a standard performance, which is determined by the performance of a large number of individuals; (3) comparison of a group's performance (performance of individuals not important) with its previous performance; (4) comparison of a group's performance with a standard group performance; and (5) presentation of individual's performance as a percentage of group's performance. The determination of which of the above should be employed is based on several considerations. One is the type of information available. Are data available on individual employee productivity, or do data represent a group effort? Another consideration is comparability of performance of different groups or individuals, e.g., are tasks similar enough to allow meaningful comparisons? Another factor is the specific type of information to be included in the feedback message, e.g., praise for appropriate performance, statements of goals, constructive criticism, and so forth.

Temporal Characteristics of Feedback

The third parameter of feedback involves the question of when and how often feedback should be provided. There are two major temporal characteristics of feedback. The first is the total duration of the feedback interaction. Duration is clearly a function of the content of as well as the mechanism employed to deliver the performance information. It may range from a short glance at a printout counter to an extensive performance analysis interview. In most cases duration plays an interdependent role with other feedback parameters, and thus is not a significant factor in and of itself in the overall effectiveness of an intervention.

The second and more significant temporal characteristic is the contiguity between performance and feedback, that is, the length of time between performance and feedback. Feedback may be provided immediately after performance of a targeted behavior or after a delay. In the latter case feedback, delivered on daily (Shook, Johnson, and Uhlman, 1978), semiweekly (Sulzer-Azaroff and deSantamaria, 1980), weekly (Andrasik and McNamara, 1977), bi- and triweekly (Komaki et al., 1977) and monthly (Miller, 1977) schedules, has been reported to be effective in changing employee target behavior. Important considerations regarding the contiguity of feedback with performance include task complexity (e.g., is feedback provided for relatively simple or complex tasks?), rate of feedback (e.g., is performance feedback scheduled as a relatively frequent or infrequent event?) and the content of feedback (e.g., outcome versus process feedback). With respect to the latter dimension, Tosti and Jackson (1981) suggest that feedback provided to change the topography of an employee's performance, a process feedback system, should only be provided when an individual has the opportunity to immediately practice or try out the new performance. For example, feedback on how to load pallets should be provided sometime during the actual working day rather than at the end of the day when employees would not have the opportunity to modify their performance based upon the feedback.

Feedback Mechanisms

Another characteristic of feedback is the type of mechanism used to deliver the performance data. Four basic feedback mechanisms (verbal, written, mechanical, and self-recorded) have been used in the organizational behavior management literature.

Verbal Feedback.   Perhaps the most common method of providing feedback within organizations has been verbal feedback in one-to-one interpersonal interactions. The following statement, cited by Eldridge, Lemasters, and Szypot (1978), describes a simple face-to-face verbal feedback interaction from a supervisor to an employee. "Today your piece yield is at 60 percent. That's higher than yesterday." As this brief example shows, the advantages of face-to-face verbal performance feedback include short duration and contiguity of feedback with performance. Yet the simplicity of verbal feedback may be deceptive. Verbal feedback intervention must take into account the interpersonal skills of individuals delivering the feedback, the past history of interpersonal interactions between the providers and recipients of feedback, and the physical proximity of recipients to providers.

Written Feedback.   Another mechanism commonly used to provide performance data to employees has been written feedback. Written feedback has been provided in a variety of ways, including written personal communications (Weitz, Antoinetti, and Wallace, 1954); memos (Kreitner, Reif, and Morris, 1977); newsletters (Patterson, Cooke, and Liberman, 1972); and public posting of performance information (Quilitch, 1975). Traditional written evaluations, typically placed in employees' files, are also a form of written feedback. Typically, publicly posted performance feedback is provided in terms of a graphical display in which quantifiable performance measures (e.g., number of days absent, total sales in dollars) are charted over time. All forms of written feedback, however, must take into account the potential advantages (e.g., employees have a record of performance to show co-workers, friends or spouses for additional reinforcement) and disadvantages (e.g., employee embarrassment and anger over public posting of low rates of performance) of permanent documentation of performance.

Mechanical Feedback. Still another method of providing performance feedback has been the delivery of performance data via mechanical devices. Examples of this type of delivery include videotape feedback (Bricker, Morgan, and Grabowski, 1972; Walter, 1975) and electromechanically operated tape printouts (Parsons, 1974). For instance, Parsons noted that the Hawthorne data demonstrated that simply providing employees with a continuous, electromechanical record of their daily output increased productivity. Although the application of mechanical devices to deliver feedback has not received much research attention, the future for mechanical feedback systems looks particularly bright. The low cost, usually continuous and immediate nature of delivery and the fact that once mechanical devices are established they are likely to be maintained are potential benefits of mechanical feedback mechanisms.

Self-Recorded Feedback. Another feedback delivery mechanism is to have employees generate their own feedback by self-recording their performance (Komaki, Blood, and Holder, 1980). This feedback mechanism, commonly called self-monitoring, has been applied to a wide range of clinical problems, but has received less attention in organizational intervention. A number of recent studies, however, have demonstrated the utility of this feedback mechanism in organizational intervention. Komaki, Blood, and Holder (1980) used a self-monitoring procedure to increase smiling and conversation between a fast food restaurant's employees and customers by having workers self-monitor their performance. Lamal and Benfield (1978) increased the punctuality and on-task behavior of an employee with self-monitoring. Prue et al. (1980) combined self-monitoring with three different types of feedback to increase employee treatment activities in a hospital. Potential advantages of self-recorded feedback include the high level of employee participation in the intervention, and its applicability to situations in which employees are not closely supervised. Its also useful when there are no physical products of the behavior of concern (e.g., number of positive comments to employees by supervisors), or when process variables play an important role in the employees' overall productivity (e.g., effective use of time). These advantages must be weighed against potential disadvantages such as employee subversion of the system, and cost of devising an independent procedure for assessing the reliability of self-report data.

Source of Feedback

The final parameter of performance feedback intervention is the source of feedback. The organizational behavior management (OBM) literature reveals that performance feedback has been effectively provided by supervisors of varying rank (Chandler, 1977; Sulzer-Azaroff and de-Santamaria, 1980). Feedback has been provided by subordinates (Hegarty, 1974), co-workers (Greller, 1980), outside consultants (Komaki et al., 1977), the targeted employees themselves (Lamal and Benfield, 1978), and a variety of mechanical devices (Ford, 1980; Parsons, 1974). Unfortunately, there have been no reports in the OBM literature of well-controlled studies comparing the outcome effectiveness and cost-efficiency of these sources of feedback upon performance measures. Further, the effects of different sources may interact with the status and power of the provider of feedback and the history of interactions between the recipients and providers of feedback.

GUIDELINES FOR DEVELOPING PERFORMANCE FEEDBACK SYSTEMS

The preceding section introduced five parameters of feedback systems and briefly described the alternatives within each. Since no single procedure for developing effective performance feedback systems exists, the purpose of this section will be to provide guidelines for designing a system that takes into account the numerous options available. This will be a best-guess effort, since very few studies have compared different feedback systems in organizational settings. References from the organizational behavior management literature will be cited to provide distinctions on the effects of the different options.

1. Feedback messages should be precise and objective (Brethower and Rummler, 1966; Hamner and Hamner, 1976). Effective feedback messages need only to convey information specific to targeted performance measures. Externally verifiable quantitative or qualitative aspects of performance, exclusive of subjective standards or bias, should always be emphasized.

2. Insure that organizational performance goals are specified and understood by feedback providers and recipients prior to implementation of any feedback system. This is important, since feedback systems have been reported to be more effective when accompanied by goal setting, a procedure for specifying performance standards whereby employees are assigned specific amounts of work to be accomplished (Kim and Hamner, 1976; Nemeroff and Cosentino, 1979).

3. Whenever possible, feedback systems should be yoked to the compensation system, i.e., pay and incentive formats, of the organization to enhance the effects of both the feedback and compensation systems.

4. Prior to developing performance feedback systems, consider the

potential of specific components to produce detrimental side effects within the organization. For example, individual feedback provided to group members often produces competition as a side effect. If interdependence exists between individual performance and the behavior of others, carefully weigh the potentially negative long-term side effects of intragroup competition against the long-term positive effects of the overall feedback program. Similarly, group feedback may have undesirable side effects. For instance, before providing group feedback to individuals with diverse but interrelated jobs, consider the potentially disadvantageous effects of groups making an individual a scapegoat for inadequate group performance. Regarding private and public dimensions of feedback intervention, consider: (1) the potential for negative employee response to public feedback (e.g., public posting) especially when baseline performance levels are low; (2) the costs to the work force of private feedback systems upon organizational resources (e.g., supervisor time); and (3) the problems involved in attempting to implement private feedback programs in organizations where feedback providers lack good interpersonal skills.

5.   Provide feedback on several relevant outcome or process measures of performance when possible. If only a single performance measure is employed in a feedback system, recipients may fail to attend to other important aspects of their jobs. This may have detrimental effects upon organizational functioning. Also, when process feedback is employed to improve the performance of work tasks, employees should be queried regarding how *they* think their performance should change. This should facilitate employee cooperation with implementation of feedback systems.

6.   Utilize multiple sources of feedback at varying levels of the organizational structure (Sulzer-Azaroff and deSantamaria, 1980). This will decrease the likelihood of feedback drift, i.e., the tendency to drift from feedback based upon objective performance standards to feedback based upon subjective bias. Participation of individuals and groups at multiple levels of the organizational structure is also likely to increase the probability of program maintenance.

7.   Whenever possible use multiple feedback mechanisms. This may increase the durability (maintenance) of feedback programs, since recipients are less likely to become overly accustomed, or habituated, to one particular feedback mechanism. For example, include both written and verbal feedback on performance. Whenever possible, use feedback mechanisms that fit within the organizational structure, e.g., feedback during regularly scheduled planning meetings, since these feedback systems are more likely to be maintained. The limitations of various approaches to delivering feedback must be taken into account when developing performance feedback systems. For example, personal individual verbal feedback may not be the feedback mechanism of choice in organizations in which supervisors and workers have little opportunity for daily face-to-face contact (e.g., truck drivers).

8.   Basic experimental literature suggests that contiguous feedback is

best for increasing performance proficiency on complex tasks (Hall, 1966). For simple tasks, however, delayed feedback appears to be effective using a variety of interval schedules, e.g., semiweekly, weekly, or monthly.

9.   Provide individual feedback when a situation calls for an individual to initiate a behavior, and when the individual has the opportunity to immediately practice the new behavior. Individual feedback appears to be especially effective in shaping new rates of performance. Also, rely on individual feedback when baseline rates of behavior are low or when providing criticism of past performance.

10.   Provide group feedback when organizational goals require cooperation or there is an interdependent function to individuals' performance. Group feedback is also the procedure of choice when it is difficult to distinguish any one individual's contribution to the total performance, and when total performance is greater than the sum of differentiated individual performances. Also, use group feedback when group affiliation, often a process measure of performance, is an important organizational consideration.

11.   Feedback should be delivered frequently, i.e., daily or semiweekly, when implementing a performance feedback system. Frequent performance feedback is recommended in order to familiarize targeted individuals and groups with the system, and more importantly, to expose them to the relationship between their performance and feedback content. As performance stabilizes at acceptable levels, the frequency of feedback often may be decreased. In point of fact, satisfactory steady-state performance may often be maintained with relatively long interfeedback intervals, e.g., monthly or bimonthly.

The following case study illustrates how these guidelines may be used to develop an effective feedback intervention system for an organizational performance problem.

Mr. Smith is the owner of a fleet of taxicabs that operate in the suburbs of a major northeastern city. He employs more than 200 drivers, many of whom work part-time afternoons, nights, and on weekends to supplement their incomes. During a recent 10-month period an increasing number of Mr. Smith's drivers were assaulted or robbed while on duty. As a result, his business had experienced a greater than usual employee turnover rate. Concurrently, he began to have problems recruiting adequate numbers of replacement drivers, which resulted in idle cabs and decreased company profits. Termination interviews with several drivers who had resigned indicated that they quit primarily out of concern for their safety. These events alarmed Mr. Smith, as he was genuinely concerned about the safety of his employees, and he knew that the success of his business depended upon maintaining a large pool of experienced part-time drivers.

Analysis of the situation by a consultant indicated that the frequency of assaults and robberies of drivers could be reduced if driver-operated safety devices were installed in each cab. At a meeting with driver representatives it was agreed that if Mr. Smith installed protective equipment in the cabs, the drivers would use them as part of their routine operating procedure. Following this agreement, he had a number of expensive safety features and protective devices installed in each of his cabs. These included a driver-operated door locking system, an impact-resistant safety glass divider between the driver and passenger compartments, a locked cash deposit box that could not be opened by the driver or removed from the cab, and a two-way intercom system for driver and passenger communication. In addition, he arranged for each driver to be trained to properly use the safety equipment. Then Mr. Smith and representatives of his drivers drafted standards and regulations for use of safety equipment by drivers.

Several months after installation of the safety devices, completion of training, and adoption of safety regulations, Mr. Smith was disappointed to learn that neither the rate of assaults upon drivers nor driver turnover rate had decreased substantially. An analysis of the circumstances surrounding each robbery or assault revealed that most of the drivers had, at the time of the robbery, failed to comply with one or more of the rules governing use of safety equipment. Although company regulations required drivers to use the devices, threats and implementation of punitive measures for violations of safety standards, such as suspension or dismissal, had little effect upon employee compliance with safety regulations. At this point, faced with seemingly interrelated problems of low rates of driver adherence to regulations regarding use of safety equipment in company cabs, high rates of assault and robbery upon drivers, and high driver attrition rates, Mr. Smith decided to consider developing and implementing an intervention program based upon the principles of performance feedback presented in this chapter.

His initial step in developing a performance feedback program was to specifically assess the suitability of this type of intervention for the organizational problems with which he was concerned. To rule out the possibility that performance decrements were primarily due to drivers' skills deficits, to structural characteristics of the job, or to misunderstood, unreasonable, or ambiguous performance goals, he followed the task analysis steps outlined earlier in this chapter. Only after determining that (1) his drivers had indeed acquired the necessary skills to utilize safety devices effectively, (2) structural characteristics of cab driving itself did not interfere with the proper use of safety devices, and (3) organizational standards and goals were clearly stated and understood by drivers, did he begin to devise a performance feedback system. His first decision involved choosing appropriate measures of performance. Specifically, he had to decide which process or outcome measures of the organizational performance problem to use in the intervention. He elected to primarily rely on a process measure of driver performance, rate of adherence to company safety regulations in the intervention. He felt strongly that the rate of adherence to safety regulations was directly related to each of the outcome measures in which he was ultimately interested. Also the outcome measures, robberies or assaults and turnover rate, occurred less frequently than the process measure of performance. However, to provide his drivers with additional relevant measures of their performance, he also gave feedback on these outcome measures.

Mr. Smith's next decision involved choosing a feedback mechanism. Should he provide performance information to his drivers using verbal, written, self-recorded, or mechanical feedback? In answering this question, he considered his proximity to the intended recipients of feedback messages, the drivers. Since he realized that he would have little opportunity for daily face to face contact with many of his drivers, he decided against using personal verbal feedback as the primary mechanism for his feedback system. Because his employees were generally unsupervised when driving their cabs, he decided to provide feedback on adherence to safety regulations by using a system that included both self-recorded and written feedback mechanisms. Regarding the former type of feedback mechanism, he designed an easy and quick "safety equipment checklist" that was completed by the driver each time a customer entered the cab. This checklist provided drivers with immediate feedback on their performance. The reliability of this self-monitoring feedback mechanism was evaluated by having trained observers pose as customers and make intermittent checks of drivers' adherence to safety regulations. One week prior to implementation of this self-monitoring feedback procedure, drivers were informed that checks would be made throughout the course of intervention. In addition to self-monitored feedback, Mr. Smith also provided his drivers with written feedback by the public display of group performance rates for the selected outcome and process measures. The content of publicly posted group feedback was selected so that overall group performance was compared with both a company performance standard and the group's previous performance. The combination of self-monitored and written feedback insured that the content of feedback messages included precise and objective information that was specific to targeted employee behavior.

With respect to the temporal characteristics of feedback, drivers' self-monitoring provided feedback that was contiguous with performance of the tasks of interest, while written group feedback was provided on a weekly basis. Following the guidelines for developing performance feedback systems that were presented in this chapter, Mr. Smith began to experiment with thinner feedback schedules once performance rates stabilized.

He also tied his performance feedback program to an incentive plan in order to enhance the effects of each. Each week that drivers met the organizational standard for compliance with safety regulations, they received a cash bonus amounting to 5 percent of their earnings for the week.

The feedback program was implemented on a trial basis for a period of one month. At the end of this period the effectiveness of the program was evaluated, and necessary adjustments were made. Mr. Smith noted a steady increase in driver adherence to safety measures during the trial period, with performance levels meeting company standards by the third week. Thus he found that he had designed a flexible performance feedback program that could be adjusted to suit the various aspects of his employee performance problem. In addition, he was pleased to find that over a several month period, robbery and assault rates had declined significantly, and employee turnover rate had ceased to be a major problem for his company.

SUMMARY

This chapter has attempted to provide a framework for developing and implementing comprehensive and effective performance feedback systems designed to fit the administrative structure of organizations. The specific components of feedback systems were delineated, and guidelines for developing and implementing flexible, efficient, and effective feedback systems were presented. These guidelines emphasized general rules that can be successfully applied to specific organizational performance problems. However, due to a lack of definitive research on the relative effectiveness of various system options, some of these guidelines might most appropriately be viewed as best-guess recommendations. Hopefully, the present chapter will serve both as a guide for developing effective feedback systems and an impetus for initiating the systematic research required to determine the necessary and sufficient components of effective performance feedback systems.

REFERENCES

Andrasik, F., and McNamara, J. R. Optimizing staff performance in an institutional behavior change system. *Behavior Modification,* 1977, *1,* 235–248.

At Emery Air Freight: Positive reinforcement boosts performance. *Organizational Dynamics,* 1973, *1,* 41–50.

Bourdon, R. D. A token economy application to management performance improvement. *Journal of Organizational Behavior Management,* 1977, *1,* 23–38.

Brethower, D. M., and Rummler, G. A. For improved work performance: Accentuate the positive. *Personnel,* September–October 1966, 40–48.

Bricker, W. A., Morgan, D. G., and Grabowski, J. G. Development and maintenance of a behavior modification repertoire of cottage attendants through T. V. feedback. *American Journal of Mental Deficiency,* 1972, *77,* 128–136.

Chandler, A. B. Decreasing negative comments and increasing performance of a shift supervisor. *Journal of Organizational Behavior Management,* 1977, *1,* 99–103.

Eldridge, L., Lemasters, S., and Szypot, B. A performance feedback intervention to reduce waste: Performance data and participant responses. *Journal of Organizational Behavior Management,* 1978, *1,* 258–266.

Ellsworth, R. B. Feedback: Asset or liability in improving treatment effectiveness? *Journal of Consulting and Clinical Psychology,* 1973, *40,* 383–393.

Ford, J. E. A classification system for feedback procedures. *Journal of Organizational Behavior Management*, 1980, *2*, 183–191.

Gilbert, T. F. *Human competence: Engineering worthy performance.* New York: McGraw-Hill, 1978.

Greller, M. M. Evaluation of feedback sources as a function of role and organizational level. *Journal of Applied Psychology*, 1980, *65*, 24–27.

Hall, B. H. Issues in assessing an organization. Paper presented at the fifth annual meeting of the Association for Behavior Analysis, Dearborn, MI, 1979.

Hall, J. F. *The psychology of learning.* Philadelphia: J. B. Lippincott Co., 1966.

Hamner, W. C., and Hamner, E. P. Behavior modification and the bottom line. *Organizational Dynamics*, Spring 1976, 3–21.

Hegarty, W. H. Using subordinate ratings to elicit behavioral changes in supervisors. *Journal of Applied Psychology*, 1974, *59*, 764–766.

Kempen, R. W., and Hall, R. V. Reduction of industrial absenteeism: Results of a behavioral approach. *Journal of Organizational Behavior Management*, 1977, *1*, 1–21.

Kim, J. S. and Hamner, W. C. Effect of performance feedback and goal setting on productivity and satisfaction in an organizational setting. *Journal of Applied Psychology*, 1976, *61*, 48–57.

Komaki, J., Barwick, K. D., and Scott, L. R. A behavioral approach to occupational safety: Pinpointing and reinforcing safe performance in a food manufacturing plant. *Journal of Applied Psychology*, 1978, *63*, 434–445.

Komaki, J., Blood, M. R., and Holder, D. Fostering friendliness in a fast food franchise. *Journal of Organizational Behavior Management*, 1980, *2*, 151–164.

Komaki, J., Waddell, W. M., and Pearce, J. G. The applied behavior analysis approach and individual employees: Improving performance in two small businesses. *Organizational Behavior and Human Performance*, 1977, *19*, 337–352.

Kreitner, R., Reif, W. E., and Morris, M. Measuring the impact of feedback on the performance of mental health technicians. *Journal of Organizational Behavior Management*, 1977, *1*, 105–109.

Lamal, P. A., and Benfield, A. The effect of self-monitoring on job tardiness and percentage of time spent working. *Journal of Organizational Behavior Management*, 1978, *1*, 142–149.

Locke, E. A., Cartledge, N., and Koeppel, J. Motivational effects of knowledge of results: A goal-setting phenomenon. *Psychological Bulletin*, 1968, *70*, 474–485.

Miller, L. M. Improving sales and forecast accuracy in a nationwide sales organization. *Journal of Organizational Behavior Management*, 1977, *1*, 39–51.

Mollenhoff, C. V. How to measure work by professionals. *Management Review*, November 1977, 39–43.

Nadler, D. A. The effects of feedback on task group behavior: A review of the experimental research. *Organizational Behavior and Human Performance*, 1979, *23*, 309–338.

Nadler, D., Mirvis, P., and Cammann, C. The ongoing feedback system: Experimenting with a new managerial tool. *Organizational Dynamics*, 1976, *4*, 63–80.

Nemeroff, W. F., and Cosentino, J. Utilizing feedback and goal setting to increase performance appraisal interview skills of managers. *Academy of Management Journal*, 1979, *22*, 566–576.

Oberg, W. Make performance appraisal relevant. *Harvard Business Review*, 1972, *50*, 61–67.

Parsons, H. M. What happened at Hawthorne? *Science*, 1974, *183*, 922–932.

Patterson, R., Cooke, C., and Liberman, R. P. Reinforcing the reinforcers: A method of supplying feedback to nursing personnel. *Behavior Therapy*, 1972, *3*, 444–446.

Pedalino, E., and Gamboa, V. U. Behavior modification and absenteeism: Intervention in one industrial setting. *Journal of Applied Psychology*, 1974, *59*, 694–698.

Prue, D. M., and Fairbank, J. A. Performance feedback in organizational behavior management: A review. *Journal of Organizational Behavior Management*, 1981, *3*, 1–16.

Prue, D. M., Krapfl, J. E., Noah, J. C., Cannon, S., and Maley, R. F. Managing the treatment activities of state hospital staff. *Journal of Organizational Behavior Management*, 1980, *2*, 165–181.

Quilitch, H. R. A comparison of three staff-management procedures. *Journal of Applied Behavior Analysis*, 1975, *8*, 59–66.

Runnion, A., Johnson, T., and McWhorter, J. The effects of feedback and reinforcement on truck turnaround time in materials transportation. *Journal of Organizational Behavior Management*, 1978, *1*, 110–117.

Shook, G. L., Johnson, C. M., and Uhlman, W. F. The effects of response effort reduction, instructions, group and individual feedback, and reinforcement on staff performance. *Journal of Organizational Behavior Management*, 1978, *1*, 206–215.

Sims, H. P., and Szilagyi, A. D. Leader reward behavior and subordinate satisfaction and performance. *Organizational Behavior and Human Performance*, 1975, *14*, 426–438.

Skinner, B. F. *Science and human behavior*. New York: MacMillan, 1953.

Stoerzinger, A., Johnston, J. M., Pisor, K., and Monroe, C. Implementation and evaluation of a feedback system for employees on a salvage operation. *Journal of Organizational Behavior Management*, 1978, *1*, 268–280.

Sulzer-Azaroff, B., and deSantamaria, M. C. Industrial safety hazard reduction through performance feedback. *Journal of Applied Behavior Analysis*, 1980, *13*, 287–295.

Tosti, D., and Jackson, S. Formative and summative feedback. Paper presented at the seventh annual meeting of the Association for Behavior Analysis, Milwaukee, WI, 1981.

Walter, G. A. Effects of videotape feedback and modeling on the behaviors of task group members. *Human Relations*, 1975, *28*, 121–138.

Weitz, J., Antoinetti, J., and Wallace, S. R. The effect of home office contact on sales performance. *Personnel Psychology*, 1954, *1*, 381–384.

Welsch, W. V., Ludwig, C., Radiker, J. E., and Krapfl, J. E. Effects of feedback on daily completion of behavior modification projects. *Mental Retardation*, 1973, *11*, 24–46.

12

Strategic Planning for Employee Productivity Improvement

BRANDON L. HALL
Wilson Learning Corporation

For some time there has been a set of effective principles of behavior and an evolving set of procedures derived from applied behavior analysis technology. The greatest difficulty has been the attempt to tie the procedures to a client's particular needs. Too frequently behavior analysts have had a solution in hand and have gone in search of a problem without full consideration of effective consulting strategies identified in the counsulting literature (Blake, Mouton, and Srygley, 1976; Hunt 1977; *Management Consulting*, 1979; Lippitt and Lippitt, 1978; Steele, 1975; Fuchs, 1975; Albert, 1980). This chapter describes a planning procedure designed to tie an improvement program to the objectives of the target organization. It is only in this way that a productivity improvement program will get sufficient attention from those in line management positions to make things happen. Their support is necessary to have the program achieve its results and to have those results maintained over time.

One of the trickier problems consultants have had has been developing ways to make a program successful when it is purchased by someone high in the organization, but where the focus is on improvement at the bottom of the organization. It is all too easy for a vice president of manufacturing to say, "Go into one of my plants and improve productivity." That makes for a difficult entry when the consultant goes knocking on a plant manager's door and says, "Hi, we are here at your boss's request to improve the way you are doing things." One alternative is to improve the situation by not stressing that it is management's mandate when the consultant arrives on site. However, this may lead to the easy option of refusing the services, or to not having sufficient influence to make the program really successful. Therefore, the better solution is to make the mandate stronger rather than simply have the appearance on-site be mandated. This involves working with top management to clarify program needs, objectives, and activities.

Let me set the tone for the chapter and preface its content by explaining the title. "Strategic planning" is a wonderful buzz-word. Who can argue with it? It suggests something long-range and implies considering all the ramifications of one's plans. "Human productivity improvement" also sounds pretty good. There was a time not long ago when productivity improvement meant fellows walking around the factory carrying stop watches and clip boards, with speed-ups and job eliminations soon to follow. Now, however, many in business, and even outside of business, realize the tremendous economic need throughout the country for greater productivity and more efficient use of our resources. We have long relied in this country on technological breakthroughs for our significant productivity improvements. However, more and more organizations are beginning to realize that they also need to implement programs to improve the productivity of their human resource. For example, General Motors has designated billions of dollars for upgrade of its plants and machinery over the next several years, but it has also set aside funds for employee productivity and quality of work life programs. Until recently, there was not an effective technology for doing this, but now human productivity improvement programs are becoming more effective.

This chapter will detail one way to work with the top management of an organization, whether that be corporate or division management or the top management group at an individual facility. It is a way to work with the top management that will translate their general notion of wanting productivity improvement to a specific plan that will identify several phases of an improvement program over a several year period. This strategic planning has four separate components, which will be described in the chapter.

1. *Mission statement.* Development of long-range organizational goals. This is the identification of the overall goals that the management group wants to work toward as an organization. This is most frequently a five-year or so look ahead, and it should take into consideration the constraints on the organization (the musts) as well as the wants of the organization.

2. *Ideal management practices.* This is the identification of those practices and procedures that need to be in place throughout the organization in order to achieve the goals identified in the mission statement. The most effective way for a consultant to help an organization over the long run is not to go in and solve any one given problem but rather to examine the management practices that are currently in place and help that organization implement new man-

agement procedures that are basic to the achievement of goals within the organization. This may include fundamental management practices such as MBO or a performance measurement system, and may also include newer practices such as quality circles.

3. *Assessment of current management practices.* This procedure is an attempt to answer the question concerning which of the ideal management practices identified above are currently in place and how well they are working. It also examines the current achievement level of the performance goals identified in the mission statement.

4. *Improvement program planning.* This is an overall, several-year plan, which is designed to reduce the difference between the ideal management practices and the current management practices to better achieve the identified performance goals. It includes priorities for improvement, programs to be implemented, and schedules for completion of successive phases. When this long-term plan is finalized, the programs and objectives for improvement for the next one-year period is specified.

This procedure is designed to improve the most significant factor in the success of the entry stage with an organization, namely, the clear linkage between the top manager who wants a productivity improvement program and a program that will achieve the results desired, survive over time, and be accepted and supported by people in the organization.

Many times programs based on behavior modification procedures, or some other type of improvement program appears to those in the organization as a "quick fix." The most important job a consultant can do is to avoid this problem by insuring that the improvement program is fully integrated into the current business objectives of the organization. Otherwise it will simply not receive the attention and support required to achieve results. If the line managers in the organization can see that this program will help them to achieve their objectives, then they will make it work rather than simply see the program as a make-work exercise.

MISSION STATEMENT

A mission statement means different things to different people. It should identify long-range goals for the organization, including specific business objectives as well as less easily quantifiable objectives such as relations with outside organizations, statements about the desired culture of the organization, and so on. It should identify those goals and objectives for the organization that are both long-range and high priority. It should identify both the area of the objectives and indicate the general level of achievement to be worked toward for that area. Most groups find that a five-year time frame for the look ahead is both reasonable and workable.

Developing a mission statement gives the top management the opportunity to communicate to the organization, and among themselves, what they expect the organization to become in the next several years. As such, it communicates to people what they should be working toward.

The form of a mission statement will vary greatly from organization to organization, based on the type of business as well as the type of group that develops the statement. It should reflect the character of the top management group and their priorities, and thus may reflect more or less of a focus on specific business objectives, or on describing the organizational characteristics and relations with outside groups. It should include goals and objectives that could be described as "musts" and "wants." The musts are the demands placed on the organization from outside groups, which may be corporate management, regulatory agencies, labor groups, and so on. The musts are generally defined as such because of the significant downside costs should these objectives not be met. The wants are the balance of the objectives. For all of the objectives the internal and external demands of the organization need to be considered. The mission statement should define where top management wants the organization to go but not how to get there. The "how" will be addressed in the following section. Defining the mission of the organization requires considerable vision and leadership of the top management group. It is up to them to consider the external demands on the organization and for them to identify the ultimate goals for the group. The mission statement provides the broadest goals that the organization can rally around, strive for, and take pride in the accomplishment of. Defining the mission of the organization is one of the most important activities for top management; no subgroup can do this job. It provides the basis from which all policies, programs, objectives, and activities should spring.

An example of a mission statement from a large manufacturing facility is given below. (This example has been adapted from several mission statements for different organizations to protect proprietary information.)

Business Performance

1. Safe work place: Provide a safe work environment for employees.
2. Environmental compliance: Perform operations in a manner that will insure compliance with environmental regulations.
3. Equal employment opportunity: Comply with all laws and regulations in regard to equal opportunity in all aspects of employment relationships.
4. Reliable production equipment: Sustain a high level of production equipment reliability to insure that we meet our production commitments and are perceived as a reliable supplier.
5. High efficiency of operations: Sustain high efficiency levels in all indexed areas, including the use of energy, utilization of workers, control of cost, and deployment of capital.

People Management

1. High job competence: Maintain an employee work force that is highly competent in the performance of the tasks required to meet our business needs.
2. Meeting corporation manpower needs: Recruit, train, and develop qualified employees to supply corporation needs, while continuing to fulfill our own organization requirements.
3. Maximize individual productivity: For all members of our organization.
4. Maximize employee involvement: Provide an environment that encourages teamwork among individuals and maximizes employee involvement.
5. High enjoyment and satisfaction: Create an environment that promotes personally satisfying work, while efficiently achieving company business objectives.

Organizational Culture

1. High management credibility and trust: Maintain a high level of credibility and trust with all employees.
2. Balance between high productivity and concern for people: Maintain a proper balance of emphasis between concern for high productivity and concern for employee job satisfaction.
3. Open communication: Establish effective multidirectional (upward, downward, and lateral) communications among all employees.
4. Commitment to and ownership of strategy: Achieve understanding and a high level of ownership of the long-range strategies by all employees.
5. Increase innovation: Increase the amount of organizational improvement activities to assist in achieving the organization's objective.
6. Strong productivity ethic: Develop organizational commitments to an ethic of high productivity, which is in the interest of each individual, our organization, the company, and the nation.
7. Nondiscriminatory ethic: Achieve dedication throughout the organization to an ethic of nondiscrimination to allow realization of each individual's full potential and self-satisfaction.

External Relationships

1. Positive relations with government agencies: Work to establish positive relationships with state and local agencies.

2. Good working relationship with corporations: Maintain an open and constructive working relationship with other corporations.

3. Good corporate citizen: Be recognized as a good corporate citizen in the community and the state.

4. Concern for employees' families: Demonstrate greater interest in employees' families through additional programs that include family participation.

How to Develop the Mission Statement

The mission statement for an organizational unit can by definition be developed only by the policy making group. It is most frequently done at the corporate level, the division level, or the individual facility (factory) level.

The statement can be developed in a structured, intensive, two-day off-site meeting. It needs to be off-site to limit interruptions and to provide an environment to encourage stepping out of the day-to-day activities to take a longer view. It should be structured, and led by a facilitator to make sure that boundaries for the discussion are set and adhered to, and that the group makes appropriate progress toward the expected outcome. It needs to be intensive because the issues cannot be addressed in a casual manner, and it needs to be accomplished as quickly as possible because there is a business to be run back at the shop. An alternative to the off-site, intensive meeting is to develop the mission statement over a period of weeks during shorter, on-site meetings. Although this allows more time for consideration, it takes longer and allows more opportunities for getting off track.

After clarification of the result to be expected, the time frame, and the ground rules for the discussion, the process begins. Although a member of the group can serve as the facilitator, it is beneficial to use a trained facilitator who has gone through the activity before, and who can be the one concerned with keeping the group on track, so that the group members can each concentrate on the content. The most effective way to proceed, if this is the first attempt at a long-range plan, is to have the group members call out areas they would like to see included in the mission statement. All of these are written on an easel pad, and additional sheets are posted on the wall as needed. After an hour or two, most distinct areas will have been listed, and further suggestions from the group will become redundant. At this point, the group identifies categories for the areas listed. This will involve some negotiation and restatement, but the group will soon come up with a number of cateogries that encompass the areas previously listed. The group then modifies lists within the category, adding or changing as appropriate. (There is no attempt to convert these general areas into sentences; this should be done by subgroups after returns from the meeting.) This process will usually take a full day. The second day will be spent on identifying the ideal management practices, to be discussed next.

IDEAL MANAGEMENT PRACTICES

The mission statement identified the long-range goals for the organization in terms of areas and levels of achievement. The ideal management practices exercise identifies basic management procedures that management wants to see in place throughout the organization. It should answer the question, "What practices need to be in place in order to consistently achieve the levels of performance we desire?" It identifies what the top management group sees as basic good management. It identifies the minimal requirements for management within the organization. It allows management to find, and really to learn, what their own and other managers' philosophy of management is. It helps them to find what management procedures they believe in, what they think are necessary and valuable, and what they want to require throughout the organization. This is often a very enlightening experience for managers. Just as there are many different views about the organization's mission and goal, so too there are often many views of what good management consists of.

In most organizations these discussions never take place. Unfortunately, there is very little training or continuing development in these areas either. It is usually assumed that once a person is promoted past the first level of supervision, he or she knows all that is needed about how to manage. In addition, people assume management practices are a reflection of individual style, and that no one can say that one set of practices is better than another set of practices. Some say that management practices need to be consistent with one's overall style and that to attempt to specify some basic procedures takes away from a manager's autonomy. It is usually assumed that managers have all the information necessary to know the best way, and are sufficiently motivated to do all they should be doing in managing their subordinates. But this is often not true. If one wants to significantly improve the effectiveness of management of an organization to more fully achieve bottom-line results, there is a need to identify the best management procedures for use in that particular environment. One also needs to insure coordination among managers in using these practices, and for these practices to become part of the overall organizational culture.

Getting basic management procedures to occur consistently throughout an organization needs to be managed just like any other activity in the organization. Management needs to define specifically what they expect; they need to make sure that their subordinates have the knowledge and skills to apply the procedures; and they need to hold those subordinates accountable for carrying out those management practices. If you look at any organization that consistently gets exceptional results, you will find that this is consistently the case. These companies have an entire language, even a subculture, around how they manage, and the things they do to assure that performance levels desired are achieved. They do not hesitate to specify how they expect subordinates to carry out the management task, and they do not leave it simply to individual whim to do so.

As part of a productivity improvement program this is even more important, because there will be changes in procedures and practices. The proper management accountability practices need to be in place to insure that these changes last over time and do not disappear when the program formally ends.

Defining the Management Practices

What are some of these ideal management practices? One must identify those procedures of management that affect the performance of people within the organization. Miller (1978) has a list of management practices that is both behavioral and managerial: behavioral in the sense that the procedures specify the activities in terms of their influence on behavior, and managerial in the sense that the procedures define currently existing practices, familiar to most managers. The practices are listed under five categories. The first three resemble the three-part behavioral paradigm of antecedents, behavior, and consequences. The remaining two categories list other activities necessary for effectiveness at work. Miller's (1978) list is provided below:

Direction.   The presentation prior to performance of stimulus events that evoke the desired performance.

> Policy communication: The communication of all policies that are intended to affect employee behavior in a manner that results in the desired performance.
>
> Planning: The process of defining performance direction and output and establishing long-term objectives based on considerations of all input or resource variables.
>
> Job description: The definition and communication of job functions in a manner that results in performance consistent with that description.
>
> Objective setting: The process of determining short-term (one year or less) measurable results, the actions required, and the date by which the results are to be achieved.
>
> Instruction: The verbal or written direction provided to employees, which directs short-term activities.
>
> Communication: The verbal interaction between the manager and employee through which information regarding job performance is given and received.
>
> Modeling: The procedure of observing a behavior or set of behavior and subsequently imitating them.

Performance Measurement and Feedback.   The measurement of behavior or results of behavior of both individuals and groups of individuals, and the presentation of that data in a manner that provides for comparison over time and between groups or individuals.

Data systems: Ongoing systems that record and report the results of performance.

Feedback systems: Ongoing systems that provide data on performance to those individuals whose behavior results in the performance.

Performance appraisal: Evaluation of an individual's performance that is comprehensive in scope, conducted periodically, and provides the feedback to the individual required for his or her professional development.

Personal feedback: That informal feedback the manager provides to his or her employees on a daily or regular basis regarding performance.

Management of Consequences. The activities of the manager that result in the presentation or withdrawl of reinforcement or punishment to the individual within the organization.

Salary determination: The procedure of determing an increase or decrease in salary, the size, frequency, and relationship between salary and performance.

Bonus determination: The procedure of determining the size, frequency, and relationship between bonus and performance.

Promotion determination: The procedure whereby promotions are awarded.

Social reinforcement: Those interactions between two individuals in the work setting that result in an increase in a work performance.

Intrinsic reinforcement: Reinforcement that is received in the course of performing the job and is the function of events directly associated with the job itself.

Correcting: Procedures that reduce the occurrence of undesirable behavior.

Problem Solving and Decision Making. Behavior engaged in by either an individual or a group of individuals to arrive at the selection of a problem solution or decision, and which has fully considered all relevant inputs, alternatives, and consequences.

Individual problem solving: The behavior in which an individual engages to select a problem solution after having fully considered the causes of the problem, inputs to a solution, alternatives, and consequences of potential solutions.

Individual decision making: The behavior in which an individual engages to select a course of action that will assure the continued effective functioning of the work process.

Group problem solving and decision making: The behavior engaged in by a group leader and members of a group to arrive at a unified consensus regarding a course of action.

Self-Management. Those activities in which an individual may engage to control other behavior that contributes to productivity.

Managerial self-management: Those activities in which a manager may engage to control his or her own behavior that contributes to his or her productivity.

Employee self-management: Those activities in which the individual employee may engage to manage his or her own behavior that contributes to his or her productivity.

In addition to the list of practices, Miller identifies several indicators, or pinpoints, for each practice, as well as analysis procedures for assessing the existence or effectiveness of the practice, training procedures for improving the practice, and reinforcement procedures to maintain the activities. Hall (1981) has identified four management practices that are necessary to insure proper accountability for performance of a manager and his or her area:

1. *Identify Key Indicators of Performance.*   The purpose is to identify and agree on those few performance data indicators that reflect the important performance areas for that individual.

No matter what may exist in terms of objectives or an MBO system, the bottom line is: What numbers (indicators) is the boss going to look at on a regular basis to tell whether that subordinate (with his or her group) is doing his or her job? These should be few in number and reflective of the major responsibilities.

All organizations have some type of data system that managers look at. But is is necessary to make sure that boss and subordinate agree on which numbers are most important.

In many cases, the problem is not that there is poor agreement on what the important data areas are, but that the data system is not very good at providing information on performance. If so, it may be necessary to revise the data system so that it provides data that is accurate, timely, and individualized for that group.

2. *Establish Monthly or Weekly Group Data Review Meetings.*   The purpose is to review progress against objectives and completion of management activities, and to identify action steps for each member of the group.

The purpose of establishing accountability meetings is to provide a cornerstone for the accountability process—where performance against objectives and completion of management activities can be reviewed, and where problem solving and action planning can take place.

These meetings should be monthly at the upper and middle levels, and weekly at the lower levels. The meetings would be similar in function to those in the team system described by Foxworthy, Ellis, and McLead (in press).

The content of these meetings for middle and upper levels of management should include the following:

(a) *Communication* of recent developments (both up and down).

(b) *Review* of performance on the key performance indicators. If improving: reinforcement and recognition. If not improving: corrective feedback and problem solving.

(c) *Action plan* for improving the performance of the group. Develop a program to improve the data. Then identify action steps to be completed between now and the next meeting (these are written down and reviewed at the next meeting).

Having meetings of this sort on a regular, frequent basis is an effective way to establish a thread of continuity among peers at each level, and from each level to other levels all the way down the line. It provides the opportunity for communication of developments, for discussion of problems or upcoming issues, for recognition and feedback, and for corrective action when necessary.

3. *Clarify Job Expectations.*   The purpose is to establish an agreement between boss and subordinate concerning the major job responsibilites, how those responsibilities should be executed, and the frequency and content of communication between the boss and subordinate.

The subordinate and superior could each write a draft of their view of job expectations for the subordinate's position, followed by a discussion and negotiation between the two, resulting in one written document. This one- to two-page written document should be discussed during the quarterly performance feedback sessions.

There may be some resistance to this clarification of job expectations among some managers. It is not as common a management activity as the others listed here, and the need for it is often not appreciated by the superior (although the subordinate usually sees a need for it). There might also be the concern that what this produces is just a job description. But a job description is a somewhat formal document that identifies work requirements for that position, whereas the job expectations document focuses on some of the more subtle aspects of the job, how the superior expects the job should be executed, how frequently he or she wants to be kept informed, areas of opportunity for the subordinate to develop and so on.

4. *Conduct Quarterly Informal Performance Feedback Sessions.*   The purpose is to provide feedback to each subordinate on his or her performance, and to develop an improvement program to be reviewed at the next feedback session.

The performance appraisal process in many organizations is so structured and infrequent that it often has little real effect on improving performance. The purpose of the more frequent, informal performance review discussion is to allow the boss to provide the subordinate with current feedback, related to the way he or she is conducting the job today, and to provide the subordinate with some specific areas for improvement.

These discussions should be informal and should occur quarterly. (At the start of these new procedures, or for someone new in a position, they need to occur monthly for the first two or three months.) The focus of discussion should be the subordinate's actual current performance on his or her objectives, and on the agreed-to job expectations, as well as other strengths or weaknesses that have become apparent since the last discussion.

An important part of the discussion should be the identification of some specific areas for improvement on which the subordinate should work. A form can be developed for listing improvement steps in a systematic way. This should then be reviewed at the next feedback discussion.

There are other procedures that can be identified by management as their ideal management practices. Many organizations have a strong concern for employee involvement and so may wish to identify participative management practices, or worker involvement through procedures such as quality circles (Bodek and Scanlan, 1981), a team system (Foxworthy, Ellis, and McLead, in press), or similar procedures.

Procedures for Identifying Ideal Management Practices

The top management group that defined the mission statement for the organization should also be the ones to begin the process of identifying the management practices.

In working with a top management group to identify ideal management practices, the following sequence of steps can be effective.

1. *Seminar on Management Practices.* Before a management group can agree on what procedures it considers valuable and worthwhile to implement, it is necessary for them to be knowledgeable about management procedures. They need to know what procedures are commonly used, what are the difficulties and benefits of various practices, and which will contribute most to the goals identified in the mission statement.

2. *Agreement on a Set of Practices.* After familiarizing themselves with management practices, the top management group needs to discuss and agree to a set of procedures for use in their organization. Any appropriate group decision making process can be used here, from simple group discussion and agreement, to rank and rating, to more sophisticated normative group techniques. The important part is that the group be satisfied that all voices have been heard and that the decision represents the best thought of the group.

If desired, one can combine the identification of ideal management practices with the development of the mission statement. The mission statement would be developed on Day 1 of the off-site meeting as described in the previous section, and the discussion and negotiation of ideal management practices would take place on Day 2 of the meeting, with the seminar on management practices in the morning and agreement on procedures in the afternoon.

ASSESSMENT

Top management has now developed the mission statement and identified the ideal management practices for the organization. However, it would be unrealistic, and probably catastrophic, to try to implement these management procedures within the organization without first gathering more information about the organization to insure a proper "fit." There are several areas of information to be collected during an organization assessment:

1. *Organization.* What is the structure of the organization? What are the reporting relationships? In what ways does each group relate to the others?

2. *Workflow.* What is the work being performed? How is this process accomplished? Which departments depend on which others to do their work? What are the critical elements in the work process?

3. *Performance Indicators.* What are the most important performance indicators for each department? For what is the department held accountable? How and to whom is this reported?

4. *Organizational Change History.* What have been the major influences in the organization in the last several years? There may be changes in the process, in personnel, in organizational structure. Of particular interest is any previous improvement effort or other work with consultants, trainers, or change agents.

5. *Common Concerns and Problems.* Every organization has its areas of concern and complaints at different levels of the organization. After all, that is frequently why a consultant is called in. A major purpose of the assessment procedure is to determine what each level or department sees as the major problems that inhibit productivity or job satisfaction within the organization.

6. *Plans and Desires for Improvement.* Each group will have their view of the problems, and many of the groups may also have plans or programs in place to correct these problems. It is important that this information be gathered so that the final recommendations to the organization take these programs into consideration.

7. *Current Management Procedures.* This area is the most important and will take up a large part of the assessment effort. It is necessary to

know what practices are currently in place, how they are being executed, the effectiveness of the results, and the view of the participants regarding these practices.

Depending on the time available and the agreements and expectations resulting from defining the ideal management practices, you may want to examine all of those practices that affect the performance of employees (see Miller's list of management practices shown above). On the other hand, you may want to examine only a few practices, such as those that contribute specifically to accountability of a manager's performance (see Hall's list shown above).

In either case the primary information collecting tool is the individual interview. All of top management should be interviewed, as well as a sampling of middle managers, supervisors, and employees. The list of questions provided below serves to collect information on those management practices defined by Miller.

Policy

1. Are there any company policies that cause problems here?
2. Are the policies administered fairly to everyone?

Job Description

1. Do you have a job description? (Ask to see it.)
2. Is it useful and up-to-date?
3. Do you know your responsibilities, or are there any gray areas?

Objectives

1. Do you have written objectives? (Ask to see them.)
2. What are your objectives?
3. Did you help set them? Are they reasonable?
4. How often are they set or adjusted?
5. Does your supervisor go over them with you at specific times? How often? Is there a completion date?
6. What happens if you do not meet your objectives?

Instructions

1. Do you get enough instructions or directions so you know what you are supposed to be doing, and how to do it?
2. When you give instructions, are they followed?

Training

1. Do you feel you were adequately trained for your present job?

2. What kind of additional training would you like to have?

3. Are your subordinates adequately trained by the company?

4. What kind of training would you like for them to have?

Communications

1. Does your supervisor listen to your suggestions and ideas?

2. When you bring up a problem with your supervisor, does he or she do all he or she can to help solve it?

3. Are you kept adequately informed? What other information would you like to have from upper management?

4. Is there adequate communication and cooperation between departments?

Data System

1. What reports do you receive? (Productivity, efficiency, quality, scrap, safety, housekeeping, absenteeism, tardiness, turnover)

2. Which of these reports are really helpful to you?

3. What other data would be helpful to you?

Feedback System

1. What kind of feedback do you get about your performance?

2. What kind of feedback do your subordinates get about how they are doing?

3. What other kind of feedback would you like about how you are doing?

4. How do you know if you are doing well in your job?

Interpersonal Feedback

1. How often does your supervisor tell you that you are doing a good job or a poor job? (Cite last time.)

2. Do you usually hear about the good things or the bad things?

3. Does he or she tell you specifically what you are doing right or wrong, and how to correct it?

4. Would you like your supervisor to give you comments about how you are doing, or how you could improve, more often?

Performance Appraisal

1. Is the performance helpful? Do you learn from it? Why or why not?
2. Is it balanced between positive and negative comments?
3. Does it tell you how to improve?

Salary

1. Are salaries reasonable here?

Bonus

1. Are you on any kind of bonus system? (Describe it.)

Promotions

1. Are the chances for advancement in this company good?
2. Are promotions awarded fairly?

Social Reinforcement

1. Does your manager usually tell you when you are doing well? (Cite last time.) How often?
2. How often do you tell your subordinates that they are doing a good job?
3. Do you feel comfortable telling an employee that he or she is doing well?
4. Is there any department-wide or division-wide recognition for outstanding performance? (Bulletin boards, newsletters, and so on.)
5. When was the last time you received a memo telling you that you did a good job?
6. Does your supervisor place more emphasis on what you do right or what you do wrong?

Correcting

1. Are some workers allowed to get by with poor work when they should be corrected or removed?
2. When workers are told they are doing poorly, are they also told how to improve?
3. Are they told in a reasonable manner, or are they sometimes yelled at?
4. Has anyone ever told you to do something better or different? When, how?

Decision Making

1. Does your boss ask for input on problems or decisions?
2. Does upper management? How often? Last time?
3. When a decision is needed, is it generally arrived at promptly?
4. Are good decisions made?
5. Are you consulted before decisions are made affecting your areas?
6. Is there adequate input on decisions that are made?
7. Are decisions usually made by one person, or by a group of people?

Meetings

1. Are there enough or too many meetings?
2. Are agendas and objectives for meetings specified?
3. Are minutes distributed when appropriate?
4. What meetings do you attend?
5. Are problems clearly defined during meetings when they are discussed?
6. Are meetings usually well conducted? Is time wasted?

Job Satisfaction

1. Do you like working here?
2. What kind of things do you like about working here?
3. Do you have enough say in what you do?
4. Are things getting better or worse around here?
5. Are you satisfied with: company? department? boss? job?
6. What do you like least about working here?

Performance

1. What areas are in need of improvement? (Productivity, quality, efficiency, attendance, turnover, safety, pilferage, scrap, tardiness, housekeeping)
2. What would you like your people to do more of? Less of?
3. What could your employees do to make things run better?
4. Do you have outstanding workers in your area? What makes them so?

Problems

1. What would you change if you were boss?
2. What do employees complain about?

3. Are there conflicts or problems between your department and other departments?

4. What other problems exist here that reduce productivity or job satisfaction?

Although all of the questions cannot be asked during the usual one-hour interview, they can serve as a "menu" from which the interviewer can select question based on the categories most relevant to that setting.

A shorter assessment can focus on the accountability practices listed above. The procedure for evaluating the current execution of these practices is defined below.

1. *Identification of Key Indicators of Performance.* Each department usually has some performance measurement system. However, there is not always agreement on which of the indicators are most important. To assess whether there is agreement on the major performance indicators, ask both the boss and subordinate independently what the six to eight most important indicators are for the subordinate area, and see if the two individuals produce the same list, in the same order.

2. *Regular Group Data Review Meetings.* To determine whether group accountability meetings are already in place and effective, ask all line managers or supervisors how often they meet with their boss, how performance is reviewed, what topics are covered, what other topics they would like to see discussed, and whether long-range problems or improvement plans are ever discussed. In some organizations there may need to be new meetings; in others, simply a revision of existing meetings.

3. *Clarification of Job Expectations.* A simple assessment of the need for clarifying job expectations includes a straightforward process of asking a few specific questions of both the superior and subordinate as in the followings:

   (a) *Ask Subordinates.* Do they feel they have a good understanding of what the boss expects them to do in this job? Are there disagreements with the boss about what they are doing (or not doing), how they are spending time, what they should keep the boss informed of, or who should be making which decisions?

   (b) *Ask Superiors.* Is the subordinate doing those activities in the job that the superior would be doing if he or she were in that job? Are there things on which subordinates should be spending time that they're not, or vice versa? Does the subordinate have the proper perspective about the position, in terms of looking for opportunities, risk taking, innovation, and so on?

If there is substantial disagreement between the two, or if there is strong concern on either side, clairfying job expectations is warranted.

4. *Regular Informal Feedback Sessions.* To determine if there is a

need for this procedure, one should ask subordinates how they think the boss would say they're doing, and what they see as their strengths and weaknesses—nothing in great depth, just the major points. This would be followed by asking the boss the same question concerning how he or she rates the subordinate. If there is good correspondence between the two, there is no problem. If not, it illustrates the need for the feedback session.

Format of the Assessment

Although the content and size of the assessment may vary, there is a basic format that should be followed. The components of this format include Planning and Communication, Data Collection, Problem Solving and Action Planning, and Assessment Report.

Planning and Communication.

   1. *Planning.* An organizational assessment requires a significant amount of resources and can have important ramifications for the members of the organization. As such, it should be adequately planned to insure that all parties have a clear understanding of what will and will not take place, and to help insure that the objectives of the assessment are met. The planning phase should include the following activities:

    (a) Identify the objectives and constraints for the services. Clarifying objectives will insure that all involved share the same expectations for the results of the assessment. A one to two hour meeting with the top management group to define and negotiate objectives should serve this need well. In addition, the same meeting can be used to define the constraints for the services. In essence, this entails stating the "ground rules" for conducting the service: what will and will not be done, what sensitivities that may exist to be aware of.

    (b) Identify and schedule the major activities for the service. This should include interviews, surveys, report writing, and other activities.

    (c) Clarify the roles and responsibilities of the managers and consultant during the assessment. If there are activities that are required of managers during the assessment, these should be specified beforehand. These may include being available for interviews, communicating the assessment activities to their departments, arranging for surveys in their areas, and so on. The role of the consultant should also be specified. This should include responsibilities for coordination of activities, reporting relationship to the management group, frequency of status updates, and so on.

   2. *Communication.* In memo or in meeting, the members of the organization should be told why the assessment is being conducted, what the outcomes from the assessment are, and who will be involved in what

activities during the assessment; and they should be introduced to those who will be conducting the assessment.

These steps will help to insure that as many people as possible know about the assessment and participate in the process and the findings.

Data Collection Activities. A number of procedures can be used to collect data, depending on the objectives and scope of the assessment. The procedures commonly used include the following:

1. *Individual Interview.* The interview process described above can be the most fruitful data collection process. It allows in-depth discussion with individuals about those topics central to the assessment purpose. Interviews should include a cross section of the organization, including members from all levels and areas.

2. *Employee Survey.* Surveys are a popular assessment tool because they allow for the collection of a large amount of information from a large number of participants, with relative ease. A survey can follow the same areas as the questions listed above, or they can address only those areas of concern to a particular group.

3. *Group Facilitation.* Working with a representative group rather than individuals has the advantage of allowing them to define the current situation in their own terms, rather than providing new data to the consultant, and having them provide the summary findings. This encourages a more participative process, which allows the participants to feel greater ownership of the process and the findings. One way to do this is to work with one representative group from each level of the organization (top management, middle management, first-line supervisors, hourly employees) to develop a statement that identifies what they see as the strengths and areas for improvement in current management practices.

4. *Direct Observation.* In addition to learning what people believe and feel about the current management practices, it is useful to collect direct data on those management procedures which are of concern. This may mean checking files for documentation of objectives, existence of performance data, frequency and quality of performance appraisals, existence of disciplinary notices and commendations in employee files, and so on. It may also be appropriate to observe any employee participation meetings, data review meetings, and so on.

Problem Solving and Action Planning. The traditional approach with an organizational assessment is for the consultant to collect data from the participants, then to use that data to draw conclusions and make recommendations on his or her own. Although the consultant may be quite expert concerning organizational problems, there is a significant drawback to this process, namely, that the conclusions and recommendations become the consultant's, not the organization's. The issues of resistance and ownership of ideas and plans become important here, and what is gained by the consultant's expertise may be lost through the organization's resistance.

The alternative is to use groups within the organization to provide input to the conclusions and the recommendations. During the data collection process, representative groups at each level are formed to provide data on current practices. These same groups can be used to provide feedback on the suggested ideal management practices, and on recommendations for implementation. This can be accomplished as follows:

1. Have the representative groups at each level evaluate the suggested ideal management practices, and have them identify potential benefits and pitfalls of the recommended practices.

2. Have the representative groups at each level identify some possible implementation steps (training, follow-up assistance, management reviews) that would be required to implement the ideal management practices for their areas.

Assessment Report. By this time in the assessment, the data collection on site has been completed, as well as the analysis of that data. The final step is to document these findings in the form of an assessment report. The report serves several purposes. First, it allows management to see the raw data that has been collected. Second, it allows the consultant the opportunity to document the analysis of that data, and finally, it allows for the written delineation of the recommendations resulting from the assessment, and any necessary explanations of those recommendations.

In addition to the above, the following documents from the assessment should be included in the report:

1. An analysis of current management practices. Based on the data collection activities, a definition of current procedures should exist, along with an analysis of the effectiveness of those procedures in helping to accomplish the organizational objectives.

2. A statement from each of the representative groups. These should describe their view of the strengths and areas for improvement of current management practices, and their view of the appropriateness of the ideal management practices for their area.

3. An action plan for each section of the organization describing how the new management practices can be implemented in that area.

IMPROVEMENT PROGRAM PLANNING

The purpose of the program planning phase is to design those implementation activities that will move the organization from where it is (according to the assessment) to where it needs to go (according to the ideal management practices). This is a complicated process. It is difficult for a group to sit down and identify who will do what to whom when they have not conducted a large-scale program like this before. It is also difficult to try to identify in this section how planning should be conducted when the content and format of a program can vary as dramatically as the type of organization one might be working with. However, a few common procedural elements can be identified. I will discuss six of these, which contribute most substantially to a successful planning phase and implementation program.

Define the Implementation Activities

The major activities in terms of what will be done as part of the implementation strategy need to be outlined. This should emphasize any training or consulting activities. An example is provided below:

1. Training sessions

    A. Managers
        Two-day seminar for managers and department heads.
        1. Overview of program.
        2. Basics of performance management.
        3. Definition of management roles and responsibilities in the program.

    B. Supervisors
        Each first and second level supervisor will attend two workshops (three days each).

        Objectives: 1. Teach supervisors how to counsel the poor performer, and how to document those discussions.
        2. Teach supervisors positive ways to motivate employees, including positive feedback and reinforcement.
        3. Teach supervisors how to establish effective accountability of employee performance.

        Content: 1. Objective setting.
        2. Specifying and measuring performance.
        3. Providing data-based feedback.
        4. Counseling and documentation of the poor performer.
        5. Use of positive reinforcement.
        6. Developing improvement projects.
        7. Communication skills.
        8. Team building skills.
        9. Group problem solving and accountability.

2. Follow-up consulting
    The activities to be accomplished in the follow-up consulting include the following:

A. Serve as a resource to current departmental meetings and to help establish data review meetings within sections.

B. Sit in on regular team meetings to help the group do the following:

Establish effective accountability practices.

Set functional and cross-functional objectives, where necessary.

Set guidelines for the improvement plans to be developed by each team member during the workshop.

Insure effective group problem solving and communication.

C. One-on-one follow-up with managers and supervisors to insure proper application of management practices and implement action plans.

D. Assist upper management in the development and maintenance of procedures to insure program success and the continued improvement of performance. These include:

Insuring upper management support and participation, including recognition of improved performance.

Initiating problem solving activities as necessary.

Monitoring program progress and performance improvement.

Define Program Results

This section indicates what results are expected from the program. This includes both changes in the process (i.e., management procedures) and changes in the accomplishment of the business objectives (results). The following is an example from a performance improvement program at a large chemical plant:

Management Practices and Procedures to be in Place by the End of the Program.

Improvement in use of business teams to manage the business of each section within the production department.

Establishment of functional operating teams within each section in production and technical, made up of second and first levels to direct day-to-day operations.

Involvement of first and second level supervisor in the objective setting process.

Establishment of an accountability system involving all management from refinery management to first level supervisor in stewarding performance on specific objectives.

Development with each supervisor of the skills necessary to manage their subordinates more effectively. These will include the following:

How to counsel the poor performer and how to document those discussions.

Positive procedures for improving the performance of employees on a day-to-day basis, through the use of positive feedback and reinforcement.

Procedures for establishing accountability among subordinates, including:

(a) Clarifying expectations and objective setting.

(b) Measurement of performance.

(c) Use of data-based feedback.

(d) Use of positive and negative management consequences for performance.

Improvement of Business Results. The skill training for supervisors and the changes in the management procedures and accountability practices, outlined above, are designed to improve the business results for the organization. Specifically, the following levels of accomplishment are expected for each area.

Business Results Area	Target Level
Safety	1.5 disabling injuries (max.) for year
Environmental	No monthly violations; one daily
Water quality	violation (max.) per month
Air quality	100% service factors on all units
Operational availability	2 (max.) unscheduled shutdowns
Of production facilities	for all production units
Production output goals	Achieve 97% of production goals each month
Energy	Attain each monthly goal
Operating expenses	Stay within 2% (+ or −) of budget

Program Review Procedures

Since many programs are designed to improve accountability practices within an organization, it is wise to have the program management procedures serve as an example of good management practices. This applies to many of these program planning and managerial procedures, but particularly to those defining program review procedures. The purpose of these procedures is to insure progress against the program objectives, and to communicate program status to those who need to be kept informed.

There are two types of review procedures that are most frequently used. These include status reports and quarterly program review meetings.

Status Reports. The status report is a written update that details program progress and status. The format and style will vary with program type and individual preference, but will usually be issued monthly. The first section should define current program status relative to the program plan, including: Are activities on schedule? Are they being implemented satisfactorily? What is some of the feedback from participants? What changes in procedure or emphasis are necessary for more effective implementation?

The next section should review the accomplishments of the past month's objectives, and a definition of next month's objectives. The final section can be used to reinforce and give group recognition to those individuals who are doing an exceptional job in the program and to recognize positive results of the work to date.

Quarterly Program Review Meetings. These meetings can be designed to serve a necessary "show and tell" function for upper management, and a recognition function for lower level participants. It is useful to include those upper levels of management who might not be directly involved in the program as a way of educating them about the implementation activities. The second half of the meeting should include a very frank discussion of program results relative to the program objectives and management's expectations. It is the best opportunity for all of those responsible for program success to exchange views with those at higher levels who are responsible for business success. It may be necessary to realign expectations or objectives based on the results to date, or to modify the implementation strategy if the results are not as expected.

Steering Committee

If a program is either complex, long term, or involving a large number of people, a steering committee may be needed to provide ongoing guidance and direction to the program. During such a program there is a continuing need for planning, review of progress, and revision of implementation and steps. It should be this group that is given the responsibility for insuring effective implementation of the agreed-to program strategy. Giving this responsibility to the group, as well as the authority to make decisions, encourages the feeling of ownership among the members for the program. They begin to recognize that it is *their* program.

If the program is very large and includes more than one autonomous division within a facility, a steering committee for each division may be appropriate. For example, in an 1800-employee chemical plant with a program designed for each of two divisions with 130 managers and supervisors each, two separate steering committees make sense.

Clarify Roles and Responsibilities

Implementing a large-scale productivity improvement program is something new and different for an organization. It involves new functions, different tasks and responsibilities, and it may involve new personnel or outside consultants. None of these changes "just happens," nor do they happen without some misunderstanding and conflict. But knowing in advance that these changes need to be implemented, the program planners can work to minimize the resulting conflict. This is done by reaching agreement on what the role and responsibilities are, and communicating them to those involved.

The difficult part is foreseeing what the major or ambiguous areas of responsibilities are to be. However, to the extent possible, the planners need to identify the important areas of responsibility, agree on who will be responsible for what, and communicate this to those who need to be informed.

A related clarification need is the reporting relationships of those working on the program. Basically, who reports to whom on what areas? What is the hierarchy of approvals for program changes? Naturally, this should follow the existing hierarchy of the organization, but steering committees, individuals with new responsibilities, and outside consultants can blur traditional lines. An important rule for outside consultants to keep in mind is not to violate the client's chain-of-command (Foxworthy, 1981). This means that instructions or mandates, or objectives for the program from upper management to lower management, should never be transmitted by the consultant. The same is true for upward communication. Program status or problems need to be communicated by the managers themselves to upper management.

Communicate the Program Plans to the Organization

People don't like change. It is a threat to their security and to their position, power, and reinforcers. Most people will say that the biggest concern is that of the unknown. Therefore, program planners should do what they can to ally these fears while giving as much information about the program as is reasonable, and showing how the members of the organization can "win" with the new changes. The first two questions that need to be answered are: What is it? How will it affect me?

The third significant concern to those in the organization is whether the improvement effort will result in any lasting, substantive changes in the organization. This is particularly true when there have been previous improvement efforts in the organization that were not very helpful and quickly passed from the scene. Questions frequently asked are "Is this going to last after the consultants are gone?" "Is upper management really committed to this?"

The final concern among individuals is whether the improvement effort will be imposed on them, or whether they will have some say in what the improvement activities will be, and how the program is to be implemented. People tend to support a program and benefit from a program much more when they are involved in some of the decision making.

Therefore, those planning the program need to define who will be informed of what, when, and how input will be collected from those lower in the organization. This is true both before the program begins and during the course of the program.

Comment. It is much easier to write about a productivity improvement program than it is to actually develop and implement one. The main reason for this is the wide range of differences among organizations. Organizations differ in geographical regions, industry, and basic organizational culture. For these and other reasons, one cannot use only a single format for planning a large scale program. The planning procedures, like the program itself, will need to be custom designed to fit the needs and the expectations of a given organization. The most one can do is keep in mind the important factors of program success, but otherwise be flexible.

The procedures identified here are a single snapshot of an evolving process. Each engagement with a client provides more information about how to implement programs most effectively, and the procedures one uses evolve over time. In addition, the procedures are somewhat arbitrary. Others use different procedures than those outlined here with good success. Therefore one should not put too much stock in any one procedural viewpoint. The important thing is to learn what you can from alternative procedures that will complement best what you already know, and what meshes satisfactorily with your own consulting style.

SUMMARY

This chapter has described one strategy for planning for employee productivity improvement. The reason such planning is necessary is to insure that whatever performance improvement procedures are installed, they do in fact address those areas of greatest concern to management, and are consistent with the business goals of the organization.

There are four components to the strategic planning process. The first of these is the identification of the organizational mission statement. This statement is a definition of the long-range organizational goals that top management wants the organization to work toward. It should entail a five-year look ahead for the organization, and should include the constraints on the organization as well as the desired business levels. The mission statement is usually developed by the top management group for the facility or division in question, and can be done most effectively by taking the management committee off site for a couple of days, and having the group led by a facilitator who can lead the group through several exercises to identify the long-range goals.

The second component of the strategic planning process is the identification of the ideal management practices. This includes procedures that need to be practiced by all managers in order to accomplish the goals identified in the mission statement. For instance, if one of the goals in the mission statement is to significantly improve quality of product, it may be appropriate to include employee participation or quality circles as one of the procedures to be implemented as part of the ideal management practices. Other procedures that may be included are a performance measurement system, a performance feedback system, an MBO system, and so on.

The third part of the strategic planning process is the assessment of current management practices. Once the ideal management practices are identified, it is necessary to determine which of these practices are currently in place, and how well they are functioning in their contribution to performance improvement.

The final component of the process is the improvement program planning. This is frequently a several year plan, which is designed to install those management procedures considered desirable but which are currently lacking according to the management assessment. It should include priorities for improvement, programs to be implemented, and schedules for completion of successive phases. After the long-range plan is developed, the improvement activities for the coming year can be identified in very specific terms.

REFERENCES

Albert, K. J. Handbook of business problem solving. New York: McGraw-Hill, 1980.

Blake, R. R., and Moulton, J. S. Consultation. Reading, MA: Addison-Wesley, 1976.

Bodek, N., and Scanlan, J., Quality control circles: A practical guide, Productivity Newsletter, 1981.

Foxworthy, R., Personal communication, 1981.

Foxworthy, R., Ellis, W. D., MeLead, C. A management team system. Journal of Organizational Behavior Management, in press.

Fuchs, Jerome H. Management consultants in action. New York: Hawthorn Books, 1975.

Hall, B. L., Accountability practices for client management. Unpublished manuscript, 1981.

Hunt, Alfred. The management consultant. New York: Ronald Press, 1977.

International Labour Office. Management consulting (rev. ed.). Geneva, 1977.

Lippitt, G., and Lippitt, R. The consulting process in action. LaJolla, CA: University Associates, Inc., 1978.

Miller, L. M. Behavior management: The new science of managing people at work. New York: Wiley, 1978.

Steele, F. Consulting for organizational change. Amherst, MA: University of Massachusetts Press, 1975.

13

Overcoming Resistance to Change

DONALD M. PRUE
*Jackson Veterans Administration Medical Center
and
University of Mississippi Medical Center*

and

LEE W. FREDERIKSEN
Virginia Polytechnic Institute and State University

The development of a variety of organizational change strategies such as organizational behavior management, job enrichment, and participative management (Baytos, 1979; Cummings, Molloy, and Glenn, 1975) has not been accompanied by specification of procedures for implementing these strategies. This is unfortunate, since implementation of organizational changes may present a more formidable challenge to consultants and in-house management personnel than the problems themselves. That is, change agents often have at their disposal well-developed strategies to solve organizational problems, but encounter resistance in making the necessary changes in organizational functioning. This chapter will describe constraints frequently encountered during the process of planned change, and will propose strategies to circumvent resistance to change.

The constraints described have been identified in our own consulting work or have been reported in the consulting literature. Two types of literature were surveyed to identify sources of resistance to innovation. The first was literature on the consultation process. This included experientially derived rules for successful consultation, case studies of successful intervention, and prescriptions for organizational change. The second type of literature surveyed consisted of case reports of unsuccessful interventions. The latter proved to be a particularly valuable source of information, since specific examples of failure are ultimately the basis for making rules about successful consulting.

Rather than simply listing the large number of problems that may be encountered in attempts at organizational change, we have organized the chapter in four stages that represent a prototypical consultation endeavor: (1) entry into the organization, (2) preparation for the intervention, (3) initiation, and (4) maintenance of the intervention. These stages are not independent. While they can be temporally defined, a more important distinction is that they circumscribe tasks or behavior required during an intervention procedure. Although the four stages may not apply equally to internal versus external consultants or human service versus business and industrial settings, they still offer a useful framework for organizing frequently encountered constraints.

Resistance during the four stages of planned change may stem from a variety of sources. Resistance from management personnel and workers are so common that these sources usually have been considered by change agents when developing intervention procedures. However, constraints can also arise from sources that are sometimes neglected during the change process. For instance, forces outside the organization can often influence planned change. Extraorganizational factors might include governmental agencies and regulatory bodies, unions, and even the local community. When the target of change is not the entire company but rather one division or work unit, external forces would also include divisions not targeted for change. Another source of constraints could be the structure of the organization with its hierarchy of authority and rules for operation. The term "bureaucracy" has become a synonym for these structural aspects of organizations. Finally, consultants themselves may constitute an important source of constraints.

The outline for the remainder of this chapter follows the four-stage consultation schema described above. Within each section a more detailed description of the stages will be provided, along with constraints likely to be encountered at that stage. We have attempted to address the problem of resistance in a manner that is independent of any particular approach to organizational change, although it is likely that our orientation, organizational behavior management, influenced the identification of constraints. Specific actions will be suggested for avoiding pitfalls that characterize each stage.

ENTRY STAGE

Entry into an organization refers to the initial contact of the external consultant with the organization or an internal consultant with an organizational subunit targeted for change. The most salient goal of the con-

sultant at the entry stage is a broad assessment of the organizational problem. The assessment includes an identification of who is defining the
problem, who hired the consultant, what has been done to try to solve
the problem, and what are members' thoughts about possible solutions.
An idealized notion of why initial contact with an organization is made
would suggest that someone within the organization identified some area
of inefficiency, then members defined the problem and determined the
best method or strategy to solve the problem. An expert in the specific
intervention strategy then was identified and hired to guide the intervention. Unfortunately, this idealized scenario of organizational problem solving seldom reflects the actual process of planned change efforts.

More often than not, a consultant is hired for reasons other than to
solve a simple problem. In fact individuals in the organization may not
even agree that a problem exists. For instance, the impetus for change
may stem from sources only indirectly associated with the organization.
Factors outside the organization often play a significant role in the identification of problem areas, specification of appropriate solutions, and
perhaps even the designation of the individual directed to "solve" the
problem. For example, EEO or OSHA guidelines can lead to organizational
problems (Ginzberg, 1978; Schneier, 1978). Or the legal system can mandate changes that might not have been considered by the organization
prior to the mandate (Ledvinka and Schoenfeldt, 1978). Another common
example of external factors affecting an organization's operations occurs
in corporate systems when, e.g., the Board of Directors of a parent company
requests changes at the division level. Likewise the home office may request changes in the way relatively autonomous branches operate. The
externally generated requests for change will create resistance when there
is disagreement between the initiator and the target of change regarding
the nature of the problem. In a more subtle way, extraorganizational mandates may lead the organization to seek the guise of change and cooperation with the consultant, yet never make any real efforts to meet those
mandates. This may be especially true if mere attempts to make changes
are sufficient to satisfy extraorganizational mandates for change.

Even when the initial request for change stems from an intraorganizational source, the consultants should still determine the impetus for
change. Intraorganizational initiation of consultant contact is not always
directed toward the solution of some problem (Miller, 1978). Often the
fact that organizations have consultants, regardless of their responsibilities, is viewed as a status symbol. Under these circumstances it is unlikely
that active intervention efforts on the part of the change agent will be
supported.

A similar result may occur when consultants have a role in completing
initial contact with an organization by marketing their services. Marketing
often involves promises of better organizational efficiency, which include
explicit descriptions of likely results but only general descriptions of what
types of intervention will be required by the organization. These promises

can later restrict appropriate intervention strategies, because individuals in the organization may be surprised when the consultant attempts to identify unnoticed organizational problems prior to initiating an intervention. If "word of mouth" or past successes with other organizations play a role in the initial contact with the organization, then preconceptions about intervention and results may define the organizational change efforts more than the nature of organizational problems. For instance, the organization may expect an intervention centered on job redesign when other types of interventions would be more appropriate.

Alternatively, organizational members may seek consultative services in order to avoid having to deal with an organizational problem (Baron, 1978). Organizational members want the consultant to take responsibility for solving the problem and not to bother them with details about the change effort. Yet it is unlikely that the change agent can be successful without organizational members' input into the design of a solution to their problem (Parks, 1978).

Lastly, a consultant may be hired when an organization is confronted with interpersonal conflicts or other hidden factors (Dorr, 1978). The consultant may be expected to "collect evidence" to aid in a predetermined solution. Under these circumstances any effort by the consultant to objectively assess problem areas and direct solutions designed to increase functioning will surely meet with resistance. The common link among all these examples is that people in the organization have preconceptions regarding both the consultant's role and the problems facing the organization.

A point that is related to why the consultant was hired involves the question of who enlisted the consultant to direct the change effort. If the decision about whom to hire was made by someone outside the organization, such as the board of directors, then the consultant may be perceived as an unwanted intruder by the management of the organization targeted for change. If management questions both the necessity for change and the selection of a change agent, there is a synergistic increase in resistance. Even when someone within the organization is responsible for the selection of the change agent, it is still important to identify that person and assess their role in the organization.

Most consultants prefer that initial contact be made with upper levels of the organization's management (Ganesh, 1978). The most obvious reason for initial contact with upper management is that their support is usually a necessary condition for change. Also an intervention without the support of the chief executives will soon be considered a farce by those in lower organizational levels. Yet the identification of the consultant with individuals in top management positions is not, in and of itself, sufficient to insure management support. The consultant may assume appropriate management support only to find that he or she has been hired by someone who has very little influence in the organization. Other, more prestigious individuals in the organization may not support either the consultant or the change effort. In other words, the failure of planned change is insured when an intervention is associated with individuals who have little formal or informal power and who are not considered instrumental to organizational functioning. All of the circumstances noted so far lead to the first action statement of the entry stage.

Action Statement 1: *Determine organizational members' preconceptions of reasons you were hired and the organizational role and status of those who were most influential in your hiring.*

As noted earlier, one objective of the entry stage is a general description of the problem. Thus the consultant must complete an initial assessment of the organization during the entry stage. In fact most of a consultant's activities during entry involve investigating perceptions of the problem at different organizational levels. Unfortunately, assessment of organizational inefficiency is seldom a straightforward process. Individuals at all levels seldom focus on the problem in the same way, since they are influenced by different factors. In other words, discrepancies in information provided the consultant cannot be avoided. The consultant simply has to insure that people at all levels have input into the conceptualization of the problem, so that the conceptualization takes into account important influences on individuals at different levels.

Gummer (1980) suggests a number of other difficulties in obtaining an evaluating information. First, individuals may provide conflicting information that is difficult to evaluate by external consultants unfamiliar with important organizational processes. In large organizations individuals can effectively minimize problems or diffuse responsibility making it difficult to identify the locus of the problem. Second, information may be withheld or selectively amassed to overwhelm the consultant during the initial assessment process. Problems and resistance may arise when selectively amassed information is presented by an effective communicator and it inordinately affects the conceptualization of the problem. Third, there is usually a lack of information regarding the interplay of individuals in organizational functioning. Although the organizational chart may be useful in identifying formal authority relations and work flow, it also omits important information. Fraser (1978) notes that formal charts do not include information on interpersonal influence, informational relations, the importance of different individuals to the overall profitability of the organization, subunits in competition for limited resources, and past histories of intraorganizational conflict. This information may be critical to an accurate conceptualization of the problem. The three factors discussed above make information collection difficult and often misleading. In spite of the difficulties in obtaining a valid preliminary assessment, it is still important to obtain one. Action Statement 2 summarizes the steps involved in increasing the liklihood of a valid assessment.

Action Statement 2: *Interviews with individuals at all organizational levels (upper management, middle level management, first line supervisors and workers) increases the likelihood of obtaining a valid assessment. Input from multiple individuals also helps insure that the problem conceptualization takes into account important variables at different organizational levels.*

Change strategies that will eventually be implemented do not play an instrumental role at entry. However, two points should be made regarding tentative strategies. First, the consultant's conceptualization of the problem determines the types of strategies that would be appropriate in an intervention. The conceptualization is based upon information gathered during initial consultant contacts, and typically should correspond with the conceptualizations of significant organizational members (Graziano, 1973). A lack of correspondence between the consultant's conceptualization and those of others may lead to resistance to change. If the consultant and the organization's members disagree regarding the cause of organizational inefficiency at this early stage of change, then it will be unlikely that requests for actual changes in functioning will be supported later. The second point, related to the first, is that tentative solutions devised by the change agent must also correspond with organizational solutions. Agreement regarding tentative solutions should be on a very general level at this point, since specification of a change strategy is premature. For instance, if a consultant considers the solution of a problem to involve hiring additional trained workers while organizational members support the creation of an apprenticeship system, the disagreement is great and should be resolved prior to further consultative efforts. Failure to resolve the lack of correspondence may lead to termination of the planned change effort. Action Statement 3 takes into consideration issues regarding initial problem conceptualizations and solutions.

Action Statement 3: *Consultants should validate their initial conceptualizations of organizational problems at multiple organizational levels and determine, in a general way, management ideas about alternative solutions.*

There is a critical source of constraints as the consultant enters the organization: the personal characteristics of the consultant. An early factor in the success of an organizational intervention has to do with perceptions of the consultant's credibility. Often interpersonal skills and credentials are the only basis for an initial assessment of credibility. Thus these factors are also critical to the consultant's initial level of power (i.e., interpersonal influence) or status in the organization. The bases for a consultant's credibility and ultimate effectiveness has been discussed by Martin (1978). He states that perceptions of the consultant's interpersonal influence stem from either expert power or referent power. Expert power is equated with organizational members' perceptions of the consultant's ability to get things done and is related to age, experience, level of education, and status (e.g., association with a prestigious consulting firm). Thus notions of expert power play a particularly important role during the entry stage. However, referent power also affects conclusions about whether or not the change agent can help the organization. Referent power refers to influence that has its basis in the interpersonal relationships between the consultant and individuals in the organization. Levels of referent power are a function of perceptions of similarity in attitude, beliefs, goals, and behavior between organizational members and the consultant. Referent power increases at the entry stage as the consultant gets to know individuals at management levels in the organization and they get to know the consultant. Martin hypothesizes that successful intervention requires both types of influence, because both determine the organization's perceptions of the consultant's skills.

Lastly, formal advanced training in management and psychology seldom equips consultants with the skills necessary to deal with individuals with a variety of norms, beliefs, and goals. Formal training, with its emphasis on the use of a technical language to describe phenomena, may actually prevent effective communication with organizational members. In other words, the change agent with technical expertise may never have the opportunity to test it. If key individuals do not think the consultant can solve the problem, then the consultant may never have the opportunity to attempt the change effort, regardless of the effectiveness of any intervention technique.

A number of factors can affect a consultant's level of influence in the organization. Influence is determined by organizational member's perceptions of how the consultant can help solve the problem confronting the organization. Therefore, it is critical during entry that the consultant be perceived as someone who can help the organization. While some factors affecting a consultant's level of influence are immutable, e.g., age or years of experience, Action Statement 4 lists others that can be attended to at the entry stage.

Action Statement 4: *The consultant should (1) identify and be associated with influential management during the entry stage, (2) stress similarities in training and experience with management personnel, (3) demonstrate an understanding of variables that are important to organizational func-*

tioning, (4) avoid the use of technical language and jargon, and (5) avoid violations of company norms and rules for appropriate behavior.

The entry stage of organizational change is completed when the consultant and organization come to agreement regarding an initial description of the problem and tentative solutions. In most cases a contract is developed that calls for a more comprehensive assessment and further delineation of the intervention prior to its implementation. The latter two tasks comprise the second stage of organizational change, the preparation stage.

PREPARATION STAGE

The preparation stage of organizational change has two primary objectives: a detailed evaluation and the development of a well-specified change strategy. Mobilization of organizational support and the removal of obstacles to the intervention are also defining characteristics of the preparation stage.

Unfortunately, critical activities during preparation (e.g., planning and mobilization of support) are usually neglected because the consultant believes that it is imperative to get things started while enthusiasm still supports the innovation efforts. However, the demise of innovations typically stems from failure to consider the importance of preparation in organizational change (Locke, Sirota, and Wolfson, 1976). The first action statement of the preparation stage considers the importance of proper preparation.

Action Statement 5: *The hallmark of successful changes have involved the balancing of pressure to act quickly and to get things going, and the competing need to take time to plan the intervention, identify likely sources of resistance, and prepare organizational members for change.*

Since a more specific proposal clarifies the impact of the planned innovation on individuals and organizational functioning, it is likely to be accompanied by increases in resistance to change. Increased resistance should be expected; it is an inevitable part of this stage of change. Up to this point the consultant had been the communicator, mediator, and objective evaluator. This role allowed the consultant to conduct an initial assessment. However, as the consultant's role becomes more sharply defined during the preparation stage, so too does an allegiance to a change strategy with explicit implications. The myriad of problems that can be encountered during the preparation stage parallel those in the entry stage in that the sources of constraints (e.g., management or consultant) remain essentially unchanged. The one exception is that the consultant has increased contact with the organizational unit targeted for change.

Again, extraorganizational factors may play a major role in the preparation stage. However, rather than simply being involved in the definition of the problem, as they were at entry, external factors may now have input into the appropriateness of specific intervention measures. Governmental, economic, community, and societal forces all play a part in defining appropriate intervention. For instance, prevailing economic conditions may have an important role in defining the acceptability of different types of interventions. During periods of rapid economic expansion and high corporate profits, human-relations-oriented techniques, such as T-groups or sensitivity training, may be acceptable modes of change. Productivity-oriented intervention, feedback systems for example, may be more popular during periods of decreasing profit margins.

External factors also play a role on a philosophical level. For instance, public response to the technology of behavior modification may be initially negative. This reaction is often based on the specificity of intervention strategies and related notions of determinism and free will. Educationally oriented intervention, on the other hand, which is usually general and not directed at individuals, may be considered appropriate. Direct modification of specific behavior e.g., decreased cigarette smoking in the asbestos industry, aimed at specific individuals, may be seen by some as an infringement of personal freedom. Thus community and societal pressure may be brought to bear on the organization to avoid employing strategies that have a philosophical basis contrary to prevailing beliefs.

Extraorganizational forces are assumed to play a greater role in public as opposed to private organizations. Yet unions, federal regulatory agencies, and public law all have vested interests in defining organizational functioning. The specification of criteria for promotion (e.g., seniority), requirements regarding productivity (e.g., import and export quotas), and laws regarding work site behavior that is within organizational control (e.g., number of hours that truck drivers can drive in a 24-hour period) are all examples of how extraorganizational factors influence organizational functioning. The extent of conflict between the planned innovation and extraorganizational interests and rules, determines whether or not extraorganizational factors will restrict change. One likely guideline in assessing the influence of external forces is to consider how these external forces benefit from the traditional manner of organizational functioning. The extent to which an intervention technique disrupts the flow of benefits to individuals outside the unit targeted for change determines the resistance expected from them. For instance, mechanization in unionized, labor-intensive industries may affect the size of unions and also limit future growth. Both of these facts have implications for the future influence of union leaders over organizational functioning, and should be expected to result in resistance. Goodman, Conlon, and Bazerman (1980) state that unions may resist change even in the face of direct benefits to their members, simply to avoid the perception of being in collusion with a company. The second action statement of the preparation stage deals with the issue of external forces affecting organizational functioning.

Action Statement 6: *A thorough assessment of the influence of extraorganizational factors and the benefits they receive from the present manner of functioning should be made to determine their investment in innovation or the maintenance of the status quo.*

Another reason to expect resistance as the intervention takes form is that change may be accompanied by fear in direct proportion to its perceived impact on the individual. Berlin (1979) suggests that change can lead to fear because it involves the unknown, provides an increased likelihood of making errors and thus appearing incompetent, and may represent a threat to job security. When change is threatening, it becomes important for the consultant to minimize factors that exacerbate the fears that can lead to resistance to change. A number of steps can be taken to reduce fear-based resistance and thereby increase support for the intervention. Perhaps the most important step in mobilizing support involves keeping management informed about the proposal as it develops, rather than surprising them with a completed proposal (Huseman, Alexander, Henry, and Denson, 1978). This can be completed by routine contact with management personnel. Continuous contact allows the consultant to increase management's understanding of the proposal's basis in organizational functioning. Routine contact also facilitates management contributions to the final proposal and thus allows management personnel to take credit for the innovation upon its establishment.

Action Statement 7: *Maintain routine contact with the organization's management and especially management personnel likely to be associated with the intervention strategy. This can be accomplished by regular meetings to keep as many people as possible informed of developments in the proposed intervention and facilitate their input in designing the strategy.*

A related concern of management personnel during preparation is the more formal assessment of organizational functioning conducted during the preparation stage. Since assessment inherently evaluates how well someone is doing or has done their job, it is a very threatening procedure (Bonoma, 1977). If the consultant can lessen the fear associated with evaluation by promising anonymity or insuring job security, then these steps should be taken. However, if these latter options are not available, the change agent should at least provide advanced notice and briefing of involved management personnel regarding the assessment procedures. The latter steps tend to limit the threat of evaluation.

As noted above, the consultant spends proportionally more time with the personnel in the organizational unit targeted for change during the preparation stage. The reason for this is that a comprehensive assessment and specific proposal must take into account the specific tasks and behavior that will require modification during the intervention. The necessity for a valid assessment demands increased contact with employees who will be most affected by the change. Furthermore, cooperation and input from middle level managers and first-line employees may be critical to the validity of conclusions based on an assessment. Evaluations and subsequent interventions are likely to threaten first-line supervisors and workers for the same reasons they threatened management, and will lead to similar resistance. The irony of this situation is that those who often have the most to lose following successful innovation are asked to be the most cooperative (Kempen and Hall, 1977).

Interpersonal characteristics of the consultant also have a significant role in successful preparation. However, qualitative changes in the style of interpersonal interactions must be made between the entry and preparation stages. During entry the change agent's contacts primarily involve upper management personnel whose backgrounds may be similar to the consultants. Also, interpersonal influence during entry is largely based on management's perception of expert power—that the consultant knows what to do. However, during preparation consultants may have to deal with individuals with backgrounds unlike their own. The basis for influence changes, for the most part, to influence based on employees' perceptions that the consultant understands the organizational environment and the workers' situation and is willing to help solve the problem because they have encountered similar problems themselves, i.e., referent power (Berlin, 1979; Martin, 1978).

The differences in these two types of influence are subtle but important to successful change. Munro (1977) and Martin (1978) have stated that an overreliance on expert power during preparation and in later stages of the change process can actually increase resistance to change. Discrepancies between the consultant's behavior and culturally defined norms and attitudes lead to perceptions of the consultant as an outsider and an associated unwillingness on the part of employees to provide the input necessary to formulate change strategies. Proverbial insinuations by employees—"He doesn't understand what is going on" or "He has never worked an assembly line and still thinks he can tell me what to do"—are fundamentally related to perceptions of the consultant's credibility to make changes. Since credibility is a precondition for actual change, organizational members may be unwilling to supply necessary information and attempt new approaches to functioning, if they do not believe the change agent has sufficient information to make suggestions regarding changes. Reppucci and Saunders (1977) suggest that the consultant understand the history of the problem they have been hired to solve as a way of circumventing resistance. A knowledge of the history of the problem indicates to workers that you have "taken the time to learn their setting" (p. 406).

Ganesh (1978) notes that consultants differ regarding the importance of notions of referent power, but agree that it is of concern to the extent that interpersonal factors at the level of change are important for successful intervention. Unfortunately, there is no simple rule regarding the need for rapport with those targeted for change. The change agent must rely on subjective evaluations of what is necessary for successful change. The consulting literature generally endorses the notion of organizational members' participation in the planning process of an intervention as a necessary condition for organizational change. In other words, consultants should include not only management, but workers and first-line supervisors as well, in the planning of change.

Finally, during initial communications with targets of the intervention, it is important to remember that new programs will almost always interrupt traditional routines, and at least initially, increase employees' work loads. This state of affairs is readily apparent to those individuals who will be most affected by the intervention. The change agent should not deny that this might occur, unless of course the intervention might actually decrease work loads. Change agents should also avoid arguing with employees regarding the appropriateness of intervention strategies. Both denial and arguments can lead to decreased consultant credibility and associated increases in resistance to the intervention (Dorr, 1978). Action Statement 8 considers the issue of worker cooperation in the preparation stage.

Action Statement 8: *A change agent should increase workers' cooperation with the intervention by routine contact with the organizational unit targeted for change, attention to important norms that govern behavior at this level, and worker participation in the planning of strategy.*

Another important factor that determined the acceptability of an intervention strategy is the nature of the proposed change. The correspondence between the ideas of organization's chief officers regarding alternative solutions and the proposed strategy plays an important role in the acceptability of innovation. Organizational executives, regardless of their ability or inability to solve a particular problem, have a philosophy that defines the appropriateness of alternative change strategies (Bonoma, 1977). The philosophy may involve a style of leadership or decision making, (e.g., democratic versus authoritarian), preferred procedures, or goals. Management philosophy is usually evidenced by the behavior of an organization's chief administrators and can be determined by examining the organization's history of problem solving. If the management philosophy is in conflict with the proposed intervention, there will be a lack of support for change. Likewise, since the management philosophy defines the organization's chain of command, a strategy that is too incongruent with typical lines of authority is likely to be deemed unacceptable by management personnel. The obvious reason for this is that the strategy may result in the consultant or proponents of the change within the organization usurping the influence of specific management personnel. For example, a strategy that proposes autonomous work groups in an organization with a hierarchically oriented authority structure will likely lead to decreased status and power for those in middle management positions. Such a change will not be viewed favorably by those who stand to lose organizational influence. The next action statement of this section implicitly addresses the issue of management philosophy in the development of a proposal.

Action Statement 9: *If possible, avoid intervention strategies that are incompatible with the management philosophy of the organization and its typical solutions to problems. For example, avoid strategies that appear to circumvent the authority of significant organizational members.*

In addition to the relationship between the proposed change and the organization's management philosophy, the change agent also has to consider organizational resources as a factor that influences the acceptability of change. An intervention strategy that requires resources far in excess of those the organization is willing to commit to change will not be supported. An intervention that requires a large initial outlay of resources based on promises of possible success will also suffer from lack of support. For instance, an airline that is faced with low occupancy rates on some routes may be willing to consider a strategy aimed at decreasing the frequency of flights, but might resist one that would call for the purchase of smaller aircraft.

The extent of proposed changes also affects their acceptability to the organization (Fairweather, Sanders, Tornatzky, and Harris, 1974). If extensive modifications of the organization are suggested, then the consultant had better insure that significant organizational power is amassed to support the change (Gummer, 1980). An extensive intervention might involve all divisions in a company, as opposed to targeting only one division at a time. It is unlikely that extensive change efforts will be acceptable because of possible disruptions in organizational functioning. Further, the problem with garnering support for extensive changes is that the greater the scope of change, the larger the number of employees and management personnel affected, and the smaller the number of personnel available to support the innovation. Less comprehensive change efforts involve less disruption and require less organizational support. Thus small-scale or pilot intervention strategies should be more attractive to a larger number of management personnel (Fairweather, et al., 1974). Action Statement 10 considers factors important in the selection of alternative change strategies.

Action Statement 10: *The scope of proposed changes should take into consideration the amount of organizational resources allocated to change and the amount of support that can be expected from organizational members. Avoid proposing large-scale change until a record of success has been developed within the organization.*

Association of a strategy with past failures, by similarity to previous attempts or by association with certain personnel supporting the change, may have a deleterious effect on the overall level of organizational support for the planned change. If an organization has not had much success with feedback intervention because of social skill deficits of many middle level managers, it is unlikely that another feedback system will be acceptable. Thus the consultant should identify prior attempts to solve organizational problems and analyze reasons for past failures.

The consultant's typical problem-solving orientation, may also inhibit improvements in efficiency. Change agents may have tried and proven solutions to organizational problems. These solutions will probably be proposed simply because they worked in the past or the consultant feels comfortable with them. But any approach that restricts evaluations of alternative strategies may inadvertently preclude selection of a strategy with a greater likelihood of success. In other words, a consultant's training, past experience, and notions of appropriate strategies interact to determine the proposed innovation. Action Statement 11 suggests a way to partially avoid the dilemma of stock solutions.

Action Statement 11: *Interventions should directly address the problems of greatest concern to the organization. If the consultant discovers that he or she has to intensively lobby for a change strategy, it may be an* *inappropriate strategy, or the consultant may be addressing the wrong problem.*

Often the change agent is tempted to modify proposed programs to meet the special demands of the organizational environment. For instance, monthly feedback, as opposed to immediate or even weekly feedback, might be considered if there is no feedback mechanism presently in operation and monthly feedback is the only arrangement that would work in the organization. The consultant may even avoid a particular intervention entirely rather than offend or alienate certain individuals in the organization. Clearly flexibility in the design of intervention strategies is called for. The technology of organizational change is not developed to the point where we can consistently point out what will work and what will not work in a given situation. The consultant has to consider what changes the organization might be willing to make to increase efficiency. However, modification of an intervention to "sell it" may ultimately lead to failure. Action Statement 12 considers the issue of modifying change strategies.

Action Statement 12: *The change agent must be careful not to lessen the potential impact of a proposed intervention when modifying it to fit organizational exigencies. While flexibility is necessary, the essential elements of an intervention must be preserved.*

The final issue that must be considered in the selection of a change strategy is the role of consultant in the intervention. Traditional notions of consultation centered on the consultant as an expert information provider or objective evaluator (Levine, 1974; Sarason, 1973). Consultative practice often took the form of educational endeavors such as workshops or advice sessions. The consultant in this type of relation was seldom held accountable for change. However, evidence of failure to find maintenance of organizational change has prompted a redefinition of consultant characteristics necessary for long-term change. Ample evidence now exists that the probability of successful change and the quality of change is a direct function of long-term consultant involvement and the consultant's proximity to the organizational setting (Berlin, 1970; Levine, 1973; Martin, 1978). Thus the issue of what role the consultant should take (information provider, catalyst, leader, and so on) may be reduced to the issue of contact and personal involvement with responsibility for change. The change agent who conceptualizes the consultant's role as an objective observer or bystander is not likely to be successful in instituting change (Munro,

1977). Likewise significant organizational change should not be expected when organizational contact is limited to a predefined time frame of short duration and infrequent contacts. Fairweather et al. (1974) notes that when change agents are forced into the latter arrangement, they must arrange for qualified individuals within the organization to assume responsibility for innovation during periods of absence. The designation of in-house responsibility is probably a good idea, regardless of how much contact the change agent intends to have with the organization (Foxworthy, Ellis, and McLeod, in press).

The question of degree of accountability is raised more often with regard to outside consultants than on-site consultants. Yet an on-site consultant's accountability may still be an issue when organizations, or the consultants themselves, define their role to exclude personal responsibility for organizational effectiveness. The final action statement of the preparation stage considers the consultant's relationship with the organization.

Action Statement 13: *The consultant should be responsible for innovation via personal involvement and investment in its outcome. Qualified employees at the organizational level targeted for change should be considered on-site liaisons and designated as responsible for the intervention.*

At this point a clear picture of the organizational problem has been developed, and an intervention strategy has been designed and agreed upon by the organization. The first day of program operations, including any training that must occur, has been designated as the beginning of the initiation stage.

INITIATION STAGE

Most problems in program initiation stem from insufficient activity during the entry and preparation stages. This fact becomes apparent to the consultant when those who had verbally agreed to the proposed change are now asked to make the required changes in their behavior. It is during the initiation stage that the behavioral implications of the proposed changes must be met by those in the organization. Improper preparation, such as minimizating the scope of change at earlier stages, can result in problems in program initiation. Yet there are also a number of constraints specific to program initiation efforts.

Successful change can be stymied by a large number of factors directly related to characteristics of a change strategy. These factors usually operate when there is a discrepancy between between the requirements of an intervention and organizational resources to implement it. One critical constraint to successful change occurs when employees do not have the skills to carry out the intervention. That is, the nature of the intervention requires skills that are not in the behavioral repertoires of workers, and no attempts are made to shape the new behavior. Brierton, Garms, and Metzger (1969) as well as Austin (1977) suggest a number of reasons for this state of affairs. First, employees may not have had the opportunity to acquire the new behavior. This would be the case when an intervention depends upon skills not previously required to complete the task in question (Kuypers, Becker, and O'Leary, 1968). Examples of this would be familiarity with the metric system, reading computer printouts, or running new machines. Employees who have not been properly trained in these new skills are unlikely to show proficiency in their usage. Occasionally skills required by an intervention strategy may be beyond the capabilities of workers (e.g., inability to read) and create insurmountable problems to the planned change effort. In such cases new strategies may have to be developed by the consultant. The second reason that workers may lack the requisite skills to implement the strategy is that the strategy is too complex. A management by objective system with multiple levels of goals (e.g., immediate, one year and five year goals) and objectives provides an example of a complex strategy that may require an extended time frame for implementation (Lasagna, 1971). The third reason that workers may not have the requisite skills stems from insufficient specification of procedures by the change agent. Most consultants can provide a host of examples where workers simply did not understand what was required of them during initial implementation of a change strategy.

Intervention strategies are sometimes implemented too rapidly or on too grand a scale (Dorr, 1978). When this occurs, organizational functioning may be disrupted to such an extent that the intervention is abandoned prior to its complete implementation. The first action statement of the initiation stage addresses the correspondence between the behavioral requirements of the intervention and worker skill repertoires.

Action Statement 14: *The change agent must thoroughly analyze the behavioral requirements of the intervention. Intervention should be matched to the skill levels or capabilities of employees. The consultant should directly monitor the intervention during its initial implementation to identify behavioral deficiencies prior to their having an adverse impact on the intervention.*

There are other ways to avoid resistance associated with deficient behavioral repertoires and rapid change.

Action Statement 15: *Interventions should be implemented in criterion-referenced fashion with progression to more sophisticated or complex* *skills after mastery of more rudimentary skills. Intervention should be piloted on a small scale to test the strategy and debug it prior to full-scale implementation.*

There still may be constraints to change even when workers have the skills to successfully complete an intervention technique. One likely constraint occurs when some aspect of the intervention interferes with other areas of organizational functioning. For instance, Runnion, Johnson, and McWhorter (1978) pointed out that the large time demands of a data collection procedure led to a decline in support of a successful intervention and its eventual termination. In the face of competing demands for limited time, it is unlikely that the organization will support innovation over more traditional ways of functioning. Thus the consultant has to be concerned with implementing a strategy that does not have a deleterious effect on routine functioning.

The consultant must also be concerned that the behavior targeted for change or the expected results of the intervention (e.g., increased quality) are not inconsistent with the traditional behavioral requirements of the job (e.g., high productivity). If there are inconsistencies between the effects of the intervention and traditional ways of functioning, then there are also likely to be competing contingencies that can decrease the probability of adopting the new behavior. An example of this might be an intervention designed to decrease the number of safety violations in a factory. The intervention might successfully decrease accidents but also result in lower productivity and lost production bonuses. In this case management would react to decreased productivity and workers to decreased compensation. Both would resist continuation of the intervention. Action Statement 16 considers the importance of designing strategies that do not disrupt organizational functioning.

Action Statement 16: *The costs of an intervention (e.g., higher work loads or decreased productivity) should not exceed the positive results (e.g., higher quality or increased safety) to be gained from improved functioning at both individual and organizational levels.*

One final point regarding the nature of the intervention involves the organizational problem to be addressed by the intervention. Consultants are often hired to solve problems that are not amenable to simple solutions. This may result in a number of unsuccessful strategies prior to identifying a strategy than can solve the problem. A change agent should be aware of this fact and make an early determination of the likelihood of success and reasons for program failure. Strategies that have only a small chance of success must be balanced with the availability of alternative solutions as well as the intransigence of the problem. If it is clear that a strategy has no chance to succeed, the consultant should assess alternative strategies. Few consultants like to admit during an intervention that initial strategies have failed and that successful change requires recycling to previous stages, but in some cases this may be the only alternative (Tomlinson, 1972).

The successful implementation and initial operation of the change effort is clearly dependent upon the continued support of the organization's management. Most organizations place a premium on smooth, uneventful operations (Kahne, 1959). Management support is likely to wane if initiation unduly disrupts operations. When disruptions come as a surprise, it may breed even greater resistance. The flip side of this situation is that management support for change can be maintained or even increased by following action statement 17.

Action Statement 17: *Management support can be maintained by keeping managers informed of the status of initiation in regular meetings. Support may be increased by providing reports of success in implementing the intervention or, if available, initial positive results of the intervention.*

In the initiation of change it is important to insure that the benefits of changes and credit for changes accrue to upper and middle managers in the organization who support the change effort (Friedlander, 1980; Parks, 1978). This is especially true if traditional sources of positive consequences to these individuals have been disrupted by the intervention. Thus the change agent should insure that management receives credit for the successful intervention. This means the consultant should avoid receiving public praise for the success of an intervention, because management personnel may feel that their source of rewards has been usurped by the change agent. These feelings could even lead to termination of the project. Rewarding management is important, because the extent to which positive consequences increase for management personnel largely determines their positive influence on the behavior of individuals at lower levels in the organization.

Unfortunately, management personnel do not always have the philosophy required for increasing positive consequences at lower levels. They may see improved performance at lower organizational levels as "individuals finally doing their job correctly" with no need for bringing about changes. Another factor that may inhibit management's trying to effect change at lower levels may involve skill deficits in delivering consequences (e.g., praising improved performance). Prue and Fairbank (1981) state that a skill deficit would make supervisory feedback sessions aversive events that would be avoided by management. In these cases modeling, training, and subsequent prompting of management contact might be required to insure interactions with lower organizational levels. Regardless of the reason, failure of management to positively influence or at least provide feedback on change to workers at lower organizational levels may result in the latter concluding that management is unconcerned about the intervention. This conclusion would be associated with a failure to fully initiate the intervention. Action Statement 18 follows from the necessity for rewarding support and behavior change at all organizational levels.

Action Statement 18: *Management support for initiation must be rewarded, and management in turn must be prompted to reward change at lower levels in the organization.*

Action Statement 18 indicates that the change agent's responsibility to reward management support during initiation is paralleled by the necessity to increase rewards for change at lower organizational levels. The burden may be greater in the latter case, when change at lower levels is associated with either increases in work loads or decreases in traditional sources of reward. The point here is that unless there is something "in it" for workers to change, they are not likely to be enthusiastic about increasing work loads or decreasing rewards (Goodman et al., 1980). The benefits lost by workers may be either tangible rewards, such as number of paid sick days, or intangible rewards, like perceptions of autonomy in job responsibilities. Regardless of the nature of rewards lost, it is instrumental to avoid an overall decline in benefits. Action Statement 19 parallels Action Statement 18, but confronts more directly the issue of rewards for first-line supervisors and workers.

Action Statement 19: *Any intervention that results in a loss of tangible or intangible rewards to organizational members targeted for change should be accompanied by rearrangement of organizational rewards to replace or exceed the benefits lost.*

As noted above, careful monitoring of the day-to-day operations of the intervention is required to insure implementation and head off disruption in organizational functioning. Kratochwill and Bergan (1978) stress the importance of monitoring to insure that the program is implemented as planned by the consultant. Failure to keep in close, periodic contact can result in incomplete initiation or unwanted variations of procedures. Additionally, if first-line supervisors and workers observe a consultant's lack of concern with the integrity of the change effort, there will be a corresponding lack of concern on their part for its implementation. Similarly, when data collection procedures are included in the organizational change, the consultant must continuously verify the data and reporting procedures. When a consultant neglects data reporting procedures, there may be a decline in the reliability and validity of data. The latter is particularly true when tangible evidence to support the self-report of workers is not available for evaluation. The bottom line with regard to monitoring implementation is that failure to maintain contact and provide feedback on critical features of the intervention will lead to employee's perceptions that the consultant has no concern or accountability for the outcome of the intervention. This perception may lead individuals targeted for change to provide the consultant with information based upon what they think the consultant wants to hear without associated changes in organizational functioning. Action Statement 20 follows directly from this line of reasoning.

Action Statement 20: *The consultant should routinely observe implementation and results at the organizational level targeted for change to insure that the intervention is implemented as planned and without undesirable variations in procedures.*

Up to this point we have deferred consideration of the most serious source of resistance at the initiation stage, the targets of the change effort. (Earlier mention was made of the importance of rewards to this group, which should be kept in mind by the reader.) Let us assume that first-line workers represent the target group, although it is obvious that an intervention can be made at any organizational level. Resistance can take many forms at this level, including inability to learn, waiting the consultant out, criticism regarding the demands of the intervention, finding ways to circumvent the necessity for change, or even outright disregard of the requested changes. However, not all criticism of an intervention should be disregarded as resistance. Failure to respond to workers' suggestions for change, and interpretation of all complaints as resistance, tends to mobilize these individuals against change that they see as mandated by the consultant and management. More importantly, workers and their supervisors often have valid criticisms of the strategy selected for change. The consultant would be wise to evaluate the basis of criticism and make appropriate changes in the intervention. Clearly workers have been doing their jobs longer than the consultant has been evaluating them. Further, timely changes based on worker input are likely to increase workers' stake in the program and affect positively their level of cooperation with the intervention. As noted earlier, the greater the level of participation in the change at all organizational levels, the more likely the change will be completed successfully. One way to insure worker input during initiation is addressed in Action Statement 21.

Action Statement 21: *Schedule periodic reviews of initiation efforts to formalize worker input, to increase their stake in of the program, to provide continuous positive feedback to shape new behavior, and to diffuse resistance before it affects implementation.*

A notable source of worker resistance involves the degree of change required by the intervention. The reason for this is that workers are probably comfortable with the traditional ways of functioning and that any change will lead to initial discomfort. When the new behavior is not in the behavioral repertoires of the workers, the change will also be aversive. Failure during initiation to provide training, time for workers to learn the new system, and shaping of desired behavior can lead to resentment of the innovation and subsequent resistance to let go of the traditional manner of functioning. Thus it is important for the change agent to increase the likelihood of new behavior via meetings, reporting requirements, modeling and imitation, and to provide feedback and positive consequences for changes in target behavior. Other chapters in this book clearly demonstrate the efficacy of consequences in influencing behavior.

Despite the best efforts of the change agent to develop additional sources of reward for change, there may still be alternative sources of rewards that are powerful enough to restrict change. One source of conflicting rewards is the peer culture. Cultural factors will sometimes lead co-workers to punish behavior targeted for change and reward those that are incompatible with the success of the program. For example, individual increases in efficiency (e.g., "rate busting") that may lead to an increase in the expected work load for the group are likely to be strongly sanctioned by co-workers. A more subtle example might involve sanctions or group norms regarding style of dress. This norm might then be expected to restrict the success of intervention strategies aimed at, e.g., the wearing of ear protectors. Since it is likely that the peer group rewards and punishes with greater frequency and more subtlety than the organizational system can (Buehler, Patterson, and Furniss, 1966; Katkin and Sibley, 1973), co-workers will have greater influence over the behavior of the individual. A strategy that is in conflict with the rewards delivered by co-workers is not likely to be initiated successfully.

An intervention considered demeaning by those targeted for change will be resisted (Carper, 1977). For instance, a management by objectives system applied to research and development workers, who traditionally function in a relatively autonomous manner, may be seen as an unwanted infringement on their professionalism. Such situations are likely to lead to high levels of resistance. One way to avoid resistance associated with competing rewards in the peer culture is to try to enlist the support of significant peer group members. Significant peers are instrumental in designating group norms. The adoption of the requested change by important group members may then lead to new norms regarding appropriate behavior and decreased peer pressure to resist change. Action Statement 22 of the initiation stage summarizes this point.

Action Statement 22: *Identify significant members of the peer group and enlist their public support during initiation.*

Also remember that commitment to new behavior increases with increased public display of the behavior (Goodman et al., 1980).

The final source of resistance to successful program initiation is the effects of initial organizational changes on those outside the target system. Often the impact of changes within an organization or organizational unit leads to changes in the work load outside the unit targeted for change. If extraorganizational factors cannot accommodate changes in functioning that are outgrowths of organizational change, then pressure will be placed on the target organization to revert back to traditional practices. For example, if changes in productivity cannot be handled by those responsible for later steps in the marketing process, e.g., transportation or sales, a bottleneck will develop with an accompanying return to traditional methods. Another way in which extraorganizational factors can restrict initiation occurs when the intervention disrupts other organizational units not targeted for change. Support units in the organization may place restrictions on the change strategy when it requires that they modify traditional operations. Examples of support services include record keeping, budgeting, reporting and billing systems, maintenance, and employee scheduling. Intervention that requires changes in these support services, only indirectly associated with the areas of product manufacturing or service delivery, can restrict the successful outcome of otherwise appropriate interventions. For instance, if an intervention designed to decrease absenteeism requires a new monitoring system to insure appropriate consequation of absence, the new system is likely to be actively or passively resisted by the organization's accounting services. Likewise, new pay systems that rely on bonuses may involve the development of budgeting systems with associated changes in traditional accounting practices. Individuals in the budgeting unit may resist the extra burden placed on them by the intervention and resist its continuation. Thus the consultant must insure the smooth operation of an intervention in the face of conflict with the operations of interdependent work units. Action Statement 23 highlights the importance of considering intraorganizational support for change.

Action Statement 23: *The consultant should identify the impact of the intervention on organizational members not targeted for change. When intervention can be expected to disrupt the operations or increase the work load of other work units, the latter should be prepared for the change.*

In closing this discussion, a brief review of initiation suggests that the consultant's efforts should involve arranging new or alternative sources of reward for employees, mobilizing workers' cooperation, and insuring the integrity of the change effort. The overall goal is to implement an intervention that will permanently solve the organizational problem. However, the writings of numerous consultants suggest that successful initiation and the long-term maintenance of change may be two distinctly different and occasionally incompatible phases of change. The final section of this chapter, the maintenance stage, examines the issue of long-term systems change and addresses organizational pressures to return to traditional ways of functioning.

MAINTENANCE STAGE

The issue of maintenance of desired changes involves the continued demonstration of procedures, skills, or behavior shaped during initiation. Distinctions between the critical steps required for maintenance and those required in earlier stages are difficult to make because many consultant or organizational members' behaviors necessary for maintenance also are important for success at earlier stages of the change effort. In fact many of the action statements given above (e.g., insure management support and the flow of records, or link new procedures with traditional organizational mechanisms) describe procedures required for maintenance. However, resistance of an intervention is more passive after its implementation and usually stems from factors related to neglect of the program. Thus there are a number of points that separate maintenance issues from concerns at entry, preparation, and initiation stages of change. (For a more comprehensive discussion of factors that affect maintenance see Goodman et al., 1980.)

The first source of constraints on program maintenance stems from the fact that programs typically begin with a great deal of hoopla. This consultant-orchestrated enthusiasm usually continues through the early period of program initiation. Hopefully, initial successes continue to fire organizational support. However, as the program increases in age there may be an associated decline in the special priority and attention that provided early support. Although it is quite natural that success would prompt the consultant and management to turn their attention elsewhere, the resultant state of affairs may undermine the maintenance of programmed change. Further, a program that continuously requires infusion of support and resources should not be maintained by the organization. Thus it is incumbent upon the consultant to arrange for the program to be maintained by more traditional organizational mechanisms (Levine, 1974). A number of changes in organizational functioning might increase the probability of maintenance. Failure to make these changes would be associated with a return to the status quo. In other words, if financial support of the program does not reflect the impact of the intervention on problem solving mechanisms and resource allocation, there will be a gradual return to traditional ways of functioning.

More specifically, an intervention effort that involves the shaping of new behavior or increased behavioral demands on workers is not likely to be maintained unless supported by increases in rewards. At the beginning it is often sufficient to initiate new behavior or increased work loads with social praise, feedback, and so on. However, social praise and feedback should also be accompanied by more formal changes in traditional organizational reward mechanisms such as raises and promotions (Roberts, 1979). If not, individuals will soon learn that old rules are still the basis for reward and punishment. Intervention strategies that do not link results and performance to compensation and promotion are likely to result in low rates of productivity, dissatisfaction, and a return to traditional ways of functioning. The first action statement of the maintenance phase specifies the necessity for rewarding employee behavior.

Action Statement 24: *Traditional organizational consequences for employee behavior should reflect the importance of the new modes of functioning to the attainment of organizational goals. Increases in work loads, productivity, and so on, should be accompanied by increased rewards to employees.*

An additional point should be noted regarding the arrangement of maintenance contingencies. Individual consequences may be the best method to establish a new mode of functioning, but may have unintended side effects that are detrimental to an organization's operations. For instance, if a cooperative effort is necessary to accomplish organizational goals, individual contingencies may lead to competitive behavior that conflicts with cooperation. In this case group contingencies may be more appropriate for the long-term maintenance of change to counteract the deleterious impact of competition in work groups (Goodman et al., 1980).

Another important objective for a consultant during maintenance is to insure that departure from the organization will not be followed by termination of the program. Termination of a program usually follows a change agent's exit, when he or she has been largely responsible for arranging a program's support and initiation (Laws, 1974). Unfortunately, the skills and behavior necessary to insure initiation (e.g., personal accountability, interpersonal influence) are to some extent incompatible with program maintenance. The dilemma that faces the change agent is that, on the one hand, the degree to which a program is associated with one individual places that program at risk for nonsupport when the individual leaves. On the other hand, individual accountability and a long-term consulting relationship are necessary conditions for successful organizational change. The next action statement of the maintenance stage suggests a way to challenge this dilemma.

Action Statement 25: *The change agent should prepare on-site personnel to assume responsibility for the program prior to termination of contact with the organization. The consultant should gradually restrict responsibility for the day-to-day operations of the new manner of functioning and slowly reduce contacts. Job descriptions or standards should be revised to include tasks associated with the intervention.*

The likelihood of program maintenance that follows from Action Statement 25 may be further increased by the designation of responsibility to individuals at multiple organizational levels. That is, individuals in both management positions and at the organizational level of change should be assigned responsibility for continuation of the program. Schefelen, Lawler, and Hackman (1971) have provided a poignant example of the importance of participation in the program at all organizational levels. These authors reported a strategy supported by workers and first-line supervisors that led to decreased absenteeism. Yet the program was terminated because middle level management personnel, who originally supported the change but were not involved in its planning, later reduced their support for the program.

Another constraint to continuation of a program, perhaps its most direct threat, is labor turnover. In the case of high labor turnover an influx of new employees who were not involved in the first three stages of organizational change creates a work force with no investment in continuation of the program. Again this source of resistance is passive, and may be partially circumvented by following Action Statements 24 and 25 above. In particular, the development of new managerial performance standards that specify continuation of the intervention insures transmission is critical (Zohar and Fussfeld, in press). It also may be diffused by the additional steps specified in Action Statement 26.

Action Statement 26: *Formal mechanisms (e.g., training seminars, employee manuals) should be developed to transmit the task requirements of the ongoing intervention to new organizational members and to communicate the relationship between these requirements and organizational contingencies such as pay and promotion.*

In other words, new organizational members should be educated regarding intervention-related responsibilities and socialized to the behavioral demands of the project. Lack of employee knowledge about the history of the intervention and its goals could result in conflict over functioning with an associated return to traditional modes of functioning. The development of formal mechanisms should insure that important information is transmitted across time in a changing work force.

Another factor that could undermine the long-term operation of a program stems from the nature of the program. Initially, a complex program with high behavioral demands on workers and management may be required to change organizational functioning. Yet once initial changes are made, continued functioning may be accomplished with a simplified strategy. For instance, a program may initially require that line supervisors closely watch workers' behavior. These supervisors may need to meet with their own immediate supervisors on a weekly basis and keep continuous records of important organizational results. As the program begins to run smoothly it is likely that both line supervisors and those above them will begin to discount the importance of these time-consuming requirements. The employees may be right in their conclusions regarding how frequently meetings should be held. They may consequently develop a pattern of missed meetings, haphazard monitoring, and incomplete data collection. A decrease in the integrity of the intervention may be followed by declining success and a return to old forms of behavior. However, if the consultant systematically reduces the behavioral requirements, the program may have a greater chance of being continued by workers. In the above example the consultant could program intermittent monitoring by line supervisors, less frequent supervisory sessions, and random assessments of outcome. This modified intervention is more likely to be continued than the high demand intervention. Action Statement 27 addresses this issue.

Action Statement 27: *The extent to which a change agent can simplify and routinize an intervention largely determines its long-term mainte-*

*nance. The consultant should strive to fit the program into other signif-
icant operations of the organization.*

The last point to be made regarding the maintenance of planned change involves the interaction of the intervention with other organizational units not targeted in the change process. As noted earlier, the initiation of an intervention usually is accompanied by enthusiasm and support from the organization's management. An unintended side effect of this extra attention is that others may perceive the target organizational unit as being special. This reaction may lead to resentment and subtle pressure on the target group to return to traditional ways of functioning. Pressure may take many forms, such as increased turnaround time in processing the target unit's sales orders or low priority in receiving maintenance support from divisions that should complement the efforts of the target unit. The point here is that there are natural interdependencies in any organization, and the fact that one particular work unit is selected for intervention is likely to result in other organizational members feeling left out.

The consultant can diffuse this state of affairs in a number of ways. Perhaps the best approach would be to insure that an intervention spreads to these other organizational units whenever possible (Fairweather et al., 1974). Another way of reducing the resentment associated with "special privilege" is open public communication regarding the change. Lastly, the change agent could insure that other organizational units are rewarded for their own efforts in supporting the intervention. In the latter case, an intervention that results in an increased work load or new behavioral demands in interdependent work units should be followed by increased rewards in these other units. Changes in task requirements of nontargeted work units should be supported in the same manner as changes in the organizational unit targeted for change. The final action statement takes into account the inter-dependencies that exist with work units targeted for change in any organization.

Action Statement 28: *The consultant must insure that individuals outside of the organizational level targeted for change support the long-term maintenance of the change effort.*

The goal of the maintenance stage is an ongoing program that is responsive to changing circumstances. The maintenance stage of organizational change ends when the consultant terminates contact with the organization. Hopefully, the program is now institutionalized, and organizational employees will resist efforts from within the organization to make changes in functioning based on whim or subjective decisions. The innovation has become an integral part of organizational functioning.

SUMMARY

This chapter has attempted to identify a number of constraints that can interfere with the process of organizational change and to describe ways of overcoming them. The issue of resistance represents a particularly bothersome but natural reaction to planned change. The consultant should not bemoan the occurrence of resistance but rather actively confront it in a systematic manner. On the positive side, the consultant should remember that if he or she is successful in making significant changes, then the same resistance will aid in the maintenance of the new strategies. Four prototypical stages of organizational interventions are identified: *entry* (from

---

Entry Stage
1. Determine why you were hired and who was behind it.
2. Obtain assessment information for all organizational levels.
3. Recheck initial conceptualizations.
4. Attempt to fit into the organizational culture.

Preparation Stage
5. Balance pressures to act quickly versus thorough preparation for change.
6. Assess extraorganizational influences.
7. Maintain routine contact with key management personnel.
8. Maintain input from units targeted for change.
9. Avoid intervention strategies that violate organizational norms or values.
10. Avoid proposing changes without adequate organizational support.
11. Address problems of greatest concern to the organization.
12. Avoid watering down the intervention.
13. Maintain personnel responsibility for the success of the change.

Initiation Stage
14. Insure that employees have the necessary skills to implement the intervention.
15. Debug the intervention prior to full-scale introduction.
16. Insure that net individual and organizational benefits outweight the costs (e.g., interference with other activities).
17. Maintain ongoing management contact.
18. Insure that change is rewarded at all organizational levels.
19. Insure the replacement of lost individual rewards.
20. Monitor to insure that the intervention is implemented as planned.
21. Schedule regular worker input.
22. Elicit public support from key peer group members.
23. Prepare organizational members not targeted for change for possible impact.

Maintenance Stage
24. Insure that traditional organizational consequences reflect the importance of the new behavior patterns.
25. Prepare on-site personnel to assume program responsibility well before termination.
26. Insure that the ongoing intervention requirements are formally transmitted to new organizational members.
27. Make the ongoing intervention a part of routine operations.
28. Solicit long-term support from individuals outside the organizational level targeted for change.

FIGURE 13-1. Consultant actions that can be used to overcome constraints to change at four stages of organizational intervention.

initial contact to the establishment of a formal or informal contract specifying procedures and desired outcomes); *preparation* (including a detailed assessment and the design and preparation for the intervention); *initiation* (from the first day of the intervention to the point of its stable operation); and *maintenance* (the ongoing operation of the program following initiation). At each of these stages, constraints may arise from management, employees, extraorganizational influences, organizational structure and rules, the behavior of the change agent, and the nature of the change proposed. It is recognized that certain constraints are more important at different stages of the intervention. For each constraint, actions that can be taken to attenuate resistance and increase the probability of successful interventions are described. These action statements specify important consultant activities and considerations and are proposed as an alternative to a happenstance approach to program implementation. They are summarized in Figure 13-1.

REFERENCES

Austin, C. J. Planning and selecting an information system. *Hospitals, J.A.H.A.*, 1977, *51*, 95–96, 100, 202.

Baytos, L. M. Nine strategies for productivity improvement. *Personnel Journal*, 1979, *58*, 449–456.

Berlin, I. N. Resistance to mental health consultation directed at change in public institutions. *Community Mental Health Journal*, 1979, *15*, 119–128.

Bonoma, T. V. Overcoming resistance to changes recommended for operating programs. *Professional Psychology*, 1977, *8*, 451–463.

Brierton, G., Garms, R., and Metzger, R. Practical problems encountered in an aide-administered token reward cottage program. *Mental Retardation*, 1969, *7*, 40–43.

Buehler, R. E., Patterson, G. R., and Furniss, J. M. The reinforcement of behavior in institutional settings. *Behavior Research and Therapy*, 1966, *4*, 157–167.

Carper, W. B. Human factors in MIS. *Journal of Systems Management*, 1977, *28*, 48–50.

Cummings, T. G., Molloy, E. S., Glen, R. H. Intervention strategies for improving productivity and the quality of work life. *Organizational Dynamics*, 1975, *4*, 52–68.

Dorr, D. Training for rapid behavioral consultation. *Professional Psychology*, 1978, *9*, 198–202.

Fairweather, G. W., Sanders, D. H., Tornatzky, L. G., and Harris, R. N. *Creating change in mental health organizations*. New York: Pergamon Press, 1974.

Foxworthy, R., Ellis, W., and McLeod, C. A management team system. *Journal of Organizational Behavior Management*, in press.

Fraser, R. Reorganizing the organization chart. *Public Administration Review*, 1978, *38*, 280–282.

Friedlander, F. The facilitation of change in organizations. *Professional Psychology*, 1980, *11*, 520–530.

Ganesh, S. R. Organizational consultants: A comparison of styles. *Human Relations*, 1978, *31*, 1–28.

Ginzberg, E. EEO's next frontier: Assignments, training, and promotion. *The Employee Relations Law Journal*, 1978, *4*, 24–33.

Graziano, A. M. Clinical innovation and the mental health power structure: A social case history. In Goldenberg, I. (Ed.), *The helping professions in the world of action*. Lexington: D. C. Health, 1973.

Goodman, P. S., Conlon, E., and Bazerman, M. Institutionalization of planned organizational change. In Straw, B. M., and Cummings, L. L. (Eds.), *Research in organizational behavior* (Vol. 2). Greenwich, CT: JAI Press, 1980.

Gummer, B. Muddling or modeling: Goal setting in organizations. *Administration in Social Work*, 1980, *4*, 107–112.

Huseman, R. C., Alexander, E. R., Henry, C. L., and Denson, F. A. Managing change through communication. *Personnel Journal*, 1978, *57*, 20–25.

Kahne, M. J. Bureaucratic structure and impersonal experience in mental hospitals. *Psychiatry*, 1959, *22*, 363–375.

Katkin, E. S., and Sibley, R. F. Psychological consultation at Attica State Prison: Post-hoc reflections on some precursors to a disaster. In Goldenberg, I. (Ed.), *The helping professions in the world of action*. Lexington: D. C. Heath, 1973.

Kempen, R. W., and Hall, R. V. Reduction of industrial absenteeism: Results of a behavioral approach. *Journal of Organizational Behavior Management*, 1977, *1*, 1–21.

Kratochwill, T. R., and Bergan, J. R. Evaluating programs in applied settings through behavioral consultation. *Journal of School Psychology*, 1978, *16*, 375–386.

Kuypers, D. S., Becker, W. C., and O'Leary, K. D. How to make a token system fail. *Exceptional Children*, 1968, *35*, 101–109.

Lasagna, J. B. Make your MBO pragmatic. *Harvard Business Review*, 1971, Nov.–Dec., 64–69.

Laws, D. R. The failure of a token economy. *Federal Probation*, 1974, 33–38.

Ledvinka, J., and Schoenfeldt, L. F. Legal developments in employee testing: Ablemarle and beyond. *Personnel Psychology*, 1978, *31*, 1–13.

Levine, M. Problems of entry in light of some postulates of practice in community psychology. In Goldenberg, I. (Ed.), *The helping professions in the world of action*. Lexington: D. C. Heath, 1973.

Locke, E. A., Sirota, D., and Wolfson, A. D. An experimental case study of the successes and failures of job enrichment in a government agency. *Journal of Applied Psychology*, 1976, *61*, 701–711.

Martin, R. Expert and referent power: A framework for understanding and maximizing consultation effectiveness. *Journal of School Psychology*, 1978, *16*, 49–55.

Miller, L. M. *Behavior management: The new science of managing people at work*. New York: Wiley, 1978.

Munro, J. D. Avoiding front-line collapse within mental retardation facilities utilizing an alternative consultative approach. *Canada's Mental Health*, 1977, *25*, 10–13.

Parks, A. W. A model for psychological consultation to community residences—Pressures, problems and program types. *Mental Retardation*, 1978, *16*, 149–152.

Prue, D. M., and Fairbank, J. A. Performance feedback in organizational behavior management: A review. *Journal of Organizational Behavior Management*, 1981, *3*, 1–16.

Reppucci, N. D., and Saunders, J. T. History, action and change. *American Journal of Community Psychology*, 1977, *5*, 399–411.

Roberts, J. C. Contextual variables that influence performance in business organizations. *Improving Human Performance Quarterly*, 1979, *8*, 227–233.

Runnion, A., Johnson, T., and McWhorter, J. The effects of feedback and reinforcement on truck turnaround time in materials transportation. *Journal of Organizational Behavior Management*, 1978, *1*, 110–117.

Sarason, S. B. Social action as a vehicle for learning. In Goldenberg, I. (Ed.), *The helping professions in the world of action*. Lexington: D. C. Health, 1973.

Scheflen, K. C., Lawler, E. E., III, and Hackman, J. R. Long-term impact of employee participation in the development of pay incentive plans: A field experiment revisited. *Journal of Applied Psychology*, 1971, *55*, 182–186.

Schneier, D. B. The impact of EEO legislation on performance appraisals. *Personnel*, 1978, *55*, 24–34.

Tomlinson, J. R. Implementing behavior modification programs with limited consultation time. *Journal of School Psychology*, 1972, *10*, 379–386.

Zohar, D., and Fussfeld, N. Modifying earplug wearing by behavior modification techniques: An empirical evaluation. *Journal of Organizational Behavior Management*, in press.

PART

Applications and Results

In this final section of the book, we present applications of OBM to specific organizational problems. In many ways this is the critical test of OBM. The most incisive theories and innovative techniques are of little value if they can't be applied to improve organizational performance. The bottom line is, "Does it work?"

The chapters in this section cover a range of important organizational concerns. While the topics are diverse, the authors' approaches to them share some common elements. Each chapter first orients the reader to the problem area. Are there special concerns or constraints associated with this topic? How serious is the problem? What must the reader know before attempting to change this behavior? The chapters then go on to show what has been done in the area. In some chapters this involves a detailed review of the behavioral literature on that topic. In others, where there is no relevant body of OBM literature, the authors draw more heavily on their own experiences in applying OBM to the problem at hand. Based on this background each chapter then presents an action plan. The purpose of this action plan is to provide the reader with a series of concrete steps to actually tackle the problem in his or her own organization. Most chapters also include case study material to illustrate key points.

The opening chapter in this section focuses on absenteeism and tardiness. Authored by R. W. Kempen, this chapter first points out that these problems often have complex causes. The literature on OBM approaches is critically reviewed. Kempen then presents a detailed six-step procedure for approaching an absenteeism or tardiness problem. He places special emphasis on the need for careful problem assessment. Through his presentation he gives a wealth of suggestions and examples that should prove invaluable in tackling this often difficult problem.

Chapter 15, authored by Hopkins and Sears, tackles the pervasive problem of productivity improvement. Starting with a basic definition of productivity, they illustrate how one must be careful in selecting targets for change. The behavioral approach to productivity improvement is placed in its historical context, and the available literature is critically reviewed. A nine-step model to attach specific productivity problems is then described and illustrated with a case example. While not intended as an organization-wide approach to productivity improvement, the model is ideally suited for specific problem areas.

Management of performance in sales organizations represents a challenge. The difficulties in this area are complex, ranging from widely held superstitions about what constitutes good sales behavior to geographically dispersed sales personnel. In Chapter 16 Bob Mirman takes a hard look at the whole field. Starting from the effects of sales training, he reviews the behavioral literature covering a range of different wholesale and retail sales situations. A plan for implementing a performance management system is then described and illustrated with a well-documented program from a national sales organization.

In an era of escalating energy and raw material costs, the effective management of resources is an important area of concern. Chapter 17, authored by Winett and Geller, covers several different aspects of this problem. After reviewing some general issues, they call upon the available literature for principles and specific techniques that are most likely to be successful in an organizational setting. They give special attention to heating and cooling, transportation management, and waste reduction and resource recovery. Finally, they present an overall plan to help organizations approach the task of more effectively managing their resources. A special feature of this chapter is the focus on often-overlooked considerations such as the terminology used to describe resource management programs, the importance of organizational commitment, and the relationship of work schedules to energy usage.

Chapter 18, authored by Beth Sulzer-Azaroff, discusses health and safety. She first points out some of the complexities involved in working with the area, such as the relative low frequency of accidents, which makes them difficult to track systematically. The behavioral strategy of enhancing safe practices rather than trying to prevent accidents is also presented. The literature that has sought to take this approach is systematically and critically reviewed. Attention is directed toward both the initial acquisition and maintenance of safe practices. An action plan is also presented and illustrated. One of the most telling points in this chapter is the section in which the author compares the features of a behavioral approach to the characteristics of companies who have the best safety records. The correspondence is close indeed.

Managing the behavior of managers is one of the newest but perhaps most important areas of OBM. In Chapter 19, Malcom Warren presents a systematic approach to this topic. He starts by pointing out how any performance management system must speak to the difficult problems of selection, management development, and measuring and planning managers' work. The performance management approach is then placed in its historical context. Since measurement and planning is a critical part of both selection and management development, the remainder of the discussion centers on these two important concerns. He first reviews traditional approaches to selection, presents a behavioral alternative, and presents a three-part action plan for managerial selection. The differing approaches to management development are then discussed, as well as the important role of instructional methodology in management development. He presents a four-step plan for developing a system and concludes the chapter with the important consideration of how these overall systems can be maintained.

Another important and innovative area of application is organization-wide intervention. The final chapter in this section, authored by Zemke and Gunkler, focuses on this topic. They start by presenting the case for treating the organization as a single system. How such an approach might be actually implemented is illustrated with a multiyear case study conducted in a theme park. The authors develop a convincing case for making organizational level systems outcome-referenced. Finally, a detailed action plan is presented to guide the development of such a system.

In some of these areas of application OBM has already developed an impressive track record. In other areas the hard outcome data is less substantial, but still very promising. In short, these chapters offer practical approaches to specific organizational problems that are likely to yield a positive answer to the bottom-line question "Does it work?"

14

Absenteeism
and Tardiness

R. W. KEMPEN
Western Electric

Absenteeism and tardiness are irritants, at best, for organizations of all sizes. Managers have to contend with problems ranging from the multi-million dollar cost of absent workers to the daily disruptions caused by chronically late subordinates. For public organizations, these problems tend to raise the cost and lower the quality of services rendered. In the private sector, they may have a telling impact on a company's ability to compete effectively.

Although absenteeism and tardiness are often considered to be two dimensions of the same problem, that is, a worker's tendency to stay away from work, there is a great disparity in the knowledge available about the two phenomena. The research literature on absenteeism is abundant; it has been the focus of investigation for dozens of researchers over a period of several decades. In contrast, little is known about tardiness. There is a paucity of published research and, compared to absenteeism, much less prescriptive literature in the popular management press. As a result of this disparate emphasis in the research literature, we do not know if tardiness is related to absenteeism, in the sense of sharing some common causes, or if it is an independent phenomenon controlled by a different set of variables. We can draw on a large data base to reach relatively firm conclusions about absenteeism and its control, but we are forced to be much more tentative about tardiness.

The difference in research attention may be a simple reflection of real-world problems. Tardiness, no matter how pervasive or chronic in an organization, cannot compete with excessive absenteeism for economic impact honors. Cruikshank (1976) estimated that the cost of absenteeism in the United States was in the range of 15 to 20 billion dollars a year, considering only wages paid for time not worked. More recently, Steers and Rhodes (1980) estimated the cost at 26.4 billion dollars, based on an average cost per day of absence of $66, including wages, fringe benefits, and loss in productivity.

This estimated daily cost of absence probably understates the cost for most large companies. The national average includes many workers who do not get paid when absent and whose fringe benefits are meager compared to an employee of a large company. Our own estimate of the average daily cost of an absence in such a company is in the range of $80 to $100 per day for wages and fringe benefits alone. In these companies wages are generally high, most absences are paid, and fringe benefit packages are handsome (and costly). To put things in organization-specific terms, the annual cost of a 5 percent absence rate in an organization of 1,000 employees, using our estimate of costs, is about one million dollars. Viewed this way, it is not surprising that absenteeism has captured more attention than tardiness among students of organizational performance.

There is an interesting footnote to the story of absence research in this country. Despite the abundance of studies and overabundance of prescriptive literature in the popular management press, absence rates have not declined during the last decade (Hedges, 1973; Hedges and Taylor, 1981; Taylor, 1979). It seems that we have not been able to convert our knowledge into effective action, at least not to the extent that it would affect national statistics. In this chapter we will try to sift through the available research data to draw useful conclusions, separate fact from folklore, and provide guidelines for cost effective management action.

DEFINITION AND MEASUREMENT

Anyone who begins an investigation of absenteeism or tardiness soon discovers that there are no common definitons to guide the way. Most studies of absenteeism, e.g., exclude paid vacation or other excused leave time from the statistics, but some do not. Some reports include enforced absences such as jury duty and annual military leaves, while others exclude such time lost. In some studies, an absence is counted only if the employee misses more than six hours out of an eight hour shift. In others, an employee who arrives for work more than two hours late is counted as absent for half a day. (Arriving less than two hours late may count as an incident of tardiness.) Sometimes absence is measured not in days but in terms of hours missed versus hours available. Still other studies provide insufficient information to determine how absences are counted and how rates are computed. The net effect is to make it difficult to compare one study to another, at least in terms of what is meant by the terms "absence" and "absence rate."

In this arena there clearly are no standards. And without standard definitions, there can be no reliable comparisons of statistics. Is your company's 5 percent average annual absence rate worse than the national average for your industry? If yours is a manufacturing company, it would appear that your rate is almost 20 percent worse than the average for your industry in 1978 (Taylor, 1979). But the national average of 4.1 percent was based on a self-report via a telephone survey of a sample of workers during May of that year. Because of seasonal variations in absence rates and differences in how absences are counted, your company's performance may be considerably better than the comparable national group. Or it could be much worse.

The first step for any organization, then, is to define for itself what it will mean by the terms "absence," "tardiness," and absence or tardiness rates. Since there are no standards to facilitate comparisons with other organizations, the definitions might as well be tailored to the organization's particular needs. A good definition will include both of the following:

A specification of when an absence has occurred, as opposed to a late arrival (tardy) or other work schedule irregularity.

A listing of what types of lost time will and will not be counted and therefore will or will not be included in the statistics or rate calculations.

A good definition provides a basis for reliable measurement. Three measures are in common use:

1. Frequency. The number of incidences or occurrences in a time period.
2. Duration. The total time away from work.
3. Severity. The average time away from work per occurrence.

Usually at least two of these measures used together are needed to obtain a balanced view of the problem. For absence diagnostic purposes, we recommend using both frequency and duration data. For tardiness, it may be sufficient to use frequency data alone.

We will return to this subject later when we discuss procedural guidelines for scoping and diagnosing an absence or tardiness problem. Before that, however, we should review the scientific literature on these subjects to determine how it can guide our efforts to develop practical solutions.

REVIEW OF THE LITERATURE

Research on absenteeism has been extensive. It can be divided roughly into two general classes: passive research, involving statistical analyses of the correlations between absenteeism and a variety of personal, work, and organizational factors, and active research that involves experimental manipulation of one or more of these or other factors in an effort to change absence rates. Most of the research on absenteeism is of the passive type, which is easiest to conduct. Much of our knowledge about this subject, therefore, comes from these studies. We have found no such studies that explored the subject of tardiness.

Active research is more difficult to conduct. It requires an experimentally controlled intervention in an organization with all the predictable problems associated with organizational change efforts. Any intervention has risks for the host organization and may meet with resistance from managers and affected employees. The presence of a union adds another complexity. Compared to a laboratory setting, field experiments are messy. If is often impossible to obtain adequate control groups, and dozens of uncontrolled (and often unidentified) variables can confound the results and the conclusions that can be drawn from such studies. It is not surprising that relatively few experimental studies have been reported in the research literature. However, those which have been reported, despite their shortcomings, add considerably to our knowledge and to our confidence in recommending action strategies for managers.

In this section we will review briefly the passive type of studies and the conclusions that seem appropriate given the limitation of such research. We will give more attention to the smaller body of active research studies, since they offer more substantial guidance. We will further subdivide the active research literature into two subgroups to even more sharply focus our attention. One subgroup of studies was not concerned with absenteeism per se; these studies reported the results of efforts to improve productivity. Absenteeism, along with turnover, was measured only as an indicator of employee satisfaction. The effects on absence and turnover rates, however, should be of interest to managers concerned with either problem. The second subgroup of active research studies are those in which absenteeism or tardiness was the direct target of the change effort. These few studies will be dissected to extract the maximum utility for our purposes.

For many of the researchers absenteeism is viewed as a symptom rather than a problem. That is, absenteeism, along with turnover, is viewed as a form of withdrawal behavior. Where turnover (i.e., resignation) is a permanent form of withdrawal, absenteeism represents a less dramatic, temporary means for a person to withdraw from the work setting. This view of absenteeism assumes that the employee is dissatisfied with some aspect(s) of organizational life and wishes to avoid the work environment; he or she, however, is unwilling to permanently sever the relationship with the organization and chooses instead to periodically go absent. In this scenario, it is unclear whether absenteeism and turnover are independent, alternative means of withdrawal or if excessive absenteeism is a preliminary step to resignation—a sort of lead indicator.

This assumption or hypothesis about absenteeism as a symptom has important implications. It has focused much research attention on a search for the causes of absence in an effort to find the variables that, if changed, would remove the sources of employee dissatisfaction and would lead to a reduction in absence rates. The search based on this hypothesis has not led us down a blind alley. As will be discussed shortly, a growing body of research indicates that changes in key work and organizational variables can produce improvements in absence and turnover rates. There is a danger however, in this medical model view: It may not be considered appropriate to treat the "symptom" directly. But the experimental research on efforts to attack absence as a problem rather than a symptom suggest that it can be treated directly without the repercussions normally thought to be the result of symptom suppression. That is, absenteeism can be reduced without creating undesirable side effects.

The view of absenteeism as a form of temporary withdrawal has a certain logical appeal. The principles of behavior suggest that if a person experiences a situation as aversive or punishing, he or she will tend to avoid it. If the person cannot escape from the setting permanently, due perhaps to economic factors, he or she may resort to a less drastic form of avoidance: periodic absenteeism. The more aversive the setting is, and the more commonly it is viewed as aversive by organization members, the higher the rate of absence we would expect.

Is this commonly held view supported by research evidence? Porter and Stiers (1973) reviewed the extensive scientific literature on both absenteeism and turnover and their relation to organizational, work, and personal factors. They found strong correlations between many of these factors and turnover. Regarding absenteeism, however, they were forced to report that:

> Much less can be concluded about the impact of these factors on absenteeism due to a general lack of available information. Sufficient evidence does exist, however, to conclude with some degree of confidence that increased unit size is strongly and directly related to absenteeism. In addition, tentative evidence suggests that opportunities for participation in decision making and increased job autonomy are inversely related to such behavior. (p. 169).

With few exceptions, the research reviewed by Porter and Stiers involved passive studies of the correlations between various factors and absence and turnover rates. Once these statistical analyses have identified a potentially useful relationship—an hypothesis about cause and effect where the hypothesized cause is under management control—the next logical step is to attempt to manipulate the supposedly causative variable and observe its effect on absence rates. The first subgroup of intervention studies mentioned earlier attempted to do just that. These studies, based on the absence-as-symptom hypothesis, were reviewed by Cummings, Molloy, and Glen (1975). In a review of the literature on productivity and the quality of work life, they found 22 studies that used absenteeism and turnover as dependent variables to assess the attitudinal effects of productivity-improvement intervention. They concluded:

> Participative management and job restructuring has the highest percentage
> of totally positive attitudinal results. . . . On the basis of these findings, the
> most obvious conclusion is that an increase in autonomy/discretion alone
> is sufficient to account for positive attitudinal results (pp. 57–58).

An analysis of these studies, then, corroborates the participation job
autonomy conclusions that Porter and Stiers reached as a result of their
review of decades of correlation studies. Summed up, management can
expect a reduction in absenteeism (and turnover) if they can provide
workers with more real job autonomy and a chance to participate in decisions that directly affect their work.

Unfortunately, in many organizations these are not viewed as immediately applicable practical solutions. In some organizations, such as the
automotive and steel industries, the capital investment in current production facilities precludes significant job redesign as a short-term goal.
In other organizations in which embedded technology is not a problem,
tradition, norms, and the attitudes of management or labor-management
relations may prevent the successful introduction of job redesign or functionally important participative management concepts. Even if such fundamental changes were made, there is no guarantee that absence problems
would disappear. At best, we might expect a reduction in overall absenteeism, the average absence rate in an organization. We would still be
faced with the issue of relative absenteeism, the problem of a minority of
employees who were still absent excessively.

The second subgroup of intervention studies may offer some guidance
here. These are studies in which the target was absence reduction itself.
Here the emphasis was on arranging the consequences to employees for
varying levels of attendance without changing autonomy/discretion or
participation. The premise of this approach was nicely summarized by
Porter, Lawler, and Hackman (1975):

> Organizations can influence attendance behavior by tying extrinsic rewards
> to coming to work and by tying penalties to being absent. . . . Organizations
> can significantly influence the connections their employees perceive be-
> tween attendance and certain outcomes by the installing of reward and
> penalty incentive systems (p. 351).

Stated this way the prescription seems simple. It describes what may
in fact be the most common approach to absence control used by management today and for decades past. Although the use of incentives is not
new (Thompson, 1952), the primary method of control seems to have been
to arrange penalties for absence, usually by withholding pay for time not
worked or by providing sanctions for excessive absence (Mann and Sparling, 1956). In some cases the pay rule was simple: no work, no pay. In
many industries today, however, employee benefit systems provide substantial protection against loss of pay due to illness, blunting the impact
of this monetary penalty. Sanctions for excessive absence, on the other
hand, are still common and may be powerful. Sanctions usually take the

form of progressive discipline, a series of formal warnings, usually including one or more disciplinary suspensions without pay, and leading eventually to termination. Secondary sanctions such as removal of advancement opportunity or wage progressions may be tied to some step in the progressive discipline process.

Although direct methods of control have been in common use for decades, there is little published research on the effects of rewards and penalties on absence or tardiness. What does exist is a handful of case studies and field experiments, which provide a positive if meager base for action recommendations. The lack of experimental controls in the case studies limits the conclusions that can be drawn from them. However, the generally positive results reported for incentives (Nord, 1970; Thompson, 1952; Wallin and Johnson, 1976) and aversive consequences (Mann and Sparling, 1956) are consistent with the findings reported in more adequately controlled field experiments. The case studies are mentioned here only because there are so few experiments, and most of these have deficiencies that limit their usefulness.

Six key field experiments on absenteeism have been reported: Kempen and Hall (1977a); Lawler and Hackman (1969); Orpen (1977); Pedalino and Gamboa (1974); Reid, Schuh-Wear, and Brannon (1978); and Shoemaker and Reid (1980). Of these, only two (Kempen and Hall; Shoemaker and Reid) described the consequence systems in use before the experiments began, and only in the Kempen and Hall studies was there an attempt to modify the penalty system as a significant part of the experiment. The remainder of the studies limited the intervention to the introduction of reward-based incentive plans. The experimental research on tardiness seems to be limited to two field experiments (Hermann, de Montez, Dominquez, Montez, and Hopkins, 1973; Lamal and Benfield, 1978), both of which used positive consequences to reduce tardiness. Figure 14-1 provides a summary of these experiments.

Although all of the studies reported strong positive results, most would best be described as demonstration projects rather than serious attempts to install and test permanent methods of control. With few exceptions, the experiments were of short duration, involved few people in a single facility, and used rewards as the primary intervention. The Lawler and Hackman experiment differed in that a one-year follow-up study was conducted to investigate the durability of the early results. Scheflen, Lawler, and Hackman (1971) found that the initial improvements in attendance had been maintained, and that similar improvements had been obtained in other groups that had shown no initial change. The other major exception was the Kempen and Hall study, which reported results for up to three years for a large group of employees dispersed over a dozen different sites. In this study a major part of the intervention was a redesign of the existing system of negative consequences for excessive absence, a component that may be critical for the long-term success of any practical solution in many organizations.

Study	Target Behavior	Subject Population	Type of Intervention	Length of Experiment	Results
Kempen and Hall (1977)	Absenteeism	43,000 production workers in 12 factories	Progressive discipline plus no-cost rewards	6 months to 3 years	20% to 50% reduction in absence rate
Lawler and Hackman (1969)	Absenteeism	66 part-time maintenance employees	Weekly or monthly small cash bonuses	16 weeks with 1 year follow-up	50% reduction in the groups (N = 27) who participated in design of the bonus system. No change in nonparticipating group
Orpen (1978)	Absenteeism	46 female factory workers	Weekly cash bonus	Two 8-week experimental periods	35% to 46% reduction in absence rate
Pedalino and Gamboa (1974)	Absenteeism	215 production workers	Weekly cash lottery incentive system with group feedback	16 weeks	18% reduction in absence rate
Reid, Schuh-Wear, and Brannon (1978)	Absenteeism	75 staff members in a state institution	Group contingency to earn preferred time off schedule	28 weeks	Average absence reduction of 2.38 percentage point in 5 of 6 units
Shoemaker and Reid (1980)	Absenteeism	15 staff members in a state institution	Counseling, commendation letters, monthly lottery with no or low-cost rewards	19 weeks	27% reduction in absence rate
Hermann, et al. (1973)	Tardiness	6 production workers	Daily small cash bonus	43 weeks	90% reduction in frequency of tardiness
Lamal and Benfield (1978)	Tardiness	1 draftsman	Self-monitoring plus supervisory inspection of data	5 weeks with follow-up check	90 minute per day reduction in tardiness

FIGURE 14-1. Summary of studies.

A further possible limitation to some of the studies is that the subjects were not representative of the typical employees of large organizations, whether public or private. They were either part-time workers (Lawler and Hackman), had less than two years of service (Pedalino and Gamboa), or were employed in institutional settings (Orpen; Reid, Schuh-Wear; Shoemaker and Reid). In another sense, however, this may be a strength of the studies taken as a whole; they do demonstrate that significant positive results can be achieved with different types of workers in a variety of settings. They clearly indicate that direct methods of control can be made to work, and if care is taken in total design, reductions in absenteeism and tardiness can be sustained beyond the initial novelty period.

Summary and Conclusions

There appear to be two alternatives to reduce lost time: remove the causes of absence and tardiness or minimize the effects of these causes by better control procedures. Removing the causes of excessive lost time may require extensive change in the organization, an option not practical in many cases, at least in the short term. In contrast, minimizing the effects of these causes through better control procedures requires only relatively simple changes in controls, a rebalancing of the consequences for attendance and absence. The emphasis in the rest of this chapter therefore will be on direct control processes, specifically, the delineation of guidelines for the diagnosis of lost time problems, and for the design, implementation, maintenance, and evaluation of absence and tardiness control programs.

This focus should not be interpreted as a devaluation of efforts to remove more fundamental causes of these problems. To the extent that sources of dissatisfaction can be eliminated and the work environment made to be less aversive, the job of control will be made easier. It will not, however, disappear. Some members of an organization will always incur an excessive amount of lost time, at least in the relative terms of comparison with their peers. Effective, positive controls may always be necessary to insure cost control and equity to organizational members. The guidelines that follow are consistent with the findings from published research and have been tested in practice. Their thoughtful use should yield economic benefits to the organization and psychological benefits to its members.

ACTION PLAN

Overview

The guidelines that follow provide a framework for practitioners in efforts to scope, diagnose, and solve lost time problems. No general, packaged solution will be offered. Instead this process approach will enable managers to tailor a solution to the specific problem that exists in their organization and insure that the solution fits the culture of that organization.

This framework or model was developed and tested in the early 1970s and was described briefly, along with the results of its initial application, by Kempen and Hall (1977b). Since that time it has been applied in the development of absence control procedures for more than 90,000 workers in 75 different sites. Some of these applications and their initial results were reported by Kempen and Hall in 1977 (1977a). In each case the applications have resulted in the development and implementation of new control plans, called attendance management systems, all of which have produced positive results. Absence rates have been reduced from 20 to 50 percent with total annual savings in the eight figure bracket. The improvements have been sustained over time, more than six years now for the earliest applications. And the improvements have been achieved without creating labor unrest or other unwanted side effects. In fact, both the need for formal discipline and the initiation of absence-related union grievances have been substantially reduced.

These applications have helped to further shape the six-step model, which will be discussed in detail after a brief overview:

1. *Scoping.* Is there really a problem? How big is it? Is it worth solving?

2. *Diagnosis.* What exactly is the problem? Isolate and define it.

3. *Design.* What should be done? Design a control program based on the principles of behavior to correct the problem that has been diagnosed.

4. *Implementation.* Take the design from the drawing board into practice, with due consideration for the target group, the union (if any), the supervisors who must administer it, and the organization's management.

5. *Maintenance.* Monitor the program over time with special emphasis on insuring that administration is carried out effectively after the novelty has worn off.

6. *Evaluation.* Assess the effectiveness of the program. Was the design implemented as intended? Is it being properly administered? Has it produced the results expected? Has it created any problems or unintended side effects?

To illustrate the application of the model, the following discussion will focus on the problem of absenteeism. The same process, however, is applicable to the problem of tardiness as well as many other behavioral problems.

Step 1: Scoping

This first step plunges the practitioner directly into some problems mentioned earlier: definition and measurement. It is necessary to define what will be meant by an absence and how absence data will be collected and assessed. Answers to questions such as the following are needed:

When is an employee considered absent? When he or she misses an hour, two hours, a half day, or only when a full day is lost? Only when the absence is unexcused, or regardless of the reason?

Will illness absences be counted, or just nonillness, personal absences? What other absences, if any, will be excluded from consideration for control purposes?

How will an absence occurrence be defined?

Will absence data be accumulated by the hour? By the half day? By full days only?

There are no right answers to these questions. Each organization must decide for itself. In many organizations current practice may already dictate the answers. A word of caution: Do not automatically accept current definitions and measures; they may not be functional for the organization.

For example, an organization's comptroller may be interested in all time not worked, regardless of cause or authorization. To the comptroller, vacations and holidays are as important as sick leave in calculating the costs of doing business. For the line manager, personnel specialist, or consultant, however, the focus should be on absences over which they may expect to exert some influence, that is, absences over which employees have at least partial control. This view argues for counting, for control purposes, only absences due to sickness, injury, and personal reasons other than those stemming from the work itself or forced by outside agencies. The purpose of excluding other types of absences from consideration is to focus attention on those types of absences that, collectively, have proven responsive to effective control efforts.

Some suggestions for definitions:

1. Define an occurrence as any uninterrupted absence regardless of length. A one-day absence due to car trouble is then one occurrence. So is a continuous 45-day absence for surgery.

2. For control purposes, exclude from consideration all absences that result from organization policy (e.g., vacations, formal holidays) or from forces over which neither the employee nor the employer has control (e.g., jury duty, military training). Also exclude those which might loosely be described as permitted, if not encouraged, by the organization as part of its culture or as the result of collective bargaining agreements. Examples might include absences for certain kinds of political work, such as running for public office, or to conduct union business. The list of exceptions may be long. An example list from one large company is shown in Figure 14-2.

3. Include all other absences for personal reasons, whether approved in advance or not. Most importantly, *include all absences due to illness or off-the-job injury.* These two categories typically represent the bulk of lost time in an organization and are absences over which the employee has some degree of control. People may not be able

Absences That Are Not Charged When Authorized in Advance by the Company

Observance of ethnic or religious holidays not covered by the contract
Performance of civic duty
Leaves of absence
Alien registration or citizenship hearing
Vacation own expense

Other Nonchargeable Absences

Holidays	Absence due to on-the-job accidents
Vacations	when recognized as such by the com-
Military leave	pany
Death in the immediate family	Insurmountable transportation failure
Quarantine	when recognized as such by the com-
Service as judges and clerks of elections,	pany
jury duty, and appearance as a witness	Absences of employees responding to
in a court case	emergencies as members of voluntary
Substantiated absences due to court ap-	fire departments, civil defense, and
pearance as plaintiff or defendant	rescue squads, when such absence is
Time off for union business	excused by the company
Work interruptions in violation of the	Voting time (when required by law)
contract, when the employee is sus-	Occupational disease
pended for his or her participation	Disciplinary suspension

FIGURE 14-2.   Examples of absences.

to avoid catching the flu or suffering a heart attack, but they do have some control over when they consider themselves healed and ready to return to work.

Having defined the measures of absenteeism, the next step is to determine if there is an absence problem worth solving. What is the current absence rate and what does it cost the organization? What is the trend in absence rates and costs? Studies of dozens of large organizations suggest that it is not unusual to find average absence rates of 5 percent or higher with an average cost of $600 or more per employee per year. And that cost represents only wages paid for time not worked. It does not include the cost of fringe benefits, which typically would add at least 25 percent to the cost. In an organization of 1,000 employees, these figures would mean that absenteeism costs about $750,000 per year, without considering its impact on productivity. The research indicates that well-designed control processes can reduce these costs by one-fourth to one-third, an annual savings of up to $250,000 in an organization of 1,000 people.

National absence rates have remained stable through the last decade (Hedges, 1973; Hedges and Taylor, 1981; Taylor, 1979), but the trend in any company or subunit may vary considerably. Even with a stable rate of absenteeism, the trend in costs is probably up. Wages and fringe benefit costs have been escalating continuously. Unless your organization has substantially lower absence rates, or your policy is to pay only for time worked, it is probably to your advantage to reexamine your costs and control methods.

One way to determine if an organization has an absence problem worth attacking is to compare its absence rate to the rates suggested by Hedges (1973) as reasonable or attainable. She suggested from an analysis of national statistics that an absence rate of 3 percent might be considered a good normal target, and that a rate of 2 percent might be the attainable minimum.

Step 2: Diagnosis

The emphasis in diagnosis is on determining what the absence problem is exactly, not on finding its causes. Causes relate to the societal, organizational, or personal variables that may be the reasons for high absenteeism. Our interest here is much narrower. We are trying to isolate and define the problem so that we may develop effective controls. We are not trying to isolate causes so that they can be removed.

An organization's absence problem can be loosely fit into one of two categories: frequency or duration. Frequency refers to a problem of employees being absent too often, without concern for the length of the absences. A high rate of one-day absences falls in this category, sometimes referred to as the Monday-Friday syndrome. Duration refers to a problem of total lost time without regard for the number of occurrences employees incur.

Before absence data are analyzed, the definition of which kind of problem an organization has is often a function of who is asked. First-line supervisors usually cite frequency as the problem. To them it is. A spate of one-day absences causes supervisors to juggle work assignments day by day to work around missing people. A long-term absence is less trouble; if a supervisor knows, e.g., that an employee will be out for several months for surgery, he or she can rebalance the work load once and get on with the job.

In contrast, top managers of the organization usually cite overall costs as the problem. They are removed from the daily difficulties faced by first-line supervisors and are more concerned with organizational results. Since the total cost of absenteeism is a function of the amount of time lost rather than the frequency of absences, top managers are usually more concerned with absence duration. Only an analysis of absence data will reveal the true nature of the organization's absence problem.

There are many ways to analyze absence data. The most common is to compare the absence rates of various subgroups in the population, such as men versus women or whites versus minorities. Also common are analyses by age groups, grade levels, length of service, department in the organization, method of pay (hourly versus salaried), and marital status. Typical findings from these analyses are that women and minorities are absent more than white men, hourly personnel are absent more than their salaried counterparts, people in lower work grades are absent more than higher grade personnel, and single persons are absent more than married employees. Analyses by age usually show that people between the ages of 25 and 55 miss about the same amount of time, while those over 55 are absent more and those under 25 are absent less. The patterns of absence usually differ by age, with older workers absent less frequently but for longer durations.

Such results generally reinforce our stereotypes, but secondary analyses often reveal a different picture. For example, if the absence rates of men and women are compared by grade level, the difference between the sexes is usually much less than the difference between the two groups as a whole. The same is often true for comparisons by race. Absenteeism may be more a function of grade level than the race or sex of the employee. The moral is to beware of drawing conclusions from simple analyses.

These common forms of analysis are interesting if only to understand where the absence problem is. They may also help to understand why the absence rates of two organizations differ. A fair comparison across organizations must take into account their demographic differences. But this type of analysis is not very helpful in determining the nature of the absence problem and therefore how to control it. There is one form of analysis that does meet this need. It is illustrated in Figures 14-3 and 14-4.

Figure 14-3 provides a cumulative summary of the number and percent of employees who were absent a certain number of days, or less, during

(A) Days Absent	(B) Number of Employees	(C) Cumulative Number of Employees	(D) Cumulative Percent of Employees	(E) Number of Days Lost (A × B)	(F) Cumulative Number of Days Lost	(G) Cumulative Percent of Days Lost
0	330	330	30.2	0	0	0
1	50	380	34.8	50	50	0.3
2	68	448	41.0	136	186	1.0
3	58	506	46.3	174	360	2.0
4	44	550	50.4	176	536	2.9
5	37	587	53.8	185	721	3.9
6	32	619	56.7	192	913	5.0
7	28	647	59.2	196	1109	6.1
8	38	685	62.7	304	1413	7.7
9	25	710	65.0	225	1638	9.0
10	29	739	67.7	290	1928	10.5
11–20	126	865	79.2	1890	3818	20.9
21–30	72	937	85.8	1800	5618	30.7
31–40	40	977	89.5	1400	7018	38.4
41–50	22	999	91.5	990	8008	43.8
51–100	49	1048	96.0	3675	11,683	63.9
101–200	44	1092	100.0	6600	18,283	100.0
Over 200	0 1092	0	0	0	0	0

FIGURE 14-3.   An analysis of the number of days absent during 1980 for production workers in a Midwestern factory.

Number of Absence Occurrences	Number of Employees	Cumulative Number of Employees	Cumulative Percent of Employees
0	330	330	30.2
1	242	572	52.4
2	175	747	68.4
3	130	877	80.3
4	83	960	87.9
5	52	1012	92.7
6	34	1046	95.8
7	20	1066	97.6
8	11	1077	98.6
9	4	1081	99.0
10	6	1087	99.5
11	2	1089	99.7
12	1	1090	99.8
13	2	1092	100.0
	1092		

FIGURE 14-4. An analysis of the number of occurrences of absence during 1980 for production workers in a Midwestern factory.

the period of the study. In this case the study period was the year 1980. Figure 14-4 provides a similar cumulative summary of the number and percent of employees who incurred a certain number of absence occurrences, or less, during the period.

This analysis will provide strong indicators about whether the problem is one primarily of absence frequency or of absence duration. The analysis ignores all the demographic variables and merely summarizes absence data in a way that permits a decision vital for design efforts: Do we need to control absence frequency, the number of absence occurrences, or do we need to control absence duration, the length of absences?

The data in Figures 14-3 and 14-4 are from a manufacturing plant in the Midwest. As shown in Figure 14-3, about 30 percent of the employees had no absences during 1980, nearly 60 percent had seven days or fewer absent, and only about 20 percent had more than 20 days absent. Some arithmetic will show that this worst attending 20 percent of employees accounted for about 80 percent of the total time lost during this year. The data in Figure 14-4 show that 80 percent of the employees incurred three or fewer absence occurrences, and no one was absent more than 13 times. In this factory it is clear that the absence problem is one of duration. People are not absent often, but when they are absent they tend to stay out a long time. Further, for the year of this study, the bulk of time lost (and cost) can be traced to a small group of people.

Further analysis of the worst attending group, the 20 percent of employees who accounted for 80 percent of the lost time, will usually reveal that many have had relatively good long-term attendance records. But others, usually less than half the group, will be found to have been absent for large amounts of time in previous years. Where absence duration is diagnosed as the problem, this small group of repeat, long duration absentees becomes the primary target for absence reduction efforts. These people are typically absent only once or twice a year, but their absences contribute significantly to the total absence costs of the organization.

The absence profile of employees at this factory is typical of the profiles found in most organizations studied. Only rarely has the analysis revealed a problem of absence frequency, and then it has always been in addition to a problem of duration. Also typical is the finding that the majority of employees have records of good attendance, although the factory used in this example has an unusually high percentage of perfect attenders.

In summary, the analysis illustrated here will help to determine the nature of the absence problem and whether it is worth solving. In this example the problem is clearly one of absence duration, not absence frequency. The absence rate in this factory was an average of 16.7 days absent per employee for the year 1980, about 7 percent assuming 240 workdays in a year. Compared to a standard of 3 percent as mentioned earlier, the problem seems worth working on. The next step in the process, then, is to design a control system to resolve the diagnosed problem.

Step 3: Design

An effective attendance management system (AMS) will consist of three main components: an absence control program, an attendance reinforcement program, and a set of administrative procedures to insure that both programs are administered properly over time. For the purpose of this discussion it will be assumed that the employees who will be affected by the AMS are represented by a union. Further, it will be assumed that the organization is large, with many supervisors who must all administer the program in the same way. If either assumption is incorrect in a given application, the task is easier.

The Absence Control Program. An absence control program (ACP) consists of a series of progressive disciplinary or warning steps leading eventually to termination of employment for employees whose absence records exceed an established criterion. An effective control plan will be based on the problem identified in Diagnosis. If the diagnosed problem is one of duration, the control plan will not identify employees as potential problem cases by counting the number of absence occurrences they have.

In the factory used to illustrate the diagnostic process, the problem was absence duration. The control plan that had been in use was designed to control absence frequency. Any employee who exceeded six occurrences of absence in the most recent 12-month period was placed on Level 1 of a five-level progressive disciplinary ladder. Each succeeding occurrence would cause the employee to progress to the next level of discipline. The first three levels involved formal warnings. The fourth and fifth levels included suspensions without pay of one and five days, respectively. Another absence led to termination.

As time passed, old occurrences would drop out of consideration because of the rolling 12-month review period. If new occurrences were not added, the employee would step down the disciplinary ladder. Based on the data examined earlier, this plan was effective in controlling absence frequency: Less than 5 percent of the population exceeded the six-occurrences criterion. However, total absenteeism rose slowly but steadily to the 7 percent level of 1980, causing management to reexamine its policies.

Where absence duration is the problem, the ACP must use total time lost as the criterion to identify employees who are absence problems. The typical control plan that has evolved in response to absence duration problems uses days of absence as the sole criterion to identify employees who have unacceptable attendance. Since the target is usually employees who miss many days per year, year after year, the ACP usually uses a multiyear criterion. For ease of administration, calendar years are most commonly chosen. The typical ACP uses a criterion of "7 and 40." That is, an employee is considered to have unacceptable attendance if he or she exceeds seven days absent in the current calendar year *and* exceeds 40 days absent in a combination of the current year to date plus the preceding three calendar years. The actual numbers in the criterion are arrived at through management judgment applied to the data used in diagnosis. The intent is to select a criterion that is reasonable, that will home in on the truly worst attenders, but which will minimize the number of employees to whom discipline must be applied. Although 7 and 40 has evolved as the most common criterion, other examples include 5 and 35, 5 and 40, 5 and 42, and 6 and 36. A retroanalysis of results suggests that the specific criterion is not critical; under any of them the truly worst attenders are addressed. The tighter the criterion, however, the larger will be the percent of employees who are placed on a level of discipline.

The criterion selected defines explicitly the boundary between acceptable and unacceptable attendance. Once an employee exceeds the criterion, he or she is placed on the first of a series of levels of progressive discipline. Each succeeding *occurrence* of absence during the remainder of the year causes the employee to move to the next level. The number of levels may vary and may include extra levels for employees with long service. Usually the progressive steps involve only progressively serious warnings, perhaps delivered by successively higher levels of management. Disciplinary suspensions seem to be disappearing. There is no evidence to show they have a positive effect, and they do seem to be counterproductive. Why treat a case of excessive absenteeism by forcing more time off?

Since the review period is usually fixed rather than rolling, an employee who is placed on a disciplinary level cannot "step down" during the year. An annual review, therefore, is provided. At the end of the year each employee's attendance record is reviewed to determine if he or she should be lowered one or more levels or removed from the program entirely. For this review only days of absence are considered, not occurrences. Usually this review is based on the most recent three years, including the one just completed. Thus the earliest year included in the "previous three years" drops out of consideration. Typical criteria used to determine what, if any, adjustments are appropriate are shown in Figure 14-5.

There is nothing scientific about the criteria in Figure 14-5. Ninety-six days of absence in a three-year period represents an average of more than 13 percent absenteeism, a rate that might be considered excessive by any objective observer. Among objective observers are assumed to be those people who serve as arbitrators for labor disputes that cannot be resolved by discussions between representatives of labor and management. The criteria shown in Figure 14-5 are those in use in a number of organizations that use the 7 and 40 criterion to define unacceptable attendance. Once these adjustments are made the new calendar year is begun, again applying the 7 and 40 or similar criterion.

In its efforts to control absenteeism, the organization is seldom challenging the legitimacy of a given absence, although that is sometimes necessary and appropriate. Rather the organization is responding to overall absence patterns and is taking corrective action when an individual's absenteeism has reached a level beyond that which the organization can tolerate and still function effectively.

The Attendance Reinforcement Program.   In any organization only a small percentage of employees will be affected by the absence control program, regardless of the type of program used. If the ACP is properly designed and administered, it will modify the attendance behavior of these few employees. However, it will affect the remaining employees only peripherally, if at all. An attendance reinforcement program (ARP), in contrast, can affect all employees in an organization. It can help excellent attenders maintain their excellence, it can encourage average attenders to improve toward excellence (rather than to play attendance roulette, maintaining attendance that hovers near but just better than the organization's definition of unacceptable), and it can encourage poor attenders to improve beyond the point needed to merely escape discipline. In short, an

Employee's Three-Year Total of Days Absent	Action
More than 96 days absent	Remain on current level
96 or fewer days but more than 60	Level 3 or current level if lower
60 or fewer days but more than 32	Level 2 or current level if lower
32 or fewer days	Off program
After Applying Above Guidelines	
If employee had seven or fewer days absent in most recent year	Lower one additional level
If employee had seven or fewer days absent in each of most recent two years	Remove from program

FIGURE 14-5.   Typical criteria for annual attendance review in absence control plans that use a days-only criterion to trigger disciplinary action.

attendance reinforcement program can be an eminently practical endeavor for management if it is designed to be cost effective.

Reinforcement programs can seldom be cost effective if the reinforcers are cash or equivalent awards made to employees based on their individual attendance records. First, all perfect attenders would receive the award, but they cannot improve on their records, and the immediate effect would be an increase in costs with no compensating cost reduction. To the extent that nonperfect but still excellent attenders might be induced to become perfect, there would be a cost savings. However, it would tend to be small. For a cash award to have sufficient incentive value to motivate the remaining employees it would have to be large, further exacerbating the up-front cost problems. The only alternative would seem to be to distribute cash awards to only a few of the qualified employees by using some type of lottery.

Cash awards may have their use, as has been illustrated in the lottery-type systems reported in some of the demonstration experiments reviewed earlier. A compelling body of evidence indicates, however, that they are not necessary. The successful intervention techniques reported by Kempen and Hall used only noncash low-cost or no-cost reinforcers. The guide used to identify reinforcers in those studies could be used in any setting. Basically it asks two questions: (1) What privileges would people like to have that they do not have now? (2) What do they find irritating or aversive in the work setting?

Answers to these questions will provide a list of items that might be used to reinforce good or improving attendance. Management can pick from the list those items it is willing to make available to employees contingent on specific levels of attendance. And answers to the questions can be obtained easily either by asking employees directly or by observing their actions or by listening to what they talk and complain about.

Common items that have surfaced as irritants for hourly workers in many settings have been the time clocks and the lack of recognition or credit given for long-term good attendance. Items such as these have formed the core of many reinforcement programs. Freedom from the requirement to punch the time clock, for example, has been granted to employees who meet any one of three criteria:

No days absent in the most recent 13 weeks.

Two or fewer days absent in the most recent 26 weeks.

Four or fewer days absent in the most recent 52 weeks.

In many ways this is a near-perfect reinforcement contingency. First, most employees dislike the time clock routine; escaping from it is reinforcing. Second, it costs little or nothing to grant the privilege. Third, no matter how bad a person's overall attendance record may be, he or she can qualify rapidly. Fourth, maintaining the privilege does not require maintaining a perfect record. Even if a person has to miss a day or two, there is a mild incentive to return quickly to maintain the no-punch privilege. Fifth, the privilege is exercised several times each day, providing frequent reinforcement for continuing good attendance. Sixth, the reinforcement is a public event; people see each other being reinforced and enjoying it. Nonqualifiers have a constant reminder that (1) most of their peers are good attenders, and (2) they are being recognized for it.

Like any potential reinforcer, the nopunch privilege will affect employee behavior only if it is made available contingent on that behavior. To grant the privilege unilaterally to all employees, perhaps by removing the time clocks, may make them happier, but it will probably not affect their attendance.

This point seems so obvious that it is a constant source of amazement how often managers ignore it. Many changes instituted by management represent opportunities to selectively reinforce employee performance. The current move toward flextime or variable work schedules is an example. Instead of making this privilege available to all employees, regardless of their relative contribution or performance, why not make it available only to those who meet a certain criterion of importance to management? It could be instituted in an organization using the same attendance criteria described above for nopunch.

To address the complaint that good long-term attendance records are often ignored when a person develops a short-term attendance problem, many organizations implemented a disciplinary immunity privilege. At the end of each year an employee can qualify for immunity from discipline during the new year if his or her long-term attendance record meets a specified criterion level. The criterion has ranged from 15 to 21 days of absence or less during the most recent three years. Employees who meet this criterion are guaranteed that they will not be placed on any level of discipline of the absence control program during the coming year, regardless of their absences during the year. Of course the absences they do incur will be counted in their records. At the end of the new year these new absences will become part of the new three-year record to determine qualification for immunity for the succeeding year.

The assumption has been that people who have been good attenders over several years will remain good attenders in the future. The assumption has proven valid. The vast majority of employees who have qualified for immunity initially have requalified year after year. Roughly half of all affected employee groups have qualified for immunity when it has first been offered. The percentage typically has increased each succeeding year.

In summary, many useful low-cost items can be found to serve as reinforcers in an attendance reinforcement program. They should be selected from items of importance to the affected employees, not those management believes they should want. They should be made available contingent on specific levels of attendance, with emphasis on reinforcing short and medium-term good records, not just long-term perfection. In this way long-term excellence can be shaped in small increments. The trick is to shorten the success interval and help people succeed.

Administrative Procedures.   No matter how well designed, the absence control and attendance reinforcement programs will break down in practice if they are not effectively administered. If a few supervisors fail to take the prescribed disciplinary action, e.g., this lack of consistency will undermine management efforts to pursue other cases of similar or worse attendance records. The key to the long-term effectiveness of any program is to insure that deviations from program-prescribed action are controlled in advance by management.

Administrative control can be achieved by a simple combination of instructions to supervisors, centralized review and approval of all deviations before they occur, and exception reporting to top management of the organization. Supervisors must be instructed that program-prescribed actions must be taken unless advance approval has been obtained for a deviation. A timely review process must then be established to permit a determination on the appropriateness of supervisors' requests for deviations. Lastly, a reporting process must be installed to identify and bring to management's attention all failures by supervisors to apply the programs' requirements consistently.

No matter how well designed and apparently equitable, there will be times when the provisions of the absence control program should not be applied by the book, a deviation is called for. For example, few people would think it appropriate to discipline an employee for an absence incurred as a result of an attempt to save the life of a fellow commuter involved in a highway accident. Most cases, however, are not so clearcut. Left on their own, first-line supervisors will differ in their judgments as to what circumstances justify withholding prescribed disciplinary action.

One solution is to review the decisions of supervisors after they have been rendered and put into action. This is generally an unsatisfactory arrangement; the decisions cannot easily be reversed if assessed as inappropriate, and supervisors may feel they have been overruled. An alternative has proven fully successful: When a supervisor believes that his or her subordinate's situation deserves a deviation, the supervisor brings the case before a small administration committee for review. The committee, composed of representatives from the various subunits in the organization, reviews the specifics of the case to determine if it justifies a deviation. The committee serves as a coordinating body for the organization, insuring that deviations which are granted are consistent with its long-term policy intent and with the cases of other employees. The committee's decisions and rationale also serve to educate line supervisors about what may and may not constitute grounds for a deviation.

In practice, such a committee needs to meet weekly to review cases in a timely manner. Experience indicates that they can conduct their business within one hour each week, once their procedures are worked out. Often, less time is required if coffee is not served.

But what about line supervisors who neither take program-prescribed action nor seek committee approval for deviations? In any large organization there will be a few supervisors who for any number of reasons choose not to implement the programs as prescribed. Left uncorrected their actions or inactions will weaken the whole control process. A simple reporting scheme has proven effective: Periodically (e.g., weekly or monthly) provide top management with a report of "supervisory failures," a list of supervisors who failed to administer the programs as intended. Since supervisors in most modern organizations have been conditioned to respond to what gets measured and reported, unauthorized deviations will soon disappear.

A final word about reports and administration. Management at all levels in the organization needs periodic reports to assess how well the programs are being administered and are working. It is often effective to provide all supervisors with reports, perhaps monthly, of the status of various aspects of the attendance management system's functioning. Reports might include charts of absence rates, the number of employees participating in the different parts of the ARP, the number of employees on each level of the ACP, the number of approved deviations granted, and the number of supervisory failures incurred. Often a single brief report can display much of this information in a way that is easily scanned and assimilated. Such reports help to keep the issue of attendance management in the organizational spotlight, where it can compete with the other measures of organizational performance.

Step 4: Implementation

After an attendance management system has been designed, it must be put into operation in the organization. This is easily said but not so easily done. To put a new system into practice smoothly requires much planning and prework. There are many constituencies in an organization whose needs must be identified and met: the employees who will be directly affected (controlled) by the system; their elected representatives, if they are unionized; the first-line supervisors who must administer the system; middle and upper management who must insure that the supervisors perform their roles effectively; the attendance review committee who will monitor supervisory performance and decide on deviation requests; other staff specialists whose actions may affect the system's effectiveness, such as the medical department and benefit administration personnel.

Orientation or training sessions are important for all of these groups. The affected employees deserve a briefing on the new system, perhaps supplemented by a concise written description of its main elements, plus encouragement to discuss questions with their supervisors. Supervisors in turn need a detailed written description of the system and their role and responsibility in its execution. It has proven most effective to have the affected employees oriented by their immediate supervisors' boss. This increases the probability that the second-level supervisor will learn the details of the system. It also signals to employees that someone beyond their immediate supervisor supports the new system. Such an orientation process also increases the likelihood that the system will be, and will be perceived to be, controlled by line supervision rather than being a program of, by, and for the personnel department.

The personnel department, however, may be responsible for the development of orientation materials and supervisory guides, as well as for training first and second level supervisors to perform their roles. In addition, they or the labor relations department, if separate, would be responsible for discussing and negotiating the new system with the union. Most union contracts contain a provision that makes working conditions a negotiable item. Absence control programs may be viewed as an element of the working conditions, and as such may require that a new or changed program be negotiated. Although a union may not wish to sign an agreement regarding absence control, it may be necessary for management to show a good-faith effort to negotiate. Negotiations may then proceed to an impasse, at which point management may have to unilaterally implement the new program. Whatever the provisions of the contract or applicable labor law, it is foolhardy to ignore the union as a source of power in the organization.

Finally, upper management and other staff groups who can influence the system's functioning should be briefed on how they can support the new system. Even if these groups do not have any direct day-to-day impact on the system, it is important that they understand its purpose and procedures. Sometimes they can do harm due to ignorance, even if they cannot make a measurably direct positive contribution.

Step 5: Maintenance

This really is not a separate step, in the sense of a discrete phase of action. Rather it involves the ongoing execution of the administrative functions established as part of the design. Maintenance functions carry no glory, yet in the long run they make all the difference in successful programs. The people charged with maintenance responsibilities therefore should be reinforced for their work. Especially important are two groups: first-line supervisors and the attendance review committee.

Ineffective supervisory performance (supervisory failures) should be overcome through the exception reporting process mentioned earlier. Unfortunately, effective supervisory performance often goes unnoticed and unreinforced. One solution is the periodic status reports described earlier; they at least serve to confirm for supervisors who are administering the programs well that they are in the majority. It would help to have effective performance recognized in more concrete ways, such as through the organization's performance appraisal program. Reinforcement does not have to be extensive, but it should exist.

Similar considerations apply to the attendance review committee. These people take on a responsibility in addition to their normal roles. The responsibility requires extra time, usually extracted from busy schedules. In one sense, the power and recognition that comes with committee membership may be reinforcement enough. But it may be well to arrange for more, perhaps through periodic meetings with upper management to report on the status of the system. Generally it has proven effective to arrange for systematic rotation of the duty as a committee person; the term is seen as finite, and more people get to benefit from the experience and perspective of committee membership.

Step 6: Evaluation

Like maintenance, evaluation is not a discrete event. It is a continuous process of collecting and evaluating a variety of data to determine if the attendance management system is functioning as intended and is delivering the results expected. Evaluation then should encompass two different issues: administration and results.

The first emphasis should be on administration. Have the system and its components been implemented as designed? Are they being administered on a day-to-day basis as intended? Do key personnel know what they should be doing, and are they doing it? Are supervisory failures, e.g., rare? Have any problems cropped up that were not anticipated? Have grievances increased? What is the general attitude of the employees: Has it improved or worsened? How about supervisors: Are they more or less satisfied with the new system compared to the old?

Sometimes a new attendance management system takes getting used to, especially if it is greatly different from the system it replaced. New is often bad in organizations until the new has been around for awhile. It may take six months or more before employees and supervisors become accustomed to the new roles and procedures. By the end of one year, however, if there is more than isolated resistance there is probably something amiss. Check it out and change procedures as needed. The guiding rule in evaluation as well as design is to make things as simple, predictable, and easy as possible, especially for the supervisor.

Once administration is going well, results should follow. But results are unpredictable. Sometimes they have been immediate and dramatic— 30 percent reductions in absence rates and more in the first month or so. In other cases they have been slow but steady—perhaps initially only a cessation in a rising trend, followed by a gradual downward slope in absence statistics.

Any case that does not produce a fairly immediate result, at least a break in trend, should be considered a danger signal. Check administration first. The early months are often plagued with administrative problems, especially if the organization is large or implementation did not go smoothly. If administration is satisfactory, wait. It may take three or four months before results begin to show, although this is rare. If absence rates do not improve—a situation we have yet to encounter—it may be that the diagnosis was faulty. Even so, the mere increase in management attention should have produced a positive effect.

Experience in applying the model has yet to yield an intervention strategy that has not produced measurable positive results within one to three months. Sometimes absence rates have improved but stabilized at a level still considered too high. It may be necessary to recycle to diagnosis and start again. Sometimes the improvement potential from the new (lower) rate of absence does not justify further effort. The new problem may not be worth solving.

If an organization has more than one division or location, an excellent means to implement and evaluate a new attendance management system is to implement it in accordance with a multiple baseline research strategy (Hall, 1975). Using this strategy, the system would be implemented in only one part of the organization—one location or one division—while attendance data is monitored for all parts of the organization. If the system produces the intended effects without creating unanticipated problems, it can then be implemented successively in the other parts of the organization.

This strategy has several practical advantages. It allows a test of the new system while limiting the risks. Any problems that arise can be solved before the whole organization becomes involved. Also the other parts of the organization act as quasi-control groups: If attendance improves in the trial site but not in the others, there is some evidence that the improvement is due to the new system rather than to some general change that might have caused an improvement anyway.

When the new system is debugged, it can be more safely implemented elsewhere. If each succeeding implementation causes an improvement, management can become more confident that the system is the cause, that it is truly working. Such evidence is not only useful for evaluation purposes; it can also be used to help convince reluctant or skeptical managers that their organization should adopt the new system.

SUMMARY

Long-term strategies for reduction of absenteeism and tardiness, to the extent that they are forms of withdrawal or avoidance behavior, should focus on organization and work design. In the interim, there are procedures that can be used by organization management to maintain absence and tardiness rates within tolerable levels. The key is objective assessment of the problem, coupled with systematic approaches to control that are based on sound behavioral principles, and evaluated with practical experimental tactics.

We have outlined a six-step model to guide practitioners in the diagnosis of lost time problems and in the design of corrective programs. Step 1, scoping, focused attention on determining whether there is a problem worth solving. Step 2, diagnosis, described an analytic process to isolate and define the problem that exists, so that in Step 3, design, efforts would be directed to develop sound, data-based programs for its correction. A three-pronged design strategy was suggested: a control program to dispense negative consequences for excessive lost time, a complementary reinforcement program to encourage employees to improve or maintain their excellent records, and a set of administrative procedures to insure that the provisions of both programs are carried out as intended. Once corrective programs are designed, the emphasis is on planning their effective implementation, Step 4, and maintenance, Step 5. All constituencies must be properly considered, and ongoing administrative routines must be established and maintained. Maintenance and evaluation (Step 6) were viewed as continuing processes rather than discrete events. Evaluation focused on two issues, administration and results; are the programs being administered as designed, and are the expected results being achieved? The results of evaluation efforts could lead to returning to an earlier step in the process, if expected results were not achieved.

Application of the model described here has consistently led to the development of attendance management systems that have reduced absenteeism significantly. In all cases the new systems have replaced older programs that were not based on a sound diagnosis of the absence problem, and whose designs were not well-grounded in the principles of behavior.

The examples used to illustrate application of the model were based on absence problems that were diagnosed as duration-type problems. This has been the most common type of problem found in practice, by an overwhelming margin. However, if the diagnosis indicates that the problem is one of absence frequency, the same systematic approach to design, implementation, maintenance, and especially evaluation should yield satisfactory results.

REFERENCES

Cruikshank, G. E. No-shows at work. High-priced headache. *Nations Business*, September 1976, 37–39.

Cummings, T. G., Molloy, E. S., and Glen, R. H. Intervention strategies for improving productivity and quality of work life. *Organizational Dynamics*, Winter 1975, 49–68.

Hall, R. V. *Managing behavior, Part II, basic principles.* Lawrence, KS: H & H Enterprises, Inc., 1975.

Hedges, J. N. Absence from work—a look at some national data. *Monthly Labor Review*, July 1973, 24–30.

Hedges, J. N., and Taylor, D. E. Fewer absences reported, but time fast remains steady. *News*, U. S. Department of Labor, Bureau of Labor Statistics, June 26, 1981.

Hermann, J. A., deMontes, A. I., Dominquez, B., Montes, F., and Hopkins, B. L. Effects of bonuses for punctuality on the tardiness of industrial workers. *Journal of Applied Behavior Analysis*, 1973, 6, 563–570.

Kempen, R. W., and Hall, R. V. Industrial absenteeism: Replication and longitudinal results of a behavioral intervention. Paper presented at the annual convention of the American Psychological Association, San Francisco, August 1977 (a).

Kempen, R. W., and Hall, R. V. Reduction of industrial absenteeism: Results of a behavioral approach. *Journal of Organizational Behavior Management*, 1977 (b), *1*, 1–21.

Lamal, P. A., and Benfield, A. The effect of self-monitoring on job tardiness and percentage of time spent working. *Journal of Organizational Behavior Management*, 1978, *1*, 142–149.

Lawler, E. E., and Hackman, J. R. Impact of employee participation in the development of pay incentive plans: A field experiment. *Journal of Applied Psychology*, 1969, *53*, 467–471.

Mann, F. C., and Sparling, J. E. Changing absence rates: An application of research findings. *Personnel*, March, 1956, 392–408.

Nord, W. R. Beyond the teaching machine: The neglected area of operant conditioning in the theory and practice of management. *Organizational Behavior and Human Performance*, 1969, *4*, 375–401.

Orpen, C. Effects of bonuses for attendance on the absenteeism of industrial workers. *Journal of Organizational Behavior Management*, 1978, *1*, 118–124.

Pedalino, E., and Gamboa, V. U. Behavior modification and absenteeism: Intervention in one industrial setting. *Journal of Applied Psychology*, 1974, *59*, 694–698.

Porter, L. W., Lawler, E. E., and Hackmann, J. R. *Behavior in organizations*. New York: McGraw Hill, 1975.

Porter, L. W., and Stiers, R. M. Organizational, work, and personal factors in employee turnover and absenteeism. *Psychological Bulletin*, 1973, *30*, 151–176.

Reid, D. H., Schuh-Wear, D. L., Brannon, M. E. Use of a group contingency to decrease staff absenteeism in a state institution. *Behavior Modification*, 1978, *2*, 251–266.

Scheflen, K. C., Lawler, E. E., and Hackmann, J. R. Long-term impact of employee participation in the development of pay incentive plans. *Journal of Applied Psychology*, 1971, *55*, 182–186.

Shoemaker, J., and Reid, D. H. Decreasing chronic absenteeism among institutional staff: Effects of a low-cost attendance program. *Journal of Organizational Behavior Management*, 1980, *2*, 317–328.

Stiers, R. M., and Rhodes, S. R. A new look at absenteeism. *Personnel*, 1980, November-December, 60–65.

Taylor, D. E. Absent workers and lost work hours, May 1978. *Monthly Labor Review*, August 1979, 49–53.

Thompson, D. M. *Controls for absenteeism*. New York: National Industrial Conference Board, 1952.

Wallin, J. A., and Johnson, R. D. The positive reinforcement approach to controlling employee absenteeism. *Personnel Journal*, August 1976, 390–392.

15

Managing Behavior for Productivity

BILL L. HOPKINS

and

JUDITH SEARS

University of Kansas

The decline over the past decade in the growth of U.S. productivity has stimulated a great deal of rhetoric, concern, and hand wringing among economists, managers, and politicans. The general consensus is that dire consequences will soon befall us unless we learn to improve productivity. In spite of or perhaps because of this interest, there is widespread disagreement about what productivity is and how it should be measured, both among experts (Siegel, 1980) and the population at large (National Commission on Productivity, 1973). It is certainly disconcerting that a topic of such importance should be so imprecisely understood.

What Is Productivity?

Webster's (1977) defines productivity as *the rate of production* or *the quantity of goods and services produced per unit of time.* We can quickly see certain shortcomings with Webster's definition. Assume that you have one person making printed circuit boards, and that this worker averages 10 boards per hour. Webster's definition would yield a 10-board per hour index of productivity.

Assume now that you hire a second person to help the first and that together they average 15 boards per hour. Webster's definition would indicate that productivity has increased 50 percent from 10 boards to 15 boards per hour. From a different perspective, however, you may not be sure that hiring an additional employee has led to increased productivity. The one worker assigned to this job produced 10 boards per person-hour worked, while two workers average only 7.5 boards per person-hour, a 25 percent decrease.

The most common usage of the term productivity among economists and business people takes into account the number of labor hours invested in a unit of production. We will adopt this convention in the working definition for this chapter. Productivity is *the number of units of goods or services produced per hour of labor.*

Before discussing the factors that affect productivity, we should acknowledge that productivity is not the bottom line for business and industry, and it should not be the bottom line for government agencies. If a business person needs a certain number of units of goods or services of a particular kind and quality, the primary interest should be in obtaining them at the lowest possible cost regardless of the implications for productivity.

Returning to our example of one or two workers making printed circuit boards, we can illustrate this point. Assume that the original employee is a skilled technician who knows and understands photography and acid etching and can make adjustments in these processes to keep a near-zero rejection rate for completed parts. You pay for this skill. Assume that this person costs you $10 per hour. The second person hired may be inexperienced and function as a helper under the supervision of the technician. Assume that you pay the helper $4 per hour. When the technician worked alone, you obtained 10 boards per hour at an average labor cost of $1 per board. After the helper is hired, they produce 15 boards per hour at an average labor cost of $0.93 per board. If plant management or ownership needs 15 printed circuit boards per hour, the addition of the helper to the work force is cost effective even if the index of productivity, the boards produced per hour of labor, has declined by 25 percent.

A related example will illustrate yet another way in which business ownership could be terribly mistaken to rely too much on estimates of productivity while ignoring costs of production. Go back to the example of the one technician producing 10 printed circuit boards per hour. A salesperson arrives on the scene with four-color pictures, specifications, and prices for a new automatic photography and etching machine that will double the technician's productivity from 10 to 20 boards per hour. Estimates indicate that the costs of purchasing and operating this machine are only $0.62 per board in excess of previous expenses. Will the 100 percent improvement in the productivity of the technician pay off for the company? Won't we obtain an extra 10 boards per hour at a cost of $0.62 per board? No. The labor costs of the 20 boards per hour will decline to $0.50 per board. However, there is the $0.62 per board cost associated with the new machine yielding a net per board cost of $1.12. You would have doubled the productivity but increased costs by 12 percent.

It should be clear that productivity and means of improving productivity are not an end in themselves, but must always be considered in the larger context of the cost of producing goods and services. And of course methods to improve productivity may have real costs, which must be offset by the value of productivity gains.

Why Is Productivity Important?

If changes in productivity must always be weighed against cost considerations, why is it even worthwhile to measure and try to improve productivity? Why wouldn't businesses simply be interested in fundamental analyses involving costs and values of goods and services produced and ignore labor productivity? There are several answers to this question, and they explain the importance of productivity.

From the broadest perspective, productivity has vast sociological importance. Everyone is familiar with the concept of the gross national product (GNP), the dollar value of all final goods and services produced in a period of time, usually a year. This is a rough index of the average physical standard of living of our people. If the GNP increases, once inflation and changes in population are accounted for, improvements are possible in the average physical standard of living. If the GNP declines, it is likely that there will be decreases in standards of living.

The annual report of the economic advisors to the president (*Economic Report of the President*, 1979) routinely provides information on estimated national productivity. National productivity is approximately the GNP divided by the sum of hours worked by the national labor force, or once again, the ratio of goods and services produced to hours worked. This economic statistic has disturbed many people in recent years, simply because it suggests that growth of productivity has been declining and that in several areas of business there has been an actual decrease in productivity (America's Restructured Economy, 1981). The implication is that we may not be able to continue to expect our accustomed gradual improvement in average standard of living, or perhaps will experience an actual decline in the average standard of living.

A related concern is that our higher labor costs contribute to pricing that makes it impossible for U.S. businesses and industries to compete with similar concerns in other countries. For example, we have seen large segments of our shoe and garment manufacturing and electronics, steel, flatware, and automobile production shift to foreign companies. A major consideration in these shifts has been labor costs. The only ways to make our labor costs more competitive are to reduce what we pay per hour worked or to increase the amount produced per hour worked, at relatively constant pay scales. The first solution is socially difficult and perhaps even impossible in a competitive labor market. The latter solution is a cost-efficient improvement in productivity.

From a narrower perspective, any person dealing with profits must be concerned about the ratio of the dollar value of the goods or services produced and eventually sold to the costs of producing them, and there is often much more money to be made in reducing costs than in increasing sales. It is not uncommon for the mark-up, the difference between the cost of an item and its sales price, to be only a few percentage points above the cost of the item. If the total costs of producing and selling printed circuit boards is $1.80 per board and you can sell them for $2, your markup is 10 percent. Your technician producing 10 boards per hour is making you $2 in profits each hour or about $16 per day or about $4,000 per year. Suppose you want to make $6,000 per year from this operation. One approach would be to try to hold your per board costs constant and increase your output and sales by 50 percent. But increasing output while holding costs constant may not be an easy matter. To do this you must increase purchasing, production, distribution, and sales all by 50 percent. Suppose, on the other hand, you find a way to reduce total costs from $1.80 per board to just $1.70 per board. That 5.5 percent reduction in costs will translate into the desired 50 percent increase in profits. Therefore, containment of the costs of producing goods and services has enormous implications for profits. Labor costs often constitute a major portion of production costs, and individual productivity is a major contributor to labor costs. Therefore, productivity improvement, if it is cost efficient, is important both to business profits and, in the long run, to the standards of living of our populace.

The Behavior Involved in Productivity

Traditionally, students of productivity have looked to engineering and technological innovations as primary sources of improvements in worker productivity. Lott (1980), to explain decreases in the labor hours required to produce an automobile, discussed process changes in metal forming and casting, automated equipment, and machines that operate at higher speeds. In discussing the prospects for productivity improvement in the currently troubled machine tool industry, DeLuca (1980) focused on technological methods such as computerized control of machinery, increases in the size and speed of machines, and economies of scale. These views of course ignore possibilities for labor contributions to improved productivity.

The point that is consistently overlooked is that human behavior is ultimately responsible for virtually all productivity. Winter (1980) provided a good example of a thoughtful analysis of nation-wide productivity that still missed this crucial point. He discussed many factors that are thought to contribute to the current declines in productivity, such as: higher taxes and stockholder demands for short-term returns on investments, which confiscate capital and thus prevent purchases of needed machinery; government regulation, which diverts money to pollution control from research and development that might lead to greater productivity; and a lack of work incentives, which creates a net short-term motivation for employees to minimize rather than maximize productivity.

Workers' outputs would generally be recognized as a behavioral problem, while the first two would probably be labeled as political or social problems. However, human behavior is involved directly or lies behind every popularly discussed factor thought to be important to productivity. Human behavior elects members of Congress, and human behavior votes tax legislation. Human behavior educates or fails to educate the general populace about the effects taxes and government regulation have on productivity, prices, and profits. Decisions that environmental pollution is a more serious threat than higher prices, or that immediate returns on investments are more important than long-range potential, are behavior. Worker behavior breaks the tool that stops production, and worker behavior is involved in finding more efficient ways to do jobs. Management behavior creates or fails to create the motivation to cause workers to be more productive with available machinery and facilities. Engineering and design behavior produces the machinery that can allow a worker to behave more productively. If business is going to come to grips with productivity and the potential it has for profits and for our collective standard of living, it must learn how to deal with these kinds of behavior. The fact that productivity is a current problem attests to the fact that sufficient knowledge about dealing with this behavior is not available, or if available, is not yet widely disseminated. This too is a behavioral problem.

Historical Perspective

Sidney Pollard, in *The Genesis of Modern Management* (1968), noted that the developing Industrial Revolution in England created enormous demands for efficient management that were apparently only haphazardly met. Some companies survived and grew, while others died or were quickly absorbed by the strong. In reviewing the history of this period, he notes that there are anecdotal accounts of practices thought to be good and poor, but there was "an absence of any attempt to generalize or rationalize the experiences of industrial management into a management science or at least a management technology" (Pollard, 1968, p. 291). Parts of the conglomerate of managerial responsibility have evolved commonly accepted principles. For example, certain principles of accountancy are almost universally employed, at least in the private sector. However, the management of human behavior, particularly the management of productive work behavior, has not generally developed into universally held principles.

Frederick Taylor's conceptualization of "scientific management" (1911) has created an enduring impact in the area popularly called time and motion study or work simplification and standard setting. However, his views on methods for motivating or rewarding work behavior are less widely held, and there are contemporary suspicions that work simplification has destroyed initiative and judgment of workers (Leavitt and Whisler, 1958).

A number of theories of human motivation (Maslow, 1954; Herzberg,

1966; McGregor, 1966) have led to considerable laboratory research, many surveys of what workers say about their jobs and about management, and a few attempts to change management and work practices in hopes of influencing productivity. However, research has not generally established the validity or the practical utility of these theories (Wabba and Bridwell, 1975; Hulin and Blood, 1968; Lawler, 1969).

The existence of these theories and the research they have prompted have led to distinct movements, including the "sociotechnical" approach to management and work organization as typified by the Volvo experiment (Gyllenhammar, 1977) and the "productivity and quality of work life" movement in the United States (Bluestone, 1977; Lawler, 1978). As a part of this movement, several large corporations have experimented with job redesign, participative management, and team building, with reports of substantial success (Poza and Markus, 1980; Fuller, 1980; Macy, 1980). Unfortunately, the empirical evidence for the utility of these programs is not available in proportion to their popularity. The literature is characterized by anecdotal reports, case histories, and imprecise descriptions of the variables involved (National Center for Productivity and Quality of Working Life, 1975). Of equal concern is the fact that the underlying assumption of the quality of work life movement seems to be that satisfaction will cause improved productivity, an assumption for which there is little evidence (Cherrington, Reitz, and Scott, 1971; Organ, 1977). While successful case studies are gratifying for those involved and invite further investigation by others, the practicing manager should understand that participation, autonomy, and satisfaction are poorly defined and probably have little effect, in themselves, on productivity (Powell and Schlacter, 1971; Locke, Sirota, and Wolfson, 1976; Orpen, 1979).

There have been a number of reports of thoroughly eclectic approaches to productivity improvement. For examples, Hornbruch (1977) reports 10 case histories in which a variety of approaches were employed to improve productivity in organizations ranging from a job shop to a government bureau to a zipper manufacturing plant. The approaches range over employee involvement, regularization of procedures, employee training, wage incentives, reorganization of the control of work scheduling, production feedback, and computerized information processing. Perhaps the consistent element in all of the cases is careful measurement of production. Such a book may present a rich source of ideas for the manager who is faced with productivity problems. However, the book leaves the reader yearning for a set of rules that would point to particular solutions for problems with certain specifications. In addition, it is unclear which of the many methods used at a particular setting were functional and which harmful or wasted effort. It represents good art, but it is not science.

Mali (1978) has written a similar book from the perspective of management by objectives. This book also provides a number of case histories in which apparent successes are reported. However, the procedures used to attack various problems are again quite eclectic, and the reasons for selection of particular procedures are not entirely clear. The consistent feature in all of the case histories is some form of consistent measurement of productivity.

This is the general context in which behavioral procedures have come to be applied to productivity problems in business and industry. The movement is about 10 years old, and the incidence of reported applications is still apparently increasing. It began in 1970 with popular accounts of Ed Feeney's work at Emery Air Freight (Organizational Dynamics, 1973).

Emery was faced with a number of familiar productivity problems. Employees were not efficiently packing containerized air freight shipments. Customer calls for service were not being properly answered. By using performance feedback and social rewards such as compliments and praise, the company in a short period of time improved their measures of work output, presumably with a relatively constant work force, and produced a dramatic savings.

Details of this project have never been reported in the literature, and it must stand as an impressive but largely artistic case history. Nevertheless, it was a beginning, and it existed in a context that was different in two important respects from the other theoretical and eclectic case histories. First, behavioral methods could be derived from a theory that was built on much more thorough evidence than most theories of human motivation. Second, the broad field of applied behavior analysis was committed to evaluation research.

The data base for behavioral theory is quite deep, so deep in fact that many behavioral scientists view the basic principles as laws rather than theoretical propositions. For example, the most fundamental principle, *that behaviors are controlled by their consequences—the rewards and punishments that follow them,* appears to be virtually universal. By 1970, many years of research (see, e.g., the *Journal of the Experimental Analysis of Behavior* or Honig, 1977) had established the broad generality of this principle. At least 10 years of research had established that methods based on this principle could usefully change many forms of human behavior that were problems (see, e.g., the *Journal of Applied Behavior Analysis*). Therefore, work on the problems of business and industry, and particularly on problems of productivity, could begin with a coherent, tested set of principles and a considerable amount of applications technology that had been developed in other areas.

The commitment to outcome research promised that fact could be gradually separated from fiction, that we would accumulate evidence about what did and did not work. In addition, applied behavior analysis had evolved a research methodology (Baer, Wolf, and Risley, 1968) that was practical and efficient: it allowed problems to be solved wherever they were found, while questions about effectiveness were being objectively answered.

LITERATURE REVIEW

Criteria of Review

Research must have certain characteristics to properly belong to the area of productivity and must meet several criteria to provide useful information to the reader. The following is a brief statement and explanation of these characteristics and criteria.

Productivity Characteristics.   Research should deal with some problem involving quantity produced, amount of work accomplished, or services performed per unit of labor to be included in this review. This characteristic will be interpreted liberally to minimize exclusion of research that might be of interest to the reader concerned about productivity.

Behavioral research reports will be examined with respect to several procedural criteria described below. The extent to which these criteria are met by a particular report determines how much the reader can depend on the information contained in the report, and influences the conclusions that can be made about the field. This analysis is similar to one employed by Andrasik (1979) for a more general review.

Specification of Background.   A behavioral research paper on productivity should provide detail on the kind of problem addressed, the business or industry and employees studied, and the behavior or products of behavior measured. This information would allow a reader to compare the similarity of the reported problem and situation to those of interest. In addition, as the method is a repeated focus of research over a period of time, this information allows for the determination of the range of problems, employees, and settings for which a particular method is useful.

Specification of Method.   The method used to improve productivity should be specified in sufficient detail that the reader could repeat it. If this detail is not provided, the reader faced by a similar problem and wishing to use the method may have to make inferences about the method with unexpected and poor results.

Objectivity of Data.   The data collected to evaluate the effects the productivity improvement method has on the targeted problem should be objective and closely related to the stated problem. Behavioral data are easily biased by the person collecting them (Azrin, Holz, Ulrich, and Goldiamond, 1961). Dependable research will safeguard against biases and will present information to help guarantee the objectivity of the data. Occasionally investigators will attack a problem, but will take data that are only tangentially related to that problem. An extreme example might be research that was aimed at improving productivity in a manufacturing department, but reported data on how much workers said they thought they were producing, rather than data on what they actually produced. Obviously the phenomenon of concern should be the phenomenon measured.

Magnitude of Effects. If productivity is measured during ongoing operations, research reports should state the extent of productivity changes or allow the reader to determine the magnitude of changes from data presented in the reports. Without this information there is no way to judge the potential importance of the new method.

Benefit: Cost Analyses. As was noted in the introduction to this chapter, there are always many ways to improve productivity. However, a large number of those ways will cost more money than they save. Therefore, research reports aimed at productivity should include some analysis of the benefits and costs of the methods used to improve productivity.

Controls. The many variables that impinge on the productivity of employees are never static. Such things as changes in the availability of parts, vacations, machine breakdowns, and even weather can strongly affect productivity and the costs per unit produced. Therefore, if a method designed to increase productivity is introduced, and the data indicate that improvements soon occur, there can be room to wonder if the improvements result from the new method or rather from the host of other variables that might affect productivity. Various research design procedures can be used to reduce the chances of attributing productivity improvements to variables that did not cause them (Hersen and Barlow, 1976). Productivity research should use control procedures to allow a safe inference that the new methods were what actually produced improvements.

Discussion

Figure 15-1 presents summaries of the research on productivity and estimates of the extent to which each of the reports meets the criteria. This figure is organized by areas of application; most of the research has been carried out on manufacturing and human service delivery problems.

The range of the specific problems that have been attacked is considerable. There have been applications to production problems such as waste in a textile spinning operation (McCarthy, 1978), material usage and output per labor hour in a photography supply department (Eldridge, LeMasters, and Szypot, 1978), trapping destructive animals on a tree farm (Latham and Dossett, 1978), truck turnaround time at different plants within a company (Runnion, Johnson, and McWhorter, 1978), and sales within a chemical firm (Miller, 1977). Much of the research on productivity in human service organizations has focused on goals for patients (e.g., Quilitch, 1975), or the extent to which institution staff engage in assigned work (e.g., Prue, Krapfl, Noah, Cannon, and Maley, 1980).

At this point there is no indication that there are any limitations on the range of people, work, or settings for which the methods can improve productivity. The vast majority of research has focused on the productivity of people in the lower strata of organizations. However, it is likely that this focus simply reflects the fact that it is politically safer for people to acknowledge productivity problems at these levels. Moreover, the pro-

Author and Year	Subjects, Setting, and Problem	Method	Objectivity of Data	Repeatability	Magnitude of Effects	Controls	Benefit: Cost Ratio
Production of Goods							
Seilaff, 1974	2 production workers; publishing firm; hourly production	Piece rate pay system	Probably, no information given	Probably no	93% increase	Minimal	Not presented
Adam, 1975	28–39 diecasters; midwestern manufacturing facility; no. of units produced; % scrap	Weekly supervisory feedback, graphic feedback, banners, shirt pencil holders	Probably, no information given	Probably no	6% performance increase; 12% scrap increase	Minimal	Presented and documented
Yukl and Latham, 1975	38 forestry crew members; SE U.S. tree farm; rate of planting trees	Bonuses contingent on production—administered for different rates of production	Probably, no information given	Probably yes	33% increase	Moderate	Presented, not documented
Yukl, Latham, and Pursell, 1976	38 forestry crew members; SE U.S. tree farm; rate of planting trees	Bonuses administered contingent on production—administered for different rates of production	Probably, no information given	Probably yes	3% increase	Moderate	Not presented
Bourdon, 1977	1500 textile employees; 2 manufacturing facilities; production and quality control	Training, goal setting, token reinforcement program, feedback	Probably, no information given	Probably no	10% and 4% increase in efficiency in respective plants; 1% and 4% increase in first quality products in respective plants	Minimal	Presented, not documented

Study	Population; setting; measure	Intervention	Baseline	Reversal	Results		Feedback
Chandler, 1977	Textile employees; manufacturing plant; rate of loads dyed	Feedback to supervisor on his behavior and on group productivity	Probably, no information given	Probably yes	30% increase	Minimal	Not presented
Dick, 1978	4 relief operators; fiberglass manufacturing; % of standard production rate	Individual feedback and social reinforcement	Probably, no information given	Probably no	7.5% increase	Minimal	Presented and documented
Eldridge, LeMasters, and Szypot, 1978	23 operators; photographic supplies manufacturing plant; units inspected, piece yield	Goal setting, individual and group feedback, middle management and support staff social reinforcement	Probably, no information given	Probably no	32% increase in piece yield; 37% increase in units per labor hour	Moderate	Presented, not documented
Emmert, 1978	32 hourly employees; fiberglass manufacturing; splices made, bobbins wound, overtime	Training for line supervisors in use of social reinforcement; group and individual feedback	Probably, no information given	Probably yes	14% increase in splices and bobbins; 50% decrease in overtime	Moderate	Presented, not documented
Latham and Dossett, 1978	14 mountain beaver trappers; reforestation site; animals trapped	Bonuses contingent on production, administered for different rates of production	Probably, no information given	Probably yes	23% increase	Moderate	Presented and documented
McCarthy, 1978	Unspecified number of hourly employees; textile manufacturing plant; faulty, high bobbins	Goal setting, graphed group feedback, verbal reinforcement, coffee contingent on meeting goal	No information given	Probably yes	90% decrease	Moderate	Not presented

FIGURE 15-1. Behavioral research in productivity.

Author and Year	Subjects, Setting, and Problem	Method	Objectivity of Data	Repeatability	Magnitude of Effects	Controls	Benefit: Cost Ratio
Miller, 1978	15 weavers; textile manufacturing; loom operation rate	Individual and group feedback; social and tangible reinforcement	Probably, machine collected data	Probably no	15–25% increase	Minimal	Presented, not documented
Frost, Conard, and Hopkins, 1981	6 production line workers; sports products manufacturing plant; rate of filling and packing rosin bags	Graphed group feedback and social reinforcement	Evidence for objectivity	Probably yes	20% increase	Substantial	Presented and documented
Materials Handling							
Komaki, Waddell, and Pearce, 1977	2 retail clerks; small grocery store; regularly stocking shelves and display cases	Instructions, individual feedback, paid time off contingent on performance	Evidence for objectivity	Probably yes	50% increase	Substantial	Not presented
Runnion, Johnson, and Mc-Whorter, 1978	Large but unspecified number of truck drivers; transport operations of textile firm; turnaround time	Weekly group feedback reduced to monthly; recognition of plants, dock workers and drivers, verbal praise	Probably, machine collected data	Probably no	15% decrease	Minimal	Not presented
Sales							
Gupton and Lebow, 1971	2 telephone solicitors; home appliance firm; number of new sales made	Opportunities to make easier sales contingent on making more difficult sales first	Probably, no information given	Probably yes	178% increase	Moderate	Not presented

Study	Subjects/Setting	Procedure	Objectivity	Effective	Results	Magnitude	Cost
Miller, 1977	17 sales people; chemical firm; increase sales	Goal setting, point system with bonuses contingent on points earned, individual feedback	Probably, no information given	Probably no	6% to 42% increase	Minimal	Not presented
Human Services							
Pomerleau, Bobrove, and Smith, 1973	12 psychiatric aides; psychiatric ward; increase patient activity	Bonuses contingent on patient activity	Evidence for objectivity	Probably yes	Up to 25% increase	Substantial	Not presented
Welsch, Ludwig, Radiker, and Krapfl, 1973	29 attendants; mental retardation ward; completion of projects	Individual and group feedback	Probably, some evidence provided	Probably yes	128% increase	Moderate	Not presented
Pommer and Streedbeck, 1974	9 staff members; residential child treatment facility; completion of jobs and new procedures implemented	Posting of assignments; token system with backup rewards	Evidence for objectivity	Probably yes	121% increase in jobs completed; 133% increase in procedures implemented	Substantial	Not presented
Burroughs and Richardson, 1975	11 venipuncture technicians; hospital; unfilled blood sample requests	Time off, contingent on no unfilled blood sample requests	Probably, no information given	Probably yes	87% decrease	Moderate	Not presented
Quilitch, 1975	80 staff members; mental retardation units; increase in patient activity	Specific assignments and individual feedback	Evidence for objectivity	Probably yes	425% increase	Substantial	Not presented

FIGURE 15-1. Continued.

Author and Year	Subjects, Setting, and Problem	Method	Objectivity of Data	Repeatability	Magnitude of Effects	Controls	Benefit: Cost Ratio
Iwata, Bailey, Brown, Foshee, and Alpern, 1976	36 attendants; retardation institution; condition of residents	Lottery for time off from work	Evidence for objectivity	Probably yes	23% to 150% increase	Substantial	Not presented
Kreitner, Reif, and Morris, 1977	8 mental health technicians; psychiatric hospital; completion of patient care tasks	Individual feedback	No information given	Probably no	100% increase	Moderate	Not presented
Ford, 1980	9 mental health professionals; residential facility for mental retardation; specifying written goals for patient rehabilitation	Individual feedback on weekly and monthly schedule	No information given	Probably no	14%–16% increase	Minimal	Presented
Prue, Krapfl, Noah, Cannon, and Maley, 1980	750 staff; psychiatric hospital; staff interaction with patients; patient participation in activities	Group feedback to administrators; public posting of group feedback	Evidence for objectivity	Probably yes	Phase 1: 78% increase in staff interaction; 95% increase in patient participation Phase 2: 160% increase in staff interaction; 200% increase in patient participation	Substantial	Not presented

FIGURE 15-1. Continued.

ductivity of persons at higher levels ultimately depends on the work of the people who sell the chemicals, treat the patients, and weave the cloth.

Measurement. Measurement of productivity and some use of the data generated by this measurement have been common ingredients in every report. At a pragmatic level, the person who would manage productivity must have some form of data to indicate that a problem exists, and only accurate data can provide assurance that new methods produce improvements or that additional efforts are needed.

While measurement of productivity is important, much of the research fails to provide detailed information about how data were collected or the objectivity of the data. This problem should be easily corrected, at least in the private sector, because businesses often take great pains to insure the reliability of many of their output measures and suffer if such data aren't accurate. Therefore, researchers can probably often provide guarantees of the objectivity of the data simply by presenting the safeguards taken by companies to insure that such data are objective.

Much of the public sector research on productivity has employed the direct observation of people or their behavior. This is probably necessary, because the major products of these endeavors are moving people and changing people's behavior. The business research, on the other hand, has typically measured products of employees' behavior, such as bags filled, dollars worth of chemicals sold, or bobbins wound. This too is appropriate because these items are the units of production of businesses. The fact that similar methods produce similar results, whether applied to behavior or behavioral products, argues for the power and generality of the methods.

Goals and Standards. Goals and standards have been used along with feedback or reinforcement in some of the studies (e.g., McCarthy, 1978; Eldridge, Lemasters, and Szypot, 1978), while very similar feedback and reinforcement methods without specific goals or standards have been applied to produce performance improvements in other cases (Yukl and Latham, 1975; Frost, Conard, and Hopkins, 1981). While it may be possible to achieve productivity improvements without specific goals or standards, it seems likely that the common methods, which include social approval and tangible or monetary rewards, demand at least some kinds of implicit criteria. In order to administer rewards and approval contingently, the behavior to be reinforced must be specified.

While there is some controversy about the relative merits of management-imposed standards and subordinates' participation in the development of goals (Latham and Yukl, 1975), the reviewed research includes standards resulting from time and motion studies, subjectively determined and management-imposed goals, and employee participation in the development of goals. None of the research provides for a determination that any of these methods are superior to others. Regardless of how they are derived, goals and standards should be reasonable and achievable.

Assignments and Training. The research by Quilitch (1975) is interesting because it provides a demonstration of the futility of the common management practice of sending memos or holding workshops to try to get more work done. Virtually all of the reported research probably began with people who had already been instructed to be productive and had been trained to do their jobs. The fact that these procedures were yielding unsatisfactory productivity argues strongly that something more is needed. The reader who is responsible for improving productivity would do well to recognize that training, job assignments, and little else is probably the norm in many organizations. While these two methods may be important, additional methods, like those reviewed, are probably also necessary to obtain good productivity.

Performance Feedback. Performance feedback is a common feature of all of the behavioral productivity research. As noted above, this feedback not only provides information about current or recent performance but usually also provides information about performance relative to goals or standards that are either implicit or explicit.

There are a host of still unsettled issues about how feedback can be most effectively used. How often should feedback be scheduled? Is group or individual feedback more effective? What are the relative merits of worker-produced and management-provided feedback? Is publicly displayed or private feedback more useful to promote productivity? These questions simply are not yet adequately answered. Furthermore, answers are likely to develop only slowly and often be idiosyncratic to the particular organizations in which they are investigated.

In the meantime, practical, rational rules of thumb may be useful. It may be prudent to provide feedback as often as is feasible. It is likely that more frequent feedback will influence performance better than less frequent feedback. At the same time there is a price for feedback. Choose some level of frequent feedback, say once per day. Estimate the costs of the feedback. Consider the possibility that more frequent feedback would give slightly better results. Would that improvement offset the costs of more frequent feedback? Consider the possibility that less frequent feedback would yield slightly worse results. Would the loss in value of the slightly reduced productivity be more than offset by the savings in the cost of the feedback?

In working with mental retardation professionals, Ford (1980) reported what is apparently the first attempt to analyze the benefits and costs of various frequencies of feedback. This investigation found that weekly feedback produced a performance that was 2.3 percent better than monthly feedback, but the weekly feedback program cost twice as much to administer. The report is not conclusive, in that assurances as to the objectivity of the data are not provided, and the study did not control well for possible individual differences affecting the results. Nevertheless, Ford has provided an illustration of the trade-offs of varying feedback frequency and the salience of benefit:cost analysis when choosing one type of feedback over another.

The Runnion, Johnson, and McWhorter (1978) report provides another possibility. Their method initially employed weekly letters to plant managers to improve truck turnaround times. After 19 weeks, they reduced the frequency of the letters to one every two weeks. After another 80 weeks, they reduced the frequency of the feedback letters to one about every four weeks. Once good performance is established with frequent feedback, it may be possible to gradually reduce the frequency of the feedback without a loss of productivity.

Other possibilities for reducing the costs and bother associated with providing feedback probably only await a creative person's inventiveness. For example, Brown (1980), referencing Currie (1979), describes a device that can be attached to a sewing machine to provide automatic and continuous feedback on the amount of work that has been done, a daily production goal, the percentage of the goal that has been met, and the amount of money earned. The data collected by Runnion, Johnson, and McWhorter (1978) were mechanically collected, but had to be transformed for feedback purposes.

In any case, the reader should recognize that some data on productivity must be collected at some cost if there is to be any reasonable management of work. Once the manager has these data, the costs of translating them into a form suitable for feedback is often quite modest.

The literature includes reports of good results that apparently rely primarily on public feedback (Prue, Krapfl, Noah, Cannon, and Maley, 1980), others that use private feedback (Chandler, 1977), and others that successfully use combinations of public and private feedback (Emmert, 1978). Similarly, superiority of feedback that reflects group (McCarthy, 1978) or individual (Miller, 1977) performances, and feedback that is based on data provided by the workers themselves (Frost, Conard, and Hopkins, 1981) or on data independently obtained by management (Eldridge, Lemasters, and Szypot, 1978) is simply not clear.

Common sense rules for these considerations might include using both group and individual feedback whenever possible. Group feedback would be expected to prompt social interaction and pressure among workers to be productive. However, group performance feedback could allow for the hiding of relatively poor performances of some workers.

Similarly, public posting of feedback would seem to maximize social exchanges about productivity, while private feedback, particularly about the performances of individual workers, might help to protect an outstanding worker from punishment by jealous co-workers or to insulate a poor but promising worker if there are strong group pressures to be immediately productive. Surely, if basic data on productivity are going to be provided by workers themselves, there should be some mechanism to insure that such data are accurate. This mechanism could be as simple as occasional, unannounced, independent samples of productivity. This kind of mechanism is often a routine quality control procedure in manufacturing.

Some of the reviewed research reports using little more than feedback as a method to improve productivity (Prue, Krapfl, Noah, Cannon, and Maley, 1980; Kreitner, Reif, and Morris, 1977). However, there is some evidence to indicate that feedback alone may have little effect on performance, unless some additional reinforcement or punishment is dependent on work output (Meyer, 1972; Harris, Bushell, Sherman, and Kane, 1975; Miller, 1978). Research that has found good effects with feedback alone possibly does so simply because the employees work in a social context that will provide reinforcement or punishment when performance data are publicly known. It is probably not safe to assume that all work environments include social groups that will function in this manner. Therefore, it seems sensible to adopt, as a working rule, the practice of always using some form of performance-dependent reinforcement or punishment in conjunction with feedback. From the above literature, it is clear that much more is known about the functional use of reinforcement than punishment. Consequently the remainder of this discussion will focus on positive reinforcement procedures.

Positive Reinforcement.   Once the decision has been made to use both feedback and reinforcement, there are many possible kinds of reinforcement. Approving and congratulatory comments and expressions of gratitude are commonplace and would probably have a place in any behavioral productivity management system. The list of reinforcers includes letters of recognition and appreciation, trophies, pictures, tangible prizes, coffee and coffee breaks, snacks, lunches and dinners, time off from work, special privileges such as preferred parking and freedom from punching time clocks, preferred work, tickets to sporting events and movies, opportunities to go home early, and of course money. Again there is no evidence to guide the selection of reinforcers to be used in conjunction with feedback. Behavioral research has generally suggested that it is better to employ many as opposed to a few reinforcers. An advantage of using money is that it can be exchanged for a very large number of things.

The productivity manager should remember that reinforcement is a functional concept. Just because something is given to a worker with the intent that it strengthen the behavior on which it is dependent does not qualify that something as a reinforcer. The behavior must actually be strengthened. In initially selecting rewards that will hopefully function as reinforcers, it may be useful to note what workers do when given the opportunity, how they spend their time, and what they say they would like to have.

The frequency with which reinforcers are given, whether they are dependent on individual or group performance, and whether they should be publicly or privately presented are important considerations just as they were for feedback. However, there is again little concrete information to guide selections among these choices. The common sense rules presented for use of feedback are also reasonable for arranging reinforcement.

Program Development and Maintenance. If every behavioral productivity management program will involve measurement, feedback, and reinforcement, and if rough practical rules exist for selection of the parameters of these methods, there are still many choices to be made about developing a productivity improvement program and integrating it into an organization. For example, should such programs be started at the line level of an organization and be gradually built up through the organization, or should they begin at the top? How can a program, once it is established in one segment of an organization, be made to articulate with the rest of the organization so that it is maintained? Answers to these questions involve the roughest of guesswork.

Generally feedback and reinforcement for productive work must flow downward from the highest levels of an organization. Productivity goals and objectives also seem to be set by higher levels for lower levels. These considerations dictate that a productivity improvement program should begin at the top of an organization and be disseminated to lower levels. However, all work directly involved with purchases, manufacturing, sales, maintenance, and provision of services is usually done by the bottom levels of organizations. The other levels simply exist to organize and manage the work of the bottom levels. Therefore, the development of specific standards of productivity must always begin at the lowest levels. There is no adequate way to set productivity standards for a department manager who is in charge of four supervisors who manage the activities of 40 line workers, until standards have been set for the workers and supervisors. Then the standard for the manager is simply the sum of the standards of all of the people who work at the lower levels in the organization. From a different perspective, the data on which feedback must be based will usually flow from the bottom of the organization towards the top. These latter considerations would seem to suggest that productivity improvement programs might build from the bottom up.

Perhaps a combination of these two approaches is reasonable. Introduction of the use of feedback and reinforcement and the setting of broad goals might begin at the highest levels of an organization and then be introduced at successively lower levels. This will at least provide for feedback and reinforcement of improvements at lower levels when they occur. Otherwise, as increased productivity occurs at lower levels, the behavior of people responsible would not be reinforced, and their efforts probably would not be maintained. In addition, this development will help to insure that each person in the organization is motivated to achieve better productivity as opportunities become available to them.

Subsequent productivity improvement work should perhaps develop from the bottom of an organization to the top. Potentially, this would allow for a more precise determination of reasonable standards and the development of better data, feedback, and reinforcement systems.

A related question is whether it is better initially to develop broad productivity improvement programs or to first focus on relatively narrow department programs. Both approaches are illustrated in the literature. Bourdon's work represents the broad approach (1977). He worked with many management-level people, gradually teaching them the principles of behavior and showing how they could be applied in their branches of the organization. The improvements in productivity he reported were not great, but they occurred on a large scale. In contrast, Eldridge, Lemasters, and Szypot (1978) focused narrowly on the problems of a homogeneous department and tailored an elaborate data, feedback, and reinforcement program to fit that department. The resulting increase in productivity was probably greater than that obtained by Bourdon, but it was of course on a much narrower scale. These two programs can also be viewed in terms of the top level to bottom level trade-off discussed earlier. Bourdon's work might be an example of the development of general feedback and reinforcement methods introduced first at higher levels of an organization, while the Eldridge, Lemasters, and Szypot program might be a good example of the more detailed and precise program development that will progress from the bottom of the organization towards the top. It seems likely that the narrower focus on the problems of a single division or department would yield methods that are tailored to that unit, and therefore produce better results. Breadth could be obtained by providing the narrow approach in many different units.

It is probably always tempting for organizations to look for quick, one-time fixes, the simple machine-like method that can be installed and forgotten. Productive human behavior is clearly not so easily managed. There are several examples in the literature that improvements of work behavior may not be maintained if feedback and reinforcement are not maintained. Therefore, whether one implements a broad or narrow program, or begins at the bottom or the top, planning for behavioral productivity programs should include provisions for the permanent installation of these methods as integral parts of an organization's routines.

Magnitude of Effects. Comparing the magnitude of effects reported by different research studies is risky. They involve different workers, settings, problems, and measurement, as well as different productivity improvement methods. The magnitudes of effects listed in Figure 15–1 have been transformed to facilitate comparisons. This transformation consisted of calculating the average preintervention productivity, and the average productivity eventually produced after the described methods were implemented. The improvement was then calculated as a percentage of increase over the preintervention level. Even though this provides a certain uniformity in reporting results, it could be misleading for the unwary reader. Some problems, no doubt, had much more room for improvement than others. For example, almost none of the retarded persons in the Quilitch (1975) report of institutional staff and management practices were active prior to the implementation of the methods. Therefore, there was abundant room for improvement in the percentage of increase in activity. Percentage of efficiency measures of productivity, e.g., Bourdon (1977) and Miller (1978), present special interpretation problems because the uniform magnitudes reported in Figure 15-1 then amount to calculated percentage changes of percentages.

Given these problems in interpreting reported data, increases in manufacturing productivity in the 15 to 30 percent range are common. Percentage decreases in wastage might be expected to be considerably greater than this, e.g., McCarthy (1978), because of the greater reasonable room for improvement. Several of the reports on improved human service productivity include increases on the order of several hundred percent, perhaps again as a result of the low levels of initial performance.

Procedural Adequacy. The literature to date is disappointing because so much of the research fails to include measurement of costs and benefits as an important part of the results. As was pointed out in the introduction to this chapter, simple improvements in labor productivity can yield net monetary losses. Anyone who would institute productivity improvement programs should include a benefit:cost analysis as an integral part of their work. More details on how this can be done will be described below. Briefly, such an analysis simply involves measuring all relevant costs and the value of all production to see if they change as the new methods are introduced.

Although there is a general trend to better procedural quality in the behavioral research on productivity, there is still much room for improvement. For example, there may be an increasing trend for researchers to report information about the objectivity of data or to deal with data that would have a good chance of being objective in many companies. One might hope that the value of precise knowledge about effects of methods would be so great in both the public and private sectors that thorough controls would be a routine requirement. However, this is clearly not the case. The literature is also lacking in thorough descriptions of the productivity improvement methods used. The manager searching for details of methods that might be adapted to his or her problems will simply be frequently disappointed by the paucity of detail to be found in many of the reports.

ACTION PLAN

A nine-step model for the systematic development, testing, and revision of behavioral productivity improvement programs will be presented below. This model has been used by the authors' work group at the University of Kansas to attack problems such as cost control, waste reduction, sales improvement, and productivity. Variations on the model have been used by so many people in the field that its origins cannot be properly attributed to any one person. It is an elaboration on a model published by Luthans and Kreitner (1975) and is similar to one described by Feeney (1976).

The model is not generally appropriate for the organization-wide introduction of behavioral productivity improvement, although it might be used systematically to identify and attack problems in areas throughout an organization. It is appropriate for attacking the problems of a circumscribed division of a company, a department, or sales force. Recognize that the use of the model on an organization-wide basis would probably entail applying the model independently in different divisions of an organization.

Measure Productivity

The first step is to develop a measuring system that will frequently and accurately reflect the numbers and costs of the units of input into the department and the numbers and values of the outputs of the department. For example, an hour of labor by a press operator is an input that might cost $8. A wound bobbin of yarn is an example of an output that has a certain value to the company.

The first step is not always this simple, however. Manufacturing departments often have difficulty in determining values of their products, because they do not directly generate income for the company. For example, how much does a paint job add to the value of a partially completed automobile that the company will eventually sell for $7,000? The department takes a partially completed product, invests certain labor, supplies, energy, and equipment into it, at costs that can usually be estimated, and thereby adds some value to the product. But that value may not be well known, because the product is never sold on the open market before and after the department has done its work.

A practical solution to this problem is to analyze historical records to determine average costs of the department's work on products. This is not the true value of that work, but it can at least provide a benchmark. If the number of products, valued at the previously determined costs, produced per labor hour can be increased with a reduction in total costs, it is reasonable to assume that there has been a cost-efficient increase in productibity.

Plot your various measures of input and output and the ratio of input to output in graphic form. Plots by days are preferred to plots by weeks, and once-a-month plots can hide so much day-to-day variation that they may be almost useless to you. You are likely to eventually use these data as the basis for feedback, and you must have a new data point for each round of feedback. Therefore, you want to update the graphs frequently. There is a common argument that establishing such a detailed measurement system is too much trouble, that the value of improved productivity will never justify the expense of developing the data system. While it may not be worthwhile to count and cost every paper towel, it will be important to have at least aggregate data. Be concerned that the manager who is very unwilling to invest his or her time in measurement is not positively motivated to improve productivity.

Identify Possibilities for Improvement

Search for where, how, and how often work is being done for instances in which productivity could be improved. A good way to spot labor inefficiencies is to rapidly scan a department several times each day and note whether each worker is or is not engaged in the assigned job. This scanning is similar to the "disc-o-tec" sampling procedure described by Norman and Bahiri (1972). If an employee is not engaged in assigned work, note whether he or she is doing something related to assigned work (such as procuring supplies or blueprints), is simply waiting for supplies or maintenance, or is nonproductive for no immediate cause. Frequent instances of the latter obviously point to the need for some methods such as those presented in this chapter. Take precautions that you don't bias these data by always conducting the scans when workers look busy or lethargic. To get a representative picture of what is going on, make yourself a schedule for conducting the scans that is either random or representative of the entire day and stick to that schedule.

If your department has good time and motion-based standards, consider work output in relation to these standards. If standards aren't available or may be inaccurate, ask yourself how efficiently you could do the work or how fast it could be done by a steady worker. Again, poor relative performance can point to a need for better motivation.

Analyze your data system. Are costs, particularly labor costs, much higher than had been planned for your department? Are there large fluctuations in output when input is relatively constant? Are there parts of your department that appear to be operating particularly inefficiently?

Analyze Current Management Methods

List the current management practices that impinge on the workers. Ask questions such as, What happens if a worker does a good job or is relatively productive for an hour or a week? What are the consequences when a worker is very unproductive for a day? Are there pressures that workers impose on each other to be nonproductive? Is there a social system that distracts workers from their jobs to swap jokes or to hear the latest stories about the kids, the wives, the weekend, or the boss's secretary?

Consider the many rewards that the company provides the workers—pay, profit sharing, desired overtime, retirement programs, health insurance, sick pay, company picnics, and recreation. Ask yourself which of these depend on good productivity or improvements in productivity?

Don't be surprised if this analysis tells you that the only consequence of hard work is a tired back and some peer pressure to not work so hard. In many companies about the only existing force for productivity is the threat of firing and perhaps an occasional chewing out. Labor markets, union pressures, and bureaucratic company policies often dictate that the threat of firing is not a very serious one. Most rewards such as pay and fringe benefits are not given for productive work but merely for being employed and showing up at the place of work.

Develop Your Method

A crucial step in developing your productivity improvement program is to translate the data you have been collecting into a graphic feedback system. Study the above discussion on what is known about how to use feedback. If you have been keeping both individual and group data in graphic form, your feedback system may be little more than presenting copies of your data to the workers. Probably you should lean towards providing both individual and group feedback and towards providing at least the group data publicly. Arrange to provide the feedback daily or at least weekly. Explain to the workers your purposes, what the graphs mean, and how they can interpret them. Solicit their suggestions and act on them when they are feasible and promising. Explain to the worker involved why a suggestion is not implemented, if this is the case. Encourage discussions and honestly answer all questions asked you.

Arrange to frequently spend time with each worker to discuss the feedback. These meetings might be kept short and conducted on the job. Generally the meetings should be kept friendly and should focus on things that can be done to improve productivity.

Be sure to develop a reinforcement system to accompany the feedback system. Compliments, praise, expressions of gratitude and thanks, and complimentary notes would seem to be basic ingredients in every reinforcement system. You can embellish on this base in whatever ways are consistent with your company's policies and resources. Notes or memos from people in superior positions in the organization are common methods. You may want to relieve workers, to provide extra breaks or arrange for free coffee during such breaks, or take someone a cup of coffee on the job. Paid time off from work or allowing workers to leave the plant early when they have met standards can be cost efficient. If company policy and union contracts allow it, consider using cash bonuses or piece rate pay systems. If your workers are going to make or save money for the company, why shouldn't they share in this gain? If you can't use bonuses, consider purchasing prizes. Be sure that there is a variety of prizes, and if possible let workers select from a number of choices so that each might get something with personal value.

As you praise or compliment people or give them privileges or rewards, remember that these should always be dependent on some work accomplishment. If you give them for nothing, that is exactly what your workers are likely to give you in return. Instead reinforce improvements in productivity, progress toward goals, and meeting or exceeding goals. Don't be stingy. If you decide not to reinforce a worker's efforts until his or her performance reaches a goal, that accomplishment is likely never to be realized. Instead reinforce improvements until the goal is reached, and then perhaps try to arrange for some extraordinary reward. Continue to reward good performances that meet or exceed goals or standards.

Even though rewarding all members of a group for group accomplishments may amount to rewarding an individual whose performance hasn't improved, this may be a good risk in some circumstances. For example, if most of the interactions among work group members are distractions in the sense that they involve reinforcement for not working, or if there are group pressures not to be productive, rewards to everyone dependent on relatively good group performance may help to produce some peer pressure and encouragement for improvements.

Predict the Magnitude and Value of Improvements

Before you implement your methods, you would like to have some estimate of whether or not they will pay off for your company. Obtaining this estimate is a two-step process, consisting of predicting the improvement in productivity you may obtain and then calculating the benefits and costs that will result if the predicted improvements are produced.

Study the research that has been published on methods that are most like the ones you are developing. Look particularly at the magnitude of productivity improvement they obtained. If the problems and circumstances to which published methods were applied are like yours, you might hope to obtain similar results. Make a conservative estimate, then, of the productivity improvement you expect to obtain. Project this change onto your input or output data. Calculate how the costs and values will change if you obtain the predicted improvements. Be sure to include, in the costs, the costs of developing and installing your new productivity improvement method. These could include the costs of your time and that of your workers, costs of rewards, and costs of supplies and computer time for your feedback system. If the ratio of new benefits to costs is better than what you are currently achieving and you can maintain a satisfactory rate of output, prepare to install your new behavior management method. If your projected changes yield a net loss, look for ways to modify your method to reduce its estimated costs or increase its projected productivity improvements.

Install Your Method

If your projections of gains or cost savings are promising, install the method you developed. Remember, though, that you can't operate an accurate feedback system until you have a functional measurement system, and you probably don't want to provide even accurate feedback for a long period of time without a functioning reinforcement method.

Evaluate the Method Frequently

Previously you estimated benefits and costs based on your predictions of improved productivity and the costs associated with production and management of the new program. Now recalculate the benefits and costs using actual data. These should be periodically updated. Don't be surprised if the net changes are negative for a few weeks. Remember, many of the improvements reported in the literature didn't develop immediately. However, if your program is going to work, your evaluations should be revealing improvements within about a month, even though the full extent of improvements may not be realized for several months.

If these evaluations should not become positive, prepare to change or supplement your methods or to look for ways to reduce the costs of the methods themselves. The evaluations may tell you ways in which your method needs to be changed. If there is no improvement in productivity, you would look for ways to strengthen your feedback or reinforcement methods. Make sure that the data on which you are basing the feedback and on which reinforcement should be dependent are accurate.

Maintain Your Method

Assuming that you obtain cost efficient improvements in productivity, be sure to continually maintain your method. Frequently check the data, feedback, and reinforcement components to make sure that they are functioning as planned. If you have obtained good gains in productivity but later have declines, suspect that there have been relapses in the faithfulness with which one or more of the components is being carried out.

Reuse the Model

Once you have successfully used the model, don't assume that there is no room for further improvements. Study your data again for indications that some areas of productivity are still less than reasonable. Survey your operations to see if there are important functions that still are not being measured by your data system. Conduct more department-wide scans to determine what percentage of the time individual employees are engaged in productive work. If your people are frequently forced to be nonproductive because of poor service from the maintenance department or stores, consider setting up data, feedback, and reinforcement to improve the services these other departments provide yours.

An Example of Application

James T. George, a graduate student at the University of Kansas, has just completed a research project that nicely illustrates the application of the model. Jim was working as a consultant to a restaurant chain, which was having trouble containing costs. In addition, customer service was sometimes indifferent. A specific cost concern was the cost of labor as a percentage of gross sales. The chain had a standard of trying to hold waitress labor costs to 7 percent of sales, but this goal was seldom met by the individual restaurants. These costs often ranged to twice the standard.

The chain kept elaborate objective data for each restaurant, but the data were computer processed and made available once a week in a tabular form that made them difficult to understand. Jim's first job was to convert the data into graphic form. He constructed graphs to reflect the number of customers, sales per customer, sales per labor hour, sales per dollar of labor cost, and waitress earnings per labor hour, and updated these weekly for each waitress in each of three restaurants. He constructed similar graphs for the totals of the restaurants.

Several possibilities for improvement were evident from casual inspections of the data. First, there were wide variations in productivity over waitresses. One might average 20 customers and $50 in sales per hour, while another waitress in the same store would average six customers and $14 per hour. There was no relationship between wages paid and waitress productivity. A very productive waitress might be paid only minimum wage, while another would be paid 50 percent over minimum and produce a very low rate of sales. The average sale per customer also varied inexplicably over waitresses. One of the stores was consistently holding labor costs as a percentage of sales close to the standard, but the other two nearly always exceeded the standard by considerable amounts. There were abundant possibilities for improvement.

Very casual observations in the restaurants suggested activities that underlaid some of the peculiarities of the data. First, some waitresses virtually ignored the customers. They collected behind the kitchen to talk, or slowly worked behind the counter while customers waited to be seated or to have their orders taken. Food waited too long in the order window before it was served. Too many waitresses would be on the job during slack afternoon and evening hours, while too few would sometimes be present during rush hours. Some waitresses tactfully made suggestions to customers about side orders or desserts to supplement basic orders, while others gave customers the briefest of opportunities to order anything.

Direct study of restaurant and store management practices and policies suggested many reasons for the problems and ways in which improvements might be made. First, no waitress was paid according to productivity. Waitresses began working at minimum wage and received raises on a scale, dependent partly on years of service and partly on recommendations of store managers. There was some indication that managers' recommendations for raises were based on something other than the productivity of the waitresses. The assignment of waitresses to work extra hours was based on their requests and on considerations other than their productivity. Preferred hours for many waitresses were slack times because they didn't have to work so hard. Assignment to slack-time hours was apparently made on the basis of the managers' personal relationships with the waitresses. Particularly during rush times, the managers busied themselves with helping the cooks, procuring foods and utensils from storage, and operating the cash register, and provided virtually no supervision for the waitresses. Never was a manager seen to give a waitress a compliment or a pat on the back for a well-done job. Restaurant managers regularly received feedback from the corporate office on the various business volume and cost data, but this feedback was always in tabular form so that week-to-week improvements or decline in any of the data were not easily recognized. No systematic reinforcement for managers was associated with the feedback. Corporate office management staff regularly talked with the restaurant managers, but specific discussions about labor productivity and costs were infrequent and buried in discussions about other matters such as menu changes and advertising campaigns.

Jim's recommended productivity improvement method was simple and straightforward. He posted feedback boards by the time clocks in each of the restaurants. The boards listed each waitress's earnings as a percentage of sales. These figures were updated each day. The pay system for the waitresses was changed from fixed hourly rates to a straight commission system, so that each waitress received pay equal to 7 percent of her sales.

The estimated weekly savings for this method, assuming constant sales, was from about $100 to $600 per restaurant.

The method was installed and had numerous effects, some of them almost immediately evident and some more delayed, but all developing within about four weeks. The number of customers waited on per labor hour increased about 24 percent. Sales per labor hour increased 25 percent. Labor costs, as a percentage of sales, decreased 12 percent. The savings to the company, projected over a year and summed over the three restaurants, was $23,000. Needless to say, the company quickly extended the method to the other restaurants in its chain, with a chain-wide savings projected at $300,000 per year.

Other interesting results occurred. Two waitresses quit work, complaining that they would have to work too hard to earn their wages. One who was about to quit to seek better-paying employment stayed on. Waitresses began requesting work during the busier times because that is when there were more customers, sales, and earnings. Some refused to work when too many people had been assigned by the manager to work a particular shift. Waitresses began eagerly capturing customers as they came in the door and providing them with quick service. Waitresses were observed, for the first time, to return unattractively prepared food to the kitchen, insisting that it be prepared properly for their customers. Opportunities for managers to play favorites, contrary to considerations of productivity, in making job assignments or recommending pay rates were eliminated. There was no longer any reason for corporate management to discuss waitress labor costs with restaurant managers. These costs were now fixed as a percentage of sales. The pay per hour of most of the waitresses increased, while the number of hours they had to work to earn a given amount of take-home pay decreased.

Reapplication of the first steps of the model indicated that food costs in all restaurants consistently ran above standards. Much food was lost, and visits in the restaurants indicated that much was wasted as a function of such practices as cooking bacon and sausage ahead of orders and cooking more than would be sold. Labor costs for cooks were generally higher than necessary, especially when it was noted that many managers devoted considerable time to helping out in their kitchens. Here was another set of problems to which the model and the methods of behavior management could be applied.

SUMMARY

Worker productivity, defined as the ratio of the number of units produced to the number of hours worked, is important on several levels. It is important to the profitability of an individual company because it is one element of costs that can be directly and quickly controlled and improved. Improving productivity and decreasing labor costs is important to a work force, because it increases the amount of money available for wages and it is necessary for increases in standards of living. It is important on a national scale, because it will partly determine the extent to which businesses in the United States can compete with foreign corporations. Productivity must have implications for the welfare of all people in the world, because the less that is produced the less there will be to eat, live in, and use.

Everyone seems to be talking and writing about productivity, but few people are doing anything concrete about it. Much of the apparently successful research on productivity has failed to provide detailed descriptions of methods, so that a reader could duplicate them with hopes of achieving similar results. Some of the more popular theories that purport to be related to productivity appear to have a very poor grounding in fact and generally have not produced fruitful results.

Behavioral research on productivity, in contrast, appears to be relatively solidly based on well-proven principles of behavior management. A sizable percentage of this research still leaves much to be desired in the areas of objectivity of data, adequate description of methods, controls to insure that apparent effects are attributable to the methods intended to promote productivity, and analyses of benefits and costs. Nevertheless, models of sound research are included in the literature. The results from all of the behavioral research are quite consistent.

The methods employed in most of the behavioral productivity research include data systems to accurately reflect worker performances, feedback systems based on the data, and systems to reinforce good and improving productivity. The manager who would use behavioral methods to improve productivity will face several choices with little empirical evidence to serve as a guide. However, rational guides for these choices may be adequate until more is known. It seems that the first order of business in most of the research reports has been to get workable combinations of the systems installed to improve immediate problems, and save refinements for later opportunities. This has been done with good success. Whenever benefit:cost analyses have been included in research, the results have been impressive.

A technology to manage productive behavior is developing. There are as yet no obvious limitations on the applicability of this technology. The systematic management of productive behavior should serve us well in the foreseeable future.

REFERENCES

Adam E. E., Jr. Behavior modification in quality control. *Academy of Management Journal,* 1975, *18,* 662–679.

America's restructured economy. *Business Week,* June 1, 1981, 56–98.

Andrasik, F. Organizational behavior modification in business settings: A methodological and content review. *Journal of Organizational Behavior Management,* 1979, *2,* 85–102.

At Emery Air Freight: Positive reinforcement boosts performance. *Organizational Dynamics,* 1973, *1,* 113–122.

Azrin, N. H., Holz, W., Ulrich, R., and Goldiamond, I. The control of the content of conversation through reinforcement. *Journal of the Experimental Analysis of Behavior,* 1961, *4,* 25–30.

Baer, D. M., Wolf, M. M., and Risley, T. R. Some current dimensions of applied behavior analysis. *Journal of Applied Behavior Analysis,* 1968, *1,* 91–97.

Bluestone, I. Implementing quality of worklife programs. *Management Review,* 1977, *66,* 43–46.

Bourdon, R. D. A token economy application to management performance improvement. *Journal of Organizational Behavior Management,* 1977, *1,* 23–37.

Brown, M. G. Behavioral engineering in the sewn products industry. *Journal of Organizational Behavior Management,* 1980, *2,* 267–268.

Burroughs, W. A., and Richardson, P. Behavior modification in a clinical laboratory. *Hospital Administration,* 1975, *20,* 54–59.

Chandler, A. B. Decreasing negative comments and increasing performance of a shift supervisor. *Journal of Organizational Behavior Management,* 1977, *1,* 99–103.

Cherrington, D. J., Reitz, H. J., Scott, W. E., Jr. Effects of contingent and non-contingent reward on the relationship between satisfaction and task performance. *Journal of Applied Psychology,* 1971, *55,* 531–536.

Currie, R. A. Production achievement monitor, or money is the true incentive. *Bobbin,* 1979, *21,* 174–178.

DeLuca, J. Machine tools. In J. E. Ullman (Ed.), *The improvement of productivity.* New York: Praeger, 1980, pp. 289–298.

Dick, H. W. Increasing the productivity of the day relief textile machine operator. *Journal of Organizational Behavior Management,* 1978, *2,* 45–57.

Economic Report of the President, 1979. Washington, DC: United States Government Printing Office.

Eldridge, L., Lemasters, S., and Szypot, B. A performance feedback intervention to reduce waste: Performance data and participant responses. *Journal of Organizational Behavior Management*, 1978, *1*, 258–266.

Emmert, G. D. Measuring the impact of group performance feedback vs. individual performance feedback in an industrial setting. *Journal of Organizational Behavior Management*, 1978, *1*, 134–141.

Feeney, E. J. *Behavioral engineering systems training*. Redding, CT: Edward J. Feeney and Associates, 1976.

Ford, J. E. A classification system for feedback procedures. *Journal of Organizational Behavior Management*, 1980, *2*, 183–191.

Frost, J. M., Conard, R. J., and Hopkins, B. L. An analysis of the effects of feedback and reinforcement on machine-paced production. *Journal of Organizational Behavior Management*, in press.

Fuller, S. H. How quality of worklife projects work for General Motors. *Monthly Labor Review*, 1980, *103*, 37–39.

Gupton, T., and LeBow, M. D. Behavior management in a large industrial firm. *Behavior Therapy*, 1971, *2*, 78–82.

Gyllenhammar, P. G. How Volvo adapts work to people. *Harvard Business Review*, July–Aug., 1977, 102–113.

Harris, V. W., Bushell, D., Jr., Sherman, J. A., and Kane, J. F. Instructions, feedback, praise, bonus payments, and teacher behavior. *Journal of Applied Behavior Analysis*, 1975, *8*, 462.

Hersen, M., and Barlow, D. H. *Single case experimental designs: Strategies for studying behavior change*. New York: Pergamon Press, 1976.

Herzberg, F. *Work and the nature of man*. Cleveland: World Publishing Company, 1966.

Honig, W. K. (Ed.). *Operant behavior: Areas of research and application*. New York: Appleton-Century-Crofts, 1977.

Hornbruch, F. W. *Raising productivity: Ten case histories and their lessons*. New York: McGraw-Hill, 1977.

Hulin, C. L., and Blood, M. R. Job enlargement, individual differences and worker responses. *Psychological Bulletin*, 1968, *69*, 41–55.

Iwata, B. A., Bailey, J. S., Brown, K. M., Foshee, T. J., and Alpern, M. A performance-based lottery to improve residential care and training by institutional staff. *Journal of Applied Behavior Analysis*, 1976, *9*, 417–431.

Komaki, J., Waddell, W. M., and Pearce, M. G., The applied behavior analysis approach and individual employees: Improving performance in two small businesses. *Organizational Behavior and Human Performance*, 1977, *19*, 337–352.

Kreitner, R., Reif, W. E., and Morris, M. Measuring the impact of feedback on the performance of mental health technicians. *Journal of Organizational Behavior Management*, 1977, *1*, 105–109.

Latham, G. P., and Dossett, D. L. Designing incentive plans for unionized employees: A comparison of continuous and variable rate reinforcement schedules. *Personnel Psychology*, 1978, *31*, 47–70.

Latham, G. P., and Yukl, G. A. A review of research on the application of goal setting in organizations. *Academy of Management Journal*, 1975, *18*, 824–846.

Lawler, E. E., III. Job design and employee motivation. *Personnel Psychology*, 1969, *22*, 426–435.

Lawler, E. E., III. The new plant revolution. *Organizational Dynamics*, 1978, *6*, 3–12.

Leavitt, H. J., and Whisler, T. L. Management in the 1980's. *Harvard Business Review*, November–December, 1958.

Locke, E. A., Sirota, D., and Wolfson, A. D. An experimental case study of the successes and failures of job enrichment in a government agency. *Journal of Applied Psychology,* 1976, *61,* 701–711.

Lott, C. W. The automobile industry. In J. E. Ullman (Ed.), *The improvement of productivity.* New York: Praeger, 1980, 245–255.

Luthans, F., and Kreitner, R. *Organizational behavior modification.* Glenview, IL: Scott, Foresman, 1975.

McCarthy, M. Decreasing the incidence of "high bobbins" in a textile spinning department through a group feedback procedure. *Journal of Organizational Behavior Management,* 1978, *1,* 150–154.

McGregor, D. *Leadership and motivation.* Cambridge: The MIT Press, 1966.

Macy, B. A. The quality of worklife project at Bolivar: An assessment. *Monthly Labor Review,* 1980, *103,* 41–43.

Mali, P. *Improving total productivity: MBO strategies for business, government, and not-for-profit organizations.* New York: Wiley, 1978.

Maslow, A. H. *Motivation and personality.* New York: Harper Bros., 1954.

Meyer, H. H. Feedback that spurs performance. In A. J. Marrow (Ed.), *The failure of success.* New York: AMACOM, 1972.

Miller, L. M. Improving sales and forecast accuracy in a nationwide sales organization. *Journal of Organizational Behavior Management,* 1977, *1,* 39–51.

Miller, L. M. *Behavior management.* New York: Wiley, 1978, pp. 153–156.

National Center for Productivity and Quality of Working Life. *Improving productivity: A description of selected company programs.* Washington, DC: Government Printing Office, 1975.

National Commission on Productivity. *Second annual report.* Washington, DC: Government Printing Office, 1973.

Norman, R. G., and Bahiri, S. *Productivity measurement and incentives.* London: Butterworths, 1972.

Organ, D. W. A reappraisal and reinterpretation of the satisfaction-causes-performance hypothesis. *Academy of Management Review,* 1977, *2,* 46–53.

Orpen, C. The effects of job enrichment on employee satisfaction, motivation, involvement and performance: A field experiment. *Human Relations,* 1979, *32,* 189–217.

Pollard, S. *The genesis of modern management.* Baltimore: Penguin, 1968.

Pomerleau, O. F., Bobrove, P. H., and Smith, R. H. Rewarding psychiatric aides for the behavioral improvement of assigned patients. *Journal of Applied Behavior Analysis,* 1973, *6,* 383–390.

Pommer, D. A., and Streedbeck, D. Motivating staff performance in an operant learning program for children. *Journal of Applied Behavior Analysis,* 1974, *7,* 217–221.

Powell, R. M., and Schlacter, J. L. Participative management: A panacea? *Academy of Management Journal,* 1971, *14,* 165–173.

Poza, E. J., and Markus, M. L. Success story: The team approach to work restructuring. *Organizational Dynamics,* 1980, *8,* 3–25.

Prue, D. M., Krapfl, J. E., Noah, J. C., Cannon, S., and Maley, R. F. Managing the treatment activities of state hospital staff. *Journal of Organizational Behavior Management,* 1980, *2,* 165–181.

Quilitch, H. R. A comparison of three staff management procedures. *Journal of Applied Behavior Analysis,* 1975, *8,* 59–66.

Runnion, A., Johnson, T., McWhorter, J. The effects of feedback and reinforcement on truck turnaround time in materials transportation. *Journal of Organizational Behavior Management,* 1978, *1,* 110–117.

Siegal, I. H. *Company productivity: Measurement for improvement.* Kalamazoo, MI: W. E. Upjohn Institute, 1980.

Sielaff, T. J. Modification of work behavior. *Personnel Journal,* 1974, *53,* 513–517.

Taylor, F. W. *The principles of scientific management.* New York: Harper and Row, 1911.

Wabba, M. A., and Bridwell, L. G. A review of research on the need hierarchy theory. In K. N. Wesley and G. A. Yukl (Eds.), *Organizational behavior and industrial psychology: Readings with commentary.* New York: Oxford University Press, 1975, 5–11.

Webster's new collegiate dictionary. Springfield, MA: G. & C. Merriam, 1964.

Welsch, W. V., Ludwig, C., Radiker, J. E., and Krapfl, J. E. Effects of feedback on daily completion of behavior modification projects. *Mental Retardation,* 1973, *11,* 24–26.

Winter, R. E. A series of articles on productivity. *Wall Street Journal,* 1980, October 13, pp. 1, 15; October 21, pp. 1, 24; October 28, p. 1, 22.

Yukl, G. A., and Latham, G. P. Consequences of reinforcement schedules and incentive magnitudes for employee performance: Problems encountered in an industrial setting. *Journal of Applied Psychology,* 1975, *60,* 294–298.

Yukl, G. A., Latham, G. P., and Pursell, E. D. The effectiveness of performance incentives under continuous and variable ratio schedules or reinforcement. *Personnel Psychology,* 1976, *29,* 221–231.

16

Performance Management in Sales Organizations

ROBERT MIRMAN
General Mills, Inc.

Darwin may groan and roll over in his resting place, but I'm convinced that in addition to the generally accepted biological characteristics we inherit, such as hair color, facial features, and a genetic craving for chocolate, we also are born with the belief that we can SELL. As a young boy, I can remember reading an ad on the back page of a *Classics Illustrated* comic book, which described the wealth and prestige I could earn by selling Christmas cards door to door. What could be easier? Almost everyone uses Christmas cards, and the prices were certainly reasonable. I decided to spend my anticipated earnings on a new baseball glove or a three-speed racer—or both. After all, this was America, the land of opportunity.

After selling only three boxes of cards in two weeks, one to my neighbor and two to my mother, I came to the only conclusion possible: the Christmas spirit was dying and I was pushing an inferior product. It wasn't until later that I realized that with my "Hi, you wouldn't wanna buy some Christmas cards, wouldya?" style, I couldn't have sold a Christmas tree to the Pope.

There is of course no telling what I could have become today had I been given some rudimentary instructions on *how* to sell those boxes of "Peace on Earth, Set III." It is apparent that the bridge between the belief that one can sell and a successful sales pitch must be a certain amount of skill training, combined with a high level of sustained motivation, for perseverance in the face of frequent rejection.

With this thought firmly in mind, the modern sales organization has invested much of its energy and resources to develop the skills of its sales force and stimulate them to use their skills frequently and appropriately. Since very few products sell themselves, and every product's sales volume can be dramatically improved by a skilled sales person, the organization's overall success is contingent upon the performance of its sales force.

Two elements that have a direct impact on successful sales performance, sales training and motivation, will be discussed in this chapter, with major emphasis on a description of performance improvement programs that take place once sales training has been completed. A successful sales improvement strategy, the performance systems approach, will be reviewed in considerable detail, and an action plan will be provided for adoption of this strategy in other sales settings.

SALES TRAINING: IS IT WORTH THE EXPENSE?

Sales training is big business. In addition to basic instruction in one-to-one selling skills, typical training seminars cover a wide range of sophisticated topics including customer psychology, product knowledge, marketing, and demographics. Long gone are the days when selling was considered an art effectively practiced by only those gifted with innate salesmanship abilities. Selling, like teaching, is not and never has been an art. It is a science, and as such can be taught, practiced, and learned. To be sure, the proliferation of firms that do nothing but design sales training programs for their clients is testimony to our perceived need for such an effort.

Although sales training is most often accepted as a necessary element in the establishment and maintenance of a successful sales organization, it is just as necessary to ask if such training is effective in improving the sales behavior of the sales force. Managers all too often prescribe training for their sales people on little more than faith alone (Hahne, 1977), and can rarely verify the cost effectiveness of such efforts. The authors of one research report candidly admitted, "We cannot really blame store management for hesitating to invest their people, time and money in [sales] training when they don't know what kind of return they will get on their investment." (Does retail training pay?, 1969). Retailers in fact have often dismissed sales training as a costly waste, because turnover of sales personnel averages 60 percent annually. (Retailers discover an old tool: Sales Training, 1980).

Emery Air Freight, one of the first companies to utilize behavioral technology to improve performance in a business environment, found that their sales people were "too often content to walk away from sales calls with promises, good will, and handshakes rather than orders." (Emery salesmen ask themselves "Why?", 1970). A training program entitled "Guide to Action" was initiated to teach Emery's sales people to become more aggressive and to work toward an observable action from each customer. An observable action could be a phone call to a superior, placement of an order, calling in an assistant to discuss Emery's proposal, and so on.

Emery found that business immediately increased up to 100 percent in all sales offices for several months, and *then decreased to previous levels.* Frustrated by these results, Emery's management initiated a test program in which additional training covering the same guide to action program was prescribed for three of the same sales offices. Once again, sales increased, stayed high for four months, and then returned to normal. It became clear that Emery's sales people had the appropriate skills in their repertoire, but were not using these skills in a sustained manner. "Like any training program," claimed Emery's national marketing manager, " 'Guide to Action' broke down once the sales people were out of the classroom and in the field." Emery's management correctly sensed that the problem was not a lack of training but a lack of proper supervision and feedback.

A system called "Post-Call Learning Cycle" was initiated. This system enabled sales people to measure their use of *specific targeted behavior* on every call. This self-administered feedback device provided immediate feedback to the sales person and stimulated additional feedback from sales managers. Following the addition of this process to the training program, sales increased as before and were sustained.

All too often, inadequate training is pinpointed as the scapegoat when sales figures fail to reach expected levels. Although Emery learned that its duplication of training efforts provided little long-term effectiveness, it cannot be assumed that poor performance is a direct result of poor training. Connellan (1978) described the efforts of one organization to convince its sales people to reduce the sales of low-profit items and increase sales of those products that brought far greater profit to the corporation. These low-margin items were priced relatively low in the marketplace, and were therefore easier to sell. Since commission payments were contingent upon overall sales volume, the performance goals of the sales force were in opposition to the goals of the company. Low sales of higher-profit items was certainly not a result of poor training, for sales people were aware of both the profit potential from higher-margin items and the company's desire to increase profitability. The firm's management correctly realized that the basic reason for this problem was an improper schedule of incentive conditions; when sales volume objectives were changed to *profitability* goals, and commissions made contingent upon this performance factor, in a short time "sales leveled off and some product lines even dropped a bit, but profits were up substantially" (p. 118).

Training versus Feedback

In a recent study by Brown, Malott, Dillion, and Keeps (1980), three department store sales people were given training in four specific sales skills: (1) approaching customers, (2) greeting customers, (3) courtesy, and (4) closing the sale. Performance in these areas was measured prior to training (baseline) and following training. Utilization of these appropriate skills, i.e., percent of opportunities in which the correct behavior was demonstrated, increased 9.6 percent after training. Through the use of a multiple baseline design, daily feedback on performance of these four kinds of behavior was then presented to each sales person. During this feedback phase, performance of these specific acts increased another 35 percent. Interestingly, a sales person who had not participated in the sales training program, but did participate in the feedback phase, showed as much improvement as those who did go through customer service training. Brown et al. suggested that the training program be reduced to a "one or two-page set of instructions prior to the implementation of the feedback procedure" (p. 263), plus four hours of instruction showing managers how to give feedback.

Moreover, when feedback was withdrawn (baseline 2), performance dropped, but returned to high levels when sales people were told their performance would be evaluated by customers. Performance remained high during the six weeks of this customer evaluation phase, even though none of the 500 customers ever bothered to return an evaluation form. The conclusion that sales behavior could be controlled by the *announcement* of impending accountability was substantiated by the fact that performance also increased dramatically for all three subjects *on the first day* of the feedback phase after being shown a graph depicting their performance during baseline, but before they had received any feedback on that particular day's performance (p. 261).

A cost analysis of this program provided additional evidence to support the advantageous cost effectiveness of the feedback procedure. Cost projections for formal customer service training on a year-long, store-wide basis (250 employees and 14 managers) indicated that a total of $5,942 would be spent for the training program, or $619 per percentage point of anticipated improvement. It was estimated that $1,637 would be spent for a feedback program covering the same time period, or $47 per percentage point of improvement. For an expenditure of only 28 percent of that necessary to operate a training exercise, the simple feedback procedure was *four times as effective.*

This study by Brown et al. is one of the very few controlled studies that provide a comparative analysis of performance and cost effectiveness of basic training versus another sales improvement startegy. Although the authors failed to account for interactive efforts, used a small sample of three sales people, and did not report on differential changes in sales volume resulting from these procedures, the combination of multiple baseline and reversal design strategies effectively verified the relative ineffectiveness of the training model and underlined the need to supplement training programs with procedures to *maintain* sales skills in the selling arena.

A sales training course attended by 100 sales people in eight Chicago Montgomery Ward department stores resulted in a 10 percent sales increase over a control group. (Retailers discover an old sales tool, 1980).

In addition, turnover dropped 68 percent, and sales people were rated as more helpful and enthusiastic. A similar program in John Wanamaker, Inc., described in the same article, also resulted in some sales gain, but managers found that sales people "were not making the multi-unit sales we expected" (p. 51). To remedy the situation, "pressure will be put on supervisors to see that employees use the skills, offer refresher courses, run sales contests, and train a crew of 'mystery shoppers' to evaluate salespeople" (p. 52). Showing people *how* to sell and getting them to continually *use* those skills are apparently separate issues, which must be separately addressed.

Another study that evaluated the comparative effectiveness of training versus a performance feedback model (Weitz, Antoinetti, and Rains, 1954) found that written weekly performance feedback to half of those insurance sales people recently attending sales training was effective in increasing sales by this group. This feedback communicated weekly individual and group sales data to each member of the experimental group. While this group demonstrated sales gains averaging 15.2 percent, the group receiving no feedback showed a 10.5 percent *decrease*. Fifty-four percent of the sales agents receiving weekly feedback showed a posttraining improvement, while this was true of only 38 percent of the group receiving training only. Although it would be unreasonable to assume that this sales training had a negative effect on sales performance, it would be more appropriate to conclude that the effect of sales training was certainly magnified by the inclusion of a follow-up strategy to insure sustained performance by sales people upon their return to their sales offices.

Sesame Street for Sales People

A training strategy that has gained recent attention is the use of behavior modeling. Sales people are typically shown a live or videotaped example of appropriate selling skills, and are required to practice the behavior used by the model. This imitation approach utilizes pinpointing of specific skills, repeated practice, reinforcement by the trainer, and other techniques commonly associated with a behavioral approach (and Sesame Street). One anecdotal report that utilized a variation of the behavior modeling approach was described by Hahne (1977) in an article entitled "How to Measure Results of Sales Training." Hahne described a sales training program that assisted sales people in developing a strategy to sell their most "unsellable customer." After participating in strategy development, role playing, and rehearsal sessions, participants later reported an 85 percent success rate in selling this targeted customer. Additionally, 84 percent of the participants increased their sales over the previous year. Although interpretation of these results is clouded by the lack of information regarding sales in similar groups not having the benefit of such training, the 85 percent success rate remains an impressive figure.

Data from the application of behavior modeling training in another large department store indicate the degree to which the performance of veteran sales people can be improved. Using nine other stores as a control, sales people participating in the behavior modeling training increased their use of the 10 pinpointed sales skills 37 percent more than their counterparts in the control stores (see Figure 16-1).

The experimental store increased sales per hour by 4.5 percent more than nine control stores, while simultaneously reducing selling costs by 3.6 percent more than the control group (Rubenstein, 1981). Although the measurement criteria were not specified, the store's productivity ranking increased from fifth to second in the company.

A similar program in a J. L. Hudson Department Store verified the effectiveness of the behavior modeling training (Harris, 1981). Post-training utilization of the 10 measured kinds of sales behavior increased 14 percent, while performance in the control group dropped 31 percent (i.e., overall difference of 45 percent). Although sales data indicated increased traffic in both the training and control departments, increased customer traffic in the control department "caused a significant deterioration in service and use of selling skills." Although the training group did improve performance in the posttraining measures, absolute levels of performance were still low in several skill categories. For instance, the training group increased its use of "feature and benefit" statements from 25 to 40 percent of the opportunities. This is certainly a strong improvement, but even 40 percent is still quite low. Another category, "thanking the customer and using his or her name," also showed an improvement from 40 to 51 percent, but again this posttraining performance is still relatively weak.

Although the behavior modeling approach was apparently effective in the cases described above, the lack of long-term follow-up data does not allow a conclusive statement to be made regarding the overall effect of such a procedure. This point is particularly significant in light of the Emery Air Freight data, which indicated a decrease in training effect over time. However, the positive effect of Emery's self-administered account-

Target Behavior	% Increase vs. Control Group
1. Greeting customers	+35%
2. Determining needs	+30
3. Showing specific merchandise	+27
4. Selling benefits	+33
5. Overcoming objections	+38
6. Closing the sale	+13
7. Suggesting additional merchandise	+113
8. Maintaining customer self-esteem	+22
9. Complimenting customer on choice	+249
10. Speed and efficiency	−22
Overall use of targeted skills	+37

FIGURE 16-1. Catagories of targeted sales skills and resulting increase over the control group following training utilizing behavior modeling (courtesy of MOHR Development, Inc., Stamford, CT, 1981).

ability system, and the observation by Brown et al. (1980) that sales performance increased after sales people were simply *told* their performance would be evaluated by shoppers, indicated that the use of "mystery shoppers" in these retail environments should very likely increase the probability of performance maintenance.

Other references in the general sales literature indicate the successful use of behavior modeling techniques. For example, Cheesebrough-Ponds, Inc. (Making sales people behave, 1979) taught sales people how to sell a new hair spray product by filmed models, and found improvements in the areas of distribution of product and speed of the first order. Once again, however, it is difficult to pinpoint sales training as the effective change element in this report, because in addition to the behavior models, formalized commitment to sales targets and follow-up accountability was also initiated. It appears that a necessary factor in insuring the long-term success of behavior modeling sales training is a measurement system that is either self-administered or in some way allows for managers to provide sales people with feedback on their performance.

Pygmalion and the Sales Person

Another element that increases the difficulty of assessing the effectiveness of sales training is the so-called "Pygmalion effect." One of the underlying purposes of any sales training program is to convince the trainee that he or she will be a more effective sales person at the completion of the training. Assuming that trainees' confidence in their ability to sell *is* increased as a function of the sales training, what effect does this change in self-confidence have on future sales performance? Jones (1979) described a study done in a British insurance agency, in which sales agents were assigned to one of three groups, each headed by a sales manager. The agents were told they had been assigned to each group on the basis of their ability (i.e., superior, average, poor). The superior group, who became known as the super staff, were asked to produce two-thirds of the premium volume achieved by the agency the previous year. Sales in the superior and poor groups increased and decreased respectively. Jones concluded that sales performance was directly related to the sales person's expectation of success. If this is indeed the case, it is not surprising that sales performance often increases immediately following graduation from a sales training program designed to convince the sales person that he or she can sell successfully.

Therefore, it becomes difficult to determine whether the improvement in sales behavior following training is due more to an increased knowledge of sales skills or to the increased expectation of success. Certainly there must be an interactive effect, but the important question must be: *If some of the change in performance is due to the Pygmalion effect, how much long-term effect can we therefore expect from sales training?* Regardless of the short-term effectiveness of sales training, how can we insure that sales people continue to use the appropriate skills on every sales occasion?

A great deal of evidence suggests that sales people do not continually use the skills they have been trained to use. Many sales managers would like to believe that their sales people, particularly those operating under commission or incentive contingencies, use all their skills appropriately on every opportunity. Although this perception is tantamount to a belief in Easter bunnies and tooth fairies, it is easy to understand how managers can develop this delusion. After all, haven't their sales people been trained well? Aren't they well paid? And most importantly, aren't they earning incentive pay contingent upon sales performance? Following this delusion further, if we accept that these conditions insure continual maximum performance, the addition of a *sales contest* to this sales environment should have little or no effect on sales performance. Right?

If you answered in the affirmative, leave your dentures under your pillow—the tooth fairy will be there *tonight!* There are only three Basic Truths of Life: (1) Santa Claus hasn't ever left the North Pole, (2) Superman only flies in the movies, and (3) most sales people will increase their sales to meet any reasonably set target in order to win a free trip to Hawaii. One national sales organization found it could generate sales increases of between 15–20 percent over expected levels by holding sales contests in which divisional winners received family vacations in Hawaii or some other desirable locations (Mirman, 1979). These sales people were already earning incentive pay based on sales, but sales volume still improved dramatically during the three-month contest period.

If Training Works, Why Use Incentives?

Actually, most managers do understand that sales people do not continually operate at full speed and occasionally need additional stimulation. In a survey of the sales managers of 396 firms (Haring and Myers, 1953), 72 percent of these managers felt that sales contests would "do the most to stimulate the average salesmen to *better* his usual or normal performance" (p. 159). An annual report covering 330 companies with over 26,000 sales people (Steinbrink, 1980) indicated that 74 percent of them operated under various types of incentive contingencies that provided increased pay contingent upon sales volume. This figure rises to 87 percent if we include "discretionary bonuses" in the definition of incentive pay. The philosophical pessimism inherent in any incentive system lends credence to the argument that sales people do not consistently work to their potential, for if they *were* consistently working at their peak, why would incentive pay be necessary at all?

Conclusions

In light of the fact that sales contests and incentive programs work so well to improve sales performance (Conference Board, 1970), it should be apparent that training programs cannot be relied upon to singularly insure high levels of sales performance. In a detailed analysis of a training failure in a retail clothing store, Connellan (1978) described five reasons why selling skills, although easily performed in the training classroom, were difficult to sustain on the selling floor (p. 26):

1. Little, if any, feedback or support from customers was typically offered on employee effectiveness.

2. An instructor was available for help in the classroom, but not on the selling floor.

3. Sales people received little or no support or reinforcement from managers or customers for behaving as suggested by the training department.

4. Some attempts to follow suggested guidelines were extremely punishing. For example, in Connellan's study, customers often became angry or upset when sales people tried to sell them related merchandise.

5. The high ratio of successful sales to opportunities in the training room (i.e., 1:1 success rate) fell to a success ratio of 1:10 when dealing with real customers. This is a particularly aversive ratio for new employees. Customer approaches that appeared practical in class did not pay off often enough on the floor. Connellan reported that sales people "began to take a more passive attitude toward helping customers" (p. 26).

Some form of sales training for new sales people is necessary in order to provide them with information about basic selling skills. However, when attempting to *improve* sales performance, the issue is not often resolved through additional training, but through procedures that stimulate sales people to do what they *already know how to do*. Since sales people tend to improve their performance under incentive and contest conditions, it is apparent that there is a gap between what they *can* do as a result of training and what they *will* do on the selling floor. For sales people, at least, the possession of appropriate skills does not always result in the appropriate use of these skills.

It appears that sales training must be supplemented by additional factors such as performance measurement and feedback, goal setting, and accountability, if the newly learned skills are to be fully utilized upon the individual's return to the selling task. To be maximally effective, sales training must be considered as one element of a system that not only shows sales people which skills are appropriate to job success but also places them within an environment that supports the frequent use of these skills.

SALES IMPROVEMENT STRATEGIES

We can't rely on training to get our people to sell. We have to keep after them, push them to their limits, and let 'em know we've got to have those orders. If push comes to shove, I know my people will squeeze blood from a stone to meet their quotas; they've just gotta be motivated, that's all. (Sales Manager at management meeting)

"They've got to be motivated, that's all." Most sales managers recognize the need for procedures to supplement sales training, and have traditionally relief heavily on a combination of negative reinforcement (i.e., fear) and monetary incentives to insure continued high levels of sales performance. The tools with which the sales manager can improve the performance of his or her sales team can be placed into two major categories, antecedent strategies and consequence strategies.

Antecedent strategies are used *prior* to the selling occasion and serve to stimulate the use of appropriate skills, for example, exhortation, review of appropriate selling points, goal and objective setting, and establishing performance measures.

Consequence strategies are used *following* the selling occasion and increase the likelihood that the appropriate skills (behavior) will be used again under similar circumstances. Some examples are data feedback, managerial feedback, public recognition, contingent performance evaluation rating, and contingent awards, salary increases, incentive pay, and so on.

The manner in which sales managers use both antecedent and consequence strategies will certainly determine their success in that role. Although there is a paucity of studies dealing specifically with the application of these behavioral strategies in the sales area, the remainder of this section will review these applications in four settings; restaurants, retail sales, wholesale sales, and telephone sales.

Restaurants

Many anecdotal reports in restaurant magazines suggest procedures to increase sales of food and liquor, but these reports typically provide no data that can be used to verify effectiveness. The two published behavioral studies in restaurant settings both deal with improving customer service, but neither provides any data on the resulting effect on sales volume. The authors of one of these studies (Komaki, Blood, and Holder, 1980) point out that sales data are not suitable measures for verifying effectiveness of customer service improvements, because "Factors other than the quality of service rendered (economic conditions, seasonality, competition, product quality) affect sales" (p. 152). In the study of Komaki et al. (1980) 11 employees of a fast-food franchise were taught to measure their own rate of smiling and talking with customers. The desired behavior was rehearsed and then reinforced by both the store manager and the reactions of customers. Employees increased their frequency of smiling at customers while at the cash register area (as measured by observers), but attempts to improve such friendliness in the dining area were mixed, due to delayed and infrequent reinforcement well as the difficulties experienced when attempting to do research in business settings—measurement and observation difficulties, managers out of town, turnover of personnel, and so on (pp. 159–163).

Another report (Customer service behavior, 1978) described improvements in 11 types of customer service behavior through the use of a poker game incentive strategy similar to the one used by Pedalino and Gamboa (1974). Daily measures were taken on such behavior as taking orders, collecting tickets, delivering meals, asking customers if they were pleased, and saying "thank you" before customers left. Use of these techniques rose from 60 to 90 percent when employees were able to draw a new card from a deck of playing cards for each day the group exceeded a specific performance standard. After five days, the employee with the highest poker hand won a "small dollar bonus" (p. 1).

There are, however, unpublished reports of restaurant programs geared specifically to increasing such factors such as dollars spent per customer, wine sales, and dessert sales. Restaurant magazines continually suggest that managers take care to teach their service personnel to use suggestive selling skills, but aside from this exhortation, no data or specific instructions are provided regarding the actual implementation of this strategy. King (1980a), in a hotel restaurant program, asked 15 waiters and waitresses to take a daily tally of the type and amount of wine sold. Supervisors held training sessions for these employees, in which they discussed techniques for increasing wine sales (and therefore tips) through suggestive selling. Weekly graphic feedback of wine sales per employee resulted in a 25 percent increase, particularly for champagne and after dinner wines. In a similar program (Hanisch, 1980), assisted a restaurant owner in the implementation of a procedure that used a combination of feedback and antecedent stimuli, such as the addition of wine glasses to the table setting, and large buttons worn by servers that said "Ask About Our Wine" in several languages. Wine sales immediately jumped from 60 to 160 gallons per month as a consequence of these antecedents and an increase in suggestive selling.

Another study conducted by this author verified the effectiveness of antecedent stimulus control on customer behavior in restaurants. After taking a baseline count of the number of dessert items ordered off the regular menu, specially designed placemats, which pictured these items along with a deliciously worded description, were substituted for the normal plain white paper placements. During the seven-week baseline period, an average of 1.3 percent of customers ordered dessert. This increased to an average of over 6 percent once the pictorial placemats were substituted.

Restaurants are fertile ground for the use of behavioral techniques for several reasons: (1) Since service personnel who effectively use suggestive selling skills reap the immediate consequence of higher tips based on a percentage of increased orders, this behavior should be easily maintained once learned; (2) since most customers do not walk into a restaurant with a specific food selection firmly in mind, the server can play a decisive role in assisting customers with their selections; (3) measurement of sales of specific high margin items (e.g., wine or liquor, desserts, and so on) has recently been made easier by the increased use of computerized cash registers, which automatically tally the number of these items sold by each server. This ability to easily measure daily sales figures is necessary if one wishes to provide immediate feedback to each sales person; (4) computerization has also increased the speed with which evaluation of the improvement strategy can be accomplished; changes in strategy can be quickly achieved as a function of up-to-the-minute data. Cost analysis of each procedure is also more easily determined.

Retail Sales

In the area of retail sales, or sales made directly to the consumer in a single setting such as department or grocery stores, several studies have been described in the first section of this chapter (Brown et al., 1980; Retailers discover an old sales tool, 1980; Rubenstein, 1981; Harris, 1981). Komaki, Waddell, and Pierce (1977) reported on a program in which a combination of procedures (employee self-measurement, behavior rehearsals, and contingent time off from work) were used to improve customer assistance (i.e., approach and courtesy) in a small grocery store. Although actual sales data were not used as a dependent variable, the frequency of appropriate customer assistance, as measured by observers, improved from 35 percent of opportunities during the baseline period to 87 percent during the intervention phase. The authors also concluded that "When attempting to modify the behavior of others, the person initiating the change should expect to alter his or her own behavior as well" (p. 349).

Self-measurement was also used as a strategy in an unpublished program (King, 1980b) designed to increased sales in a jewelry store. Sales personnel were trained to maintain frequency counts on tally cards of three sales skills:

1. Percent of opportunities in which jewelry was taken off the shelf for presentation to customers.
2. Percent of opportunities in which an alternative item was suggested.
3. Following a rebuff by customer, percent of opportunities in which customers were asked to describe the occasion for which they were contemplating a jewelry purchase.

It was assumed that frequent use of this success-related behavior (SRB) would increase the probability of a sale. Unfortunately, no data were maintained by the store, so evaluation of this procedure was not possbile. However, anecdotal reports from store management indicated that these SRBs increased in frequency.

The strength of sales employee participation in establishing appropriate sales procedures was demonstrated by Neider (1980) in a program conducted in four department stores. Hypothesizing that sales performance would increase when sales personnel more clearly perceived (1) the effort-performance linkage, and (2) a direct relationship between performance and consequences, Neider found that performance was highest when employees both participated in the identification of appropriate sales behavior and received tangible incentives for increased sales. An incentive-only condition increased sales more than "participation only," but was not as effective as a combination of these approaches. This suggests that asking sales people to assist in the identification of critical sales *behavior* is an effective antecedent stimulus for increasing the use of these skills, but is more powerful when used in combination with some type of reinforcing consequence.

The potential effectiveness of behavioral procedures in the sales area was aptly demonstrated by Warren (1978) in a program designed to increase the average amount of sale per customer in the men's accessories department of a Dayton-Hudson department store. After rejecting frequency of sale as a dependent variable due to variable customer counts, seasonality, and so on, Warren identified a 20 percent improvement in average amount of sale as the program's objective. Historical data showed a $19 average sale per customer prior to the program's initiation. Sales people were informed of this baseline figure and the $23 objective, and were asked to circle (on the sales receipt) sales totals that exceeded $19. Graphic feedback on average dollars was posted for each sales person, in addition to the self-monitoring procedure. Managerial reinforcement was offered:

1. For improvements over the prior day.
2. Intermittently, when the sales average approximated the $23 objective.
3. On a regular basis when department performance was reviewed with the sales team.
4. Individual *public* recognition for improvement.

The average sale amount showed an immediate increase, reached the objective of $23 within five weeks, and "maintained for as long as it was tracked" (p. 56). Warren did not specify the length of the measurement period, nor did he describe the level of this performance once the measurement was eliminated. Hopefully, a procedure that demonstrated such control over sales behavior was not discontinued. Warren also commented that "the impact of training (i.e., for suggestive selling skills) was relatively low, since the selling skills were largely present" (p. 56).

These studies indicate that the effect of basic sales training can be sustained in retail settings through the use of such behavioral procedures as: (1) feedback from customers, managers, and mystery shoppers, (2) self-measurement, and (3) objective setting. In fact the effectiveness of sales training should be more easily sustained in a retail setting than in whole-sale or "insurance selling" situations for several reasons:

1. *Opportunity for Repeated Practice.* The traffic flow in most retail stores provides multiple opportunities for the sales person to practice the sales skills learned in training. These daily opportunities for practice and feedback far exceed the number of prospective opportunities an insurance agent might have in an entire week. Whereas a retail clothing sales person in a department store might approach 50 potential customers per day, a food products sales person for a large manufacturer averages only seven calls per day.

2. *Opportunity for Managerial Feedback.* Although Connellan (1978) pointed out that one of the problems with transference of training to the selling floor was the general unavailability of managerial feedback, the likelihood for managerial feedback is still greater for the retail person than for his or her counterpart in the insurance or food products business. Assuming 50 customer contacts per day, even if the department manager witnesses only 10 percent of the sales person's customer contacts, there are still five opportunities for feedback from the manager. Because whole-sale sales people are making their presentations in various locations, the frequency of sales manager observations is quite low. In food product sales, e.g., the district sales manager accompanies the sales representative on an average of approximately one per 100 calls. The close proximity of retail managers increases the probability of feedback and therefore main-tenance of training effect.

3. *Opportunity for Customer Feedback.* As described above, retail operations have successfully utilized the services of "mystery shoppers," who are specifically trained to evaluate the performance of sales people. Although it would be awkward to ask clients and customers of wholesale and insurance sales people to provide a written evaluation of the sales person's skills, this procedure is often used in department store settings (Brown et al., 1980). This opportunity to unobtrusively evaluate the per-formance of retail sales people allows for an increased level of feedback and accountability.

4. *Opportunity for Peer Modeling.* Retail sales people have the op-portunity to observe their peers in action. This is the ultimate in realistic behavior modeling and is rarely available to the wholesale sales person who operates alone.

From the "what-if-all-else-fails department": Dress your sales people in conservative business suits and ties, or conservative dresses in good taste. A recent study by the department of psychology of Emory University (Brooks Brothers braun, 1981) verified that department store salesmen dressed in old-fashioned traditional suits outsold colleagues in informal dress, even in the low-priced departments. Maybe George Bernard Shaw and Clark Kent were right: clothes *do* make the man!

Wholesale Sales

In addition to the studies described earlier in this chapter (Emery salesmen ask themselves "Why?", 1970; Connellan, 1978; Hahne, 1977; Making salespeople behave, 1979; Jones, 1979), several reports describe the use of behavioral procedures in various wholesale sales settings, including chemicals, textiles, medical equipment, food products, paint, hosiery, electronic equipment, and telephone equipment.

Miller (1977) described a program that used a point system to increase sales volume and improve sales forecasting, i.e., sales people's estimates of future sales volume. After finding that a chemical firm's sales people were being loosely evaluated and paid bonuses based on subjective criteria, Miller convinced sales management to initiate a tighter accountability system, in which performance requirements were clearly delineated for each sales person. These five categories were weighted according to importance:

1. Sales volume (30 points).
2. New business (20 points).
3. Forecast accuracy (20 points).
4. Administrative reports (15 points).
5. Miscellaneous (5 points).

Points were awarded monthly (instead of the previous yearly evaluation period) based on performance against predetermined objectives, and were the sole criteria for awarding bonus payments. In addition to earning points for successful sales, sales people also earned "new business" points for SRBs, such as number of client calls, obtaining sample orders, entertaining clients, and making appointments.

Prior to this arrangement, no feedback had been provided on sales people's forecast accuracy. When monthly feedback was offered in addition to points awarded for improved accuracy, forecasting error decreased significantly for the three products being measured. Consistency in forecasting also improved. Sales volume of all three products also increased significantly more than the industry trend.

Miller reported that sales managers thought the point system provided a better means of direction and control. They particularly liked the ability to identify and emphasize priorities through the weighted points. Sales people commented that they "knew where they stood" in relation to performance evaluations and bonus potential. Miller pointed out several benefits of such a point system:

1. Increased specificity of managerial direction and priorities.

2. Improved objectivity of evaluation and bonus awards.
3. Increased frequency of direction and feedback. This is particularly important for sales people who have infrequent contact with managers.
4. Improved performance.

Several reports in business magazines describe the results of behavioral applications in sales settings without providing very much procedural detail:

> In one case (At Bio-Dynamics, cash boosts systems sales, 1979), sales of medical test equipment increased 20 percent when sales people were offered variable cash bonuses from $25–$105 for each "systems" sale. The bonus award was tripled if a client was converted from a competitor's product. To insure management involvement, field sales managers were given smaller cash awards contingent upon their subordinates' sales.
>
> A brief report entitled "Performance feedback boosts efficiency and ups sales dramatically" (1976) provided data showing increases in "sales versus allocation" by awarding tangible reinforcers (i.e., gift certificates) contingent upon increased sales.
>
> In another instance (Performance management pays off for 3M Canada, 1979), two sales managers used frequent reinforcement and graphic displays of performance data to increase sales performance by 30 to 40 percent. It is interesting to note that these managers had projected increases of only 10–20 percent. An important facet of this program was the fact that *these managers were accountable for reporting the results of these projects to top management on a quarterly basis.*

A program in which attention was focused primarily upon SRBs was successful in increasing paint sales for Mobil Oil Corporation in South America (Reinforcement: Its effect on paint sales, 1979). Reinforcement, in the form of managerial feedback, public display of data at sales meetings, and monetary awards, were provided to sales personnel who demonstrated improved performance of four critical SRBs:

1. Frequency of sales calls.
2. Providing specified information on calls made.
3. Frequency of calls to local wholesale sales people to train them in Mobil sales techniques and procedures.
4. Providing information on these training calls.

Monthly sales meetings were held in which each sales person would publicly review his or her performance during the previous month; monetary awards were made at the end of each meeting. During the baseline period, an average of 43,450 gallons of paint were sold; this increased 28 percent to an average of 55,616 gallons during the intervention phase.

A major hosiery manufacturer also utilized a graphic feedback procedure to increase sales calls and sales of in-store product displays, and improve the cleanliness and arrangement of these in-store displays (Howard, 1981). After receiving training in behavior management techniques such as objective setting, feedback, and reinforcement, sales managers provided private and public recognition for improvements and posted graphs showing individual and group performance. Tangible reinforcers or cash awards were not used. Howard reported that sales of displays increased to 100 percent of opportunities, although specific baseline data were not available. Display conditions showed negligible improvement and sales calls increased from 92 to 95 percent of planned frequency. Weekly variability in the percent of planned sales calls also decreased dramatically, demonstrating better control by sales people over their business.

Connellan (1978) described a program, initiated by the sales management of one Bell System region office, to increase sales of telephone services (e.g., WATS lines, PBX equipment). Managers were trained to use shorter (monthly) periods for goal setting and provide more frequent feedback (shaping procedure), particularly to new and problem performers. Although the most dramatic improvements occurred with low-level performers, even excellent employees demonstrated remarkable improvements in the percent of total items sold versus opportunities to sell. Connellan described two sales people who improved from 110 to 140 percent and from 120 to 160 percent. This improvement potential for high performers is often overlooked by most sales managers who tend to concentrate only on low performers. An additional critical factor in this program was the reinforcement provided by sales managers for accomplishment of specific SRBs, particularly for those sales representatives who were not able to reach their sales goals.

One major national corporation instituted the use of behavioral procedures throughout its entire sales organization of 550 salespeople (Mirman, 1979). One hundred fifty managers from 20 sales regions, which included 72 districts, were trained to use behavior management techniques as part of their ongoing system of management. Goal setting, performance measurement and feedback, performance evaluations, and the sales incentive plan were upgraded and fine-tuned to become much more immediate and contingent. Most programs included immediate graphic feedback as an independent variable, and most of these were self-monitored. Improvements were reported in such performance areas as sales volume, quality of promotional support from client accounts, submission of administrative reports from sales people, and speed of initital orders on new products. A complete description of this large-scale program is provided in the final section of this chapter, including detailed data from three additional sales improvement projects.

The only report of a behavioral sales program that failed was provided in Miller's (1978) book *Behavior Management*. Prior to the program's initiation in a sportswear sales company, sales people were found to be unaware of their lack of success in meeting sales targets. They consistently overestimated their success due to lack of contact with available sales objectives and performance data. Miller reported that the management consultant attempted to initiate a point system (Miller, 1977) with increased feedback against monthly sales targets. Unfortunately, managers resisted the behavior management training, as did the vice president of sales. Managers paid no attention to the performance graphs, and complained about the lack of time to fool with data collection and feedback. As a consequence, the consultant terminated the program. The lesson from this program failure was described by Miller (p. 238):

> The primary failure of this program was the failure to initiate change at the right level of the organization. The first behavior that should have been changed were those of the President and Vice President. They set the model for the managers.. . . The program procedures must be incorporated into the routine management practice. They must, therefore, be used by line managers, and not the consultant or trainer.

Telephone Sales

There isn't a man or woman in these United States who hasn't been bothered at least once by a telephone sales person at some unreasonable hour of the night. Although we should urge government funding of research to devise procedures to eliminate the nuisance of 10 p.m. telephone calls in which one is urged to purchase necessary items such as lettuce spinners and subscriptions to *Mushroom Growers' Quarterly*, such research efforts are not, unfortunately, available for review at this time. However, since many products are sold by telephone, it is important to present data that demonstrate the effectiveness of behavioral procedures in this widely used sales area.

In one of the first published reports of a behavioral application in a business setting, Gupton and LeBow (1971) described the use of a Premack procedure to increase telephone sales of service contracts on new household appliances. Sales people were required to sell renewal contracts as well as convince new buyers to purchase service contracts. Since renewal contract calls and sales were emitted at a higher rate than new service contract calls and sales, the opportunity to sell five renewal contracts was made contingent upon one new service contract *sale*. As a result, sales for both types of contracts increased when this contingency was in effect, and decreased when this contingency was removed. Using a reversal (ABA) design, this program verified that the opportunity to engage in a high probability behavior can be used to reinforce completion of low probability tasks.

Although not strictly falling into the category of telephone sales, a study by Kreitner and Golab (1978) demonstrated the effectiveness of small monetary incentives in increasing sales people's required telephone calls to their home office. A reversal (ABA) design verified the effectiveness of a $0.30 per day award if the sales person met the standard of three calls per day. Phone calls increased from an average of 18.9 per day during baseline to 30.0 during the monetary award phase. and then dropped to 24.6 (and decreasing) during the reversal to baseline conditions. The authors pointed to the strength of an apparently insignificant amount of money as the critical element in this success, but one must wonder what affect the additional attention and probable increase in reinforcement had on these data, irrespective of the monetary reinforcers.

Much work has been done with the passenger reservations agents of major airlines, but little of this data has been available, publicly. In their book *Behavior Analysis and Training*, Rackham and Morgan (1977) devoted an entire chapter to a description of their efforts to increase sales by these agents (i.e., first class bookings, hotel and rental car bookings, number of sales of flights versus opportunities, and so on). Although no data were reported demonstrating a successful intervention, this report was nevertheless an excellent study of the process one must go through to (1) identify key behavior (SRBs), (2) measure these SRBs, and (3) provide immediate feedback. Preprogram data analyses pointed out that only 10–15 percent of all calls to the airline represented sales opportunities; reservation sales agents "suggestive selling" on only 18 percent of these opportunities. Interviews with these agents clarified that *they were not sure if they were supposed to be selling or simply taking orders.* Many agents functioned only as information givers and receivers. This ambiguity of role definition can also be used to describe the position of most waiters, waitresses, and bartenders, as well as sales clerks in bookstores, gift shops, and most areas of any department store in which sales personnel are not on direct commission.

The only published report of a successful behavioral program with passenger reservation agents was described in the quarterly newsletter of a management consulting company (The Tarkenton Performance Improvement Strategy, 1981). Although the "best available sales training" had been provided, and incentive programs had been used occasionally, all of the sales managers of this large national airline agreed that "sales agents were capable of selling more business if they would only try" (p. 3). Questionnaires returned by the sales agents revealed that they were never given feedback on their individual performance. Substantial sales performance data were available to management, but had not been used to provide feedback to the sales agents.

Agents were asked to increase sales by 5 percent over their previous three-months' revenues. Daily feedback on the amount of revenue sold was provided to each agent within 24 hours. Individual and group graphs were posted in the office and supervisors were requested to comment positively, if possible, on each graph at least once per week.

Although costing the airline only $5,000 to implement this program, an additional $3.15 *million* was earned. Revenues increased an average of 11 percent per agent, and an extra 9,500 segments (i.e., one "leg" in a trip) were sold at an average of $322 each. Although these results are certainly dramatic, this outcome is not unusual, and the potential for similar percentage gains exist in any industry in which the sales person can exert stronger control over the sales situation.

Conclusions

It is evident that the performance of sales personnel can be improved significantly with the proper combination of antecedent and consequence strategies. The most effective strategy appears to be the use of performance feedback for outcome measures (sales) and input measures (SRBs). Individualized graphic feedback is a commonly and successfully utilized tactic, in addition to face-to-face managerial feedback.

It is also evident that there is a critical need for such programs to include a major emphasis on insuring the *active* support from managers at all levels. In addition to the comments previously described regarding the importance of this issue (Komaki, Pierce, and Waddell, 1977; Miller, 1978; Performance management pays off for 3M Canada, 1979), the authors of a study dealing with the establishment of feedback systems (Stoerzinger, Johnston, Pisor, and Monroe, 1978) point out that the largest problem in their feedback program for salvage employees was the lack of support by the firm's operations director. As a result, they strongly suggested that "A major training effort for all levels of management personnel should be implemented prior to the introduction of any feedback systems" (p. 278).

ACTION PLAN: DEVELOPING A SALES PERFORMANCE SYSTEM

Although most successful organizations have created elaborate technologies based upon scientific research and precision implementation to help minimize the problems associated with the technical aspects of production, the control of the human factor has remained somewhat elusive. In a sales organization this human factor is a critical variable; the organization is successful to the extent that it can account for and control the performance of its sales force. In short, the motivation of sales people has always been a primary objective, as well as a problem, for sales managers.

One district sales manager recently told me that his motivation problems would be greatly reduced if he could only hire people who met his requirements for the professional sales person. After asking what these requirements were, I was handed a document that included a list of 19 "success" traits, including loyalty, aggressiveness, dependability, industriousness, honesty, courtesy, tact. Apparently, one way of becoming a successful manager is to only hire deities—or Boy Scouts.

Since most businesses cannot afford the luxury of waiting around for the "right" sales person to walk in the door, sales managers must learn to effectively use the talent currently at their disposal. The performance systems approach was designed to improve sales management effectiveness and therefore sales performance.

Regardless of the type of sales organization, the performance systems action plan utilizes five major components:

Phase 1: Region Assessment

Prior to the initiation of the program in each region or sales office, the program director visits each major location to analyze the operation, style, and management philosophy of the location's management team. Management systems, e.g., performance measurement, feedback, evaluation, and use of the incentive sytem, and performance effectiveness are assessed. Management priorities and potential performance improvements are also identified.

Phase 2: Development of Management Skills

A workshop (see Figure 16-2) is held for each region's management team to discuss the assessment and review guidelines for maximizing the effect of the region's performance systems (see Figure 16-3) on sales performance.

Phase 3: Adjustments to Management Systems

Activity in this phase centers on convincing managers to adjust their performance evaluation and incentive pay systems to become much more specific to the job requirements, and to adjust the perceived purpose of the performance evaluation from a rating device to a motivating tool that has a measurable effect on performance levels. This is the most critical phase of the program, because performance improvement cannot be sustained over time unless the performance systems elements (see Figure 16-3) are integrated into these ongoing management systems.

Accountability models
Performance analysis (Mager and Pipe, 1970)
Antecedent strategies
   Pinpointing success-related behavior (SRBs)
   Objective setting
   Performance measurement
Consequence strategies
   Reinforcement
   Use of data feedback
   Punishment
   Performance evaluation
Development of action plan

FIGURE 16-2. Topics covered in management workshop.

Manager-Controlled Systems

    Objective setting
    Performance measurement
    Performance feedback
    Performance reviews and evaluations
    Reinforcement

Corporate-Controlled Systems

    Incentive pay
    Compensation pay
    Sales contests

FIGURE 16-3. Performance systems elements.

Phase 4: Follow-up Consultation

To insure management compliance with the systems' adjustments and the guidelines developed during the region workshop, the program director returns to each region several times to meet individually with each manager. Additional guidance and feedback on the initiation of the program, as well as assistance in dealing with individual performance concerns, is also provided during this phase.

Phase 5: Program Maintenance

Managers are held more tightly accountable for reporting progress to their superiors on performance against key objectives. They are also responsible for maintaining frequent use of reinforcement and data feedback.

PERFORMANCE SYSTEMS:
APPLICATION IN A LARGE SALES ORGANIZATION

In 1977, General Mills, Inc., initiated a pilot program in two of its 20 grocery products sales regions to determine the potential for increasing sales through a systematic program utilizing behavioral strategies to improve management's use of goal setting, performance measurement and feedback, recognition, performance evaluations, and the incentive pay system. The data resulting from this test revealed that improvements in these strategies directly influenced overall sales performance by affecting both outcome measures (i.e., sales volume) and process measures (i.e., sales calls per day, number of displays sold, shelf facings gained, and so on). As a consequence, the performance systems department was established within the sales division in 1978 and given the responsibility of upgrading all organizational systems and management behavior that influenced sales volume.

Program Objectives

The performance systems department was established to fulfill several major objectives.

1. To improve sales performance by improving mangers' utilization of the elements of their Performance System (see Figure 16-3). Primary emphasis was given to those manager-controlled systems that directly affect day-to-day performance.
2. To increase sales people's perception that a strong relationship exists between performance and consequences.
3. To provide sales managers with the behavioral skills necessary to improve the performance of their people and insure that they use these skills.
4. To develop the concept of a positive accountability system (PAS) in which objectivity-measured accountabilities were specified, positive consequences (recognition, feedback, salary increases, improved ratings) awarded as these accountabilities were achieved, and negative consequences (warnings, memos, probation, termination) were provided following unsatisfactory performance. This was somewhat different from most accountability models, which have acquired a negative connotation due to an overreliance on the use of negative consequences.

The Sales Organization

The Grocery Product Sales Division of General Mills is responsible for over $1 billion in food sales to grocery stores of all sizes, from small Mom and Pop independents to national chains. The 550 salespeople and 150 field managers are spread out nationally across 20 sales regions, each containing three to five districts, with six to ten sales people per district. Regions are divided geographically into three zones, each headed by a zone director who reports directly to the Vice President, General Manager of Sales (see Figure 16-4).

The sales division is not a profit center, but is responsible for sales volume, i.e., cases of product. Recent years have seen case volume in excess of 70 million, averaging over 120,000 cases per sales person. Best sellers such as Gold Medal Flour, Wheaties, Cheerios, and Bisquick make up some of the 250 food products sold by the sales force.

Sales Force Priorities

The basic responsibility of the grocery products sales person was to convince the store manager or chain store (i.e., account) buyer to purchase promotional items offered at a reduced price by the manufacturer in exchange for in-store displays or newspaper advertisements of the product

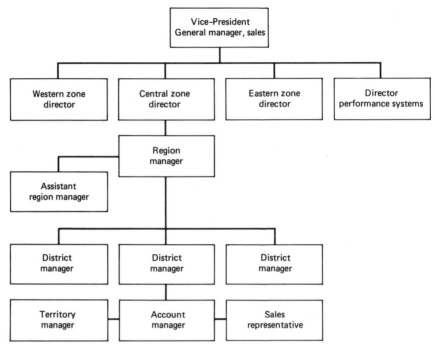

FIGURE 16-4. Organizational chart of sales division detailing typical region structure.

as its regular or reduced price during the promotional period (several weeks). The sales person had two priorities:

1. Convince the buyer to purchase sufficient quantities of product at a reduced price during the promotion period.
2. Convince the buyer to pass along these savings to the consumer.

For example, if the account was offered an allowances of $0.10 for every package of Betty Crocker Super Moist Cake Mix purchased during the promotional period, the salesperson would in many accounts actively attempt to convince the buyer to pass this entire $0.10 savings along to the consumer by reducing the price of the cake mix an equal amount. This represented 100 percent pass-through of the promotional allowance and would have a positive impact on sales volume. In addition, the sales person tried to convince the account to advertise these promotional items in the local newspapers to further stimulate sales volume.

The sales person also had accountabilities in such areas as sales of new products, increased distribution of established products, additional facings (shelf space) for established products, and submission of required administrative reports on such things as competitive activity, sales calls, and performance against sales objectives. Performance in these areas was formally evaluated semiannually using a format established by the corporate headquarters. This format listed specific accountabilities, weighted according to importance. Although regional autonomy allowed for minor changes to this basic format, it was most often followed.

The overall yearly evaluation rating was used to determine frequency and amount of salary increase, promotion potential, and yearly cash incentive award. This yearly incentive award was based on a combination of factors, including total region sales, the individual's performance rating, and position title. Turnover within the sales force averaged approximately 10 percent each year for the past five years, which was slightly more than half the industry average.

Organizational Constraints

Regardless of the successful pilot program initiated in two of the 20 sales regions, there were many constraints that restricted the implementation of a similar program on a national scale. These constraints were primarily created by the very nature of the sales division's structure and responsibilities.

Geographical Separation.   By definition, a national sales force covers the territory from Key West to Puget Sound, and from Northern Maine to the beaches of Southern California. A district sales manager (DSM) in the Dallas Region might live 500 miles from the region office and several hundred miles from several of his or her sales people. The excessive time required to visit these sales people, combined with the fact that gasoline was approaching $1.50 a gallon (which may sound inexpensive by the time you have finished reading this chapter) made it necessary to keep person-to-person contacts to a minimum in such widely scattered areas. As a result, the DSM depended heavily upon the telephone to maintain contact with field activities and provide feedback on performance. The DSM also invested heavily in AT&T common stock.

The distance between managers and sales representatives often made it difficult for the manager to frequently observe the sales person's actual performance. Performance feedback therefore was often based on outcome measures for which performance data were readily available (Miller, 1977). Managers in metro-urban areas, however, were able to witness actual sales presentations more often, and as a result were able to provide more feedback on use of SRBs, in addition to sales results. Since the frequency of feedback has been shown to directly affect performance improvement and the attitude of the employee (Cook, 1968, Doyle and Shapiro, 1980), the inability to provide immediate feedback on sales performance must be viewed as an impediment to performance improvement. This constraint was diluted, however, by this program's emphasis on increased written and phoned feedback based on performance measurements made by sales people and sent to the DSM, and by emphasis on the *quality* of the feedback communication, i.e., specificity, personalization, brevity, and so on.

Since the large distance between members of a district eliminated the need for a district office, sales people worked out of offices in their homes. Contact between district members was therefore limited.

Distance was also a factor in considering the design of the performance systems program. Since this program was tailored to the specific conditions existing in each region, it was mandatory that the program director spend time meeting with region management personnel to develop program strategies, and provide training with follow-up consultation. This was certainly a labor-intensive task, best done face to face, and required much travel if it was to be done correctly. The time needed to introduce this program to a large sales force was excessive. In this case it took the program director over two and one-half years to initiate the program in a stair-step fashion to 20 sales regions.

Measurement Problems.   Many of the sales person's responsibilities were difficult to measure, and as a result, resistance to new manual measurement procedures was often stiff due to the time required to obtain these measures. The perceived burden of manual measurement made it more difficult to sell the program to managers.

Although computerized data were available for major sales outcome variables, shelf share, sales volume, and distribution, reports on these data often had a latency period of up to 90 days. Manual, self-monitored data systems, i.e., measured by sales personnel, were developed in order to collect immediate data on performance of SRBs, as well as performance of relatively small outcome measures (i.e., new shelf facings sold, number of benefits given during sales pitch).

Although objections to such systems were frequently expressed, mostly by managers who expected resistance from their sales people, the immediacy of such record keeping allowed these managers to provide frequent feedback for important behavior. On the negative side, these self-monitored data were found to be unreliable on several occasions; managers had to be careful to accept only correct data. Intermittent audits by managers eliminated this problem.

Regional Differences.   Due to variations existing between sales regions as a consequence of their differing account philosophies, market conditions and requirements, and particularly sales management approaches, it was impossible to develop a prepackaged program that could be easily adopted in all regions. Most of the program director's time was spent assisting managers in tailoring the procedures to fit their needs. This included the development of measurement systems that were applicable only within one sales region.

These regional differences also dictated a different set of performance priorities within each region organization. The decentralized nature of the sales division provided each region manager with a great deal of autonomy to develop individualized approaches and systems. In essence, each region was like a separate organization. These differences also made it impossible to equitably compare regions on any given performance variable, and even made it extremely difficult to compare performance across sales territories.

Lack of Controllability.   The nature of this sales task was such that sales people's success or failure in selling was not always a function of their sales expertise. For example, if an account's marketing philosophy was structured so as to limit the number of products stocked, it would be difficult to hold the sales representative accountable for dramatically increasing the number of items in distribution. On the other hand, accountabilities could not be totally forgiven; after all, the sales person's job was to sell products to difficult customers. Perceived lack of control over critical accountabilities was a sensitive issue, particularly at performance evaluation time.

As an example, a military commissary capriciously discontinued 26 products from its stores. Although sales people were inevitably responsible for distribution levels in their stores, should the performance rating of the sales person responsible for this account have been lowered as a consequence of this account's actions? Quick thinking and excellent selling by the sales person convinced the account to reinstate 18 items two months later. The basic question is, for what do we hold sales people responsible—sales volume (output) or excellence in selling *activities*, which, if done well, should lead to additional sales volume?

Another major uncontrollable factor was the extremely *competitive environment* in the food products business. A sales person's selling activities could in fact be outstanding, but if the competition offered more financial support to the grocer for stocking their competitive products, the sales person's activities might have little effect on the grocer's buying decision. Should the sales person be evaluated on the outcome, i.e., the lost sale, or on the performance of selling activities? The ambiguity of this issue became an important factor in establishing performance standards and objectives, and was a roadblock until an equitable solution was developed. (See Case Study 3.)

More importantly, performance excellence has been found to be linked to the degree of "task clarity" evident in the selling position (Neider, 1980; Doyle and Shapiro, 1980). Task clarity refers to the "perceived relationship between effort and results." These studies found that measured effort was highest for those sales jobs in which the sales person could easily discern the relationship between his or her effort and sales results:

> If a sales task is unclear (i.e., low perceived relationship between effort and results), selling can be frustrating. In such a situation, the salesperson will not know where he/she stands and will not be able to pinpoint the results of his/her own efforts. Good performance seems to be a random occurrence in no way related to effort. This lack of connection is discouraging and dampens the pride that might otherwise come from accomplishment. (Doyle and Shapiro, 1980, p. 136)

A major responsibility of the performance systems program was to clarify the perceived relationship between effort and results by: (1) improving performance measurement approaches, and (2) identifying the degree of uncontrollability in specific sales situations.

Management Resistance. As in most programs of this type, regardless of the industry, many managers perceived the performance systems program as a threat to their autonomy. Some even took it personally—"Someone must think I'm not doing a good job." Managers often resisted efforts to institute changes in their operations or management style and rationalized this resistance by saying such things as:

The program requires an excessive amount of my people's time.

My sales people are out there to sell, not collect data.

We already give feedback here.

There is no need for all this measurement. I already know who my best sales people are.

The name of the game is sales volume; everything else is secondary.

We pay 'em well and give them good training. They oughta wanna do well.

We've tried that before and it didn't work.

Passive resistance, or smiling and going through the motions for the benefit of top management, also occurred. Being an autonomous leader of a large sales organization, the region manager set the tone for the rest of the region. On at least two occasions, the region sales manager professed support for the program in the presence of his superiors and the program director, but then privately talked down the program to his staff. On other occasions, the region manager had other priorities and offered little attention to, or support for, the program. The large degree of autonomy present within each region did not allow the program to be legislated to all regions, nor would it be a good idea to do so. Since program success was largely a function of the region manager's support and active involvement, each manager had to be *sold* by the program director. Unfortunately, not everyone bought the program. C'est la vie.

Systems Constraints. Years ago, when implementing behavioral programs in other industries, we rather naively believed that all we had to do to improve performance was to teach managers to use contingent social reinforcement. "Catch 'em being good" was the main battle cry of behavioral consultants, and the result was a general failure to maintain program success over the long term. Without support from the performance evaluation, incentive, and salary administration systems, this program was bound to meet the same fate as many of its predecessors in other industries. Program maintenance could not be assured if these major management control systems were allowed to continue to provide noncontingent consequences (i.e., salary increases and incentive pay) for performance; changes in the corporate philosophy that determined the use of these systems were also required as part of this program. This was the most difficult step in this performance systems approach.

Proof Data.   Since there have been very few behaviorally based programs developed within sales organizations, data that verified the success of such procedures in the sales area were scarce. When shown data from other industries to demonstrate the effectiveness of behavioral procedures, sales managers respond to data in much the same way that plant managers respond to data from other types of manufacturing facilities: "Sure it worked in 'X', but we're 'Y' and this is a unique situation!"

Selling behavioral procedures to field sales managers was difficult until a suitable data base had been established. Once collected, however, these "success stories" generated strong interest and prompted managers to utilize these procedures and improve on what other regions had done. The palatability of previous data was a key ingredient in insuring a successful kickoff in each region. A presentation of data from previous regions helped establish the positive expectation that, "If Jim in Cincinnati can do it, so can I!" Nothing melted resistance and objections faster than hard data showing how a good friend and fellow manager successfully handled a similar performance problem.

PERFORMANCE SYSTEMS: IMPLEMENTATION

The costs involved in the selling process have risen dramatically over the past few years. The latest available figures (1979) show that the average cost of each sales call for 188 national companies was $71.90, up 22 percent from 1977 (Steinbrink, 1980). A large national firm with over 500 sales people averaging six or seven sales calls per day, approximately 750,000 calls per year or over $50 million in sales costs, must therefore use several strategies to increase the return from its sales efforts. Companies concerned about improvements in sales productivity have traditionally directed their energies to four strategies:

1. *Marketing Effectiveness.*   This includes improvements through better market research, demographic studies, data systems, regional marketing plans, and improved integration of marketing and sales operations.

2. *Technology Innovation.*   The most rapidly changing sector of the sales business is an increasing reliance on computerized information systems leading to improvements in efficiency of all aspects of the sales function. This includes a reduction in ordering cycles and administrative time loads, and improved customer service through more timely and accurate data tracking systems.

3. *Product Improvements.* Improvements in the quality of established products and the introduction of novel or time-saving products are critical to the maintenance of sales volume, particularly in the food business where national volume trends have been flat for a few years.

4. *Work Force Productivity.* The emphasis here has been on specialized training and motivational programs such as incentive pay plans and sales contests. The number of sales companies moving toward commission, incentive, and bonus pay plans has been increasing (Steinbrink, 1980).

The continually increasing costs resulting from capital investments in the first three items above have forced sales management to focus more clearly on employee productivity. General Mills has long been a leader in the development of innovative technology and management systems. This firm provided B. F. Skinner, in 1942–43, with the funds, laboratory space, and engineering assistance to develop the ill-fated "pigeon-guided" air-to-ground missile (Skinner, 1960), and sponsored George Odiorne's early efforts in the development of the MBO concept within General Mills in the late 1950s (Odiorne, 1965). As one of the top three marketing organizations for graduating MBAs, General Mills has consistently maintained a competitive edge in a highly competitive market. The performance systems program was viewed as a means of sharpening that edge.

Implemented over a 2½ year period in a stair-step fashion to 20 national sales regions, the performance systems program was comprised of five component phases. To assist the reader in the utilization of the performance systems strategy within other sales organizations, the following section will provide details on the implementation of the five-phase approach and the effects of this program on three sales improvement programs.

Phase 1: Region Assessment

In the first phase, the program staff should collect information about each region's operations in order to tailor the workshop and program agenda to meet the needs of the management team.

In General Mills, this information was collected by various means:

1. Reports on many major sales variables (volume, incentive earnings, product distribution, new product sales, and so on) were available in the Minneapolis national office. These data were used to evaluate region effectiveness relative to other comparable regions; charts and graphs were often developed to analyze trends, and for use in the workshop.

2. Individual interviews were held with key management personnel and in some instances sales personnel. Managers were asked to

describe and show examples of their systems for objective setting, performance measurement, feedback, and reinforcement.

In a political sense, this initial meeting also provided an opportunity to explain the purpose of the program to the region manager and defuse any potential anxiety surrounding the large-scale program that had been unceremoniously dropped in his lap. Although the vice president of sales had described the purpose of the program at the national sales meeting, a considerable amount of uncertainty about time demands, additional work loads, meeting scheduling, program effectiveness, and accountabilities still existed.

3. Personnel files were initially reviewed to determine the actual frequency of written feedback memos, but due to the consistently low level of positive memos found in the first few regions' files, this effort was discontinued.

4. Important intraregional reports were analyzed to determine their degree of effectiveness in controlling sales performance: Who collected the data? Who received copies? What feedback was offered as a consequence of changes noted in the data?

5. The region's performance evaluation system was scrutinized to determine its effectiveness in controlling performance: What were sales people being held accountable for? Were these accountabilities being measured? Were specific measurable objectives set? Did the sales person participate in the negotiation of these objectives? Were universal standards used for all sales people in the region, or were these standards individualized to take territorial differences into consideration? How often was the evaluation review held? Did the evaluation ratings distinguish between poor, average and outstanding performers, or was there little differentiation in ratings? How much district manager subjectivity was tolerated in the formulation of the rating?

In most regions, the performance evaluation process was characterized by excessive subjectivity, lack of participatory objective setting, regional standards that were inflexible to territorial differences, and a narrow range of ratings that inadequately distinguished the average from the above-average performer. We concluded that it would be difficult for a sales person to perceive a strong relationship between actual performance and eventual ratings. More importantly, since incentive pay was heavily determined by one's performance rating, the perceived relationship between performance and pay was therefore weakened. In fact some regions typically split their incentive "pot," determined by region performance against quota, evenly among all sales people, with little or no differentiation for excellent or inadequate performers.

6. To verify the conclusions regarding problems associated with the inadequacies of evaluation and incentive plans, and to gather additional information for management, a 75-question survey was sent

to each sales person in the region asking for opinions on such issues as frequency of management feedback, equity and frequency of performance evaluations, effectiveness of sales training, satisfaction with salaries, and perception of the relationship between performance and salary-incentive pay-promotions.

7. Managers were also asked to identify specific sales performance areas in need of improvement. These areas would later serve as preliminary targets during the management workshop (Phase 2).

Phase 2: Development of Management Skills

Phase II of a performance systems program should be a workshop for the managers of each region. Regions can be combined in the workshop only if their systems, procedures, and market conditions are very similar.

At General Mills, a concentrated, three-day workshop (Figure 16-2) was held for all region management personnel. Participants included the region sales manager, assistant region sales manager, district sales managers (3–5), region sales assistant (i.e., manager-in-training), and the region office manager. Office managers, responsible for a staff of 6–10 people and all administrative functions including order processing, accounts receivable, and so on, fully participated in this program and developed procedures for improving many areas of office performance. (See Figure 16–5) In some cases an office supervisor also attended the workshop. The success of these office programs was often dramatic, particularly in the area of accounts receivable reductions.

For the procedural topics listed in Figure 16-2, guidelines were provided for maximizing the effect of each procedure. These guidelines were then compared to the procedure's actual utilization, as determined during the assessment. For example, managers were given guidelines showing how to set sales objectives in such a way as to increase the likelihood these objectives would be met. Managers were then given the opportunity to compare their current objective-setting procedures to these guidelines and develop improved performance objectives during the workshop.

Primary emphasis was given to a review of the consequence strategies listed in Figure 16-2. Data resulting from the use of such procedures in other regions were presented to gain credibility, stimulate interest, and demonstrate the application process. These procedures were discussed in respect to the great geographic distances that often existed between managers and their sales people. Emphasis was placed on improving the frequency and quality of written and telephone feedback.

The final day of the workshop included a detailed review of the questionnaire completed by the region's sales people, and an identification of pinpointed objectives by managers. Rather than simply provide information on behavioral procedures and hope the managers would follow these guidelines on their return to the field, each sales manager was required to identify at least one targeted performance concern for each of his or her sales people. To identify this area of concern, the sales manager frequently reviewed the sales person's most recent performance evaluation and selected the lowest rated category as the targeted performance. An action plan for improving this target area was then developed.

Managerial reactions to these workshops were directly related to the amount of data presented from successful programs in other regions. Managers in the initial workshops were more passive and skeptical, while managers in the last 14 or 15 regions became increasingly positive, openly supportive, and enthusiastic. This increase in workshop effectiveness was also a function of the program director's increasing understanding of the intricacies of the sales operation.

Case Study 1.   As part of his action plan developed in the workshop, one district sales manager determined to improve his district's timely submission of performance proofs, i.e., evidence that the account had qualified for the discount on the General Mills product by advertising the sale price—copies of the newspaper ad or evidence of display support or shelf price reduction. Prior to this program, the district sales manager typically sent reminders to his people when these proofs were overdue. Negative

---

Performance Targets

Sales Force: Sales Targets

Sales of displays	Open-ended questions asked
Shelf share vs. market share	during presentation
Cases sold per call	Facings vs. competition
Calls per day	New product acceptance
Adherence to planned coverage	Distribution
Ad features sold	Promotions sold
Pricing parity	Suggested selling
Pass-through of allowance	Order filing speed

Sales Force: Administrative Targets

Sales forecast accuracy	Expense report timeliness
Quality off business review	Contract timeliness
Number of negative comments	Orders meeting guidelines
Quality of sales presentation	Unitized shipments
Competitive Reports	Expense reductions
Performance proofs submitted	

Office Staff: Administrative Targets

Accounts Receivable ($) (30 and 90 days)	Overdue contracts
Accounts Receivable Number of items (30	Expense report errors
and 90 days)	Order errors
Invoice corrections	

FIGURE 16-5. Sample of measurable performance targets successfully improved by sales and office personnel. This list represents a small sample of total number of areas improved. Note that most sales force targets are *activities* that lead to sales volume.

feedback, warnings, and threats had also been used to improve this administrative performance, but during the previous year, an average of 11.7 new contracts were submitted late each month.

Based on the information reviewed in the workshop, the district sales manager discontinued the use of all types of negative feedback and required his sales people to graph their "percent on-time submission" performance each month. A copy of this graph was also submitted to the district sales manager monthly. The district sales manager then provided sales people with positive reinforcement, verbally or in writing, with occasional copies of these memos to the region manager. Six of the eight district members hung the graph over their home office desks, thereby allowing the graph to serve as both an antecedent stimulus and a feedback device.

In the 34 months since the initiation of this feedback approach, submission of late proofs has declined 51 percent, to an overall average of 5.7 per month (see Figure 16-6). A major result of this program was the reduction in time spent by the district sales manager and office personnel to track down these overdue proofs.

Phase 3.   Adjustments to Management Systems

The third and most critical phase of the performance systems program should involve the fine tuning (or development) of those management control systems that will insure long-term maintenance of the gains posted during the formal implementation period. Key to this effort should be adjustments to the performance evaluation and incentive pay systems.

Following a detailed analysis during the assessment phase and a complete review during the workshop, each General Mills region's performance evaluation system was improved in four major areas.

1. *Performance standards were objectified.*   Although measures for performance variables often existed, performance standards had not always been developed. Qualitative standards were added to these quantitative measures already in existence.

2. *Performance standards were individually established on the basis of the account's history and sales potential.*   Although volume quotas had always been set differentially, region standards for other accountabilities were most often based on a universal standard for all accounts, regardless of account conditions or merchandising philosophy. The punishing aspect of a rigid system, which subjected all salespeople to the same standards, had been frequently discussed by managers and salespeople, but managers had been concerned about the time and effort necessary to convert to a more equitable system that would evaluate each person against recent (baseline) performance within his or her account, rather than against a universal region standard.

The establishment of individualized standards allowed managers to reinforce improvements; this was particularly important for new sales

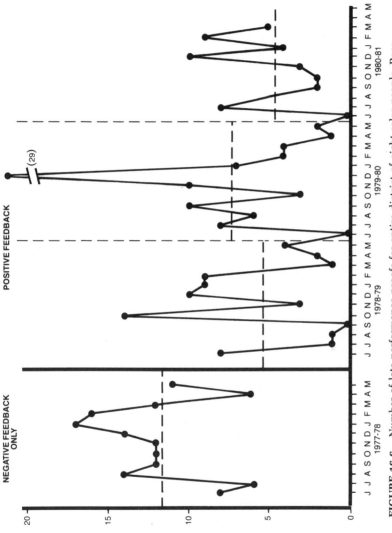

FIGURE 16-6. Number of late performance proofs for entire district of eight sales people. Baseline = 11.7 per month. Feedback phase (34 months) = 5.7 per month (51 percent improvement).

people or in situations where the sales person's past performance had been quite low (i.e., shaping procedure).

3. *Performance evaluation standards were often negotiated with each sales person.* Although sales volume quotas continued to be assigned to each territory, individual performance standards for sales activities such as distribution, promotion sales, and shelf share were negotiated with sales personnel. It was felt that this negotiation process would increase the sales person's commitment and sense of accountability for the accomplishment of the objective. The sales person therefore became an active agent, rather than a passive object in the performance evaluation process (McGregor, 1972).

4. *The relationship between potential performance levels and the eventual evaluation rating was specified prior to the performance period.* In an effort to increase the perception of a relationship between performance and consequences, it was necessary to change the nature of the evaluation process. Prior to this change, performance ratings were assigned to each sales representative by the district manager at the end of the six-month evaluation period. This allowed for too much subjectivity, uncertainty, and anxiety for managers and subordinates.

To eliminate most of this uncertainty, it was decided that the goal of the performance evaluation process was: *Under no circumstances should a sales person be surprised by any aspect of his or her performance evaluation.* As reviewed above, the likelihood of surprise was reduced by: (1) establishing measurable standards that were objectively set on the basis of territory conditions, (2) requiring input from each sales person, and (3) requiring sales people to continually measure their own performance. The final element in this process was to prespecify the relationship between potential performance results and evaluation ratings.

Cast Study 2. Rather than telling people that their objective was to "convince grocers to set up end-aisle displays of a new product," specific parameters were assigned to potential performance ratings at the beginning of the six-month evaluation period (see Figure 16-7).

The establishment of Level (3) objectives allowed sales people to evaluate their own performance. It also removed much of the "judicial" responsibility from the shoulders of the sales manager and placed the responsibility for determining evaluation ratings right where it belonged— on the sales person.

In the case described in Figure 16-7, the sales person tracked and graphed his own performance on a monthly basis, thereby providing a means of immediate feedback even in the absence of his DSM. The self-monitored Level (3) approach allowed this sales person to know exactly where he stood against the potential evaluation ratings and reduced any ambiguities in the evaluation process.

During the baseline phase of introducing six new products, this sales person had sold displays to only 24 percent of his retail stores. Once the

Impact of Objective Setting
Format on Probability of Achievement

LOW ——————— HIGH

| Level (1) objective: Sell as many displays as you can. |

| Level (2) objective: Sell displays to 90 percent of your stores. |

Level (3) objective: Display Sales

Standard	Rating
80–100% of Stores	5
50–74%	4
25–49%	3
0–24%	2

FIGURE 16-7.   Effect of objective setting format on probability of achievement (case study).

evaluation system was changed to include this Level (3) objective, performance immediately increased to 94 percent over the next nine products (see Figure 16-8). This represented an increase in display placements of almost 400 percent by a veteran sales person with over 20 years sales experience. This was an impressive gain, particularly considering that data collected by *Progressive Grocer* magazine (How in-store merchandising can boost sales, 1981) showed that in-store displays boost sales volume from 100–500 percent over normally expected sales, depending on the location of the display in the store.

The success of this program prompted the district sales manager to initiate a similar program with all the members of his district. Overall district performance on displays sold increased from 36 to 92 percent of opportunities and has been maintained for almost two years.

After convincing several regions to experiment with this evaluation approach on one or two major accountabilities, it became relatively easy to sell this concept to the remaining regions. Performance improvements from these first regions were often so dramatic that the data were almost unbelievable. Consequently, managers of these first regions were asked to provide a written summary of their programs, which could then be distributed at other region workshops.

The major advantage of this evaluation system, other than its affect on performance, was that it allowed the performance evaluation system to become the focal point of the program rather than only the series of individual projects initiated by each manager. It also helped absorb the program's behavioral procedures and principles into the ongoing management system. Most importantly, this focus provided a framework in which to cover the basic bahavioral procedures of objective setting, measurement, feedback, and reinforcement. In essence, the development of a behaviorally oriented evaluation process helped to insure the continued

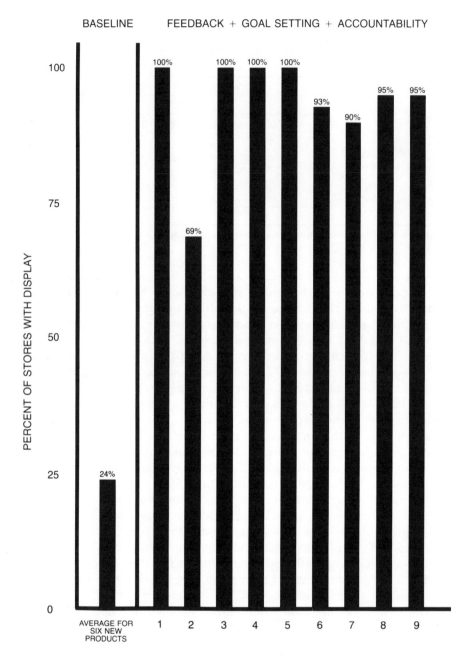

NEW PRODUCT DISPLAY OPPORTUNITIES

FIGURE 16-8. New product display opportunities. Percent of retail stores that set up displays for new product introduction. Baseline (six products) = 24 percent; accountability phase = 94 percent; overall improvement = 392 percent.

high levels of performance identified as the overall goal of the performance systems program.

In addition, the incentive system was adjusted to provide more weight to the sales person's evaluation rating, and less weight to the performance of the region.

Phase 4: Follow-up Consultation

Following each manager's development of an action plan in the management workshop, the manager should later be contacted to review his or her implementation procedures. The purpose of these meetings should be to clarify areas discussed in the workshop, assist managers to adjust their implementation strategies, and provide feedback on steps already completed.

Three to four weeks after the workshop, the program director returned to each region and met individually with each of the workshop participants to review steps for implementing their action plan. Prior to this initial meeting, each DSM was to have:

1. Finalized selection of performance targets for each sales person.
2. Collected baseline data to show past and current levels of performance for each targeted area, or defined a measurement system to collect data in those areas for which baseline data was not available.
3. Established preliminary performance goals for each targeted performance.
4. Reviewed steps 1–3 with the region manager.

Each of these sessions lasted 2–3 hours; most of this time was spent assisting the manager in the development of new, individualized measurement systems to collect data on performance areas not previously tracked. Feedback strategies were pinpointed, and performance objectives were integrated into the evaluation system when appropriate. Managers were also counseled on techniques to use when negotiating performance objectives with their sales people.

Following each meeting, a summary of the DSM's updated action plan was submitted to the region manager. When appropriate, a reinforcing memo was sent to the DSM, with a copy to his or her region manager, complimenting the DSM on proficiency in developing this action plan.

Phase 5: Program Maintenance

To further insure long-term maintenance of program effect, managers must be held accountable for the progress of their subordinates. Systems must be implemented that insure continued use of managerial feedback and recognition and provide organizational consequences contingent upon performance.

Although less of a problem than in most conventional performance improvement models, program maintenance in behaviorally based programs has traditionally been a major concern. Maintenance of effect has been difficult, because too often the program was directed entirely at changing the behavior of people without making corollary adjustments to the *systems* that direct and control the behavior of these people, i.e., performance evaluation and incentive systems. The program must be accepted as a part of the current system, a way of managing, and not just another "here today, gone tomorrow" motivational program.

To show that the performance systems program was not to be used to simply gain a temporary increase in performance, heavy emphasis was placed on the integration of the principles of objective setting, performance measurement, and feedback within the formal performance evaluation system. Although performance improvement would certainly result from managers' increased use of feedback and reinforcement, the program director rather pessimistically assumed that the proper level of managerial feedback would not be sustained over time, even though these managers would be occasionally reinforced for their efforts by the improved performance of their sales people. An evaluation rating system that utilized individualized, measurable, negotiated, and self-monitored objectives, and prespecified relationships between potential performance and subsequent ratings served as the strongest element in insuring continual improvements in performance.

The DSM was responsible for providing the region manager with monthly status reports summarizing the progress of each sales person against priority objectives identified in the action plan. The purpose of these reports was to provide an accountability framework, as well as to stimulate feedback from the region manager. Copies were frequently sent to the zone director.

DSMs were also accountable for increasing the frequency of feedback given for performance improvement. To insure continued use of managerial feedback and reinforcement, some regions required DSMs to track the number of occasions in which positive feedback was given, although most regions simply required DSMs to frequently send copies of reinforcing memos to the region manager. These reinforcing memos were extremely effective because: (1) they reinforced specific behavior or sales results, (2) they let the sales person know that his or her performance was important enough to inform the region manager, and (3) they helped bridge the gap created by the lack of personal contact time between manager and sales person.

The program director was responsible for presenting the results of the performance systems program to the Consumer Foods Group Executive Committee and to all sales managers at the yearly national sales conference. These presentations allowed for ample opportunity to publicly reinforce individual managers for their appropriate use of the procedures described in this chapter. In addition, the program director intermittently sent copies of graphs or other data to top management in order to stimulate their use of reinforcement. To increase the likelihood that these executives would send reinforcing memos to sales managers, the program director often sent "suggested" reinforcing memos for their signature.

Case Study 3.   The sales managers in one region had always stressed that their 33 sales people were responsible for convincing their accounts to increase pass-through of promotional monies to consumers, i.e., promotional discounts offered to grocers in exchange for advertising or displaying the manufacturer's product; but they had never tied this responsibility to a measurable accountability system. Sales performance had traditionally been measured only by the percent of promotions accepted by grocers, with no qualitative elements.

As a function of the region manager's action plan, developed in the management workshop, it was decided to measure sales effectiveness by including percentage of pass-through as the qualitative measure, in addition to percentage of promotions accepted. As an example, General Mills might offer the grocer a discount of $0.10 per package in exchange for advertising or display support for a specific product. Instead of passing this $0.10 on to the consumer by reducing the advertised price at least $0.10, the grocer might decide to reduce the price by only $0.01, and use the balance to finance his or her own private label products or to support other areas of the store's operation. This is a perfectly legitimate and well-accepted practice in a business in which the profit margin of the average store is *less than 1 percent!* Higher pass-through, i.e., a lower advertised price, results in higher sales volume.

Prior to implementing this program with the region's sales force, the previous year's sales records were analyzed, and pass-through data were summarized for each of the Region's 56 key accounts. The average percentage of pass-through for these accounts was found to be 105.9 percent, with a range from 24 to 253 percent. These data were given to each sales person, along with an explanation of the new pass-through evaluation system. Each sales person was asked to identify a pass-through performance objective for the upcoming six-month evaluation period, which would be equivalent to a "fully satisfactory" rating (i.e., 3 on a 5-point scale). They were also requested to determine a performance level equivalent to a 1 and 5 rating. These objectives were then negotiated with the DSM and a *performance contract* drawn to formalize this agreement (see Figure 16-9).

As discussed earlier in this chapter, the issue of controllability was a major concern in the development of these objectives. However, three major steps were taken to reduce this concern:

1.   Objectives were individualized to reflect account conditions. Universal standards, which in essence discriminated against sales people whose accounts' merchandising philosophies did not allow

high pass-through, were eliminated in favor of objectives based on the accounts' immediate past performance. A sales person whose account had been operating at a 50 percent pass-through level might now have an objective of 55 percent to earn a fully satisfactory (3) rating and an objective of 75 percent to earn a 5 rating. The purpose of this approach was to *reinforce improvement* and allow each sales person an opportunity to earn a strong rating. This also enabled managers to evaluate the *sales person* rather than the account's merchandising philosophy.

2. The performance contract stipulated that adjustments would be made to the evaluation standards contingent upon uncontrollable occurrences such as store closings, weather conditions, and windfalls (new stores). However, it was up to the sales person to request an adjustment *prior* to the end of the evaluation period. If no such request was made, the evaluation standards stood as agreed. This was done to keep the DSM from becoming a watchdog, and placed the responsibility for recognizing changing conditions on each sales person.

3. The evaluation period was kept at six months rather than 12 months. This short period not only reduced the likelihood of uncontrollable occurrences within the evaluation period, but reduced the effect of such occurrences on overall performance measures.

Performance Contract: Major Promotion Support

NAME: Harry Humble   ACCOUNT: Food Masters, Inc.

LAST YEAR: PERCENT PASS-THRU = 130.8% (CPR = 3)
EVALUATION STANDARDS (JUNE–NOVEMBER, 1980):

% PASS-THRU	RATING
110 or below	1
120	2
132	3
142	4
154 +	5

THE UNDERSIGNED AGREE TO USE THESE STANDARDS FOR DETERMINATION OF THE CPR RATING FOR MAJOR PROMOTIONS AND UNDERSTAND THAT THESE STANDARDS ARE SUBJECT TO ADJUSTMENTS RESULTING FROM UNCONTROLLABLE SITUATIONS SUCH AS EXTREME WEATHER, STORE CLOSINGS, WINDFALLS, ETC.

Region Manager   Account Manager, Sales Rep.

District Manager

FIGURE 16-9. Sample of performance contract negotiated between the sales person and district sales manager.

Sales people were required to track their pass-through on a monthly basis, graph their cumulative performance, and send a copy of this graph to their DSM at the end of each month. The DSM then summarized their results on a district graph and submitted this to the region manager. On an intermittent basis, the region manager sent a region or district status report to all sales people, and took care to identify several sales people whose performance had shown improvement. Copies of this report were sent to the zone director.

As a consequence of this program, pass-through increased significantly (see Figure 16-10) and has exceeded the baseline level for six consecutive quarters (1½ years). The average of 131 percent pass-through during this period represented a 23.7 percent improvement over baseline. Management and sales people reported a high degree of satisfaction for this performance contract approach; at least three other regions have since adopted this same procedure and have achieved similar results.

DISCUSSION

There are only two productive groups within any organization: those who make a product and those who sell it. The viability of every firm is therefore heavily dependent upon its sales managers' ability to maintain high-level performance from its sales force. In most sales organizations, managers are selected from among the ranks of the most successful sales people. Their sales experience does of course make them very knowledgeable about the technical aspects of the sales operation: integration of marketing and sales functions, promotional strategies, shipment and delivery scheduling, sales presentation skills, account histories, and so on. They probably also know a good deal about the management function simply by observing other managers, much like the parents of a new baby know something about parenting by observing other parents raising their children. However, regardless of their knowledge level about the job of sales manager, their skill level may not be comparable.

Since it was assumed that an efficient sales force is a function of efficient managers and management control systems, the purpose of the performance systems program was to assist sales managers in fine tuning those management skills directly related to insuring strong performance from their sales people. In addition, the control systems used on a day-to-day basis by these managers were adjusted to tighten the relationship between sales performance and consequences. The success of this approach verifies that performance is, after all, directly related to the degree of accountability exercised by management.

Two unique factors greatly enhanced the success of this program. First, the heavy reliance placed on self-measurement (1) required sales people to learn more about management's expectations, (2) increased the credibility of sales performance data, (3) served as a stimulus for appropriate behavior, (4) provided accurate and individualized feedback on perfor-

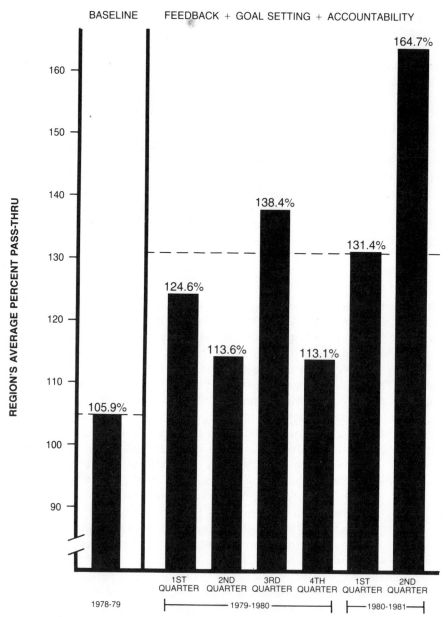

FIGURE 16-10. Region's average pass-through of promotional allowances for all accounts on all promotions. Baseline (one year) = 105.9 percent; accountability phase (1½ years) = 131.0 percent; overall improvement = 23.7 percent.

mance for salespeople, sales management, and marketing, and (5) served to stimulate reinforcement by sales and marketing managers. The effect of this technique on performance was often immediate and dramatic. The reason for the effectiveness of self-measurement was perhaps best explained by a sales person who had been tracking the number of new shelf facings he sold each day. When asked by his district manager to explain the recent increase in facings sold, the sales person said: "I just hated to put down a O." Regardless of whether this can be interpreted as positive or negative reinforcement, *performance improved.*

Second, managers were trained to reinforce *improvement.* Although reinforcement had been a commonly used procedure prior to this program, it was most often given to those sales people who generated the big sales or worked with the large accounts. Sales people who increased sales within smaller accounts were not typically afforded the same degree of recognition. The individualization of performance objectives and standards forced managers to evaluate each salesperson's performance relative to past performance within that specific territory. Consequently, recognition and performance ratings were awarded contingent upon relative improvement, rather than against universal or absolute standards. The primary benefit of such a change was that sales people began to report that they felt more "control" over their performance ratings.

Managers also reported a greater degree of control over their subordinates' performance. In a status report to top management, one district manager stated, "These objectives would probably have been achieved without the performance systems program, but it would have taken a great deal more time by the district manager, and the results would have been *much* slower." In a similar report, a region office manager added, "In conclusion, I would add that the performance systems concept, with self-imposed deadlines, performance graphing, and the reinforcement technique, has convinced me, an original skeptic, that we now have a *positive* mechanism here to improve our overall performance."

SUMMARY

Sales training, although a necessary element in the growth and development of sales personnel, cannot be relied upon alone to insure high levels of sales performance. Critical sales behavior such as customer approach, suggestive selling, and closing statements are difficult to sustain even following concentrated training sessions; the possession of appropriate skills does not always result in the appropriate use of these skills.

Evidence from various sales environments, including department stores and insurance sales, indicate the general failure of sales training efforts in insuring sustained use of appropriate selling skills. Based on data documenting the effectiveness of incentive plans and sales contests, as well as surveys that showed strong management support for the use of various incentives and contests, it is apparent that sales people do not typically work to their potential performance level, and that factors other than training have a strong impact on sales success.

Data from four different sales settings (restaurants, retail, wholesale, and telephone sales) suggest that sales training effectiveness can be increased through the use of such posttraining or performance systems strategies such as goal setting, performance measurement and feedback, increased accountability through contractual performance evaluations, and positive reinforcement. Data were presented to show that this behavioral approach was successfully used to improve performance in such areas as wine and dessert sales, average customer transaction, customer assistance, sales forecasting, sales call frequency, sales of telephone services, and airline reservations.

The most effective strategy for insuring use of appropriate sales skills was an increased frequency and specificity of performance feedback. Face-to-face and graphic feedback of performance data were common strategies in these studies and often had dramatic effects on both outcome measures (sales) and input measures (success related behavior).

Based on the evidence supporting the success of the behavioral approach in sales settings, the performance systems program was successfully introduced within a large national grocery products sales force. Sales managers were trained to improve performance measurement, feedback, and evaluation procedures, and documented their increased effectiveness by completing sales improvement projects that graphically demonstrated increases in sales or behavior leading to sales.

The performance systems program introduced the positive accountability model, which included seven major elements:

1. Specific success-related behaviors or critical sales results were defined in measurable terms.

2. In order to establish baseline levels of performance, data were collected for each of these variables. Although historical data were often available, it was sometimes necessary to develop new measures. Old measurement systems were updated to include more frequent measures of individual rather than group performance.

3. Baseline data were used to develop performance objectives; these objectives were negotiated between the sales person and district manager.

4. When appropriate, each objective was integrated into the performance evaluation process. Potential ratings were prespecified and tied directly to various performance parameters.

5. Performance levels were continually monitored, but most often by the salesperson; frequent status reports were submitted to the district manager.

6. The self-monitoring process provided immediate data-based feedback to each sales person. In those cases for which self-monitoring

was not feasible, data feedback was given to each sales person via manual or computerized reports monitored at the region of national level.

7. Frequent positive reinforcement for individual accomplishments was provided verbally or via memos by district, region, and national management.

As an indication of the overall acceptance of this approach, the performance systems program has been extended company-wide and is now being introduced throughout all operating divisions and subsidiaries, including manufacturing facilities, purchasing, data processing, marketing, retail stores, and distribution centers. In addition, at the request of the vice president of grocery products sales, a behaviorally oriented performance improvement program entitled *Make Performance Matter* (Mirman, 1981) was developed for use by grocery store managers.

These types of programs will continue to be used successfully, because employees work better and are more satisfied when they feel that their performance *matters* to the organization. This can best be described by a memo recently sent by a veteran salesman to his district manager:

Pete–

Thanks for your phone call Friday afternoon about the Donutz introduction. Even after 18 years of selling—grey hair, overweight and failing eyesight—it still feels damn good to get a pat on the back every now and then. Thanks for noticing.

Ray

REFERENCES

"At Bio-Dynamics, cash boosts system sales," *Sales and Marketing Management*, September 17, 1979, 49.

Brooks Brothers braun, *Creative Management*, Business Research Publications, Inc., Plainview, NY, March 1981, 4.

Brown, M. G., Malott, R. W., Dillon, M., J., and Keeps, E. J. Improving customer service in a large department store through the use of training and feedback, *Journal of Organizational Behavior Management*, 1980, 2, 251–265.

Connellan, T. K. *How to Improve Human Performance: Behaviorism in Business and Industry.* New York: Harper and Row, 1978, pp. 118, 170–174.

Customer Service Behavior, *Behavior Improvement News.* Champaign, IL: Research Press Co., 2, February 1978, 1.

Does retail training pay? Reprinted from *Training in Business and Industry.* Gallert Publishing Corporation, Februrary 1969.

Doyle, S. X., and Shapiro, R. P. What counts most in motivating your sales force? *Harvard Business Review*, May–June 1980, 133–140.

Emery salesmen ask themselves "Why?" *Sales Management*, September 15, 1970.

Gupton, T., and LeBow, M. Behavior management in a large industrial firm, *Behavior Therapy*, 1971, *2*, 78–82.

Hahne, C. E. How to measure results of sales training, *Training and Development Journal*, November 1977, 3–7.

Hanisch, D., personal communication, 1979.

Haring, A., and Myers, R. H. Special incentives for salesmen, *Journal of Marketing*, October 1953, 155–159.

Harris, M., personal communication, March 31, 1981.

Incentive plans for salesmen, *The National Industrial Conference Board, Inc.*, New York: 1970.

Jones, L. Prediction is the performance, *Education and Training*, Association of Business Executives, London, England, January 1979, 30–31.

King, Henria, Personal Communication, November, 1980 (a)

King, Henria, Personal Communication, 1980(b)

Komaki, J., Blood, M. R., and Holder, D. Fostering friendliness in a fast food franchise, *Journal of Behavior Management*, 1980, *2*, 151–164.

Komaki, J., Woddell, W., and Pearce, G., The applied behavior analysis approach and individual employees: Improving performance in two small businesses, *Organizational Behavior and Human Performance*, 1977, *19*, 337–352.

Kreitner, R., and Golab, M., Increasing the rate of salesperson telephone calls with a monetary refund, *Journal of Behavior Management*, 1978, *1*, 192–195.

Mager, R. F., and Pipe, P. *Analyzing Performance Problems or "You Really Oughta Wanna"*. Belmont, CA: Fearon-Pittman Publishing, Inc., 1965.

Making sales people behave, *Sales and Marketing Management*, July 9, 1979, 16–17.

McGregor, D., An uneasy look at performance appraisal, *Harvard Business Review*, September–October, 1972, 133–138.

Miller, L. M. *Behavior Management*. New York: Wiley, 1978, pp. 232–239.

Miller, L. M., Improving sales and forecast accuracy in a nationwide sales organization, *Journal of Organizational Behavior Management*, 1977, *1*, 39–51.

Mirman, R. Behavior management for sales managers: Breakfast of champions. Presentation at Association for Behavior Analysis, Chicago, May 1979.

Mirman, R. *Make Performance Matter*, General Mills, Minneapolis, MN, 1981. This behavioral training program was developed for and based on an idea by Mr. Howard L. Ross, vice president and general manager, grocery products sales division. This package includes a 20-minute 16MM film with three manuals for group or self-instruction.

Neider, L. L., An experimental field investigation utilizing an expectancy theory view of participation. *Journal of Organizational Behavior and Human Performance*. 1980, *26*, 425–442.

Odiorne, G. S., *Management by Objectives*. Belmont, CA: Fearon-Pitman Publishers, Inc., 1965.

Pedalino, E., and Gamboa, V. U. Behavior modification and absenteeism: Intervention in one industrial setting, *Journal of Applied Psychology*, 1974, *59* 694–698.

Performance management pays off for 3M Canada, *Training*, January 1979, 36.

Rackham, N., and Morgan, T. The behavior of telephone sales agents, *Behavior Analysis and Training*. London: McGraw Hill, 1977, 220–247.

Reinforcement: Its effect on paint sales, *Behavior Improvement News*, January 1979, 4.

Rubenstein, F. D., personal communication, April 1981.

Skinner, B. F. Pigeons in a Pelican, *American Psychologist*, 1960, *15*, 28–37.

Steinbrink, J. P., *Compensation of salesmen: Dartnell's 20th Biennial Survey*. Chicago, IL: The Dartnell Corporation, 1980.

Stoerzinger, A., Johnston, J., Pisor, K., and Monroe, C., Implementation and evaluation of a feedback system for employees in a salvage operation, *Journal of Organizational Behavioral Management*, 1978, *1*, 268–280.

The Tarkenton Productivity Update, Case Study #2, Tarkenton and Co. Newsletter, Vol. *1*, 1981.

Warren, M. W. Using Behavioral Technology to improve sales performance, *Training and Development Journal*, July 1978, 54–56.

Weitz, J., Antoinetti, J., and Wallace, S. R. The effect of home office contact on sales performance, *Personnel Psychology*, 1954, *1*, 381–384.

17

Resource Management
in Organizational Settings

RICHARD A. WINETT

and

E. SCOTT GELLER

Virginia Polytechnic Institute and State University

Industry is characterized by constant self-awareness. Ever greater effort goes into computing and comparing, in order to better allocate resources, balance processes, and improve products. In other words, industry has a bottom line and profits are its final test. (Stobaugh and Yergin, 1979, p. 153)

In this chapter we emphasize one major point. In an era of escalating costs and concerns about productivity, an important way for a firm or organization to remain or become more competitive is to reduce costs for resources involved in production, services, or maintenance of the organization. While the specific mix of resources used will vary from setting to setting, the point applies to virtually every setting. A large insurance firm can become more competitive if resources used for heating, cooling, hot water, lighting, and equipment could be reduced by 30 percent. A trucking company may be able to charge less than competitors and thus increase business or simply clear more profits, if its fleet's gasoline consumption were decreased by 10 percent. A university may be able to hire additional staff if most of its paper were recycled. A manufacturing industry could capture a larger share of a market if the resources used to produce a product were reduced, and hence the cost of the product to the consumer decreased.

While the reduction of resource use from the perspective of the organization or firm, and indeed the entire country, is a laudable goal, the

477

question is, how can this be done? Are the initial costs so high and the payback period so long that an investment in efficiency and conservation is really not cost effective? In this chapter we show that considerable savings of resources can be achieved with virtually no capital investments. That is, the first step any organization or firm should take involves good housekeeping—the adoption of low cost or no cost resource management strategies. Most often these strategies entail better maintenance procedures and the effective management of human behavior.

Evidence for this perspective comes from case studies reported in Stobaugh and Yergin (1979). Firms including Burger King, Lockheed, Tenneco, Colgate-Palmolive, Exxon, and Western Electric from the years 1972–77 were able to reduce energy consumption by a mean of 29 percent primarily through good housekeeping procedures. While larger savings are possible through other types of conservation strategies, e.g., through extensive recovery of waste and technological innovation, housekeeping procedures should be the first priority because of cost considerations. In this chapter we focus on housekeeping and simple resource recovery procedures. The combination of these low technology strategies, while offering no panacea-like technical fix, can lead to very substantial savings. Conservation strategies for transportation management are also discussed.

Problems in resource management have traditionally been approached through engineering and design interventions, i.e., the modification of physical environment or structure. Obviously for many problems this is entirely appropriate. Better designed buildings and more fuel efficient cars and trucks can greatly reduce resource consumption. But most firms or organizations are not in a position to construct new buildings, to extensively retrofit their present buildings, or to replace their fleet. However, a considerable body of research from numerous field projects indicates that everyday problems of resource management can be approached through the application of behavioral technology (Cone and Hayes, 1980; Geller, Winett, and Everett, 1982). Quite often the most effective approach is a combination of physical and behavioral technology. For example, in the residential sector, simple physical retrofits can markedly reduce the energy requirements of many homes (Socolow, 1978). The main problem, however, is developing and implementing marketing campaigns to expedite adoption of simple retrofit technology. A similar situation exists in the industrial and government sectors of the community.

To date, most of the behavioral resource management work has not been conducted in organizations or industries (Geller et al., 1982). For example, almost all of the projects on energy conservation have been conducted in the residential sector. We will review procedures that have been used to modify resource consumption behavior in different settings and sectors, discuss special problems and considerations, and then discuss how these procedures can be applied in an organization by providing a step-by-step blueprint for action. A procedure based on behavioral principles can be easily tailored to fit virtually any setting.

The resource management targets in this chapter include heating and cooling, solid waste disposal, transportation, and equipment efficiency. Behavioral strategies can be divided into two broad categories, antecedent and consequence strategies. Antecedent procedures are introduced prior to specified behavior in order to try to increase the occurrence of desirable behavior or decrease the probability of undesirable behavior. In this category are included various prompting, modeling, and informational approaches. Consequences, positive or negative, follow the occurrence or nonoccurrence of the target behavior and are designed to increase or decrease the target behavior. In this category are included various feedback and reinforcement procedures.

The hallmarks of the behavioral approach in resource management have been the careful and continuous assessment and monitoring of the resource target, the implementation of specified procedures, and the continuous evaluation of the effectiveness of the procedures. After describing specific strategies and case examples evaluated in this way, we conclude with an outline of an action plan for an organization based on behavioral procedures and evaluation methodology.

RESULTS VERSUS PROCESS

With many resource management problems, it is possible to focus on specific processes, results, or both. Procedures can be developed to assure compliance with thermostat guidelines (process); incentives can be given contingent on reduced energy consumption (outcome); or a combination of procedures can be used. While it is apparent that the bottom line is always an outcome measure (e.g., energy saved), there are important reasons for focusing on processes. In some settings specific processes account for most of the resource expenditure. For example, in the residential sector, 79 percent of energy consumption is attributable to space heating and cooling, and heating hot water. Therefore an effective residential energy conservation program must concentrate on thermostat control for spatial heating and cooling, and for heating hot water, and on retrofit strategies designed to reduce energy consumption connected with heating and cooling. Consumers should receive specific information and procedures to modify heating, cooling, and hot water practices, and also be shown exactly how much energy (outcome) they are saving by engaging in these processes. Without specific information, consumers may continue inappropriate practices and not optimize resource conservation. For example, they may mistakenly turn off lights while not employing thermostat setbacks. Turning off lights accounts for minimal savings, while thermostat setbacks account for highly significant savings (Beckey and Nelson, 1981).

This example suggests that an *assessment* needs to be made of the practices that contribute most to resource expenditure, and how such practices can be inexpensively modified. Without such information, a program must focus solely on results, and these are likely to be less substantial and probably less cost effective than a program that concentrates on both processes and results.

Behavioral intervention in resource management has traditionally been concerned with either processes or results. In residential energy conservation, most of the early studies were concerned with demonstrating that a particular behavioral technique such as feedback could reduce energy consumption. Less attention was given to the careful delineation of specific conservation practices. The shortcomings of this approach were probably attributable to the limited interaction of behavioral scientists with engineers, and perhaps the need of behavioral scientists to demonstrate that they had something unique to contribute to resource management (Geller et al., 1982). Specific practices in the home that needed to be modified, e.g., thermostat control, were simply not made public.

For other problems, the research started with processes. In programs designed to reduce dependence on the automobile, commuters were given incentives for riding a bus, generally at the point at which they boarded the bus (Everett and Hayward, 1974). Obviously this is a highly specific public behavior that can be rewarded immediately. These same commuters did not, e.g., receive feedback on how much energy they were saving by not driving their cars and by taking the bus. While bus ridership seems to be an example of a highly specific process, other assessments and intervention have called attention to deficits in transportation companies' route information and subsequent consumer awareness of optimal commuting routes, and the need to implement strategies that provide for more convenience, such as van pooling.

In the next section we review behavioral strategies designed to reduce energy consumption in the home. The work in residential energy conservation is quite extensive and does provide consistent data on effective and ineffective strategies and results that have been replicated in other developed areas of behavioral resource management, such as litter control (see reviews by Geller, 1980; Osborne and Powers, 1981), recycling (see reviews by Geller, 1980, 1981b), and transportation energy conservation (see reviews by Everett, 1980; Reichel and Geller, 1981).

APPLICATIONS FOR RESIDENTIAL ENERGY CONSERVATION

The largest number of behavioral projects have intended to reduce energy used for heating and cooling in the residential sector, since in that sector 65 percent of energy consumption is attributable to heating and cooling. Many conclusions from that work appear applicable to organizations, as has been substantiated by recent research (Shippee and Gregory, in press).

Antecedent Strategies

With some exceptions, antecedent strategies, such as giving people written information on energy savings practices, have not yielded reductions in energy consumption (Hayes and Cone, 1977; Winett, Kagel, Battalio, and

Winkler, 1978; Winett and Neitzel, 1975). That is, providing your employees with brochures, memos, and even informational meetings and workshops will probably be an unsuccessful approach to resource management (Geller et al., 1982) if these approaches are used alone. A likely outcome is that employees will become more knowledgeable about, and perhaps more favorably disposed toward, effective resource management, but will not increase their practice of resource management (Wicker, 1969). Informational approaches should be one component of resource management programs, but by themselves are usually not sufficient to promote change.

Two promising antecedent strategies are modeling and prompting. Modeling involves the actual live or videotaped demonstration of resource management strategies. In two studies, specially developed videotapes demonstrating conservation strategies dealt entirely with heating and cooling practices (thermostat control) in the home, and were found to be effective in promoting average overall energy savings of about 20 percent on energy used for heating or cooling, even when shown only once to consumers (Winett, Hatcher, Fort, Leckliter, Love, Riley, and Fishback, unpublished). However, these programs had some special attributes that were probably critical determinants of program success. Specifically, the videotapes used actors whose demographic characteristics were similar to the audience, and who were depicted in everyday situations in a home setting virtually identical to the viewers' homes. Programs were seen in groups, and people received some written material on conservation strategies. The videotape programs depicted and emphasized specific behavior.

It is possible, however, to extrapolate this method to an organizational setting. That is, programs demonstrating specific conservation practices relevant to a setting can be produced on location and shown to groups of employees, who also receive specific written information and discuss the practical implementation of the strategies shown. The combination of video programs and group discussions, termed the "media forum," has been considered an effective behavior change strategy (Rogers and Shoemaker, 1971).

Signs, messages, blinking lights, or sounds can serve as prompts to perform specific behavior. Prompts have been infrequently used alone because, as has been shown in other areas (e.g., solid waste management), they tend to have more limited and transient effects (Geller, 1980a, 1980b, 1981b). That is, only a minority of employees will probably respond to prompts and only for a minimal time period. Prompts, however, can be made more effective by specifically indicating the target behavior and by locating them in close proximity to opportunities for the target response. It has been found that large signs located at the exit doorways, which indicate when and by whom lights should be turned off in unoccupied areas, were far more effective than stickers placed on light switches that noted generally the need to save a watt (Winett, 1978). With the typical sticker, lights were left on in an unoccupied area on 100 percent of observations. With the large, well-placed signs, lights were only left on 40 percent of the time. A similar procedure can probably be effective when applied to turning off unused equipment. Here again it appears that delineating specific and appropriate processes results in more beneficial results.

Prompts can probably also be made more effective if they are more obtrusive. In one residential study a blinking blue light was connected to the air conditioning thermostat and an outside thermometer (Becker and Seligman, 1978). The light would blink if the air conditioning was on and if it was 68°F or below outside. This procedure was instituted because many consumers rarely check to see if it has cooled off outside; they simply close all windows and doors and leave the air conditioning on. In this study the light would not stop blinking until the consumer turned the air conditioning off. This procedure yielded a 15 percent saving on overall electricity consumption. Larger savings could have been achieved if a higher outdoor temperature criteria was chosen (such as 75°F).

If a firm or organization is located in a building where the windows can open, a similar strategy to the blinking light can be adopted. Unfortunately, in most buildings, heating or cooling systems are set 24 hours a day, with minimal or no regard for outdoor temperature. In a later part of this section, we discuss data relevant to comfort and the thermal environment. However, we here note that simply modifying thermostat settings in buildings, and using natural ventilation where possible can reduce heating and cooling cost by at least 30 percent.

To return to the antecedent strategy of prompting, general recommendations and conclusions from the research are that prompts specify or signify a target behavior, be strategically placed, and be obtrusive without being aversive (in the latter case, employees will probably sabotage the prompt; see reviews by Geller, 1980a, 1980b, 1982). Prompts should also be embedded in other types of programs. For example, a consequence strategy may be even more effective if employees are consistently reminded about the more effective strategies for saving heating and cooling energy.

Consequence Strategies

Consequence strategies involve applying rewards or giving information following engagement in a certain behavior in order to maintain or increase its frequency of occurrence. The most frequently used consequence strategies have been monetary rebates and feedback. Interestingly, most research in this area has focused on outcome rather than process. Early studies (Hayes and Cone, 1977; Winett, Kaiser, and Haberkorn, 1977; Winett and Nietzel, 1975; Winett et al., 1978) showed that receiving a specific amount of money contingent on specified reductions of energy consumption was a successful resource management strategy. In the residential sector, this strategy has been conceptualized as a price change manipulation or a rate change strategy (Winett et al., 1978). One problem in using this strategy on a broad scale in the residential sector is that, until recently, rates for energy have not been high enough to make rebates cost effective (Winett and Neale, 1979).

However, within an organizational setting rebates may indeed be a very cost-effective approach. If parts of an organization's or firm's building were on different energy meters, then savings on energy from expected figures could be rebated to employees. The part of the building recording the largest savings could receive a proportion of allocated funds for energy, with the company saving the rest. On the other hand, savings could be passed on to all employees, or winners could be picked in a lottery, with one or several large prizes. Commodities produced by the industry could be used instead of monetary rebates. Obviously feedback and incentive procedures must be tailored to the organization's traditions and practices.

Similar approaches have been used in master-metered apartment buildings, with reductions ranging from 3 to 15 percent (McClelland and Belsten, 1980; Slavin, Wodarski, and Blackburn, 1981). These rebate procedures can be made more effective in two ways: first, by focusing on group, unit, or department identity and cohesion, and perhaps competitiveness; second, by identifying and prompting certain behavior, as used in heating, cooling, or water heating.

A variation of the rebate strategy involves the use of milieu checks and a payment on the spot. For example, if a department or part of the building had all thermostats set at appropriate temperatures, and all unused equipment were turned off, then the department might receive $10 toward a party fund. A similar procedure was found to be quite effective in master-metered apartments (Walker, 1979).

Consequence procedures are not restricted to rebates or material rewards. Studies in the residential sector have shown that frequent feedback on energy consumption combined with explicit, difficult, but reachable conservation goals can consistently reduce overall energy consumption by about 15 percent (Becker, 1978; Hayes and Cone, 1977; Seligman and Darley, 1977; Winett, Neale, and Grier, 1979; Winett, Neale, Williams, Yokley, and Kauder, 1979). In these studies consumers received written information several times per week on how much energy they used, generally in the energy unit (kilowatt hours) and as a percent increase or decrease of a prior baseline period, which took into account a weather correction factor (Winett et al., 1979). With residential consumers the cost of giving written feedback is less than the cost of energy that would have been expended, but was saved; and with discontinuation of feedback, consumers actually maintained their savings (Winett et al., 1979a; 1979b). However, in the residential sector, giving frequent feedback to millions of households is not very practical. This has led to the development of different kinds of automated feedback devices, by the U.S. Department of Energy and by the commercial sector. Studies testing the efficacy of these devices have yielded equivocal results (Becker, 1978; McClelland and Cook, 1980). This may be because some of the dimensions of the written feedback procedures (goal setting and weather correction) have not been incorporated into mechanized feedback.

It is conceivable that frequent feedback can be a very effective strategy for resource management in organizations. The cost of delivering feedback can be considerably more cost effective than in the residential sector. Few energy meter readings would be necessary, but these meters would represent the considerable energy expenditure of a setting and its many employees. For example, maintenance people could regularly read meters, calculate energy expenditures and savings, and post feedback in highly visible places. Depending upon the metering of separate sites, various department or parts of a firm can compete with each other. Important aspects of feedback would still have to be included in this plan, including credible and frequent information, difficult but achievable goals, and the particular use of feedback during peak consumption periods. Specifying energy saving processes and creating commitment to energy saving and group identify can also enhance the impact of feedback.

Special Considerations: Comfort, Clothing, and Energy

Probably the simplest, no cost, and most effective energy saving procedure for buildings involves thermostat settings during the time that a building is occupied and when it is not occupied. Changing standard thermostat settings when a building is occupied lead to questions of human comfort. Considerable research on comfort has been conducted under the auspices of the American Society for Heating, Cooling, and Refrigeration Engineers; much of the research follows one particular laboratory paradigm (Rohles, 1981). In human comfort studies, subjects in small groups were placed in environmental chambers where temperature, humidity, and clothing worn by subjects could be rigorously controlled. Subjects then used nine-point scales to vote anonymously on how comfortable they were at different temperatures. It has been found in these studies that when wearing apparel equivalent to an insulation value of .80 clo (underwear, shoes, socks, shirt, pants, light sweater), the mean comfortable temperature is 75°F.

Recent work has challenged both the methodology and findings of laboratory comfort studies, particularly with respect to recommended winter temperatures (Winett et al., unpublished). Winett et al. noted that self-reports of comfort can be influenced by cultural and social expectancies and information, and by consequences such as the cost of comfort. Comfort studies had not been conducted in field settings over long periods of time, thus reducing the generality of the laboratory studies.

In studies conducted with all-electric apartment and townhouse dwellers, hygrothermographs that continuously and very accurately measure temperature and humidity were placed at table-top height, several feet from the thermostat of each household. Participants in winter and summer studies saw the videotape program described previously in this chapter or received daily feedback on energy consumption. Dependent measures included continuous temperature and humidity, daily electricity use (from meters), and frequent reports from participants on perceived comfort and (actual) clothing worn. In addition, household's mean baseline temperature when the home was occupied was used to create an individualized thermostat change schedule. The schedule called for a one-degree drop in temperature each week when the home was occupied, and setbacks to the mid-50° (F) range at night or when the home was unoccupied.

It was found that in the winter the combination of procedures resulted in a 15 percent savings on overall electricity use, and a 26 percent savings on electricity used for heating. The hygrothermographs indicated that the mean temperatures in homes during the six-week intervention period (February to mid-March) was 62°F, yet participants reported they were comfortable and were only wearing clothing that totaled a mean of .75 clo (underwear, shirt, pants, light sweater). Thus these field data challenged conclusions from laboratory studies, and suggested that in most settings people will be comfortable at 65°F with minimal change in clothing. In other words, it appears that former, mandatory thermostat settings were entirely appropriate.

In this study, about 80 percent of energy savings were attributable to the setbacks. Any organization that only occupies a building on certain days and hours can drastically reduce energy used for heating and cooling by putting heating and cooling systems on set-back timers.

In the summer study, it was found that simple procedures such as closing all windows, drapes, and shades in the morning, turning off air conditioning when doors or windows are open, using window fans in the evening (which use 16 percent as much energy as air conditioning), and making only slight thermostat changes resulted in mean savings of 34 percent of electricity used for cooling, with savings as high as 45 percent. Modeling programs and feedback were used to promote these conservation practices. These simple housekeeping procedures yielded large energy savings with virtually no change in interior temperature and maintenance of comfort.

Participants reported comfort at a mean temperature of about 77°F. However, this was with a mean clo value of .37 (light pants, light shirt). One of the simplest ways for any organization to reduce the use of energy used for cooling is by modifying dress codes. For each degree that the air conditioning thermostat is raised in the summer, a savings of about 7 to 8 percent on energy used for cooling is achieved. Reducing clo value from .75 to .35 can account for about four degrees of cooling and about 30 percent savings!

Summary

Considerable savings in buildings are possible by implementing behavioral strategies to support simple housekeeping, dress code changes, and thermostat control strategies. To the list of energy savings strategies described here should be added turning the hot water thermostat from 160° to 130° (U.S. Department of Housing and Urban Development, 1980). Data indicate that these conservation strategies can save from 30 to 40 percent on overall energy used in a home, with no cost and no loss in comfort. The amount saved in other buildings by adopting these strategies will vary as a function of building occupancy time, type of business, and equipment used. The no-cost factor indicates that *every* organization or firm should adopt aspects of these procedures.

Unlike the situation in the residential sector, conservation practices in the industrial sector can be readily made public. Therefore, within organizations and firms, it is relatively easy to prompt and provide consequences for energy saving practices. It is also possible to simply implement changes (e.g., thermostat settings) by decree. However, as with other organizational changes, intervention techniques are likely to be more effective when managers and employees participate in the planning and implementation of change, and receive feedback and other tangible evidence of the value of their effort.

TRANSPORTATION MANAGEMENT

The use of the automobile as the dominant means of transportation has resulted in a host of environmental problems including: increasing our dependence on foreign oil; using up valuable land for parking and roads, and using up other natural resources for automobile production; contributing substantially to air and noise pollution; and decreasing the aesthetic quality of the environment. While these problems are of obvious national concern and affect any organization or firm, why should an organization or firm be concerned with the commuting practices of its employees? For several reasons: (1) Mounting transportation costs mean that employees will have to be increasingly drawn from areas in close proximity to a firm, unless alternative means of transportation are developed; (2) Capital expenditures for expanding or improving facilities to accommodate the automobile may be completely avoided if transportation modes are modified; (3) Considerable personal stress is associated with contemporary commuting (Stokols, Novaco, Stokols, and Campbell, 1978), and such stress can diminish productivity on the job.

In this section we describe antecedent and consequence strategies for modifying transportation behavior, particularly commuting. We also review recent behavioral work on increasing driving efficiency, such as increasing miles per gallon or decreasing unnecessary driving. An increase in driving efficiency should be of direct relevance to firms that have fleets of vehicles or are involved in shipping.

Changing Transportation Modality

Car pools, van pools, and use of public transportation are considerably more energy efficient than the single-occupant car. It has been estimated that the single-occupant car uses 14,190 BTUs per passenger mile compared to 2410 BTUs per passenger mile for van pools.

Car Pooling. Attempts to promote car pooling have primarily involved either alone or in combination preferential treatment of car poolers and efforts to organize car pool programs. The development of priority lanes for car poolers provides an obvious example of the combination of physical design and behavioral technology. Priority lanes are set aside to be used only by buses and carpools; sometimes reduced toll fares are also available for car pools (MacCalden and Davis, 1972). The priority lane is generally less congested and faster moving than other lanes, thus providing a mechanism to reinforce use of car pools. Evaluations of priority lanes suggest that they are somewhat effective in increasing car pooling, but rather difficult to manage (Geller et al., 1982; Reichel and Geller, 1981).

Preferential parking for car poolers and extra parking fees for solo drivers have also been employed to increase ride sharing. An evaluation of these techniques indicated that the combination, compared to preferential parking alone, was effective in decreasing solo driving and increasing car pooling (Hirst, 1976). Other reports suggest that monetary payments for employee use of public transportation and free parking or differential payments contingent on number of employees in a car pool are effective strategies (Letzku and Scharfe, 1975).

A second strategy for promoting car pooling has involved organizational efforts to apply computer technology for matching potential car poolers with information on employees' work schedules, address, and interest in car pooling. This antecedent approach is similar to other informational strategies described previously, and it is not surprising that a tentative conclusion is that matching services alone are not sufficient to increase car pooling (Geller et al., 1982). Matching procedures can, however, help maximize the impact of incentive approaches. Additional research indicates that commuters' perceptions of lost time and inconvenience may be important factors to dispel in any promotional campaign for car pooling (Horowitz and Sheth, 1977), and that acquaintance with potential car poolers and social skills may also be involved in willingness to car pool (Barkow, 1974; Dueker and Levin, 1976).

These findings suggest that organizations or firms should take a more personalized approach to car pooling with company time given, e.g., for potential car pool employees to meet. Such a procedure has been followed by the Hewlett Packard Company, which allowed its employees extended coffee breaks to meet other employees from nearby residential areas in order to plan and negotiate car pools (Pratsch, 1975). In this way the company clearly indicated its commitment to ride sharing, and as a result, 40 percent of the employees participated in car pools.

Van Pooling. Van pooling is a second major form of ride sharing that appears to have some advantages over car pooling. An exemplary program was developed by the 3M Company for its headquarters in St. Paul, Minnesota. The primary reason for instituting the program was the high costs associated with building new parking facilities. The program started on a pilot basis in 1973 with six 12-passenger vans; presently there are 86 vans with more being added.

The program includes: (1) selection of van-pool coordinators based on special interviews of individuals from specific residential areas; (2) designation of the coordinators' job including driving the van, training backup drivers, billing riders, keeping records, and parking over night; (3) contingencies to encourage coordinator participation, including a free ride to and from work, personal use of the van for 7¢ per mile, the receipt of all passenger fares over the minimum requirement of eight, and convenient parking; (4) completion of monthly vouchers to determine the amount due the company and the coordinator.

Evaluations of the program indicated considerable employee satisfaction, and the income generated by the program paid for the cost of the program (Owens and Sever, 1977). About half the van-pool passengers previously commuted to work by single-occupant car. Fares in the program were based on operating cost (vehicle maintenance and gasoline) and on fixed cost (e.g., depreciation, insurance, licensing). This program also illustrates the principle of *reciprocal reinforcement*: all parties, the company, the coordinator, and passengers were rewarded in this program. The van-pool program has been also implemented at two other 3M sites. Estimates by Owens and Sever (1977) on savings were: 2.25 million vehicle miles per year; 190,00 gallons of gasoline; and 735 parking places at 3M headquarters. This program should become even more cost effective as the cost of gasoline and building increases.

Mass Transit.   Behavioral research by Everett and his colleagues (as reviewed in Everett, 1980; Geller et al., 1982; Reichel and Geller, 1981) and demonstration projects by municipalities have been carried out to try to increase ridership on mass transit, primarily on buses. The major technique in these projects has been the reinforcement of ridership through: (1) reduced fares for short periods of time, (2) free transit to certain areas or during certain times, (3) redeemable coupons, usable for a free bus trip or other commodities, and (4) combinations of these procedures. Such programs have not always been carefully evaluated, and at times the focus has been on inappropriate target behavior, e.g., receiving coupons for attending a talk on bus ridership. A general conclusion of demonstration projects is that in the short run, bus ridership was markedly increased (Geller et al., 1982).

Experimental studies indicated that reinforcement of bus ridership by redeemable coupons, either for a free ride or commodities by local merchants, successfully increased ridership, and that this plan was more cost effective when a partial reinforcement schedule was followed, such as reinforcement of every third rider (Deslauriers and Everett, 1977). Experiments with free ridership have also indicated that the condition of a free fare generally increases ridership, but that parameters of the free-ride schedule can influence ridership patterns. For example, the length of time that coupons are redeemable and the contingency between ridership and receipt of more coupons are important parameters influencing ridership rate (Everett, Gurtler, and Hildebrand, 1981).

Many free transit programs can be supported by merchants on the basis of free advertising, bringing customers to their stores, and reducing the costs of building parking facilities. A firm or organization can also contribute to free transit programs in lieu of constructing parking accommodations, to reduce employee stress, and to draw employees from a wide geographical area.

While the research on reinforcing bus ridership is promising, there are several caveats. First, it appears that middle and upper class drivers of single-occupant cars may not have been affected by the measures. It might be possible to draw such drivers to mass transit by the provision of more luxurious buses that increase the prestige of ridership and by rewards that involve large payoffs (e.g., coupons for a community lottery). Second, the research needs to be directed toward other variables that presumably influence ridership, such as ride quality, service frequency, and trip flexibility. Third, programs need to be implemented that are aimed at long-term maintenance of transit behavior.

Special Considerations: Flexible Work Schedules

Flexible work schedules, or flexitime, is an organizational change strategy that could alleviate commuting problems and also improve work productivity and extra-work activities. One of the major problems of commuting in urban areas is the morning and afternoon rush hours. Because most people work similar hours, they commute to and from work at about the same time resulting in traffic congestion, inefficient use of fuel (e.g., from "stop and go" driving), and considerable personal stress (Stokols et al., 1978). Large capital expenditures are needed to make transit modalities capable of accommodating rush hours. During off-peak hours, most transit modalities are virtually empty (Geller et al., 1982).

An obvious approach to this problem is to spread out the rush hour peaks by changing work hours either through staggered work schedules or through flexitime. With flexitime, workers can choose within guidelines when they want to start and end work. Usually workers are still required to work an eight-hour day, although under some plans, they need only total a specified number of hours at the end of a week or pay period. While other organizational procedures need to be instituted with flexitime to assure adequate coverage and supervison, and not all jobs or organizations are suitable for flexitime, there are specific benefits from flexitime: (1) the potential to decrease commuting congestion, since workers will be arriving and departing at somewhat different times; (2) an increase in hours of operation of a facility, because of differing schedules that can potentially provide greater customer service, and greater contact with areas of the county on different time zones, or even with other countries: (3) a possible increase in productivity, since by giving employees greater participation in arranging and controlling their work schedule, increases in morale and job satisfaction have been recorded (Nollen, 1979), factors possibly linked to productivity; and (4) flexitime may be particularly suitable for the contemporary work force, which values participation in leisure and family life (Best, 1978), and which is increasingly composed of women with school-age children (Johnson, 1980). Recent studies have shown that flexitime can alleviate some work-family conflicts and allow more time for family life (Winett, Neale, and Williams, 1982).

Clearly, one possibility for firms and organizations is to combine the programs discussed here. A company can promote van pools, offer reduced or free transit fares, and institute flexible work schedules. Such an approach may be the optimal strategy (Remak and Rosenbloom, 1976). Employees could then commute in relatively comfortable buses or quickly moving vans following a work schedule more suitable to them.

Reduction of Vehicle Miles and Increasing Miles per Gallon

For organizations or firms that have fleets of vehicles, two prime objectives are reduction of vehicle miles driven (VMD) and increasing miles per gallon (MPG). Reducing VMD is perhaps the most direct approach to reducing energy consumption of vehicles. A relatively small reduction in VMD would have a dramatic effect on demand for gasoline and hence imported oil (Federal Energy Administration, 1977). Obviously an organization or firm with a fleet of vehicles that can reduce unnecessary VMD will also accrue savings.

While behavioral research is not extensive in this area, some studies have indicated that procedures similar to those used to decrease energy in homes can be effective in decreasing VMD. Monetary rebates or payments contingent on reduced VMD (Foxx and Hake, 1977; Hake and Foxx, 1978), feedback with specified goals or self-monitoring strategies (Hake and Foxx, 1978), and public competitions and public feedback (Reichel and Geller, 1980) have all reduced VMD. Possibly as a function of low gasoline costs at the time of the study, written feedback alone did not appear effective in reducing VMD (Everett and Hayward, 1974), although such feedback procedures might be effective under present gasoline prices. It may also be possible, however, to increase the effectiveness of rebate, feedback, and other procedures by incorporating a "leader" variable. For example, managers and line supervisors could be incorporated into VMD programs to prompt and motivate employees and to provide competitive work units (Hake and Foxx, 1978; Reichel and Geller, 1981). As in other programs, firms and organizations need to calculate the amount of rebates and the costs of the program against savings. The escalating costs of gasoline suggest that such programs should be cost effective in the future.

Increasing MPG is a second way to save transportation energy. This strategy has been primarily promoted through the development of more fuel-efficient engines. For example, it is likely that within the next five years, some passenger cars will be capable of 75 MPG. Minimal attention has been directed toward strategies to modify driver behavior so as to increase MPG. Although several oil companies publish driving guides and have driving exhibits, it is unlikely that this information strategy by itself promotes changes in driving behavior.

Coupling information on efficient driving behavior (e.g., accelerate slowly, maintain constant speed, avoid stop and go driving, release the accelerator when going downhill, and reduce idling time) with consequence procedures is a more promising strategy. Lauridsen (1977) reported a successful program that reduced MPG in utility company vehicles by the combination of feedback on MPG or gallons per hour from fuel-flow meters installed in the cars, and a lottery whereby the number of chances and amount of winnings was contingent on the increase in MPG.

Runnion, Watson, and McWhorter (1978) reported the efforts by one of the top 10 textile companies in America to increase the miles per gallon of its long-haul and intermill drivers, and to increase the amount of fuel that its drivers obtained at company terminals rather than at more expensive commercial service stations. These results were seen as the product of several kinds of behavior by the drivers including driving patterns (e.g., speed, idling time, gear-shifting practices, braking procedures) and trip planning so that gasoline purchases could be made at company stations. The study was conducted with 195 drivers who had an average driving experience of six years. These drivers covered about six million miles per year while delivering freight between 58 company sites in a three-state area (intermill drivers) and throughout 32 state (long-haul drivers). Job satisfaction was reportedly high, with turnover low prior to the start of the study; and while communication between managers, supervisors, and drivers was also reportedly good, no individual or group feedback procedures had been used before being implemented in the study.

The department measure in the first two studies was MPG, computed on a daily basis for intermill drivers and on a trip basis for long-haul drivers. The data was derived from fuel tickets and odometer readings. In addition, a mechanical disc was connected to each vehicle as another measure of miles driven. In the third study, fuel tickets obtained at company or commercial stations were the basis for the dependent measure, percent fuel obtained at company terminals.

Each study had a brief baseline followed by the introduction of the intervention package, including specific instructions on how to improve the target behavior and publicly graphed, highly visible, individual and group feedback. Drivers also received occasional praise from supervisors, managers, and other company officials for improvement, plus occasional letters of commendation, and specified goals (i.e., six miles per gallon in Study 1), which if reached, would give a driver a chance to receive a small prize (e.g., key and pen sets) or a free dinner. The studies were conducted over a two-year period.

The results of the studies indicated an increase in miles per gallon for the intermill drivers of about 4.6 percent (5.7 MPG at baseline to about 6.0 MPG during intervention); an increase of about 5.5 percent for long-haul drivers (4.8 MPG to about 5.1 MPG); and an increase of from 30 to 48 percent for fuel obtained at company stations. While the results for MPG seem small, because over six million miles per year were traveled by the drivers, even small changes led to highly significant savings. Enough money was saved in the second year of both MPG studies to run the company fleet for one month at no cost. Additional saving were accrued by drivers purchasing fuel at company stations. The studies are also note-worthy because of the simplicity of the procedures and the long-term results, with apparent maintenance up to four years (Runnion et al., 1978).

WASTE REDUCTION AND RESOURCE RECOVERY

Waste reduction refers to decreasing the generation of waste by reducing the consumption of environmental resources, whereas resource recovery refers to the extraction of resources from discarded materials used for manufacturing (Geller, 1980b; 1981b). In addition, resource recovery pro-grams can also be distinguished by their focus on using wastes to produce the original commodity (recycling) or changing wastes into other materials (reclamation or conversion). Therefore, recycling includes the use of waste paper to produce paper, re-refined oil to produce lubricants, crushed glass to make glass, and scrap iron to produce steel. Reclamation or conversion includes burning garbage to generate energy and using crushed glass for road building.

Ideally waste reduction and resource recovery can be combined. For example, packaging material for a product may be reduced, but packaging can also be produced from recycled paper. The successful use of this combined strategy is illustrated by a report from the president of the Pillsbury Company, that from 1965–75 the company reduced the amount of metal used in packaging by 36 percent, and each year the company uses about 50 million pounds of recycled paper (Peterson, 1975).

High and low technology strategies for resource recovery can also be distinguished. In a high technology approach, which is quite expensive, nonseparated garbage is collected and transported to a plant, where paper, glass, aluminum, and metal are mechanically separated, and the remaining refuse burned with other energy sources to produce steam for electricity generation or oil by a process called pyrolysis. The disadvantages of the high technology approach include: high initial and maintenance costs; high energy costs to operate a facility; air pollution as a by-product of the process; the use of a waste quota for municipalities and a concomitant fee for missing the quota, creating a disincentive to reduce waste; the lack of a dependable technology for aluminum and glass separation; finding a stable market for the resources produced by the plants; fire hazards as-sociated with the operation; and the need to separate paper and organic material (comprising 55 to 75 percent of the municipal solid waste), which are more valuable when recycled than burned for BTUs.

The low technology approach requires consumer or employee separation of the garbage into reusable materials at the place where the waste was produced. The low technology approach is less convenient for the consumer or employee, but is more economical. The low technology approach primarily entails the implementation of psychological strategies to prompt and motivate consumers to discard or reuse waste products properly.

It is beyond the scope of this chapter to detail programs for each type of waste or recyclable product. Instead strategies are outlined that are generally applicable to this problem and that are based on field research. For some firms or organizations, attention might be directed at a manufacturing process or product (e.g., excess packaging), while for others the emphasis might be on employee use and discard of resources (e.g., paper).

Based on the research literature (Geller, 1980b, 1981b; Geller et al., 1982), an effective waste reduction or resource recovery program should: assess what products or resources are the most important to save or recover; design a convenient area, container, or other apparatus where resources can be separated by employees (e.g., the Environmental Protection Agency uses a small desk top container for employees to deposit high quality paper); establish goals for waste reduction and recycling; use written and visual prompts, public and individual feedback, and incentives to promote sustained employee efforts. Note, however, that the use of goals, feedback, and incentives requires a sensitive monitoring system to be developed for target products or resources (Stoerzinger, Johnston, Pisor, and Craig, 1978). These points are illustrated in the following study description.

Eldridge, LeMasters, and Szypot (1978) reported the results of a project at Eastman Kodak in Rochester, New York, to reduce waste in a 23-employee department. The job of these employees (operators) involved cutting and inspecting photographic sheets. After cutting and inspecting the sheets, workers packed the passed sheets (based on stipulated criteria) for shipping, while discarding the rejected ones. A sample from each packed unit was sent to a quality control inspector. Operators affected waste by making very conservative judgments, i.e., discarding borderline products. There were no consequences for discarding borderline products, but considerable negative consequences for packing a defective product, including repacking and reinspecting the product and public awareness by all the operators of the deficient employee. An examination prior to the study indicated that about 20 percent of the rejected products actually met acceptable criteria and should have been packed.

The program was started by first developing a new measure and a form to keep track of the measure. The measure, piece yield, was the number of units packed each day divided by the maximum possible units. Note that this unit places emphasis on positive products. Baseline data indicated that piece yield was about 58 percent and a piece-yield goal (obviously also dependent on the quality of incoming material) was set at 75 percent. The intervention consisted of explaining the measure and goals to supervisors and employees, measuring each employee's and the department's piece yield per day, charting individual data daily, posting the department's data, comparing the data among individual employees, and giving individual feedback and praise according to piece yield data.

The results of the program showed that within four weeks the goal of 75 percent piece yield was reached. During the first year of the waste reduction program, it was estimated the $105,000 was saved with virtually no cost in company time or material. A standard measure of productivity for the department (units per labor hour) increased by about 25 percent. More qualitative evaluations also indicated favorable employee responses to the feedback program.

RESEARCH SUMMARY

Figure 17-1 summarizes the behavioral research presented in this chapter. The table includes indications of effective and ineffective antecedent and consequence strategies and special points or considerations for a particular resource management problem. Some areas such as energy consumption have been rather heavily researched, while other areas such as driving behavior are just beginning to receive attention. Work on litter control and water conservation using similar principles has been detailed elsewhere (Geller et al., 1982). We now turn to an overview of steps that need to be taken in order to implement a resource management program.

ACTION PLAN

Organizational Response

In this section we discuss important facets in the development and implementation of a behavioral resource program. First we describe an overall organizational response for promoting conservation. An analysis by Stobaugh and Yergin (1979) of effective conservation programs suggested that a response and commitment is necessary at three levels in an organization: (1) senior management; (2) a conservation unit composed of engineers and managers with the authority of senior management behind them so that the unit can implement changes; and (3) at the employee level so that conservation becomes part of employees' daily work behavior. There are some excellent examples of corporate responsiveness to conservation. For example, DOW (as reported in Stobaugh and Yergin, 1979) in the late 1950s and early 1960s correctly interpreted market signals and trends, and managed over a 10-year period to reduce its energy consumption per pound of product by 40 percent! Some of the behavioral aspects of the programs instituted by DOW included: specific goals for amount of energy expended per pound of product; an accurate monitoring system; a daily reporting procedure, and the use of results of energy savings for job performance reviews and merit raises.

Resource Management Problem	Antecedent Strategies		Consequence Strategies		Special Considerations
	Ineffective	Effective	Ineffective	Effective	
Energy consumption for heating, cooling, and other functions	Information only in various formats General prompts Aversive prompts	Modeling and demonstration Specific and strategically placed prompts Goal setting	Infrequent feedback† Low rebates	Frequent feedback Self-monitoring High rebates On-the-spot payment	New data on comfort; dress codes; set-backs; potential of feedback in an organization; relationship between water and energy
Transportation Modality change (car and van pools, mass transit)	Information only in various formats Matching riders only	Acquaintance with other riders Detailed planning of van pools More understandable route maps*	Priority lanes, preferential parking, and payments for car pooling when each procedure is used alone (minimally effective)	The combination of priority lanes, preferential parking, and payments for car pooling Free bus ridership Reduced fares Free ridership coupons contingent on ridership	Benefits to organizations include less capital costs; wider geographical area to choose employees; less stressed employees; reciprocal reinforcement; flexitime
Modification of vehicular miles and miles per gallon	Information only in various formats	Use of a leader Goal setting	Some types* of written feedback	Frequent or continuous feedback Self-monitoring Public posting Praise from supervisors Rebates Lotteries	Studies need replication under current prices
Waste reduction and resource recovery	Information only in various formats Inconvenient, infrequent areas for collection	Convenient and numerous areas for collection Goal setting	Payments not contingent on specification of unit	Frequent feedback Public feedback Praise from supervisors	Low technology approach as inexpensive, high technology as expensive

†Data are equivocal
*Data are minimal

FIGURE 17-1. Effective and ineffective antecedent and consequence resource management strategies plus special points for each problem.

DOW's program also stressed doing the easiest, simplest, and cheapest strategies first (i.e., good housekeeping), followed by retrofitting strategies, and finally the construction of more efficient plants. The DOW program makes a very dramatic point. With relatively little capital investment, DOW was able to increase the productivity of its energy inputs by 40 percent, and make a substantial contribution to corporate profits. In summarizing the DOW program, Stobaugh and Yergin (1979) noted that:

> Several lessons emerge from the DOW experience. There is a strong need for accurate measurement of energy consumption in order to establish targets, evaluate results, and assess managerial responsibility. Commitment must come from the top to make clear that conservation is a bottom-line concern and not a public relations ploy (Stobaugh and Yergin, 1979; p. 165).

Terminology.   One point that overrides the action plan's initial development and implementation concerns the use of terms to describe the program. We suggest that the term "demonstration project" be used instead of "experiment." The latter term implies such factors as nonpermanence, uncertainty, ultrascientific approach, and so on, which may undermine the program and its administration. Nevertheless, the program should be implemented within the true spirit of experimentation, e.g., rigorous evaluation and refinement.

Based on our experience, certain words in resource management have negative connotations for many people. The word "conservation" has become unfortunately associated with sacrifice and poor economic conditions (Winett and Geller, 1981). Certainly a major point in this chapter is that there is nothing sacrificial about the modification of the target practices or procedures recommended in this chapter. Organization-wide conservation should improve the economic condition of employees, managers and executives, and collectively the nation. To avoid the potential problems of faulty preconceptions of a program, we suggest that the term "efficiency" be used instead of conservation. This term simply has more positive connotations. An example of the benefit of close attention to terminology is the modeling videotape used in residential energy conservation programs. In the 21-minute summer videotape program, which was highly rated by project participants and resulted in significant energy savings in the home, the term efficiency was used 19 times, while the term conservation was never used.

Thus, probably the first step in the design and promotion of a resource management program involves attention to the terms used to describe it. The proper use of language can enhance a program's acceptance, and possibly effectiveness, while some terminology may undermine a program.

Behavioral Strategies

The behavioral strategies described in this chapter are completely compatible with the successful approaches followed at DOW. The steps in an action plan include:

1. *Obtain Commitment.* Commitment is necessary at the various levels of the organization. Recent managerial (Ouchi, 1981) and behavioral literature (Becker, 1978) suggest that the participation of managers and employees from all levels in the formulation of organization policy can facilitate results, in this case resource conservation. Representatives from the different organizational levels and in-house experts can participate on a "resource-management unit."

2. *Delineate Target Practices.* We recommend that an organization or firm pick one or more important kinds of costly and visible target behavior. That is, although the eventual goal is the development of a comprehensive resource management program, it will probably be easier to start with one important target behavior. This strategy also allows the program developers and the organization a chance to experiment with the various facets of a program. It may also be advisable to limit a first endeavor to part of a facility. Again this strategy allows experimentation and fine tuning of an intervention strategy without the overcommitment of organizational resources. However, it should be clear to all parties from the outset that the eventual goal is a comprehensive, organization-wide program.

3. *Monitor Process and Outcome.* The outcome of the target behavior, e.g., KWH consumption, and if possible the target behavior itself (e.g., the processes of thermostat control, equipment use), should be frequently and reliably monitored, daily if possible. It is necessary prior to the start of behavioral programs to be sure that the monitoring system is accurate and sensitive to change. In the case of water management, water meters are subject to considerable error and must be verified before implementing a program (Erickson and Geller, 1981). The KWH consumption of an entire facility would be a poor measure to use to monitor and assess the impact of an electricity conservation program in one department or section of that facility. An example of a good monitoring system could include the random checking of thermostat settings and equipment use. In a number of instances, however, a monitoring system may not need to be specifically developed for a new program, if indeed the present recording system provides frequent, accurate, and sensitive feedback.

If such an information system has not been in place, or even if a recording system meeting the criteria noted above has been operational, but not closely monitored, a baseline period should precede the implementation of a program. The baseline period, as a comparison data set, allows for accurate program evaluation and is the basis for program feedback. Also, for many problems in resource management, seasonal factors influence consumption. Therefore, a monitoring system may also need to include a seasonal adjustment factor. Such procedures have been used in prior behavioral research and are described in detail elsewhere (Geller, 1982; Geller et al., 1982; Winett, Neale, and Grier, 1979).

4. *Implement Intervention Strategies.* Multiple antecedent and consequence strategies should be initially used. The first priority in an or-

ganizational setting should be to institute a reasonably cost-effective set of procedures that maximize outcome (Azrin, 1977). We therefore recommend that a behavioral resource management program include specific information and demonstrations of appropriate target behavior; the delineation of specific goals; specific, frequent, and public prompting of target behavior; frequent (daily, if possible) feedback on the target behaviors or results; and where feasible, the implementation of social and tangible reinforcers contingent on desirable program feedback. Reinforcers can be as simple as praise to employees by management or be more complex, such as rebate and lottery systems. However, consistent with a plan to involve different levels of the organization is the notion that multiple levels should be subjected to the program's goals and contingencies, i.e., reciprocal reinforcement. For example, including the attainment of a program's goals in periodic reviews for managerial promotion or raises will assure active managerial involvement in the program. Likewise, daily program feedback received by executives can form the basis for interpersonal communication between executives and between executives and manager.

5. *Evaluate.* An adequate information feedback system provides the means to continuously evaluate the program and fine tune program components. Indeed the program should be viewed as an experiment, although perhaps called by a different term, e.g., "demonstration project." The goal of the program and monitoring system is to develop the most cost-effective program by refining the program over time. For example, with a sensitive monitoring system, the effects of changing target practices, or decreasing the frequency of feedback, or changing from a system that reinforces every employee to a lottery system can be assessed. The appropriate designs and procedures for evaluating different program components are described elsewhere in this text.

The goal of this fine tuning is not only to develop the most cost-effective strategies for the particular target behavior and procedures but also to develop approaches usable for other target behavior and other sites. Plans will probably have to be somewhat modified and tailored to fit a particular resource problem and site. Knowledge of behavioral principles is not an adequate substitute for knowledge and assessment of the particular resource management problems. However, starting at a relatively small level should provide the experience and skill to adapt the basic program to different conditions and different problems.

Figure 17-2 provides a schema for implementing an organizational action plan. The two-way arrows in the figure indicate input, feedback, and potential modification of a step in the problem solution process. Thus the resource management unit composed of in-house experts and managerial and employee representatives can have a plan shaped and modified by input and feedback from different levels in the organization. The plans of the resource management unit are directed to the eight specific steps noted in the figure, but the two-way arrows indicate that plans should be

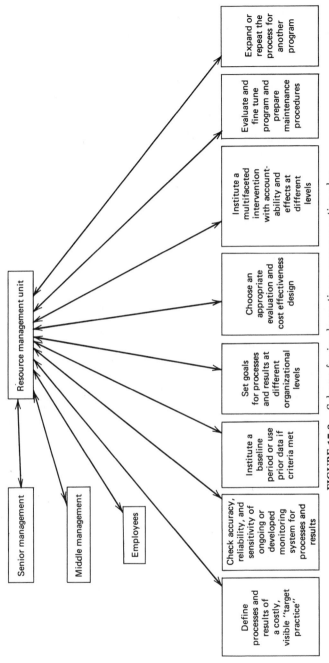

FIGURE 17-2. Schema for implementing a resource action plan.

499

developed and modified on the basis of data feedback accruable from each step of the process. For example, assessment at Step 1 may indicate inappropriate selection of target practices; baseline data (Step 3) can help formulate or modify resource management goals.

SUMMARY

In this chapter, we have reviewed behavioral strategies that have been used to decrease energy for space heating or cooling and water heating, to increase equipment efficiency, to modify transportation methods and driving behavior, to reduce waste and increase recycling practices. It should be clear from the description of the behavioral procedures and results that an organization can considerably reduce costs for resources with minimal capital investment and minimal, if any, employee discomfort or inconvenience. Typically, studies have shown resource savings of 10 to 15 percent, but there are studies in the literature showing savings of a much greater magnitude. This appears to be particularly the case when procedures have a number of components and there is careful attention to both process and results. Where costs and benefits have been analyzed, it appears that costs of behavioral programs are less, and often considerably less, than the costs of wasting the resource. This should be even more true in the future, when resources become more expensive.

This is not to suggest that implementation of a behavioral resource management program is simple, with guaranteed savings. We have stressed that an effective behavioral resource management program involves knowledge and assessment of target practices; an overall organizational commitment including employee participation; expertise in behavioral management; continuous, accurate monitoring and evaluation of target practices and results; fine tuning of procedures; and where possible, implementation of reciprocal reinforcement strategies. We have also emphasized starting a program with a costly and visible resource management problem that does not involve large capital investment. Following demonstrated cost effectiveness, the program can be expanded to handle other resource-management problems. However, a comprehensive resource management program should still adhere to the principle of modifying the easiest and less expensive practices first.

Organizations and firms that follow these principles should become more competitive and productive by reducing costs through modifying operations to reflect the realities of the 1980s. Attention to these plans by organizations across the country can appreciably decrease our dependence on foreign countries for resources, and hence improve our national and international economic condition.

REFERENCES

Azrin, N. H. A strategy for applied research: Learning based but outcome oriented. *American Psychologist*, 1977, *32*, 140–149.

Barkow, B. *The psychology of car pooling*. Ontario, Ministry of Transportation and Communications, 1974.

Becker, L. J. The joint effect of feedback and goal setting on performance: A field study of residential energy conservation. *Journal of Applied Psychology*, 1978, *63*, 228–233.

Becker, L. J., and Seligman, C. Reducing air-conditioning waste by signalling it is cool outside. *Personality and Social Psychology Bulletin*, 1978, *4*, 412–415.

Beckey, T., and Nelson, L. W. Field test of energy savings with thermostat setback. *ASHRAE Journal*, *87*, 1981, 67–70.

Best, F. Preferences on worklife scheduling and work-leisure tradeoffs. *Monthly Labor Review*, June 1978, 31–37.

Cone, J. D., and Hayes, S. C. *Environmental problems: Behavioral solutions*. Monterey, CA: Brooks/Cole Publishing Company, 1980.

Deslauriers, B. C., and Everett, P. B. Effects of intermittent and continuous token reinforcement on bus ridership. *Journal of Applied Psychology*, 1977, *62*, 369–375.

Dueker, K. J., and Levin, I. P. *Car pooling: Attitudes and participation (Technical Report No. 81)*. Iowa City: University of Iowa, Center for Urban Transportation Studies, 1976.

Eldridge, L., LeMasters, S., and Szypot, B. A performance feedback intervention to reduce waste: Performance data and participant responses. *Journal of Organizational Behavior Management*, 1978, *1*, 258–267.

Erickson, J., and Geller, E. S. Applications of educational versus engineering strategies to promote residential water conservation. Final Report for Grant #NSF SPI-8003981 from the National Science Foundation, March 1981.

Everett, P. B. A behavioral approach to transportation systems management. In D. Glenwick and L. Jason (Eds.), *Behavioral community psychology: Progress and prospects*. New York: Praeger Publishers, 1980, pp. 284–319.

Everett, P. B., Gurtler, M. D., and Hildebrand, M. G. Free Transit: How much—how long? *Transportation Research*, 1981 (in press).

Everett, P. B., Hayward, S. C., and Meyers, A. W. Effects of a token reinforcement procedure on bus ridership. *Journal of Applied Behavior Analysis*, 1974, *7*, 1–9.

Foxx, R. M., and Hake, D. F. Gasoline conservation: A procedure for measuring and reducing the driving of college students. *Journal of Applied Behavioral Analysis*, 1977, *10*, 61–74.

Geller, E. S. Increasing desired waste disposals with instructions. *Man-Environment Systems*, 1975, *5*, 125–128.

Geller, E. S. Applications of behavioral analysis for litter control. In D. Glenwick and L. Jason (Eds.), *Behavioral community psychology: Progress and prospects*. New York: Praeger Publishers, 1980(a), pp. 254–283.

Geller, E. S. The energy crisis and behavioral science: A conceptual framework for large scale intervention. In A. W. Childs and G. B. Melton (Eds.), *Rural Psychology*. New York: Plenum Press, 1982.

Geller, E. S. Evaluating energy conservation programs: Is verbal report enough. *Journal of Consumer Research*, (in press), 1981 (a).

Geller, E. S. Saving environmental resources through waste reduction and recycling: How the behavioral community psychologist can help. In G. L. Martin and J. G. Osborne (Eds.), *Helping in the community: Behavioral applications*. New York: Plenum Press, 1980(b), pp. 55–102.

Geller, E. S. Waste reduction and resource recovery: Strategies for energy conservation. In A. Baum and J. E. Singer (Eds.), *Advances in environmental psychology, Vol. 3: Energy Conservation: Psychological perspectives*. Hillsdale, NJ: Erlbaum Associates, 1981(b), pp. 115–154.

Geller, E. S., Winett, R. A., and Everett, P. B. *Preserving the environment: New strategies for behavior change*. Elmford, NY: Pergamon Press, 1982.

Hake, D. F., and Foxx, R. M. Promoting gasoline conservation: The effects of reinforcement schedules, a leader and self-recording. *Behavior Modification*, 1978, *2*, 339–369.

Hayes, S. C., and Cone, J. D. Reducing residential electrical use: Payments, information, and feedback. *Journal of Applied Behavior Analysis*, 1977, *10*, 425–435.

Hirst, E. Transportation energy conservation policies. *Science*, 1976, *192*, 15–20.

Horowitz, A. D., and Sheth, J. N. *Ridesharing to work: A psychosocial analysis.* Warren, MI: General Motors Corporation, 1977.

Johnson, B. Marital and family characteristics of workers: March, 1979. *Monthly Labor Review*, April 1980, 48–52.

Lauridsen, P. K. Decreasing gasoline consumption in fleet-owned automobiles through feedback and feedback-plus-lottery. Unpublished thesis manuscript, Duke University, Department of Psychology, 1977.

Letzkus, T., and Scharfe, V. Employer incentive program. *Proceedings of the 1975 National Conference of Areawide Carpooling.* Houston, TX, December 1975, Washington, DC: Federal Highway Administration, Urban Planning Division, 1975.

MacCalden, M., and Davis, C. *Report on priority lane experiment on the San Francisco-Oakland Bay Bridge.* California Department of Public Works, 1972.

McClelland, L., and Belsten, L. Prompting energy conservation in university dormitories by physical, policy, and resident behavior changes. *Journal of Environmental Systems*, 1980, *9*, 29–38.

McClelland, L., and Cook, S. W. Energy conservation effects of continuous in-home feedback in all-electric homes. *Journal of Environmental Systems*, 1980, *9*, 169–173.

Nollen, S. *New patterns of work.* Scarsdale, NY: Work in America Institute, Inc., 1979.

Osborne, J. G., and Powers, R. B. Controlling the litter problem. In G. L. Martin and J. G. Osborne (Eds.), *Helping in the community: Behavioral applications.* New York: Plenum Press, 1980, pp. 102–168.

Ouchi, W. *Theory Z.* New York: Addison-Wesley, 1981.

Owens, R. D., and Sever, H. L. *The 3M commute-a-van program* (Progress Report II). St. Paul: 3M Company, 1977.

Peterson, J. R. Environmental protection and productivity. *Proceedings, 1975 Conference on Waste Reduction.* U. S. Environmental Protection Agency, Washington, DC, 1975, 41–44.

Powers, R. B., Osborne, J. G., and Anderson, E. G. Positive reinforcement of litter removal in the natural environment. *Journal of Applied Behavior Analysis*, 1973, *6*, 579–586.

Pratsch, L. *Carpool and buspool matching guide* (4th ed.). Washington, DC: U.S. Department of Transportation, Federal Highway Administration, January 1975.

Reichel, D. A., and Geller, E. S. Group vs. individual contingencies to conserve transportation energy. Paper presented at the 26th Annual Meeting of the Southeastern Psychological Association, Washington, DC, March 1980.

Reichel, D. A., and Geller, E. S. Attempts to modify transportation behavior of energy conservation: A critical review. In A. Baum and J. E. Singer (Eds.), *Advances in environmental psychology, Vol. 3: Energy conservation: Psychological perspectives.* Hillsdale, NJ: Erlbaum Associates, 1981, pp. 53–91.

Remak, R., and Rosenbloom, R. *Solutions to peak-period travel congestion.* Report prepared for the National Cooperative Research Program, Transportation Research Board, National Research Council, Washington, DC, 1976.

Rogers, E. M., and Shoemaker, F. F. *Communication of innovations.* New York: Free Press, 1971.

Rohles, F. H. Thermal comfort and strategies for energy conservation. *Journal of Social Issues*, 1981, *37*, 132–149.

Runnion, A., Watson, J. D., and McWhorter, J. Energy savings in interstate transportation through feedback and reinforcement. *Journal of Organizational Behavior Management*, 1978, *1*, 180–191.

Seligman, C., and Darley, J. M. Feedback as a means of decreasing residential energy consumption. *Journal of Applied Psychology*, 1977, *62*, 363–368.

Shippee, G., and Gregory, W. L. Public commitment and energy conservation. *American Journal of Community Psychology*, in press.

Slavin, R. E., Wodarski, J. S., and Blackburn, B. L. A group contingency for electricity conservation in master-metered apartments. *Journal of Applied Behavior Analysis*, 1981, in press.

Socolow, R. H. *Saving energy in the home*. Cambridge, MA: Ballinger Publishing Company, 1978.

Stobaugh, R., and Yergin, D. *Energy Future: Report of the energy project of The Harvard Business School*. New York: Random House, 1979.

Stoerzinger, A., Johnston, J. M., Pisor, K., and Craig, M. Implementation and evaluation of a feedback system for employees in a salvage operation. *Journal of Organizational Behavior Management*, 1978, *1*, 268–281.

Stokols, D., Novaco, R. W., Stokols, J., and Campbell, J. Traffic congestion, type A behavior and stress. *Journal of Applied Psychology*, 1978, *63*, 467–480.

U. S. Department of Housing and Urban Development, *Energy efficient home study*. Washington, DC, USHUD, 1980.

Walker, J. M. Energy demand behavior in a master-meter apartment complex: An experimental analysis. *Journal of Applied Psychology*, 1979, *64*, 190–196.

Wicker, A. W. Attitudes vs. actions: The relationship of verbal and overt behavioral responses to attitude objects. *Journal of Social Issues*, 1969, *25*, 41–78.

Winett, R. A. Prompting turning out lights in unoccupied rooms. *Journal of Environmental Systems*, 1978, *6*, 237–241.

Winett, R. A., and Geller, E. S. Comment on psychological research and energy policy. *American Psychologist*, 1981, *36*, 425–426.

Winett, R. A., Hatcher, J. W., Fort, T. R., Leckliter, I. N., Love, S. Q., Riley, A. W., and Fishback, J. F. The effects of videotape modeling and feedback on residential electricity conservation, interior temperature and humidity, clothing worn and perceived comfort. Unpublished manuscript, Psychology Department, Virginia Polytechnic Institute and State University, Blacksburg, VA 24061.

Winett, R. A., Kagel, J. H., Battalio, R. C., and Winkler, R. C. Effects of monetary rebates, feedback and information on residential electricity conservation. *Journal of Applied Psychology*, 1978, *63*, 73–78.

Winett, R. A., Kaiser, S., and Haberkorn, E. The effects of monetary rebates and daily feedback on electricity conservation. *Journal of Environmental Systems*, 1977, *5*, 327–338.

Winett, R. A., and Neale, M. S. Psychological framework for energy conservation in buildings: Strategies, outcomes, directions. *Energy and Buildings*, 1979, *2*, 101–116.

Winett, R. A., Neale, M. S., and Grier, H. C. The effects of self-monitoring and feedback on residential electricity consumption. *Journal of Applied Behavior Analysis*, 1979, *12*, 173–184 (a).

Winett, R. A., Neale, M. S., and Williams, K. R. The effects of flexible work schedules on urban families with young children: Quasi-experimental, ecological studies. *American Journal of Community Psychology*, 1982, in press.

Winett, R. A., Neale, M. S., Williams, K. R., Yokley, J., and Kauder, H. The effects of individual and group feedback on residential electricity consumption: Three replications. *Journal of Environmental Systems*, 1979, *8*, 217–233 (b).

Winett, R. A., and Nietzel, M. Behavioral ecology: Contingency management of residential use. *American Journal of Community Psychology*, 1975, *3*, 123–133.

18

Behavioral Approaches to Occupational Health and Safety[1]

BETH SULZER-AZAROFF

University of Massachusetts, Amherst

According to *Accident facts*, 1979, a publication of the National Safety Council, accidents are a leading cause of death and injury—fourth across the full age range, after heart disease, cancer, and stroke. For ages one through 44 years, accidents are the *leading* cause of death. Not only did accidents account for a death rate of 47.7 per 100,000 population in the year 1978 but they cost a total of $68.7 billion during that year, taking into account loss of wages, medical expenses, insurance administration costs, property damage, and related expenses.

Among various classes of accidents in 1978, those involving motor vehicles accounted for the highest death rate and cost ($34.3 billion). Accidents at work came next, at a cost of $23 billion, while home and public accidents cost $7.1 and $5.6 billion, respectively. One death takes place every 40 minutes in the work setting.

The picture was even grimmer in the past. Since 1912 there has been a gradual decline in deaths due to accidents in the United States, and since 1968 the overall reduction was 44 percent. In the work place, accidental deaths have declined by 22 percent. Undoubtedly advances in public policy, technology, and social awareness have contributed to this

[1]I would like to express my appreciation to the Department of Psychology at the University of Connecticut for providing the space for preparation of this manuscript during my sabbatical, and to the following individuals who have assisted in the preparation and editing of the manuscript: Leonid Azaroff, Lenore Azaroff, Denise Fellner, Anne Peterson, and Jayne Sullivan.

improvement. A close investigation of the most recent evidence is disquieting, however, because a reversal of this downward trend appears to be taking place. While some occupational accidents may be prevented by new engineering developments and advances in design and materials, we need to concentrate more on the behavioral aspects if this problem is to be addressed adequately. We need to identify effective behavioral strategies for preventing and reducing accidents in general and particularly in the work place.

How are effective strategies for preventing and reducing rates of occupational accidents to be developed? One approach is to examine theories of accident causation, e.g., Hale and Hale (1970), Strasser, Aaron, Bohn, and Eales (1964). But few direct links between accidents and their causes have been established. Much of the research on the prevention of occupational accidents has been correlational. For example, decreases in occupational deaths and injuries since 1970 are correlated with the enactment of the Occupational Safety and Health Act. While it is very likely that the legislation directly influenced the results, demonstrating a correlation does not permit identification of specific causal factors. We cannot tell which event caused what to happen, or if changes were related to some other influence. According to the National Safety Council, there is a relation between the size of a plant and the rate of accidents. Large plants have fewer accidents per worker than smaller ones. Is this because accident-prone people tend to work in small plants? Because something about small plants causes the accidents? Or is there some other reason? A good hypothesis is that large plants have well established safety programs and can afford to hire experts. One way to be sure would be to institute and subsequently withdraw a program to see if accident rates change accordingly. In other words, conduct an experiment.

By conducting experiments, organizational behavior management has recently begun to discover some of the conditions that directly influence safe and unsafe practices in the work place. Events or conditions thought to influence a particular act are systematically managed to see if the behavior changes directly as a result; if as expected, *when and only when* selected conditions are managed performances change reliably; when those conditions are withheld or delayed, no such change is noted.

In its attempt to identify those controlling conditions, organizational behavior management looks at performance, examining its components closely. Then it considers the conditions that appear to follow, precede, or accompany the performance (see Figure 18-1). Some workers in a noisy plant use earplugs regularly, while others do not. "What are the components of the safe practice and how are they sequenced?" asks the analyst. One worker fails to insert the plugs correctly, or another uses them only when he has a headache. Various events follow the safe and unsafe practices. Some may specifically be arranged to promote the use of plugs, while others occur without any formal planning. According to a prearranged schedule, the supervisor may visit those workers who are wearing their earplugs and pat them on the back, thereby signaling his or her approval. The same positive consequence could also occur without any planning at all. But those consequences are only two among many. There can be unplanned negative consequences as well. The safe practice could be ridiculed by fellow workers, or it might be a nuisance to go through

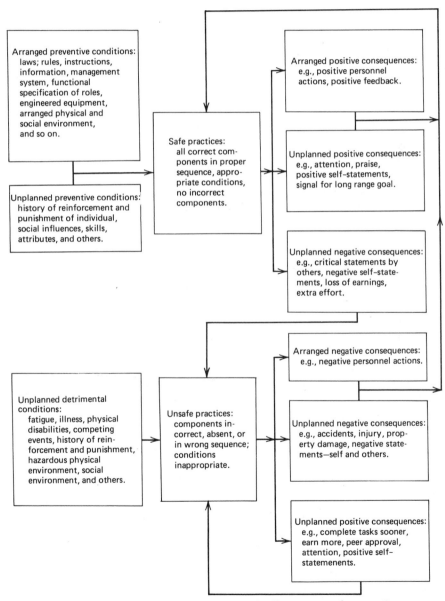

FIGURE 18-1.   Arranged and unplanned influences on safety practices.

the process of inserting and removing the plugs. From a behavioral perspective, the positive consequences, whether planned or not, should promote the practice, while the negative consequences should reduce it. Similarly, an unsafe practice can be followed by various arranged or unplanned events, which influence it for better or for worse.

No matter how many incentives are promised or aversive consequences threatened, rules proclaimed, or prompts supplied, if workers have never learned how to perform a safe practice in the first place, they must first learn it. A worker may never have learned exactly how to adjust goggles, how to position a metal to be pressed or ground, where and how far back to stand, and so on. In fact he or she may be under the mistaken impression that his or her unsafe practices are safe. Correcting such a situation requires instruction sufficient to produce the sequence as it should be practiced correctly.

Any events that precede or accompany safe and unsafe practices may be influential. Some are intentionally arranged to promote safe performance: a mounted sign reminding workers to protect their hearing; training in the use of earplugs; threats, warnings, and appeals from supervisors or loved ones. But other *unplanned* prior events play a role as well. The worker who was irregular about safety practices might quickly come around after observing a highly respected fellow worker adhering regularly to the practice. As we know, the story is incomplete without recognizing the whole realm of unplanned detrimental events that set the stage for unsafe acts: being tired or distracted, having been reinforced for engaging in the unsafe act in the past, and many others.

Once controlling events are discovered by means of experimental analysis, it should be possible to arrange conditions purposely to reduce or prevent accidents. For example, important missing prior conditions may be supplied, protective clothing provided, hazardous arrangements rearranged, the physical or psychological status of the worker altered, prompts or cues provided. Or the components of unsafe practices may be altered by teaching different aspects of the response, or the consequences may be modified. For instance, a positive consequence may be presented only when the practice is safely performed, or a negative consequence presented when it or one of its component elements is performed unsafely, so that the sequence is interrupted before the injury, death, or property damage occurs.

Thus it appears that a promising way to proceed is through experimental analysis of controlling conditions. The findings are subsequently used in purposely arranging those conditions that cause accidents to be reduced or prevented altogether. In the following pages, each of the main elements of occupational safety will be addressed. First, we shall focus on the practice itself, emphasizing how the organizational behavior management approach is applied to examining and specifying safe practices. Next we shall turn to methods for arranging consequences in order to promote safe practices. Then we'll see how unsafe practices are corrected and safe ones taught. Afterwards we shall examine how antecedent conditions may be arranged to prevent unsafe and promote safe practices. Finally, a case study will illustrate a set of action guidelines that may be used to promote occupational safety in general.

DEFINING SAFE PRACTICES

Behavioral practitioners recognize how important it is to define a complex skill in precise detail (Mager, 1961; 1972) and to identify all of the subcomponents of that skill (Gagne, 1970). The definition of a skill permits objectives to be unambiguously specified, making very clear exactly what act is to occur under what conditions. The analysis of the skill or task into its components reveals the sequence of steps to be followed. By comparing the requirements for completing each step with the repertoire— the learned skills—of each learner, necessary adjustments can be made. One learner with an advanced repertoire may skip initial steps, while another, stumbling over a particularly difficult step, may overcome the barrier when that step is further dissected into its component parts, each to be mastered separately. This method resembles "Systems Safety Analysis" (Sasser, 1970), but is different in the sense that the latter focuses on events that cause accidents rather than on safe practices.

The value of using behavioral definitions for personnel management began to be recognized about a decade ago, as writings such as Odiorne's Management by Objectives (1965) began to appear on the scene. Now we are beginning to see instances of applications of these techniques within the area of occupational health and safety. In their work on reducing workers' exposure to styrene, Hopkins, Conrad, and Duellman (1980) identified seven broad categories of safe work practices. Each work practice was then broken down into sets of specific work procedures of such a size and level of complexity that workers should experience little difficulty in mastering each. For example, one of the broad categories was "personal protective clothing and equipment"; one practice was labeled "covering body." The rationale for the practice was then presented in a brief paragraph. Then a series of 16 procedures was listed, for example:

> Wear splash-proof safety goggles which comply with CFR 1910, 133 in any
> location where eye contact with styrene could occur. Purpose: To prevent
> eye irritation or damage. . . . Wear face shields. Purpose: To avoid irritation
> and absorption. . . . (p. 159)

In some of our own work, we invested a substantial amount of time in identifying and defining safe and unsafe practices. Among the methods we used were: examining accident reports; interviewing safety experts, supervisors, and workers; referring to written regulations; and observing, recording, and measuring performances and physical arrangements of equipment and materials. We were confident we were on our way to identifying important practices when those we had consulted agreed with

our choices, and when we found that observers, armed with the definitions, closely agreed when they independently recorded the presence or
absence of the practice or arrangement.

The accomplishment of this crucial step permits a decision to be made.
The practices are observed and assessed for level of compliance. If compliance is high but not high enough, the test may be simply to provide
consequences to increase safe and decrease unsafe practices. Very low
rates of compliance may mean that either more powerful consequences
need to be arranged, perhaps along with a rearrangement of antecedent
conditions, or it may mean that the practices need to be taught anew. In
the sections to follow we shall discuss some of the methods that practitioners of organizational behavior management have or might use to accomplish those tasks.

ARRANGING CONSEQUENCES

Experimental evidence has repeatedly demonstrated how consequences
of behavior influence its subsequent occurrence. Certain events, *reinforcing events*, increase the likelihood that the behavior will be repeated.
Others, punishers or aversive stimuli, decrease the likelihood of reoc-
currence. But a number of critical variables influence the relationship.
These include the amount of time that passes between the behavior and
the related consequences, the frequency of the consequence, its intensity,
and competing consequences.

Consider how these features relate to safety practices. The practice may
be safe or unsafe. Many unsafe practices probably persist because they
are in some way naturally reinforced. The task may be completed faster,
perhaps resulting in higher earnings, or praise and admiration from peers
or supervisors; or completion may signal the end of a less preferred task,
which in turn permits a shift to a more preferred activity such as going
home, doing a different job, or time for a break. It is also reinforcing to
accomplish a given task with less effort. Operating a press with one instead
of two hands or mixing chemicals at the lab table rather than moving to
the vent hood and turning it on would be tempting because less effort
would be required. Reinforcing events of that type tend to occur often
and with minimal delay.

There are also natural punishers for unsafe practices: accidents, injury,
damage, disapproval from others and oneself—"It really isn't very smart
of me to be doing this. One day it might catch up with me." But the natural
negative consequences may be weak, delayed, and infrequent. The likelihood of an accident occurring following a particular unsafe act may be
very low. Many unsafe acts probably continue to be practiced because
they are overlooked by peers and supervisors or by the person doing them.

If the negative consequences are mild, they will do little to overcome
the influence of more powerful positive reinforcers. If completing a laboratory experiment early permits Sarah to arrive home in time to watch

the evening news, something she really enjoys, and the only danger in mixing her chemicals away from the vent hood is that she could possibly get a slight headache, she might skip the preventive step. Conversely, if she knew that mixing the chemicals would produce highly toxic fumes, she's be more apt to use the hood. Although natural consequences may be the best teachers, from the practical perspective, permitting the natural consequences of unsafe practices would usually be considered foolish, dangerous, or unethical. One can hardly design a safety program that permits injury or damage, even if the negative consequence were to reduce the probability that the behavior would reoccur. An equivalently difficult problem is the corollary: substitute safe for unsafe practices and let the natural consequences take over. What are the natural consequences of safe practices? The absence of injury or damage? Hardly effective reinforcing events, since the absence of a rare event is apt to exert little influence. The absence of the damage or injury would have to be supplemented by some less natural or *contrived* reinforcers: laudatory statements by others or oneself—"Good. You (I) used your (my) earplugs. You'll (I'll) be less likely to suffer a hearing impairment"—or even tangible rewards such as money or prizes.

So we see that an analysis of consequential conditions requires that a number of factors be considered: whether they are positive, aversive, or potentially very dangerous; whether they are immediate or delayed; whether they occur frequently or infrequently; and whether they are mild or intense. When natural conditions are such that an unsafe act regularly results in immediate, strong reinforcement, and that any potential punishing events are irregular, delayed, and generally not very intense, conditions are hazardous. In cases in which all or some of those conditions prevail, it is necessary to arrange consequences by design. Here are some of the methods that might be used: an ideal positive approach would be to make the safe practice more reinforcing by presenting powerful positive consequences regularly and with minimal delay. An effective negative approach would be regularly to present intense negative consequences immediately following unsafe acts. Or the two could be combined. Here we discuss and illustrate each of these methods, used separately or in combination.

Arranging Positively Reinforcing Consequences

Incentives have been used in business and occupational settings to encourage productivity, attendance, and other practices for longer than recorded history. The system of paying wages for work performed or for time on the job is familiar to everyone. In the area of occupational safety too, incentive systems have long been employed. In a textbook on occupational safety, Blake (1943), in a chapter entitled "Methods of Promoting Safe Practice," cites the "desire for gain" as one of several motivating characteristics for workers: "Offer rewards in pay, bonuses, cash prizes, objects of value for good safety performance or safety suggestions. The rewards should have a reasonable relationship to the effect involved and be large enough to be attractive" (p. 226). Principles of behavior are currently being incorporated with many motivational or incentive programs. In a talk to the National Safety Congress in 1979, Shirmer (1979) discussed how his organization was able to reduce injuries by 23 percent. He summarized the approach in a series of steps:

1. Determine your positive goal.
2. Select the performance (behavior) you want.
3. Divide the performance goal into steps or levels.
4. Select the reinforcements to be used: This is simply the reward the worker will receive for demonstrating proper performance. They can range from a simple expression of recognition to some form of material reward, such as notes or letters regarding the worker's accomplishment in a personnel folder. A point system, used to reward certain steps within the desired behavior, is another example.
5. Reinforce the desired performance. This means to start looking for the performance you are trying to accomplish, and recognize it immediately as it occurs.
6. Keep it up. Human motivation is somewhat like walking up a down escalator; the minute you stop you start going backward (pp. 6–7).

Mining has a particularly high rate of accidents, and many work days are lost as a result. David K. Fox (1976) presented a paper describing the incentive system that had been implemented at an open pit mining site in Utah. According to the level of risk of their particular job assignment, participants in the program were awarded a specific number of trading stamps as a consequence of the safety record of their unit each month. Bonus stamps were also awarded for safety suggestions that were adopted by the project, for acts that prevented injury or death to a fellow worker, acts that prevented accidents or property damage, and other special efforts. Over the four years in which the program had been in operation, there were some dramatic results. Injuries were substantially reduced, from a rate of more than one per year per employee to only 16 percent of the employees. Simultaneously, compensation cases, cost incurred, lost time, and damage to equipment dropped precipitously, saving the company considerably more money than the expenditures incurred by the incentive program.

A similar incentive system was used by Ritschl, Mirman, Hall, Sigler, and Hopkins (1976) to reduce accidents in a chemical plant. Again rewards were delivered as a consequence of no injuries serious enough to require lost days. The incentive system was called "Protective Poker." Workers who did not lose any days due to injuries during the past month were awarded five numbers, each of which corresponded to a playing card.

Additional numbers were awarded for additional months in which no lost days due to injuries had occurred. Using the rules of poker, the best hands won the opportunity to select a prize from a reinforcing menu. Ten workers and one supervisor were chosen as winners each month. Although the authors have subsequently found that the system requires careful monitoring and verification of reporting, they did report a decline in frequency and severity of accidents after the system was implemented.

In an effort to reduce accidents among bus drivers in a large Midwestern city, an incentive system based on team competition was established (Haynes, unpublished). Four teams of drivers were selected by means of a drawing. Accidents were classified according to whether or not they were avoidable. Points were then assigned for damage to equipment and passenger accidents. After each two-week period points were compared, and the team with the lowest number of points was designated the winner. Each member of the team then selected items of their choice from a reinforcing menu, which consisted of small cash prizes, gift certificates, passes, and other items of about $5 each in value. Team captains were also personally congratulated by the general manager of the transit authority, and there was a bonus of a double prize if during the two-week period the team had not been assigned any points at all.

A control group was used in the Haynes study, in order that seasonal variations could be considered in the analysis. Seasonal fluctuations in vehicular accidents do occur, especially as a function of snow and ice and other weather conditions. Once the intervention was implemented, the number of accidents among members of the incentive group declined substantially below that of the control group. Surprisingly, when the six-month intervention period ended, and incentives were no longer awarded, the group differences persisted. Drivers in the experimental group continued to practice safe driving skills, possibly motivated by the natural reinforcing consequences of low accident rates and attention for good safety records.

At an automobile assembly plant in Mexico, a different sort of incentive system was implemented, as one aspect of a more complex system, to be discussed below (Hermann, 1978). In this instance there was a reluctance to use too many costly tangible rewards, such as frequent prizes or cash. Instead safety performance was audited weekly, and at the end of seven weeks the group of workers whose safety performance had improved were publicly recognized as a group. Each was presented with a photograph of all the workers around a Christmas tree that had been decorated with engine parts. Four months later seven circus tickets were raffled among department workers whose performance met a set criteria for improvement. In both cases workers were told that the rewards were in recognition for their improved safety performance.

In each of the cases reported here, systematically delivering rewards substantially improved safe performance. Even rewards delivered with delays up to several months and with varying probabilities of payoff produced positive results. Valuable incentives, such as trading stamps and cash prizes, do have a powerful effect, but those with much subtler value such as group recognition also have been shown to exert control. (Later we shall see how reinforcers as mild and unobtrusive as feedback for positive performance may also have a substantial impact.) However, in each of the instances described here the safe practices (or unsafe practices or conditions) were very clearly identified and communicated. Also precise observational recording systems were used. The degree to which those conditions may have contributed to the outcome is difficult to determine, yet it is likely that their influence is not totally negligible.

Incentive systems are not universally effective. In fact Ritschl et al. (1976) found that "the Protective Poker Incentive Program had no significant effect on employees with *high* frequencies of injuries attributed in part or in total to unsafe acts (p. 2)." Was this a function of the delay or irregularity with which incentives were delivered, or of the weakness of the reinforcing conditions? Is it necessary to add negative consequences for unsafe practices to strengthen the procedure? Would punishment of unsafe practices alone or in conjunction with reinforcement of safe acts produce better results? These questions remain largely unanswered, although recently completed studies are beginning to shed some light on this issue. These studies include penalties for unsafe acts or present a combination of positive and negative consequences.

Arranging Aversive Consequences

As noted earlier, the natural consequences of an accident are aversive, with death, injury, or damage the ultimate result of the sequence. Theoretically that fact should be sufficient to limit unsafe conditions or acts, but in reality it is not. The aversive consequences are too infrequent, intermittent, delayed, and often of mild intensity. Aversive consequences should function most effectively when they occur regularly, and immediately following unsafe acts. Nor should the unsafe act yield any reinforcement. Rather behavior that is not compatible with the unsafe act should be reinforced (Azrin and Holz, 1966). The discrepancy between actual and optimal conditions is obvious. That probably explains why, despite their potential danger, people commit unsafe acts as often as they do. To overcome the discrepancy and improve results, various attempts have been made to *arrange* aversive consequences.

Society has long attempted to reduce accidents by applying aversive consequences to unsafe acts or directly as a consequence of accidents. Termination of employment, temporary suspension from work, loss of wages, required restitution for damaged equipment, fines, and prison sentences represent some of the various methods that have been applied. As with less than optimal reinforcement conditions, these arrangements do apparently prevent recklessness to some extent. But if aversive consequences are to be used, then they can be applied, as we have noted, far more effectively.

A few studies have attempted to analyze the use of aversive consequences arranged to more closely match the rules of effective application, although such research must be seriously restricted. First, optimal applications of aversive consequences would probably cause harm to the subject, since it would be necessary to present intensive aversive consequences following every instance of the unsafe behavior. That leads to the second major difficulty—the ethics of causing someone discomfort. Third is a practical problem, the difficulty and expense that would be involved in monitoring individuals continuously to catch and apply aversive consequences following each unsafe act. So if arranged aversive consequences are to be studied, there will usually have to be some compromises. The research on the use of aversive consequences, to be described here, does include such compromises.

In several studies, aversive consequences are delivered following a delay period, say at the end of a monthly or weekly period. When Ritschl et al. (1976) found that a group of employees at a chemical plant continued to have high rates of injuries, a set of aversive procedures was arranged. Workers with a record of an injury due to an unsafe act were to have their names posted each quarter for a period of one year. An additional injury due to an unsafe act would result in public posting of the record and a required biweekly meeting with the safety director to discuss the employee's safety record, performance, or progress. Warning letters, suspension, and eventual termination were consequences for successively more injuries. At the time of this writing, the results of this study have not been published, but it will be interesting to find out how effectively they are functioning.

Aversive consequences are often arranged to follow the unsafe acts, rather than waiting for the accident and then administering the aversive consequences. Fines, penalties, or reprimands may be presented following events such as: skipping segments of the safe practice, as in neglecting to don protective clothing, or utilizing venting hoods, guards, or double hand switches; permitting hazardous conditions to prevail, such as unstable piles of materials, obstructions, or improperly guarded operating equipment. Another compromise is simulating real accidents.

Among the aversive consequences that have been used in experimental research on safety have been threats of dismissal (Larson, Schnelle, Kirchner, Carr, Domash, and Risley, 1980), sounding a loud klaxon (Leslie and Adams, 1973), emitting a jet of water (Rubinsky and Smith, 1973), a cold pressor (immersing the hand in ice water) (Parsons, 1979), muscular exertion (Parsons, 1976), timeout from music (Ritschl, Mongrella, and Presbie, 1972), and others.

Forty percent of police vehicles from 59 police departments surveyed were involved in at least one accident during the year 1976, according to data reported by Larson et al. (1980). Because high accident rates and negligent abuse of police cars were identified as a serious problem by the Nashville police department, a behavioral study was undertaken. The intervention consisted of placing a tachograph in the vehicle. "A tachograph is a clock-driven recording device which provides a permanent record of such vehicle functions as speed, distance traveled, non-movement and use of emergency equipment" (p. 3). Officers were threatened with dismissal for noncompliance with rules, regulations, and policies, including safe driving practices. When the tachograph charts were inspected by the officers in the higher chains of command and feedback was delivered to drivers, there was a major, systematic reduction in speed, accidents, and injuries across different vehicular units. Vehicle repair costs were also substantially reduced, saving many thousands of dollars over a one and one-half year period.

Some types of occupational accidents are prevented by teaching operators of equipment where to stand or how to properly position their hands. Failure to follow safe practice in placing the material in a punch press may cause injuries to hands and fingers. Leslie and Adams (1973) designed a punch press simulator that electronically measured the occurrence of simulated accidents as well as the production of substandard parts. Although the device was designed to compare the effectiveness of several different training programs, regardless of program, there was a decrease in rates of simulated accidents. This might be explained by the fact that, when a simulated accident was measured, a loud klaxon was sounded. The sound may have functioned as an aversive stimulus, reducing the rates of unsafe practices.

One of the dangers in using a bench grinder is that the wheel can explode and injure anyone standing within the plane of rotation. In a series of three studies, Rubinsky and Smith (1973) used a water jet to simulate an "accident," either by a demonstration or by providing the trainee a direct experience. They found that trainees who directly experienced the jet of water exhibited the fewest accidents during retention sessions, when compared against those who did not have the modeled experience or had no exposure to it at all. It would be interesting to see if these training effects also extend outside of the experimental training setting, particularly in the actual work setting.

Arranging a Combination of Positive and Negative Consequences

With the risk of injury or death at stake, optimal preventive methods must be sought. This means that positively reinforcing consequences should be arranged to follow safe practices *and* simultaneously aversive consequences should be arranged to follow unsafe practices. Workers in a noisy factory are given earplugs. To follow use of the plugs with approbation and failure to use the plugs with disapproval from a respected co-worker would be much more powerful than either separately. (Figure 18-1 depicts how these two classes of consequences may combine to influence practices.)

McKelvey and his colleagues (1973) have arranged combinations of positive and negative consequences to promote safe practices. Subjects operated a punch press that permitted accidents to occur and be recorded. These accidents were rendered harmless through the addition of special protective parts. A vigilance component was also activated from time to time. The subject was to note a red light and press a button beneath it to demonstrate alertness to safety conditions independent of the operation of the machine. For example, a press operator needs to attend closely while working the machine, but must also be alert as to potentially hazardous conditions in the environment such as the ringing of a fire alarm. As anticipated, those subjects who worked under no incentive conditions worked slowly and had few accidents. Those who earned money for working quickly worked faster and had quite a few accidents. Those who earned money for working quickly but who lost the opportunity to earn for five minutes for failing to press the button when the red light was activated worked at a moderate rate and had a moderate number of accidents. Those who experienced the same consequence plus a loss of five minutes for each accident worked at a moderate rate; their accident rate was very low.

Combinations of positive and negative consequences are usually intrinsic to systems in which informational feedback is delivered. Feedback may be delivered as a consequence of accidents or injuries (Roberts, 1977; Kim and Hamner, 1976) or of safe or unsafe acts or their products (Komaki, Barwick, and Scott, 1979; Komaki, Heinzmann, and Lawson, 1980; Sulzer-Azaroff, 1978; Sulzer-Azaroff and de Santamaria, 1980). In the Larson et al. (1980) study mentioned earlier, tachograph records were presented to the drivers of police vehicles. Presumably if the records matched those of a properly operated vehicle, the feedback would constitute positive reinforcing consequences, while indicated deviations from accepted practice should be aversive, particularly since unjustified risk taking could result in suspension.

Zohar, Cohen, and Azar (1980) have reported a dramatically successful program of informational feedback to increase use of ear protectors in a noisy metal fabrication plant. Workers in the experimental group were given audiograms before and after their work shifts. Records indicated a visible loss of hearing acuity at the end of the shift among workers who did not use the ear protectors. While workers whose tenure on the job was short showed a recovery in acuity in the next preassessment, those who had extensive exposure to the noise showed no such recovery. The records clearly demonstrated that long-term exposure to noise had produced permanent damage. These audiograph records were posted in a public place, and their implications explained to workers viewing their own records. Data collected four months later showed that although the control group showed no improvement, 90 percent of the workers in the experimental group were using the protectors, even though there had been a major employee turnover. Apparently the example of widespread use was sufficient to prompt new employees to establish the habit themselves.

Would informational feedback alone, without any clearly apparent correlated incentives or aversive consequences be sufficient to influence safety performance? Several recent studies are permitting this question to be examined. Kim and Hamner (1976) studied the influence of feedback combined with goal setting on several measures, including a number of episodes requiring first aid. A different procedure was applied in each of four plants: on-the-job feedback, given weekly, on achievement of goals set the previous week plus praise by the supervisor for goals accomplished; goals set within work groups plus self-ratings; a combination of both procedures and goal setting alone by the group members. The results suggested an improvement in safety for all four groups, with the weakest effect demonstrated for the goal-setting-only group, and the strongest for the maximum-feedback group, although differences between groups were not significant.

A food manufacturing plant, a wholesale bakery, was the setting of the study conducted by Komaki et al. (1979). There had been an alarming increase in accidents, and the program was instituted to reverse the trend. Unsafe and safe practices were analyzed into their component operations. During a baseline phase the percentage of safe performances was measured reliably across two different departments. Following several weeks of observation, an intervention of instruction and feedback was implemented. It consisted of teaching workers to distinguish safe from unsafe practices. For each practice two slides were prepared: one showing the unsafe practice, the other the safe practice. Workers were asked to differentiate them. A graph of the safety performance was posted in a conspicuous place, and data from each observation session were added as soon as they were gathered. Supervisory personnel were also instructed to praise workers periodically for safe performance, and to record their own compliance in doing so.

Data were collected over 25 weeks, for 65 recording sessions. The intervention was implemented with the first department on the twentieth session and with the second on the fiftieth. In each case there was a rapid, dramatic, and sustained improvement in the percentage of safe performances. On the sixty-second session the feedback system, the posted graph, was withdrawn and practices immediately deteriorated. The resultant data were apparently so compelling that the system was quickly reinstated and maintained. Within a year the injury frequency had stabilized at less than 10 lost time accidents per million hours worked, a relatively low figure, particularly when compared with the 53.8 for the year preceding the study. It was particularly interesting that supervisors generally failed to comply with the request that they deliver and record their delivery of praise. It seems that the posted graphic feedback was primarily responsible for the noted improvement. This finding was later supported by Rhoton (1980), who achieved similarly effective results by conducting random weekly inspections to assess ventilation violations in an underground coal mine. When miners were given graphic feedback on violations, there was a drop from 2.6 violations per month to 10 months without any violations.

A similar intervention system was used in a set of two studies I conducted with my colleagues (Sulzer-Azaroff, 1978; Sulzer-Azaroff and de Santamaria, 1980). The major difference was that not safety practices but their products, *safety hazards,* were the main focus of change. The first was conducted at a University Materials Research Institute. The Institute contained 30 laboratories in which analyses ranged from radiological to chemical, thermal, mechanical, electrical, biological and other forms of study of the properties of various materials. Accident rates *per se* were quite low, due in part to the fact that members were not continuously engaged in hazardous activities. Yet safety conditions could stand improvement. A tour of the facility indicated several hazardous conditions such as unsecured gas cylinders, frayed electrical cords, overloaded circuits, unlabeled and improperly stored chemicals, unguarded fan belts, and other electrical, chemical, and mechanical hazards. Occasionally personnel were observed operating equipment without using adequate protective clothing devices: safety glasses, lab coats, and so forth.

Again an objective and reliable observation system was devised. Each hazardous condition or unsafe act was defined clearly and assigned a code number. These were placed on a recording sheet, which also contained a generic layout map. On the map some landmark of the lab, such as the main entry or a window, could be indicated to orient the reader. Extensive baseline measurements were collected for each laboratory over a period of several months by members of the safety committee (faculty, administrative, and technical staff) and by a special research assistant. This assistant was not informed as to the intervention conditions in effect in any laboratory, and it was the data that he collected that were used for feedback and for analysis of results.

Observations conducted each three to four weeks indicated an average of over four hazardous conditions or unsafe acts recorded per laboratory. The goal was to bring this down substantially. The intervention, consisting of a very simple feedback system, was implemented sequentially several months apart across three groups of the laboratories. Observation forms were copied and distributed to the laboratory supervisor, along with a cover sheet that suggested methods for improving conditions and practices. On a couple of occasions the director of the institute distributed notices supporting the safety program and requested continued cooperation.

The frequency of hazards declined in parallel with the introduction of the feedback system, in each of the three groups, to an average level of less than two per laboratory. Subsequent to the study the system was modified somewhat, by the addition of other categories and a more detailed cover sheet containing a place for commenting on improvements demonstrated over time. Improvement has continued.

The second study (Sulzer-Azaroff and de Santamaria, 1980) used essentially the same procedure, this time in a small factory in which plastic products were custom fabricated. In this case observations were conducted daily, and during the intervention phases the resultant feedback was given more regularly—twice a week. The cover sheet accompanying the form also included praise statements for improvement that had been measured.

Results were also similar, with major reductions in hazardous conditions noted during the intervention phases. Follow-up measures taken after several months showed that the reduced levels persisted or even improved further, and the plant manager reported that the system was being maintained independently of the research team. Two years afterwards, although many changes had taken place, we found conditions to have remained at the same improved level. In both studies, accident rates were so low prior to and during intervention phases that they could not be used as sensitive measures of change. To what extent the reduced frequency of hazards may have contributed to the continued low accident rate, therefore, is unknown.

A study by Komaki and her colleagues (1980) was designed to separate out the differential contributions of training and feedback. Using a set of observational procedures similar to those used previously, a city's vehicle maintenance department was the locus of the study. Training was provided initially without feedback. Feedback was only added several sessions later. In each of four departments, training resulted in improvements ranging from slight to substantial. Adding the feedback component, however, resulted in a much greater level of performance. When feedback was temporarily discontinued (and appropriate safety procedures continued to be posted), there was a slight drop in performance. Reinstatement of the feedback less regularly than during the first feedback phase resulted in a general recovery in performance. The rate of accidents also declined substantially compared with its level prior to the study.

Issues Related to Arranging Consequences

Although reinforcing and aversive consequences have been studied intensively for their influence on a broad range of performances, their influence on occupational safety has only recently begun to be analyzed systematically. As this new focus begins to expand, various questions and issues are beginning to emerge. For example: How frequently should the consequences be applied? Might increases in rates of production produced by incentive conditions be accompanied by increases in accidents? When given the choice of either positive consequences for safe practices or aversive consequences for unsafe practices, which should be selected?

We have seen that specific feedback can effectively improve safety conditions. One associated issue that emerges is: "What is the optimal schedule for the delivery of consequences such as feedback?" The frequency with which the feedback has been delivered has ranged from several times a week to as infrequently as once a month. Yet each schedule seemed to have a positive effect. As expected, the more rapid effects accompanied the more frequent feedback. Yet very frequent feedback may not be cost efficient. Also, as noted in the Komaki et al. (1980) article, a discernable reduction in the frequency of feedback seemed to result in a slight deterioration in performance among some subjects. Apparently one should avoid any abrupt reductions in the frequency with which consequences are presented. Rather a schedule should be selected that is shown to be effective now, and that later might be reasonably maintained over extended periods. Otherwise great care needs to be taken to reduce the frequency very gradually so that the changes taking place are almost imperceptible.

Do incentive conditions for increases in productivity create safety risks? Will more rapid performance result in more accidents? The answer is "perhaps." Adam (1975) conducted a study in which supervisors of a die casting operation were instructed to systematically administer praise and admonishment based on operator performance. Increases in production were not accompanied by a deterioration in quality. Conversely, McKelvey, Engen, and Peck (1973) used an incentive system to increase the rate of operation of a punch press simulator. They found that increases in incentive conditions not only led to more work responses but also a significantly increased rate of error. However, as we shall see, this increase in errors was probably a function of increases in rate produced by a set of conditions that neglected to consider the accuracy element.

An analogy may be drawn from the data on students' academic performance in school. Consider the case (Semb and Semb, 1975) in which two different methods of assigning work to students were compared. Children were either required to work on an assignment for a particular period of time, or they were asked to complete the problems on a specific number of pages, before being permitted recreation time. While the page-completion condition resulted in higher rates of items completed, sometimes those increases in rates were accompanied by increases in the error rate. The children were getting more answers right per unit of time, but they were also getting more wrong answers. It seems that in their effort to finish in a hurry they grew careless. This need not necessarily be the case. In research in which students earned incentives for increasing the number of items they completed in reading and spelling (Sulzer, Hunt, Ashby, Koniarski, and Krams, 1971), error rates were not found to increase when incentives were based on both the number of correct items and for meeting a specific percentage criterion for overall performance.

We note a parallel effect in the occupational safety literature. McKelvey et al. (1973) awarded a cash incentive to workers performing on a modified power press. Again the group that received a straight cash incentive for productivity experienced the largest number of simulated accidents. When, however, additional features were included, such as turning off the machine for five minutes if corrective action were not taken following the activation of a warning device, coupled with a warning regarding accidents, accident rates dropped to extremely low levels.

It is clear from the above experiences that increasing the rates of performance of potentially hazardous tasks can be somewhat risky. When designing such procedures, other conditions should be included to assure that errors do not begin to creep in. Possible steps include: rewarding accuracy in and of itself; punishing errors; or teaching the response to such a level of precision that, even when it is practiced at high rates, it does not tend to deteriorate and permit errors to emerge.

We have seen that either positive or aversive consequences may help promote safe practices. Given a choice, which is preferable? The answer is based on a number of considerations. Which would be easier to use? Which would tend to be used more consistently and enduringly? Which would be more acceptable to supervisory staff or workers? What are the potential side effects of each?

There is a natural tendency to turn to negative consequences when one observes the performance of an unsafe act or encounters hazardous conditions. Angered by the event, the tendency is to penalize, correct, scold, or present some other sort of aversive consequence. Aversive consequences, promptly delivered, also tend to have an immediately salutory effect. And as we know from other realms of research (Hutchinson, 1977), dishing out punishment under such conditions can be very reinforcing to the punisher! There is of course a logical association between an immediate negative consequence for engaging in unsafe acts and the delayed potential consequence—an accident—which is even more aversive. One could argue that delivering a mild aversive consequence immediately is preferable to encouraging a possibly much more serious delayed aversive consequence.

Many supervisory personnel appear reluctant to apply any sort of positive consequence. Although I am not familiar with any research to support this conviction, it is apparently very easy to teach people to reprimand, correct, or penalize. All that is generally needed is to ask them to do so. For many, however, a substantial effort must be made to teach them to use positive consequences regularly. Initially they may report feeling "phoney" when they praise and uncomfortable about smiling or providing other forms of positive feedback. Only after much practice and coming in contact with the evidence of improved performance do they start to use such procedures comfortably.

Overcoming this apparent natural reluctance by some persons to use positive consequences requires a little more creativity. What is a positive consequence to one person under one condition is not necessarily the same to the next. In fact for some workers a statement from a supervisor such as "what a wonderful job you're doing" could conceivably have a negative rather than a positive effect. On the other hand, a hearty "Hey, O.K." could be effective. Identifying potentially effective positive consequences may require careful observation of the social milieu, so that those that are normally dispensed are identified. Once identified, they can be tested and, if found effective, substituted for any less natural positive consequence.

If no reasonable amount of effort is successful in promoting the consistent and enduring application of positive consequences for safe practices, turning to the use of aversive consequences for unsafe acts may be the only answer. In making such judgments, keep in mind that consistency, above all, is the key. Whatever consequences are selected, positive, aversive, or combinations, they should be delivered regularly and with as minimal delay as possible for them to be effective.

Should the decision be to select only aversives, though, it should be recognized that, as basic research has shown (Azrin and Holz, 1966), there is a potential for such negative side effects as escape, avoidance, and aggression. In the literature on the management of students in schools there is an informative series of studies about Los Angeles County (Mayer and Butterworth, 1979; Mayer, Jones, and Butterworth, 1979). Ten experimental and nine control schools had experienced high rates of vandalism. In the experimental schools, the staff were trained to use positive reinforcement effectively, and the school programs were modified to include various positively reinforcing practices and activities, while the control schools continued their regular practices. Data on subsequent vandalism costs indicated that for the second year of the project the experimental schools experienced about one sixth the cost suffered by the control schools.

The proportion of occupational accidents that may be influenced by acts of vandalism or sabotage disguised as accidents is unknown. Yet on the basis of studies such as these, one might presume that a commission of such acts of revenge is much more apt to take place in settings in which aversive as opposed to positive management techniques are used.

TEACHING SAFE PRACTICES

The field of safety education historically has focused on teaching safe practices. Written instructions, training films, lectures, and apprenticeship experiences are among the many methods that have been extensively applied. We can even see some elements of *programmed instruction* incorporated into some of those materials. (Programmed instruction divides material to be learned into small bits of information; it involves the learner actively by requiring a response to each piece of information, prompted during initial stages, and provides immediate feedback as to correctness.) An example is a *Safe Driver Kit* (1974) published by the Travelers Insurance Company. Users are instructed to read a set of rules, then *to respond actively* by checking the condition of their vehicle and by filling in the blanks with statements about the practices they are supposed to be following.

As instructional specialists with sophistication in behavioral methodology are becoming involved in designing curricula to teach safe practices, we are beginning to see a broader range of effective training methods and more precise measures of progress. Accident simulators are being used to train people to operate equipment safely. Leslie and Adams (1973) developed a punch press simulator that recorded the occurrence of "accidents," as one component of a more sophisticated instructional safety training system. Rubinsky and Smith (1973) included a bench grinder that was designed to simulate accidents. The device was more effective in teaching safe practices than a simple demonstration of tbe accident. Another study (Smith and Rubinsky, 1972) showed that a single training session with the simulator led to retention of safe use of the grinder over a six-month period.

Principles of behavioral instruction are being used to teach *concepts* of safe practices as well. As part of our laboratory safety program, e.g., prior to being permitted to begin to work in a laboratory, each staff member must read and demonstrate mastery of the information contained in a safety manual. Hopkins, Conrad, and Duellman (1980) have proposed using principles of behavioral instruction in programs designed to reduce occupational health hazards.

The work of Komaki et al. (1980) suggests that simply knowing what to do may be insufficient to assure acceptably safe levels of performance. In that study workers were shown slides and discussed instances of safe and unsafe practices. Although the workers demonstrated their ability to separate good and bad practices, this knowledge improved their performance on the job only marginally. It was not until feedback was delivered following on-the-job performance that practices improved to any substantial extent.

A promising approach is to break practices down into their component elements. The elements may then be taught by instructions, questions, demonstrations, and guided practice and feedback. Such a technique was found effective in teaching children to cross streets safely (Yeaton and Bailey, 1978) and could well be applicable to training safe practices in the work place. Some of these components are already incorporated within training programs for public safety personnel such as fire fighters, police officers, water safety instructors, and practitioners of first aid. Some major insurance underwriters use many of these procedures to teach occupational safety personnel. In one (Aetna, Life Insurance Company, 1979), for instance, training is conducted in simulated work settings in which trainees are taught proper use of safety devices. It would also be natural and unobtrusive to include demonstrations, instructions, questions and answers, discussions, and guided practice within an apprenticeship. The safe practices would simply be incorporated within the full job sequence as they are currently in high risk occupations such as coal mining and construction. Construction workers see their fellow workers and supervisors don their hard hats before they enter the construction area. New workers are usually oriented to and given an opportunity to discuss the rationale for that precautionary measure, and it is likely that they receive guided practice in donning the hat properly. It is in occupations in which the risks are not so apparent that training and conformance tend to be inconsistent. We found, for example, that adherence to the use of protective clothing and devices in a materials research laboratory was inconsistent until other more formal measures were taken to promote compliance (Sulzer-Azaroff, 1978).

A major concern in occupational safety is whether reinforcement for working rapidly, especially when reinforcement is based on productivity, jeopardizes safe performance. As noted above, it is unlikely that practices that have been mastered thoroughly will deteriorate with moderate increases in performance rates. But increases in rate could cause problems when the components of a behavior have been insufficiently mastered and integrated into a smooth, unitary sequence. Components might fail to occur, occur improperly, or occur out of sequence. Taking the operation of a drill press as an example, inexpert workers attempting to increase their rate might fail to remove their fingers altogether, position the material improperly, and use their fingers to reposition it at the wrong time, or operate tbe press before removing their fingers.

The best remedy for problems of this kind is to insure that each and every component *and* the integrated sequence is fully mastered. To accomplish the latter, we may turn to the principles of what is called *chaining*, the term for grouping a series of acts into a unitary sequence: Components are first taught, or *shaped*, by consistently reinforcing the behavior so that it resembles the specified component more and more closely. Each newly mastered component then is added to those previously mastered and the newly constituted series repeatedly practiced and reinforced. Additional components are added one by one. Again the combined components are reinforced as a unit, until a thorough mastery of the complex skill is demonstrated over repeated trials.

Sequences of behavior that prove particularly difficult may be taught by the *backward chaining procedure*: The final component of the sequence is mastered initially, with the next to final component added next, and so on. The rationale is that the completion of the sequence is the closest in time to the reinforcing event, completing the practice successfully, so it would be acquired most expeditiously. In the drill press example, training could begin with the operation of the press, the materials having been placed in position by the trainer. After that segment has been mastered, the next one, removing one's hands, is linked into the sequence, and so on. Because the component "removing one's hands" is the hazardous portion of the response, it should be learned to a particularly high level of perfection, or *overlearned* in educational parlance. Perhaps the criterion for mastering such a response should be very high, e.g., no errors for a few hundred trials over several days in a row. Thus, should something unforeseen happen to disrupt the sequence, it would be less likely that this particular component would be improperly practiced. (See Sulzer-Azaroff and Mayer, 1977, for an extensive discussion of behavioral approaches to teaching by shaping and chaining.)

ARRANGING ANTECEDENT CONDITIONS

Many of the conditions and events that precede and accompany occupational practices influence job safety, whether by design or happenstance. Safe practices are promoted when rules of operation are clearly specified; when supportive management systems are in place; when staff roles are clearly delineated and arranged so that practices are monitored and consequences are regularly applied; when equipment is engineered for optimally safe performance; and when the physical and social environment is arranged to minimize risks. Conversely, various unplanned conditions may prove detrimental: an inauspicious learning history, illness, poor model examples, and others.

This section focuses on some of the research that specifically relates to arranging antecedent conditions to promote safe work practices. Much has been derived from applications in areas other than occupational safety. This is due to the relative paucity of published experimental studies of the antecedents to safe practices, although some are beginning to be conducted. Within the field of occupational safety in particular, tbe influence of such antecedents as the availability and use of protective equipment, rules and how compliance is promoted, and ways that safe performance may be modeled and guided effectively are considered next.

Protective Equipment

The use of protective clothing (Jones, 1971; Woodson and Conover, 1964) and equipment has long been prescribed in safety codes and guidelines. A number of behavioral studies of safety also have included these elements in their procedures. Increased compliance with rules for using protective clothing and equipment has been the target of several behavioral studies: inhalation masks (Hopkins et al., 1980), ear protectors (Zohar et al., 1980), and safety glasses and laboratory coats (Sulzer-Azaroff, 1978). But the availability of such protective items is no guarantee that they will be used. In fact, in each of the studies cited above, protective items were freely available, yet were used irregularly. Only when consequences such as feedback on hearing loss (Zohar et al., 1980) or positive or corrective feedback (Sulzer-Azaroff, 1978) were added did compliance increase to an acceptable level. This strongly suggests that appropriate consequences need to be supplied along with protective equipment and clothing.

Signs, Rules, and Instructions

Does it make sense to post signs or request compliance with safety or health practices? The data to date say "maybe." Two representative investigations found that signs may promote adherence to rules of safe performance. Laner and Sell (1960) explored the influence of safety posters on the degree to which the chain slings were hooked back on crane hooks while not in use, by displaying three posters either simultaneously or sequentially. (Unsecured chain slings present a danger to people and equipment). Data were collected periodically over 20 weeks; it was found that in many cases, when the poster was displayed, adherence increased. Interestingly, the influence tended to endure over the 20-week duration. Nevertheless, there were several instances in which the poster appeared to exert no influence at all.

What are some of the factors that may influence the effectiveness of written or oral instructions? Probably one is the type of information conveyed. Some signs may communicate more "hazard association value" than others. Bresnahan and Bryk (1975), for example, found that different colors and signal words were judged to have greater hazard values than others. Probably the social context also exerts quite an influence. In a series of studies on strategies for avoiding other people's tobacco smoke, Jason, Clay, and Martin (1979–80) noted that posted requests not to smoke did exert some influence. A far more effective procedure was a direct request that the smoker desist. (However, at the time Jason was a university faculty member, and his requests were within his university milieu, where presumably he is known and where other social elements were apt to play a role.)

The level of specificity of rules and instructions may influence their effectiveness. The field of behavioral instruction (Becker, Engelmann, and Thomas, 1975) suggests that the more specific an instruction or rule, the more likely it is to be carried out appropriately. Translating this into the occupational safety area, we would expect that a rule such as "operate venting hood while mixing chemicals" would produce better complaince than "safety first."

The social source of the material is probably critical to the success with which rules and instructions are obeyed. Information communicated by those within an organization who have prestige or power is more likely to influence behavior than that communicated by those with less social status. Although this assumption remains to be documented, it stands to reason that powerful and prestigious individuals have control of important consequences that they have delivered in the past and that they may again deliver in the future. When a supervisor who has responsibility for recommending promotions, raises, preferred assignments, or termination of employment is the individual who communicates the information, probably that information will affect the behavior of a subordinate.

As indicated above, critical to success of any accident prevention program is that the appropriate safe practice has been adequately mastered in the first place. No amount of exhortation will be effective if the rules that are to govern behavior have not been learned. For this reason, mastery-based learning systems hold so much promise. Instances of the application of mastery learning are beginning to emerge in the occupational safety area. As noted above, mastery learning requires that each of the components of a concept or skill must be demonstrated by the trainee to have reached a preset criterion level of 90 percent or better (or 100 percent for hazardous performance), before being allowed to proceed (Johnson and Ruskin, 1977). For instance, Sweitzer (1979) reports using programmed instruction as an element of the Honeywell Occupational Environment Health Program, and we continuously use mastery learning at a university research laboratory in our efforts to promote compliance.

Modeling and Guiding

Behavioral psychology has studied the influence of demonstrations, physical or verbal, and other prompting strategies. Bandura (1968) has investigated how various factors influence imitation. This has major importance in the area of occupational safety, since imitation of modeled performance may or may not occur by design or happenstance. A program of training designed to encourage a safe practice, such as the proper way to lift a heavy object, may include a live or filmed demonstration. The objective is for the observer to imitate that modeled behavior. Workers may also imitate the unsafe practices of those around them. It seems that all that needs to happen for a cumbersome safety practice to be discarded is for one or two key people to visibly fail to carry it out. Just let Joe, the supervisor, defeat the device requiring two-handed operation of a press by jamming one of the buttons with a pin, and before long half of the press operators are doing the same thing. Recognizing the factors that influence imitation are obviously important to the management of effective safety programs.

Among the variables that have been found to promote imitation are these: the similarity of the model to the imitator; the prestige of the model; whether or not the imitator has learned the behavior; whether the model's behavior has been observed to have been reinforced; and whether the imitator's behavior is reinforced when it matches that of the model. (See Sulzer-Azaroff and Mayer, 1977, for an extensive discussion of these factors.) Assuming that these principles apply equally in occupational settings, then when imitation is desired, models should be selected who share characteristics in common with those who are to imitate their behavior; but those who are to imitate should already have acquired the components of the desired response. The models should also have a reasonable amount of prestige, and the behavior to be imitated should be visibly reinforced. The model might display visible pleasure with the performance or be given reinforcing attention or even something more tangible, such as special notice, a preferred assignment, or an award. Those who are observed imitating the model's performance should also receive positive rewards. Conversely, high prestige workers who are visibly reinforced for unsafe practices need to be identified and those practices modified. Perhaps just making them aware of their pernicious influence on their fellow workers may be sufficient. Otherwise alternative measures have to be taken to assure that either the modeled practices are altered or that they are not visible to others who might be adversely influenced by them.

A promising method for training precise physical movements has recently been described by Allison and Ayllon (1980). The method incorporates some modeling features to coach skills in football, gymnastics, and tennis. It consists of five steps: (1) The trainee is instructed to execute the play (or move). (2) The coach decides whether or not the move was executed correctly. If so, the move is permitted to be completed and is followed by a statement of praise. If not, the coach yells "freeze" and the trainee is to immediately stop action. (3) As the trainee remains in the frozen position the coach describes the incorrect position, (4) demonstrates the correct position, and then (5) instructs the trainee to imitate the correct position, making appropriate positive comments when that position is assumed. Although reaction to the method was mixed (some liked it, others didn't), the measured improvement in *skills* was dramatic. This fact could be critical when training the safe operation of a difficult or complex skill.

Minimizing Errors Through Physical Guidance

There is some evidence that actions learned without errors are less likely to be performed imprecisely than those that have been learned with errors in the first place (Terrace, 1966). The individual who frequently operates a bench grinder from the incorrect position during the initial stages of learning is thus more likely to do so in the future. Conversely, the person who learns to operate a piece of equipment without ever making an error is more likely to perform safely in the future. For this reason it is imperative to train potentially hazardous operations correctly from the start.

Recent advances in behavioral technology have shown how this may be accomplished. The graduated guidance procedure, investigated by Foxx and Azrin (1973), is eminently suited to this purpose. In graduate guidance, the learner is physically guided through a movement with the minimum intensity required to permit the movement to be correctly executed. As the learner begins to assume increasing control over the correct movement, the intensity is gradually diminished. Errors are not permitted to occur. Suppose an apprentice were to learn to operate a lathe by this method. The trainer might stand behind, hands positioned on those of the trainee. The initial movements would be fully guided. As the trainer discerns that the proper movements are being exercised by the trainee, the amount of pressure on the hands would be reduced, and little by little guidance would be withdrawn. Ultimately operation would be fully independent. In order to insure against forgetting, several sessions might be conducted, backing up a degree or two to a level of guidance slightly greater than that offered at the very end of the last training session.

Pairing Consequences When Antecedent Conditions Are Arranged

Although this point has been mentioned earlier, it bears repeating. Knowing just how antecedent conditions acquire their ability to influence behavior is especially important if they are to be included in a program of occupational safety. From basic and applied experimental analysis of behavior we have learned just how important it is to arrange consequences to follow the antecedent-performance combination. If behavior is performed subsequent to a particular antecedent, such as the presentation of a rule, and the combination is followed by a reinforcing event, the behavior is more likely to reoccur in response to that rule in the future. If the consequence of that combination is aversive, the rule will be less likely to be followed, but if there are no consequences, the antecedent-performance combination will not be strengthened.

For the aforementioned reasons, management and training programs should provide regular reinforcement when the trainees perform appropriately in the presence of the antecedent. Praise, positive feedback, or other rewarding events should be arranged to follow performance that has been identified as safe. In case it is difficult to be around often enough to catch such instances, some mechanism should be incorporated within the management strategy. This could include frequent audits or systems of self-monitoring in which the worker records the appropriate performance (verified intermittently). It might also involve special workshops or training sessions that could be scheduled periodically so that the appropriate action in the presence of the antecedent can be given the appropriate consequence.

ACTION PLAN

Still in its infancy in terms of its application to problems of occupational safety, the field of organization behavior management nevertheless is beginning to formulate some promising strategies. In this section we draw upon current knowledge to suggest a plan of action that is designed to lead to safer performance in the work place. Accompanying each suggested step is a brief discussion and some illustrative examples from our own safety studies.

Demonstrate Need

The need to institute a behavioral program can arise from various sources: new regulations, results of inspections, increases in accident rates, critical incidents, a cost-benefit analysis indicating that accidents are costly, concerns with workers' quality of life, time, profit margins, and others.

One of our settings has been a university science research complex consisting of approximately 30 laboratories. We were prompted to examine the safety program there after a student in another laboratory on campus, neglecting to wear safety glasses, lost the vision in one eye due to a small explosion. The need was recognized on the basis of that one critical incident.

Identify the Safe and Unsafe Practices that Relate to the Need

These are presented as the actions to be performed and not to be performed under given conditions. A criterion of acceptability is also specified. For completeness and increased compliance, input should be solicited from workers, managers, and safety specialists.

At the research complex, a safety committee, consisting of administrators, technologists, scientists, and students, decided to focus on a reduction in hazardous conditions. Specific safe practices and hazardous conditions were listed, and a criterion of success of one or fewer hazards per laboratory was set.

Define Practices and Components

List all safe and unsafe practices, telling exactly how they can be distinguished from one another. If the practice is complex, divide it into its component acts.

Safe and unsafe practices were listed under several headings: chemical storage, electrical equipment, safe laboratory practices, and so on. These were then broken down into subcategories, e.g., bottles clearly labeled, safety glasses worn.

Design a Recording System

This may be a checklist, a time-based recording system, a recording instrument or some other device. (See Sulzer-Azaroff and Mayer, 1977, for various methods of recording performance directly.) The system is then checked to verify that it operates accurately. If performance is directly recorded, two or more observers should record it simultaneously and independently. The records are then compared to determine if the same performance was recorded at the same time. Should agreement not be very high, the system is refined until ambiguities are ironed out.

Using definitions and a map of the laboratory, the presence and location of specific hazards were marked on the map. Checking to see how closely evaluations by members of the team agreed, we continued revising our definitions until agreement was almost perfect.

Record Performances or the Results of Performances

This is done repeatedly over several sessions until it can be assumed that a typical estimate of performance (a baseline) is obtained. Usually the results are plotted session by session on a graph. The points are connected to form a picture of typical performance, prior to arranging any changes.

In order to find out just how well members of the research complex were performing, all laboratories were observed over a period of several months. At that point we agreed that we had attained a reasonably valid estimate of the current status of our selected safety practices.

Plan a System of Change

Arrange or rearrange consequences or antecedents, using the record of baseline performance as a guide.

1. If the safe performance needs to be practiced more consistently, select some effective consequences and apply them regularly and often when the performance occurs.
2. If the safe performance is practiced infrequently, check to see if necessary equipment is available. Try to prompt, cue, instruct, model; apply some strong positive consequences when it does occur, and possibly some strong aversive consequences whenever unsafe practices are noted.
3. If improvement is not noted, check to see if the worker knows how to perform the safe practice correctly. Ask for the rules and for a demonstration. Perhaps it will become apparent that additional training is required.

Noting a high rate of some categories of unsafe practice, we developed a safety manual that was supplied to all laboratories. We also provided specific corrective instructions to staff on feedback sheets that consisted of a copy of the observational recording for that laboratory. Safe practices and improvements were also noted and praised.

Test Out Planned Changes

Implement the changes, preferably with only one group of workers at first. Then later, if records show improvement with the first group, apply the procedures to the next one and so on.

We applied our feedback system to about ⅓ of the laboratories at first. Noting a sustained improvement over several months, we felt more confident about instituting the program with a second group and a few months later, a third group. The records demonstrated quite convincingly that it was the feedback procedures and not some other event that caused the improvement.

Evaluate the Complete Results of the Program

If safety improves and other data such as favorable cost-benefit ratios and satisfaction of managers and workers support the value of the system, take steps to incorporate it into the regular operation of the organization. Minor modifications are allowed as long as performance continues to be recorded and records show no deterioration.

At the end of two years, we judged that our feedback system had been a success. At that time a few new practices were added to the list, and audits of laboratories were scheduled to occur somewhat less often. The safety committee adopted the program as a regular activity and now, several years later, it remains in effect. Occasionally one hears a gripe, but on the whole everyone approves. More importantly, no one has been seriously hurt in the building over that entire period of time.

COMMENTARY

The deliberate application of behavioral principles and methods to problems of occupational safety is a relatively recent phenomenon. As with all fields of endeavor, however, elements of effective behavioral procedures have been utilized successfully over a much longer time span. Audits and inspections, safety awards, training modules, and many other accident prevention procedures certainly antedate organizational behavior management. Yet it is the behavioral approach that is enabling safety programs to be designed with greater precision. Behavioral methods permit us to analyze problematic performances and to identify the factors that exert a controlling influence upon them. They guide us toward optimal procedural revisions and pinpoint practices that may need to be discarded. We have shown how such systems operate by referring to numerous examples throughout this chapter.

In 1975 a report was published under the auspices of the National Institute for Occupational Safety and Health (Cohen, Smith, and Cohen) that identified a set of program practices in companies having low (as compared to others with high) accident rates. Consider the attributes shared by the companies with low accident rates, and see how the behavioral approach relates.

"1.   Greater stature and staff commitment given to direction of company safety efforts." (The behavioral model recognizes the importance of managing contingencies effectively and, as we see, administrative support tends to be incorporated into organizational behavior management programs.)

"2.   Greater utilization of outside influences in instilling safety consciousness into workers." (The behaviorist often operates as a consultant and, whether operating from within or outside of the organization, utilizes various instructional and management resources. As a scientist, the behavior analyst tries to remain abreast of developments that they may have implications for the field of occupational safety.)

"3.   More concerted use of a variety of safety promotional and incentive techniques." (Numerous instances of promotional and incentive techniques have been discussed in this chapter.)

"4.   Greater opportunities for general and specialized job safety training with supplemental modes of instruction for all production personnel." (Many examples of specialized training have been cited here, including those that make use of accident simulators and other refined training methods.)

"5.   More humanistic approaches in disciplining risk-takers and violators of safety rules." (By emphasizing the positive consequences for safe practices, the behavioral approach minimizes recourse to disciplining. In those instances in which disciplining is incorporated into the program, there is a continuum of consequences, proceeding from the least aversive (e.g., written feedback of conditions or practices to be changed) to only gradually increasing aversiveness (Ritschl, 1976).)

"6.   More frequent and less formal inspections of the workplace as a supplement to or instead of formal inspections at lengthy intervals." (The use of frequent, regular inspections has been discussed above. The frequency with which the consequences of performance occur has been found to be an important factor in the degree to which behavior is influenced.)

"7.   A safety program emphasizing better balance between engineering and non-engineering approaches toward accident prevention and control." (In the programs cited in the chapter, a broad variety of approaches were utilized. Here I have focused on changing human performance, which can be programmed along with the engineering of equipment and machinery.)

"8.   More stable qualities in the make-up of the workforce, i.e., more older, married workers with longer time on the job" (pp. x–xi).

This last item is not a programmatic approach, but rather a condition of the organization. As such, it cannot be directly managed as a facet of a safety program. Yet it may well be, that if behavioral approaches are increasingly incorporated within occupational safety programs, a more stable work force will result. With its emphasis on the positive and on the development of increasingly more effective strategies for improving performance, organizational behavior management should enable more workers to remain safe and enjoy a better quality of life in a more conducive work place.

SUMMARY

Although accidents on the job have dropped dramatically since the early years of the twentieth century, there are signs that the trend has begun to level off. A main contributor to continuing occupational accidents is human performance. According to the organizational behavior management models, managing human performance to promote safe and suppress unsafe acts depends on empirically based analyses. Antecedent and consequential conditions and events that influence those acts are examined, as well as the components of the acts themselves. Practitioners of organizational behavior management analyze these elements by first operationally defining specific safe and unsafe practices and identifying the conditions under which they should and should not occur. The natural contingencies in operation are also studied to determine how they are functioning to support or impair safety. Often it is necessary to rearrange contingencies by adding positive consequences regularly, and as soon as possible to follow proper performance and aversive consequences to follow incorrect actions. Positive consequences that have been applied in this fashion have included incentives such as cash or prizes, praise, attention, and public recognition. Aversive consequences have consisted of events such as simulated accidents, fines, reprimands, and temporary or permanent removal from the job. The two may also be combined, as in the application of *performance feedback:* workers or supervisors are systematically informed of the results of their action and may be complimented for improvements and requested to make necessary corrections. Enough studies of the use of feedback to improve job safety have been conducted to document its efficacy. Yet many unanswered questions remain about tbe systematic arrangement of consequences, such as "How often they should be delivered?" "Whether or under what circumstances changes in production rates influence accident rates?" "Should positive consequences for safe or aversive for unsafe practices be selected, or is there an optimal combination of both?"

Behavioral approaches have also contributed towards teaching safe practices from the beginning, by utilizing such methods as shaping, chaining, and programmed instruction. The arrangement of antecedent conditions, such as utilization of protective equipment, signs, rules and instructions, modeling, guiding, and other prompting and training strategies are also being analyzed to assess their functional properties. If safe practices are brought about by the management of antecedent conditions, they must also be regularly followed by the application of effective consequences.

Progress by organizational behavior management in occupational safety has been sufficient to permit a strategic action plan to be conceived: (1) Demonstrate the need for a behavioral safety program; (2) identify related safe and unsafe practices; (3) define practices and components; (4) design a recording system; (5) record performances or results of performances; (6) plan a system of change; (7) test it out; (8) evaluate the complete results of the program. Hopefully, by following systematic approaches of this kind, it should be possible to decrease those accidents and injuries on the job that stem from human performance.

REFERENCES

Adam, E. E. Behavior modification in quality control. *Academy of Management Journal,* 1975, *18,* 662–679.

Aetna Life Insurance Company, personal communication, 1979.

Allison, M. G., and Ayllon, T. Behavioral coaching in the development of skills in football, gymnastics and tennis. *Journal of Applied Behavior Analysis,* 1980, *13,* 297–314.

Azrin, N. H., and Holz, W. C. Punishment. In W. K. Honig (Ed.), *Operant behavior: Areas of research and application.* New York: Appleton-Century-Crofts, 1966.

Bandura, A. Social learning theory of identificatory processes. In D. A. Goslin and D. C. Glass (Eds.), *Handbook of socialization theory and research.* Chicago, IL: Rand McNally, 1968.

Becker, W. C., Engelmann, S., and Thomas, D. R. *Teaching: Cognitive learning and instruction.* Chicago: Science Research Associates, 1975.

Blake, R. P. *Industrial Safety.* Englewood Cliffs, NJ: Prentice-Hall, 1943.

Bresnahan, T. F., and Bryk, J. The hazard association values of accident-prevention signs. *Professional Safety,* 1975, *15,* 17–25.

Cohen, A., Smith, M., and Cohen, H. H. Safety program practices in high versus low accident rate companies: An interim report (Questionnaire phase). *HEW Publication No. (NIOSH) 75-185.* Washington, DC: Government Printing Office, 1975.

Fox, D. K. *Effects of an incentive program on safety performance in open pit mining at Utah's Shirley Basin Mine, Wyoming.* Paper presented at the meeting of the Midwestern Association of Behavior Analysis, Chicago, May 1976.

Foxx, R. M., and Azrin, N. H. The elimination of autistic self-stimulatory behavior by overcorrection. *Journal of Applied Behavior Analysis,* 1973, *6,* 1–14.

Gagne, R. M. *The conditions of learning* (2nd ed.). New York: Holt, Rinehart, and Winston, 1970.

Hale, A. R., and Hale, M. Accidents in perspective. *Occupational Psychology,* 1970, *44,* 115–121.

Haynes, R. *A behavioral approach to the reduction of accidents of city bus operators.* Unpublished manuscript, University of Kansas.

Hermann, J. A. *Effects of a safety program on the accident frequency and severity rate of automobile workers.* Unpublished manuscript.

Hopkins, B. L., Conrad, B. C., and Duellman, D. L. *Work practices and procedures to reduce workers' occupational exposure to styrene.* Unpublished manuscript, 1980.

Hutchinson, R. R. By-products of aversive control. In W. K. Honig and J. E. R. Staddon (Eds.), *Handbook of operant behavior.* Englewood Cliffs, NJ: Prentice-Hall, 1977.

Jason, L. A., Clay, R., and Martin, M. Reducing cigarette smoking in supermarkets and elevators. *Journal of Environmental Systems,* 1979–80, *9,* 57–66.

Johnson, K. R., and Ruskin, R. S. *Behavioral instruction: An evaluative review.* Washington, DC: American Psychological Association, 1977.

Jones, R. G. Guarding man at his machine. *Environmental Control and Safety Management,* 1971, *141,* 20–23.

Kim, J. S., and Hamner, W. C. Effect of performance feedback and goal setting on productivity and satisfaction in an organizational setting. *Journal of Applied Psychology,* 1976, *61,* 48–57.

Komaki, J., Barwick, K. K., and Scott, L. R. A behavioral approach to occupational safety. *Professional Safety,* 1979, 19–28.

Komaki, J., Heinzmann, A. T., and Lawson, L. Effect of training and feedback: Component analysis of a behavioral safety program. *Journal of Applied Psychology,* 1980, *65,* 261–270.

Laner, S., and Sell, R. G. An experiment on the effect of specially designed safety posters. *Occupational Psychology,* 1960, *34,* 153–169.

Larson, L. D., Schnelle, J. F., Kirchner, R. E., Jr., Carr, A. F., Domash, M., and Risely, T. R. Reduction of police vehicle accidents through mechanically aided supervision. *Journal of Applied Behavior Analysis,* 1980, *13,* 571–581.

Leslie, J. H., and Adams, S. K. Programmed safety through programmed learning. *Human Factors,* 1973, *15,* 223–236.

Mager, R. F. *Preparing objectives for programmed instruction.* San Francisco: Fearon, 1961.

Mager, R. F. *Goal analysis.* Belmont, CA: Lear Siegler/Fearon, 1972.

Mayer, G. R., Jones, J., and Butterworth, T. W. *Reducing school violence and vandalism: A two year experimental study.* Unpublished paper, 1979.

Mayer, G. R., and Butterworth, T. W. A preventive approach to school violence and vandalism: An experimental study. *Personnel and Guidance Journal,* 1979, *57,* 436–441.

McKelvey, R. K., Engen, T., and Peck, M. Performance efficiency and injury avoidance as a function of positive and negative incentives. *Journal of Safety Research,* 1973, *5,* 90–96.

National Safety Council. *Accident facts.* Chicago: 1979.

Odiorne, G. S. *Management by objectives.* New York: Pitman Publishing Co., 1965.

Parsons, H. M. *Behavior analysis in highway safety.* Invited address at the annual meeting of the Association for Behavior Analysis, Dearborn, MI, June 1979.

Parsons, H. M. Caution behavior and its conditioning in driving. *Human Factors,* 1976, *18,* 397–407.

Rhoton, W. W. A procedure to improve compliance with coal mine safety regulations. *Journal of Organizational Behavior Management,* 1980, *2,* 243–249.

Ritschl, C., Mongrella, J., and Presbie, R. L. Group time-out from rock and roll music and out-of-seat behavior of handicapped children while riding a school bus. *Psychological Reports,* 1972, *31,* 967–973.

Ritschl, E. R., Mirman, R. I., Hall, R. V., Sigler, J. R., and Hopkins, B. L. *Personal safety program: A behavioral approach to industrial safety.* Unpublished manuscript, 1976.

Roberts, R. M. Feedback game aimed at serious accidents. *Professional Safety,* 1977, 29–39.

Rubinsky, S., and Smith, N. Safety training by accident simulation. *Journal of Applied Psychology,* 1973, *57,* 63–73.

Safe Driver Kit. Hartford, CT: Travelers Insurance Company, 1974.

Sasser, J. R., Jr. Systems safety for unsystematic people. *Environmental Control Management,* February 1979, *69,* 57–59.

Semb, G., and Semb, S. A comparison of fixed-page and fixed-time reading assignments in elementary school children. E. E. Ramp and G. Semb (Eds.), *Behavior analysis: Areas of research and application.* Englewood Cliffs, NJ: Prentice-Hall, 1975, 223–243.

Shirmer, G. J. *Behavioral motivation.* Paper presented at 67th National Safety Congress, Chicago, 1979.

Smith, N. F., and Rubinsky, S. Long term retention of safety procedures learned through accident simulation. *DHEW Publication No. (HSM) 72-10016,* Washington, DC: Government Printing Office, 1972.

Strasser, M. K., Aaron, J. E., Bohn, R. C., and Eales, J. R. *Fundamentals of safety education.* New York: Macmillan, 1964.

Sulzer-Azaroff, B. Behavioral ecology and accident prevention. *Journal of Organizational Behavior Management,* 1978, *2,* 11–44.

Sulzer-Azaroff, B., and de Santamaria, C. Industrial safety hazard reduction through performance feedback. *Journal of Applied Behavior Analysis,* 1980, *13,* 287–295.

Sulzer, B., Hunt, S., Ashby, E., Koniarski, C., and Krams, M. Increasing rate and percentage correct in reading and spelling in a class of slow readers by means of a token system. In E. Ramp and B. L. Hopkins (Eds.), *A new direction for education: Behavior analysis.* University of Kansas, Department of Human Development, 1971.

Sulzer-Azaroff, B., and Mayer, R. G. *Applying behavior analysis procedures with children and youth.* New York: Holt, Rinehart and Winston, 1977.

Sweitzer, R. L. *Applications of occupational safety and health programs.* (Honeywell's approach to occupational safety and health.) Paper presented at the 67th National Safety Congress, Chicago, 1979.

Terrace, H. S. Stimulus control. In W. K. Honig (Ed.), *Operant behavior: Areas of research and application.* New York: Appleton, 1966, pp. 271–344.

Woodson, W. E., and Conover, D. W. *Human engineering guide for equipment designers.* Berkeley, CA: University of California Press, 1964.

Yeaton, W. H., and Bailey, J. S. Teaching pedestrian safety skills to young children: An analysis and one-year follow-up. *Journal of Applied Behavior Analysis,* 1978, *11,* 315–329.

Zohar, D., Cohen, A., and Azar, N. Promoting increased use of ear protectors in noise through information feedback. *Human Factors,* 1980, *22,* 69–79.

19

Performance Management and Management Performance

MALCOLM W. WARREN

Performance Technologies, Inc.

The spreading application of technologies rooted in behaviorism does not stem from agreement with behavioral theories. Rather it grows from recognition that to be productive, an organization requires workable management processes that lead to predictable results. A workable management process is a set of activities, procedures, and tools that can be used by people assigned the tasks of managing. The processes must be readily usable without the need for a specialized body of knowledge. In short, managers turn to behavioral technologies because they fit their own experience and knowledge. They do not require an unreasonable effort, and they produce desired results.

The term "performance management" is a convenient label for the systematic application of processes that center on optimizing human performance in an organization. Since performance management has a demonstrable and positive impact on individual task performance, it becomes an attractive approach for managing managerial performance. It grows from the continuing need to address and resolve some critical issues relating to the management of a productive organization.

CRITICAL ISSUES

These issues fall into three areas: first, management selection; second, management training and development; and, third, managing the performance of incumbent managers (which is an integrated part of the first two).

Selection

The ability of an organization to select and acquire management talent is usually of vital concern to its members. The high cost of management turnover and the impact of poor management behavior on an organization's survival makes important the search for a systematic, effective management selection process.

The first issue confronting the organization is the identification of qualified candidates both at the entry level and for middle and upper level assignments. Before selection can take place, the organization must identify its criteria for management assignment. The problem is to figure out what the candidate must be able to do if placed in the position in question. What must a controller do? Or a plant manager? Or a district sales manager? The issue is not one of identifying responsibilities. Scope of responsibility is of little help in identifying a qualified candidate for a position. The challenge is to somehow select a candidate who can effectively carry out the activities required to produce some known set of outputs. If this issue is resolved, the organization faces the problem of matching a candidate against these job requirements. In most cases a candidate has not held the position in question. The district sales manager candidate for the position of regional manager has never managed a region. The controller of Company A who is a candidate for the controllership of Company B has never worked for Company B. The organization must somehow identify the knowledge, skills, and experience in the candidate's repertorie and then have the means for matching that repertoire against tbe requirements of the position to be filled.

But there is another problem: even if we are somehow able to identify required knowledge, skill, and experience and select accordingly, the candidate can fail in the new position. There appear to be some normative activities required in every organization that are not directly task related. Other terms used are "style" or "values." The individual who does not fit into the organization will carry a higher probability of failure than one who does. The problem is to find a systematic means of describing and measuring these factors as well as those of knowledge, skill, and experience.

The next problem the organization faces is locating candidates. The continuing issue of internal or external search raises a series of curious dilemmas. The organization finds no internal candidate fully qualified and goes to the outside, only to have the passed over candidate leave, go to another organiztion for that same promotion, and become successful in the competing company. Another organization brings in an external candidate only to find after a year or so that critical task skills are lacking, even though the person's prior track record was outstanding. A third organization seeking to hire the very best people searches far and wide for talent, only to experience increased turnover of competent people within their own organization. As an organization evaluates people within the system, they apparently see only weaknesses and limitations, but when looking outside they look only at successes and strengths. The organization must find a systematic and objective means for selection that does not discriminate against either the internal candidate or the external one.

Having located candidates, the organization now confronts its next challenge. It must develop some consistency in its selection processes, both in its selection methodology and the system it uses to screen potential candidates. The best available method for selection, and the one most often used, proves excessively costly: to find someone who looks good and put the person into the position for a few years to see whether he or she succeeds or fails. A better method of selection would pick the right candidate at the start. Tests, simulations, interviews, reference checks— all these are employed by management, yet they continually wonders why their selection system gives results barely better than chance. The organization also seeks a discipline for the screening process that will reliably evaluate all available candidates quickly and equitably.

Having the means to identify qualified candidates does not resolve the issue of management selection. The organization must still attract and retain managerial talent. It is certainly not enough to identify the candidate; the desired candidate must be induced to join the organization and stay with it. Each organization competes in the marketplace not only with its business competitors but with all organizations seeking talent. The most obvious problem is that of attracting entry level talent. How does an organization identify and make available the desirable consequences sought by potential candidates?

Even if the organization finds the means to attract qualified candidates and places them appropriately, it still must retain its management core. Maintaining the right people in the right assignments is not simply a matter of effective initial selection. The needs of the marketplace, technology, and the total working environment continually change the requirements of any management position. All thing being equal, it is desirable to the organization to be able to keep competent managers in positions for as long a time as possible, moving them to other positions only in the organization's best interest. The competent manager also seeks and expects upward mobility and the enhancement of his or her personal career. The organization must seek a balance between the two requirements. The issue is further complicated by social factors. How does the organization meet its managerial needs while still accepting its obligations for advancing minority members and females at a faster rate than white male managers? This is not only a social issue; it is also an economic one. Current legislation imposes upon the organization the need to be able to defend the selection decisions against accusations of discrimination. Selection methodology is in question, as are the criteria for selection.

Several of the issues relating to management selection have to do with predicting long-term potential early in the game. This is clearly a problem at the entry level, but it is also recognized as a problem in selecting middle managers. Like effective selection, accurate assessment of potential directly affects the cost of management, and in the long run results obtained by management. The organization must somehow develop an assessment methodology that can predict longer-term success. The methodology chosen must have the capability of isolating predictors of future performance and be able to apply those predictors in a consistent and systematic evaluation technique. Both the predictors and the assessment technique must reflect the needs of the organization and be congruent with whatever planning for the future the organization requires. If assessments are made following some systematic practice, the organization must decide what to do with the information. Should assessment information and management planning data be open to the members of the organization? Some members of management hold that disclosure of this kind of information will produce expectations that may not be fulfilled. They worry about the creation of "crown princes" and its impact upon those identified as having high potential, as well as the impact on other ambitious managers not so anointed. They are also concerned with those not labeled high potential, but who have value to the organization. With all of this, however, the top management of an organization seeks to resolve the issue of selecting and retaining an effective management group, a necessity to the survival and growth of the organization.

Data collection and recording is another issue for organizations today. The organization must determine what data to collect and how often. First, in the case of assessment, how often should reevaluation take place? Can the organization assume that individuals learn and change, or are the indicators of potential absolute? The organization must also discover how assessment data can be used both by the organization and the individual involved in managing career growth. The organization must decide what data are relevant to their needs. How much do they need to know about individuals? When do the needs of the organization outweigh the individual's need for privacy? What are the legal limits of inquiry? Finally, the organization must be able to determine the best sources for the data they wish to collect—not only the means and processes for collection, but the least expensive, most convenient sources for accurate and relevant information.

Management Development

If management selection is an inadequate science or an imperfect art, the processes used to train and develop managers are a costly frustration. The organization begins with the problem of figuring out how to measure the effectiveness of whatever management development processes they use. Even if the organization's top management assumes that the programs they employ do indeed train and develop managers, they find it difficult if not impossible to measure the development impact on the organization. Was it the program that led to improvement? Were there intervening variables? Are "developed" candidates more qualified than those who did not go through the organization's management development program? How does the organization determine the relationship between the cost of management development and the benefit provided by having the program or programs in place?

The second issue relating to management development is the selection of curriculum. The organization searches for some means to identify relevant content. At the bottom of this issue is the question of whether management is or is not a profession. If it is, then somewhere there must be a discipline or body of knowledge that can be acquired and that qualifies one as a manager. Or are the skills required in Organization A different from those needed in Organization B? Or—another prevalent point of view—is success as a manager dependent not on a professional body of knowledge or series of techniques, but rather on a broad knowledge of humanities and social sciences?

The third issue confronting the organization is deciding when to place individuals into the development process. Should managers be trained as managers after they are selected, or should development take place prior to assignment and directed towards a specific planned appointment? Is it more efficient to develop entry level management trainees, or should the organization invest in preparing middle managers for top management? If the organization chooses to develop at all levels, it must decide what is to be taught. Indeed the organization must decide whether or not there is a difference in required knowledge or skill between managers at lower levels in the organization and those at the top.

Another issue relates to the selection of people for development. The organization must decide who is to be developed for the best interests of the organization. With limited investment, can the organization more effectively use its available funds by developing the broad middle group, or should it concentrate on those with demonstrable high potential? One organization may decide that all exempt employees be developed towards management. Another may reserve its funding only for those who have shown success as management incumbents. Which has greater value to the organization, to enhance strengths or to correct weaknesses?

Finally, the management must obtain support throughout the organization for whatever management development takes place. The issue is integrating development processes into the organization in such a way that they are not intrusive. The organization must overcome the problem faced by the individual returning from a management development program whose supervisor tells him or her to forget that academic nonsense and get back to work! Program content and timing have strong impact on the relevance of the program for the individual participant returning to the job.

Measurement and Planning

The organization's third area of concern is the planning and measurement of management work. We assume that an organization selects or develops individuals for management positions with some purpose. Management positions are filled in order to produce some benefit to the organization. In order to measure the value of the manager, the organization must be able to objectively measure the manager's outputs, or at least the manager's direct impact on organizational outputs. If an organization chooses to evaluate its members in terms of their productivity, it must be able to resolve those issues relating to measurable productivity of managers.

If managers are to be measured, the organization must be able to identify what it is they do when they manage. Few organizations bave found it helpful to define managing in terms of "leadership," "motivation," or even terms like "directing" or "decision making." Further issues arise for tbe organization in undertaking to define how managers are to manage. These issues of values or style further cloud the organization's ability to systematically and predictably increase the probability of the organization's survival or to produce the benefits sought by its stakeholders.

As we shall see, the concern for planning and measurement of managerial work is not separable from issues of selection and managerial development. Consequently our discussions of measurement and planning will be integrated with the sections on managerial selection and development.

THE HISTORIC CONTEXT

The compelling need to resolve these issues of selection, development, and measurement leads organizations to seek workable management processes. Since the beginning of the twentieth century we have observed a continuous experimental movement towards an understandable and workable set of management disciplines. Initially the focus was on the management of activities. Scientific management approached the management process as an engineering problem. It sought to identify the best way to do the job. It assumed that if a task were correctly designed, simplified, and made efficient, the organiztion's production could be maximized. Tasks were broken down into measurable increments, and those increments were assembled into an efficient sequence. Tools were designed to enhance the efficiency of the worker. The manager was viewed as an engineer, the worker as a tool. This approach assumed a rational and willing work force with attention focused on the individual worker, with the manager as designer and overseer.

The organization of work became the next focus. Bureaucratic management examined the division of labor, moving away from the individual worker and looking at the organization as a productive system. The tools of scientific management were inadequate for this job; new ones were devised. The organization was given social structure with roles established for managers and managers of managers. Organizations were designed according to a formal logic, an abstract idea of how labor should be divided and controlled. Areas of responsibility were established with power and authority structurally defined. The linking together of tasks into jobs, jobs into departments, departments into divisions, and divisions into companies proceeded in a disciplined fashion. The military concepts of staff and line were expanded and applied to the industrial setting. The organization was viewed as static, and it was assumed that a manager once assigned to a position of responsibility and given appropriate authority had the competence to direct and control the work force. The correctness of structure and the division of labor were considered key enabling factors in an organization's survival and success.

Building on Taylor and Fayol and their followers, organizations began to focus on expertise. Technical management expanded the ideas of bureaucratic management and scientific management to address the technologies necessary to run an organization. The success of an organization appeared to need more than correct structure and division of labor. Competence was not automatic. The organization looked for the knowledge and skills needed by each of the organization's functions. It looked for learnable and transferable bodies of knowledge for production, financial control, materials management, marketing, and sales. It sought workable procedures for each function that could guide them to desired results. These bodies of knowledge were taught in our schools of business. Rather than being static, the organization was assumed to be a closed dynamic system. It was also assumed that there was a best way for its component parts to function.

It was discovered that all members of organizations did not behave rationally all of the time. The psychology of the individual performer became the next focus in the search for an effective management process. Human relations management looked at the individual with the eye of the social scientist. It looked at the role of the manager not as an engineer, bureaucrat, or technician but rather as a human relations expert. Sometimes a psychoanalytic approach was used to attempt to identify internal forces at work within the performer and with that knowledge to attempt to motivate workers to be productive. To be effective, a manager was required to consider the nonrational side of people and to become a leader.

From a concentration on the forces internal to the worker, it seemed natural enough for organizations to turn their attention to the forces internal to the organization. Organization process management provided an approach that examined the dynamics of group behavior. Learning to lead individuals did not resolve all the issues of management. The organization itself was examined as a social group or community, and the individual performer was perceived as having power in various ways within that community. The skills of managing now centered on ways to build a synergy out of separate and disparate parts. The manager was expected to also be concerned for the values of the organization, as well as for his or her own ethics. The disciplines provided by organization development (organization process management) were descriptive, with individual freedom and participation part of the definition. A successful organization leadership was defined in terms of integrating the activities of others and sharing the power to direct.

To the bewilderment of managers who have grown up with this upsurge of management discipline, there must be a sense of frustration. As the game of management has become more complicated and erudite, its impact on the productivity of the organization has been irregular and unpredictable. It was stated earlier that the interest in the technologies rooted in behaviorism does not come from agreement with its theory base. Its attraction stems from a need for workable management processes that produce predictable results. Performance management places its initial focus on the results desired by an organization and those actually obtained. As a behavioral approach, it begins by observing the behavior of individuals and groups in terms of stimulus-response and consequence. It presumes no prescriptive model, but rather tends to provide a framework for managing based upon the organization's stakeholders. Beginning with systematic inquiry, it attempts to look at managing as a set of activities that can be described and measured. Viewing the organization as an open system of changing, dynamic relationships, it tries to furnish the organization with short-term effects rather than generalized remedies. Often the remedies it does propose are simplistic, but since it makes no claims beyond that of being a workable management process, it continues to attract the attention of organizations.

SELECTION

Approaches to Selection

Traditionally there have been three approaches to selection of managers. The first approach takes the point of view that the best doer makes the best manager of doers. The second takes the position that there are a set of intrinsic traits required to have management potential. The third operates from a kind of social determinism with ethnic background, family upbringing, and school attendance as the bases for selection.

The "best doer" approach leads the organization to search out the outstanding performer for promotion to management. The best salesperson becomes the top candidate for sales manager; the outstanding accountant is promoted to accounting supervisor. This approach concludes that management success is dependent upon the manager's ability to perform the tasks of his or her subordinates. It assumes that the organization structure will provide the necessary power and support for the manager.

The intrinsic traits approach operates with a set of personality and character factors that determine management potential. These traits may be genetic or the products of early learning, but are held to be unchanging and able to discriminate between success and failure potential. The factors used include intelligence, motivation, psychological health or normalcy, and individual interests or preferences.

Those organizations that practice social determinism make selection decisions based on the idea that if the "right kind" of person from the "right background," a graduate of the "right school," is selected, success is assured. Prior to the Civil Rights Act of 1964, this meant that an organization tended to have a management group from the same alumni club and fraternity as its top managers. At the extreme, the organization also recognized the need for a "Jewish bookkeeper, a "German Engineer," and an "Irish public relations manager." This approach still lingers, with interest in Harvard MBAs in one area of the country and Stanford graduates in another.

The systems used to select managers were shaped by these traditional approaches. Boss nomination has been the most commonly used system of selection, and it remains in common practice today. The factory manager with an opening for a production superintendent chooses from among his or her general supervisiors, hopefully selecting the best practitioner. This approach reflects the best doer as best manager. In similar fashion, should a manager go from Organization A to Organization B in a similar or higher capacity, he or she looks to his old organization to fill positions in the new one. Selection based on seniority is another commonly practiced system. Where the alumni club is important, tenure and loyalty are also key selection factors. Promotion becomes inevitable in time, unless the individual is obviously counterproductive. As we observe organizations and their selection systems, we find seniority a principal factor at the lowest and highest levels of management.

Organizations with a more contemporary point of view of the selection process tend towards task-based or certification-based systems. With a test-based system, the organization seeks to objectively select on the basis of those intrinsic traits or factors it feels necessary to insure success. Objectivity is insured by employing an outside testing agency or practicing psychologist. Sometimes initial nomination is made by the boss from among his or her most senior practitioners. In order to be selected, however, one must "pass the test." A certification-based system goes one step further with roots in all three of the traditional approaches to management selection. Its decisions are based upon some certification attesting to management capability. This is most frequently carried out at the entry level, where the organization looks for a Masters degree in business administration. Other certification may be required in the middle ranks, particularly in the professional or quasi-professional functions such as finance, personnel, or engineering. In this way a controllership may be dependent upon holding a CPA designation.

A Behavioral Alternative

In order to describe a behavioral approach to selection and the selection systems derived from that approach, it is useful to compare the assumptions with some historical assumptions about management. Historically we have assumed that there is a conceptual nature of management, that an ideal model of a manager exists. This concept of a manager includes a listing of management functions such as planning, organizing, controlling, coordinating, communicating, and motivating. It also includes a listing of the internal characteristics of a manager, such as being achievement-oriented, self-starting, objective, and decisive. The behavioral approach assumes that there is no conceptual nature of management. It also assumes that the only way to derive a model of management is to observe the actual behavior of managers. This difference in assumptions tends to lead to descriptive rather than normative selection criteria.

A second difference comes from the traditional assumption that the prediction of future success as a manager is essentially subjective. It is the belief that management is an art, and that artistic talent cannot be measured or compared. The behaviorist assumes that the prediction of future management success can be made objectively. Therefore, the behavioral approach tends to look for data-based criteria. Following this is the traditional assumption that management must be taken as a whole, that it cannot be broken into discrete elements or behavior. This assumption leads to the conclusion that all managers are the same. The behavior of a supervisor is the same as the behavior exhibited by a plant manager or the president of a company. The behaviorist assumes that each position or set of tasks has its own specific performance or selection criteria. Skills appropriate in one position are inappropriate in another. The behaviorist also assumes that specific behavior can be identified and that managing is not holistic, but rather a set of discrete measurable behavior.

Historically we have assumed that a set of general attributes is required for all managers. This leads to the notion that a manager is a manager is a manager. Thus the criteria for selecting a general sales manager in Organization A are the same as those in Organization B. The practitioner following a behavioral approach assumes that the behavior required of a manager is culture bound, and that the criteria required for selecting managers varies from organization to organization.

Perhaps the most important difference in assumption is the departure from the historical notion that there is a cognitive profile of a manager. We have assumed that an individual can be selected for a management position based upon his or her knowledge. The behaviorist assumes instead that there is an operational profile of a manager. The behavioral approach is less concerned with what a candidate needs to know in order to fill a position than with what a successful incumbent is required to do. To a behaviorist, knowledge or skill acquisition is relevant to the degree that that knowledge or skill is demonstrably required for the performance of the manager's tasks. Thus interpersonal skills are relevant as a selection criteria only when their application has been proven necessary, and then the specific skills must be related to the specific situations in which they will be used.

Because of its assumptions, the behavioral approach seeks to identify the behavior required of a successful incumbent in the position under consideration, and then to identify similar behavior in the repertoire of the candidates. The more closely the candidate's past behavior compares to the required behavior, the more likely he or she is to be successful. Historically, past performance is always considered to be a factor in predicting future performance. To the behaviorist, past performance is the only predictor of future performance.

ACTION PLAN: SELECTION

Using a behavioral approach, we will now examine selection as a system. This system has three elements: selection criteria, the nomination system, and the screening and selection system. Given our assumptions about observable behavior, data-based criteria, and specificity, a systematic inquiry is required to develop usable selection critera.

Step 1: Selection Criteria

The investigation begins with the position to be filled. The objective is to obtain a descriptive profile of the position against which candidates can be compared. We begin with those results expected by the organization if the position is filled and the standards of performance met. Results are those benefits derived by the organization from having tasks performed. They are the final results of activities and outputs that can be objectively measured and have value in terms of the organization's survival or growth. For the organization that intends to provide its stakeholders with a return on their investment, the results will be economic. Nonprofit organizations may seek other than economic results, usually in terms of specified social or personal benefits. In any case, the results to be derived from having the position filled ultimately determine the activities to be performed and the outputs to be produced.

Let us develop a descriptive profile for a regional sales manager of a field sales organization. We will discover that there are three primary results, all of which contribute to the larger organization's total goal. The first of these can be expressed in terms of dollar volume of sales, either in relation to an objective plan or as a percentage of growth against prior performance in the region to be managed. The second outcome is gross margin expressed either as dollars or as a percent of sales. Finally, cost is identified either as dollars or a percentage of gross margin. These three results combined contribute to the organization's overall net profit outcome, and from that to a return on investment for its stakeholders. But what about the sales training manager of this national sales force? What results are derived from that position? From the point of view of performance management, the answer is quite clear: sales representatives who meet or exceed their volume, margin, and expense standards. In each case, results define the result of having the position filled.

With results defined, we examine the outputs necessary to produce the results. Outputs are the measurable product of activity. The regional sales manager, e.g., must produce a number of outputs if the desired results are to be achieved: purchase orders from existing accounts, receivables, payments, contracts with new accounts, and so on. Determining outputs for the sales training manager is more difficult. His or her outputs relate to the performance of the sales representatives that have undergone training processes. Thus outputs are determined by the performance of the sales representatives in the field. Outputs provide the objective standards of performance against which an incumbent will be measured. Outputs also determine the activities that need to be performed. An individual who correctly performs all of these activities needed to produce all required outputs will fully meet standards of the position. The regional sales manager position will include such activities as the assignment of sales representatives to territories, monitoring their call performance and providing them with feedback, making calls, writing orders, presenting programs, allocating expense budgets, and so on. The sales training manager position will include such activities as deciding on training schedules, evaluating instructional designs, purchasing outside resources, and so on.

From activities we move to an analysis of the knowledge, skills, and experiences most needed to correctly perform the activities. A regional sales manager should probably be able to observe a sales call by a representative and evaluate that person's performance of that activity. He or she should probably also know how to give feedback based on his or her observations. The sales training manager should know how to tell the difference between a good training design and a poor one.

We now have the ingredients of a descriptive profile for a position to be filled. We have identified results, specified outputs, described activities, and listed the knowledge, skills, and experience needed for those activities. All of the data collected has been related to desired results. We can have a reasonable degree of certainty that if the candidate selected has the knowledge, skills, and experience we have identified, the activities will be correctly performed, the outputs produced, and the results realized. Our inquiry will require a range of data sources. Data relating to results and outputs will come from upper levels of management and from the administrative systems they maintain to inform them about organizational performance, such as divisional or departmental profit and loss statements. These profit and loss statements, together with relevant performance appraisal records, will provide information about the performance of current and past incumbents so that we can verify that the desired results and required outputs are obtainable. In order to obtain information about activities, we will identify successful performers and through observation or interview draw data relating to the activities they perform. If we are careful, we will be able to discriminate between the activities performed by successful incumbents and those performed by unsuccessful ones. As we profile the position, we will be cataloging these key discriminators. In the same manner, we will examine historical information relating to successful and unsuccessful incumbents and through observation and interview gather data about the knowledge, skills, and experience most probably needed.

One area of our profile has not been covered as yet. We have examined and described only task-related criteria; that is, we have looked at those skills and activities required to produce a specified set of outputs. Nontask-related behavior may also affect the success or failure of an incumbent. For example, we may discover that in Organization A, regional sales managers who verbally and openly criticize the behavior or competence of their superiors will fail. Behavior that conforms to the values of an organization will be required if a candidate is to be successful once placed. This behavior will also be specific to given positions within an organization, as well as specific to the organization. Gathering data relating to nontask behavior is often difficult. Management is often reluctant to expose biases and values when they cannot be related to on-the-job performance. This aspect of our descriptive profile cannot be ignored, however. Our selection criteria will include all required task activities as well as critical nontask behavior and will list the knowledge, skills, or experience required to correctly perform the activities or exhibit the needed nontask behavior.

Step 2: Nomination Systems

In performance management, nomination systems are designed or selected to produce qualified candidates in the shortest time and at the lowest cost. Since the quality and completeness of selection criteria affect the efficiency of the nomination system, the development of selection criteria is the most important aspect of a selection system. From the selection criteria, jobs are identified in which potential candidates would most likely have built a repertoire of skills and knowledge that closely match those identified. The primary focus of the search and recruitment elements of the nomination system is potential candidates within the organization. External search is secondary.

Given a clear and complete set of selection criteria, open bidding becomes one of the more effective nomination systems available. The potential candidate reviews his or her own skills and experience repertoire against the criteria list and self-nominates. This means that selection criteria must be exposed to anyone wishing to enter into candidacy. A second nomination system in regular use employs a continually updated resumé file. The resumé or profile is constructed as a matching file to position criteria. Using some kind of data processing system, resumés are scanned against selection criteria, and qualified candidates are pulled automatically for further screening. This system requires less disclosure of criteria to the work force, but it requires a systematic updating of the profile information in a form that permits easy retrieval and matching to selection criteria. Both systems required specific and complete selection criteria.

External search is by its nature more generalized and less efficient.

Matching repertoire to criteria requires more inference, since reliable data is more difficult to collect. Therefore, from a behavioral point of view, we cannot expect to be very effective in predicting success or failure in the new position.

Step 3: Selection System

A number of methods are employed by performance management in its screening and selection systems. A guiding principle in choosing selection methodology is the method's ability to obtain and use objective and relevant behavioral data. We look first for evidence that a candidate has demonstrated a required skill in a similar position or assignment. For example, a skill requirement for a middle manager of a manufacturing facility might be evaluation of a production variance and deciding on corrective action. There are a number of positions that could demonstrate this skill, including production manager, shift superintendent, production control manager, and industrial engineering manager. All of these positions offer the opportunity to apply this specific type of decision-making skill. Oddly enough, the first line supervisor on the midnight shift will probably apply it more frequently than the production manager three levels above.

The second step is to look for demonstration of a skill that is analogous to one required in the position. A field sales manager must be able to review, evaluate, and provide corrective feedback to field sales representatives on the efficiency of their territory coverage. A sales representative who efficiently covers assigned territory may be demonstrating a skill analogous to the one required of the manager. We guess that some of the elements of reviewing and correcting are present if the individual is independently managing the territory. From a behavioral point of view, there are some dangers in selecting on the basis of analogous skills. In this example we will want to support our selection decision by identifying the candidate's demonstration of giving feedback and in discriminating between effective and ineffective territory coverage.

Where direct evidence is unavailable, performance management turns to simulation as a means of demonstrating skill. At this third level, the assessment center process can be employed as a selection method. The use of simulation is most frequently made at the first level of supervision and for top management. At the entry level it is often the best method, because candidates have had little opportunity to demonstrate required skills. It is useful at higher levels in the organization for skill applications that are unique. For example, a vice president of manufacturing maybe required to decide on plant location or relocation. Although the organization requires its chief manufacturing executive to make this decision correctly 100 percent of the time, it is a skill infrequently employed. It also requires the ability to analyze complex and confusing data. Simulation may be the only way to identify the presence or absence of this skill.

The fourth method employed in a selection system is, in performance management, considered the least effective: the selection interview. At best, an interview is inferential. That is, the candidate is asked to respond to questions, the answers to which will describe rather than demonstrate behavior. Even here, given clear and complete selection criteria, the interviewer can develop data that might not be available from any other method. Obviously, when the candidate comes from outside the organization, very little more verifiable information is available. Even using the extension of the interview, the reference check, the information obtained is inferential.

Performance management tends to provide the organization with reliable data-based decision making. It therefore tends to reject selection information that cannot be supported by observable behavior or that does not relate to specific performance requirements of the position under consideration. Further, it does not usually bring about decisions based upon a "best" candidate, but rather tries to identify the most cost-effective qualified candidate. Decisions relating to the selection of managers are approached in the same manner as decisions relating to the physical, technical, or financial resources of the organization.

A critical element in the development of a reliable and cost-effective system is career path analysis. The objective of career path analysis is to identify progression paths that insure that candidates acquire skills needed for success in positions. Job assignments are seen both as a means for a candidate to demonstrate skills and as a means to acquire new skills. Career path analysis requires the mapping of historical successions and the development of required skill repertoires for each position. Behaviorally, career path analysis is more than simply identifying the historical lines of progression in an organization. The analysis also examines specific skills, position by position, both vertically and hoizontally within the organization. We do not assume that the only career path to a chief marketing executive is through sales. Frequently the array of skills needed for this position can be acquired in other paths. Further, the position by position analysis permits us to identify more cost-effective progression paths, particularly when the needs of the organization are in a state of change. By using a data-based performance and skill profile, new positions can be defined with some accuracy. The same methods used in developing criteria for existing positions can be used to define new positions or modify existing ones. It can also affect organization structure and relationships by developing new ways of integrating and coordinating management skills.

MANAGEMENT DEVELOPMENT

So far we have discussed performance criteria as the basis of behaviorally based selection. It is also the basis of a performance centered management development system. Performance management considers management development as a strategy for making more qualified candidates available for selection.

Traditional Approaches

In traditional approaches to the development of managers, there have been three points of view. First is the notion that management's development is really a process of natural selection—"Cream rises to the top of the bottle." This attitude of course precludes any planned or systematic management development. It is still a prevalent attitude.

A second traditional approach views management as a science taught in school. In this view, a bachelor's or master's degree in business administration is the correct prerequisite for one's entire career. Going to extremes, it views midcareer developmental actions as irrelevant and wasteful in time and money. Often this approach goes hand in hand with the idea of natural selection.

A third traditional approach to management development is that it is a matter of experience. It rejects planned development actions, because the only way to learn how to manage is to do it, and doing it takes time. Organizations that place a great deal of stress upon tenure are demonstrating the view that managing is a matter of experience.

Against these traditional views, larger organizations have attempted to create and maintain organized activities directed towards the development of management talent. Many of the organizations that have undertaken systematic management development have found it disturbing that there is a lack of recognizable correlation between participation in a formal development program and success in performance. The chances of success or failure on a new job appear no different for the person who went to the executive development program than for the person who did not. There also appears to be no difference between the impact of an academic program and one developed within the organization.

The search for an effective approach providing qualified candidates for management positions has been clouded by several issues. Disagreement exists as to whether actions should be taken primarily to improve performance on a present job or to prepare for future positions. Is the manager trained or developed after appointment or in preparation for appointment? Are the actions taken to provide skill acquisition, or should the actions provide processes for personal growth? Considerable disagreement exists as to what skills should be taught and whether management is indeed a repertoire of acquirable skills. Another major issue is that of leadership. Considerable time and effort both in the research community and by practitioners has been expended in trying to define and describe leadership, either because being a good leader is critical to being a manager, or because management is itself defined in terms of leadership. It remains a major issue. The questions arising out of the issue of definition and content are made more complicated by the difficulty of measuring management development results. If the purpose of management development activity is to enhance personal growth or build leadership qualities, then reasonable measurement is impossible. If, however, the organization derives some outcome from the investment in the development of managers, the need for measurement is imperative, if only to evaluate the efficiency of development actions.

A Behavioral Alternative

Since performance management considers management development as a strategy for making more qualified candidates available for selection, its overall goal is the design of a system in which learning processes related to management or executive development can be made more efficient and more effective. Increased efficiency requires development activities significantly less costly than acquiring candidates from outside the organization. It also means a system that can provide candidates when and where they are needed, with some assurance that once placed the new incumbent will be successful at a rate greater than chance.

As in the case of management selection, it is useful to compare some of the historical assumptions about management development with the assumptions of performance management. Historically we have assumed that there is a set of content that applies to all manager learners. The set may be generic: planning, organizing, directing, controlling, coordinating. It may be functional: finance, production, marketing, personnel, engineering. Or it may be a set of processes: problem solving, decision making, interpersonal relations, motivation. No matter how the set is put together, the assumption is the same—that there is a content that all managers need to learn. A behavioral point of view holds that most of what a manager-learner needs to acquire is unique to that person and to the situation in which the person will be placed. There is no set of content that is generally appropriate or relevant. It may be as yet that management is not a profession in the sense that there is a definable discipline. There appears instead to be a wide array of content, some of which is relevant at one time for one person. What a developing manager needs to learn and the sequence in which he or she needs to learn it varies with the specific criteria that will be used to select that individual for a given position.

The second assumption is that decisions relating to development activities are best made by experts. Most of the time the experts are in the training or development functions of an organization. Sometimes the organization looks to experts in an academic institution. Performance management assumes instead that decisions relating to development activities are best made by the participant. The person with the greatest interest in his or her career development is that individual. Experience also seems to indicate that the person being developed has the most accurate notions about the organization's short-term future estimate of his or her personality. The person being developed also appears to have the most accurate information about the specific skill and knowledge needed. These are rarely seen as generic or functional, but rather as discrete "how to" needs.

The third assumption relates to the organization's model of career progress. It has been assumed that every useful individual views career growth in the same way as does the organization. The managers who make decisions relating to development assume that every successful performer judged to have potential for growth wants to follow a progression pattern congruent with the one the organization feels is right and best. As decisions are made about management development, the organization follows its norms as though they were the only possible views. Other views are not considered valid or useful to the organization.

Performance management assumes that each person views his or her own growth in a unique way. Each individual creates a unique model of goals and growth. Although this model is modified by the person's experience with organizational norms, it remains unique to the individual and to his or her situation. Frequently the developing manager's views are in conflict with the organization. This is the sort of conflict faced by the "high potential" sales manager, who views his or her growth in terms of success as a professional leading a growing and effective marketing force, while the organization has set up norms that will only permit rewards and advancement to someone who wants general management.

The fourth assumption is that the participant must undergo formal educational experiences in order to be developed. Management development activities are assumed to require a program. Development programs, like other educational programs, have carefully chosen content framed in a well-designed medium supplied to the learner in the proper sequence. The contrary assumption is that development is a continuous process with many elements; behavior is constantly being modified, and change is inevitable. For many manager learners, formal programs are unnecessary.

A corollary to this assumption has been that educational experiences are different from other kinds of experience. One must learn to manage apart from the working environment, preferably in an environment especially set aside for learning how to manage. With this goes the idea that work interferes with learning about management, adding the need to prevent the contact with work situations. Performance management takes the position that learning experiences are effective when integrated with other relevant activities. Learning must be a normal activity, as much a part of an individual's job as any other element. The appropriate linking of behavior and consequences can only be achieved in the working environment.

Management developers have historically assumed that the primary influence on an individual's career growth is what the person knows. A person is entered into a management development program because of performance or because of anticipated performance. The program is then expected to produce a developed person ready for additional responsibilities. The individual's superiors, peers, and subordinates are not expected to affect the person's growth, nor are task assignments, resources, or work environment. In opposition, performance management assumes that the amount of knowledge an individual holds has little direct influence on career growth. Completion of a course or program rarely influences a management to give a person additional responsibilities. The task being performed and the perceptions of the individual's superiors, peers, and subordinates are the primary influences on his or her career growth. Indeed knowledge about managing as opposed to technical knowledge about specialized functions may inhibit career movement. It is not always helpful to appear smarter than one's superiors or peers except in technical areas.

These assumptions and those made about instructional methodology profoundly affect the way in which developmental activities are designed and implemented. Each set of assumptions builds a set of conditions for development action, which may or may not support career growth or suitability for a specific position.

Instructional Methodology

Historically the first condition that occurs is a formal curriculum, essentially academic in nature. The curriculum is imposed upon participants with rigid time and format constraints. The participant is selected by some mechanism such as time on the job, boss nomination, performance evaluation, or level attained in the organization. He or she is advised of the program to be attended and the start and stop date of the program. The participant arrives and participates in the set curriculum and then returns to the job.

A second condition that proceeds from the historically held assumptions is a lack of influence by the participant on his or her development. The experts have chosen the content, and the instructors who deliver it make all the key decisions relating to the development process. The participant may choose not to acquire the planned learning, but most people selected would perform the activities required by the program. Each participant will undertake the same educational experience as the others without prior assessment of needs or consideration of the specific position for which the participant is being nominated.

Failure to provide a means for integrating what is learned in the program with the participants' "real world" is a third condition. Separation begins by taking the participant to a classroom setting. It is likely that the class will be located some distance from the participant's work place. It will be designed for the purpose of education and for the efficiency and convenience of the instructors. It will contain the best and newest artifacts of the education business. The curriculum followed and the media used will necessarily be generalized enough to build a homogeneous classroom out of the diverse individuals present. If noncompany resources are used, such as a university, trade association, or commercial firm, the materials will be drawn from the instructor's repertoire, and will be abstract enough or simple enough to lead diverse participants to a common conclusion through common activities. If the program is run "in company" and the materials drawn from actual company situations, they are usually modified to match the instructor's views of what the materials should teach a homogeneous group.

The fourth condition is the lack of relevant feedback and reinforcement to the participant. Because the candidate is there to learn, he or she is expected to be learning what the instructor believes is correct. If the participant fails to learn or fails to demonstrate what he or she is supposed to learn when on the job, something is wrong with the learner. The more sophisticated management educator may attribute the learner's failure to something in the work environment. Either the job assignment is wrong, or the supervisor does not support application of what is learned. The management educator in this situation sees his or her responsibility as limited to the delivery of learning. Failure to receive it or to apply it is not a problem of the development program.

Finally, there is a lack of relevant feedback to the participant's organization. The manager or managers who will make decisions about the candidate's promotability get little useful information about the changes brought about in the program and no information to assist on the job. The management development program is a separate experience and is not related to other activities.

The second set of assumptions, those made in performance management, result in a very different set of conditions. These assumptions, together with a behaviorally based learning technology, tend to produce specific and relevant skill acquisition.

First, the orientation is nonacademic. A broad range of activities are used as learning media. Formal academic programs are part of an individual's development, but they are specific to the participant's needs. For example, one individual will participate in a short seminar on the use of financial data for decision making in a manufacturing operation, while a colleague is attending a workshop in selling price analysis and its application to product manufacture. Special projects and participation in task groups are frequent developmental activities. Temporary job assignments are employed. Two elements are integral to this nonacademic orientation. First, specific learning objectives are set for every developmental activity, and some sort of learning or information mapping process is used. A learning map describes the knowledge and skills and performance standards judged as required for a specific career objective, relevant to the participant's work and time constraints. At best the mapping process is formal, but even when informal is recognized as an integral element of the development system.

The second condition is the active involvement of the participant and the participant's supervisor in every part of the development process. The involvement is continous and planned. Decisions as to objectives, content, scheduling, and measures are made by the participant and the supervisor.

Participation in this part of the process by individuals responsible for management selection and development is frequent.

There is a means for the participant to specify his or her own learning requirment. The learner is able to describe the performance or knowledge required to meet the specific goal in mind, plus the kinds of content and the skills that must be acquired to achieve the performance described. Performance criteria and selection criteria are available, which accurately specify what is required of a successful incumbent. There is information available about success and failure factors. Accurate data is available about realistic career paths and career decision points. There is also a means for the participant to learn how to use the knowledge and skills, evaluate programs, and set learning objectives.

Finally, the learner's career goal and learning objectives are endorsed by the organization. The individual or group who will make selection decisions for future assignments also believes that the performance or knowledge specifications described by the participant are indeed required and desirable.

ACTION PLAN: MANAGEMENT DEVELOPMENT

To satisfy these conditions, the management development system requires that four elements be in place and working. First, there must be a set of consistent processes and procedures for identifying learning needs in relation to the candidate's current repertoire and selection criteria. Second, there must be a planning system that integrates development activities with work force plans, organization requirements, and individual needs. Third, the system requires processes for managing developmental activities, identifying and evaluating resources, and providing learning assistance to the participant. Finally, there must be a set of effective feedback and evaluation processes both for the participant and the organization.

Step 1: Needs Assessment

Three types of data are required for needs assessment. First, information relating to the participant's career path up to the point of the current assessment is used to examine prior career decisions, success or failure factors, changing directions, prior learning acquisitions, and current learning needs. The data can be obtained in various ways, but commonly is developed through structured interviews or through self-administered questionnaires. The second kind of data needed relates to the participant's current performance. An objectives-based performance appraisal system is probably the best source of information. Historical performance data stored electronically or manually is helpful in providing information about skill acquisition and skill repertoire. Both of these kinds of data focus on the individual, the first with the person's career decisions and personal growth, and the second with the person's observed performance. These data are combined to form the profile used for skill matching and management selection decisions. The third kind of data focuses on the organization. Part of this information describes work force needs and forecasts; another part consists of the organization "rules of the game," that is, those policies and procedures that accurately present the way in which an organization will cope with its people and their development.

These data are combined and used to identify the most productive career path alternatives for the individual being developed. It enables the participant to specify his or her existing skill repertoire and identify the skill, knowledge, and experience needs that must be satisfied in the new set of selection criteria.

After completing this analysis process, the participant should be able to make short-term decisions about what to learn, how to learn it, and when to take action. The final step in needs assessment is a means for getting the organization's concurrence to the participant's decisions.

Step 2: Planning

The second element required is a system that will integrate the work force and organization planning with the development activities. There is little hope of success in creating and maintaining a development system unless changes in organization and work force requirements are known both to the development function and to the individuals being developed. In many cases, changes in organization structure are not communicated or put together with work force plans. As a result, there is little relationship between the kinds of development actions going on and the real needs of the organization. Some sort of succession charting that will bring to the surface probable promotions, transfers, retirements, terminations, and so on on a regular basis is probably the most effective way of integrating work force planning with development. Unless the organization is very large, a manual system is probably quite adequate for this purpose.

Step 3: Managing Developmental Activities

The third element consists of systems for managing the developmental activities witb focus on identifying resources and providing learning assistance for the participants. The primary objective of this system is to provide learning experiences tailored to the individual needs of the participants, not the design and implementation of formalized programs. This means that the major effort is in the identification of both internal and external resources and providing the learner with access to those resources.

Step 4: Feedback and Evaluations

The fourth element has as its objective the most important piece of the process, that of providing information to the participant and to the organization about how well that participant is doing and what skills are being acquired. It is probable that even if no other element of the development were present, effective feedback and evaluation would result in more qualified candidates for available positions. There are a number of ways this element might work. Formal and regular development reviews are probably the simplest approach. During regular meetings with the participant, the participant's supervisor and some coordinator review progress and evaluate skill level. Another possibility is a formal record of progress maintained by the participant or the organization, which is regularly reviewed with the supervisor and made available for selection purposes.

Since the primary objective of management development is insuring an adequate supply of qualified candidates for positions that will become open in the future, integration with both business planning and organization planning processes is important. Both the operational and strategic plans of the organization must be considered. Selection and development criteria are affected by the organization's operational planning, since the accomplishment or failure to accomplish short-term results dramatically affects the performance standards established for each position in the organization. In similar fashion, the organization's longer range strategic plans project changes in the makeup of the existing positions and establishment of new ones as the organization considers future technological change or changes in its marketing environment. The interface between the organization's business planning system and its selection and development systems is in its organization planning process. As business operational and strategic plans are formulated, they are translated into positions, jobs, and tasks. If organization plans consist of chart models of the organization without establishing performance or selection criteria for its projections, those plans have little utility. In a performance management approach, organization planning develops performance models for the organization. These performance models define the specific performance criteria required to meet the organization's operational and strategic plans.

The performance management approach takes organization planning a step further. Not only is the future organization designed in terms of performance requirements, but the performance requirements are defined in terms of individual performance standards, objectives, and goals. An effective "management by objectives" system is implicit in any application of performance management. Whether the MBO is based upon upward participation or downward direction is not critical. What is critical is that short and long term performance requirements are accurately and clearly defined in terms of individual performance criteria.

Once an effective set of standard-setting mechanisms are in place, performance management looks to the organization's processes for performance feedback. In the behavior model, feedback is required by the performer in order to compare current behavior to desired behavior. Performance management extends this idea to the provision of feedback to the organization, so that it may compare both individual and total organization performance against its planned goals and objectives. Annual performance appraisals become summary comparisons of actual performance to required performance for the purpose of identifying developmental needs. Periodic performance reviews become the primary feedback medium. The primary purpose of the periodic review is to provide information that will permit closer approximations to desired performance at a time when those adjustments can still be made. End of year appraisals do not satisfy the requirements of usable feedback. Nor does the annual appraisal provide the organization with timely and useful feedback for this reason. Performance management systems usually include a systematic feedback process, which provides information both about individual performance and about unit or organization performance at frequent intervals during an operational year.

SYSTEM MAINTENANCE

A major concern of any behavioral approach to management is the way in which the organization distributes consequences. The selection and development system described here requires considerable investment in time by the participants, superiors, and those individuals in the organization who will provide informational or developmental resources. Performance management searches out and implements positive consequences for those involved. A number of potentially negative consequences ensue for a manager whose subordinate is participating in a development process, and especially if that subordinate is selected for another position. First of all, the manager will lose the services of that subordinate from time to time while he or she undergoes developmental programs, and finally, when the manager loses the person, he or she will have to go through the process of selecting a replacement and then spend the time to integrate that new individual into the department. Positive consequences for the boss can result if the development and promotion of subordinates is made a measurable and rewardable part of his or her performance criteria.

For all of those involved in the development and selection system, measurable performance standards are established, feedback is periodically provided, and a recognizable portion of their rewards are based upon those elements of their job. For the participants in the development activities, the long-term positive consequence is of course assignment to a desired position. Unfortunately, this does not always happen at the right time, and failure to achieve it appears to have a strong negative impact both upon the individual candidate and other potential candidates. The solution offered by performance management is to provide positive consequences for becoming qualified. These interim rewards range from a minimum of public recognition through special assignments to dollar reward. In summary, the performance management approach requires that consequences be systematically designed and provided to maintain the selection and development systems. The activities required to make this system work will be executed only if the individuals involved are rewarded. The organization cannot be the sole beneficiary.

Comments

The selection and development processes are part of a single system integrated with the organization's management processes. Selection criteria match the organization's performance criteria. Just as performance management demands that individual performance standards be measurable, it also requires that selection and development criteria be measurable and in the same terms. In the same way, performance feedback must be provided, both to the organization and to those involved in the maintenance of the selection and development system. Finally, the organization's consequence management processes must not only support desired task performance but must also reinforce the maintenance of the selection and development system.

Performance management requires that the organization's culture support the activities executed. Thus organizational development actions are centered on developing a set of values that support performance rather than on a predetermined social model. The values of the organization support and reinforce behavior that produces the results desired by and planned for the organization and its stakeholders.

SUMMARY

Performance management is a systematic application of processes based on behavioral research to human performance in an organization. When these processes are applied to managerial performance, three areas of concern are attacked: management selection, management training and development, and managing the task performance of incumbents. These three concerns cannot be treated as separate systems. They are not merely linked, but rather are integrated as a single system designed and managed to produce planned results, or benefits, to the stakeholders of the organization.

From known results, expectation can be established. Whether in the form of goals, objectives, standards, or describable behavior, the establishment of expectation for each performer is the first positive action of performance management. In management selection, it provides the criteria for selection and the means for matching candidates' repertoires to position requirements. In management development, it provides the means for identifying skill, knowledge, and experience needs. In managing incumbents, it provides the basis of performance evaluation and the means of identifying performance discrepancies.

Management selection is a systematic process for identifying candidates whose repertoires most closely match established expectations. Screening is done against prepared criteria. Screening first searches out prior demonstration of skills that meet criteria, and next demonstration of analagous skills. Failing these, it may seek skill demonstration in simulation, or by interview or reference check. In any case, matching is done against known criteria.

Management development is a strategy for providing qualified candidates for management assignments. It is, in effect, a recruitment system. Setting performance expectations remains the first positive action. Development needs are identified by matching repertoire against criteria and identifying voids or shortfalls.

Management development also requires a congruence between development actions and organization requirements. Organization planning and management development must be linked so that the repertoires being acquired are those the organization can use.

This link between organization needs and indiviudals' repertoires is extended to task management. The planning of management work, monitoring of activities, and the measurement and rewards of performance are based on outcome, expectation, and demonstration. Results are identified; individual performance expectations are established; task activities are audited, and interim feedback is given to the performer; performance checkpoints are set, and performance is reviewed when checkpoints are reached. Finally, the performer is rewarded by the accomplishment of his or her expectations.

20

Organization-Wide Intervention

RONALD E. ZEMKE

Performance Research Associates

and

JOHN W. GUNKLER

Wilson Learning Corporation

The principles and techniques of organizational behavior management have proved an effective methodology for directing and changing the behavior of individuals, small groups, and organizational subsystems. In our experience, it is both possible and practical to treat whole organizations as single entities, using the principles and techniques of organizational behavior management that have proved so useful in suborganizational contexts. There are three prerequisites to treating organizations as single systems:

1. The development of a measurement system that tracks desired organizational results, but that at the same time provides information that can be confirming or corrective of individual and subgroup performance.

2. The development of a system for making organizational performance and outcome information available to subgroups and individuals.

3. The establishment of contingent relationships between organizational results (outcomes) and reinforcement for individual behavior.

These key principles are largely prefigured in the literature on the effects of organizational feedback and token reinforcement systems. Nadler (1976) and Nadler et al. (1976) have demonstrated that collecting and feeding back performance data to members of an organization can be an effective approach to changing organizational performance at a variety of levels. Feedback has been associated with changes in employee attitudes and perceptions of the organization (Klein et al., 1971), with changes in specific and observable behavior (Johnston et al., 1978), and with desired organizational results (Emmert, 1978).

Feedback that includes an implied goal has more impact on work performance than explicit goal setting and is as effective as feedback plus explicit goal setting (Dockstader et al., 1977). But the literature also shows that feedback alone is usually much less effective than feedback combined with other organizational intervention techniques (Annett, 1969).

Some of the intervention techniques that have been shown to be highly effective combined with the systematic feedback of performance data include: token reinforcers (see the seminal work by Birnbrauer and Lawler, 1964; Ayllon and Azrin, 1965, 1968; Phillips, 1968; Hunt and Zimmerman, 1969; Henderson and Scoles, 1970; and the review by Kazdin and Bootzin, 1972); social approval (Atthowe and Krasner, 1968; Locke, 1969; Kazdin and Klock, 1973; but also see Quay and Hunt, 1965, for a reminder that social approval isn't for everybody).

It is logical, then, that most reported successful organizational behavior management applications tend to be multiple intervention techniques. Komaki et al. (1977) have shown that job description and goal clarification, self-monitoring, posted feedback, and time off can affect worker presence, customer assistance, and maintenance of display products in a retail store. Bourdon (1977) reports increasing employee attendance, efficiency, and product quality in a textile factory using job description clarification, goal setting, training of supervisors in organizational behavior management, a token economy, social reinforcers, and public display of performance data. Connellan and Martin (1981) report substantial change in employee attendance, machine down time, scrap rates, product quality, customer satisfaction, and job satisfaction measures in the Fisher Body Fleetwood plant of General Motors through the use of performance feedback, goal-setting

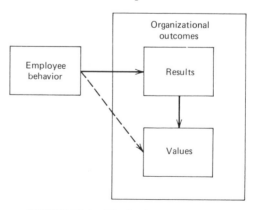

FIGURE 20-1. The business proposition.

activities, a social reinforcement strategy, supervisory training, and team-building training. And Luthans and Schweizer (1979) showed the impact of contingent time off, feedback, and social reinforcers on productivity, error rate, and quality in a small factory.

We wish to describe how an actual organization-wide intervention works. There is a simple model that may be helpful in understanding the principles. We call this model "the business proposition" (see Figure 20-1), because in any organization there is someone who carries it around in their head as their understanding of how the organization should look when it is functioning well. The business proposition involves several inferential links: "If people PERFORM in a certain manner, we will achieve certain organizational RESULTS, and they will return a profit or VALUE to us." Into the inferential category go both the link between results and value, and the link between behavior and results. Some managers skip a factor and carry around a model that links how people perform directly with profits or value. Others focus only on the results-values link.

As Zemke and Larsen (1981) have discovered, this business proposition is often the standard by which senior management consciously or unconsciously recognizes and rewards the actions of middle managers. Whether those actions actually lead to organizational success, or value, is less important (because it is not made immediately evident) than whether the actions conform to the business proposition (i.e., produce the results). So if the business proposition is that "If we make steel-reinforced buggy whips better than anyone else, we can sell millions of them at 7¢ (12 for 79¢)," then the message to subsystem managers is clear: You had better find ways to produce the best quality steel-reinforced buggy whips you possibly can! Eventually the business proposition will be tested by the exigencies of the marketplace (we'll actually try to peddle the buggy whips), and those who managed by it will either keep their jobs or be looking for other work.

Most of us who work in organizational behavior management spend our time helping subsystem managers understand and actualize the roles they are to play within the business proposition. We don't usually have the luxury of evaluating that proposition. But if it fails, the line managers won't be the only ones looking for work. In an organization-wide system, the key is to make organizational results and their values more immediately evident and usable. Then we can use measures of those results as referents for managing the behavior of employees. This way, either the adequacy of the business proposition will become evident, or employee behavior will correct for its errors. Let's look at an example.

CASE STUDY: AN ORGANIZATIONAL-RESULTS-REFERENCED PERFORMANCE MANAGEMENT SYSTEM

Background

For three years we acted as consultants to a medium-sized, upper Midwest theme park on the design, development, installation, and management of an organizational-results-referenced performance management system. Theme parks, since the advent of Disneyland, are highly sophisticated, highly profitable, results-oriented businesses. They are made all the more remarkable by the fact that, outside the sun belt, they are staffed primarily by 17- to 20-year-old students working for spending money or tuition. Partly because of their seasonal nature, partly due to heavy turnover, they have to be staffed anew every summer. In addition, theme parks are essentially fixed-market service institutions, so they are dependent upon repeat business for their survival.

The particular theme park we consulted with (we'll refer to it as "Countryfair") employed 800–1000 people at the height of their season. Countryfair is a mixed attraction park; that is, it has a mixture of thrill rides, stage shows, game areas, and food service. Like most theme parks, Countryfair charges a fixed entry fee that entitles guests to free access to all rides, stage shows, and attractions. Food, gifts, and games cost extra. The running bottom-line indicator in the industry (and it is quite a sensitive one) is gross dollar revenue divided by guest count, or "per-cap" (for per-capita expenditure). It is a common goal to try to induce the average guest to spend an amount on food, gifts, and games equal to the fixed entrance fee.

Our work with Countryfair began as a training consultancy prior to the first year of actual operation. The management team, veterans of Disney, Marriott, and Six Flags parks, brought with them a very strong training-and-development ethic. Such managers are very conscious of guest satisfaction, and are used to spending time and money on the training of front-line employees in customer service and customer relations. And the Disney system veterans especially are quite used to paying close attention to the details of on-the-job behavior of employees, particularly the interactions between guests (customers) and hosts and hostesses (employees). So our consulting work quickly matured beyond training and embraced the more comprehensive goals of assisting management with a complete system for managing performance of employees and organizational results.

Our three-year involvement can be divided into the three Countryfair seasons and labeled: Phase 1—design, develop, test; Phase 2—implement and tune; Phase 3—run and refine. In fact, we are able to report on a fourth season, the year after our involvement ended, which may be labeled: Phase 4—return to baseline.

Phase 1: Design, Develop, Test

During our first season, we worked primarily on the design, development, and testing of results-referenced feedback system, and the pilot testing of a rudimentary system-wide token economy (reinforcement system).

Among our first actions was to hold a series of lengthy discussions with senior management to specify, behaviorally, their model of what the business looked like when it was operating to their satisfaction. This business proposition was deceptively simple when finally we wrote it down. In part it reads: "Our success depends on repeat business. When guests come to Countryfair, they expect to have a good time, to have fun. When this expectation is met they tell others and, more importantly, they come back themselves."

We then worked with management to define more precisely what they thought they meant by "fun," so that we could try to develop some measures of this conception of customer satisfaction. Eventually, an operational model coalesced around four keys to guests having fun:

1. *Friendliness.* This meant that customer contact employees were perceived by the guests as smiling and being slightly assertive.

2. *Cleanliness.* When walkways, rest rooms, eating areas, and parking lots were perceived to be neat and clean by guests, this criterion was fulfilled.

3. *Service.* This meant that guests perceived employees to be helpful: food orders taken and delivered in a reasonable time, shop clerks attentive and available when guests arrived, and requests attended to quickly and without rancor.

4. *Show.* This most elusive of the four criteria refers in general to guests' enjoyment of the shows, rides, and attractions. Perceived quality of food and beverages, movement of queues (especially at the rides), and attractiveness of employee costumes all contributed.

Armed with this model, we developed a pool of 48 items to survey guest perceptions of the park's performance. Initial testing over nine days with 222 guests, and factor analysis, resulted in 36 Likert-type items we were confident would reliably measure park results against the four criteria.

Where possible, we subsequently tested the validity of these scales by comparing changes in guest perception ratings to measurable changes within the park. For instance, we tested the cleanliness scale by experimentally manipulating the amount of trash allowed to accumulate and by changes in the number of cleanings a specific facility received. We found, in the parking lot, that when the clean-up crew was halved, scores on items asking for guest perceptions of parking lot cleanliness sagged.

The nine days of initial item testing, plus five more days of sampling of guest perceptions using tbe factor-analyzed scales (we item sampled, so no guest had to answer more than nine questions), formed a baseline for comparison when we began posting organizational feedback and awarding of tokens.

As Figure 20-2 suggests, the display of organizational performance information (feedback alone) had minimal effect on subsequent guest perceptions during this first phase and, by inference, little effect on employee performance. But the institution of a rudimentary token economy did appear to gradually have an effect on guest perceptions and satisfaction. This early token system consisted of providing supervisors and managers

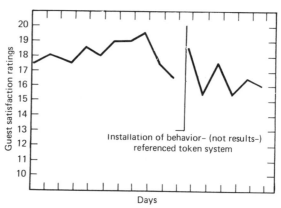

FIGURE 20-2.   Season 1—design and test phase.

with tokens they handed out to employees who they believed were "help-ing guests enjoy their day." These tokens were redeemable for pizzas, blue jeans, and records.

Phase 2: Implement and Tune

During the second season of operation at Countryfair, the following pro-cedures were instituted in an effort to make the results-referenced system a viable management tool.

1. A 50-foot-long by 10-foot-high wall next to the time clock was turned into a graph for displaying guest perceptions. On this wall we charted a running average of guest ratings on each of the four factors, as well as an "overall guest satisfaction" measure (the sum of the averages of the four factors). Nearly every employee walked past this wall twice a day. Preceding any display of data, we ran a five-day baseline sampling of guest perceptions.

2. Detailed, item-by-item averages of survey results were also dis-played, but in numerical rather than graphic form.

3. The token economy was expanded in a number of ways, and all managers, supervisors, and line employees were trained in the nu-ances of this new system. A commercial incentives company was retained to provide a point-based menu for redeeming earned to-kens.

4. The guest satisfaction measurement system was linked with the token economy. Specifically, each token awarded in the park bore a face value. However, the redemption value of any token depended in a specified way on the level of current overall guest satisfaction. For example, an overall guest satisfaction level of 17 (out of a pos-sible 20 points) multiplied the face value of tokens redeemed that

day by 160 percent. So a 10-point token was worth 16 points, but only so long as overall guest satisfaction remained at least at 17.

Employees developed a jargon for talking about the system in which the overall guest satisfaction rating was referred to as the "Countryfair Dow Jones Average." Tokens played the role of "stock" that was traded, bought, sold, and otherwise used as the script for an economic subsystem. If anything, this increased the effectiveness of the token economy for its intended purposes.

5. Guest attendance and per-cap figures were also posted publicly. Although they were not attended by so much fanfare as the "Dow Jones," the per-caps became the second half of the results-reference system.

6. A system manager was appointed to manage the token economy and the data gathering and displaying activities. This person become the sole arbiter for disputes concerning token awarding, redemption, and value setting. In addition, we trained the system manager to design and activate suborganizational intervention strategies within the token system to meet short-term needs. He subsequently devised and ran some 30 special performance improvement projects during the second season.

7. Managers and line supervisors were assigned specific token-awarding responsibilities. To insure use of the token system, managers were assigned a minimum number of tokens to award each shift. Line supervisors were given training in the use of tokens to reinforce appropriate behavior and then assigned a criterion level of tokens to be awarded each week. These supervisors were brought together weekly to exchange ideas and experiences related to the use of tokens to foster performance improvement.

8. Multiple backup reinforcement systems were developed and implemented.
   (a) Tokens were modified so that supervisors could write on their backs a description of the specific behavior for which they were being awarded.
   (b) Every fiftieth guest was given an envelope containing two tokens called "Special Thanks Awards." The tokens, small (2¾" by 3¾") colored cards, asked guests to give the tokens to any employees at Countryfair who made a special effort to make the guest's visit enjoyable.
   (c) Employees were given the right to award their earned tokens to fellow employees and to supervisors.
   (d) As tokens were earned, employees also received small, colored furry balls (or "Fuzzies") to indicate their accumulation of tokens. Different colors represented different totals of token

points. These Fuzzies were glued to employees' name tags and employees wore them like badges of excellence, which they were. Later we found that these colored Fuzzies allowed us to tell, at a glance, which employees and which park areas were not being reinforced.

(e) To address the major management concern about employee absenteeism and turnover, especially toward the end of the summer when the students had a "jingle in their jeans" and saw the start of school looming ever larger, we added another wrinkle. Employee time cards were placed in a lottery drum, and prize drawings were held every month. The better your attendance, the more chances you had to win. The value of lottery prizes was increased over the course of the season. Employees who worked all assigned days for the entire season were eligible for a year-end lottery that had, among other big prizes, an automobile and college scholarships.

As Figure 20-3 shows, the guest perception measures proved to be sensitive to changes in the token economy. We think four features are of special interest.

1. The first 16 data points were gathered prior to data display but *with* the token system in effect. This pseudo-baseline extends over 32 days of park operation.
2. During the "tokens given and data displayed" period, guest satisfaction ratings grew quite steadily. This period extended over 50 days of park operation.

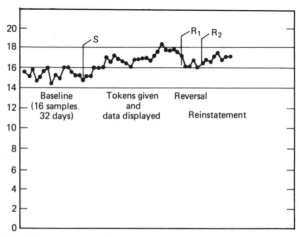

FIGURE 20-3. Guest satisfaction ratings, second year of park operations.

3. At the point labeled "R1," an accidental reversal of conditions occurred. Because of a glitch in the token accounting method, the system manager suspended all awarding and redemption of tokens for eight operating days. Guest perception data continued to be collected. The accounting problem was resolved and the token system resumed at "R2."

4. The accident reversal between R1 and R2 gave us evidence that the organizational results measures we were using were in fact functionally related to the token economy. We also noted that the results during reinstatement of tokens never again reached the levels attained prior to the reversal. We believe this was due in part to the "run on the bank" that occurred at R2, when token redemption was reinstated. Tokens that had been hoarded over the course of the season had been steadily increasing in value because of the upward trend of the Dow Jones. Thus employees had a vested interest in guest perception measures that grew with the number of tokens they owned. When a large number of tokens were redeemed, the amount of vested interest generally decreased across the park.

At the same time we were sensitive to what the guest perception measures were doing, we were paying close attention to the per-cap measures where appropriate. As we mentioned, the per-cap results (values in dollars and cents) were meaningful only for those areas where additional fees were charged after gate admission. These areas were the game areas, gift shops, and food and beverage areas.

Figure 20-4 shows the per-cap results for the games area for a 15-week period. Each data point represents a weekly per-cap average, computed

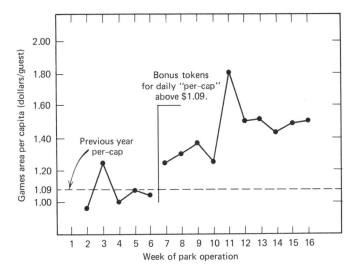

FIGURE 20-4. Per capita expenditures by park guests.

as total dollars taken in at the 10 game area booths, divided by the total park attendance for that seven-day period. As you can see from the graph, during Weeks 2–6 (baseline), per-capita expenditures were almost identical to those in the previous season ($1.08 versus $1.09).

In an effort to increase the per-cap in the games area, the division manager decided to make extra, specially colored tokens available to employees continget upon the daily per-cap on their shift. These tokens, provided by us, were referred to as "bonus" tokens, because they were earnable above and beyond any other tokens available. This bonus system was put in effect in the seventh week of the park's second season of operation.

During the 10 weeks of the bonus token availability, the per-cap averaged $1.43. The per-cap was never lower than $1.25 during this period, and at one point reached $1.80. (Bonus tokens were not awarded the final four weeks of the season because the park was only open weekends during this period and staffed by part-time people and managers.)

While we present the per-cap data in a weekly format in Figure 20-4, bonus tokens were awarded to employees daily. At the beginning of each shift, supervisors announced to employees the previous day's per-cap and awarded tokens. They too only *posted* results on a weekly basis.

The 35 employees in the games area earned a total of 28,944 bonus points, which were redeemed at an average value of about $.10 a point. So the bonus system cost about $2,894 in redeemed tokens (for an average $82.66 per employee). Payoff was based on improvement over the past year's per-cap. The difference in average per-cap during the bonus period and the past year's per-cap was $1.43 minus $1.09, or $.34. Since the average attendance during the 10-week bonus period was 30,500 people, the improvement in per-capita expenditure was worth $10,375. This translates into better than a 360 percent return on investment in a results-referenced system.

Phase 3: Run and Refine

At the end of the third season, the system manager, who was also the personnel manager, made a series of comparisons using personnel costs and attitude measures. Although our focus is, and was then, on organizational results and their primary indicators, these more indirect measures are of interest.

As Figure 20-5 indicates, there were significant changes in a number of personnel measures following the first season, when the system was piloted, and in subsequent seasons. We suppose there are reasonable alternative explanations for these results; however, it can also be argued that the results-referenced system was contributory. We'll highlight three features of the system manager's analysis.

1. Employment costs (the costs of finding, employing, and retraining employees) were much lower than expected and were budgeted in seasons

	Season 1	Season 2	Season 3
Employment costs (percent of budget)	113%	70%	73%
Hires to jobs	1.83:1	1.25:1	1.28:1
Actual turnover	81%	52%	53%
Employees completing employment contracts	18%	38%	41%
Employees requesting reemployment consideration	18%	35%	44%
Employees judged eligible (desirable) for rehire	42%	82%	81%

FIGURE 20-5. Indirect measures of system effectiveness.

two and three. Savings in these employment costs (approximately $30,000) offset nearly half the budgeted cost of the results-referenced system (which was $62,000). Such savings almost doubled in the third season, since the increase in proportion of employees requesting to be rehired made college recruiting unnecessary. This savings is not reflected in Season 3 "percent of budget" figures, since the college recruiting efforts did not become a budgeted line item.

2. Typically, employees in the theme park industry sign a contract promising to work a specified part of the season. Because of the high proportion of college students employed, a 5–10% bonus is usually paid for fulfiling the terms of the contract. Just as typically, this bonus is not very effective. While Countryfair shared the industry experience during the first season, they did much better during subsequent seasons after the full results-referenced system went into effect.

3. Low turnover rates during Seasons 2 and 3, employee requests for subsequent season rehiring, and supervisory evaluation of employees' suitability for rehiring suggest that there was a good employee relations climate in the park. The system manager believed this was a result of the "positive nature" of a system geared toward measuring, acknowledging, and rewarding performance and success rather than toward remediating problems.

Phase 4: Return to Baseline

During the fourth season of operation, Countryfair was acquired by an entertainment conglomerate. Though new management expressed interest in the feedback part of the system, the token economy was considered too complicated and unorthodox to be "useful as a management technique." The $62,000 price tag was considered too high for an "employee motivation program," and the results being tracked seemed trivial to the new management team. In our earlier language, they brought with them a different business proposition. This did afford us an unwelcome chance to see a complete reversal of conditions.

The title and labels of Figure 20-6 are somewhat misleading. Season 1, our initial "baseline" period, was not a true baseline. During the brief 35 days, with only 16 measurement periods, guest satisfaction results were displayed and experimented with. And Season 4, the return to baseline, was not exactly a return to baseline. In fact, guests were surveyed for six weeks, 18 measurements of guest perceptions were taken, and the data were displayed in the park. Measurement and display were halted by the new park management when it became evident that guest satisfaction ratings were below those of the previous seasons. But working with the data we have, it is plausible to argue that a management system referenced to overall organizational results deserves consideration as an adjunct to intervention techniques referenced solely to individual or small-group results.

We do not consider an organizational-results-referenced system to be a panacea. It does not obviate the need to train managers in behavior management principles and techniques. Nor is it a substitute for all subsystem, small-group, or individual behavior management systems and projects. We view the results-referenced system as a meta-system that provides an arena for suborganizational efforts.

ACTION PLAN: INSTALLING AN ORGANIZATIONAL-RESULTS-REFERENCED PERFORMANCE MANAGEMENT SYSTEM

As we have said, organizations are driven by the conceptions (business propositions) of certain members, usually managers. But they are dependent upon the performance of individuals, groups, and subsystems for the fulfillment of that guiding organizational concept. It is the purpose of a results-referenced system to bridge the gap between the critical behavior and the "bottom line" that validates or vitiates the business proposition. Our experience suggests some guidelines for establishing a results-referenced meta-management system.

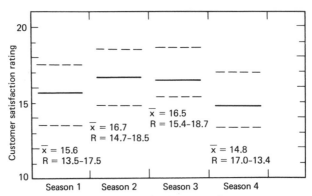

FIGURE 20-6. Four years of primary results measurement.

1. *Determine the organizational strategy, plan, or model in effect in the organization.* We take our lead from Henry Mintzberg, Robert Doktor, and other strategic thinking and planning experts, who see senior management's most critical responsibility to be holistic, strategic thinking. To further that end, we spend considerable time capturing the business proposition that senior managers hold about what a well-functioning organization (or branch, department, division) looks like—that is, what people will be doing when the organization is being maximally effective.

2. *Negotiate a measurement that reports, on a regular, short-term basis, organizational outcome indicators.* In the theme park case, we negotiated the measurement of overall guest satisfaction and four indicators of that result. In addition, we were able to roll down several direct dollar measures of the value of achieving that result. Our measures in this case happened to be mostly of customer perceptions and satisfaction. We have had equal success in organizations in which the critical organizational measures were less "soft." For instance, key indicators in other instances have been percentage of auto repairs satisfactorily completed the first time, percent of on-time deliveries, and units sold. The trick is to develop significant indicators of organizational performance that are directly related, in management's view, to the primary business proposition.

In the theme park case, we sampled the client population every other day throughout the season. In high-turn public contact organizations, this frequent sampling is useful. When clients come in smaller numbers, or performance cycles are longer, longer schedules work fine. For example, in sales situations we have used weekly and bimonthly cycles for surveying and posting.

3. *Measure key management variables so as to provide information in sizes usable by subunits.* In the theme park case, we were able to develop a pool of customer perception survey items that not only were summed, but individually had utility at the level of small areas within the park and in some cases for individual performers. It is also sometimes possible to work with existing management information systems to break down indicator data already being collected into a size usable by suborganizational units. Regardless of the source, "usable size" has tended to mean that the measure can be noticeably affected by members of the unit and bears a direct, easily inferable (face valid) relationship to unit results or individual behavior.

4. *Make results-indicator data available to all members of the organization.* It is unfortunately nearly axiomatic of organizations that those individuals with least access to performance data are the people who need it most and who, through their individual efforts, can affect it most.

In the theme park, we were able to post organizational performance data in one central location, a locale nearly all employees passed by twice a day. In this location, near the time clock, results of guest satisfaction surveys were posted every other day, as were daily attendance and per-capita guest expenditure figures. In sales and dispersed manufacturing settings, both unit and organization-wide results have been displayed. The important point is that up-to-date information must be made regularly and widely available.

5. *Establish a "psychoeconomic system" that can reinforce individuals for both individual performance and organizational results.* In the theme park, individual and subgroup accomplishment garnered tokens for employees, while organizational results levels established the exchange value of the tokens. This approach kept tokens available to subsystem managers for discretionary but contingent reinforcement of individual performance, while maintaining a contingent relationship between token value and organizational results. This dual contingency system increases the reinfrocement potential of tokens and maintains a safety factor when creativity in devising suborganizational projects is encourgaed.

6. *Get a "multiple-hit" from your reinforcers.* We have often been able to find ways for the system to reinforce one instance of good performance again and again. Perhaps this in some way makes up for the thin schedule necessitated by the economics of token redemption and our inability to notice a large portion of the instances of good performance. In the theme park, one instance of good performance could provide at least five reinforcement occasions:

1. When the token was initially given.
2. When the Fuzzy earned by the token was displayed on the name tag.
3. When guests asked about the Fuzzies on the name tag.
4. When the Dow Jones was posted (an occasion when people thought about their own already earned tokens).
5. When the tokens were redeemed for prizes.

And, in the case of supervisor-given tokens (because the behavior for which it was earned was written on the back of the token), there was a sixth occasion reported by many employees to be important to them:

6. When, perhaps at a time when things were not going so well for you, you took out your hoard of tokens and reread the nice comments on the back.

This multiple hit principle has also been effective for us in manufacturing and sales situations.

7. *Define a clear relationship between organizational results measurement and token values.* Ayllon and Azrin (1968) and Schaefer and Martın (1969) emphasıze the necessity for clear, concise rules, not only

for how tokens are to be exchanged but for the behavior by which they are to be earned and lost. These rules tie token earning precisely to well-specified behavior. We found, in a results-referenced intervention, that it was effective for token-earning behavior to be left unspecified, in fact, left up to the discretion of supervisors and guests. But it was important that the exchange value of the tokens be clearly and precisely related to the organizational results measures. In the theme park, token redemption values could as much as double if organizational measures improved dramatically, and fall if customer satisfaction fell. This direct tie to organizational results makes it relatively safe to be imprecise in the definition of token-earning behavior. Behavior that does not lead to improved organizational results will be reflected in a lowering of the value of the tokens—a self-correcting effect. Further, the guests who handed out the tokens are the ones who have the best information about (and the most vested interest in) the effectiveness of the behavior that is earning them. This is in contrast to the usual token economy in which the token givers (ward workers in an institution, training people, and so on) are usually people who have no direct vested interest in the resulting behavior of the token earners.

8. *Encourage complexity.* Another rationale for not precisely specifying token-earning behavior is that rigid earn-loss rules rob the manager and supervisor of flexibility and interfere with the organization's ability to adapt to changing conditions and new situations. To make the most of behavior management's power, systems should give managers and supervisors new management options and flexibility. The results-referenced system provides a supportive arena for supervisor-developed short-term behavior change projects. Employees too had flexibility in determining how best to achieve the desired organizational results. The system rewarded their creativity, provided they were effective.

Because our system used a common-based scrip whose availability was under the control of the system manager, it was also possible to vary the "density" of tokens in areas of the park. We were able to fine tune results by, e.g., increasing the density of tokens available in one park area when the previous day's results indicated performance was lagging. Because this "new money" was backed up by a consistent redemption formula (we were on a kind of "gold standard," unlike the U.S. economy), we did not experience any "inflation," but found rather that making more tokens available produced more of the desired behavior. We encouraged creative uses of the power and complexity built into the system, so long as they were consistent with the business proposition of management. Such complexity, which we only began to explore, leads us to believe that calling this a "psychoeconomic system" is not overstating the broad utility and impact it can have.

9. *Program the environment.* Most attempts to influence real work behavior have used artifical settings for the brunt of the intervention (such as by training people in classrooms, or in institutions). This invariably

leads to what the literature refers to as the problem of transfer, or generalization, to the work setting (see the review by Kazdin and Bootzin, 1972). The solution offered is to program the environment into which participants will go and in which they are expected to behave differently after the intervention. As should be obvious, in the theme park the brunt of the intervention occurred in the park, with only a little training occurring in artificial settings, such as part of new-employee orientation. And there was no such thing as "after" the intervention, since so long as the park was running the intervention was running, too.

Even the training that was provided was, as often as possible, done in the park itself rather than in a classroom. While we do not wish to discount the importance of orienting employees and training supervisors and managers in token-awarding and some behavior management principles, most of our efforts went into programming the park itself to provide the feedback and reinforcers necessary to sustain or improve employee performance.

In addition, we used the interactions of park employees with us, during the natural course of things, to contribute to the transfer of behavior onto the job. This was essentially a modeling activity. By training and prompting supervisors to model the use of tokens, using tokens ourselves within job-skills training sessions, and by making sure we and the senior managers gave out tokens within the plain view of others, we sensitized individuals in the environment to the use of tokens.

Ongoing, week-to-week environmental programming focused on keeping the system fresh and attended to by employees. The organization held special small-group training sessions to instruct employees in the niceties of the system: how tokens were likely to be earned, how organizational results measures affected token redemption values, and how tokens could be redeemed. In addition, the company newspaper carried stories of unusual ways individuals earned tokens and how people felt about the system.

10. *Provide a way for people to escape the contingencies.* Another problem typically encountered in token economies is that participants find ways to avoid or escape from the contingencies of the system. This can mean they cheat on the token-earning or losing rules. We did not have rigid rules relating behavior to reinforcers, which made it nearly impossible to cheat in this way. This problem also can mean that participants contrive ways so that they can avoid being subject to the token system. We realized very early that it is unrealistic to expect smiling, cheerful, helpful employees for eight straight hours every day. Therefore, we arranged for off-stage areas within the park. (Places where guests come into contact with employees are referred to as "on-stage" areas.) The off-stage areas were hidden from guests by fences and gates. There employees could go to blow off a little steam, swap "terrible guest" stories with other employees, take scheduled breaks, and generally not be in the public eye nor subject to the token system. We even installed a hanging rubber tire,

with "Dump Your Bucket" painted on it and a baseball bat nearby, for taking out aggressions physically.

11. *Prime the system regularly.* Just as people beginning a work day in a skilled job need a set-up period to ready the tools, supplies, and machines of their trade, managers and employees working within a results-referenced structure need some "make ready" activities. In the theme park, the system manager personally reported previous days' results to other managers, suggested targets for the day (goals), and personally modeled token-awarding behavior afresh each day. The system manager would, for example, stand in the hallway near the large "Dow Jones" results chart and engage employees in conversation about the trends at least one morning a week. His role was to congratulate (give social reinforcement) to line employees and line supervisors when results were high or improving, and to solicit improvement ideas when results were below standard. Priming has been a part of sales management's repertoire for years; organizational behavior management brings a new precision to such a routine.

12. *Keep the system fair and clean.* It has been our observation that organizational behavior management systems, be they results- or activity-referenced, tend to experience entropy, or go into eclipse, for one of two reasons: stimulus satiation and system injustice. We addressed the satiation problem tbrough priming, by the variety of ways performance got reinforced, and by encouraging creativity within the complexity of the system. Justice, as fairness, is defined by Homme and Tosti (1972) to mean that the terms of the contract, found on opposite sides of the agreement, must be of relatively equal weight. In general, one must try to relate the amount of reinforcement to the amount of performance."

We have found that disputes over rules and changes in contract conditions can have a highly detrimental effect on system effectiveness. Better to live with a system tipped in favor of line employees, or negotiate adjustments, than to renege on preestablished conditions. In the theme park, only one individual (the system manager) could make any changes in token base values, redemption conditions, or daily token availability (density). The system manager's working guideline was simply to protect the integrity of the system from any suspicion. Hence disputes were negotiated on a case-by-case basis instead of continually rewriting system rules. We learned this "rule" during the second year of the theme park system's operation, when a confusion over redemption rules literally caused a "market panic" and a run on the redemption center.

SUMMARY

As many who have worked within organizations can attest, there are constraints imposed upon what can be attempted, by the business proposition within which intervention strategies take place, and even more constraints on what can be accomplished and what you can take credit for. It is rare in a subsystem intervention to be able to bring to bear the authority of organizational results in designing, testing, verifying, and running behavior management programs. Because of that, the conventional wisdom seems to be: don't take the blame (but of course don't refuse the credit) for bottom-line results. In many situations that is good advice; there are a lot of things under heaven and earth that are not included in your program and that could interfere with the bottom line royally.

What we hope to have shown is how an organization-wide intervention provides an arena within which subsystem, small group, and individual behavior management projects can flourish. Further, with some ongoing feedback of organizational results, and a psychoeconomic system rewarding people on the basis of those results, you have a checks-and-balances system that keeps errant subsystem intervention strategies from going too far astray. This should allow a freer, more creative hand with subsystem intervention strategies. Management who believes in the organizational results is more likely to say, "Sure, try it; just as long as those results keep coming."

In addition, having a results-referenced system permits ongoing evaluation of the efficacy of subsystem projects. This is good news for us who like to do behavior management projects. It is also good news for line managers, who can keep an eye on us through watching the organizational impact of those projects.

The message is simple: don't be afraid to go after organization-wide results to use as referents for behavior management projects. (For example, trust customers to know when they are satisfied or, as Skinner once said, "Trust your pigeon.") Pin down the business proposition and work it. Make sure the outcome measures are credible and widely publicized. Set up contingencies between actions and their organizational results. And believe us, it is a lot more fun out in the job setting than it is in board rooms and other institutions.

REFERENCES

Annett, J. Feedback and human behaviour: The effects of knowledge of results, incentives, and reinforcement on learning and performance. Baltimore: Penguin Books, 1969.

Atthowe, J. M., and Krasner, L. Preliminary report on the application of contingent reinforcement procedures (token economy) on a "chronic" psychiatric ward. Journal of Abnormal Psychology, 1968, 73, 37–43.

Ayllon, T., and Azrin, N. H. The measurement and reinforcement of behavior of psychotics. Journal of the Experimental Analysis of Behavior, 1965, 8, 357–383.

Ayllon, T., and Azrin, N. H. The token economy: A motivational system for therapy and rehabilitation: New York: Appleton-Century-Crofts, 1968,

Birnbrauer, J. S., and Lawler, J. Token reinforcement for learning. Mental Retardation, 1964, 2, 275–279.

Bourdon, R. D. A token economy application to management performance improvement. Journal of Organizational Behavior Management, 1977, 1, 23–37.

Connellan, T. K., and Martin, J. EFG: A practical three-factor approach to improved productivity. Unpublisbed project report, 1981.

Dockstader, S. L., et al. *The effects of feedback and an implied standard on work performance.* San Diego: Naval Personnel and Training Research Lab Report NPRDC-TR-77-45, 1977.

Emmert, G. D. Measuring the impact of group performance feedback versus individual performance feedback in an industrial setting. *Journal of Organizational Behavior Management*, 1978, *1*, 134–141.

Hall, R. V., Lund, D., and Jackson, D. Effects of teacher attention on study behavior. *Journal of Applied Behavior Analysis*, 1968, *1*, 1–12.

Henderson, J. D., and Scoles, P. E. A community-based behavioral operant environment for psychotic men. *Behavior Therapy*, 1970, *1*, 245–251.

Homme, L., and Tosti, D. *Behavior technology: Motivation and contingency management.* San Rafael, CA: Individualized Learning Systems, 1972.

Hunt, J. G., and Zimmerman, J. Stimulating productivity in a simulated sheltered workshop setting. *American Journal of Mental Deficiency*, 1969, *74*, 43–49.

Johnston, J. M., Duncan, P. K., Monroe, C., Stephenson, H., and Stoerzinger, A. Tactics and benefits of behavioral measurement in business. *Journal of Organizational Behavior Management*, 1978, *1*, 164–178.

Kazdin, A. E., and Bootzin, R. R. The token economy: An evaluative review. *Journal of Applied Behavior Analysis*, 1972, *5*, 343–372.

Kazdin, A. E., and Kock, J. The effect of nonverbal teacher approval on student attentive behavior. *Journal of Applied Behavior Analysis*, 1973, *6*, 643–654.

Kelin, S. M., Kraut, A. I., and Wolfson, A. Employee reactions to attitude survey feedback: A study of the impact of structure and process. *Administrative Science Quarterly*, 1971, *16*, 497–514.

Komaki, J., Waddell, W. M., and Pearce, M. E. The applied behavioral analysis approach and individual employees: Improving performance in two small businesses. *Organizational Behavior and Human Performance*, 1977, *19*, 337–352.

Locke, B. Verbal conditioning with retarded subjects: Establishment or reinstatement of effective reinforcing consequences. *American Journal of Mental Deficiency*, 1969, *73*, 621–626.

Luthans, F., and Schweizer, J. O.B. Mod, in a small factory: How behavior modification techniques can improve total organizational performance. *Management Review*, September 1979, *68*, 43–50.

Nadler, D. A. Using feedback for organizational change: Promises and pitfalls. *Group and Organizational Studies*, 1976, *1*, 177–186.

Nalder, D. A., Mirvis, P. H., and Cammann, C. The ongoing feedback system: Experimenting with a new managerial tool. *Organizational Dynamics*, 1976, *4*, 63–80.

Phillips, E. L. Achievement place: Token reinforcement procedures in a home-style rehabilitation setting for "predelinquent" boys. *Journal of Applied Behavior Analysis*, 1968, *1*, 213–223.

Quay, H. C., and Hunt, W. A. Psychopathy, neuroticism and verbal conditioning: A replication and extension. *Journal of Consulting Psychology*, 1965, *29*, 283.

Schaefer, H. H., and Martin, P. L. *Behavioral therapy.* New York: McGraw-Hill, 1969.

Zemke, R. E., and Larsen, D. Organizational mission: A new look at managerial thinking. Unpublished, 1981.

Author Index

Subject Index